ETHICS & LIFE

An Interdisciplinary Approach to Moral Problems

Elaine E. Englehardt
Utah Valley Community College

Donald D. Schmeltekopf
Baylor University

Wm. C. Brown Publishers

Book Team

Editor *Meredith M. Morgan*
Production Editor *Scott Sullivan*
Visuals/Design Freelance Specialist *Barbara J. Hodgson*
Photo Editor *Lori Gockel*
Permissions Editor *Gail Wheatley*
Visuals Processor *Andréa Lopez-Meyer*

Wm. C. Brown Publishers

President *G. Franklin Lewis*
Vice President, Publisher *Thomas E. Doran*
Vice President, Operations and Production *Beverly Kolz*
National Sales Manager *Virginia S. Moffat*
Group Sales Manager *Eric Ziegler*
Executive Editor *Edgar J. Laube*
Director of Marketing *Kathy Law Laube*
Marketing Manager *Kathleen Nietzke*
Managing Editor, Production *Colleen A. Yonda*
Manager of Visuals and Design *Faye M. Schilling*
Production Editorial Manager *Julie A. Kennedy*
Production Editorial Manager *Ann Fuerste*
Publishing Services Manager *Karen J. Slaght*

WCB Group

President and Chief Executive Officer *Mark C. Falb*
Chairman of the Board *Wm. C. Brown*

Cover background: H. Armstrong Roberts; Left: © Lionel Delevinge/
Stock Boston; Middle: © H. Armstrong Roberts; Right: © Michael
Dwyer/Stock Boston

Cover and interior design Kay D. Fulton/Fulton Design

Printed in the United States of America by Wm. C. Brown Publishers,
2460 Kerper Boulevard, Dubuque, IA 52001

10 9 8 7 6 5 4 3 2 1

CONTENTS

PREFACE   vi

PART ONE   *The Nature of Ethics*   1

1   *Foundations of Ethics*   7

READINGS:

The Bible: The Ten Commandments,
Exodus 20:1–17   13
The Sermon on the Mount,
Matthew 5–7   13

Thomas Hobbes, "Convention," from
Leviathan   17

Immanuel Kant, "The Categorical
Imperative," from *Foundations of the
Metaphysics of Morals*   26

John Stuart Mill, "Social Benefit," from
Utilitarianism   36

Aristotle, "Virtuous Activity," from
Nicomachean Ethics, Books I and II   44

Carol Gilligan, "Images of Relationship,"
from *In a Different Voice*   54

PART TWO   *Ethics and Life*   61

2   *Abortion*   63

THE ISSUE:

Justice Harry A. Blackmun, Majority
Opinion in *Roe v. Wade*   68

Ronald Reagan, "Abortion and the
Conscience of the Nation"   74

Linda Bird Francke, "Abortion:
a Personal Moral Dilemma," from
The Ambivalence of Abortion   80

PHILOSOPHICAL POSITIONS:

Judith Jarvis Thomson, "A Defense of
Abortion"   86

Kathryn Pyne Addelson, "Moral
Revolution"   98

Mary B. Mahowald, "Abortion and
Equality"   106

RELIGIOUS PERSPECTIVES:

Pope Paul VI, Humane Vitae   108

Daniel C. Maguire, "A Catholic
Theologian at an Abortion Clinic"   124

Fred Rosner, "Jewish Attitude Toward
Abortion," from *Modern Medicine
and Jewish Ethics*   130

Basim F. Mussallam, "Why Islam Permitted
Contraception," from *Sex and Society in Islam:
Birth Control Before the 19th Century*   142

LITERARY TREATMENTS:

A. J. Cronin, "Doctor, I can't . . . I won't
have a child"   148

Gwendolyn Brooks, "The Mother"   152

Ernest Hemingway, "Hills Like White
Elephants"   156

Elaine Englehardt, "The Silent Partner"   160

HISTORICAL PERSPECTIVES:

Michael J. Gorman, "The Pagan World,"
from *Abortion and the Early Church*   164

Linda Gordon, "The Prohibition on Birth
Control" and "The Criminals," from
*Woman's Right, Woman's Body: A Social
History of Birth Control in America*   168

Suggested Readings   182

3   *War and Nuclear War*   183

THE ISSUE:

Mikhail S. Gorbachev, "Nuclear
Disarmament by the Year 2000,"   188

Carl Sagan, "The Nuclear Winter"   192

Colin S. Gray and Keith Payne, "Victory is
Possible"   198

PHILOSOPHICAL POSITIONS:

Burton M. Leiser, "War Crimes
and Crimes Against Humanity,"
from *Liberty, Justice, and Morals*   206

Douglas P. Lackey, "Missiles and Morals: A
Utilitarian Look at Nuclear Deterrence"   212

James P. Sterba, "Just War Theory
and Nuclear Strategy"   220

RELIGIOUS PRONOUNCEMENTS:

*The National Conference of Catholic
Bishops*, "Nuclear Weapons and Nuclear
Deterrence," from *The Challenge of Peace:
God's Promise and Our Response*   232

D. E. Carroll et al., Response to the U.S.
Bishops' Second Draft of a Proposed Pastoral
Letter on War, Armaments and Peace   242

David Novak, "The Threat of Nuclear War:
Jewish Perspectives"   252

Victor Danner, "The Holy War"   262

Ayatollah Ruhollah Khomeini,
"Islam is not a Religion of Pacifists,"
from *Holy Terror* ed. by Amir Taheri   266

Gholam-Reza Fada'i Araqi,
"Death is Not an End, but a Continuation,"
from *Holy Terror* ed. by Amir Taheri   266

LITERARY TREATMENTS:

Czeslaw Milosz, "American Ignorance
of War"   270

Luigi Pirandello, "War"   274

Richard Lovelace, "To Lucasta, Going
to the Wars"   278

Mark Twain, "The War Prayer"   280

Isaac Asimov, "Silly Asses"   284

Lewis Thomas, Late Night
Thoughts on Listening to Mahler's
Ninth Symphony   286

HISTORICAL PERSPECTIVES:

Arata Osada, Children of
Hiroshima (selections)   290

Marion Yass, "The Decision
to Bomb Japan," from *Hiroshima*   302

Suggested Readings   310

4   *Corporate Responsibility*   311

THE ISSUE:

Milton Friedman, "The Social Responsibility
of Business is to Increase Its Profits"   316

John DeLorean, "How Moral Men Make
Immoral Decisions," from *On a Clear Day You
Can See General Motors*   322

Robert D. Hay and Edmund R. Gray,
"Introduction to Social Responsibility,"
from *Business and Society:
Cases and Text*   336

PHILOSOPHICAL PERSPECTIVES:

*Kenneth E. Goodpaster and John B.
Matthews, Jr.*, "Can a Corporation have
a Conscience?"   348

Melvin Anshen, "Changing the Social
Contract: A Role for Business"   358

*John G. Simon, Charles W. Powers, and
Jon P. Gunnemann*, "The Responsibilities
of Corporations and Their Owners"   364

RELIGIOUS PERSPECTIVES:

The National Conference of Catholic Bishops, Economic Justice for All: A Pastoral Message   372

Robert Benne, "The Bishops' Letter: A Protestant Reading"   386

Ronald Green, "The Bishops' Letter: A Jewish Reading"   394

Yusuf Al-Qaradawi, "The Halal and the Haram in the Daily Life of the Muslim," from The Lawful and the Prohibited in Islam   406

LITERARY PERSPECTIVES:

Niccolo Machiavelli, "The Qualities of the Prince," from The Prince   412

Edwin Arlington Robinson, "Richard Cory"   420

Howard Fast, "The Cold, Cold Box"   422

Henrik Ibsen, An Enemy of the People   430

HISTORICAL PERSPECTIVES:

Robert Almeder, "Morality in the Marketplace"   436

Neil W. Chamberlin, "The Uncertain Relation between Business and Society"   444

Suggested Readings   451

INDEX   453

PREFACE

This book is designed for an introductory course in ethics that links both theoretical and practical concerns. The readings in the book are interdisciplinary and challenge students to read critically a variety of works in philosophy, religion, literature, and history. Interdisciplinary examination is an exceptional way for students to become acquainted with the study of ethics. Through the four disciplines, students will benefit from a holistic perspective on ethical questions and dilemmas. Moreover, this book should engage students in serious reflection on moral issues that relate to their own lives.

The book begins with a short essay on the nature of ethics. The first part of the book introduces the student to ethical theory through the works of selected philosophers and religious writings. This section focuses on five ethical traditions: duty, rights, utility, virtue, and caring relations. The writings from the Ten Commandments, the Sermon on the Mount, and Immanuel Kant provide varying accounts of an ethic of duty. Thomas Hobbes's ethical approach is naturalistically based, but it also establishes the rudiments of an ethic of rights. The principle of utility is presented through an essay from John Stuart Mill. The reading from Aristotle introduces the student to the notion of ethics as virtue. And, an ethic based on caring relationships, an emerging theoretical perspective, is articulated by Carol Gilligan, a professor of education at Harvard University.

Each of these ethical approaches is a legitimate part of our cultural heritage, but each can and often does conflict with others in certain respects. As students work through the book, they should determine the perspectives of the writers, for such understanding will shape the analysis of and recommended responses to ethical dilemmas. Students also should confront the question of why they are inclined to one ethical system over another. Why does one author or philosopher appeal to them over others? Are their choices explained merely by what their parents, their peers, or their religious communities believe? Or, are their choices the result of independent judgments that respect the moral views of others—including their parents, peers, and clergy—but are ultimately formed autonomously and with a full sense of personal accountability? In short, how firm and well-grounded are the students' ethical points of view? Are the students really capable of publicly justifying their ethical positions, both those they might hold in an academic sense and those they live by? These are questions that should help push students not only to think carefully about ethical matters, but also to live lives reflecting well-considered moral behavior.

The next three chapters of the book focus on moral dilemmas, again using interdisciplinary material. We have selected the topics of abortion, war and nuclear war, and corporate social responsibility as three of the most important ethical problems of our time. Each chapter opens with an introductory essay by the editors that indicates the central ethical issues connected with each area and presents an overview of all the readings in the section. The readings begin with an explanation of and an orientation to the issue by various authorities. We next present the dilemma from a philosophical perspective, paying attention to the variety of viewpoints offered by different philosophers. Religious writings also add a helpful dimension to the ethical study of these dilemmas. Religions concern themselves with questions of applied ethics, but, in addition, their leaders and sacred writings have a special authority for their adherents. We have selected perspectives from three important world religions: Christianity, Judaism, and Islam.

The discipline of literature brings an additional and distinctive contribution to moral reflection through its special focus on the human factor. Through short stories, poems, essays, and plays, literature helps the reader envision a dilemma through strong description, captivating plot lines, and, above all, emotion and feeling. The final discipline, history, brings out yet another viewpoint on ethical concerns. It is important that students understand moral dilemmas from the perspective of those who have actually experienced them in all their complexity and depth, often as an occasion of genuine suffering. Actual stories relating to abortion, war, and corporate irresponsibility confront us in a special way with the ambiguity and the harsh reality of what we sometimes do. Human experience, both direct and indirect, can be a master "teacher" of the moral point of view.

An important function of this book is to enable students to confront themselves with respect to ethical matters and examine critically all of the issues of moral dilemmas. Moreover, students should recognize possible inconsistencies in their own ethical views as well as the implications of their actual moral beliefs and actions. In the classroom, this can be done through strong discussion and the writing of papers on ethical subjects. At the end of each reading, we have six questions designed to promote discussion and to encourage the intellectual stimulation needed for interesting essays and papers.

- The first question relates to some aspect of the content of the specific reading.
- The second question asks the student to examine the soundness of the essay and the intent of the author.
- The third question focuses on personal interpretation and asks for a response to the moral issue at hand or to related issues.
- The fourth question asks for a response to the reading using ethics as the focus.
- The fifth question involves the specific discipline reflected in the reading and how this discipline relates to the ethical dilemma.
- The final question examines how the study of ethics might be influenced by a variety of disciplinary perspectives.

Finally, we hope this book will help students understand the humanities as well as the specific topic of ethics. We have not meant to teach students a specific skill, but rather to help them be individuals of a special kind— who think critically and constructively, who know how to evaluate problems, who discuss issues civilly, who communicate well orally and in writing, and who care about and strive to do what is morally right. These abilities and developed characteristics compose, we believe, much of the goal of teaching and learning in the humanities.

Acknowledgements

Many individuals have assisted us in various ways in the preparation of this book. We are indebted especially to Robert Baird, Eugene Baker, William F. Cooper, Eldon Eliason, Harriet Eliason, Cleo Hinckley, Judy Jeffrey Howard, Donald G. Jones, W. J. Kilgore, Jonathan Lindsey, William Newell, JoEllen Olsen, Kerry Romesburg, Robert Solomon, and Lucille Stoddard. We are also grateful to our expert colleagues at Wm. C. Brown Publishers, Meredith Morgan and Scott Sullivan.

Although no grant was made to support this publication, the idea for the manuscript grew out of a curriculum-development project at Utah Valley Community College, funded by the National Endowment for the Humanities. The project resulted in the establishment of a core-humanities course entitled "Ethics and Values."

We dedicate this book to Judy and Kirk.

Elaine E. Englehardt, Utah Valley Community College
Donald D. Schmeltekopf, Baylor University

PART 1

THE NATURE OF ETHICS

"**M**orality is made for man, not man for morality."[1] This statement aptly suggests what morality is about: a system of guidance designed to assist us in the living of our lives. This practical assistance, however, has a distinctive quality to it. In contrast to nonmoral guides, morality ultimately rests on self-sacrifice and the curbing of our inclination to want and to do anything that pleases us. The primary goal of morality is to establish appropriate constraints on human behavior—constraints made necessary by self-aggrandizement and conflicting interests. We would not need morality if the human situation were otherwise, if people lived together peaceably and without harming one another. The fact that we do not so live is the major condition requiring morality.

Ethics is the study of morality and moral behavior. That is, ethics is the philosophical discipline dealing with our moral choices, actions, and judgments, and their rational justifications. The main reason we engage in ethical reflection is for practical guidance on what we ought to or ought not to do. But while the analysis of some of our moral behavior yields clear-cut answers (e.g., it was wrong of X to kill Y in cold blood), the analysis of much of our moral behavior produces answers that are not always definite (e.g., it was wrong of X to abort Y). The latter kinds of situations are moral dilemmas, where desirable or undesirable alternatives conflict and where both sides seem equally justifiable. In moral dilemmas, it is not clear what the right course of action is. The study of morality—ethics—assists conscientious people in establishing the right thing to do in both definite and indefinite situations.

To a great extent, this book is arranged with moral dilemmas in mind. The proper moral choices, actions, and judgments concerning abortion, corporate responsibility, and war and nuclear conflict are not always well-defined. There is considerable moral disagreement about these matters, but the study of morality can help us make better and wiser decisions in these areas and, at the very minimum, help us know why we disagree.

We said that ethics is the disciplined study of the rational justification of moral principles and moral behavior. This means, first, that ethics is a discipline like history or psychology. As a discipline, ethics involves schools of thought (e.g., consequentialism and non-consequentialism—more on these later.) As a discipline, ethical inquiry produces theories, distinctive concepts and principles, and its own methodology. And, of course, it has its own peculiar language: "(moral) right and wrong," "good and evil," "ought and obligation," "duty," "(human) rights," "freedom and responsibility," and the like. When one engages in the study of ethics, one needs to be familiar with the history, norms, and semantics of the field, just as with other disciplines.

Second, ethics has to do with what is *moral*—with the moral domain of human behavior. The study of ethics involves reflection on *moral* behavior in contrast to prudential, legal, or even religious behavior, although they may be related. What are the fundamental, distinguishing characteristics or properties of moral behavior? Two of these characteristics are harm and mutual aid. Morality, and its study through ethics, is important to us because of our basic and universal aversion to harm, either physical or

---

[1]William K. Frankena, *Ethics* (Englewood Cliffs, N.J.: Prentice-Hall, Inc., 1963), 98.

psychological. No one wants to be harmed (killed, maimed, inflicted with pain, deprived of freedom and opportunity, etc.), and no one submits to harm unless there is an overriding reason. What specifically is harm? It is the experience of pain, suffering, or deprivation—*against our will*—that results from the willful or negligent act of another person. From the moral point of view, harm is wrongful injury as a result of human action and should be seen as an aspect of evil.

To say that no one desires to be harmed seems to be a fact of life, a truism about our common humanity. Another such truth, however, is that most, if not all, humans inflict harm from time to time on others without the others' consent. We need not agree with Thomas Hobbes's pessimistic version of the state of war among us to agree, nevertheless, that life would be intolerable without a formidable constraint on our inclination to inflict harm on others. These coexistent realities—the universal human aversion to harm and the universal human tendency to inflict harm—are the conditions that make morality necessary. This explains why the central issue of ethical reflection is the problem of harm and its appropriate constraint.

Avoiding harm, of course, is not the only distinguishing characteristic of moral behavior. Moral behavior also involves assisting others in their lives by contributing to their well-being or benefit. The concept of the "good Samaritan" captures this characteristic in classic fashion. Surely morality would be incomplete without this positive side of obligation to others. The phrase "do good and avoid evil" readily summarizes both distinctive characteristics of *moral* behavior and establishes the basic subject matter of ethics.

Morality in the sense indicated has both an individual and a social dimension. What we have said thus far assumes the preeminence of the individual as moral agent, in keeping with most moral traditions of the Western world. But morality is also a social system, sometimes understood or referred to as the "moral institution of life."

The "moral institution of life" refers to the pervasive societal framework that perpetuates morality within any given social order. Morality is not invented anew by each generation, nor is it limited to actions of individuals. Rather, as William K. Frankena observes, "like one's language, state, or church, it exists before the individual, who is inducted into it and becomes more or less of a participant in it, and it goes on existing after him."[2] Morality is a social enterprise that involves a system of rules, ideals, and sanctions, and thereby serves the essential social functions of harmony and cooperation. However, morality as a social institution *needs*, from time to time, the critical judgment of the autonomous moral agent. This criticism has the potential of contributing, over time, to a measure of moral progress within the social order.

Since morality has a social dimension, it certainly applies to institutions, institutional arrangements and policies, and the behavioral norms of various cultures and groups. Thus, the study of ethics encompasses *moral norms* applicable to business corporations, political bodies, medical organizations, colleges and universities, churches, sects, and so on, as well as individuals *qua* individuals. While moral theories and concepts are designed to deal primarily with individuals, moral categories can be sensibly applied to these various institutions and groups, although in a secondary sense. Manufacturing firms have an obligation to produce safe products because individuals working within firms can and are obligated to produce safe products in the first place.

---

[2]*Ibid.*, 5.

Third, the focus of our definition of ethics is on *behavior* rather than motives, intentions, or character. Experiences of harm and mutual aid occur primarily because of concrete actions that are committed or are not committed. Moral motivation and intention are certainly of interest to us, as is evident in the judgments we make about the reasons behind certain actions. We also have strong interest in the character of people because one's disposition to act in a certain way has predictive value in moral behavior. But, in the end, what people actually do or don't do is what counts most of all, morally speaking. The pain of actually being maimed, without our consent, is far worse than whatever intentions someone might have entertained with respect to us. Moreover, many intentions are never acted on, whereas each moral action may count as either harm or help.

A final component of our definition of ethics concerns the concept of *rational justification.* As a philosophical enterprise, work in the field of ethics is based ultimately on reason and its power to justify beliefs. Philosophers generally hold that while reason is not the only guide to truth, it provides the best direction. And, one of the areas to which reason can give guidance is morality. One aspect, then, of the nature of ethics is our *analysis* of and *reflection* on moral choices and judgments.[3] Of particular interest in this regard is the rational justification of our moral beliefs. To justify a belief—a position, a viewpoint, or a conclusion—is to give sufficient grounds for it; it is to show that an idea is warranted. There are various kinds of backings— in experience, in religion, and in reason—for a warranted moral belief, but in philosophy, the decisive kind of evidence is found in reason. In the study of ethics, both theoretical and practical, one constantly seeks the theory or principle(s) that is most convincing and that action which, all things considered, would be the best thing to do.

Our understanding of ethics may be further clarified by distinguishing morality or moral behavior from law, etiquette, customary morality, and religion. The law, of course, reflects various moral rules, ideals, and sanctions of a society. However, obedience to the law is not an adequate moral standard because the law cannot cover all acts or intentions, nor does the law prescribe for *all* acts of mutual aid. Moreover, the law occasionally runs contrary to morality—is unjust—and hence, may justifiably be disobeyed *in exceptional cases.*

Etiquette refers to the forms of behavior that are associated with social and official life. Examples of good etiquette are the use of proper language in public (and bad etiquette, the use of obscene or offensive language in public), appropriate eating habits (and bad etiquette, the slurping of one's food), and appropriate deference to others. Judgments about matters of etiquette are often expressed in moral-like language, as in, "It's wrong that he curses on the tennis court." In these matters, however, such words as "wrong," "bad," "right," and "good" convey judgments about manners or taste, not ethics. What is of primary importance in etiquette is public behavior that is socially acceptable.

---

[3]An important part of ethical analysis and reflection that is not dealt with in this book is called "meta-ethics." Meta-ethics relates to those questions of ethics that concern the language and the logic of moral belief. For example, what is the meaning of terms such as "right" and "wrong"? More basic, however, is the problem of the logic of moral beliefs. For example, do moral beliefs reflect some objective truth, or are they the product essentially of personal desires and attitudes? These examples indicate that while meta-ethics is only *about* morality, meta-ethical issues are nevertheless of fundamental importance in moral argumentation. Indeed, they may be seen as logically prior to normative considerations, which have to do with the content of moral principles and their justification. In spite of the importance of meta-ethical issues, they are beyond the immediate scope of this book.

Customary morality and religion also use the moral categories of ethics. Both propose action-guides and appropriate sanctions in the interest of a better life in the community or within the religious group. The problem with both, however, is that they may prescribe actions in the name of custom or deity that violate fundamental morality. For example, customary morality in various societies has condoned and even advocated slavery, systematic discrimination against certain groups (religious, sexual, and racial), and caste systems. Religions, too, sometimes require their followers to engage in practices that seemingly inflict gratuitous harm on others, as in holy wars, human sacrifices, and the deprivation of possessions. Indeed, there is no necessary connection between religion and morality. "God forbids rape because rape is wrong, but it is not God's forbidding rape that makes it wrong."[4] In all cultures, irrespective of religious traditions, actions such as rape are wrong from a moral point of view. It should be recognized, however, that in the established social systems of morality that exist in all cultures, religion is one of the most important pillars in the "moral institution of life."

In the history of ethics or moral philosophy, the main interest of philosophers has been to construct normative theories of morality and to comment on theories already proposed. While there are many such theories, it is convenient to group them into two broad schools of thought, consequentialism and non-consequentialism. These two schools of thought are frequently referred to as teleological and deontological ethical theories, the first stressing consequences and the second the nature of actions themselves. What all ethical theories ultimately have in common is that each tries to give a persuasive account of what constitutes right and wrong action, and how that conclusion is determined. From this main concern follows another: What we and others should do in concrete situations. We are interested in normative theories to help us know both what to do ourselves and how to make judgments, if appropriate, about what others do.

The basic idea of all consequentialist theories is that right and wrong action, and judgments about these, are determined by the results produced. Are the results good or bad? The standard for this, in turn, is the nonmoral value brought into consideration. This nonmoral value is generally spoken of as the "good" (whatever it may otherwise be called). That which is conducive to the "good" (or end) is called "right" action on our part; the action that inhibits the attainment of this end is considered "wrong."

For consequentialists, the particular nonmoral value brought into being is all-important. This "good" is considered worthful in its own right; it is intrinsically or inherently valuable. It is not a means to anything else. What might such a value be? In the history of moral philosophy, the prevailing views have been pleasure (hedonism), self-interest (egoism), maximization of happiness (utilitarianism), and happiness and self-realization (Aristotelianism). These are nonmoral values, each called the "good," that are viewed as inherently valuable. Depending on the nature of the "good," consequentialist ethical theories often produce codes of conduct that are broader in scope than our definition of ethics allows. That is, according to some consequentialist theories, one may be morally obligated to engage in certain behaviors even though these have no clear connection with harm or mutual aid (e.g., exercising or dieting). According to our definitions, these behaviors are justified on prudential grounds, not moral ones.

---

[4]William H. Shaw and Vincent Barry, *Moral Issues in Business*, 4th ed., (Belmont, California: Wadsworth Publishing Company, 1989), 11.

Non-consequentialist or deontological theories, on the other hand, maintain that rightness, wrongness, and obligation are based upon certain features of the act itself, not necessarily the results produced by the act. Non-consequentialist ethics, then, is primarily concerned with action that is right in-and-of-itself, irrespective of other considerations. The rightness or wrongness of the act is the crucial point. Thus, for example, promise keeping, truth telling, and respecting the rights of others are the kinds of behaviors advocated by non-consequentialists, not because these acts are guaranteed to bring about good results (indeed, the opposite may occur), but because these acts possess a certain moral character. Once this common character is understood, these acts command our respect and confront us as moral duties. The most influential non-consequentialist in the history of moral thought is Immanuel Kant.

While philosophical ethics and religiously based ethics need to be distinguished, it is, nevertheless, the case that the tradition of ethical reflection has been significantly influenced by religious teachings. Indeed, we cannot do justice to an adequate understanding of the history of ethics without a familiarity with action-guides that are religiously based. For those of us in the Western world, this means primarily a knowledge of the Mosaic Law, especially the Ten Commandments, and the moral teachings of Jesus. The crucial differentiating feature of religious moral systems is that they are ultimately based on divine authority rather than exclusively on human experience and reason. Often, however, these two approaches prescribe and proscribe similar codes of conduct. The final test for the adequacy of all moral systems and ethical theories—religious and natural—is whether or not they help us to prevent or to mitigate human harm and to maximize human benefit. Authentic morality, in practice and theory, must always be for us, not against us.

Donald D. Schmeltekopf
Baylor University

chapter 1

FOUNDATIONS OF ETHICS

You are leaving a parking lot. As you back out, you accidently hit the car next to you, leaving a dent in its door. You get out of your car, assess the damages at about five hundred dollars, and leave a note on the car's windshield. What does your note say?

One version of the note may leave a phone number, driver's license number, and an offer to pay the damages. Another may rationalize by saying, "I only have enough money to pay for your car or to go to school. I think it is more important for me to go to school." Or, you may write, "I'm leaving this note to satisfy the people around me. I sure hope you have insurance to pay for this dent, because I'm not paying for it. It was just an accident anyway."

It was just an accident? How would you feel had *your* car been damaged? Would you want a student to pay tuition instead of repairs? Would you want someone to leave a note to appease witnesses? Or, would you want the individual to offer to pay for the damage to your car? The choice is obvious when the tables are turned. How could someone harm you financially and not offer to compensate you?

This example, which happens daily in parking lots across the country, demonstrates some of the basic issues involved in morality. Every day we are faced with moral dilemmas, some momentous, some rather insignificant.

Calvin & Hobbes Copyright 1989 Universal Press Syndicate, Reprinted with permission. All rights reserved.

How do we make decisions? How do we know what is right and wrong, good and evil? These are fundamental questions of ethics, and they may be among the hardest of life's puzzles to solve.

Philosophers and others throughout history have given much thought to the important subject of ethics. Simply stated, ethics is the study of moral behavior, its underlying moral principles, and their rational justifications. Ethics involves critical reflection on and self-confrontation with the moral choices that arise daily. The choices can be as ordinary as borrowing your roommate's bicycle without permission, or as far-reaching as a decision involving the life of a family member who is suffering a terminal disease and wants to die now. Perhaps an opportunity to make money that appears a bit too easy comes your way. Maybe you will face a decision on the aborting of a fetus.

What should your decision be in each of these circumstances? Whatever your decisions are in these and countless other situations involving questions of right and wrong, they should reflect an understanding of sound moral principles and the importance of rational justification for choices and actions. The attempt to justify actions from the standpoint of moral considerations is one that has engaged the best thinkers and writers throughout human history. In this book we use interdisciplinary studies through writers in philosophy, religion, literature, and history to show the necessity both for ethical reflection and for the critical examination of moral choices. This opening chapter of the book, which deals with ethical foundations, presents religious and philosophical readings only.

The chapter begins with excerpts from the Bible. One foundation of ethics in our society comes from the Mosaic Law, commonly known in abbreviated form as the Ten Commandments. As a context for this passage, keep in mind that the Israelites and their ancestors had been in Egyptian bondage for approximately four hundred years. As slaves, the Israelites had been in a condition of dependency and, consequently, were not sure how to behave with their newfound religious and moral freedom. Through Moses, the Israelites believed God gave them commandments or duties to guide their lives. These commands state either "thou shalt" or "thou shalt not"! This codicil form suggests that the commands are absolute and must always be obeyed. The Ten Commandments, and the Mosaic Law generally, remain today some of the strongest moral guidelines in the world.

The main body of the ethical teachings of Jesus are found in the Sermon on the Mount, here given from Matthew: 5–7. Jesus is not content with people merely abstaining from wrongdoing; he commands them, in addition, to love one another. Instead of saying "don't kill," Jesus tells his followers to not even get angry with others. Instead of hating one's enemies, Jesus says to "love your enemies." To Jesus, the virtue of love between human beings is to have no less than the same self-giving quality love has in the relationship between God and human beings.

Moving from an ethic based on religious authority to an ethic examining the psychological condition of man, we turn to Thomas Hobbes, a fifteenth-century English philosopher. Hobbes proposes a naturalistic foundation of ethics in an excerpt from *Leviathan*. In this passage, Hobbes argues that people are by nature selfish, individualistic creatures in a constant state of war with all others. In Hobbes's "state of nature," human beings are equal in their self-seeking proclivities and live out lives that are "solitary, poor, nasty, brutish, and short." To escape this native anarchy, men contract with each other, relinquishing certain rights in order to secure peace in a created state. In the newly created state, the ruler determines what is right and wrong, just and unjust. People are willing to agree to this state of affairs because of their fear of mutual self-destruction. In essence, Hobbes's ethical system is based on the concept of rational self-preservation.

The next excerpt is from Immanuel Kant, who stresses that we must always act on the basis of a universal moral principle or law. Kant insists that moral principles are commands of reason rather than commands of God. Kant proposes that ethical judgments are essentially based on faith in a necessary moral law, discovered by reason, and that this moral law is the same for everyone. Kant names this supreme moral law the "categorical imperative," and sees it expressed basically in three forms. Form one is, "act as if the maxim from which you act were to become through your will a universal law of nature." Form two says "so act as to treat humanity whether in your own person or that of another in every case as an end in itself, never merely as a means." Form three states "act always as a legislating member of the universal kingdom of ends." The term "categorical" means in every instance; "imperative" means an obligation that must be performed. The "categorical imperative" applies to all persons. Under a test of lawfulness, Kant wants us to create moral rules of conduct that we would want everyone to follow under all circumstances.

The perspective of utilitarian ethics is presented in an excerpt from John Stuart Mill. This ethical system is based on the intrinsically valuable goal of the "greatest happiness of the greatest number." That is, utilitarians believe that an act may be judged morally right if it produces pleasure or alleviates pain for most people. An act is wrong if it decreases pleasure or brings about pain. Mill wonders, however, if social benefit can be defined purely in terms of increase of pleasure and decrease of pain, or if there are higher values that take precedence over pleasure and pain. He believes that scientific progress, social freedom, and even artistic creativity may take precedence on occasion. Mill further acknowledges the superiority of mental pleasure over physical pleasure.

The writing from Aristotle discusses the meaning of happiness and its relationship to the virtuous life. According to Aristotle, virtue is an activity of the human soul, the rational and non-rational part of our inward being. He understands virtue to be of two kinds, moral and intellectual. Moral virtue concerns our passions, actions, and developed character traits. Complete happiness, however, is found in intellectual virtue, which is the use of our rational faculties in contemplative activity.

An ethical system based on relationships is articulated in a fresh way by Carol Gilligan. This perspective involves making decisions based on a network of relationships and the principle of caring. According to Gilligan, moral dilemmas can be solved by caring persons operating over time within a web of relationships. Gilligan, a contemporary scholar interested in women's research and analysis, holds that women have been thought to be ethically inferior to men because women tend to make decisions based on caring, sharing, and their networks of relationships. The excerpt in this book presents Gilligan's analysis of Lawrence Kohlberg's "Heinz's dilemma" from a relationship perspective. She emphasizes that women's moral reasoning skills are not superior or inferior to those of men, just different on occasion.

THE TEN COMMANDMENTS &
THE SERMON ON THE MOUNT

◆◆◆

T*he Hebrew name for the Ten Commandments is the Ten Words, hence the name Decalogue. It is believed they were engraved on two tablets of stone. There is a difference of opinion as to the way in which the Commandments are divided into ten. The Ten Commandments are found in Exodus 20:1–17, and in Deuteronomy 5:6–21. Because of their wide acceptance, the Ten Commandments are often used as a standard for fundamental morality.*

The Sermon on the Mount is a discourse by Jesus to his disciples who were about to be sent forth to preach his gospel. This excerpt, found in Matthew 5–7, is similar in some respects to a sermon recorded in Luke 6:20–49. Matthew's account includes more succinct references to the law and the prophets. Jesus explains that his teachings transcend some of the aspects of the Ten Commandments. Particularly important to his teaching is the charge to love one another. ◆

The Ten Commandments:
Exodus 20:1–17

Chapter 20   And God spake all these words, saying,

2 I *am* the Lord thy God, which have brought thee out of the land of E′gȳpt, out of the house of bondage.

3 Thou shalt have no other gods before me.

4 Thou shalt not make unto thee any graven image, or any likeness *of any thing* that *is* in heaven above, or that *is* in the earth beneath, or that *is* in the water under the earth:

5 Thou shalt not bow down thyself to them, nor serve them: for I the Lord thy God *am* a jealous God, visiting the iniquity of the fathers upon the children unto the third and fourth *generation* of them that hate me;

6 And shewing mercy unto thousands of them that love me, and keep my commandments.

7 Thou shalt not take the name of the Lord thy God in vain; for the Lord will not hold him guiltless that taketh his name in vain.

8 Remember the sabbath day, to keep it holy.

9 Six days shalt thou labour, and do all thy work:

10 But the seventh day *is* the sabbath of the Lord thy God: *in it* thou shalt not do any work, thou, nor thy son, nor thy daughter, thy manservant, nor thy maidservant, nor thy cattle, nor thy stranger that *is* within thy gates:

11 For *in* six days the Lord made heaven and earth, the sea, and all that in them *is*, and rested the seventh day: wherefore the Lord blessed the sabbath day, and hallowed it.

12 Honour thy father and thy mother: that thy days may be long upon the land which the Lord thy God giveth thee.

13 Thou shalt not kill.

14 Thou shalt not commit adultery.

15 Thou shalt not steal.

16 Thou shalt not bear false witness against thy neighbour.

17 Thou shalt not covet thy neighbour's house, thou shalt not covet they neighbour's wife, nor his manservant, nor his maidservant, nor his ox, nor his ass, nor any thing that *is* thy neighbour's.

Source: from *The Holy Bible*, authorized King James Version, The World Publishing Company, Cleveland and New York.

The Sermon on the Mount:
Matthew 5–7

Chapter 5   And seeing the multitudes, he went up into a mountain: and when he was set, his disciples came unto him:

2 And he opened his mouth, and taught them, saying,

3 Blessed *are* the poor in spirit: for their's is the kingdom of heaven.

4 Blessed *are* they that mourn: for they shall be comforted.

5 Blessed *are* the meek: for they shall inherit the earth.

6 Blessed *are* they which do hunger and thirst after righteousness: for they shall be filled.

7 Blessed *are* the merciful: for they shall obtain mercy.

8 Blessed *are* the pure in heart: for they shall see God.

9 Blessed *are* the peacemakers: for they shall be called the children of God.

10 Blessed *are* they which are persecuted for righteousness' sake: for their's is the kingdom of heaven.

11 Blessed are ye, when *men* shall revile you, and persecute *you*, and shall say all manner of evil against you falsely, for my sake.

12 Rejoice, and be exceeding glad: for great *is* your reward in heaven: for so persecuted they the prophets which were before you.

13 Ye are the salt of the earth: but if the salt have lost his savour, wherewith shall it be salted? It is thenceforth good for nothing, but to be cast out, and to be trodden under foot of men.

14 Ye are the light of the world. A city that is set on an hill cannot be hid.

15 Neither do men light a candle, and put it under a bushel, but on a candlestick; and it giveth light unto all that are in the house.

16 Let your light so shine before men, that they may see your good works, and glorify your Father which is in heaven.

17 Think not that I am come to destroy the law, or the prophets: I am not come to destroy, but to fulfill.

18 For verily I say unto you, Till heaven and earth pass, one jot or one tittle shall in no wise pass from the law, till all be fulfilled.

19 Whosoever therefore shall break one of these least commandments, and shall teach men so, he shall be called the least in the kingdom of heaven: but whosoever shall do and teach *them*, the same shall be called great in the kingdom of heaven.

20 For I say unto you, That except your righteousness shall exceed *the righteousness* of the scribes and Phăr'-i-sĕe̊s, ye shall in no case enter into the kingdom of heaven.

21 Ye have heard that it was said by them of old time, Thou shalt not kill; and whosoever shall kill shall be in danger of the judgment:

22 But I say unto you, That whosoever is angry with his brother without cause shall be in danger of the judgment: and whosoever shall say to his brother, Rā'-că, shall be in danger of the council: but whosoever shall say, Thou fool, shall be in danger of hell fire.

23 Therefore if thou bring thy gift to the altar, and there rememberest that thy brother hath ought against thee;

24 Leave there thy gift before the altar, and go thy way; first be reconciled to thy brother, and then come and offer thy gift.

25 Agree with thine adversary quickly, whiles thou art in the way with him; lest at any time the adversary deliver thee to the judge, and the judge deliver thee to the officer, and thou be cast into prison.

26 Verily I say unto thee, Thou shalt by no means come out thence, till thou hast paid the uttermost farthing.

27 Ye have heard that it was said by them of old time, Thou shalt not commit adultery:

28 But I say unto you, That whosoever looketh on a woman to lust after her hath committed adultery with her already in his heart.

29 And if thy right eye offend thee, pluck it out, and cast *it* from thee: for it is profitable for thee that one of thy members should perish, and not *that* thy whole body should be cast into hell.

30 And if thy right hand offend thee, cut it off, and cast *it* from thee: for it is profitable for thee that one of thy members should perish, and not *that* thy whole body should be cast into hell.

31 It hath been said, Whosoever shall put away his wife, let him give her a writing of divorcement:

32 But I say unto you, That whosoever shall put away his wife, saving for the cause of fornication, causeth her to commit adultery: and whosoever shall marry her that is divorced committeth adultery.

33 Again, ye have heard that it hath been said by them of old time, Thou shalt not forswear thyself, but shalt perform unto the Lord thine oaths:

34 But I say unto you, Swear not at all; neither by heaven; for it is God's throne:

35 Nor by the earth; for it is his footstool: neither by Jĕ-rû'-să-lĕm; for it is the city of the great King.

36 Neither shalt thou swear by thy head, because thou canst not make one hair white or black.

37 But let your communication be, Yea, yea; Nay, nay: for whatsoever is more than these cometh of evil.

38 Ye have heard that it hath been said, An eye for an eye, and a tooth for a tooth:

39 But I say unto you, That ye resist not evil: but whosoever shall smite thee on thy right cheek, turn to him the other also.

40 And if any man will sue thee at the law, and take away thy coat, let him have *thy* cloke also.

41 And whosoever shall compel thee to go a mile, go with him twain.

42 Give to him that asketh thee, and from him that would borrow of thee turn not thou away.

43 Ye have heard that it hath been said, Thou shalt love thy neighbour, and hate thine enemy.

44 But I say unto you, Love your enemies, bless them that curse you, do good to them that hate you, and pray for them which despitefully use you, and persecute you;

45 That ye may be the children of your Father which is in heaven; for he maketh his sun to rise on the evil and on the good, and sendeth rain on the just and on the unjust.

46 For if ye love them which love you, what reward have ye? do not even the publicans the same?

47 And if ye salute your brethren only, what do ye more *than others?* do not even the publicans so?

48 Be ye therefore perfect, even as your Father which is in heaven is perfect.

Chapter 6   Take heed that ye do not your alms before men, to be seen of them: otherwise ye have no reward of your Father which is in heaven.

2 Therefore when thou doest *thine* alms, do not sound a trumpet before thee, as the hypocrites do in the synagogues and in the streets, that they may have glory of men. Verily I say unto you, They have their reward.

3 But when thou doest alms, let not thy left hand know what thy right hand doeth:

4 That thine alms may be in secret: and thy Father which seeth in secret himself shall reward thee openly.

5 And when thou prayest, thou shalt not be as the hypocrites *are:* for they love to pray standing in the synagogues and in the corners of the streets, that they may be seen of men. Verily I say unto you, They have their reward.

6 But thou, when thou prayest, enter into thy closet, and when thou hast shut thy door, pray to thy Father which is in secret; and thy Father which seeth in secret shall reward thee openly.

7 But when ye pray, use not vain repetitions, as the heathen *do:* for they think that they shall be heard for their much speaking.

8 Be not ye therefore like unto them: for your Father knoweth what things ye have need of, before ye ask him.

9 After this manner therefore pray ye: Our Father which art in heaven, Hallowed be thy name.

10 Thy kingdom come. Thy will be done in earth, as *it is* in heaven.

11 Give us this day our daily bread.

12 And forgive us our debts, as we forgive our debtors.

13 And lead us not into temptation, but delivery us from evil: For thine is the kingdom, and the power, and the glory, for ever. Ä'-měn.

14 For if ye forgive men their trespasses, your heavenly Father will also forgive you:

15 But if ye forgive not men their trespasses, neither will your Father forgive your trespasses.

16 Moreover, when ye fast, be not, as the hypocrites, of a sad countenance: for they disfigure their faces, that they may appear unto men to fast. Verily I say unto you, They have their reward.

17 But thou, when thou fastest, anoint thine head, and wash thy face;

18 That thou appear not unto men to fast, but unto thy Father which is in secret: and thy Father, which seeth in secret, shall reward thee openly.

19 Lay not up for yourselves treasures upon earth, where moth and rust doth corrupt, and where thieves break through and steal:

20 But lay up for yourselves treasures in heaven, where neither moth nor rust doth corrupt, and where thieves do not break through nor steal:

21 For where your treasure is, there will your heart be also.

22 The light of the body is the eye: if therefore thine eye be single, thy whole body shall be full of light.

23 But if thine eye be evil, thy whole body shall be full of darkness. If therefore the light that is in thee be darkness, how great *is* that darkness!

24 No man can serve two masters: for either he will hate the one, and love the other; or else he will hold to the one, and despise the other. Ye cannot serve God and măm'-mon.

25 Therefore I say unto you, Take no thought for your life, what ye shall eat, or what ye shall drink; nor yet for your body, what ye shall put on. Is not the life more than meat, and the body than raiment?

26 Behold the fowls of the air: for they sow not, neither do they reap, nor gather into barns; yet your heavenly Father feedeth them. Are ye not much better than they?

27 Which of you by taking thought can add one cubit unto his stature?

28 And why take ye thought for raiment? Consider the lilies of the field, how they grow; they toil not, neither do they spin:

29 And yet I say unto you, That even Sŏl'-ŏ-mon in all his glory was not arrayed like one of these.

30 Wherefore, if God so clothe the grass of the field, which to day is, and to morrow is cast into the oven, *shall he* not much more *clothe* you, O ye of little faith?

31 Therefore take no thought, saying, What shall we eat? or, What shall we drink? or, Wherewithal shall we be clothed?

32 (For after all these things do the Gěn'-tileś seek:) for your heavenly Father knoweth that ye have need of all these things.

33 But seek ye first the kingdom of God, and his righteousness; and all these things shall be added unto you.

34 Take therefore no thought for the morrow: for the morrow shall take thought for the things of itself. Sufficient unto the day *is* the evil thereof.

Chapter 7   Judge not, that ye be not judged.

2 For with what judgment ye judge, ye shall be judged: and with what measure ye mete, it shall be measured to you again.

3 And why beholdest thou the mote that is in thy brother's eye, but considerest not the beam that is in thine own eye?

4 Or how wilt thou say to thy brother, Let me pull out the mote out of thine eye; and, behold, a beam *is* in thine own eye?

5 Thou hypocrite, first cast out the beam out of thine own eye; and then shalt thou see clearly to cast out the mote out of thy brother's eye.

6 Give not that which is holy unto the dogs, neither cast ye your pearls before swine, lest they trample them under their feet, and turn again and rend you.

7 Ask, and it shall be given you; seek, and ye shall find; knock, and it shall be opened unto you:

8 For every one that asketh receiveth; and he that seeketh findeth; and to him that knocketh it shall be opened.

9 Or what man is there of you, whom if his son ask bread, will he give him a stone?

10 Or if he ask a fish, will he give him a serpent?

11 If ye then, being evil, know how to give good gifts unto your children, how much more shall your Father which is in heaven give good things to them that ask him?

12 Therefore all things whatsoever ye would that men should do to you, do ye even so to them: for this is the law and the prophets.

13 Enter ye in at the strait gate; for wide *is* the gate, and broad *is* the way, that leadeth to destruction, and many there be which go in thereat:

14 Because strait *is* the gate, and narrow *is* the way, which leadeth unto life, and few there be that find it.

15 Beware of false prophets, which come to you in sheep's clothing, but inwardly they are ravening wolves.

16 Ye shall know them by their fruits. Do men gather grapes of thorns, or figs of thistles?

17 Even so every good tree bringeth forth good fruit; but a corrupt tree bringeth forth evil fruit.

18 A good tree cannot bring forth evil fruit, neither *can* a corrupt tree bring forth good fruit.

19 Every tree that bringeth not forth good fruit is hewn down, and cast into the fire.

20 Wherefore by their fruits ye shall know them.

21 Not every one that saith unto me, Lord, Lord, shall enter into the kingdom of heaven; but he that doeth the will of my Father which is in heaven.

22 Many will say to me in that day, Lord, Lord, have we not prophesied in thy name? and in thy name have cast out devils? and in thy name done many wonderful works?

23 And then will I profess unto them, I never knew you: depart from me, ye that work iniquity.

24 Therefore, whosoever heareth these sayings of mine, and doeth them, I will liken him unto a wise man, which built his house upon a rock:

25 And the rain descended, and the floods came, and the winds blew, and beat upon that house; and it fell not: for it was founded upon a rock.

26 And every one that heareth these sayings of mine, and doeth them not, shall be likened unto a foolish man, which built his house upon the sand:

27 And the rain descended, and the floods came, and the winds blew, and beat upon that house; and it fell: and great was the fall of it.

28 And it came to pass, when Jē′-süs had ended these sayings, the people were astonished at his doctrine:

29 For he taught them as *one* having authority, and not as the scribes.

Writing and Discussion Topics

Questions 1–6 address content, critical analysis, personal choices, ethical options, specific discipline, and interdisciplinary alternatives, respectively.

1. Which commandments could be placed in a category of man's relationship to man? Explain in detail each of these commandments. Are any of these commandments irrelevant today?

2. Examine the Sermon on the Mount. What is the strongest ethical counsel presented in this writing?

3. Which passage in the Sermon on the Mount is most helpful to your code of personal ethics? Is this passage found anywhere in the Ten Commandments?

4. Explain the fundamental differences between the Ten Commandments and the Sermon on the Mount.

5. What is an ethic based on duty? Why do the Ten Commandments fit into this system of ethics?

6. Why are the Ten Commandments and the Sermon on the Mount viewed as foundational ethics? Do philosophers base their views on these writings?

Thomas Hobbes

CONVENTION
———◆◆◆———

Thomas Hobbes (1588–1679) was a famous English philosopher who took great interest in mathematics, physics, and the current rationalism. When his political writings placed him in disfavor in England, he moved to France. In France he also found numerous critics of his political philosophy. He eventually returned to England where he lived peacefully. Among his important works are Leviathan, De Cive, De Corpore Politico, De Homine, and Behemoth. This excerpt is from Leviathan. ◆

Of the Natural Condition of Mankind, as Concerning Their Felicity and Misery

Nature hath made men so equal in the faculties of body and mind as, though there be found one man sometimes manifestly stronger in body or of quicker mind than another, yet, when all is reckoned together, the difference between man and man is not so considerable as that one man can thereupon claim to himself any benefit to which another may not pretend as well as he. For as to the strength of body, the weakest has strength enough to kill the strongest, either by secret machination or by confederacy with others that are in the same danger with himself.

And as to the faculties of the mind (setting aside the arts grounded upon words, and especially that skill of proceeding upon general and infallible rules called Science, which very few have and but in few things, as being not a native faculty born with us nor attained, as Prudence, while we look after somewhat else), I find yet a greater equality among men than that of strength. For Prudence is but Experience, which equal time equally bestows on all men in those things they equally apply themselves unto. That which may perhaps make such equality incredible is but a vain conceit of one's own wisdom, which almost all men think they have in a greater degree than the Vulgar—that is, than all men but themselves and a few others whom by Fame, or for concurring with themselves, they approve. For such is the nature of men that howsoever they may acknowledge many others to be more witty, or more eloquent, or more learned, yet they will hardly believe there be many so wise as themselves; for they see their own wit at hand and other men's at a distance. But this proves rather that men are in that point equal than unequal. For there is not ordinarily a greater sign of the equal distribution of any thing than that every man is contented with his share.

From this equality of ability ariseth equality of hope in the attaining of our Ends. And therefore if any two men desire the same thing, which nevertheless they cannot both enjoy, they become enemies and in the way to their End (which is principally their own conservation, and sometimes their delectation only) endeavor to destroy, or subdue, one another. And from hence it comes to pass that where an Invader has no more to fear than another man's single power, if one plant, sow, build, or possess a convenient Seat, others may probably be expected to come prepared with forces united to dispossess and deprive him not only of the fruit of his labor but

also of his life or liberty. And the Invader again is in the like danger of another.

And from this diffidence of one another, there is no way for any man to secure himself so reasonable as Anticipation—that is, by force or wiles to master the persons of all men he can . . . till he see no other power great enough to endanger him—and this is no more than his own conservation requires and is generally allowed. Also because there be some that take pleasure in contemplating their own power in the acts of conquest, which they pursue farther than their security requires, if others, that otherwise would be glad to be at ease within modest bounds, should not by invasion increase their power, they would not be able long. . . , by standing only on their defense, to subsist. And by consequence, such augmentation of dominion over men being necessary to a mass conservation, it ought to be allowed him.

Again, men have no pleasure (but on the contrary a great deal of grief) in keeping company where there is no power able to over-awe them all. For every man looks that his companion should value him at the same rate he sets upon himself: And upon all signs of contempt to undervaluing naturally endeavors, as far as he dares (which amongst them that have no common power to keep them in quiet is far enough to make them destroy each other), to extort a greater value from his contemners, by dommage, and from others, by the example.

So that in the nature of men, we find three principal causes of quarrel. First, Competition; secondly, Diffidence; thirdly, Glory.

The first makes men invade for Gain; the second, for Safety; and the third, for Reputation. The first use Violence, to make themselves Masters of other men's persons, wives, children, and cattle; the second, to defend them; the third for trifles, as a word, a smile, a different opinion, and any other sign of undervalue, either direct in their Persons, or by reflection in their Kindred, their Friends, their Nation, their Profession, or their Name.

Hereby it is manifest that during the time men live without a common Power to keep them all in awe, they are in that condition which is called War, and such a War as is of every man *against every man*. For *war* consists not in Battle only, or the act of fighting, but in a tract of time wherein the Will to contend by Battle is sufficiently known; and therefore the notion of *Time* is to be considered in the nature of War as it is in the nature of Weather. For as the nature of Foul weather lies not in a shower or two of rain but in an inclination thereto of many days together, so the nature of War consists not in actual fighting but in the known disposition thereto during all the time there is no assurance to the contrary. All other time is Peace.

Source: Thomas Hobbes, "The Nature of Man," from *Leviathan*, Part I, Chapters XII–XV, London, 1651.

Whatsoever therefore is consequent to a time of War, where every man is Enemy to every man, the same is consequent to the time wherein men live without other security than what their own strength and their own invention shall furnish them with. In such condition there is no place for Industry because the fruit thereof is uncertain, and consequently no culture of the Earth, no Navigation nor use of the commodities that may be imported by Sea, no commodious Building, no Instruments of moving and removing such things as require much force, no Knowledge of the face of the Earth, no account of Time, no Arts, no Letters, no Society, and, which is worst of all, continual fear and danger of violent death; And the life of man, solitary, poor, nasty, brutish, and short.

It may seem strange to some man that has not well weighed these things that Nature should thus dissociate and render men apt to invade and destroy one another: and he may therefore, not trusting to his Inference made from the Passions, desire perhaps to have the same confirmed by Experience. Let him therefore consider with himself [that] when taking a journey, he arms himself and seeks to go well accompanied; when going to sleep, he locks his doors; when even in his house, he locks his chests; and this when he knows there be Laws and public Officers, armed to revenge all injuries shall be done him; what opinion he has of his fellow subjects, when he rides armed; of his fellow Citizens, when he locks his doors; and of his children and servants, when he locks his chests. Does he not there as much accuse man's nature in it? The Desires and other Passions of man are in themselves no sin. No more are the Actions that proceed from those Passions, till they know a Law that forbids them, which till Laws be made they cannot know, nor can any Law be made till they have agreed upon the Person that shall make it.

It may peradventure be thought, there was never such a time nor condition of war as this, and I believe it was never generally so, over all the world; but there are many places where they live so now. For the savage people in many places of *America*—except the government of small Families, the concord whereof depends on natural lust—have no government at all and live at this day in that brutish manner as I said before. Howsoever, it may be perceived what manner of life there would be where there were no common Power to fear by the manner of life which men that have formerly lived under a peaceful government use to degenerate into a civil War.

But though there had never been any time wherein particular men were in a condition of war one against another, yet in all times, Kings and Persons of Sovereign authority, because of their independence, are in continual jealousy and in the state and posture of Gladiators, having their weapons pointing and their eyes fixed on one another—that is, their Forts, garrisons, and Guns upon the Frontiers of their Kingdoms, and continual spies upon their neighbors—which is a posture of War. But because they uphold thereby the Industry of their Subjects, there does not follow from it that misery which accompanies the Liberty of particular men.

To this war of every man against every man, this also is consequent: that nothing can be Unjust. The notions of Right and Wrong, Justice and Injustice, have there no place. Where there is no common Power, there is no Law; where no Law, no Justice. Force, and Fraud are in War the two Cardinal virtues. Justice and Injustice are none of the Faculties neither of the Body nor Mind. If they were, they might be in a man that was alone in the world, as well as his Senses and Passions. They are Qualities that relate to Men in Society, not in Solitude. It is consequent also to the same condition that there be no Propriety, no Dominion, no *Mine* and *Thine* distinct, but only that to be every man's that he can get and for so long as he can keep it. And thus much for the ill condition which Man by mere Nature is actually placed in, though with a possibility to come out of it, consisting partly in the Passions, partly in his Reason.

The Passions that incline men to Peace, are Fear of Death, Desire of such things as are necessary to commodious living, and a Hope by their Industry to obtain them. And Reason suggests convenient articles of Peace, upon which men may be drawn to agreement. These Articles are they which otherwise are called the Laws of Nature, whereof I shall speak more particularly, in the two following Chapters.

Of the First and Second Natural Laws and of Contracts

The Right of Nature, which Writers commonly call *Jus Naturale*, is the Liberty each man has to use his own power, as he will himself, for the preservation of his own Nature—that is to say, of his own Life—and consequently of doing anything which in his own Judgment and Reason he shall conceive to be the aptest means thereunto.

By Liberty is understood, according to the proper signification of the word, the absence of external Impediments, which Impediments may oft take away part of a man's power to do what he would but cannot hinder him from using the power left him, according as his judgment and reason shall dictate to him.

A Law of Nature *(Lex Naturalis)* is a Precept, or general rule, found out by Reason, by which a man is forbidden to do that which is destructive to his life or takes away the means of preserving the same, and to omit that by which he thinks it may be best preserved. For though they that speak of this subject . . . confound *Jus* and *Lex*, *Right* and *Law*, yet they ought to be distinguished, because Right consists in liberty to do, or to forbear, Whereas Law determines and binds to one of them; so that Law and Right differ as much as Obligation and Liberty, which in one and the same matter are inconsistent.

And because the condition of Man (as hath been declared in the preceding Chapter) is a condition of War of everyone against everyone, in which case everyone is governed by his own Reason and there is nothing he can make use of that may not be a help unto him in preserving his life against his enemies, it follows that in such a condition every man has a Right to everything, even to one another's body. And therefore, as long as this natural Right of every man to everything endures, there can be no Security to any man, (how strong or wise soever he be) of living out the time which Nature ordinarily allows men to live. And consequently it is a precept, or general rule of Reason, *That every man ought to endeavor Peace, as far as he has hope of obtaining it, and when he cannot obtain it, that he may seek and use, all helps and advantages of War.* The first branch of which Rule contains the first and Fundamental Law of Nature, which is to *seek peace and follow it.* The Second, the sum of the Right of Nature, . . . is, *By all means we can, to defend ourselves.*

From this Fundamental Law of Nature, by which men are commanded to endeavor Peace, is derived this second Law: *That a man be willing, when others are so too, as far as for peace, and defense of himself he shall think it necessary, to lay down this Right to all things and be contented with so much Liberty against other men as he would allow other men against himself.* For as long as every man hold this Right of doing anything he likes, so long are all men in the condition of War. But if other men will not lay down their Right, as well as he, then there is no Reason for anyone to divest himself of his; for that were to expose himself to Prey (which no man is bound to) rather than to dispose himself to Peace. This is that Law of the Gospel: *Whatsoever you require that others should do to you, that do ye to them.* And that Law of all men: *Quod tibi fieri non vis, alteri ne feris.*

To *lay down* a man's *Right* to anything is to *divest* himself of the *Liberty* of hindering another of the benefit of his own Right to the same. For he that renounces or passes away his Right gives not to any other man a Right which he had not before, because there is nothing to which every man had not Right by Nature, but only stand out of his way, that he may enjoy his own original Right without hindrance from him, not without hindrance from another. So that the effect which redounds to one man by another man's defect of Right is but so much diminution of impediments to the use of his own Right original.

Right is laid aside either by simply Renouncing it or by transferring it to another—By *Simply Renouncing,* when he cares not to whom the benefit thereof redounds; *By Transferring,* when he intends the benefit thereof to some certain person, or persons. And when a man has in either manner abandoned or granted away his Right, then is he said to be Obliged, or bound, not to hinder those to whom such Right is granted, or abandoned, from the benefit of it; and that he *ought,* and it is his *duty,* not to make void that voluntary act of his own: and that such hindrance is *injustice,* and injury, as being *Sine Jure,* the Right being before renounced, or transferred. So that *Injury,* or *Injustice,* in the controversies of the world, is somewhat like to that which in the disputations of Scholars is called *Absurdity.* For as it is there called an Absurdity to contradict what one maintained in the Beginning, so in the world it is called Injustice and Injury voluntarily to undo that which from the beginning he had voluntarily done. The way by which a man either simply Renounces or Transfers his Right is a Declaration, or Signification, by some voluntary and sufficient sign, or signs, that he does so Renounce, or Transfer, or has so Renounced, or Transferred the same, to him that accepts it. And these Signs are either Words only, or Actions only, or (as it happens most often) both Words and Actions. And the same are the *bonds* by which men are bound and obliged—Bonds that have their strength not from their own Nature (for nothing is more easily broken than a man's word) but from Fear of some evil consequence upon the rupture.

Whensoever a man Transfers his Right or Renounceth it, it is either in consideration of some Right reciprocally transferred to himself or for some other good he hopes for thereby. For it is a voluntary act, and of the voluntary acts of every man, the object is some *Good to himself.* And therefore there be some Rights which no man can be understood by any words or other signs to have abandoned or transferred—As, first, a man cannot lay down the right of resisting them that assault him by force, to take away his life, because he cannot be understood to aim thereby at any Good to himself. The same may be said of Wounds, and Chains, and Imprisonment, both because there is no benefit consequent to such patience as there is to the patience of suffering another to be wounded or imprisoned, [and] also because a man cannot tell, when he sees men proceed against him by violence whether they intend his death or not. And, lastly, the motive and end for which this renouncing, and transferring of Right is introduced is nothing else but the security of a man's person, in his life, and in the means of so preserving life, as not to be weary of it. And therefore if a man by words or other signs seems to despoil himself of the End, for which those signs were intended, he is not to be understood as if he meant it, or that it was his will, but that he was ignorant of how such words and actions were to be interpreted.

The mutual Transferring of Right is that which men call Contract.

Of Other Laws of Nature

From that law of Nature by which we are obliged to transfer to another such Rights as, being retained, hinder the peace of Mankind, there followeth a Third, which is this, *That men perform their Covenants made*— without which, Covenants are in vain and but Empty Words and, the Right of all men to all things remaining, we are still in the condition of War.

And in this law of Nature consists the Foundation and Original of Justice. For where no Covenant has preceded, there has no Right been transferred, and every man has right to everything, and consequently no action can be Unjust. But when a Covenant is made, then to break it is Unjust; And the definition of Injustice is no other than *the not Performance of Covenant.* And whatsoever is not Unjust is Just.

But because Covenants of mutual trust where there is a fear of not performance on either part (as had been said in the former Chapter) are invalid, though the Original of Justice be the making of Covenants, yet Injustice actually there can be none till the cause of such fear be taken away, which while men are in the natural condition of War cannot be done. Therefore before the names of Just and Unjust can have place, there must be some coercive power to compel men equally to the performance of their Covenants by the terror of some punishment greater than the benefit they expect by the breach of their Covenant, and to make good that propriety which by mutual contract men acquire in recompence of the universal Right they abandon. And such Power there is none before the erection of a Commonwealth. And this is also to be gathered out of the ordinary definition of Justice in the Schools; For they say the *Justice is the constant Will of giving to every man his own.* And therefore where there is no *Own*— that is, no Propriety—there is no injustice; and where there is no coercive Power erected—that is, where there is no Commonwealth—there is no Propriety, all men having Right to all things. Therefore where there is no Commonwealth, there nothing is Unjust. So that the Nature of Justice consists in keeping of valid Covenants; but the Validity of Covenants begins not but with the Constitution of a Civil Power sufficient to compel men to keep them. And then it is also that Propriety begins.

All Justice depends on Antecedent Covenant; so does *Gratitude* depend on Antecedent Grace—that is to say, Antecedent Free Gift—and is the fourth Law of Nature, which may be conceived in this Form: *That a man which receives Benefit from another of mere Grace Endeavor that he which gives it have no reasonable cause to repent him of his good will.* For no man gives but with intention of Good to himself, because Gift is Voluntary, and of all Voluntary Acts, the object is to every man his own Good, of which if men see they shall be frustrated, there will be no beginning of benevolence, or trust, nor consequently of mutual help, nor of reconciliation of one man to another; and therefore they are to remain still in the condition of *War,* which is contrary to the first and Fundamental Law of Nature, which commandeth men to *seek Peace.* The breach of this Law is called Ingratitude and hath the same relation to Grace that Injustice hath to Obligation by Covenant.

A fifth Law of Nature is *Complaisance*—that is to say, *That every man strive to accommodate himself to the rest.* For the understanding whereof we may consider that there is in men's aptness to Society a diversity of Nature, rising from their diversity of Affections, not unlike to that we see in stones brought together for building of an Edifice. For as that stone which by the asperity and irregularity of Figure takes more room from others than itself fills and for the hardness cannot be easily made plain and thereby hinders the building is by the builders cast away as unprofitable, and troublesome, so also a man that by asperity of Nature will strive to retain those things which to himself are superfluous and to others necessary and for the stubbornness of his Passions cannot be corrected is to be left or cast out of Society as cumbersome thereunto. For seeing [that] every man, not only by Right but also by necessity of Nature, is supposed to endeavor all he can to obtain that which is necessary for his conservation, He that shall oppose himself against it, for things superfluous, is guilty of the war that thereupon is to follow and therefore does that which is contrary to the fundamental Law of Nature, which commands *to seek Peace.* The observers of this Law may be called *Sociable* (the Latins call them *Commodi*); The contrary, *Stubborn, Unsociable, Forward, Intractable.*

A sixth Law of Nature is this: *That upon caution of the Future time, a man ought to pardon the offenses past of them that, repenting, desire it.* For Pardon is nothing but granting of Peace, which, though [when] granted to them that persevere in their hostility be not Peace but Fear, yet [when] not granted to them that give caution of the Future time is sign of an aversion to Peace and therefore contrary to the Law of Nature.

A seventh is: *That in Revenge* (that is, retribution of Evil for Evil) *Men look not at the greatness of the evil past but the greatness of the good to follow*—whereby we are forbidden to inflict punishment with any other design than for correction of the offender, or direction of others. For this Law is consequent to the next before it, that commands Pardon upon security of the Future time. Besides, Revenge without respect to the Example and profit to come is a triumph or glorying in the hurt of another, tending to no end (for the End is always somewhat to Come); and glorying to no end is vain-glory and contrary to reason; and to hurt without reason tends to the introduction of War, which is against the Law of Nature and is commonly styled by the name of *Cruelty.*

And because all signs of hatred, or contempt, provoke to fight, insomuch as most men choose rather to hazard their life than not to be revenged, we may in the eight place, for a Law of Nature, set down this Precept: *That no Man by deed, word, countenance, or gesture, declare Hatred or Contempt of another*—The breach of which Law is commonly called Contumely.

The question who is the better man has no place in the condition of mere Nature, where (as has been shewn before) all men are equal. The inequality that now is, has been introduced by the civil laws. I know that Aristotle in the first Book of his *Politics,* for a foundation of this doctrine, makes men by Nature some more worthy to command, meaning the wiser sort (such as he thought himself to be for his Philosophy), others to serve (meaning those that had strong bodies but were not Philosophers as he), as if Master and Servant were not introduced by consent of men but by difference of Wit, which is not only against reason but also against experience. For there are very few so foolish that had not rather govern themselves than be governed by others. Nor when the wise in their own conceit contend by force with them who distrust their own wisdom do they always, or often, or almost at any time get the Victory. If Nature therefore has made men equal, that equality is to be acknowledged, or if Nature has made men unequal; yet because men that think themselves equal will not enter into conditions of Peace but upon Equal terms, such equality must be admitted. And therefore for the ninth Law of Nature I put this: *That every man acknowledge another for his Equal by Nature.* The breach of this precept is *Pride.*

On this law, dependeth another: *That at the entrance into conditions of Peace, no man require to reserve to himself any Right which he is not content should be reserved to everyone of the rest.* As it is necessary for all men that seek peace, to lay down certain Rights of Nature—that is to say, not to have liberty to do all they list—so it is necessary for man's life to retain some, as right to govern their own bodies, enjoy air, water, motion, ways to go from place to place, and all things else without which a man cannot live, or not live well. If in this case, at the making of Peace, men require for themselves that which they would not have to be granted to others, they do contrary to the precedent Law that commands the acknowledgement of natural equality and therefore also against the Law of Nature. The observers of this law are those we call *Modest*, and the breakers, *Arrogant* men. The Greeks call the violation of this law πλεονεξια—that is, a desire of more than their share.

Also if *a man be trusted to judge between man and man*, it is a precept of the Law of Nature *that he deal Equally* between them. For without that, the Controversies of men cannot be determined but by War. He therefore that is partial in judgment does what in him lies to deter men from the use of Judges and Arbitrators and consequently (against the fundamental Law of Nature) is the cause of War.

The observance of this Law, from the equal distribution to each man of that which is reason belongs to him, is called *Equity*, and (as I have said before) distributive Justice; the violation, *Acception of persons*.

And from this follows another law: *That such things as cannot be divided be enjoyed in Common, if it can be, and if the quantity of the thing permit, without Stint; otherwise Proportionately to the number of them that have Right*. For otherwise the distribution is Unequal, and contrary to Equity. . . .

These are the Laws of Nature, dictating Peace, for a means of the conservation of men in multitudes, and which only concern the doctrine of Civil Society. There are other things tending to the destruction of particular men, as Drunkenness and all other parts of Intemperature, which may therefore also be reckoned among those things which the Law of Nature hath forbidden, but are not necessary to be mentioned nor are pertinent enough to this place.

And though this may seem too subtle a deduction of the Laws of Nature to be taken notice of by all men, whereof the most part are too busy in getting food and the rest too negligent to understand, yet to leave all men unexcusable, they have been contracted into one easy sum, intelligible even to the meanest capacity; and that is: *Do not that to another which thou would not have done to thy self;* which shows him that he has no more to do in learning the Laws of Nature but when, weighing the actions of other men with his own, they seem too heavy, to put them into the other part of the balance and his own into their place, that his own passions and self-love may add nothing to the weight; and then there is none of these Laws of Nature that will not appear unto him very reasonable.

The Laws of Nature oblige in *foro interno*—that is to say, they bind to a desire they should take place; but *in foro externo*—that is, to the putting them in act—not always. For he that should be modest and tractable and perform all the promises in such time

and place where no man else should do so, should but make himself a prey to others and produce his own certain ruin, contrary to the ground of all Laws of Nature, which tend to Nature's preservation. And again, he that, having sufficient Security that others shall observe the same Laws towards him, observes them not himself, seeks not Peace but War and consequently the destruction of his Nature by Violence. . . .

The Laws of Nature are Immutable and Eternal, For Injustice, Ingratitude, Arrogance, Pride, Iniquity, Acception of persons, and the rest can never be made lawful. For it can never be that War shall preserve life, and Peace destroy it.

The (same) Laws, because they oblige only to a desire and endeavor—I mean an unfeigned and constant endeavor—are easy to be observed. For in that they require nothing but endeavor, he that endeavors their performance, fulfills them; and he that fulfills the Law, is Just.

And the Science of them is the true and only Moral Philosophy, For Moral Philosophy is nothing else but the Science of what is *Good* and *Evil* in the conversation and Society of mankind. *Good* and *Evil* are names that signify our Appetites and Aversions, which in different tempers, costumes, and doctrines of men are different. And divers men differ not only in their Judgment on the senses of what is pleasant and unpleasant to the taste, smell, hearing, touch, and sight, but also of what is conformable or disagreeable to Reason in the actions of common Life. Nay, the same man in divers times differs from himself; and one time praises—that is, calls Good—what another time he dispraises and calls Evil, from whence arise disputes, Controversies, and at last War. And therefore so long as man is in the condition of mere Nature, (which is a condition of War) as private Appetite is the measure of Good and Evil. And consequently all men agree on this, that Peace is Good, and therefore also the way or means of Peace, which (as I have showed before) are *Justice, Gratitude, Modesty, Equity, Mercy,* & the rest of the Laws of Nature, are good—that is to say, *Moral Virtues*—and their contrary *Vices*, Evil. Now the science of Virtue and Vice is Moral Philosophy; and therefore the true doctrine of the Laws of Nature is the true Moral Philosophy. But the writers of Moral Philosophy, though they acknowledge the same Virtues and Vices, yet not seeing wherein consist their Goodness nor that they come to be praised as the means of peaceable, sociable, and comfortable living, place them in a mediocrity of passions, as if not the

Cause but the Degree of daring made Fortitude, or not the Cause, but the quantity of a gift, made Liberality.

These dictates of Reason men used to call by the name of Laws, but improperly, for they are but Conclusions or Theorems concerning what conduces to the conservation and defense of themselves; whereas Law properly is the word of him that by right has command over others. But yet if we consider the same Theorems as delivered in the word of God, that by right commandeth all things, then are they properly called Laws.

Writing and Discussion Topics

Questions 1–6 address content, critical analysis, personal choices, ethical options, specific discipline, and interdisciplinary alternatives, respectively.

1. Why does Hobbes believe that, in a state of nature, the life of man is "solitary, poor, nasty, brutish, and short"?

2. In Hobbes's theory, when people create a state, they form a compact. As part of the compact, they must submit absolutely to the sovereign. Why is the sovereign important in this state?

3. You are living in Hobbes's century. You have just come out of feudalism and you are finally given some freedom. If a group of individuals were to take some of your possessions, would you be more inclined to be at war with these people or to solve the problem peacefully? What does Hobbes suggest?

4. Why could this ethic be termed the beginning of a social contract ethic? Examine which of Hobbes's principles give rights and equality to individuals.

5. Examine some of the reasons that Hobbes gives for war and the avoidance of war. Which of these reasons still apply in today's world?

6. Compare and contrast Hobbes's philosophy on the nature of man with that of Christian teachings.

Immanuel Kant

THE CATEGORICAL IMPERATIVE

◆◆◆

I mmanuel Kant (1724–1804) was a Prussian and a Pietist. His life
was spent in the East Prussian port city of Königsberg. He was a
professor of logic and metaphysics and achieved wide renown through his
writings and teachings. In 1781, he published The Critique of Pure
Reason; *in 1785,* Foundations of The Metaphysics of Morals *was*
published. The reading that follows is from this short text. He next wrote
The Critique of Practical Reason *in 1788, and in 1790,* The Critique
of Judgment. *The results of Kant's works are incalculable. His theories*
have been influential in philosophy, science, psychology, and religion. All
of his important works have been translated into English and other
languages. ◆

Part One

Nothing in the whole world, or even outside of the world, can possibly be regarded as good without limitation except a *good will*. No doubt it is a good and desirable thing to have intelligence, sagacity, judgment, and other intellectual gifts, by whatever name they may be called; it is also good and desirable in many respects to possess by nature such qualities as courage, resolution, and perseverance; but all these gifts of nature may be in the highest degree pernicious and hurtful, if the will which directs them, or what is called the *character*, is not itself good. The same thing applies to *gifts of fortune*. Power, wealth, honour, even good health, and that general well-being and contentment with one's lot which we call *happiness*, give rise to pride and not infrequently to insolence, if a man's will is not good; nor can a reflective and impartial spectator ever look with satisfaction upon the unbroken prosperity of a man who is destitute of the ornament of a pure and good will. A good will would therefore seem to be the indispensable condition without which no one is even worthy to be happy.

A man's will is good, not because the consequences which flow from it are good, nor because it is capable of attaining the end which it seeks, but it is good in itself, or because it wills the good. By a good will is not meant mere well-wishing; it consists in a resolute employment of all the means within one's reach, and its intrinsic value is in no way increased by success or lessened by failure.

This idea of the absolute value of mere will seems to extraordinary that, although it is endorsed even by the popular judgment, we must subject it to careful scrutiny.

If nature had meant to provide simply for the maintenance, the well-being, in a word the happiness, of beings which have reason and will, it must be confessed that, in making use of their reason, it has hit upon a very poor way of attaining its end. As a matter of fact the very worst way a man of refinement and culture can take to secure enjoyment and happiness is to make use of his reason for that purpose. Hence there is apt to arise in his mind a certain degree of *misology*, or hatred of reason. Finding that the arts which minister to luxury, and even the sciences, instead of bringing him happiness, only lay a heavier yoke on his neck, he at length comes to envy, rather than to despise, men of less refinement, who follow more closely the promptings of their nat-

ural impulses, and pay little heed to what reason tells them to do or to leave undone. It must at least be admitted, that one may deny reason to have much or indeed any value in the production of happiness and contentment, without taking a morose or ungrateful view of the goodness with which the world is governed. Such a judgment really means that life has another and a much nobler end than happiness, and that the true vocation of reason is to secure that end.

The true object of reason then, in so far as it is practical, or capable of influencing the will, must be to produce a will which is *good in itself*, and not merely good *as a means* to something else. This will is not the only or the whole good, but it is the highest good, and the condition of all other good, even of the desire for happiness itself. It is therefore not inconsistent with the wisdom of nature that the cultivation of reason which is essential to the furtherance of its first and unconditioned object, the production of a good will, should, in this life at least, in many ways limit, or even make impossible, the attainment of happiness, which is its second and conditioned object.

To bring to clear consciousness the conception of a will which is good in itself, a conception already familiar to the popular mind, let us examine the conception of *duty*, which involves the idea of a good will as manifested under certain subjective limitations and hindrances.

I pass over actions which are admittedly violations of duty, for these, however useful they may be in the attainment of this or that end, manifestly do not proceed *from* duty. I set aside also those actions which are not actually inconsistent with duty, but which yet are done under the impulse of some natural inclination, although *not a direct inclination* to do these particular actions; for in these it is easy to determine whether the action that is consistent with duty, is done *from duty* or with some selfish object in view. It is more difficult to make a clear distinction of motives when there is a *direct* inclination to do a certain action, which is itself in conformity with duty. The preservation of one's own life, for instance, is a duty; but, as everyone has a natural inclination to preserve his life, the anxious care which most men usually devote to this object, has no intrinsic value, nor the maxim from which they act any moral import. They preserve their life *in accordance with* duty, but not *because of* duty. But, suppose adversity and hopeless sorrow to have taken away all desire for life; suppose that the wretched man would welcome death as a release, and yet takes means to prolong his life simply from a sense of duty; then his maxim has a genuine moral import.

Source: *The Philosophy of Kant: As Contained in Extracts From His Own Writings.* Copyright © 1927 Jackson, Wylie & Co., Glasgow, Scotland.

But, secondly, an action that is done from duty gets its moral value, *not from the object* which it is intended to secure, but from the maxim by which it is determined. Accordingly, the action has the same moral value whether the object is attained or not, if only the *principle* by which the will is determined to act is independent of every object of sensuous desire. What was said above makes it clear, that it is not the object aimed at, or, in other words, the consequences which flow from an action when these are made the end and motive of the will, that can give to the action an unconditioned and moral value. In what, then, can the moral value of an action consist, if it does not lie in the will itself, as directed to the attainment of a certain object? It can lie only in the principle of the will, no matter whether the object sought can be attained by the action or not. For the will stands as it were at the parting of the ways, between its *a priori* principle, which is formal, and its *a posteriori* material motive. As so standing it must be determined by something, and, as no action which is done from duty can be determined by a material principle, it can be determined only by the formal principle of all volition.

From the two propositions just set forth a third directly follows, which may be thus stated: *Duty is the obligation to act from reverence for law.* Now, I may have a natural *inclination* for the object that I expect to follow from my action, but I can never have *reverence* for that which is not a spontaneous activity of my will, but merely an effect of it; neither can I have reverence for any natural inclination, whether it is my own or another's. If it is my own, I can at most only approve of it; if it is manifested by another, I may regard it as conducive to my own interest, and hence I may in certain cases even be said to have a love for it. But the only thing which I can reverence or which can lay me under an obligation to act, is the law which is connected with my will, not as a consequence, but as a principle; a principle which is not dependent upon natural inclination, but overmasters it, or at least allows it to have no influence whatever in determining my course of action. Now if an action which is done out of regard for duty sets entirely aside the influence of natural inclination and along with it every object of the will, nothing else is left by which the will can be determined but objectively the *law* itself, and subjectively *pure reverence* for the law as a principle of action. Thus there arises the maxim, to obey the moral law even at the sacrifice of all my natural inclinations.

The supreme good which we call moral can therefore be nothing but the *idea of the law* in itself, in so far as it is this idea which determines the will, and not any consequences that are expected to follow. Only a *rational* being can have such an idea, and hence a man who acts from the idea of the law is already morally good, no matter whether the consequences which he expects from his action follow or not.

Now what must be the nature of a law, the idea of which is to determine the will, even apart from the effects expected to follow, and which is therefore itself entitled to be called good absolutely and without qualification? As the will must not be moved to act from any desire for the results expected to follow from obedience to a certain law, the only principle of the will which remains is that of the conformity of actions to universal law. In all cases I must act in such a way *that I can at the same time will that my maxim should become a universal law.* This is what is meant by conformity to law pure and simple; and this is the principle which serves, and must serve, to determine the will, if the idea of duty is not to be regarded as empty and chimerical. As a matter of fact the judgments which we are wont pass upon conduct perfectly agree with this principle, and in making them we always have it before our eyes.

May I, for instance, under the pressure of circumstances, make a promise which I have no intention of keeping? The question is not, whether it is prudent to make a false promise, but whether it is morally right. To enable me to answer this question shortly and conclusively, the best way is for me to ask myself whether it would satisfy me that the maxim to extricate myself from embarrassment by giving a false promise should have the force of a universal law, applying to others as well as to myself, And I see at once, that, while I can certainly will the lie, I cannot will that lying should be a universal law. If lying were universal, there would, properly speaking, be no promises whatever. I might say that I intended to do a certain thing at some future time, but nobody would believe me, or if he did at the moment trust to my promise, he would afterwards pay me back in my own coin. My maxim thus proves itself to be self-destructive, so soon as it is taken as a universal law.

Duty, then, consists in the obligation to act from *pure* reverence for the moral law. To this motive all others must give way, for it is the condition of a will which is good *in itself,* and which has a value with which nothing else is comparable.

There is, however, in man a strong feeling of antagonism to the commands of duty, although his reason tells him that those commands are worthy of the highest reverence. For man not only possesses reason, but he has certain natural wants and inclinations, the complete satisfaction of which he calls happiness. These natural inclinations clamorously demand to have their seemingly reasonable claims respected; but reason issues its commands inflexibly, refusing to promise anything to the natural desires, and treating their claims with a sort of neglect and contempt. From this there arises a *natural dialectic*, that is, a disposition to explain away the strict laws of duty, to cast doubt upon their validity, or at least, upon their purity and stringency, and in this way to make them yield to the demands of the natural inclinations.

Thus men are forced to go beyond the narrow circle of ideas within which their reason ordinarily moves, and to take a step into the field of *moral philosophy*, not indeed from any perception of speculative difficulties, but simply on practical grounds. The practical reason of men cannot be long exercised any more than the theoretical, without falling insensibly into a dialectic, which compels it to call in the aid of philosophy; and in the one case as in the other, rest can be found only in a thorough criticism of human reason.

Part Two

So far, we have drawn our conception of duty from the manner in which men employ it in the ordinary exercise of their practical reason. The conception of duty, however, we must not suppose to be therefore derived from experience. On the contrary, we hear frequent complaints, the justice of which we cannot but admit, that no one can point to a single instance in which an action has undoubtedly been done purely from a regard for duty; that there are certainly many actions which are not *opposed* to duty, but none which are indisputably done *from* duty and therefore have a moral value. Nothing indeed can secure us against the complete loss of our ideas of duty, and maintain in the soul a well-grounded respect for the moral law, but the clear conviction, that reason issues its commands on its own authority, without caring in the least whether the actions of men have, as a matter of fact, been done purely from ideas or duty. For reason commands inflexibly that certain actions should be done, which perhaps never have been done; actions, the very possibility of which may seem doubtful to one who bases everything upon experience. Perfect disinterestedness in friendship, for instance, is demanded of every man, although there may never have been a sincere friend; for pure friendship is bound up with the idea of duty as duty, and belongs to the very idea of a reason which determines the will on *a priori* grounds, prior to all experience.

It is, moreover, beyond dispute, that unless we are to deny to morality all truth and all reference to a possible object, the moral law has so wide an application that it is binding, not merely upon man, but upon all *rational beings,* and not merely under certain contingent conditions, and with certain limitations, but absolutely and necessarily. And it is plain, that no experience could ever lead us to suppose that laws of this apodictic character are even possible.

There is, therefore, no genuine supreme principle of morality, which is not independent of all experience, and based entirely upon pure reason. If, then, we are to have a philosophy of morality at all, as distinguished from a popular moral philosophy, we may take it for granted without further investigation, that moral conceptions, together with the principles which flow from them, are given *a priori* and must be presented in their generality (*in abstracto*).

Such a metaphysic of morality, which must be entirely free from all admixture of empirical psychology, theology, physics and hyperphysics, and above all from all occult or, as we may call them, hypophysical qualities, is not only indispensable as a foundation for a sound theory of duties, but it is also of the highest importance in the practical realization of moral precepts. For the pure idea of duty, unmixed with any foreign ingredient of sensuous desire, in a word, the idea of the moral law, influences the heart of man much more powerfully through his reason, which in this way only becomes conscious that it can of itself be practical, than do all the motives which have their source in experience. Conscious of its own dignity, the moral law treats all sensuous desires with contempt, and is able to master them one by one.

From what has been said it is evident, that all moral conceptions have their seat and origin in reason entirely *a priori*, and are apprehended by the ordinary reason of men as well as by reason in its purely speculative activity. We have also seen that it is of the greatest importance, not only in the construction by speculative reason of a theory of morality, but also with a view to the practical conduct of life, to derive the conceptions and laws of morality from pure reason, to present them pure and unmixed, and to mark out the sphere of this whole practical or pure knowledge of reason. Nor is it permissible, in seeking to determine the whole faculty of pure practical reason, to make its principles dependent upon the peculiar nature of human reason, as we were allowed to do, and sometimes were even forced to do, in speculative philosophy; for moral laws must apply to every rational being, and must therefore be derived from the very conception of a rational being as such.

To show the need of advancing not only from the common moral judgments of men to the philosophical, but from a popular philosophy, which merely gropes its way by the help of examples, to a metaphysic of morality, we must begin at the point where the practical faculty of reason supplies general rules of action, and exhibit clearly the steps by which it attains to the conception of duty.

Everything in nature acts in conformity with law. Only a rational being has the faculty of acting in conformity with the *idea* of law, or from principles; only a rational being, in other words, has a will. And as without reason actions cannot proceed from laws, will is simply practical reason. If the will is infallibly determined by reason, the actions of a rational being are subjectively as well as objectively necessary; that is, will must be regarded as a faculty of choosing *that only* which reason, independently of natural inclination, declares to be practically necessary or good. On the other hand, if the will is not invariably determined by reason alone, but is subject to certain subjective conditions or motives, which are not always in harmony with the objective conditions; if the will, as actually is the case with *man*, is not in perfect conformity with reason; actions which are recognized to be objectively necessary, are subjectively contingent. The determination of such a will according to objective laws is therefore called *obligation*. That is to say, if the will of a rational being is not absolutely good, we conceive of it as capable of being determined by objective laws of reason, but not as by its very nature necessarily obeying them.

The idea that a certain principle is objective, and binding upon the will, is a command of reason, and the statement of the command in a formula is an *imperative*.

All imperatives are expressed by the word *ought*, to indicate that the will upon which they are binding is not by its subjective constitution necessarily determined in conformity with the objective law of reason. An imperative says, that the doing, or leaving undone of a certain thing would be good, but it addresses a will which does not always do a thing simply because it is good. Now, that is practically *good* which determines the will by ideas of reason, in other words, that which determines it, not by subjective influences, but by principles which are objective, or apply to all rational beings as such. *Good* and *pleasure* are quite distinct. Pleasure results from the influence of purely subjective causes upon the will of the subject, and these vary with the susceptibility of this or that individual while a principle of reason is valid for all.

A perfectly good will would, like the will of man, stand under objective laws, laws of the good, but it could not be said to be under an *obligation* to act in conformity with those laws. Such a will by its subjective constitution could be determined only by the idea of the good. In reference to the Divine will, or any other holy will, imperatives have no meaning; for here the will is by its very nature necessarily in harmony with the law, and therefore *ought* has no application to it. Imperatives are formulae, which express merely the relation of objective laws of volition in general to the imperfect will of this or that rational being, as for instance, the will of man.

Now, all imperatives command either *hypothetically* or *categorically*. A hypothetical imperative states that a certain thing must be done, if something else which is willed, or at least might be willed, is to be attained. The categorical imperative declares that an act is in itself or objectively necessary, without any reference to another end.

Every practical law represents a possible action as good, and therefore as obligatory for a subject that is capable of being determined to act by reason. Hence all imperatives are formulae for the determination of an action which is obligatory according to the principle of a will that is in some sense good. If the action is good only because it is a means to *something else*, the imperative is *hypothetical*; if the action is conceived to be good *in itself*, the imperative, as the necessary principle of a will that in itself conforms to reason, is *categorical*.

An imperative, then, states what possible action of mine would be good. It supplies the practical rule for a will which does not at once do an act simply because it is good, either because the subject does not know it to be good, or because, knowing it to be good, he is influenced by maxims which are opposed to the objective principles of a practical reason.

The hypothetical imperative says only that an action is good relatively to a certain *possible* end or to a certain *actual* end. In the former case it is *problematic*, in the latter case *assertoric*. The categorical imperative, which affirms that an action is in itself or objectively necessary without regard to an end, that is, without regard to any other end than itself, is an *apodictic* practical principle.

Whatever is within the power of a rational being may be conceived to be capable of being willed by some rational being, and hence the principles which determine what actions are necessary in the attainment of certain possible ends, are infinite in number.

Yet there is one thing which we may assume that all finite rational beings actually make their end, and there is therefore one object which may safely be regarded, not simply as something that they *may* seek, but as something that by a necessity of their nature they actually *do* seek. This object is *happiness*. The hypothetical imperative, which affirms the practical necessity of an action as the means of attaining happiness, is *assertoric*. We must not think of happiness as simply a possible and problematic end, but as an end that we may with confidence presuppose *a priori* to be sought by everyone, belonging as it does to the very nature of man. Now skill in the choice of means to his own greatest well-being may be called *prudence*, taking the word in its more restricted sense. An imperative, therefore, which relates merely to the choice of means to one's own happiness, that is, a maxim of prudence, must be hypothetical; it commands an action, not absolutely, but only as a means to another end.

Lastly, there is an imperative which directly commands an action, without presupposing as its condition that some other end is to be attained by means of that action. This imperative is *categorical*. It has to do, not with the matter of an action and the result expected to follow from it, but simply with the form and principle from which the action itself proceeds. The action is essentially good if the motive of the agent is good, let the consequences be what they may. This imperative may be called the imperative of *morality*.

How are all these imperatives possible? The question is not, How is an action which an imperative commands actually realized? but, How can we think of the will as placed under obligation by each of those imperatives? Very little need be said to show how an imperative of skill is possible. He who wills the end, wills also the means in his power which are indispensable to the attainment of the end. Looking simply at the act of will, we must say that this proposition is analytic. If a certain object is to follow as an effect from my volition, my causality must be conceived as active in the production of the effect, or as employing the means by which the effect will take place. The imperative, therefore, simply states that in the conception of the willing of this end there is directly implied the conception of actions necessary to this end. No doubt certain synthetic propositions are required to determine the particular means by which a given end may be attained, but these have nothing to do with the principle or act of the will, but merely state how the object may actually be realized.

Were it as easy to give a definite conception of happiness as of a particular end, the imperatives of prudence would be of exactly the same nature as the imperatives of skill, and would therefore be analytic. For, we should be able to say, that he who wills the end wills also the only means in his power for the attainment of the end. But, unfortunately, the conception of happiness is so indefinite, that, although every man desires to obtain it, he is unable to give a definite and self-consistent statement of what he actually desires and wills. The truth is, that, strictly speaking, the imperatives of prudence are not commands at all. They do not say that actions are objective or *necessary*, and hence they must be regarded as counsels (*consilia*), not as commands (*praecepta*) of reason. Still, the imperative of prudence would be an analytic proposition, if the means to happiness could only be known with certainty. For the only difference in the two cases is that in the imperative of skill the end is merely possible, in the imperative of prudence it is actually given; and as in both all that is commanded is the means to an end which is assumed to be willed, the imperative which commands that he who wills the end should also will the means, is in both cases analytic. There is therefore no real difficulty in seeing how an imperative of prudence is possible.

The only question which is difficult of solution, is, how the imperative of morality is possible. Here the imperative is not hypothetical, and hence we cannot derive its objective necessity from any presupposition. Nor must it for a moment be forgotten, that an imperative of this sort cannot be established by instances taken from experience. We must therefore find out by careful investigation, whether imperatives which seem to be categorical may not be simply hypothetical imperatives in disguise.

One thing is plain at the very outset, namely, that only a categorical imperative can have the dignity of a practical *law*, and that the other imperatives, while they may no doubt be called *principles* of the will, cannot be called laws. An action which is necessary merely as a means to an arbitrary end, may be regarded as itself contingent, and if the end is abandoned, the maxim which prescribes the action has no longer any force. An unconditioned command, on the other hand, does not permit the will to choose the opposite, and therefore it carries with it the necessity which is essential to a law.

It is, however, very hard to see how there can be a categorical imperative or law of morality at all. Such a law is an *a priori* synthetic proposition, and we cannot expect that there will be less difficulty in showing how a proposition of that sort is possible in the sphere of morality than we have found it to be in the sphere of knowledge.

In attempting to solve this problem, we shall first of all inquire, whether the mere conception of a categorical imperative may not perhaps supply us with a formula, which contains the only proposition that can possibly be a categorical imperative. The more difficult question, how such an absolute command is possible at all, will require a special investigation, which must be postponed to the last section.

If I take the mere conception of a hypothetical imperative, I cannot tell what it may contain until the condition under which it applies is presented to me. But I can tell at once from the very conception of a categorical imperative what it must contain. Viewed, apart from the law, the imperative simply affirms that the maxim, or subjective principle of action, must conform to the objective principle or law. Now the law contains no condition to which it is restricted, and hence nothing remains but the statement, that the maxim ought to conform to the universality of the law as such. It is only this conformity to law that the imperative can be said to represent as necessary.

There is therefore but one categorical imperative, which may be thus stated: *Act in conformity with that maxim, and that maxim only, which you can at the same time will to be a universal law.*

Now, if from this single imperative, as from their principle, all imperatives of duty can be derived, we shall at least be able to indicate what we mean by the categorical imperative and what the conception of it implies, although we shall not be able to say whether the conception of duty may not itself be empty.

The universality of the law which governs the succession of events, is what we mean by *nature*, in the most general sense, that is, the existence of things, in so far as their existence is determined in conformity with universal laws. The universal imperative of duty might therefore be put in this way: *Act as if the maxim from which you act were to become through your will a universal law of nature.*

If we attend to what goes on in ourselves in every transgression of a duty, we find, that we do not will that our maxim should become a universal law. We find it in fact impossible to do so, and we really will that the opposite of our maxim should remain a universal law, at the same time that we assume the liberty of making an exception in favour of natural inclination in our own case, or perhaps only for this particular occasion. Hence, if we looked at all cases from the same point of view, that is, from the point of view of reason, we should see that there was here a contradiction in our will. The contradiction is, that a certain principle is admitted to be necessary objectively or as a universal law, and yet is held not to be universal subjectively, but to admit of exceptions. What we do is, to consider our action at one time from the point of view of a will that is in perfect conformity with reason, and at another time from the point of view of a will that is under the influence of natural inclination. There is, therefore, here no real contradiction, but merely an antagonism of inclination to the command of reason. The universality of the principle is changed into a mere generality, in order that the practical principle of reason may meet the maxim half way. Not only is this limitation condemned by our own impartial judgment, but it proves that we actually recognize the validity of the categorical imperative, and merely allow ourselves to make a few exceptions in our own favour which we try to consider as of no importance, or as a necessary concession to circumstances.

This much at least we have learned, that if the idea of duty is to have any meaning and to lay down the laws of our actions, it must be expressed in categorical and not in hypothetical imperatives. We have also obtained a clear and distinct conception (a very important thing) of what is implied in a categorical imperative which contains the principle of duty for all cases, granting such an imperative to be possible at all. But we have not yet been able to prove *a priori*, that there actually is such an imperative; that there is a practical law which commands absolutely on its own authority, and is independent of all sensuous impulses; and that duty consists in obedience to this law.

In seeking to reach this point, it is of the greatest importance to observe, that the reality of this principle cannot possibly be derived from the *peculiar constitution of human nature.* For by duty is meant the practically unconditioned necessity of an act, and hence we can show that duty is a law for the will of all human beings, only by showing that it is applicable to all rational beings, or rather to all rational beings to whom an imperative applies at all.

The question, then, is this: Is it a necessary law *for all rational beings* that they must always estimate the value of their actions by asking whether they can will that their maxims should serve as universal laws? If there is such a law, it must be possible to prove entirely *a priori*, that it is bound up with the very idea of the will of a rational being. To show that there is such a connection we must, however reluctantly, take a step into the realm of metaphysic; not, however, into the realm of speculative philosophy, but into the metaphysic of morality. For we have here to deal with objective practical laws, and therefore with the relation of the will to itself, in so far as is it determined purely by reason. All relation of the will to what is empirical is excluded as a matter of course, for if reason determines the relation *entirely by itself*, it must necessarily do so *a priori*.

Will is conceived of as a faculty of determining itself to action *in accordance with the idea of certain laws.* Such a faculty can belong only to a rational being. Now that which serves as an objective principle for the self-determination of the will is an *end*, and if this end is given purely by reason, it must hold for all rational beings. On the other hand, that which is merely the condition of the possibility of an action the effect of which is the end, is called the *means.* The subjective ground of desire is natural inclination, the objective ground of volition is a motive; hence there is a distinction between subjective ends, which depend upon natural inclination, and objective ends, which are connected with motives that hold for every rational being. Practical principles that abstract from all subjective ends are *formal*; those that presuppose subjective ends, and therefore natural inclinations, are *material*. The ends which a rational being arbitrarily sets before himself as material ends to be produced by his actions, are all merely relative; for that which gives to them their value is simply their relation to the peculiar susceptibility of the subject. They can therefore yield no universal and necessary principles, or practical laws, applicable to all rational beings, and binding upon every will. Upon such relative ends, therefore, only hypothetical imperatives can be based.

Suppose, however, that there is something the existence of which has in itself an absolute value, something which, *as an end in itself*, can be a ground of definite laws; then, there would lie in that, and only in that, the ground of a possible categorical imperative or practical law.

Now, I say, that man, and indeed every rational being in such, *exists* as an end in himself, *not merely as a means* to be made use of by this or that will, and therefore man in all his actions, whether these are directed towards himself or towards other rational beings, must always be regarded as an end. No object of natural desire has more than a conditioned value; for if the natural desires, and the wants to which they give rise, did not exist, the object to which they are directed would have no value at all. So far are the natural desires and wants from having an absolute value, so far are they from being sought simply for themselves, that every rational being must wish to be entirely free from their influence. The value of every object which human action is the means of obtaining, is, therefore, always conditioned. And even beings whose existence depends upon nature, not upon our will, if they are without reason, have only the relative value of means, and are therefore called *things.* Rational beings, on the other hand, are called *persons*, because their very nature shows them to be ends in themselves, that is, something which cannot be made use of simply as a means. A person being thus an object of respect, a certain limit is placed upon arbitrary will. Persons are not purely subjective ends, whose existence has a value *for us* as the effect of our actions, but they are *objective ends*, or beings whose existence is an end in itself, for which no other end can be substituted. If all value were conditioned, and therefore contingent, it would be impossible to show that there is any supreme practical principle whatever.

If, then, there is a supreme practical principle, a principle which in relation to the human will is a categorical imperative, it must be an *objective* principle of the will, and must be able to serve as a universal practical law. For, such a principle must be derived from the idea of that which is necessarily an end for every one because it is an *end in itself.* Its foundation is this, that *rational nature exists as an end in itself.* Man necessarily conceives of his own existence in this way, and so far this is a *subjective* principle of human action. But in this way also every other rational being conceives of his own existence, and for the very same reason; hence the principle is also *objective*, and from it, as the highest practical ground, all laws of the will must be capable of being derived. The practical imperative will therefore be this: *Act so as to use humanity, whether in your own person or in the person of another, always as an end, never as merely a means.*

The principle, that humanity and every rational nature is an end in itself, is not borrowed from experience. For, in the first place, because of its universality it applies to all rational beings, and no experience can apply so widely. In the second place, it does not regard humanity subjectively, as an end of man, that is, as an object which the subject of himself actually makes his end, but as an objective end, which ought to be regarded as a law that constitutes the supreme limiting condition of all subjective ends, and which must therefore have its source in pure reason. The objective ground of all practical laws consists in the *rule* and the form of universality, which makes them capable of serving as laws, but their *subjective* ground consists in the *end* to which they are directed. Now, by the second principle, every rational being, as an end in himself, is the subject of all ends. From this follows the third practical principle of the will, which is the supreme condition of its harmony with universal practical reason, namely, the idea of *the will of every rational being as a will which lays down universal laws of action.*

This formula implies, that a will which is itself the supreme lawgiver cannot possibly act from interest of any sort in the law, although no doubt a will may stand under the law, and may yet be attached to it by the bond of interest.

At the point we have now reached, it does not seem surprising that all previous attempts to find out the principle of morality should have ended in failure. It was seen that man is bound under law by duty, but it did not strike anyone, that the *universal* system of laws to which he is subject are laws which he *imposes upon himself,* and that he is only under obligation to act in conformity with his own will, a will which by the purpose of nature prescribes universal laws. Now so long as man is thought to be merely subject to law, no matter what the law may be, he must be regarded as stimulated or constrained to obey the law from interest of some kind; for as the law does not proceed from *his own* will, there must be *something external* to his will which compels him to act in conformity with it. This perfectly necessary conclusion frustrated every attempt to find a supreme principle of duty. Duty was never established,

but merely the necessity of acting from some form of interest, private or public. The imperative was therefore necessarily always conditioned, and could not possibly have the force of a moral command. The supreme principle of morality I shall therefore call the principle of the *autonomy* of the will, to distinguish it from all other principles, which I call principles of *heteronomy.*

The conception that every rational being in all the maxims of his will must regard himself as prescribing universal laws, by reference to which himself and all his actions are to be judged, leads to a cognate and very fruitful conception, that of a *kingdom of ends.*

By *kingdom,* I mean the systematic combination of different rational beings through the medium of common laws. Now, laws determine certain ends as universal, and hence, if abstraction is made from the individual differences of rational beings, and from all that is peculiar to their private ends, we get the idea of a complete totality of ends combined in a system; in other words, we are able to conceive of a kingdom of ends, which conforms to the principles formulated above.

All rational beings stand under the law, that each should treat himself and others, *never simply as means,* but always as *at the same time ends in themselves.* Thus there arises a systematic combination of rational beings through the medium of common objective laws. This may well be called a kingdom of ends, because the object of those laws is just to relate all rational beings to one another as ends and means. Of course this kingdom of ends is merely an ideal.

Morality, then, consists in the relation of all action to the system of laws which alone makes possible a kingdom of ends. These laws must belong to the nature of every rational being, and must proceed from his own will. The principle of the will, therefore, is, that no action should be done from any other maxim than one which is consistent with a universal law. This may be expressed in the formula: *Act so that the will may regard itself as in its maxims laying down universal laws.* Now, if the maxims of rational beings are not by their very nature in harmony with this objective principle, the principle of a universal system of laws, the necessity of acting in conformity with that principle is called practical obligation or *duty.* No doubt duty does not apply to the sovereign will in the kingdom of ends, but it applies to every member of it, and to all in equal measure. *Autonomy* is thus the foundation of the moral value of man and of every other rational being.

The three ways in which the principle of morality has been formulated are at bottom simply different statements of the same law, and each implies the other two.

An absolutely good will, then, the principle of which must be a categorical imperative, will be undetermined as regards all objects, and will contain merely the *form of volition* in general, a form which rests upon the *autonomy* of the will. The one law which the will of every rational being imposes upon itself, and imposes without reference to any natural impulse or any interest, is, that the maxims of every good will must be capable of being made a universal law.

Writing and Discussion Topics

Questions 1–6 address content, critical analysis, personal choices, ethical options, specific discipline, and interdisciplinary alternatives, respectively.

1. What is the "categorical imperative"? What are the differences between a categorical imperative and a hypothetical imperative?
2. Why does Kant think that moral and natural laws are not incompatible? How could this be the thesis for this excerpt?
3. Kant says it is never acceptable to lie. Can you think of a situation in which it may be acceptable to lie? Do you agree with Kant's stand on lying?
4. What is a duty? How is Kant's ethical theory based on what one "ought" to do?
5. What are the three forms of the categorical imperative? Explain the importance of each. Are any of these similar to Jesus' admonition, "Do unto others as you would have them do unto you"? Explain.
6. How are religious commandments different from Kant's categorical imperative?

SOCIAL BENEFIT

John Stuart Mill (1806–1873) was an English philosopher and economist. He was educated privately by his father, James Mill. In 1823 he abandoned the study of law and began exploring political reform and philosophy. He is best known as an ethicist in his writings, On Liberty and Utilitarianism. While married to Harriet Taylor, he wrote On the Subjugation of Women. He constantly advocated political and social changes such as proportional representation, emancipation of women, and the development of labor organizations and farm cooperatives. This piece is from Utilitarianism. ♦

What Utilitarianism Is

The creed which accepts as the foundation of morals, Utility, or the Greatest Happiness Principle, holds that actions are right in proportion as they tend to promote happiness, wrong as they tend to produce the reverse of happiness. By happiness is intended pleasure, and the absence of pain; by unhappiness, pain, and the privation of pleasure. To give a clear view of the moral standard set up by the theory, much more requires to be said; in particular, what things it includes in the ideas of pain and pleasure; and to what extent this is felt an open question. But these supplementary explanations do not affect the theory of life on which this theory of morality is grounded—namely, that pleasure, and freedom from pain, are the only things desirable as ends; and that all desirable things (which are as numerous in the utilitarian as in any other scheme) are desirable either for the pleasure inherent in themselves, or as means to the promotion of pleasure and the prevention of pain.

Now, such a theory of life excites in many minds, and among them in some of the most estimable in feeling and purpose, inveterate dislike. To suppose that life has (as they express it) no higher end than pleasure—no better and nobler object of desire and pursuit—they designate as utterly mean and grovelling: as a doctrine worthy only of swine, to whom the followers of Epicurus were, at a very early period, contemptuously likened; and modern holders of the doctrine are occasionally made the subject of equally polite comparisons by its German, French, and English assailants.

When thus attacked, the Epicureans have always answered, that it is not they, but their accusers, who represent human nature in a degrading light; since the accusation supposes human beings to be capable of no pleasures except those of which swine are capable. If this supposition were true, the charge could not be gainsaid, but would then be no longer an imputation: for if the sources of pleasure were precisely the same to human beings and to swine, the rule of life which is good enough for the one would be good enough for the other. The comparison of the Epicurean life to that of beasts is felt as degrading, precisely because a beast's pleasures do not satisfy a human being's conceptions of happiness. Human beings have faculties more elevated than the animal appetites, and when once made conscious of them, do not regard anything as happiness which does not

include their gratification. I do not, indeed, consider the Epicureans to have been by any means faultless in drawing out their scheme of consequences from the utilitarian principle. To do this in any sufficient manner, many Stoic, as well as Christian elements require to be included. But there is no known Epicurean theory of life which does not assign to the pleasures of the intellect, of the feelings and imagination, and of the moral sentiments, a much higher value as pleasures than to those of mere sensation. It must be admitted, however, that utilitarian writers in general have placed the superiority of mental over bodily pleasures chiefly in the greater permanency, safety, uncostliness, &c., of the former—that is, in their circumstantial advantages rather than in their intrinsic nature. And on all these points utilitarians have fully proved their case; but they might have taken the other, and, as it may be called, higher ground, with entire consistency. It is quite compatible with the principle of utility to recognise the fact, that some *kinds* of pleasure are more desirable and more valuable than others. It would be absurd that while, in estimating all other things, quality is considered as well as quantity, the estimation of pleasures should be supposed to depend on quantity alone.

If I am asked, what I mean by difference of quality in pleasures, or what makes one pleasure more valuable than another, merely as a pleasure, except its being greater in amount, there is but one possible answer. Of two pleasures, if there be one to which all or almost all who have experience of both give a decided preference, irrespective of any feeling of moral obligation to prefer it, that is the more desirable pleasure. If one of the two is, by those who are competently acquainted with both, placed so far above the other that they prefer it, even though knowing it to be attended with a greater amount of discontent, and would not resign it for any quantity of the other pleasure which their nature is capable of, we are justified in ascribing to the preferred enjoyment a superiority in quality, so far outweighing quantity as to render it, in comparison, of small account.

Now it is an unquestionable fact that those who are equally acquainted with, and equally capable of appreciating and enjoying, both, do give a most marked preference to the manner of existence which employs their higher faculties. Few human creatures would consent to be changed into any of the lower animals, for a promise of the fullest allowance of a beast's pleasures; no intelligent human being would consent to be a fool, no instructed person would be

---

Source: John Stuart Mill, *Social Benefit.*

an ignoramus, no person of feeling and conscience would be selfish and base, even though they should be persuaded that the fool, the dunce, or the rascal is better satisfied with his lot than they are with theirs. They would not resign what they possess more than he, for the most complete satisfaction of all the desires which they have in common with him. If they ever fancy they would, it is only in cases of unhappiness so extreme, that to escape from it they would exchange their lot for almost any other, however undesirable in their own eyes. A being of higher faculties requires more to make him happy, is capable probably of more acute suffering, and is certainly accessible to it at more points, than one of an inferior type; but in spite of these liabilities, he can never really wish to sink into what he feels to be a lower grade of existence. We may give what explanation we please of this unwillingness; we may attribute it to pride, a name which is given indiscriminately to some of the most and to some of the least estimable feelings of which mankind are capable; we may refer it to the love of liberty and personal independence, an appeal to which was with the Stoics one of the most effective means for the inculcation of it; to the love of power, or to the love of excitement, both of which do really enter into and contribute to it: but its most appropriate appellation is a sense of dignity, which all human beings possess in one form or another, and in some, though by no means in exact, proportion to their higher faculties, and which is so essential a part of the happiness of those in whom it is strong, that nothing which conflicts with it could be, otherwise than momentarily, an object of desire to them. Whoever supposes that this preference takes place at a sacrifice of happiness—that the superior being, in anything like equal circumstances, is not happier than the inferior—confounds the two very different ideas, of happiness, and content. It is indisputable that the being whose capacities of enjoyment are low, has the greatest chance of having them fully satisfied; and a highly-endowed being will always feel that any happiness which he can look for, as the world is constituted, is imperfect. But he can learn to bear its imperfections, if they are at all bearable; and they will not make him envy the being who is indeed unconscious of the imperfections, but only because he feels not at all the good which those imperfections qualify. It is better to be a human being dissatisfied than a pig satisfied; better to be Socrates dissatisfied than a fool satisfied. And if the fool, or the pig, is of a different opinion, it is because they only know their own side of the question. The other party to the comparison knows both sides.

It may be objected, that many who are capable of the higher pleasures, occasionally, under the influence of temptation, postpone them to the lower. But this is quite compatible with a full appreciation of the intrinsic superiority of the higher. Men often, from infirmity of character, make their election for the nearer good, though they know it to be the less valuable; and this no less when the choice is between two bodily pleasures, than when it is between bodily and mental. They pursue sensual indulgences to the injury of health, though perfectly aware that health is the greater good. It may be further objected, that many who begin with youthful enthusiasm for everything noble, as they advance in years sink into indolence and selfishness. But I do not believe that those who undergo this very common change, voluntarily choose the lower description of pleasures in preference to the higher. I believe that before they devote themselves exclusively to the one, they have already become incapable of the other. Capacity for the nobler feelings is in most natures a very tender plant, easily killed, not only by hostile influences, but by mere want of sustenance; and in the majority of young persons it speedily dies away if the occupations to which their position in life has devoted them, and the society into which it has thrown them, are not favourable to keeping that higher capacity in exercise. Men lose their high aspirations as they lose their intellectual tastes, because they have not time or opportunity for indulging them; and they addict themselves to inferior pleasures, not because they deliberately prefer them, but because they are either the only ones to which they have access, or the only ones which they are any longer capable of enjoying. It may be questioned whether any one who has remained equally susceptible to both classes of pleasures, ever knowingly and calmly preferred the lower; though many, in all ages, have broken down in an ineffectual attempt to combine both.

From this verdict of the only competent judges, I apprehend there can be no appeal. On a question which is the best worth having of two pleasures, or which of two modes of existence is the most grateful to the feelings, apart from its moral attributes and from its consequences, the judgment of those who are qualified by knowledge of both, or, if they differ, that of the majority among them, must be admitted as final. And there needs be the less hesitation to accept this judgment respecting the quality of pleasures, since there is no other tribunal to be referred to even on the question of quantity. What means are there of determining which is the acutest of two pains, or the intensest of two pleasurable sensations, except the general suffrage of those who are familiar with both? Neither pains nor pleasures are homogeneous, and pain is always heterogeneous with pleasure. What is there to decide whether a particular pleasure is worth purchasing at the cost of a particular pain, except the feelings and judgment of the experienced? When, therefore, those feelings and judgment declare the pleasures derived from the higher faculties to be preferable *in kind,* apart from the question of intensity, to those of which the animal nature, disjoined from the higher faculties, is susceptible, they are entitled on this subject to the same regard.

I have dwelt on this point, as being a necessary part of a perfectly just conception of Utility or Happiness, considered as the directive rule of human conduct. But it is by no means an indispensable condition to the acceptance of the utilitarian standard; for that standard is not the agent's own greatest happiness, but the greatest amount of happiness altogether; and if it may possibly be doubted whether a noble character is always the happier for its nobleness, there can be no doubt that it makes other people happier, and that the world in general is immensely a gainer by it. Utilitarianism, therefore, could only attain its end by the general cultivation of nobleness of character, even if each individual were only benefitted by the nobleness of others, and his own, so far as happiness is concerned, were a sheer deduction from the benefit. But the bare enunciation of such an absurdity as this last, renders refutation superfluous.

According to the Greatest Happiness Principle, as above explained, the ultimate end, with reference to and for the sake of which all other things are desirable (whether we are considering our own good or that of other people), is an existence exempt as far as possible from pain, and as rich as possible in enjoyments, both in point of quantity and quality; the test of quality, and the rule for measuring it against quantity, being the preference felt by those who, in their opportunities of experience, to which must be added their habits of self-consciousness and self-observation, are best furnished with the means of comparison. This, being, according to the utilitarian opinion, the end of human action, is necessarily also the standard of morality; which may accordingly be defined, the rules and precepts for human conduct, by the observance of which an existence such as has been described might be, to the greatest extent possible, secured to all mankind, and not to them only, but, so far as the nature of things admits, to the whole sentient creation.

Against the doctrine, however, rises another class of objectors, who say that happiness, in any form, cannot be the rational purpose of human life and action; because, in the first place, it is unattainable: and they contemptuously ask, What right hast thou to be happy? a question which Mr. Carlyle clenches by the addition, What right, a short time ago, hadst thou even *to be?* Next, they say, that men can do *without* happiness; that all noble human beings have felt this, and could not have become noble but by learning the lesson of *Entsagen,* or renunciation; which lesson, thoroughly learnt and submitted to, they affirm to be the beginning and necessary condition of all virtue.

The first of these objections would go to the root of the matter were it well founded; for if no happiness is to be had at all by human beings, the attainment of it cannot be the end of morality, or of any rational conduct. Though, even in that case, something might still be said for the utilitarian theory; since utility includes not solely the pursuit of happiness, but the prevention or mitigation of unhappiness; and if the former aim be chimerical, there will be all the greater scope and more imperative need for the latter, so long at least as mankind think fit to live, and do not take refuge in the simultaneous act of suicide recommended under certain conditions by Novalis. When, however, it is thus positively asserted to be impossible that human life should be happy, the assertion, if not something like verbal quibble, is at least an exaggeration. If by happiness be meant a continuity of highly pleasurable excitement, it is evident enough that this is impossible. A state of exalted pleasure last only moments, or in some cases, and with some intermissions, hours or days, and is the occasional brilliant flash of enjoyment, not its permanent and steady flame. Of this the philosophers who have taught that happiness is the end of life were as fully aware as those who taunt them. The happiness which they meant was not a life of rapture; but moments of such, in an existence made up of few and transitory pains, many and various pleasures, with a decided predominance of the active over the passive, and having as the foundation of the whole, not to expect more from life than it is capable of bestowing. A life thus composed, to those who have been fortunate enough to obtain it, has always appeared worthy of the name of happiness. And such an existence is even now the lot of many, during some considerable portion of their lives. The present wretched education, and wretched social arrangements, are the only real hindrance to its being attainable by almost all.

The objectors perhaps may doubt whether human beings, if taught to consider happiness as the end of life, would be satisfied with such a moderate share of it. But great numbers of mankind have been satisfied with much less. The main constituents of a satisfied life appear to be two, either of which by itself is often found sufficient for the purpose: tranquillity, and excitement. With much tranquillity, many find that they can be content with very little pleasure: with much excitement, many can reconcile themselves to a considerable quantity of pain. There is assuredly no inherent impossibility in enabling even the mass of mankind to unite both; since the two are so far from being incompatible that they are in natural alliance, the prolongation of either being a preparation for, and exciting a wish for, the other. It is only those in whom indolence amounts to a vice, that do not desire excitement after an interval of repose; it is only those in whom the need of excitement is a disease, that feel the tranquillity which follows excitement dull and insipid, instead of pleasurable in direct proportion to the excitement which preceded it. When people who are tolerably fortunate in their outward lot do not find in life sufficient enjoyment to make it valuable to them, the cause generally is, caring for nobody but themselves. To those who have neither public nor private affections, the excitements of life are much curtailed, and in any case dwindle in value as the time approaches when all selfish interests must be terminated by death: while those who leave after them objects of personal affection, and especially those who have also cultivated a fellow-feeling with the collective interests of mankind, retain as lively an interest in life on the eve of death as in the vigour of youth and health. Next to selfishness, the principal cause which makes life unsatisfactory, is want of mental cultivation. A cultivated mind—I do not mean that of a philosopher, but any mind to which the foundations of knowledge have been opened, and which has been taught, in any tolerable degree, to exercise its faculties—finds sources of inexhaustible interest in all that surrounds it; in the objects of nature, the achievements of art, the imaginations of poetry, the incidents of history, the ways of mankind past and present, and their prospects in the future. It is possible, indeed, to become indifferent to all this, and that too without having exhausted a thousandth part of it; but only when one has had from the beginning no moral or human interest in these things and has sought in them only the gratification of curiosity.

Now there is absolutely no reason in the nature of things why an amount of mental culture sufficient to give an intelligent interest in these objects of contemplation, should not be the inheritance of everyone born in a civilised country. As little is there an inherent necessity that any human being should be a selfish egotist, devoid of every feeling or care but those which centre in this own miserable individuality. Something far superior to this is sufficiently common even now, to give ample earnest of what the human species may be made. Genuine private affections, and a sincere interest in the public good, are possible, though in unequal degrees, to every rightly brought up human being. In a world in which there is so much to interest, so much to enjoy, and so much also to correct and improve, everyone who has this moderate amount of moral and intellectual requisites is capable of an existence which may be called enviable, and unless such a person, through bad laws, or subjection to the will of others, is denied the liberty to use the sources of happiness within his reach, he will not fail to find this enviable existence, if he escape the positive evils of life, the great sources of physical and mental suffering—such as indigence, disease, and the unkindness, worthlessness, or premature loss of objects of affection. The main stress of the problem lies, therefore, in the contest with these calamities, from which it is a rare good fortune entirely to escape; which, as things now are cannot be obviated, and often cannot be in any material degree mitigated. Yet no one whose opinion deserves a moment's consideration can doubt that most of the great positive evils of the world are in themselves removable, and will, if human affairs continue to improve, be in the end reduced within narrow limits. Poverty, in any sense implying suffering, may be completely extinguished by the wisdom of society, combined with the good sense and providence of individuals. Even that most intractable of enemies, disease, may be indefinitely reduced in dimensions by good physical and moral education, and proper control of noxious influences; while the progress of science holds out a promise for the future of still more direct conquests over this detestable foe. And every advance in that direction relieves us from some, not only of the chances which cut short our own lives, but, what concerns us still more, which deprive us of those in whom our happiness is wrapt up. As for vicissitudes of fortune, and other disappointments connected with worldly circumstances, these are principally the effect either of gross imprudence, of ill-regulated desires, or of bad or imperfect social institutions. All the grand sources, in short, of human suffering are in a great degree, many of them almost entirely, conquerable by human

care and effort; and though their removal is griev-
ously slow—though a long succession of generations will perish in the breach before the conquest
is completed, and this world becomes all that, if will
and knowledge were not wanting, it might easily be
made—yet every mind sufficiently intelligent and
generous to bear a part, however small and incon-
spicuous, in the endeavour, will draw a noble enjoyment from the contest itself, which he would not for
any bribe in the form of selfish indulgence consent
to be without.

And this leads to the true estimation of what is
said by the objectors concerning the possibility and
the obligation, of learning to do without happiness.
Unquestionably it is possible to do without happiness. It is done involuntarily by nineteen-twentieths
of mankind, even in those parts of our present world
which are least deep in barbarism; and it often has
to be done voluntarily by the hero or the martyr, for
the sake of something which he prizes more than his
individual happiness. But this something, what is it,
unless the happiness of others, or some of the requisites of happiness? It is noble to be capable of resigning entirely one's own portion of happiness or
chances of it, but after all, this self-sacrifice must be
for some end. It is not its own end; and if we are told
that its end is not happiness but virtue, which is
better than happiness, I ask, would the sacrifice be
made if the hero or martyr did not believe that it
would earn for others immunity from similar sacrifices? Would it be made if he thought that his renunciation of happiness for himself would produce
no fruit for any of his fellow creatures, but to make
their lot like his, and place them also in the condition of persons who have renounced happiness? All
honor to those who can abnegate for themselves the
personal enjoyment of life, when by such renunciation they contribute worthily to increase the amount
of happiness in the world; but he who does it, or
professes to do it, for any other purpose is no more
deserving of admiration than the ascetic mounted
on his pillar. He may be an inspiriting proof of what
men *can* do, but assuredly not an example of what
they *should*.

Though it is only in a very imperfect state of the
world's arrangements that anyone can best serve the
happiness of others by the absolute sacrifice of his
own, yet so long as the world is in that imperfect
state, I fully acknowledge that the readiness to make
such a sacrifice is the highest virtue which can be
found in man. I will add that in this condition of
the world, paradoxical as the assertion may be, the
conscious ability to do without happiness gives the

best prospect of realizing such happiness as is attainable. For nothing except that consciousness can
raise a person above the chances of life, by making
him feel that, let fate and fortune do their worst, they
have no power to subdue him, which, once felt, frees
him from excess of anxiety concerning the evils of
life and enables him, like many a Stoic in the worst
times of the Roman Empire, to cultivate in tranquillity the sources of satisfaction accessible to him
without concerning himself about the uncertainty of
their duration any more than about their inevitable
end.

Meanwhile, let us utilitarians never cease to claim
the morality of self devotion as a possession which
belongs by as good a right to them as either to the
Stoic or to the Transcendentalist. The utilitarian
morality does recognize in human beings the power
of sacrificing their own greatest good for the good
of others. It only refuses to admit that the sacrifice
is itself a good. A sacrifice which does not increase,
or tend to increase, the sum total of happiness, it
considers as wasted. The only self-renunciation
which it applauds is devotion to the happiness, or
to some of the means of happiness, of others—either
of mankind collectively or of individuals within the
limits imposed by the collective interests of mankind.

I must again repeat what the assailants of utilitarianism seldom have the justice to acknowledge,
that the happiness which forms the utilitarian standard of what is right in conduct is not the agent's
own happiness but that of all concerned. As between his own happiness and that of others, utilitarianism requires him to be as strictly impartial as
a disinterested and benevolent spectator. In the
golden rule of Jesus of Nazareth, we read the complete spirit of the ethics of utility. To do as you would
be done by and to love your neighbour as yourself
constitute the ideal perfection of utilitarian morality. As the means of first making the nearest approach to this ideal, utility would enjoin, first, that
laws and social arrangements should place the happiness or (as speaking practically it may be called)
the interest of every individual as nearly as possible
in harmony with the interest of the whole and, secondly, that education and opinion, which have so
vast a power over human character, should so use
that power as to establish in the mind of every individual an indissoluble association between his own
happiness and the good of the whole—especially between his own happiness and the practice of such
modes of conduct, negative and positive, as regard
for the universal happiness prescribes—so that not
only he may be unable to conceive the possibility of

happiness to himself consistently with conduct opposed to the general good, but also that a direct impulse to promote the general good may be in every individual one of the habitual motives of action and the sentiments connected herewith may fill a large and prominent place in every human being's sentient existence. If the impugners of the utilitarian morality represented it to their own minds in this its true character, I know not what recommendation possessed by any other morality they could possibly affirm to be wanting to it, what more beautiful or more exalted developments of human nature any other ethical system can be supposed to foster, or what springs of action, not accessible to the utilitarian, such systems rely on for giving effect to their mandates.

The objectors to utilitarianism cannot always be charged with representing it in a discreditable light. On the contrary, those among them who entertain anything like a just idea of its disinterested character sometimes find fault with its standard as being too high for humanity. They say it is exacting too much to require that people shall always act from the inducement of promoting the general interests of society. But this is to mistake the very meaning of a standard of morals and confound the rule of action with the motive of it. It is the business of ethics to tell us what are our duties or by what tests we may know them, but no system of ethics requires that the sole motive of all we do shall be a feeling of duty; on the contrary, ninety-nine hundredths of all our actions are done from other motives, and rightly so done, if the rule of duty does not condemn them. It is the more unjust to utilitarianism that this particular misapprehension should be made a ground of objection to it, inasmuch as utilitarian moralists have gone beyond almost all others in affirming that the motive has nothing to do with the morality of the action, though much with the worth of the agent. He who saves a fellow creature from drowning does what is morally right, whether his motive be duty or the hope of being paid for his trouble; he who betrays the friend that trusts him is guilty of a crime, even if his object be to serve another friend to whom he is under greater obligations. But to speak only of actions done from the motive of duty and in direct obedience to principle, it is a misapprehension of the utilitarian mode of thought to conceive it as implying that people should fix their minds upon so wide a generality as the world, or society at large. The great majority of good actions are intended not for the benefit of the world but for that of individuals, of which the good of the world is made up; and the thoughts of the most virtuous man need not on these occasions travel beyond the particular persons concerned, except so far as is necessary to assure himself that in benefiting them he is not violating the rights, that is, the legitimate and authorized expectations, of anyone else. The multiplication of happiness is, according to the utilitarian ethics, the object of virtue. The occasion on which any person (except one in a thousand) has it in his power to do this on an extended scale—in other words, to be a public benefactor—are but exceptional, and on these occasions alone is he called on to consider public utility; in every other case, private utility, the interest or happiness of some few persons, is all he has to attend to. Those alone the influence of whose actions extends to society in general need concern themselves habitually about so large an object. In the case of abstinences indeed—of things which people forbear to do from moral considerations, though the consequences in the particular case might be beneficial—it would be unworthy of an intelligent agent not to be consciously aware that the action is of a class which, if practised generally, would be generally injurious and that this is the ground of the obligation to abstain from it. The amount of regard for the public interest implied in this recognition is no greater than is demanded by every system of morals, for they all enjoin to abstain from whatever is manifestly pernicious to society.

The same considerations dispose of another reproach against the doctrine of utility, founded on a still grosser misconception of the purpose of a standard of morality and of the very meaning of the words right and wrong. It is often affirmed that utilitarianism renders men cold and unsympathizing; that it chills their moral feelings towards individuals; that it makes them regard only the dry and hard consideration of the consequences of actions, not taking into their moral estimate the qualities from which those actions emanate. If the assertion means that they do not allow their judgment respecting the rightness or wrongness of an action to be influenced by their opinion of the qualities of the person who does it, this is a complaint not against utilitarianism but against having any standard of morality at all; for certainly no known ethical standard decides an action to be good or bad because it is done by a good or bad man, still less because done by an amiable, a brave, or a benevolent man, or the contrary. These considerations are relevant not to the estimation of actions but of persons; and there is nothing in the utilitarian theory inconsistent with the fact that there are other things which interest us in persons besides the rightness and wrongness of their actions. The Stoics, indeed, with the paradoxical misuse of language which was part of their system and by which they strove to raise themselves above all concern about anything but virtue, were fond of saying that he who has that has everything, that he, and only he, is rich, is beautiful, is a king. But no claim of this description is made for the virtuous man by the utilitarian doctrine. Utilitarians are quite aware that there are other desirable possessions and qualities besides virtue and are perfectly willing to allow to all of them their full worth. They are also aware that a right action does not necessarily indicate a virtuous character and that actions which are blamable often proceed from qualities entitled to praise. When this is apparent in any particular case, it modifies their estimation, not certainly of the act but of the agent. I grant that they are, notwithstanding, of the opinion that in the long run the best proof of a good character is good actions and resolutely refuse to consider any mental disposition as good of which the predominant tendency is to produce bad conduct. This makes them unpopular with many people; but it is an unpopularity which they must share with everyone who regards the distinction between right and wrong in a serious light, and the reproach is not one which a conscientious utilitarian need be anxious to repel.

If no more be meant by the objection than that many utilitarians look on the morality of actions, as measured by the utilitarian standards, with too exclusive a regard and do not lay sufficient stress upon the other beauties of character which go towards making a human being lovable or admirable, this may be admitted. Utilitarians who have cultivated their moral feelings but not their sympathies nor their artistic perceptions do fall into this mistake; and so do all other moralists under the same conditions. What can be said in excuse for other moralists is equally available for them—namely, that, if there is to be any error, it is better that it should be on that side. As a matter of fact, we may affirm among utilitarians, as among adherents of other systems, there is every imaginable degree of rigidity and of laxity in the application of their standard: some are even puritanically rigorous, while others are as indulgent as can possibly be desired by sinner or by sentimentalist. But on the whole, a doctrine which brings prominently forward the interest that mankind have in the repression and prevention of conduct which violates the moral law, is likely to be inferior to no other in turning the sanctions of opinion against such violations. It is true, the question, What does violate the moral law? is one on which those who recognize different standards of morality are likely now and then to differ. But difference of opinion on moral questions was not first introduced into the world by utilitarianism, while that doctrine does supply, if not always an easy, at all events a tangible and intelligible mode of deciding such differences.

Writing and Discussion Topics

Questions 1–6 address content, critical analysis, personal choices, ethical options, specific discipline, and interdisciplinary alternatives, respectively.

1. Is one pleasure more valuable than another? Do you agree with Mill's claim that some pleasures are qualitatively, not quantitatively, more valuable?

2. Mill believes heroism that does not better society has no moral value. Can you think of a case of useless self-sacrifice? Can you think of a case that involves needed self-sacrifice? What are the fundamental differences, according to Mill?

3. Do you agree with the statement by Mill, "It is better to be a human being dissatisfied than a pig satisfied; better to be Socrates dissatisfied than a fool satisfied. And if the fool, or the pig, are of a different opinion, it is because they only know their own side of the question." Explain how Mill's perspective corresponds to the way you live your life.

4. Explain the basic principles of utilitarianism. Consider the following: a. What is the greatest of all pleasures? b. Is the greatest good self-centered?

5. Examine the concept of hedonism. Neither Plato nor Aristotle thought that hedonism was an acceptable theory. They did not believe that good could be defined in terms of pleasure. Use the following quote to compare Aristotle's views with those of John Stuart Mill:

   > He [Plato] argues that pleasant life is more desirable with wisdom than without, and that if the mixture is better, pleasure is not the good; for the good cannot become more desirable by the addition of anything to it. Now it is clear that nothing else, any more than pleasure, can be the good if it is made more desirable by the addition of any of the things that are good in themselves. (*Aristotle, Nicomachean Ethics*, 1172b, 29–33)

6. How do you think Jesus would view the utilitarian ethic? How does it differ from the Christian view of the ethic of duty?

Aristotle

VIRTUOUS ACTIVITY

◆◆◆

Aristotle (384–322 B.C.) was born in northern Greece. His father was physician to King Phillip of Macedonia. Aristotle studied with Plato for eighteen years and, after Plato's death, set up his own school in Athens. He formulated a vision of the good life through happiness. He tells us that happiness has many meanings to people because humans are endowed with many capacities and skills. The bulk of Aristotle's writings, which are numerous, consists of either his lecture notes or other unpublished treatises used by his students. ◆

Book I: The Good for Man

Subject of Our Inquiry

All human activities aim at some good: some goods subordinate to others.

1. Every art and every inquiry, and similarly every action and pursuit, is thought to aim at some good; and for this reason the good has rightly been declared to be that at which all things aim. But a certain difference is found among ends; some are activities, others are products apart from the activities that produce them. Where there are ends apart from the actions, it is the nature of the products to be better than the activities. Now, as there are many actions, arts, and sciences, their ends also are many; the end of the medical art is health, that of shipbuilding a vessel, that of strategy victory, that of economics wealth. But where such arts fall under a single capacity—as bridle making and the other arts concerned with the equipment of horses fall under the art of riding, and this and every military action under strategy, in the same way other arts fall under yet others—in all of these the ends of the master arts are to be preferred to all the subordinate ends; for it is for the sake of the former that the latter are pursued. It makes no difference whether the activities themselves are the ends of the actions, or something else apart from the activities, as in the case of the sciences just mentioned.

The science of the good for man is politics.

2. If, then, there is some end of the things we do, which we desire for its own sake (everything else being desired for the sake of this), and if we do not choose everything for the sake of something else (for at that rate the process would go on to infinity, so that our desire would be empty and vain), clearly this must be the good and the chief good. Will not the knowledge of it, then, have a great influence on life? Shall we not, like archers who have a mark to aim at, be more likely to hit upon what is right? If so, we must try, in outline at least to determine what it is, and of which of the sciences or capacities it is the object. It would seem to belong to the most authoritative art and that which is most truly the master art. And politics appears to be of this nature; for it is this that ordains which of the sciences should be studied in a state, and which each class of citizens should learn and up to what point they should learn them; and we see even the most highly esteemed of capacities to fall under this, for example, strategy, economics, rhetoric; now, since politics uses the rest of the sciences, and since, again, it legislates as to what we are to do and what we are to abstain from, the end of this science must include those of the others, so that this end must be the good for man. For even if the end is the same for a single man and for a state, that of the state seems at all events something greater and more complete whether to attain or to preserve; though it is worthwhile to attain the end merely for one man, it is finer and more godlike to attain it for a nation or for city-states. . . .

Nature of the Science

We must not expect more precision than the subject-matter admits of. The student should have reached years of discretion.

3. Our discussion will be adequate if it has as much clearness as the subject matter admits of, for precision is not to be sought for alike in all discussions, any more than in all the products of the crafts. Now fine and just actions, which political science investigates, admit of much variety and fluctuation of opinion, so that they may be thought to exist only by convention, and not by nature. And goods also give rise to a similar fluctuation because they bring harm to many people; for before now men have been undone by reason of their wealth, and others by reason of their courage. We must be content, then, in speaking of such subjects and with such premises to indicate the truth roughly and in outline, and in speaking about things which are only for the most part true and with premises of the same kind to reach conclusions that are no better. In the same spirit, therefore, should each type of statement be *received;* for it is the mark of an educated man to look for precision in each class of things just so far as the nature of the subject admits; it is evidently equally foolish to accept probable reasoning from a mathematician and to demand from a rhetorician scientific proofs.

Now each man judges well the things he knows, and of these he is a good judge. And so the man who has been educated in a subject is a good judge of that subject, and the man who has received an all-round education is a good judge in general. Hence a young man is not a proper hearer of lectures on political science; for he is inexperienced in the actions that occur in life, but its discussions start from these and are about these; and, further, since he

Reprinted from Aristotle: *The Nicomachean Ethics* translated by W. D. Ross (1925) by permission of Oxford University Press.

tends to follow his passions, his study will be vain and unprofitable, because the end aimed at is not knowledge but action. And it makes no difference whether he is young in years or youthful in character; the defect does not depend on time, but on his living, and pursuing each successive object, as passion directs. For to such persons, as to the incontinent, knowledge brings no profit; but to those who desire and act in accordance with a rational principle knowledge about such matters will be of great benefit. . . .

What is the Good for Man?

It is generally agreed to be happiness, but there are various views as to what happiness is. What is required at the start is an unreasoned conviction about the facts, such as is produced by a good upbringing.

Let us resume our inquiry and state, in view of the fact that all knowledge and every pursuit aims at some good, what it is that we say political science aims at and what is the highest of all goods achievable by action. Verbally there is very general agreement; for both the general run of men and people of superior refinement say that it is happiness, and identify living well and doing well with being happy; but with regard to what happiness is they differ, and the many do not give the same account as the wise. For the former think it is some plain and obvious thing, like pleasure, wealth, or honor; they differ, however, from one another—and often even the same man identifies it with different things, with health when he is ill, with wealth when he is poor; but, conscious of their ignorance, they admire those who proclaim some great ideal that is above their comprehension. Now some thought [for example, Plato] that apart from these many goods there is another which is self-subsistent and causes the goodness of all these as well. To examine all the opinions that have been held were perhaps somewhat fruitless; enough to examine those that are most prevalent or that seem to be arguable.

The good must be something final and self-sufficient. Definition of happiness reached by considering the characteristic function of man.

7. Let us again return to the good we are seeking, and ask what it can be. It seems different in different actions and arts; it is different in medicine, in strategy, and in the other arts likewise. What then is the good of each? Surely that for whose sake everything else is done. In medicine this is health, in strategy victory, in architecture a house, in any other sphere something else, and in every action and pursuit the end; for it is for the sake of this that all men do whatever else they do. Therefore, if there is an end for all that we do, this will be the good achievable by action, and if there are more than one, these will be the goods achievable by action.

So the argument has by a different course reached the same point; but we must try to state this even more clearly. Since there are evidently more than one end, and we choose some of these (for example, wealth, flutes, and in general instruments) for the sake of something else, clearly not all ends are final ends; but the chief good is evidently something final. Therefore, if there is only one final end, this will be what we are seeking, and if there are more than one, the most final of these will be what we are seeking. Now we call that which is in itself worthy of pursuit more final than that which is worthy of pursuit for the sake of something else, and that which is never desirable for the sake of something else more final than the things that are desirable both in themselves and for the sake of that other thing, and therefore we call final without qualification that which is always desirable in itself and never for the sake of something else.

Now such a thing happiness, above all else, is held to be; for this we choose always for itself and never for the sake of something else, but honor, pleasure, reason, and every virtue we choose indeed for themselves (for if nothing resulted from them we should still choose each of them), but we choose them also for the sake of happiness, judging that by means of them we shall be happy. Happiness, on the other hand, no one chooses for the sake of these, nor, in general, for anything other than itself.

From the point of view of self-sufficiency the same result seems to follow; for the final good is thought to be self-sufficient. Now by self-sufficient we do not mean that which is sufficient for a man by himself, for one who lives a solitary life, but also for parents, children, wife, and in general for his friends and fellow citizens, since man is born for citizenship. But some limit must be set to this; for if we extend our requirement to ancestors and descendants and friends' friends we are in for an infinite series. Let us examine this question, however, on another occasion; the self-sufficient we now define as that which when isolated makes life desirable and lacking in nothing; and such we think happiness to be; and further we think it most desirable of all things, without being counted as one good thing among others—if it were so counted it would clearly be made more desirable by the addition of even the least of goods; for that which is added becomes an excess of goods, and of goods the greater is always more desirable. Happiness, then, is something final and self-sufficient, and is the end of action.

Presumably, however, to say that happiness is the chief good seems a platitude, and a clearer account of what it is is still desired. This might perhaps be given, if we could first ascertain the function of man. For just as for a flute player, a sculptor, or any artist, and, in general, for all things that have a function or activity, the good and the "well" is thought to reside in the function, so would it seem to be for man, if he has a function. Have the carpenter, then, and the tanner certain functions or activities, and has man none? Is he born without a function? Or as eye, hand, foot, and in general each of the parts evidently has a function, may one lay it down that man similarly has a function apart from all these? What then can this be? Life seems to be common even to plants, but we are seeking what is peculiar to man. Let us exclude, therefore, the life of nutrition and growth. Next there would be a life of perception, but *it* also seems to be common even to the horse, the ox, and every animal. There remains, then, an active life of the element that has a rational principle; of this, one part has such a principle in the sense of being obedient to one, the other in the sense of possessing one and exercising thought. And, as "life of the rational element" also has two meanings, we must state that life in the sense of activity is what we mean; for this seems to be the more proper sense of the term. Now if the function of man is an activity of soul which follows or implies a rational principle, and if we say "a so-and-so" and "a good so-and-so" have a function which is the same in kind, for example, a lyre player and a good lyre player, and so without qualification in all cases, eminence in respect of goodness being added to the name of the function (for the function of a lyre player is to play the lyre, and that of a good lyre player is to do so well): if this is the case, [and we state the function of man to be a certain kind of life, and this to be an activity or actions of the soul implying a rational principle, and the function of a good man to be the good and noble performance of these, and if any action is well performed when it is performed in accordance with the appropriate excellence: if this is the case,] human good turns out to be activity of soul in accordance with virtue, and if there are more than one virtue, in accordance with the best and most complete.

But we must add "in a complete life." For one swallow does not make a summer, nor does one day; and so too one day, or a short time, does not make a man blessed and happy . . . [Also, a happy man] needs the external goods as well; for it is impossible, or not easy, to do noble acts without the proper equipment. In many actions we use friends and riches and political power as instruments; and there are some things the lack of which takes the luster from happiness, as good birth, goodly children, beauty; for the man who is very ugly in appearance or ill born or solitary and childless is not very likely to be happy, and perhaps a man would be still less likely if he had thoroughly bad children or friends or had lost good children or friends by death. . . .

Division of the faculties, and resultant division of virtue into intellectual and moral.

13. Since happiness is an activity of soul in accordance with perfect virtue, we must consider the nature of virtue; for perhaps we shall thus see better the nature of happiness. The true student of politics, too, is thought to have studied virtue above all things; for he wishes to make his fellow citizens good and obedient to the laws. As an example of this we have the lawgivers of the Cretans and the Spartans, and any others of the kind that there may have been. And if this inquiry belongs to political science, clearly the pursuit of it will be in accordance with our original plan. But clearly the virtue we must study is human virtue; for the good we were seeking was human good and the happiness human happiness. By human virtue we mean not that of the body but that of the soul; and happiness also we call an activity of soul. But if this is so, clearly the student of politics must know somehow the facts about soul, as the man who is to heal the eyes or the body as a whole must know about the eyes or the body; and all the more since politics is more prized and better than medicine; but even among doctors the best educated spend much labor on acquiring knowledge of the body. The student of politics, then, must study the soul, and must study it with these objects in view, and do so just to the extent which is sufficient for the questions we are discussing; for further precision is perhaps something more laborious than our purposes require.

Some things are said about it, adequately enough, even in the discussions outside our school, and we must use these; e.g., that one element in the soul is irrational and one has a rational principle. Whether these are separated as the parts of the body or of anything divisible are, or are distinct by definition but by nature inseparable, like convex and concave in the circumference of a circle, does not affect the present question.

Of the irrational element one division seems to be widely distributed, and vegetative in its nature, I mean that which causes nutrition and growth; for it is this kind of power of the soul that one must assign to all nurslings and to embryos, and this same power to full-grown creatures; this is more reasonable than to assign some different power to them. Now the excellence of this seems to be common to all species and not specifically human . . . let us leave the nutritive faculty alone, since it has by its nature no share in human excellence.

There seems to be also another irrational element in the soul—one which in a sense, however, shares in a rational principle. For we praise the rational principle of the continent man and of the incontinent, and the part of their soul that has such a principle, since it urges them aright and towards the best objects; but there is found in them also another element naturally opposed to the rational principle, which fights against and resists that principle. For exactly as paralyzed limbs when we intend to move them to the right turn on the contrary to the left, so is it with the soul; the impulses of incontinent people move in contrary directions. But while in the body we see that which moves astray, in the soul we do not. No doubt, however, we must none the less suppose that in the soul too there is something contrary to the rational principle, resisting and opposing it. In what sense it is distinct from the other elements does not concern us. Now even this seems to have a share in a rational principle, as we said, at any rate in the continent man it obeys the rational principle—and presumably in the temperate and brave man it is still more obedient; for in him it speaks, on all matters, with the same voice as the rational principle.

Therefore the irrational element also appears to be twofold. For the vegetative element in no way shares in a rational principle, but the appetitive, and in general the desiring element in a sense shares in it, insofar as it listens to and obeys it; this is the sense in which we speak of "taking account" of one's father or one's friends, not that in which we speak of "accounting" for a mathematical property. That the irrational element is in some sense persuaded by a rational principle is indicated also by the giving of advice and by all reproof and exhortation. And if this element also must be said to have a rational principle, that which has a rational principle (as well as that which has not) will be twofold, one subdivision having it in the strict sense and in itself, and the other having a tendency to obey as one does one's father.

Virtue too is distinguished into kinds in accordance with this difference; for we say that some of the virtues are intellectual and others moral, philosophic wisdom and understanding and practical wisdom being intellectual, liberality and temperance moral. For in speaking about a man's character we do not say that he is wise or has understanding but that he is good tempered or temperate; yet we praise the wise man also with respect to his state of mind; and of states of mind we call those which merit praise virtues.

Book II: Moral Virtue

Moral Virtue, How Produced, in what Medium and in what Manner Exhibited

Moral Virtue, like the arts, is acquired by repetition of the corresponding acts.

1. Virtue, then, being of two kinds, intellectual and moral, intellectual virtue in the main owes both its birth and its growth to teaching (for which reason it requires experience and time), while moral virtue comes about as a result of habit, whence also its name *ethike* is one that is formed by a slight variation from the word *ethos* (habit). From this it is also plain that none of the moral virtues arises in us by nature; for nothing that exists by nature can form a habit contrary to its nature. For instance the stone which by nature moves downwards cannot be habituated to move upwards, not even if one tries to train it by throwing it up ten thousand times; nor can fire be habituated to move downwards, nor can anything else that by nature behaves in one way be trained to behave in another. Neither by nature, then, nor contrary to nature do the virtues arise in us; rather we are adapted by nature to receive them, and are made perfect by habit.

Again, of all the things that come to us by nature we first acquire the potentiality and later exhibit the activity (this is plain in the case of the senses; for it was not by often seeing or often hearing that we got these senses, but on the contrary we had them before we used them, and did not come to have them by using them); but the virtues we get by first exercising them, as also happens in the case of the arts as well. For the things we have to learn before we can do them, we learn by doing them, e.g., men become builders by building and lyre players by playing the lyre; so too we become just by doing just acts, temperate by doing temperate acts, brave by doing brave acts.

The differentia of moral virtue: it is a disposition to choose the mean.

6. We must . . . not only describe [moral] virtue as a state of character, but also say what sort of state it is. We may remark, then, that every virtue or excellence both brings into good condition the thing of which it is the excellence and makes the work of that thing be done well; e.g., the excellence of the eye makes both the eye and its work good; for it is by the excellence of the eye that we see well. Similarly the excellence of the horse makes a horse both good in itself and good at running and at carrying its rider and at awaiting the attack of the enemy. Therefore, if this is true in every case, the virtue of man also will be the state of character which makes a man good and which makes him do his own work well.

How this is to happen we have stated already, but it will be made plain also by the following consideration of the specific nature of virtue. In everything that is continuous and divisible it is possible to take more, less, or an equal amount, and that either in terms of the thing itself or relatively to us; and the equal is an intermediate between excess and defect. By the intermediate in the object I mean that which is equidistant from each of the extremes, which is one and the same for all men; by the intermediate relatively to us that which is neither too much nor too little—and this is not one, nor the same for all. For instance, if ten is many and two is few, six is the intermediate, taken in terms of the object; for it exceeds and is exceeded by an equal amount; this is intermediate according to arithmetical proportion. But the intermediate relatively to us is not to be taken so; if ten pounds are too much for a particular person to eat and two too little, it does not follow that the trainer will order six pounds; for this also is perhaps too much for the person who is to take it, or too little—too little for Milo [a famous Greek athlete], too much for the beginner in athletic exercises. The same is true of running and wrestling. Thus a master of any art avoids excess and defect, but seeks the intermediate and chooses this—the intermediate not in the object but relatively to us.

Virtue, then, is a state of character concerned with choice, lying in a mean, i.e., the mean relative to us, this being determined by a rational principle, and by that principle by which the man of practical wisdom would determine it. Now it is a mean between two vices, that which depends on excess and that which depends on defect; and again it is a mean because the vices respectively fall short of or exceed what is right in both passions and actions, while virtue both finds and chooses that which is intermediate. Hence in respect of its substance and the definition which states its essence virtue is a mean, with regard to what is best and right an extreme.

But not every action nor every passion admits of a mean; for some have names that already imply badness, e.g., spite, shamelessness, envy, and in the case of actions adultery, theft, murder; for all of these and suchlike things imply by their names that they are themselves bad, and not the excesses or deficiencies of them. It is not possible, then, ever to be right with regard to them; one must always be wrong. Nor does goodness or badness with regard to such things depend on committing adultery with the right woman, at the right time, and in the right way, but simply to do any of them is to go wrong. It would be equally absurd, then, to expect that in unjust, cowardly, and voluptuous action there should be a mean, an excess, and a deficiency; for at that rate there would be a mean of excess and of deficiency, an excess of excess, and a deficiency of deficiency. But as there is no excess and deficiency of temperance and courage because what is intermediate is in a sense an extreme, so too of the actions we have mentioned there is no mean nor any excess and deficiency, but however they are done they are wrong; for in general there is neither a mean of excess and deficiency, nor excess and deficiency of a mean.

The above proposition illustrated by reference to particular virtues.

7. We must, however, not only make this general statement, but also apply it to the individual facts. For among statements about conduct those which are general apply more widely, but those which are particular are more genuine, since conduct has to do with individual cases, and our statements must harmonize with the facts in these cases. We may take these cases from our table. With regard to feelings of fear and confidence courage is the mean; of the people who exceed, he who exceeds in fearlessness has no name (many of the states have no name), while the man who exceeds in confidence is rash, and he who exceeds in fear and falls short in confidence is a coward. With regard to pleasures and pains—not all of them, and not so much with regard to the pains—the mean is temperance, the excess self-indulgence. Persons deficient with regard to the pleasures are not often found; hence such persons also have received no name. But let us call them "insensible."

With regard to giving and taking of money the mean is liberality, the excess and the defect prodigality and meanness. In these actions people exceed and fall short in contrary ways; the prodigal exceeds in spending and falls short in taking, while the mean man exceeds in taking and falls short in spending. . . . With regard to money there are also other dispositons—a mean, magnificence (for the magnificent man differs from the liberal man; the former deals with large sums, the latter with small ones), an excess, tastelessness and vulgarity, and a deficiency, niggardliness. . . .

With regard to honor and dishonor the mean is proper pride, the excess is known as a sort of "empty vanity," and the deficiency is undue humility; and as we said liberality was related to maginificence, differing from it by dealing with small sums, so there is a state similarly related to proper pride, being concerned with small honors while that is concerned with great. For it is possible to desire honor as one ought, and more than one ought, and less, and the man who exceeds in his desires is called ambitious, the man who falls short unambitious, while the intermediate person has no name. The dispositions also are nameless, except that that of the ambitious man is called ambition. Hence the people who are at the extremes lay claim to the middle place; and we ourselves sometimes call the intermediate person ambitious and sometimes unambitious, and sometimes praise the ambitious man and sometimes the unambitious. The reason of our doing this will be stated in what follows; but now let us speak of the remaining states according to the method which has been indicated.

With regard to anger also there is an excess, a deficiency, and a mean. Although they can scarcely be said to have names, yet since we call the intermediate person good tempered let us call the mean good temper; of the persons at the extremes let the one who exceeds be called irascible, and his vice irascibility, and the man who falls short an inirascible sort of person, and the deficiency inirascibility.

Book VI: Intellectual Virtue

. . . We divided the virtues of the soul and said that some are virtues of character and others of intellect. Now we have discussed in detail the moral virtues; with regard to the others let us express our view as follows, beginning with some remarks about the soul. We said before that there are two parts of the soul—that which grasps a rule or rational principle, and the irrational; let us now draw a similar distinction within the part which grasps a rational principle. And let it be assumed that there are two parts which grasp a rational principle—one by which we contemplate the kind of things whose originative causes are invariable, and one by which we contemplate variable things; for where objects differ in kind the part of the soul answering to each of the two is different in kind, since it is in virtue of a certain likeness and kinship with their objects that they have the knowledge they have.

The proper object of contemplation is truth; that of calculation is truth corresponding with right desire

2. The virtue of a thing is relative to its proper work. Now there are three things in the soul which control action and truth—sensation, reason, desire. Of these sensation originates no [moral] action; this is plain from the fact that the lower animals have sensation but no share in [such] action.

What affirmation and negation are in thinking, pursuit and avoidance are in desire; so that since moral virtue is a state of character concerned with choice, and choice is deliberate desire, therefore both the reasoning must be true and the desire right, if the choice is to be good, and the latter must pursue just what the former asserts. Now this kind of intellect and of truth is practical; of the intellect which is contemplative, not practical nor productive, the good and the bad state are truth and falsity respectively (for this is the work of everything intellectual); while of the part which is practical and intellectual the good state is truth in agreement with right desire.

The origin of [moral] action—its efficient, not its final cause—is choice, and that of choice is desire and reasoning with a view to an end. This is why choice cannot exist either without reason and intellect or without a moral state; for good action and its opposite cannot exist without a combination of intellect and character. Intellect itself, however, moves nothing, but only the intellect which aims at an end and is practical; for this rules the productive intellect as well, since everyone who makes makes for an end, and that which is made is not an end in the unqualified sense (but only an end in a particular relation, and the end of a particular operation)—only that which is *done* is that; for good action is an end, and desire aims at this. Hence choice is either desiderative reason or ratiocinative desire, and such an origin of action is a man.

. . . This is why some say that all the virtues are forms of practical wisdom. . . . Socrates in one respect was on the right track while in another he went astray; in thinking that all the virtues were forms of practical wisdom he was wrong, but in saying they implied practical wisdom he was right. This is confirmed by the fact that even now all men, when they define virtue, after naming the state of character and its objects add "that (state) which is in accordance with the right rule"; now the right rule is that which is in accordance with practical wisdom. All men, then, seem somehow to divine that this kind of state is virtue, viz., that which is in accordance with practical wisdom. But we must go a little further. For it is not merely the state in accordance with the right rule, but the state that implies the *presence* of the right rule, that is virtue; and practical wisdom is a right rule about such matters. Socrates, then, thought the virtues were rules or rational principles (for he thought they were, all of them, forms of scientific knowledge), while we think they *involve* a rational principle.

Book X

Happiness in the highest sense is the contemplative life

7. If happiness is activity in accordance with virtue, it is reasonable that it should be in accordance with the highest virtue; and this will be that of the best thing in us. Whether it be reason or something else that is this element which is thought to be our natural ruler and guide and to take thought of things noble and divine, whether it be itself also divine or only the most divine element in us, the activity of this in accordance with its proper virtue will be perfect happiness. That this activity is contemplative we have already said.

Now this would seem to be in agreement both with what we said before and with the truth. For, firstly, this activity is the best (since not only is reason the best thing in us, but the objects of reason are the best of knowable objects); and, secondly, it is the most continuous, since we can contemplate truth more continuously than we can *do* anything. And we think happiness has pleasure mingled with it, but the activity of philosophic wisdom is admittedly the pleasantest of virtuous activities; at all events the pursuit of it is thought to offer pleasures marvelous for their purity and their enduringness, and it is to be expected that those who know will pass their time more pleasantly than those who inquire. And the self-sufficiency that is spoken of must belong most

to the contemplative activity. For while a philosopher, as well as a just man or one possessing any other virtue, needs the necessaries of life, when they are sufficiently equipped with things of that sort the just man needs people towards whom and with whom he shall act justly, and the temperate man, the brave man, and each of the others is in the same case, but the philosopher, even when by himself, can contemplate truth, and the better the wiser he is; he can perhaps do so better if he has fellow workers, but still he is the most self-sufficient. And this activity alone would seem to be loved for its own sake; for nothing arises from it apart from the contemplating, while from practical activities we gain more or less apart from the action. And happiness is thought to depend on leisure; for we are busy that we may have leisure, and make war that we may live in peace. Now the activity of the practical virtues is exhibited in political or military affairs, but the actions concerned with these seem to be unleisurely. Warlike actions are completely so (for no one chooses to be at war, or provokes war, for the sake of being at war; anyone would seem absolutely murderous if he were to make enemies of his friends in order to bring about battle and slaughter); but the action of the statesman is also unleisurely, and—apart from the political action itself—aims at despotic power and honors, or at all events happiness, for him and his fellow citizens— a happiness different from political action, and evidently sought as being different. So if among virtuous actions political and military actions are distinguished by nobility and greatness, and these are unleisurely and aim at an end and are not desirable for their sake, but the activity of reason, which is contemplative, seems both to be superior in serious worth and to aim at no end beyond itself, and to have its pleasure proper to itself (and this augments the activity), and the self-sufficiency, leisureliness, unweariedness (so far as this is possible for man), and all the other attributes ascribed to the supremely happy man are evidently those connected with this activity, it follows that this will be the complete happiness of man, if it be allowed a complete term of life (for none of the attributes of happiness is *incomplete*).

But such a life would be too high for man; for it is not insofar as he is man that he will live so, but insofar as something divine is present in him; and by so much as this is superior to our composite nature is its activity superior to that which is the exercise of the other kind of virtue. If reason is divine, then, in comparison with man, the life according to it is divine in comparison with human life. But we must not follow those who advise us, being men, to think of human things, and, being mortal, of mortal things, but must, so far as we can, make ourselves immortal, and strain every nerve to live in accordance with the best thing in us; for even if it be small in bulk, much more does it in power and worth surpass everything. This would seem, too, to be each man himself, since it is the authoritative and better part of him. It would be strange, then, if he were to choose not the life of his self but that of something else. And what we said before will apply now; that which is proper to each thing is by nature best and most pleasant for each thing; for man, therefore, the life according to reason is best and pleasantest, since reason more than anything else *is* man. This life therefore is also the happiest.

Writing and Discussion Topics

Questions 1–6 address content, critical analysis, personal choices, ethical options, specific discipline, and interdisciplinary alternatives, respectively.

1. According to Aristotle, what are the distinctions between moral virtue and intellectual virtue?

2. Aristotle gives a definition of happiness through the eyes of one in the Golden Age of ancient Greece. Is his definition still relevant today? If not, why not? Is pleasure the source of happiness, happiness the source of pleasure, or are they identical?

3. Aristotle said that young people, probably college students, haven't had enough experience to know what is good. Do you agree with him? Why or why not? Explain the need for self-control in making ethical judgments.

4. Can ethics be an exact science? What does Aristotle say? Explain why and why not.

5. According to Aristotle, how do we know if something is to be praised or valued?

6. Are our desires ever rational? Aristotle says the appetitive part of the soul, also known as the faculty of desire, is irrational but to some extent, in a "derivative sense," rational. Would some of our classical novelists agree with Aristotle? Find an author who would agree with this concept and one who would disagree.

Carol Gilligan

IMAGES OF RELATIONSHIP

◆◆◆

C arol Gilligan is a professor in the Graduate School of Education
at Harvard University. Her work in relationship ethics is highly
published. This essay is an excerpt from her book, In a Different Voice.
The book discusses the inferior treatment in the scholarship of the
psychological development of women. It further advances the idea that
ethical approaches do not need to be based on logic alone, but that
caring, sharing, and relationships are essential in making moral
choices. ◆

In 1914, with his essay "On Narcissism," Freud swallows his distaste at the thought of "abandoning observation for barren theoretical controversy" and extends his map of the psychological domain. Tracing the development of the capacity to love, which he equates with maturity and psychic health, he locates its origins in the contrast between love for the mother and love for the self. But in thus dividing the world of love into narcissism and "object" relationships, he finds that while men's development becomes clear, women's becomes increasingly opaque. The problem arises because the contrast between mother and self yields two different images of relationships. Relying on the imagery of men's lives in charting the course of human growth, Freud is unable to trace in women the development of relationships, morality, or a clear sense of self. This difficulty in fitting the logic of his theory to women's experience leads him in the end to set women apart, marking their relationships, like their sexual life, as "a 'dark continent' for psychology" (1926, p. 212).

Thus the problem of interpretation that shadows the understanding of women's development arises from the differences observed in their experience of relationships. To Freud, though living surrounded by women and otherwise seeing so much and so well, women's relationships seemed increasingly mysterious, difficult to discern, and hard to describe. While this mystery indicates how theory can blind observation, it also suggests that development in women is masked by a particular conception of human relationships. Since the imagery of relationships shapes the narrative of human development, the inclusion of women, by changing that imagery, implies a change in the entire account.

The shift in imagery that creates the problem in interpreting women's development is elucidated by the moral judgments of two eleven-year-old children, a boy and a girl, who see, in the same dilemma, two very different moral problems. While current theory brightly illuminates the line and the logic of the boy's thought, it casts scant light on that of the girl. The choice of a girl whose moral judgments elude existing categories of developmental assessment is meant to highlight the issue of interpretation rather than to exemplify sex differences per se. Adding a new line of interpretation, based on the imagery of the girl's thought, makes it possible not only to see development where previously development was not

Reprinted by permission of the publishers from *In a Different Voice: Psychological Theory and Women's Development* by Carol Gilligan, Cambridge, Mass.: Harvard University Press, Copyright © 1982 by Carol Gilligan.

discerned but also to consider differences in the understanding of relationships without scaling these differences from better to worse.

The two children were in the same sixth-grade class at school and were participants in the rights and responsibilities study, designed to explore different conceptions of morality and self. The sample selected for this study was chosen to focus the variables of gender and age while maximizing developmental potential by holding constant, at a high level, the factors of intelligence, education, and social class that have been associated with moral development, at least as measured by existing scales. The two children in question, Amy and Jake, were both bright and articulate and, at least in their eleven-year-old aspirations, resisted easy categories of sex-role stereotyping, since Amy aspired to become a scientist while Jake preferred English to math. Yet their moral judgments seem initially to confirm familiar notions about differences between the sexes, suggesting that the edge girls have on moral development during the early school years gives way at puberty with the ascendance of formal logical thought in boys.

The dilemma that these eleven-year-olds were asked to resolve was one in the series devised by Kohlberg to measure moral development in adolescence by presenting a conflict between moral norms and exploring the logic of its resolution. In this particular dilemma, a man named Heinz considers whether or not to steal a drug which he cannot afford to buy in order to save the life of his wife. In the standard format of Kohlberg's interviewing procedure, the description of the dilemma itself—Heinz's predicament, the wife's disease, the druggist's refusal to lower his price—is followed by the question, "Should Heinz steal the drug?" The reasons for and against stealing are then explored through a series of questions that vary and extend the parameters of the dilemma in a way designed to reveal the underlying structure of moral thought.

Jake, at eleven, is clear from the outset that Heinz should steal the drug. Constructing the dilemma, as Kohlberg did, as a conflict between the values of property and life, he discerns the logical priority of life and uses that logic to justify his choice:

> For one thing, a human life is worth more than money, and if the druggist only makes $1,000, he is still going to live, but if Heinz doesn't steal the drug, his wife is going to die. (*Why is life worth more than money?*) Because the druggist can get a thousand dollars later from rich people with cancer, but Heinz can't get his wife again. (*Why not?*) Because people are all different and so you couldn't get Heinz's wife again.

Asked whether Heinz should steal the drug if he does not love his wife, Jake replies that he should, saying that not only is there "a difference between hating and killing," but also, if Heinz were caught, "the judge would probably think it was the right thing to do." Asked about the fact that, in stealing, Heinz would be breaking the law, he says that "the laws have mistakes, and you can't go writing up a law for everything that you can imagine."

Thus, while taking the law into account and recognizing its function in maintaining social order (the judge, Jake says, "should give Heinz the lightest possible sentence"), he also sees the law as man-made and therefore subject to error and change. Yet his judgment that Heinz should steal the drug, like his view of the law as having mistakes, rests on the assumption of agreement, a societal consensus around moral values that allows one to know and expect others to recognize what is "the right thing to do."

Fascinated by the power of logic, this eleven-year-old boy locates truth in math, which, he says, is "the only thing that is totally logical." Considering the moral dilemma to be "sort of like a math problem with humans," he sets it up as an equation and proceeds to work out the solution. Since his solution is rationally derived, he assumes that anyone following reason would arrive at the same conclusion and thus that a judge would also consider stealing to be the right thing for Heinz to do. Yet he is also aware of the limits of logic. Asked whether there is a right answer to moral problems, Jake replies that "there can only be right and wrong in judgment," since the parameters of action are variable and complex. Illustrating how actions undertaken with the best of intentions can eventuate in the most disastrous of consequences, he says, "like if you give an old lady your seat on the trolley, if you are in a trolley crash and that seat goes through the window, it might be that reason that the old lady dies."

Theories of developmental psychology illuminate well the position of this child, standing at the juncture of childhood and adolescence, at what Piaget describes as the pinnacle of childhood intelligence, and beginning through thought to discover a wider universe of possibility. The moment of preadolescence is caught by the conjunction of formal operational thought with a description of self still anchored in the factual parameters of his childhood world—his age, his town, his father's occupation, the substance of his likes, dislikes, and beliefs. Yet as his self-description radiates the self-confidence of a child who has arrived, in Erikson's terms, at a favorable balance of industry over inferiority—competent, sure of himself, and knowing well the rules of the game—so his emergent capacity for formal thought, his ability to think about thinking and to reason things out in a logical way, frees him from dependence on authority and allows him to find solutions to problems by himself.

This emergent autonomy follows the trajectory that Kohlberg's six stages of moral development trace, a three-level progression from an egocentric understanding of fairness based on individual need (stages one and two), to a conception of fairness anchored in the shared conventions of societal agreement (stages three and four), and finally to a principled understanding of fairness that rests on the free-standing logic of equality and reciprocity (stages five and six). While this boy's judgments at eleven are scored as conventional on Kohlberg's scale, a mixture of stages three and four, his ability to bring deductive logic to bear on the solution of moral dilemmas, to differentiate morality from law, and to see how laws can be considered to have mistakes points toward the principled conception of justice that Kohlberg equates with moral maturity.

In contrast, Amy's response to the dilemma conveys a very different impression, an image of development stunted by a failure of logic, an inability to think for herself. Asked if Heinz should steal the drug, she replies in a way that seems evasive and unsure:

> Well, I don't think so. I think there might be other ways besides stealing it, like if he could borrow the money or make a loan or something, but he really shouldn't steal the drug—but his wife shouldn't die either.

Asked why he should not steal the drug, she considers neither property nor law but rather the effect that theft could have on the relationship between Heinz and his wife:

> If he stole the drug, he might save his wife then, but if he did, he might have to go to jail, and then his wife might get sicker again, and he couldn't get more of the drug, and it might not be good. So, they should really just talk it out and find some other way to make the money.

Seeing in the dilemma not a math problem with humans but a narrative of relationships that extends over time, Amy envisions the wife's continuing need for her husband and the husband's continuing concern for his wife and seeks to respond to the druggist's need in a way that would sustain rather than sever connection. Just as she ties the wife's survival to the preservation of relationships, so she considers the value of the wife's life in a context of relationships, saying that it would be wrong to let her die because, "if she died, it hurts a lot of people and it hurts her." Since Amy's moral judgment is grounded in the belief that, "if somebody has something that would keep somebody alive, then it's not right not to give it to them," she considers the problem in the dilemma to arise not from the druggist's assertion of rights but from his failure of response.

As the interviewer proceeds with the series of questions that follow from Kohlberg's construction of the dilemma, Amy's answers remain essentially unchanged, the various probes serving neither to elucidate nor to modify her initial response. Whether or not Heinz loves his wife, he still shouldn't steal or let her die; if it were a stranger dying instead, Amy says that "if the stranger didn't have anybody near or anyone she knew," then Heinz should try to save her life, but he should not steal the drug. But as the interviewer conveys through the repetition of questions that the answers she gave were not heard or not right, Amy's confidence begins to diminish, and her replies become more constrained and unsure. Asked again why Heinz should not steal the drug, she simply repeats, "Because it's not right." Asked again to explain why, she states again that theft would not be a good solution, adding lamely, "if he took it, he might not know how to give it to his wife, and so his wife might still die." Failing to see the dilemma as a self-contained problem in moral logic, she does not discern the internal structure of its resolution; as she constructs the problem differently herself, Kohlberg's conception completely evades her.

Instead, seeing a world comprised of relationships rather than of people standing alone, a world that coheres through human connection rather than through systems of rules, she finds the puzzle in the dilemma to lie in the failure of the druggist to respond to the wife. Saying that "it is not right for someone to die when their life could be saved," she assumes that if the druggist were to see the consequences of his refusal to lower his price, he would realize that "he should just give it to the wife and then have the husband pay back the money later." Thus she considers the solution to the dilemma to lie in making the wife's condition more salient to the druggist or, that failing, in appealing to others who are in a position to help.

Just as Jake is confident the judge would agree that stealing is the right thing for Heinz to do, so Amy is confident that, "if Heinz and the druggist had talked it out long enough, they could reach something besides stealing." As he considers the law to "have mistakes," so she sees this drama as a mistake, believing that "the world should just share things more and then people wouldn't have to steal." Both children thus recognize the need for agreement but see it as mediated in different ways—he impersonally through systems of logic and law, she personally through communication in relationship. Just as he relies on the conventions of logic to deduce the solution to this dilemma, assuming these conventions to be shared, so she relies on a process of communication, assuming connection and believing that her voice will be heard. Yet while his assumptions about agreement are confirmed by the convergence in logic between his answers and the questions posed, her assumptions are belied by the failure of communication, the interviewer's inability to understand her response.

Although the frustration of the interview with Amy is apparent in the repetition of questions and its ultimate circularity, the problem of interpretation is focused by the assessment of her response. When considered in the light of Kohlberg's definition of the stages and sequence of moral development, her moral judgments appear to be a full stage lower in maturity than those of the boy. Scored as a mixture of stages two and three, her responses seem to reveal a feeling of powerlessness in the world, an inability to think systematically about the concepts of morality or law, a reluctance to challenge authority or to examine the logic of received moral truths, a failure even to conceive of acting directly to save a life or to consider that such action, if taken, could possibly have an effect. As her reliance on relationships seems to reveal a continuing dependence and vulnerability, so her belief in communication as the mode through which to resolve moral dilemmas appears naive and cognitively immature.

Yet Amy's description of herself conveys a markedly different impression. Once again, the hallmarks of the preadolescent child depict a child secure in her sense of herself, confident in the substance of her beliefs, and sure of her ability to do something of value in the world. Describing herself at eleven as "growing and changing," she says that she "sees some things differently now, just because I know myself really well now, and I know a lot more about the world.'' Yet the world she knows is a different world from that refracted by Kohlberg's construction of Heinz's dilemma. Her world is a world of relationships and psychological truths where an awareness of the connection between people gives rise to a recognition of responsibility for one another, a perception of the need for response. Seen in this light, her understanding of morality as arising from the recognition of relationship, her belief in communication as the mode of conflict resolution, and her conviction that the solution to the dilemma will follow from its compelling representation seem far from naive or cognitively immature. Instead, Amy's judgments contain the insights central to an ethic of care, just as Jake's judgments reflect the logic of the justice approach. Her incipient awareness of the "method of truth," the central tenet of nonviolent conflict resolution, and her belief in the restorative activity of care, lead her to see the actors in the dilemma arrayed not as opponents in a contest of rights but as members of a network of relationships on whose continuation they all depend. Consequently her solution to the dilemma lies in activating the network by communication, securing the inclusion of the wife by strengthening rather than severing connections.

But the different logic of Amy's response calls attention to the interpretation of the interview itself. Conceived as an interrogation, it appears instead as a dialogue, which takes on moral dimensions of its own, pertaining to the interviewer's uses of power and to the manifestations of respect. With this shift in the conception of the interview, it immediately becomes clear that the interviewer's problem in understanding Amy's response stems from the fact that Amy is answering a different question from the one the interviewer thought had been posed. Amy is considering not *whether* Heinz should act in this situation ("*should* Heinz steal the drug?") but rather *how* Heinz should act in response to his awareness of his wife's need ("Should Heinz *steal* the drug?"). The interviewer takes the mode of action for granted, presuming it to be a matter of fact; Amy assumes the necessity for action and considers what form it should take. In the interviewer's failure to imagine a response not dreamt of in Kohlberg's moral philosophy lies the failure to hear Amy's question and to see the logic in her response, to discern that what appears, from one perspective, to be an evasion of the dilemma signifies in other terms a recognition of the problem and a search for a more adequate solution.

Thus in Heinz's dilemma these two children see two very different moral problems—Jake a conflict between life and property that can be resolved by logical deduction, Amy a fracture of human relationship that must be mended with its own thread. Asking different questions that arise from different conceptions of the moral domain, the children arrive at answers that fundamentally diverge, and the arrangement of these answers as successive stages on a scale of increasing moral maturity calibrated by the logic of the boy's response misses the different truth revealed in the judgment of the girl. To the question, "What does he see that she does not?" Kohlberg's theory provides a ready response, manifest in the scoring of Jake's judgments a full stage higher than Amy's in moral maturity; to the question, "What does she see that he does not?" Kohlberg's theory has nothing to say. Since most of her responses fall through the sieve of Kohlberg's scoring system, her responses appear from his perspective to lie outside the moral domain.

Yet just as Jake reveals a sophisticated understanding of the logic of justification, so Amy is equally sophisticated in her understanding of the nature of choice. Recognizing that "if both the roads went in totally separate ways, if you pick one, you'll never know what would happen if you went the other way," she explains that "that's the chance you have to take, and like I said, it's just really a guess." To illustrate her point "in a simple way," she describes her choice to spend the summer at camp:

> I will never know what would have happened if I had stayed here, and if something goes wrong at camp, I'll never know if I stayed here if it would have been better. There's really no way around it because there's no way you can do both at once, so you've got to decide, but you'll never know.

In this way, these two eleven-year-old children, both highly intelligent and perceptive about life, though in different ways, display different modes of moral understanding, different ways of thinking about conflict and choice. In resolving Heinz's dilemma, Jake relies on theft to avoid confrontation and turns to the law to mediate the dispute. Transposing a hierarchy of power into a hierarchy of values, he defuses a potentially explosive conflict between people by casting it as an impersonal conflict of claims. In this way, he abstracts the moral problem from the interpersonal situation, finding in the logic of fairness an objective way to decide who will win the dispute. But this hierarchical ordering, with its imagery of winning and losing and the potential for violence which it contains, gives way in Amy's construction of the dilemma to a network of connection, a web of relationships that is sustained by a process of communication. With this shift, the moral problem changes from one of unfair domination, the imposition of property over life, to one of unnecessary exclusion, the failure of the druggist to respond to the wife. . . .

Writing and Discussion Topics

Questions 1–6 address content, critical analysis, personal choices, ethical options, specific discipline, and interdisciplinary alternatives, respectively.

1. Does Gilligan believe that women have been treated fairly in the history of scholarship? Explain some of Gilligan's findings. Do you agree or disagree?

2. What is Lawrence Kohlberg's major contention with respect to a woman's moral development? How does Gilligan disagree or agree with Kohlberg? Examine which psychologist, Lawrence Kohlberg or Carol Gilligan, is more relevant in contemporary society and indicate why.

3. Do men think with their heads and women with their hearts? Assess this statement through the eyes of Gilligan and through your own perspective. Is there an implication in the question that is demeaning to women?

4. An ethical approach based on caring, sharing, and relationships is being called an "emerging ethic." Cite thinkers in the past who have recognized the need for passion and feeling in the making of ethical decisions.

5. How is developmental psychology linked to philosophy? Find other philosophers who cite psychology as part of ethics.

6. Gilligan claims that Sigmund Freud has inaccurately traced women in "the development of relationships, morality or a clear sense of self." Through this alleged inaccuracy, Freud called women "a dark continent for psychology." Who is correct, Freud or Gilligan? Examine this controversy with sources from ethics, feminist study, or psychology.

PART 2

◆◆◆

ETHICS & LIFE

chapter 2

ABORTION

Thought by some to be our new "civil war," the concerns surrounding abortion are having a divisive effect in the United States, the likeness of which has not been seen since the era of the Vietnam war. Pro-life and pro-choice camps are waging a battle over the rights of the unborn and over the rights of women. The issue of abortion was not always so divisive. Indeed, in ancient Greece and Rome abortions were practiced as a means of birth control. In western Europe, especially during the Middle Ages, abortion was accepted in the early months of pregnancy.

By the nineteenth century, however, attitudes regarding abortion began to change, partly under the influence of the Christian religion. The doctrine of the sanctity of all human life became a driving idea in the debate regarding abortion. This teaching led some, particularly the leaders of the Roman Catholic Church, to insist that the human soul is a part of the fetus at the moment of conception. Hence, the unborn must be protected, both by the church and by the state. This belief helped bring about the passage of strict anti-abortion laws in the United States and England by the middle of the nineteenth century.

Pro-life supporters.   Source:
UPI/Bettmann.

The latter part of the twentieth century saw a distinct liberalization of
abortion attitudes, resulting in the legalization of abortion in many
countries of the world, including the United States. On January 22, 1973,
the Supreme Court ruled that states could not prevent a woman from
having an abortion during the first six months of pregnancy. As this ruling
was implemented in various states, however, a new wave of opposition
began to rise from various people and groups, some religious and some not.
In general, those who opposed abortion began to call themselves "pro-life;"
those who supported abortion came to refer to themselves as "pro-choice."

From the standpoint of ethics, the fundamental questions to be addressed
are, under what conditions, if any, may abortions be justified? And, what are
the criteria applied that make the conditions justifiable? The questions are
so stated because it is arguable that the fetus has at least a prima facie right
to life, hence the burden of proof rests with the one seeking an abortion.
But it seems equally clear that the fetus's right to life is not absolute, hence
there must be sufficient circumstances or conditions that may override the
prima facie right to life of the fetus. According to *Roe v. Wade*, one of these
conditions is a woman's right to her own reproductive freedom.

A rigorous pro-life advocate believes that abortions are justified only
when the life of the mother is demonstrably at stake. It does not matter if
the fetus was conceived in an act of rape, incest, or even incestuous rape.
Since a fetus is a human being, it must be protected and granted its rightful
life, although that right may be overridden by the equal right to life of the
mother. A true pro-choice advocate, on the other hand, condones abortion
for a variety of reasons through the second trimester of pregnancy.
Whatever, if any, moral or human standing the fetus may have can always

Pro-choice rally.   Source: UPI/
Bettmann.

be overridden by the woman's right to decide what happens to her body. Society cannot prescribe for her conditions under which she must maintain an unwanted pregnancy.

There is a middle ground in this debate, a so-called moderate position. While those who advocate a moderate view may tend toward pro-life or pro-choice positions, in general they hold that abortions may be justified up to a certain stage of fetal development for morally permissible reasons. The morally permissible reasons are varied and may include a pregnancy caused by rape or incest, a pregnancy that results in serious psychological damage to the mother, a pregnancy that produces a profoundly deformed fetus, even a failure of birth control and so on. Whatever the reasons, the issue for the moderate is to decide what rights or claims of the mother justifiably override the putative right to life of the fetus.

This chapter helps us consider abortion from several points of view. First, we will examine the issues involved, followed by the philosophical positions and the religious perspectives. A literature section helps to reveal some of the deep issues from a fictional point of view, and the readings conclude with a compelling look at abortion from historical material.

The issue of abortion is established with the Supreme Court case, *Roe v. Wade.* Justice Harry Blackmun writes the majority opinion in the case. Blackmun holds that a woman has a right to privacy, and this right includes her reproductive freedom. He further finds that a woman has the right to a safe abortion. He states, however, that abortion after the second trimester should be performed only if the mother's life is in danger. At this point, the state has a tenable interest in safeguarding the mother's health and the possible life of the fetus.

Former President Ronald Reagan is emphatic in proclaiming that abortion is wrong. He refers to abortion as a battle that America is losing. Life begins at conception, according to Reagan, and therefore the value of human life is corrupted by legalizing abortion.

Linda Francke is a pro-choice advocate who had an abortion and is haunted by the experience. She was in favor of abortion for the sake of her career as well as the career of her husband. After the abortion, she came to the view that while abortion may be acceptable for other women, it is not so for her. It undermined her sense of self-respect and her relationship with her husband.

In the next section, three philosophers add their insights into the abortion debate. Judith Jarvis Thomson develops a moderate view of abortion in her essay. She avoids the question of when human life begins by granting that the fetus in the late stages of pregnancy is a human being. She argues, however, that abortion is justifiable in the instances of danger to the mother's health, rape, incest, and birth-control failure. She uses insightful analogies to exemplify the situations akin to an unwanted pregnancy. She then explores the concept of what a "minimally decent Samaritan" would do in each of these situations.

Kathryn Pyne Addelson disagrees with Thomson's approach to abortion. She argues that the concerns for rights and justice do not properly focus on the real issue of abortion. Addelson believes the focus of abortion should be on actual cases and social change. She introduces us to "Jane," a clinic that was established in Chicago before abortion was legalized. The focus of the clinic was on the issues surrounding the subservience, and its consequences, of women to a medical system that, she argues, was based on the biases of men. The clinic functioned on a system of women helping one another in a variety of ways, including counseling and medical assistance. The women at "Jane" found they could provide all the medical care needed for an abortion, regardless of wealth, social status, race, religion, or marital situation.

Abortion can be a source of social change when a woman rejects the expectations of society and does what she believes is best for her and the fetus. In light of these possibilities, Mary Mahowald believes that abortion must be understood in more ways than pro-life and pro-choice. To discuss fully the many social, personal, financial, and political ramifications of abortion, Mahowald proffers inclusive attitudes on abortion: pro-choice, pro-life, pro-abortion, pro-woman, and pro-fetus.

Moving from philosophy to religion, viewpoints on abortion from Islamic, Christian, and Jewish perspectives are discussed. This segment begins with Pope Paul VI summarizing the official Roman Catholic stance against abortion. Pope Paul asserts that since abortion can be used as a form of birth control, it interferes with the procreation of children, and hence, God's overall purpose. Thus, according to Pope Paul, abortion is evil. He further argues that abortion undermines the family, impairs society, and transgresses humanity.

Daniel Maguire, a Roman Catholic theologian who disagrees with the position of the papacy on abortion, spent time at an abortion clinic to observe women who were contending with unwanted pregnancies. He examines the causes of these unwanted pregnancies, and determines that poverty, sexual repression, and sexism are at the crux of the abortion problem. He questions placing the life of a "mass of cells" above the quality of life for a woman. He wonders why society should be able to interfere with a woman's reproductive freedom, suggesting that in some circumstances, abortion can be more pro-life than continuing a pregnancy.

Jewish perspectives on abortion differ significantly with those of most Christians, whether they support abortion or not. Fred Rosner indicates that ancient Jewish law held that an unborn fetus is not regarded as a person with a soul until it breathes its first breath outside the womb. Rosner points out that even a newborn baby does not have full adult rights for the first thirty days. The embryo, according to Jewish thought, has no identity of its own; it does not move and is dependent on its mother's body for life. Abortion is invariably allowed before "quickening" (the first movement of the fetus felt by the mother), but permitted only in certain cases thereafter.

Islamic attitudes on abortion, explained by Basim F. Mussallam, need to be seen in relation to Islamic views on marriage and sexual relations. The Islamic outlook on marriage differs from Western views in that Muslims perceive marriage as impermanent and polygamous. Divorce is easy and acceptable for men. In the Islamic religion, emphasis is placed on procreation and having many children. Historically, sexual intercourse, however, has not been confined to marriage and the goal of procreation. Sexual relations are permitted outside of marriage by the husband with his concubines as a means of sexual expression. In this reading, different Muslim jurists have presented conditions for abortion. There are a variety of acceptable reasons for abortion; however, women have few rights, and men will usually decide on reproduction issues.

Literature gives life and form to the debates surrounding abortion. A. J. Cronin recounts the experience of a wealthy woman who refuses to give birth to an unwanted child. Her physician is repulsed by the woman and her "selfishness." He treats his patient harshly after she has a botched abortion. It is important to examine both the actions of the doctor and the patient in this selection.

Gwendolyn Brooks introduces us to the life and emotions of a woman who has had abortions. The woman ponders life that was not lived, and she wonders about love she could not give to lives that are gone. In another selection, Ernest Hemingway writes about a woman who would like to keep a pregnancy that her lover believes will complicate his freedom. In "Hills Like White Elephants," Hemingway contrasts the security of and the commitment to a mother-child relationship for a woman with a "simple operation" and a lack of obligation for a man. And, Elaine Englehardt develops the complicated life of a single, thirty-five-year-old woman who suffers the torment of an unwanted pregnancy. She believes giving birth to a child is not in her best interests.

Historical perspectives provide insight on abortion in the ancient world of Athens and Rome and in the United States. Michael Gorman, writing about ancient Athens and Rome, identifies their rather ordinary practice of abortion and notes that Greek philosophers, such as Plato and Aristotle, favored abortion for the common good. At the time, many Greek city-states were overpopulated, poor, and weak. Even infanticide was a common practice done in order to strengthen society and to produce the proper male-female ratio needed to fortify the population.

Linda Gordon reviews social controls over contraception and abortion. Her historical findings reveal that culture and family have often regulated sexual activity, the role of women, and the morality of population control. Gordon finds that prior to the nineteenth century, Roman Catholic and Protestant churches in the United States accepted abortions before "quickening." New economic and social circumstances, she claims, were important reasons for the changes in social attitudes regarding abortion. As a result, social institutions came to have more control over the abortion question.

Justice Harry Blackmun

MAJORITY OPINION IN *ROE V. WADE*

◆◆◆

H arry Blackmun, an associate justice of the United States Supreme Court, is a graduate of Harvard Law School. He is noted nationally for extensive scholarship in the field of law. He also distinguished himself in Minnesota where he was an attorney, law professor, and judge. For twenty years he acted as legal counsel to the Mayo Clinic. He has been on the Supreme Court bench since 1970. ◆

It is . . . apparent that at common law, at the time of the adoption of our Constitution, and throughout the major portion of the 19th century, abortion was viewed with less disfavor than under most American statutes currently in effect. Phrasing it another way, a woman enjoyed a substantially broader right to terminate a pregnancy than she does in most States today. At least with respect to the early stage of pregnancy, and very possibly without such a limitation, the opportunity to make this choice was present in this country well into the 19th century. Even later, the law continued for some time to treat less punitively an abortion procured in early pregnancy. . . .

Three reasons have been advanced to explain historically the enactment of criminal abortion laws in the 19th century and to justify their continued existence.

It has been argued occasionally that these laws were the product of a Victorian social concern to discourage illicit sexual conduct. Texas, however, does not advance this justification in the present case, and it appears that no court or commentator has taken the argument seriously. . . .

A second reason is concerned with abortion as a medical procedure. When most criminal abortion laws were first enacted, the procedure was a hazardous one for the woman. This was particularly true prior to the development of antisepsis. Antiseptic techniques, of course, were based on discoveries by Lister, Pasteur, and others first announced in 1867, but were not generally accepted and employed until about the turn of the century. Abortion mortality was high. Even after 1900, and perhaps until as late as the development of antibiotics in the 1940's, standard modern techniques such as dilatation and curettage were not nearly so safe as they are today. Thus it has been argued that a State's real concern in enacting a criminal abortion law was to protect the pregnant woman, that is, to restrain her from submitting to a procedure that placed her life in serious jeopardy.

Modern medical techniques have altered this situation. Appellants and various *amici* refer to medical data indicating that abortion in early pregnancy, that is, prior to the end of first trimester, although not without its risk, is now relatively safe. Mortality rates for women undergoing early abortions, where the procedure is legal, appear to be as low as or lower than the rates for normal childbirth. Consequently, any interest of the State in protecting the woman from an inherently hazardous procedure, except when it would be equally dangerous for her to forgo

it, has largely disappeared. Of course, important state interests in the area of health and medical standards do remain. The State has a legitimate interest in seeing to it that abortion, like any other medical procedure, is performed under circumstances that insure maximum safety for the patient. This interest obviously extends at least to the performing physician and his staff, to the facilities involved, to the availability of after-care, and to adequate provision for any complication or emergency that might arise. The prevalence of high mortality rates at illegal "abortion mills" strengthens, rather than weakens, the State's interest in regulating the conditions under which abortions are performed. Moreover, the risk to the woman increases as her pregnancy continues. Thus the State retains a definite interest in protecting the woman's own health and safety when an abortion is performed at a late stage of pregnancy.

The third reason is the State's interest—some phrase it in terms of duty—in protecting prenatal life. Some of the argument for this justification rests on the theory that a new human life is present from the moment of conception. The State's interest and general obligation to protect life then extends, it is argued, to prenatal life. Only when the life of the pregnant mother herself is at stake, balanced against the life she carries within her, should the interest of the embryo or fetus not prevail. Logically, of course, a legitimate state interest in this area need not stand or fall on acceptance of the belief that life begins at conception or at some other point prior to live birth. In assessing the State's interest, recognition may be given to the less rigid claim that as long as at least *potential* life is involved, the State may assert interests beyond the protection of the pregnant woman alone.

Parties challenging state abortion laws have sharply disputed in some courts the contention that a purpose of these laws, when enacted, was to protect prenatal life. Pointing to the absence of legislative history to support the contention, they claim that most state laws were designed solely to protect the woman. Because medical advances have lessened this concern, at least with respect to abortion in early pregnancy, they argue that with respect to such abortions the laws can no longer be justified by any state interest. There is some scholarly support for this view of original purpose. The few state courts called upon to interpret their laws in the late 19th and early 20th centuries did focus on the State's interest in protecting the woman's health rather than in preserving the embryo and fetus. . . .

Source: United States Supreme Court, 410 U.S. 113 (1973).

The Constitution does not explicitly mention any right of privacy. In a line of decisions, however, going back perhaps as far as *Union Pacific R. Co. v. Botsford* (1891), the Court has recognized that a right of personal privacy, or a guarantee of certain areas or zones of privacy, does exist under the Constitution. In varying contexts the Court or individual Justices have indeed found at least the roots of that right in the First Amendment, . . . in the Fourth and Fifth Amendments . . . in the penumbras of the Bill of Rights . . . in the Ninth Amendment . . . or in the concept of liberty guaranteed by the first section of the Fourteenth Amendment. . . . These decisions make it clear that only personal rights that can be deemed "fundamental" or "implicit in the concept of ordered liberty," . . . are included in this guarantee of personal privacy. They also make it clear that the right has some extension to activities relating to marriage, . . . procreation, . . . contraception, . . . family relationships, . . . and child rearing and education. . . .

This right of privacy, whether it be founded in the Fourteenth Amendment's concept of personal liberty and restrictions upon state action, as we feel it is, or, as the District Court determined, in the Ninth Amendment's reservation of rights to the people, is broad enough to encompass a woman's decision whether or not to terminate her pregnancy. . . .

. . . [A]ppellants and some *amici* argue that the woman's right is absolute and that she is entitled to terminate her pregnancy at whatever time, in whatever way, and for whatever reason she alone chooses. With this we do not agree. Appellants' arguments that Texas either has no valid interest at all in regulating the abortion decision, or no interest strong enough to support any limitation upon the woman's sole determination, is unpersuasive. The Court's decisions recognizing a right of privacy also acknowledge that some state regulation in areas protected by that right is appropriate. As noted above, a state may properly assert important interests in safe-guarding health, in maintaining medical standards, and in protecting potential life. At some point in pregnancy, these respective interests become sufficiently compelling to sustain regulation of the factors that govern the abortion decision. The privacy right involved, therefore, cannot be said to be absolute. . . .

We therefore conclude that the right of personal privacy includes the abortion decision, but that this right is not unqualified and must be considered against important state interests in regulation.

We note that those federal and state courts that have recently considered abortion law challenges have reached the same conclusion. . . .

Although the results are divided, most of these courts have agreed that the right of privacy, however based, is broad enough to cover the abortion decision; that the right, nonetheless, is not absolute and is subject to some limitations; and that at some point the state interests as to protection of health, medical standards, and prenatal life, become dominant. We agree with this approach. . . .

The appellee and certain *amici* argue that the fetus is a "person" within the language and meaning of the Fourteenth Amendment. In support of this they outline at length and in detail the well-known facts of fetal development. If this suggestion of personhood is established, the appellant's case, of course, collapses, for the fetus' right to life is then guaranteed specifically by the Amendment. The appellant conceded as much on reargument. On the other hand, the appellee conceded on reargument that no case could be cited that holds that a fetus is a person within the meaning of the Fourteenth Amendment. . . .

All this, together with our observation, *supra*, that throughout the major portion of the 19th century prevailing legal abortion practices were far freer than they are today, persuades us that the word "person," as used in the Fourteenth Amendment, does not include the unborn. . . . Indeed, our decision in *United States v. Vuitch* (1971) inferentially is to the same effect, for we there would not have indulged in statutory interpretation favorable to abortion in specified circumstances if the necessary consequence was the termination of life entitled to Fourteenth Amendment protection.

. . . As we have intimated above, it is reasonable and appropriate for a State to decide that at some point in time another interest, that of health of the mother or that of potential human life, becomes significantly involved. The woman's privacy is no longer sole and any right of privacy she possesses must be measured accordingly.

Texas urges that, apart from the Fourteenth Amendment, life begins at conception and is present throughout pregnancy, and that, therefore, the State has a compelling interest in protecting that life from and after conception. We need not resolve the difficult question of when life begins. When those trained in the respective disciplines of medicine, philosophy, and theology are unable to arrive at any consensus, the judiciary, at this point in the development of man's knowledge, is not in a position to speculate as to the answer.

It should be sufficient to note briefly the wide divergence of thinking on this most sensitive and difficult question. There has always been strong support for the view that life does not begin until live birth. This was the belief of the Stoics. It appears to be the predominant, though not the unanimous, attitude of the Jewish faith. It may be taken to represent also the position of a large segment of the Protestant community, insofar as that can be ascertained; organized groups that have taken a formal position on the abortion issue have generally regarded abortion as a matter for the conscience of the individual and her family. As we have noted, the common law found greater significance in quickening. Physicians and their scientific colleagues have regarded that event with less interest and have tended to focus either upon conception or upon live birth or upon the interim point at which the fetus becomes "viable," that is, potentially able to live outside the mother's womb, albeit with artificial aid. Viability is usually placed at about seven months (28 weeks) but may occur earlier, even at 24 weeks. . . .

In areas other than criminal abortion the law has been reluctant to endorse any theory that life, as we recognize it, begins before live birth or to accord legal rights to the unborn except in narrowly defined situations and except when the rights are contingent upon live birth. . . . In short, the unborn have never been recognized in the law as persons in the whole sense.

In view of all this, we do not agree that, by adopting one theory of life, Texas may override the rights of the pregnant woman that are at stake. We repeat, however, that the State does have an important and legitimate interest in preserving and protecting the health of the pregnant woman, whether she be a resident of the State or a nonresident who seeks medical consultation and treatment there, and that it has still *another* important and legitimate interest in protecting the potentiality of human life. These interests are separate and distinct. Each grows in substantiality as the woman approaches term and, at a point during pregnancy, each becomes "compelling."

With respect to the State's important and legitimate interest in the health of the mother, the "compelling" point, in the light of present medical knowledge, is at approximately the end of the first trimester. This is so because of the now established

medical fact . . . that until the end of the first trimester mortality in abortion is less than mortality in normal childbirth. It follows that, from and after this point, a State may regulate the abortion procedure to the extent that the regulation reasonably relates to the preservation and protection of maternal health. Examples of permissible state regulation in this area are requirements as to the qualifications of the person who is to perform the abortion; as to the licensure of that person; as to the facility in which the procedure is to be performed, that is, whether it must be a hospital or may be a clinic or some other place of less-than-hospital status; as to the licensing of the facility; and the like.

This means, on the other hand, that, for the period of pregnancy prior to this "compelling" point, the attending physician, in consultation with his patient, is free to determine, without regulation by the State, that in his medical judgment the patient's pregnancy should be terminated. If that decision is reached, the judgment may be effectuated by an abortion free of interference by the State.

With respect to the State's important and legitimate interest in potential life, the "compelling" point is at viability. This is so because the fetus then presumably has the capability of meaningful life outside the mother's womb. State regulation protective of fetal life after viability thus has both logical and biological justifications. If the State is interested in protecting fetal life after viability, it may go so far as to proscribe abortion during that period except when it is necessary to preserve the life or health of the mother. . . .

To summarize and repeat:

1. A state criminal abortion statute of the current Texas type, that excepts from criminality only a *life saving* procedure on behalf of the mother, without regard to pregnancy stage and without recognition of the other interests involved, is violative of the Due Process Clause of the Fourteenth Amendment.
    a. For the stage prior to approximately the end of the first trimester, the abortion decision and its effectuation must be left to the medical judgment of the pregnant woman's attending physician.
    b. For the stage subsequent to approximately the end of the first trimester, the State, in promoting its interest in the health of the mother,

may, if it chooses, regulate the abortion procedure in ways that are reasonably related to maternal health.

   c. For the stage subsequent to viability the State, in promoting its interest in the potentiality of human life, may, if it chooses, regulate, and even proscribe, abortion except where it is necessary, in appropriate medical judgment, for the preservation of the life or health of the mother.

2. The State may define the term "physician," as it has been employed [here], to mean only a physician currently licensed by the State, and may proscribe any abortion by a person who is not a physician as so defined.

   . . . The decision leaves the State free to place increasing restrictions on abortion as the period of pregnancy lengthens, so long as those restrictions are tailored to the recognized state interests. The decision vindicates the right of the physician to administer medical treatment according to his professional judgment up to the points where important state interests provide compelling justifications for intervention. Up to those points the abortion decision in all its aspects is inherently, and primarily, a medical decision, and basic responsibility for it must rest with the physician. If an individual practitioner abuses the privilege of exercising proper medical judgment, the usual remedies, judicial and intraprofessional, are available. . . .

Writing and Discussion Topics

Questions 1–6 address content, critical analysis, personal choices, ethical options, specific discipline, and interdisciplinary alternatives, respectively.

1. What are the major arguments given by Blackmun in removing states' rights from the abortion debate? How does the 1989 Webster case affect Blackmun's findings?

2. Blackmun believes states have an obligation to protect a pregnant woman's health. What are Blackmun's arguments? Why do you agree or disagree with those arguments?

3. Assume you are ten weeks pregnant. This is an unwanted pregnancy that would cause enormous distress in your life and in the lives of others. Would you have an abortion? What arguments would you use to help you defend your decision?

4. Blackmun holds that women have the right to a safe abortion up to the point of the viability of the fetus. Why does he believe that a woman's right to her own reproductive system overrides the rights of the fetus prior to viability? Explain why you agree or disagree.

5. Did Blackmun use historical perspectives in making his decision? If so, which perspectives did he use, and which did he exclude?

6. Abortion is sometimes seen as a question of medical ethics. Should an opinion centered on abortion be made by the medical community instead of the legal community or by individuals themselves? Fully support your views.

ABORTION AND THE CONSCIENCE OF THE NATION

◆◆◆

Ronald Reagan Source: UPI/ Bettmann.

Ronald Reagan was governor of California prior to becoming the fortieth president of the United States. He was regarded as an effective communicator for his ability to reach the American people with his political views. Reagan's conservative philosophy was often broadcast on radio prior to, during, and after his two terms as president. His political life was preceded by a career in the movie industry. ◆

The 10th anniversary of the Supreme Court decision in *Roe v. Wade* is a good time for us to pause and reflect. Our nationwide policy of abortion-on-demand through all nine months of pregnancy was neither voted for by our people nor enacted by our legislators—not a single State had such unrestricted abortion before the Supreme Court decreed it to be a national policy in 1973. But the consequences of this judicial decision are now obvious: since 1973, more than 15 million unborn children have had their lives snuffed out by legalized abortions. That is over ten times the number of Americans lost in all our nation's wars.

Make no mistake, abortion-on-demand is not a right granted by the Constitution. No serious scholar, including one disposed to agree with the Court's result, has argued that the framers of the Constitution intended to create such a right. Shortly after the *Roe v. Wade* decision, Professor John Hart Ely, now Dean of Stanford Law School, wrote that the opinion "is not constitutional law and gives almost no sense of an obligation to try to be." Nowhere do the plain words of the Constitution even hint at a "right" so sweeping as to permit abortion up to the time the child is ready to be born. Yet that is what the Court ruled.

As an act of "raw judicial power" (to use Justice White's biting phrase), the decision by the seven-man majority in *Roe v. Wade* has so far been made to stick. But the Court's decision has by no means settled the debate. Instead, *Roe v. Wade* has become a continuing prod to the conscience of the nation.

Abortion concerns not just the unborn child, it concerns every one of us. The English poet, John Donne, wrote: " . . . any man's death diminishes me, because I am involved in mankind; and therefore never send to know for whom the bell tolls; it tolls for thee."

We cannot diminish the value of one category of human life—the unborn—without diminishing the value of all human life. We saw tragic proof of this truism last year when the Indiana courts allowed the starvation death of "Baby Doe" in Bloomington because the child had Down's Syndrome.

Many of our fellow citizens grieve over the loss of life that has followed *Roe v. Wade*. Margaret Heckler, soon after being nominated to head the largest department of our government, Health and Human Services, told an audience that she believed abortion

to be the greatest moral crisis facing our country today. And the revered Mother Teresa, who works in the streets of Calcutta ministering to dying people in her world-famous mission of mercy, has said that "the greatest misery of our time is the generalized abortion of children."

Over the first two years of my Administration I have closely followed and assisted efforts in Congress to reverse the tide of abortion—efforts of Congressmen, Senators and citizens responding to an urgent moral crisis. Regrettably, I have also seen the massive efforts of those who, under the banner of "freedom of choice," have so far blocked every effort to reverse nationwide abortion-on-demand.

Despite the formidable obstacles before us, we must not lose heart. This is not the first time our country has been divided by a Supreme Court decision that denied the value of certain human lives. The *Dred Scott* decision of 1857 was not overturned in a day, or a year, or even a decade. At first, only a minority of Americans recognized and deplored the moral crisis brought about by denying the full humanity of our black brothers and sisters; but that minority persisted in their vision and finally prevailed. They did it by appealing to the hearts and minds of their countrymen, to the truth of human dignity under God. From their example, we know that respect for the sacred value of human life is too deeply engrained in the hearts of our people to remain forever suppressed. But the great majority of the American people have not yet made their voices heard, and we cannot expect them to—any more than the public voice arose against slavery—*until* the issue is clearly framed and presented.

What, then, is the real issue? I have often said that when we talk about abortion, we are talking about two lives—the life of the mother and the life of the unborn child. Why else do we call a pregnant woman a mother? I have also said that anyone who doesn't feel sure whether we are talking about a second human life should clearly give life the benefit of the doubt. If you don't know whether a body is alive or dead, you would never bury it. I think this consideration itself should be enough for all of us to insist on protecting the unborn.

The case against abortion does not rest here, however, for medical practice confirms at every step the correctness of these moral sensibilities. Modern medicine treats the unborn child as a patient. Medical pioneers have made great breakthroughs in treating the unborn—for genetic problems, vitamin deficiencies, irregular heart rhythms, and other medical conditions. Who can forget George Will's moving account of the little boy who underwent brain surgery six times during the nine weeks before he was born? Who is the *patient* if not that tiny unborn human being who can feel pain when he or she is approached by doctors who come to kill rather than to cure?

The real question today is not when human life begins, but, *What is the value of human life?* The abortionist who reassembles the arms and legs of a tiny baby to make sure all its parts have been torn from its mother's body can hardly doubt whether it is a human being. The real question for him and for all of us is whether that tiny human life has a God-given right to be protected by the law—the same right we have.

What more dramatic confirmation could we have of the real issue than the Baby Doe case in Bloomington, Indiana? The death of that tiny infant tore at the hearts of all Americans because the child was undeniably a live human being—one lying helpless before the eyes of the doctors and the eyes of the nation. The real issue for the courts was *not* whether Baby Doe was a human being. The real issue was whether to protect the life of a human being who had Down's Syndrome, who would probably be mentally handicapped, but who needed a routine surgical procedure to unblock his esophagus and allow him to eat. A doctor testified to the presiding judge that, even with his physical problem corrected, Baby Doe would have a "non-existent" possibility for "a minimally adequate life"—in other words, that retardation was the equivalent of a crime deserving the death penalty. The judge let Baby Doe starve and die, and the Indiana Supreme Court sanctioned his decision.

Federal law does not allow Federally-assisted hospitals to decide that Down's Syndrome infants are not worth treating, much less to decide to starve them to death. Accordingly, I have directed the Departments of Justice and HHS to apply civil rights regulations to protect handicapped newborns. All hospitals receiving Federal funds must post notices which will clearly state that failure to feed handicapped babies is prohibited by Federal law. The basic issue is whether to value and protect the lives of the handicapped, whether to recognize the sanctity of human life. This is the same basic issue that underlies the question of abortion.

The 1981 Senate hearings on the beginning of human life brought out the basic issue more clearly than ever before. The many medical and scientific witnesses who testified disagreed on many things, but not on the *scientific* evidence that the unborn child is alive, is a distinct individual, or is a member of the human species. They did disagree over the *value* question, whether to give value to a human life at its early and most vulnerable stages of existence.

Regrettably, we live at a time when some persons do *not* value all human life. They want to pick and choose which individuals have value. Some have said that only those individuals with "consciousness of self" are human beings. One such writer has followed this deadly logic and concluded that "shocking as it may seem, a newly born infant is not a human being."

A Nobel Prize winning scientist has suggested that if a handicapped child "were not declared fully human until three days after birth, then all parents could be allowed the choice." In other words, "quality control" to see if newly born human beings are up to snuff.

Obviously, some influential people want to deny that every human life has intrinsic, sacred worth. They insist that a member of the human race must have certain qualities before they accord him or her status as a "human being."

Events have borne out the editorial in a California medical journal which explained three years before *Roe v. Wade* that the social acceptance of abortion is a "defiance of the long-held Western ethic of intrinsic and equal value for every human life regardless of its stage, condition, or status."

Every legislator, every doctor, and every citizen needs to recognize that the real issue is whether to affirm and protect the sanctity of all human life, or to embrace a social ethic where some human lives are valued and others are not. As a nation, we must choose between the sanctity of life ethic and the quality of life ethic.

I have no trouble identifying the answer our nation has always given to this basic question, and the answer that I hope and pray it will give in the future. America was founded by men and women who shared a vision of the value of each and every individual. They stated this vision clearly from the very start in the Declaration of Independence, using words that every schoolboy and schoolgirl can recite:

> We hold these truths to be self-evident, that all men are created equal, that they are endowed by their Creator with certain unalienable rights, that among these are life, liberty, and the pursuit of happiness.

We fought a terrible war to guarantee that one category of mankind—black people in America—could not be denied the inalienable rights with which their Creator endowed them. The great champion of the sanctity of all human life in that day, Abraham Lincoln, gave us his assessment of the Declaration's purpose. Speaking of the framers of that noble document, he said:

> This was their majestic interpretation of the economy of the Universe. This was their lofty, and wise, and noble understanding of the justice of the Creator to His creatures. Yes, gentlemen, to all His creatures, to the whole great family of man. In their enlightened belief, nothing stamped with the divine image and likeness was sent into the world to be trodden on . . . . They grasped not only the whole race of man then living, but they reached forward and seized upon the farthest posterity. They erected a beacon to guide their children and their children's children, and the countless myriads who should inhabit the earth in other ages.

He warned also of the danger we would face if we closed our eyes to the value of life in any category of human beings:

> I should like to know if taking this old Declaration of Independence, which declares that all men are equal upon principle and making exceptions to it where will it stop. If one man says it does not mean a Negro, why not another say it does not mean some other man?

When Congressman John A. Bingham of Ohio drafted the Fourteenth Amendment to guarantee the rights of life, liberty, and property to all human beings, he explained that *all* are "entitled to the protection of American law, because its divine spirit of equality declares that all men are created equal." He said the rights guaranteed by the amendment would therefore apply to "any human being." Justice William Brennan, writing in another case decided only the year before *Roe v. Wade*, referred to our society as one that "strongly affirms the sanctity of life."

Another William Brennan—not the Justice—has reminded us of the terrible consequences that can follow when a nation rejects the sanctity of life ethic:

> The cultural environment for a human holocaust is present whenever any society can be misled into defining individuals as less than human and therefore devoid of value and respect.

As a nation today, we have *not* rejected the sanctity of human life. The American people have not had an opportunity to express their view on the sanctity of human life in the unborn. I am convinced that Americans do not want to play God with the value of human life. It is not for us to decide who is worthy to live and who is not. Even the Supreme Court's opinion in *Roe v. Wade* did not explicitly reject the traditional American idea of intrinsic worth and value in all human life; it simply dodged this issue.

The Congress has before it several measures that would enable our people to reaffirm the sanctity of human life, even the smallest and the youngest and the most defenseless. The Human Life Bill expressly recognizes the unborn as human beings and accordingly protects them as persons under our Constitution. This bill, first introduced by Senator Jesse Helms, provided the vehicle for the Senate hearings in 1981 which contributed so much to our understanding of the real issue of abortion.

The Respect Human Life Act, just introduced in the 98th Congress, states in its first section that the policy of the United States is "to protect innocent life, both before and after birth." This bill, sponsored by Congressman Henry Hyde and Senator Roger Jepsen, prohibits the Federal government from performing abortions or assisting those who do so, except to save the life of the mother. It also addresses the pressing issue of infanticide which, as we have seen, flows inevitably from permissive abortion as another step in the denial of the inviolability of innocent human life.

I have endorsed each of these measures, as well as the more difficult route of constitutional amendment, and I will give these initiatives my full support. Each of them, in different ways, attempts to reverse the tragic policy of abortion-on-demand imposed by the Supreme Court ten years ago. Each of them is a decisive way to affirm the sanctity of human life.

We must all educate ourselves to the reality of the horrors taking place. Doctors today know that unborn children can feel a touch within the womb and that they respond to pain. But how many Americans are aware that abortion techniques are allowed today, in all 50 states, that burn the skin of a baby with a salt solution, in an agonizing death that can last for hours?

Another example: two years ago, the *Philadelphia Inquirer* ran a Sunday special supplement on "The Dreaded Complication." The "dreaded complication" referred to in the article—the complication feared by doctors who perform abortions—is the *survival* of the child despite all the painful attacks during the abortion procedure. Some unborn children *do survive the late-term abortions* the Supreme Court has made legal. Is there any question that these victims of abortion deserve our attention and protection? Is there any question that those who *don't* survive were living human beings before they were killed?

Late-term abortions, especially when the baby survives, but is then killed by starvation, neglect, or suffocation, show once again the link between abortion and infanticide. The time to stop both is now. As my Administration acts to stop infanticide, we will be fully aware of the real issue that underlies the death of babies before and soon after birth.

Our society has, fortunately, become sensitive to the rights and special needs of the handicapped, but I am shocked that physical or mental handicaps of newborns are still used to justify their extinction. This Administration has a Surgeon General, Dr. C. Everett Koop, who has done perhaps more than any other American for handicapped children, by pioneering surgical techniques to help them, by speaking out on the value of their lives, and by working with them in the context of loving families. You will not find his former patients advocating the so-called quality of life ethic.

I know that when the true issue of infanticide is placed before the American people, with all the facts openly aired, we will have no trouble deciding that a mentally or physically handicapped baby has the same intrinsic worth and right to life as the rest of us. As the New Jersey Supreme Court said two decades ago, in a decision upholding the sanctity of human life, "a child need not be perfect to have a worthwhile life."

Whether we are talking about pain suffered by unborn children, or about late-term abortions, or about infanticide, we inevitably focus on the humanity of the unborn child. Each of these issues is a potential rallying point for the sanctity of life ethic. Once we as a nation rally around any one of these issues to affirm the sanctity of life, we will see the importance of affirming this principle across the board.

Malcolm Muggeridge, the English writer, goes right to the heart of the matter: "Either life is always and in all circumstances sacred, or intrinsically of no account; it is inconceivable that it should be in some cases the one, and in some the other." The sanctity of innocent human life is a principle that Congress should proclaim at every opportunity.

It is possible that the Supreme Court itself may overturn its abortion rulings. We need only recall that in *Brown v. Board of Education* the Court reversed its own earlier "separate-but-equal" decision. I believe if the Supreme Court took another look at *Roe v. Wade,* and considered the real issue between the sanctity of life ethic and the quality of life ethic, it would change its mind once again.

As we continue to work to overturn *Roe v. Wade,* we must also continue to lay the groundwork for a society in which abortion is not the accepted answer to unwanted pregnancy. Pro-life people have already taken heroic steps, often at great personal sacrifice, to provide for unwed mothers. I recently spoke about a young pregnant woman named Victoria, who said, "In this society we save whales, we save timber wolves and bald eagles and Coke bottles. Yet, everyone wanted me to throw away my baby." She has been helped by Sav-a-Life, a group in Dallas, which provides a way for unwed mothers to preserve the human life within them when they might otherwise be tempted to resort to abortion. I think also of House of His Creation in Coatesville, Pennsylvania, where a loving couple has taken in almost 200 young women in the past ten years. They have seen, as a fact of life, that the girls are *not* better off having abortions than saving their babies. I am also reminded of the remarkable Rossow family of Ellington, Connecticut, who have opened their hearts and their home to nine handicapped adopted and foster children.

The Adolescent Family Life Program, adopted by Congress at the request of Senator Jeremiah Denton, has opened new opportunities for unwed mothers to give their children life. We should not rest until our entire society echoes the tone of John Powell in the dedication of his book, *Abortion: The Silent Holocaust,* a dedication to every woman carrying an unwanted child: "Please believe that you are not alone. There are many of us that truly love you, who want to stand at your side, and help in any way we can." And we can echo the always-practical woman of faith, Mother Teresa, when she says, "If you don't want the little child, that unborn child, give him to me." We have so many families in America seeking to adopt children that the slogan "every child a wanted child" is now the emptiest of all reasons to tolerate abortion.

I have often said we need to join in prayer to bring protection to the unborn. Prayer and action are needed to uphold the sanctity of human life. I believe it will not be possible to accomplish our work, the work of saving lives, "without being a soul of prayer." The famous British Member of Parliament, William Wilberforce, prayed with his small group of influential friends, the "Clapham Sect," for *decades* to see an end to slavery in the British empire. Wilberforce led that struggle in Parliament, unflaggingly, because he believed in the sanctity of human life. He saw the fulfillment of his impossible dream when Parliament outlawed slavery just before his death.

Let his faith and perseverance be our guide. We will never recognize the true value of our own lives until we affirm the value in the life of others, a value of which Malcolm Muggeridge says: ". . . however low it flickers or fiercely burns, it is still a Divine flame which no man dare presume to put out, be his motives ever so humane and enlightened."

Abraham Lincoln recognized that we could not survive as a free land when some men could decide that others were not fit to be free and should therefore be slaves. Likewise, we cannot survive as a free nation when some men decide that others are not fit to live and should be abandoned to abortion or infanticide. My Administration is dedicated to the preservation of America as a free land, and there is no cause more important for preserving that freedom than affirming the transcendent right to life of all human beings, the right without which no other rights have any meaning.

Writing and Discussion Topics

Questions 1–6 address content, critical analysis, personal choices, ethical options, specific discipline, and interdisciplinary alternatives, respectively.

1. Are Reagan's arguments logical? Cite where Reagan gives an argument that is both emotional and logical. Explain why you agree or disagree with the passage you selected.
2. Does Reagan include all human life in his argument, or does he exclude babies with severe deformities? What premise is he assuming? Do you support it?
3. Do you believe that your views on abortion amount to very little when sweeping court cases and legislative decisions control this issue? Can you have an effect on your legislature or the Supreme Court?
4. Reagan says the majority of Americans oppose abortion. Is this correct? Has the extent of this opposition changed since 1973? Does the Supreme Court have a role in infusing the Constitution with social questions?
5. Reagan concludes by saying that "there is no cause more important for preserving freedom than offering the transcendent right to life of all human beings, the right without which no other rights have any meaning." Do you agree with his implication that the fetus has a God-given right to life, and that this right overrides all rights of the mother except her right to life?
6. Is it a fair analogy for Reagan to compare *Roe v. Wade* to the Dred Scott decision of 1857? Why or why not?

Linda Bird Francke

ABORTION: A PERSONAL MORAL DILEMMA

◆◆◆

*L*inda Bird Francke *has enjoyed a notable career as journalist,
author, and broadcast commentator. She only attended college for
one year, yet became an editor for the* New Yorker *and* Newsweek
magazines before becoming a columnist for the New York Times. *She
has written several books including* The Ambivalence of Abortion. *The
following reading is excerpted from this work. She also has written or
collaborated on* Growing Up Divorced, First Lady of Plains, *and*
Ferraro: My Story. ◆

"Jane Doe," thirty-eight, had an abortion in New York City in 1973. The mother of three children, then three, five, and eleven, Jane had just started a full-time job in publishing. She and her husband, an investment banker, decided together that another baby would add an almost unbearable strain to their lives, which were already overfull. What Jane had not anticipated was the guilt and sadness that followed the abortion. She wrote about the experience shortly thereafter and filed the story away. Three years later she reread it and decided it might be helpful to other women who experience the ambivalence of abortion. The *New York Times* ran it on their Op-Ed page in May 1976. This is what she wrote:

We were sitting in a bar on Lexington Avenue when I told my husband I was pregnant. It is not a memory I like to dwell on. Instead of the champagne and hope which had heralded the impending births of the first, second and third child, the news of this one was greeted with shocked silence and Scotch. "Jesus," my husband kept saying to himself, stirring the ice cubes around and around. "Oh, Jesus."

Oh, how we tried to rationalize it that night as the starting time for the movie came and went. My husband talked about his plans for a career change in the next year, to stem the staleness that fourteen years with the same investment-banking firm had brought him. A new baby would preclude that option.

The timing wasn't right for me either. Having juggled pregnancies and child care with what freelance jobs I could fit in between feedings, I had just taken on a full-time job. A new baby would put me right back in the nursery just when our youngest child was finally school age. It was time for *us*, we tried to rationalize. There just wasn't room in our lives now for another baby. We both agreed. And agreed. And agreed.

How very considerate they are at the Women's Services, known formally as the Center for Reproductive and Sexual Health. Yes, indeed, I could have an abortion that very Saturday morning and be out in time to drive to the country that afternoon. Bring a first morning urine specimen, a sanitary belt and napkins, a money order or $125 cash—and a friend.

My friend turned out to be my husband, standing awkwardly and ill at ease as men always do in places that are exclusively for women, as I checked in at nine A.M. Other men hovered around just as anxiously, knowing that they had to be there, wishing they weren't. No one spoke to each other. When I would be cycled out of there four

hours later, the same men would be slumped in their same seats, locked downcast in their cells of embarrassment.

The Saturday morning women's group was more dispirited than the men in the waiting room. There were around fifteen of us, a mixture of races, ages and backgrounds. Three didn't speak English at all and a fourth, a pregnant Puerto Rican girl around eighteen, translated for them.

There were six black women and a hodge-podge of whites, among them a T-shirted teenager who kept leaving the room to throw up and a puzzled middle-aged woman from Queens with three grown children.

"What form of birth control were you using?" the volunteer asked each of us. The answer was inevitably "none." She then went on to describe the various forms of birth control available at the clinic, and offered them to each of us.

The youngest Puerto Rican girl was asked through the interpreter which she'd like to use, the loop, diaphragm, or pill. She shook her had "no" three times. "You don't want to come back here again, do you?" the volunteer pressed. The girl's head was so low her chin rested on her breastbone. "Si," she whispered.

We had been there two hours by that time, filling out endless forms, giving blood and urine, receiving lectures. But unlike any other group of women I've been in, we didn't talk. Our common denominator, the one which usually floods language and economic barriers into familiarity, today was one of shame. We were losing life that day, not giving it.

The group kept getting cut back to smaller, more workable units, and finally I was put in a small waiting room with just two other women. We changed into paper bathrobes and paper slippers, and we rustled whenever we moved. One of the women in my room was shivering and an aide brought her a blanket.

"What's the matter?" the aide asked her. "I'm scared," the woman said. "How much will it hurt?" The aide smiled. "Oh, nothing worse than a couple of bad cramps," she said. "This afternoon you'll be dancing a jig."

I began to panic. Suddenly the rhetoric, the abortion marches I'd walked in, the telegrams sent to Albany to counteract the Friends of the Fetus, the Zero Population Growth buttons I'd worn, peeled away, and I was all alone with my microscopic baby. There were just the two of us there, and soon, because it was more convenient for me and my husband, there would be one again.

How could it be that I, who am so neurotic about life that I step over bugs rather than on them, who spend hours planting flowers and vegetables in the spring even though we rent out the house and never see them, who make sure the children are vaccinated and inoculated and filled with vitamin C, could so arbitrarily decide that this life shouldn't be?

"It's not a life," my husband had argued, more to convince himself than me. "It's a bunch of cells smaller than my fingernail."

But any woman who has had children knows that certain felling in her taut, swollen breasts, and the slight but constant ache in her uterus that signals the arrival of life. Though I would march myself into blisters for a woman's right to exercise the option of motherhood, I discovered there in the waiting room that I was not the modern woman I thought I was.

When my name was called, my body felt so heavy the nurse had to help me into the examining room. I waited for my husband to burst through the door and yell "stop," but of course he didn't. I concentrated on three black spots in the acoustic ceiling until they grew in size to the shape of saucers, while the doctor swabbed my insides with antiseptic.

"You're going to feel a burning sensation now," he said, injecting the Novocaine into the neck of the womb. The pain was swift and severe, and I twisted to get away from him. He was hurting my baby, I reasoned, and the black saucers quivered in the air. "Stop," I cried. "Please stop." He shook his head, busy with his equipment. "It's too late to stop now," he said. "It'll just take a few more seconds."

What good sports we women are. And how obedient. Physically the pain passed even before the hum of the machine signaled that the vacuuming of my uterus was completed, my baby sucked up like ashes after a cocktail party. Ten minutes from start to finish. And I was back on the arm of the nurse.

There were twelve beds in the recovery room. Each one had a gaily flowered draw sheet and a soft green or blue thermal blanket. It was all very feminine. Lying on these beds for an hour or more were the shocked victims of their sex, their full wombs now stripped clean, their futures less encumbered.

It was a very quiet room. The only voice was that of the nurse, locating the new women who had just come in so she could monitor their blood pressure, and checking out the recovered women who were free to leave.

Juice was being passed about, and I found myself sipping a Dixie cup of Hawaiian Punch. An older woman with tightly curled bleached hair was just getting up from the next bed, "That was no goddamn snap," she said, resting before putting on her miniskirt and high white boots. Other women came and went, some walking out as dazed as they had entered, others with a bounce that signaled they were going right back to Bloomingdales's.

Finally then, it was time for me to leave. I checked out, making an appointment to return in two weeks for an IUD insertion. My husband was slumped in the waiting room, clutching a single yellow rose wrapped in a wet paper towel and stuffed into a baggie.

We didn't talk the whole way home, but just held hands very tightly. At home there were more yellow roses and a tray in bed for me and the children's curiosity to divert.

It had certainly been a successful operation. I didn't bleed at all for two days just as they had predicted, and then I bled only moderately for another four days. Within a week my breasts had subsided and the tenderness vanished, and my body felt mine again instead of the eggshell it becomes when its protecting someone else.

My husband and I are back to planning our summer vacation and his career switch.

And it certainly does make more sense not to be having a baby right now—we say that to each other all the time. But I have this ghost now. A very little ghost that only appears when I'm seeing something beautiful, like the full moon on the ocean last weekend. And the baby waves at me. And I wave at the baby. "Of course, we have room," I cry to the ghost. "Of course, we do."

I am "Jane Doe." Using a pseudonym was not the act of cowardice some have said it was, but rather an act of sympathy for the feelings of my family. My daughters were too young then to understand what an abortion was, and my twelve-year-old son (my husband's stepson) reacted angrily when I even broached the subject of abortion to him. Andrew was deeply moralistic, as many children are at that age, and still young enough to fell threatened by the actions of adults; his replies to my "suppose I had an abortion" queries were devastating. "I think abortion is okay if the boy and girl aren't married, and they just made a mistake," he said. "But if you had an abortion, that would be different. You're married, and there is no reason for you not to have another baby. How could you just kill something—no matter how little it is—that's going to grow and have legs and wiggle its fingers?"

"I would be furious with you if you had an abortion. I'd lose all respect for you for being so selfish. I'd make you suffer and remind you of it all the time. I would think of ways to be mean. Maybe I'd give you the silent treatment or something."

"If God had meant women to have abortions, He would have put buttons on their stomachs."

I decided to wait until he was older before we discussed it again.

There were other considerations as well. My husband and I had chosen not to tell our parents about the abortion. My mother was very ill at the time and not up to a barrage of phone calls from her friends about "what Linda had written in the newspaper." And there were my parents-in-law, who had always hoped for a male grandchild to carry on the family name. So I avoided the confessional and simply wrote what I thought would be a helpful piece for other women who might have shared my experience.

The result was almost great enough to be recorded on a seismograph. Interpreting the piece as an anti-abortion grist, the Right-to-Lifers reproduced it by the thousands and sent it to everyone on their mailing lists. In one Catholic mailing, two sentences were deleted from the article: one that said I was planning to return to the clinic for an IUD insertion, and the other the quote from a middle-aged woman, "That was no goddamn snap." Papers around the country and in Canada ran it, culminating in its appearance in the Canadian edition of the *Reader's Digest*, whose staff took it upon their editorial selves to delete the last paragraph about the "little ghost" because they considered it "mawkish." They also changed the title from "There Just Wasn't Room in Our Lives for Another Baby" to "A Successful Operation" in the hopes that it would change their magazine's pro-abortion image.

Hundreds of letters poured into the *New York Times*, some from Right-to-Lifers, who predictably called me a "murderer," and others from pro-choice zealots who had decided the article was a "plant" and might even have been written by a man. Women wrote about their own abortions, some of which had been positive experiences and some disastrous. One woman even wrote that she wished her own mother had had an abortion instead of subjecting her to a childhood that was "brutal and crushing." Many of the respondents criticized me, quite rightly, for not using birth control in the first place. I was stunned, and so was the *New York Times*. A few weeks later they ran a sampling of the letters and my reply, which follows:

The varied reactions to my abortion article do not surprise me at all. They are all right. And they are all wrong. There is no issue so fundamental as the giving of life, or the cessation of it. These decisions are the most personal one can ever make and each person facing them reacts in her own way. It is not black-and-white as the laws governing abortion are forced to be. Rather it is the gray area whose core touches our definition of ourselves that produces "little ghosts" in some, and a sense of relief in others.

I admire the woman who chose not to bear her fourth child because she and her husband could not afford to give that child the future they felt necessary. I admire the women who were outraged that I had failed to use any form of contraception. And I ache for the woman whose mother had given birth to her even though she was not wanted, and thus spent an empty, lonely childhood. It takes courage to take the life of someone else in your own hands, and even more courage to assume responsibility for your own.

I had my abortion over two years ago. And I wrote about it shortly thereafter. It was only recently, however, that I decided to publish it. I felt it was important to share how one person's abortion had affected her, rather than just sit by while the pro and con groups haggled over legislation.

The effect has indeed been profound. Though my husband was very supportive of me, and I, I think, of him, our relationship slowly faltered. As our children are girls, my husband anguished at the possibility that I had been carrying a son. Just a case of male macho, many would argue. But still, that's the way he feels, and it is important. I hope we can get back on a loving track again.

Needless to say, I have an IUD now, instead of the diaphragm that is too easily forgotten. I do not begrudge my husband his lack of contraception. Condoms are awkward. Neither do I feel he should have a vasectomy. It is profoundly difficult for him to face the possibility that he might never have that son. Nor do I regret having the abortion. I am just as much an avid supporter of children by choice as I ever was.

My only regret is the sheer irresponsibility on my part to become pregnant in the first place. I pray to God that it will never happen again. But if it does, I will be equally thankful that the law provides women the dignity to choose whether to bring a new life into the world or not.

I had obviously and unintentionally touched a national nerve. With abortion becoming an everyday occurrence since the Supreme Court ruling in 1973, which overturned the right of individual states to intervene in a woman's decision to abort in the first

trimester (twelve weeks) of pregnancy and to intervene in the second trimester (twenty-four weeks)
only to ensure medical practices "reasonably related
to maternal health," American women of all ages,
races, and backgrounds were facing the same sort of
dilemma I had. . . .

. . . So much has happened in the short time since
abortion was legalized that only now is there an opportunity to draw breath and begin to evaluate what
the 1973 Supreme Court decision has wrought, and
what repercussions the 1977 Supreme Court decision upholding states' rights to withhold abortion
funding for the poor will have. Abortion is not new
by any means. But confronting the fact of it without
furtiveness and danger is. The quantum leap from
women's age-old need and desire to control their reproductive lives to their sanctioned ability finally to
do so has raised questions of ethics and morality that
have yet to be answered. Perhaps they never will be.

Writing and Discussion Topics

Questions 1–6 address content, critical analysis,
personal choices, ethical options, specific discipline, and
interdisciplinary alternatives, respectively.

1. Francke received thousands of letters in
   response to this article when it was
   originally printed. What is so compelling
   about this piece? Does it alter your views
   on abortion? If so, how?
2. Does Francke assume that human life
   begins at conception? Is her assumption
   valid?
3. Do you believe that someone who is
   personally and emotionally secure, such as
   Francke, has an obligation to bear and
   nurture an unwanted child? Compare
   Francke's circumstances to those of an
   impoverished, unmarried seventeen-year-
   old.
4. Francke insists she still supports a woman's
   option to have an abortion. Does this
   contradict, from an ethical standpoint,
   what she says in her story?
5. What paragraphs show Francke as a gifted
   writer? What techniques does she use in
   her writing style to stir emotions?
6. Compare and contrast Francke's
   "personal" approach to abortion with
   Blackmun's Supreme Court ruling.

Judith Jarvis Thomson

A DEFENSE OF ABORTION

◆◆◆

J udith Jarvis Thomson is a well-known scholar and writer in philosophy. She is a professor of philosophy at the Massachusetts Institute of Technology. Her writings include Acts and Other Events. This reading, which examines the sanctity of human life, is one of the most cited pieces on abortion. ◆

Most opposition to abortion relies on the premise that the fetus is a human being, a person, from the moment of conception. The premise is argued for, but, as I think, not well. Take, for example, the most common argument. We are asked to notice that the development of a human being from conception through birth into childhood is continuous; then it is said to draw a line, to choose a point in this development and say "before this point the thing is not a person, after this point it is a person" is to make an arbitrary choice, a choice for which in the nature of things no good reason can be given. It is concluded that the fetus is, or anyway that we had better say it is, a person from the moment of conception. But this conclusion does not follow. Similar things might be said about the development of an acorn into an oak tree, and it does not follow that acorns are oak trees, or that we had better say they are. Arguments of this form are sometimes called "slippery slope arguments"—the phrase is perhaps self-explanatory—and it is dismaying that opponents of abortion rely on them so heavily and uncritically.

I am inclined to agree, however, that the prospects for "drawing a line" in the development of the fetus look dim. I am inclined to think also that we shall probably have to agree that the fetus has already become a human person well before birth. Indeed, it comes as a surprise when one first learns how early in its life it begins to acquire human characteristics. By the tenth week, for example, it already has a face, arms and legs, fingers and toes; it has internal organs, and brain activity is detectable.[1] On the other hand, I think that the premise is false, that the fetus is not a person from the moment of conception. A newly fertilized ovum, a newly implanted clump of cells, is no more a person than an acorn is an oak tree. But I shall not discuss any of this. For it seems to me to be of great interest to ask what happens if, for the sake of argument, we allow the premise. How, precisely, are we supposed to get from there to the conclusion that abortion is morally impermissible? Opponents of abortion commonly spend most of their time establishing that the fetus is a person, and hardly any time explaining the step from there to the impermissibility of abortion. Perhaps they think the step too simple and obvious to require much comment. Or perhaps instead they are simply being economical in argument. Many of those who defend abortion rely on the premise that the fetus is not a person, but only a bit of tissue that will become a person at birth; and why pay out more arguments than you have to? Whatever the explanation, I suggest that the step they take is neither easy nor obvious, that it calls for closer examination than it is commonly given, and that when we do give it this closer examination we shall feel inclined to reject it.

I propose, then, that we grant that the fetus is a person from the moment of conception. How does the argument go from here? Something like this, I take it. Every person has a right to life. So the fetus has a right to life. No doubt the mother has a right to decide what shall happen in and to her body; everyone would grant that. But surely a person's right to life is stronger and more stringent than the mother's right to decide what happens in and to her body, and so outweighs it. So the fetus may not be killed; an abortion may not be performed.

It sounds plausible. But now let me ask you to imagine this. You wake up in the morning and find yourself back to back in bed with an unconscious violinist. A famous unconscious violinist. He has been found to have a fatal kidney ailment, and the Society of Music Lovers has canvassed all the available medical records and found that you alone have the right blood type to help. They have therefore kidnapped you, and last night the violinist's circulatory system was plugged into yours, so that your kidneys can be used to extract poisons from his blood as well as your own. The director of the hospital now tells you, "Look, we're sorry the Society of Music Lovers did this to you—we would never have permitted it if we had known. But still, they did it, and the violinist now is plugged into you. To unplug you would be to kill him. But never mind, it's only for nine months. By then he will have recovered from his ailment, and can safely be unplugged from you." Is it morally incumbent on you to accede to this situation? No doubt it would be very nice of you if you did, a great kindness. But do you *have* to accede to it? What if it were not nine months, but nine years? Or longer still? What if the director of the hospital says, "Tough luck, I agree, but you've now got to stay in bed, with the violinist plugged into you, for the rest of your life. Because remember this. All persons have a right to life, and violinists are persons.

From Judith Jarvis Thomson, "A Defense of Abortion," *Philosophy & Public Affairs* Vol. I, No. I (Fall 1971). Copyright © 1971 by Princeton University Press. Reprinted by permission of Princeton University Press.

[1] Daniel Callahan, *Abortion: Law, Choice and Morality* (New York, 1970), p. 373. This book gives a fascinating survey of the available information on abortion. The Jewish tradition is surveyed in David M. Feldman, Birth Control in Jewish Law *(New York, 1968)*, Part 5, the Catholic tradition in John T. Noonan, Jr., "An Almost Absolute Value in History," in *The Morality of Abortion*, ed. John T. Noonan, Jr. (Cambridge, Mass., 1970).

Granted you have a right to decide what happens in and to your body, but a person's right to life outweighs your right to decide what happens in and to your body. So you cannot ever be unplugged from him." I imagine you would regard this as outrageous, which suggests that something really is wrong with that plausible-sounding argument I mentioned a moment ago.

In this case, of course, you were kidnapped; you didn't volunteer for this operation that plugged the violinist into your kidneys. Can those who oppose abortion on the ground I mentioned make an exception for a pregnancy due to rape? Certainly. They can say that persons have a right to life only if they didn't come into existence because of rape; or they can say that all persons have a right to life, but that some have less of a right to life than others, in particular, that those who came into existence because of rape have less. But these statements have a rather unpleasant sound. Surely the question of whether you have a right to life at all, or how much of it you have, shouldn't turn on the question of whether or not you are the product of a rape. And in fact the people who oppose abortion on the ground I mentioned do not make this distinction, and hence do not make an exception in case of rape.

Nor do they make an exception for a case in which the mother has to spend the nine months of pregnancy in bed. They would agree that would be a great pity, and hard on the mother; but all the same, all persons have a right to life, the fetus is a person, and so on. I suspect, in fact, that they would not make an exception for a case in which, miraculously enough, the pregnancy went on for nine years, or even the rest of the mother's life.

Some won't even make an exception for a case in which continuation of the pregnancy is likely to shorten the mother's life; they regard abortion as impermissible even to save the mother's life. Such cases are nowadays very rare, and many opponents of abortion do not accept this extreme view. All the same, it is a good place to begin: a number of points of interests come out in respect to it.

1. Let us call the view that abortion is impermissible even to save the mother's life "the extreme view." I want to suggest first that it does not issue from the argument I mentioned earlier without the addition of some fairly powerful premises. Suppose a woman has become pregnant, and now learns that she has a cardiac condition such that she will die if she carries the baby to term. What may be done for her? The fetus, being a person, has a right to life, but

as the mother is a person too, so she has a right to life. Presumably they have an equal right to life. How is it supposed to come out that an abortion may not be performed? If mother and child have an equal right to life, shouldn't we perhaps flip a coin? Or should we add to the mother's right to life her right to decide what happens in and to her body, which everybody seems to be ready to grant—the sum of her rights now outweighing the fetus' right to life?

The most familiar argument here is the following. We are told that performing the abortion would be directly killing[2] the child, whereas doing nothing would not be killing the mother, but only letting her die. Moreover, in killing the child, one would be killing an innocent person, for the child has committed no crime, and is not aiming at his mother's death. And then there are a variety of ways in which this might be continued. (1) But as directly killing an innocent person is always and absolutely impermissible, an abortion may not be performed. Or, (2) as directly killing an innocent person is murder, and murder is always and absolutely impermissible, an abortion may not be performed.[3] Or, (3) as one's duty to refrain from directly killing an innocent person is more stringent than one's duty to keep a person from dying, an abortion may not be performed. Or, (4) if one's only options are directly killing an innocent person or letting a person die, one must prefer letting the person die, and thus an abortion may not be performed.[4]

Some people seem to have thought that these are not further premises which must be added if the conclusion is to be reached, but that they follow from the very fact that an innocent person has a right to

---

[2]The term "direct" in the arguments I refer to is a technical one. Roughly, what is meant by "direct killing" is either killing as an end in itself, or killing as a means of some end, for example, the end of saving someone else's life. See footnote 5, for an example of its use.

[3]Cf. *Encyclical Letter of Pope Pius XI on Christian Marriage*, St. Paul Editions (Boston, n.d.), p. 32: "however much we may pity the mother whose health and even life is gravely imperiled in the performance of the duty allotted to her by nature, nevertheless what could ever be a sufficient reason for excusing in any way the direct murder of the innocent? This is precisely what we are dealing with here." Noonan (*The Morality of Abortion*, p. 43) reads this as follows: "What cause can ever avail to excuse in any way the direct killing of the innocent? For it is a question of that."

[4]The thesis in (4) is in an interesting way weaker than those in (1), (2), and (3): they rule out abortion even in cases in which both mother *and* child will die if the abortion is not performed. By contrast, one who held the view expressed in (4) could consistently say that one needn't prefer letting two persons die to killing one.

life.[5] But this seems to me to be a mistake, and perhaps the simplest way to show this is to bring out that while we must certainly grant that innocent persons have a right to life, the theses in (1) through (4) are all false. Take (2), for example. If directly killing an innocent person is murder, and thus is impermissible, then the mother's directly killing the innocent person inside her is murder, and thus is impermissible. But it cannot seriously be thought to be murder if the mother performs an abortion on herself to save her life. It cannot seriously be said that she *must* refrain, that she *must* sit passively by and wait for her death. Let us look again at the case of you and the violinist. There you are, in bed with the violinist, and the director of the hospital says to you, "It's all most distressing, and I deeply sympathize, but you see this is putting an additional strain on your kidneys, and you'll be dead within the month. But you *have* to stay where you are all the same. Because unplugging you would be directly killing an innocent violinist, and that's murder, and that's impermissible." If anything in the world is true, it is that you do not commit murder, you do not do what is impermissible, if you reach around to your back and unplug yourself from that violinist to save your life.

The main focus of attention in writings on abortion has been on what a third party may or may not do in answer to a request from a woman for an abortion. This is in a way understandable. Things being as they are, there isn't much a woman can safely do to abort herself. So the question asked is what a third party may do, and what the mother may do, if it is mentioned at all, is deduced, almost as an afterthought, from what it is concluded that third parties may do. But it seems to me that to treat the matter in this way is to refuse to grant to the mother that very status of person which is so firmly insisted on for the fetus. For we cannot simply read off what a

person may do from what a third party may do. Suppose you find yourself trapped in a tiny house with a growing child. I mean a very tiny house, and a rapidly growing child—you are already up against the wall of the house and in a few minutes you'll be crushed to death. The child on the other hand won't be crushed to death; if nothing is done to stop him from growing he'll be hurt, but in the end he'll simply burst open the house and walk out a free man. Now I could well understand it if a bystander were to say, "There's nothing we can do for you. We cannot choose between your life and his, we cannot be the ones to decide who is to live, we cannot intervene." But it cannot be concluded that you too can do nothing, that you cannot attack it to save your life. However innocent the child may be, you do not have to wait passively while it crushes you to death. Perhaps a pregnant woman is vaguely felt to have the status of house, to which we don't allow the right of self-defense. But if the woman houses the child, it should be remembered that she is a person who houses it.

I should perhaps stop to say explicitly that I am not claiming that people have a right to do anything whatever to save their lives. I think, rather, that there are drastic limits to the right of self-defense. If someone threatens you with death unless you torture someone else to death, I think you have not the right, even to save your life, to do so. But the case under consideration here is very different. In our case there are only two people involved, one whose life is threatened, and one who threatens it. Both are innocent: the one who is threatened is not threatened because of any fault, and the one who threatens does not threaten because of any fault. For this reason we may feel that we bystanders cannot intervene. But the person threatened can.

In sum, a woman surely can defend her life against the threat to it posed by the unborn child, even if doing so involves its death. And this shows not merely that the theses in (1) through (4) are false; it shows also that the extreme view of abortion is false, and so we need not canvass any other possible ways of arriving at it from the argument I mentioned at the outset.

2. The extreme view could of course be weakened to say that while abortion is permissible to save the mother's life, it may not be performed by a third party, but only by the mother herself. But this cannot be right either. For what we have to keep in mind is that the mother and the unborn child are not like

---

[5]Cf. the following passage from Pius XII, *Address to the Italian Catholic Society of Midwives:* "The baby in the maternal breast has the right to life immediately from God.—Hence there is no man, no human authority, no science, no medical, eugenic, social, economic or moral 'indication' which can establish or grant a valid juridical ground for a direct deliberate disposition of an innocent human life, that is a disposition which looks to its destruction either as an end or as a means to another end perhaps in itself not illicit.—The baby, still not born, is a man in the same degree and for the same reason as the mother" (quoted in Noonan, *The Morality of Abortion*, p. 45).

two tenants in a small house which has, by an unfortunate mistake, been rented to both: the mother *owns* the house. The fact that she does adds to the offensiveness of deducing that the mother can do nothing from the supposition that third parties can do nothing. But it does more than this: it casts a bright light on the supposition that third parties can do nothing. Certainly it lets us see that a third party who says "I cannot choose between you" is fooling himself if he thinks this is impartiality. If Jones has found and fastened on a certain coat, which he needs to keep him from freezing, but which Smith also needs to keep from freezing, then it is not impartiality that says "I cannot choose between you" when Smith owns the coat. Women have said again and again "This body is *my* body!" and they have reason to feel angry, reason to feel that it has been like shouting into the wind. Smith, after all, is hardly likely to bless us if we say to him, "Of course it's your coat, anybody would grant that it is. But no one may choose between you and Jones who is to have it."

We should really ask what it is that says "no one may choose" in the face of the fact that the body that houses the child is the mother's body. It may be simply a failure to appreciate this fact. But it may be something more interesting, namely the sense that one has a right to refuse to lay hands on people, even where it would be just and fair to do so, even where justice seems to require that somebody do so. Thus justice might call for somebody to get Smith's coat back from Jones, and yet you have a right to refuse to be the one to lay hands on Jones, a right to refuse to do physical violence to him. This, I think, must be granted. But then what should be said is not "no one may choose," but only "*I* cannot choose," and indeed not even this, but "*I* will not *act*," leaving it open that somebody else can or should, and in particular that anyone in a position of authority, with the job of securing people's rights, both can and should. So this is no difficulty. I have not been arguing that any given third party must accede to the mother's request that he perform an abortion to save her life, but only that he may.

I suppose that in some views of human life the mother's body is only on loan to her, the loan not being one which gives her any prior claim to it. One who held this view might well think it impartiality to say "I cannot choose." But I shall simply ignore this possibility. My own view is that if a human being has any just, prior claim to anything at all, he has a just, prior claim to his own body. And perhaps this needn't be argued for here anyway, since, as I mentioned, the arguments against abortion we are looking at do grant that the woman has a right to decide what happens in and to her body.

But although they do grant it, I have tried to show that they do not take seriously what is done in granting it. I suggest the same thing will reappear even more clearly when we turn away from cases in which the mother's life is at stake, and attend, as I propose we now do, to the vastly more common cases in which a woman wants an abortion for some less weighty reason than preserving her own life.

3. Where the mother's life is not at stake, the argument I mentioned at the outset seems to have a much stronger pull. "Everyone has a right to life, so the unborn person has a right to life." And isn't the child's right to life weightier than anything other than the mother's own right to life, which she might put forward as ground for an abortion?

This argument treats the right to life as if it were unproblematic. It is not, and this seems to me to be precisely the source of the mistake.

For we should now, at long last, ask what it comes to, to have a right to life. In some views having a right to life includes having a right to be given at least the bare minimum one needs for continued life. But suppose that what in fact *is* the bare minimum a man needs for continued life is something he has no right at all to be given? If I am sick unto death, and the only thing that will save my life is the touch of Henry Fonda's cool hand on my fevered brow, then all the same, I have no right to be given the touch of Henry Fonda's cool hand on my fevered brow. It would be frightfully nice of him to fly in from the West Coast to provide it. It would be less nice, though no doubt well meant, if my friends flew out to the West Coast and carried Henry Fonda back with them. But I have no right at all against anybody that he should do this for me. Or again, to return to the story I told earlier, the fact that for continued life that violinist needs the continued use of your kidneys does not establish that he has a right to be given the continued use of your kidneys. He certainly has no right against you that *you* should give him continued use of your kidneys. For nobody has any right to use your kidneys unless you give him such a right; and nobody has the right against you that you shall give him this right—if you do allow him to go on using your kidneys, this is a kindness on your part, and not something he can claim from you as his due. Nor has he any right against anybody else that *they* should give him continued use of your kidneys. Certainly he had no right against the Society of Music Lovers that they should plug him into you in the first place. And if you start to unplug yourself, having learned that you will otherwise have to spend nine years in bed with him, there is nobody in the world who must try to prevent you, in order to see to it that he is given something he has a right to be given.

Some people are rather stricter about the right to life. In their view, it does not include the right to be given anything, but amounts to, and only to, the right not to be killed by anybody. But here a related difficulty arises. If everybody must refrain from killing that violinist, then everybody must refrain from doing a great many different sorts of things. Everybody must refrain from slitting his throat, everybody must refrain from shooting him—and everybody must refrain from unplugging you from him. But does he have a right against everybody that they shall refrain from unplugging you from him? To refrain from doing this is to allow him to continue to use your kidneys. It could be argued that he has a right against us that *we* should allow him to continue to use your kidneys. That is, while he had no right against us that we should give him the use of your kidneys, it might be argued that he anyway has a right against us that we shall not now intervene and deprive him of the use of your kidneys. I shall come back to third-party interventions later. But certainly the violinist has no right against you that *you* shall allow him to continue to use your kidneys. As I said, if you do allow him to use them, it is a kindness on your part, and not something you owe him.

The difficulty I point to here is not peculiar to the right to life. It reappears in connection with all the other natural rights; and it is something which an adequate account of rights must deal with. For present purposes it is enough just to draw attention to it. But I would stress that I am not arguing that people do not have a right to life—quite to the contrary, it seems to me that the primary control we must place on the acceptability of an account of rights is that it should turn out in that account to be a truth that all persons have a right to life. I am arguing only that having a right to life does not guarantee having either a right to be given the use of or a right to be allowed continued use of another person's body—even if one needs it for life itself. So the right to life will not serve the opponents of abortion in the very simple and clear way in which they seem to have thought it would.

4. There is another way to bring out the difficulty. In the most ordinary sort of case, to deprive someone of what he has a right to is to treat him unjustly. Suppose a boy and his small brother are jointly given a box of chocolates for Christmas. If the older boy takes the box and refuses to give his brother any of the chocolates, he is unjust to him, for the brother has been given a right to half of them. But suppose that, having learned that otherwise it means nine years in bed with that violinist, you unplug yourself from him. You surely are not being unjust to him, for you gave him no right to use your kidneys, and no one else can have given him any such right. But we have to notice that, in unplugging yourself, you are killing him; and violinists, like everybody else, have a right to life, and thus in the view we were considering just now, the right not to be killed. So here you do what he supposedly has a right you shall not do, but you do not act unjustly to him in doing it.

The emendation which may be made at this point is this: the right to life consists not in the right not to be killed, but rather in the right not to be killed unjustly. This runs a risk of circularity, but never mind: it would enable us to square the fact that the violinist has a right to life with the fact that you do not act unjustly toward him in unplugging yourself, thereby killing him. For if you do not kill him unjustly, you do not violate his right to life, and so it is no wonder you do him no injustice.

But if this emendation is accepted, the gap in the argument against abortion stares us plainly in the face: it is by no means enough to show that the fetus is a person, and to remind us that all persons have a right to life—we need to be shown also that killing the fetus violates its right to life, i.e., that abortion is unjust killing. And is it?

I suppose we may take it as datum that in a case of pregnancy due to rape the mother has not given the unborn person a right to the use of her body for food and shelter. Indeed, in what pregnancy could it be supposed that the mother has given the unborn person such a right? It is not as if there were unborn persons drifting about the world, to whom a woman who wants a child says "I invite you in."

But it might be argued that there are other ways one can have acquired a right to the use of another person's body than by having been invited to use it by that person. Suppose a woman voluntarily indulges in intercourse, knowing of the chance it will issue in pregnancy, and then she does become pregnant; is she not in part responsible for the presence, in fact the very existence, of the unborn person inside her? No doubt she did not invite it in. But doesn't her partial responsibility for its being there itself give it a right to the use of her body?[6] If so, then her aborting it would be more like the boy's taking away the chocolates, and less like your unplugging yourself from the violinist—doing so would be depriving it of what it does have a right to, and thus would be doing it an injustice.

And then, too, it might be asked whether or not she can kill it even to save her own life: If she voluntarily called it into existence, how can she now kill it, even in self-defense?

The first thing to be said about this is that it is something new. Opponents of abortion have been so concerned to make out the independence of the fetus, in order to establish that it has a right to life, just as its mother does, that they have tended to overlook the possible support they might gain from making out that the fetus is *dependent* on the mother, in order to establish that she has a special kind of responsibility for it, a responsibility that gives it rights against her which are not possessed by any independent person—such as an ailing violoinist who is a stranger to her.

On the other hand, this argument would give the unborn person a right to its mother's body only if her pregnancy resulted from a voluntary act, undertaken in full knowledge of the chance a pregnancy might result from it. It would leave out entirely the unborn person whose existence is due to rape. Pending the availability of some further argument, then, we would be left with the conclusion that unborn persons whose existence is due to rape have no right to the use of their mothers' bodies, and thus that aborting them is not depriving them of anything they have a right to and hence is not unjust killing.

And we should also notice that it is not at all plain that this argument really does go even as far as it purports to. For there are cases and cases, and the details make the difference. If the room is stuffy, and I therefore open a window to air it, and a burglar climbs in, it would be absurd to say, "Ah, now he can stay, she's given him a right to the use of her house—for she is partially responsible for his presence there, having voluntarily done what enabled him to get in, in full knowledge that there are such things as burglars, and that burglars burgle." It would be still more absurd to say this if I had had bars installed outside my windows, precisely to prevent burglars from getting in, and a burglar got in only because of a defect in the bars. It remains equally absurd if we imagine it is not a burglar who climbs in, but an innocent person who blunders or falls in. Again, suppose it were like this: people-seeds drift about in the air like pollen, and if you open your windows, one may drift in and take root in your carpets or upholstery. You don't want children, so you fix up your windows with fine mesh screens, the very best you can buy. As can happen, however, and on very, very rare occasions does happen, one of the screens is defective; and a seed drifts in and takes root. Does the person-plant who now develops have a right to the use of your house? Surely not—despite the fact that you voluntarily opened your windows, you knowingly kept carpets and upholstered furniture, and you knew that screens were sometimes defective. Someone may argue that you are responsible for its rooting, that it does have a right to your house, because after all you *could* have lived out your life with bare floors and furniture, or with sealed windows and doors. But this won't do—for by the same token anyone can avoid a pregnancy due to rape by having a hysterectomy, or anyway by never leaving home without a (reliable!) army.

It seems to me that the argument we are looking at can establish at most that there are *some* cases in which the unborn person has a right to the use of its mother's body, and therefore *some* cases in which abortion is unjust killing. There is room for much discussion and argument as to precisely which, if any. But I think we should sidestep this issue and leave it open, for at any rate the argument certainly does not establish that all abortion is unjust killing.

5. There is room for yet another argument here, however. We surely must all grant that there may be cases in which it would be morally indecent to detach a person from your body at the cost of his life. Suppose you learn that what the violinist needs is not nine years of your life, but only one hour: all you need to do to save his life is to spend one hour in that bed with him. Suppose also that letting him use your kidneys for that one hour would not affect your health in the slightest. Admittedly you were kidnapped. Admittedly you did not give anyone permission to plug him into you. Nevertheless it seems to me plain you *ought* to allow him to use your kidneys for that hour—it would be indecent to refuse.

---

[6]The need for a discussion of this argument was brought home to me by members of the Society for Ethical and Legal Philosophy, to whom this paper was originally presented.

Again, suppose pregnancy lasted only an hour, and constituted no threat to life or health. And suppose that a woman becomes pregnant as a result of a rape. Admittedly she did not voluntarily do anything to bring about the existence of a child. Admittedly she did nothing at all which would give the unborn person a right to the use of her body. All the same it might well be said, as in the newly emended violinist story, that she *ought* to allow it to remain for that hour—that it would be indecent in her to refuse it.

Now some people are inclined to use the term "right" in such a way that it follows from the fact that you ought to allow a person to use your body for the hour he needs, that he has a right to use your body for the hour he needs, even though he has not been given that right by any person or act. They may say that it follows also that if you refuse, you act unjustly toward him. This use of the term is perhaps so common that it cannot be called wrong; nevertheless it seems to me to be an unfortunate loosening of what we would do better to keep a tight rein on. Suppose that box of chocolates I mentioned earlier had not been given to both boys jointly, but was given only to the older boy. There he sits, stolidly eating his way through the box, his small brother watching enviously. Here we are likely to say "You ought not to be so mean. You ought to give your brother some of those chocolates." My own view is that it just does not follow from the truth of this that the brother has any right to any of the chocolates. If the boy refuses to give his brother any, he is greedy, stingy, callous—but not unjust. I suppose that people I have in mind will say it does follow that the brother has a right to some of the chocolates, and thus that the boy does act unjustly if he refuses to give his brother any. But the effect of saying this is to obscure what we should keep distinct, namely the difference between the boy's refusal in this case and the boy's refusal in the earlier case, in which the box was given to both boys jointly, and in which the small brother thus had what was from any point of view clear title to half.

A further objection to so using the term "right" that from the fact that A ought to do a thing for B, it follows that B has a right against A that A do it for him, is that it is going to make the question of whether or not a man has a right to a thing turn on how easy it is to provide him with it; and this seems not merely unfortunate, but morally unacceptable. Take the case of Henry Fonda again. I said earlier that I had no right to the touch of his cool hand on my fevered brow, even though I needed it to save my life. I said it would be frightfully nice of him to fly in from the West Coast to provide me with it, but that I had no right against him that he should do so. But suppose he isn't on the West Coast. Suppose he has only to walk across the room, place a hand briefly on my brow—and lo, my life is saved. Then surely he ought to do it, it would be indecent to refuse. Is it to be said "Ah, well, it follows that in this case she has a right to the touch of his hand on her brow, and so it would be an injustice in him to refuse"? So that I have a right to it when it is easy for him to provide it, though no right when it's hard? It's rather a shocking idea that anyone's rights should fade away and disappear as it gets harder and harder to accord them to him.

So my own view is that even though you ought to let the violinist use your kidneys for the one hour he needs, we should not conclude that he has a right to do so—we should say that if you refuse, you are, like the boy who owns all the chocolates and will give none away, self-centered and callous, indecent in fact, but not unjust. And similarly, that even supposing a case in which a woman pregnant due to rape ought to allow the unborn person to use her body for the hour he needs, we should conclude that she is self-centered, callous, indecent, but not unjust, if she refuses. The complaints are no less grave; they are just different. However, there is no need to insist on this point. If anyone does wish to deduce "he has a right" from "you ought," then all the same he must surely grant that there are cases in which it is not morally required of you that you allow that violinist to use your kidneys, and in which he does not have a right to use them, and in which you do not do him an injustice if you refuse. And so also for mother and unborn child. Except in such cases as the unborn person has a right to demand it—and we were leaving open the possibility that there may be such cases—nobody is morally *required* to make large sacrifices, of health, of all other interests and concerns, of all other duties and commitments, for nine years, or even for nine months, in order to keep another person alive.

6. We have in fact to distinguish between two kinds of Samaritan: the Good Samaritan and what we might call the Minimally Decent Samaritan. The story of the Good Samaritan, you will remember, goes like this:

> A certain man went down from Jerusalem to Jericho, and fell among thieves, which stripped him of his raiment, and wounded him, and departed, leaving him half dead.

And by chance there came down a certain priest that way; and when he saw him, he passed by on the other side.

And likewise a Levite, when he was at the place, came and looked on him, and passed by on the other side.

But a certain Samaritan, as he journeyed, came where he was; and when he saw him he had compassion on him.

And went to him, and bound up his wounds, pouring in oil and wine, and set him on his own beast, and brought him to an inn, and took care of him.

And on the morrow, when he departed, he took out two pence, and gave them to the host, and said unto him, "Take care of him; and whatsoever thou spendest more, when I come again, I will repay thee."

(Luke 10:30–35)

The Good Samaritan went out of his way, at some cost to himself, to help one in need of it. We are not told what the options were, that is, whether or not the priest and the Levite could have helped by doing less than the Good Samaritan did, but assuming they could have, then the fact they did nothing at all shows they were not even Minimally Decent Samaritans, not because they were not Samaritans, but because they were not even minimally decent.

These things are a matter of degree, of couse, but there is a difference, and it comes out perhaps most clearly in the story of Kitty Genovese, who, as you will remember, was murdered while thirty-eight people watched or listened, and did nothing at all to help her. A Good Samaritan would have rushed out to give direct assistance against the murderer. Or perhaps we had better allow that it would have been a Splendid Samaritan who did this, on the ground that it would have involved a risk of death for himself. But the thirty-eight not only did not do this, they did not even trouble to pick up a phone to call the police. Minimally Decent Samaritanism would call for doing at least that, and their not having done it was monstrous.

After telling the story of the Good Samaritan, Jesus said "Go, and do thou likewise." Perhaps he meant that we are morally required to act as the Good Samaritan did. Perhaps he was urging people to do more than is morally required of them. At all events it seems plain that it was not morally required of any of the thirty-eight that he rush out to give direct assistance at the risk of his own life, and that it is not morally required of anyone that he give long stretches of his life—nine years or nine months—to

sustaining the life of a person who has no special right (we were leaving open the possibility of this) to demand it.

Indeed, with one rather striking class of exceptions, no one in any country in the world is *legally* required to do anywhere near as much as this for anyone else. The class of exceptions is obvious. My main concern here is not the state of the law in respect to abortion, but it is worth drawing attention to the fact that in no state in this country is any man compelled by law to be even a Minimally Decent Samaritan to any person; there is no law under which charges could be brought against the thirty-eight who stood by while Kitty Genovese died. By contrast, in most states in this country women are compelled by law to be not merely Minimally Decent Samaritans, but Good Samaritans to unborn persons inside them. This doesn't by itself settle anything one way or the other, because it may well be argued that there should be laws in this country—as there are in many European countries—compelling at least Minimally Decent Samaritanism.[7] But it does show that there is a gross injustice in the existing state of the law. And it shows also that the groups currently working against liberalization of abortion laws, in fact working toward having it declared unconstitutional for a state to permit abortion, had better start working for the adoption of Good Samaritan laws generally, or earn the charge that they are acting in bad faith.

I should think, myself, that Minimally Decent Samaritan laws would be one thing. Good Samaritan laws quite another, and in fact highly improper. But we are not here concerned with the law. What we should ask is not whether anybody should be compelled by law to be a Good Samaritan, but whether we must accede to a situation in which somebody is being compelled—by nature, perhaps—to be a Good Samaritan. We have, in other words, to look now at third-party interventions. I have been arguing that no person is morally required to make large sacrifices to sustain the life of another who has no right to demand them, and this even where the sacrifices do not include life itself; we are not morally required to be Good Samaritans or anyway Very Good Samaritans to one another. But what if a man cannot extricate himself from such a situation? What if he appeals to us to extricate him? It seems to me plain

---

[7]For a discussion of the difficulties involved, and a survey of the European experience with such laws, see *The Good Samaritan and the Law*, ed. James M. Ratcliffe (New York, 1966).

that there are cases in which we can, cases in which a Good Samaritan would extricate him. There you are, you were kidnapped, and nine years in bed with that violinist lie ahead of you. You have your own life to lead. You are sorry, but you simply cannot see giving up so much of your life to the sustaining of his. You cannot extricate yourself, and ask us to do so. I should have thought that—in light of his having no right to the use of your body—it was obvious that we do not have to accede to your being forced to give up so much. We can do what you ask. There is no injustice to the violinist in our doing so.

7. Following the lead of the opponents of abortion, I have throughout been speaking of the fetus merely as a person, and what I have been asking is whether or not the argument we began with, which proceeds only from the fetus' being a person, really does establish its conclusion. I have argued that it does not.

But of course there are arguments and arguments, and it may be said that I have simply fastened on the wrong one. It may be said that what is important is not merely the fact that the fetus is a person, but that it is a person for whom the woman has a special kind of responsibility issuing from the fact that she is its mother. And it might be argued that all my analogies are therefore irrelevant—for you do not have that special kind of responsibility for that violinist, Henry Fonda does not have that special kind of responsibility for me. And our attention might be drawn to the fact that men and women both *are* compelled by law to provide support for their children.

I have in effect dealt (briefly) with this argument in section 4 above; but a (still briefer) recapitulation now may be in order. Surely we do not have any such "special responsibility" for a person unless we have assumed it, explicitly or implicitly. If a set of parents do not try to prevent pregnancy, do not obtain an abortion, and then at the time of the birth of the child do not put it out for adoption, but rather take it home with them, then they have assumed responsibility for it, they have given it rights, and they cannot *now* withdraw support from it at the cost of its life because they now find it difficult to go on providing for it. But if they have taken all reasonable precautions against having a child, they do not simply by virtue of their biological relationship to the child who comes into existence have a special responsibility for it. They may wish to assume responsibility for it, or they may not wish to. And I am suggesting that if assuming responsibility for it would require large sacrifices, then they may refuse. A Good Samaritan would not refuse—or anyway, a Splendid Samaritan, if the sacrifices that had to be made were enormous. But then so would a Good Samaritan assume responsibility for that violinist; so would Henry Fonda, if he is a Good Samaritan, fly in from the West Coast and assume responsibility for me.

8. My argument will be found unsatisfactory on two counts by many of those who want to regard abortion as morally permissible. First, while I do argue that abortion is not impermissible, I do not argue that it is always permissible. There may well be cases in which carrying the child to term requires only Minimally Decent Samaritanism of the mother, and this is a standard we must not fall below. I am inclined to think it a merit of my account precisely that it does *not* give a general yes or a general no. It allows for and supports our sense that, for example, a sick and desperately frightened fourteen-year-old schoolgirl, pregnant due to rape, may *of course* choose abortion, and that any law which rules this out is an insane law. And it also allows for and supports our sense that in other cases resort to abortion is even positively indecent. It would be indecent in the woman to request an abortion, and indecent in a doctor to perform it, if she is in her seventh month, and wants the abortion just to avoid the nuisance of postponing a trip abroad. The very fact that the arguments I have been drawing attention to treat all cases of abortion, or even all cases of abortion in which the mother's life is not at stake, as morally on a par ought to have made them suspect at the outset.

Secondly, while I am arguing for the permissibility of abortion in some cases, I am not arguing for the right to secure the death of the unborn child. It is easy to confuse these two things in that up to a certain point in the life of the fetus it is not able to survive outside the mother's body; hence removing it from her body guarantees its death. But they are importantly different. I have argued that you are not morally required to spend nine months in bed, sustaining the life of that violinist; but to say this is by no means to say that if, when you unplug yourself, there is a miracle and he survives, you then have a right to turn round and slit his throat. You may detach yourself even if this costs him his life; you have no right to be guaranteed his death, by some other means, if unplugging yourself does not kill him.

There are some people who will feel dissatisfied by this feature of my argument. A woman may be utterly devastated by the thought of a child, a bit of herself, put out for adoption and never seen or heard of again. She may therefore want not merely that the child be detached from her, but more, that it die. Some opponents of abortion are inclined to regard this as beneath contempt—thereby showing insensitivity to what is surely a powerful source of despair. All the same, I agree that the desire for the child's death is not one which anybody may gratify, should it turn out to be possible to detach the child alive.

At this place, however, it should be remembered that we have only been pretending throughout that the fetus is a human being from the moment of conception. A very early abortion is surely not the killing of a person, and so is not dealt with by anything I have said here.

Writing and Discussion Topics

Questions 1–6 address content, critical analysis, personal choices, ethical options, specific discipline, and interdisciplinary alternatives, respectively.

1. Why is the parable of the good Samaritan a central point of this essay? What did the good Samaritan do that placed his own life in danger? Does Thomson believe a woman must be a good Samaritan?

2. Is a comparison between a violin player and a fetus an appropriate analogy? How does this analogy bear on the rest of the essay?

3. Consider that someone is drowning in a raging river. Do you have an obligation to risk your life to save that person? Explain the possible consequences of your actions. How does this compare to the abortion issue?

4. Does a pregnant woman have a moral obligation to the fetus? Does it make a difference if the pregnancy is the result of rape? Could a "marginally decent Samaritan" have an abortion in the case of rape?

5. Thomson calls a law "insane" that would not allow an abortion to a fourteen-year-old rape victim. How has she defended this claim?

6. Compare and contrast Blackmun's findings with the philosophy expressed by Thomson.

Kathryn Pyne Addelson

MORAL REVOLUTION

◆◆◆

*K*athryn Pyne Addelson is a professor of philosophy at Smith
College. She is also a scholar in the field of sociology and often
integrates the two disciplines in her writings. Her work has been widely
published. Her articles include "Nietzsche and Moral Change" and
"Man of Professional Wisdom." ◆

Jane

In 1969, most state laws prohibited abortion unless the life of the pregnant woman was threatened. A few states had reformed their abortion laws to allow abortion by doctors in hospitals in cases of threat to the health of the woman, threat of fetal deformity, or rape. In the mid-1960s, the estimated death rate for abortions performed in hospitals was 3 deaths per 100,000 abortions, the rate for illegal abortions was guessed to be over eight times that—30 deaths per 100,000 abortions was a rough estimate and almost certainly conservative. For minority and poorer women, it was certainly very much higher.

The women's liberation movement was in its infancy in 1969. In that year, a group of Chicago women who had been active in radical politics formed an organization called Jane. Over the next year and a half, Jane evolved from an abortion counseling and referral service to a service in which abortions were actually performed by the Jane members themselves. By 1973 when they closed the service, over 12,000 abortions had been performed under Jane's auspices. The medical record equalled that of abortions done under legal, licensed conditions by physicians in hospitals. The service charged on a sliding scale; eventually all abortions were cheaper than the going rate, and some women paid nothing. Jane served many poor women, black women, and very young women who could not have had an abortion otherwise.

My discussion of Jane is based on one newspaper series and an interview with one member. Perhaps not all Jane members will agree with this member's interpretation, but that isn't the point here because I'm not doing a sociological study. I am investigating patterns of moral thinking and acting which the Judith Thomson tradition makes invisible. The fact that one person's thinking and action are concealed is enough to show bias . . . .

What Jane Did   This is the way Jane operated, as reported in the June 1973 Hyde Park-Kenwood *Voices* article on the organization: "Jane was the pseudonym we chose to represent the service. A phone was opened in her name and an answering service secured, later replaced by a tape recorder. Jane kept all records and served as control-center." "Jane"

was not a particular woman but the code name for whichever counselor was taking calls and coordinating activities on a given day.

> For four years, Jane kept the same phone number . . . . At first she received only eight to ten calls a week. A year later she was receiving well more than 100 calls a week.
>
> All phoned-in messages were returned the same day: "Hello, Marcia, This is Jane from women's liberation returning your call. We can't talk freely over the phone, but I want you to know that we can help you."
>
> Then Jane would refer the name to a counselor, who would meet personally with the woman and talk with her at length about available alternatives.
>
> The counselor would also help the woman arrange finances and, whenever possible, collect a $25 donation for the service loan fund. The counseling session was also a screening process for detecting conflicts and potential legal threats.

Jane worked with several male abortionists. One of these was "Dr. C." Dr. C worked alone with his nurse in motel rooms until the day an abortion was interrupted by a pounding on the door and a man's voice shouting, "Come on out of there, baby killer!" After a wild chase between buildings and down alleys, Dr. C escaped the irate husband. When he caught his breath, he decided that it might be better to quit working in motels.

Jane members then began renting apartments for Dr. C and his nurse to work in. Jane describes the first day they used a rented apartment: "Seven women were done that day, in a setting where they could relax and talk with other women in a similar predicament. And when the first woman walked out of the bedroom, feeling fine and no longer pregnant, the other six were noticeably relieved. They asked her questions and got firsthand answers." Another advantage of the new arrangement was that Jane counselors were with a woman during the abortion, giving her psychological and moral support and explaining what was going on to her. Still another was that the counselors gradually began assisting Dr. C in the abortion itself, and he began training them in the abortion procedures.

After a few months of operation, members of Jane had begun inducing miscarriages for women more than twelve weeks pregnant. During this time, Dr. C was teaching the women of Jane more and more about the process of doing direct abortions. Finally, some counselors were doing the entire direct abortion themselves, under Dr. C's eye. In the midst of all this, they learned that Dr. C was no doctor at all, but just a man who had become an expert in the giving of abortions. Later, they broke off the relationship with Dr. C and began doing all of their own abortions. For good or ill, this meant that they had a sudden abundance of funds, since the abortion fee went to Jane instead of to Dr. C. In the eyes of the law, they became full-fledged abortionists: "We could no longer hide behind the label of 'counselor' or expect 'Dr. C' to act as a buffer, with his know-how and ready cash for dealing with a bust." Jane members were arrested only once, although they were harassed by the police.

The change in the abortion service meant that Jane members had to accept the full consequences of what they were doing—even if it resulted in illness, personal tragedy, or death—and they had to bear this without the protection that the doctor's professionalism gives him. They worked under these conditions until 1 April 1973. Then, two months after the United States Supreme Court passed its opinion on the constitutionality of restrictive abortion laws, Jane officially closed.

What Jane Meant   In describing what Jane did, I selected data to a certain purpose. It was a selection different in many respects form the selection someone in Judith Thomson's tradition would have made. I didn't, however, use any special technical concepts or categories from some philosophical theory. In this section, I shall use Jane as a basis for discussing a moral theory which competes with theories of the Judith Thomson tradition, in order to reveal value implications of bias in that tradition.

Jane was an abortion clinic, and the women of Jane were working out moral and political beliefs and activities, not constructing a theory. I want to try to give a fragment of a theory which is able to capture their thinking and their work. The theory should be taken as *hypothesis* about what Jane meant, subject to correction through future investigation of Jane and groups like Jane, and through seeing what comes of acting on the theory. I believe the theory is based on anarchist, or anarchist-feminist principles, but I won't discuss that. Instead I'll call the tradition out of which the theory arises the Jane tradition, to contrast with the Judith Thomson tradition.

In March 1977, I interviewed one of the founders of Jane. She said that the women who founded the organization had been active in civil rights or anti-war work in the late 1960s. They wanted to begin work in the newly born women's liberation movement. But how should they begin? What should they do? Someone suggested abortion as an issue. It was a difficult decision, and they struggled over it for months. Deciding on an issue required an analysis of a network of larger issues, and of the place of the abortion issue in that network. According to the woman I interviewed, the question was one of a woman's opportunities for life choices: "It was a question of free choice about reproduction, free choice about life style, because the old roles for women weren't viable any more. In frontier times, childbearing was valuable and important. So was housework. But that role is gone. The old ways are gone. We felt nothing *could* come in to replace them unless women could make a choice about childbearing. That seemed necessary for any other choice." These alternatives had to be *created* within our social system. The members of Jane hoped that other groups within the women's movement would work on other alternatives—offering alternative living arrangements, working on ways that women could become economically independent, and so on—while Jane members tried to offer the alternative of choosing not to have the child by aborting. That is, they thought in terms of a division of labor among women working to change the society so that women would have real alternatives for meaningful lives.

. . . the concept of a *meaningful life* (more often called "a good life") has traditionally been a central concept in moral philosophy. The pattern of thinking Jane members use requires a holistic analysis of the society in terms of the resources it actually offers for women to have meaningful lives, plus an analysis of how to change the society so that it can offer such resources. . . .

In offering the alternative of abortion, Jane was offering a service that was badly needed. The alternative was open to all kinds of women—rich and poor, older and young, white and nonwhite, but it was a service most desperately needed by the poorer, younger, and minority women. One author says:

> In a comparison of blacks and whites, both for premarital and marital conceptions, we find that whites have higher percentages ending in induced

abortions at the lower educational levels, while at the higher educational levels there is little or no difference between blacks and whites . . . the data point to the greater reliance upon abortion on the part of whites over blacks and on the part of the more affluent or more educated over the less affluent and less educated.

When they did turn to illegal abortion methods, poorer and nonwhite women came out far worse. Nationally in 1968, the black death rate from abortion was six times that of the white death rate. In New York in the early 1960s, 42 percent of the pregnancy-related deaths resulted from illegal abortions; and of those women who died, half were black and 44 percent were Puerto Rican. Only 6 percent were white.

More affluent women were also able to pay the high fees which all good, illegal abortionists charged. Jane overcame this by calculating fees on a sliding scale according to income. Some women paid nothing.

Jane's purpose, however, was not simply to provide a service for women, however valuable that service might be. The Jane group could not provide abortions to all Chicago women who needed them. More than that, Jane members knew that when abortion was legalized, their service would have to disappear. Jane's purpose was to show women a much broader alternative than simply not having a baby, to show that by acting together, women can change society so that all women can have an opportunity to choose a meaningful life. They tried to show this in different ways. One way was through the sliding scale for fees. Counselors explained to a woman paying $300 that she was helping pay the cost for a woman who could pay only $5.00. She was, in a small way, helping to undercut the unfairness of a society which would allow her an abortion but not the poorer woman.

Jane itself was the most dramatic demonstration of an alternative for women acting together. Jane members were themselves future or past candidates for abortion, and in the present, they were doing something dangerous, exhausting, and illegal for the sake of changing society for all women. Jane showed that women could take change into their own hands. By coming to Jane for their abortions, other women were also acting for this change. They were trusting women to do things which traditionally were done by men in their society, and legally done only by doctors (overwhelmingly male) within the rigid, hierarchically ordered medical profession. This was a leap of trust.

In the structure of their service, Jane members were trying to build an alternative kind of medical structure as well.

> We—the counselors—we learned the medical mystiques are just bullshit. That was a great up for us. Do you know, you're required to have a license as a nurse just to give a shot. Nurses can't even give an intravenous on their own. That takes a different kind of license. We would just explain to our workers how you had to fill the syringe, and how to be certain there was no air in it, and why that was important, and so on. We'd spend a lot of time explaining it. Then we would say to the patient, "Well this is the first time that Sue is giving anyone a shot. Maybe you can help her, and be patient with her." The patient was part of what was happening too. Part of the whole team.
>
> Sometimes in the middle of an abortion, we would switch positions to show that everyone in the service could do things, to show that the woman who was counseling could give a shot, and the one who was giving a shot could counsel too. We did it to make people see that they could do it too. They have the power to learn to counsel and give a shot. They have the power to change things and build alternatives.

We here come to the central analysis within the Jane tradition, as it is expressed in Jane's practice. The analysis operates in a very general way to criticize our society and to offer direction to move toward change. Let me state it first in terms of the social structure of the institution of medicine in the United States today.

In the United States, medical people operate within a hierarchical system of dominance and subordination. Those higher in the hierarchy have power which those lower do not have—and the power to order those lower ones around is the least of it. One key aspect of that power is what Howard Becker calls "the right to define the nature of reality." He uses the notion of a "hierarchy of credibility". "In any system of ranked groups, participants take it as given that members of the highest group have the right to define the way things really are." I would argue that this "right of definition" means not only that the word of the higher has heavier weight than that of the lower (teacher over student, doctor over intern or aide) but that the very categories and concepts that are used, the "official" descriptions of reality, are descriptions from the point of view of the dominant persons in the hierarchy. What counts as knowledge itself is defined in terms of that viewpoint, and the definition further legitimates the power of the dominant person.

The power of those in dominant positions in the hierarchy is *legitimate authority*. This contrasts with the *natural authority* of a person who, regardless of position, happens to have a great deal of knowledge, experience, or wisdom about a subject. A doctor's authority is legitimated by the criteria, standards, and institutions which control access to his place in the hierarchy. These criteria and requirements for training on the one hand are aimed at insuring that those with legitimate authority in the hierarchy also have the natural authority required to do the jobs they are doing. Although we all know there are incompetent doctors, these criteria do operate to screen out incompetence *as defined from the top of the hierarchy*. Do they insure that those at the top have natural authority? I think not, and that is because *legitimate authority* carries with it a definition of what counts as knowledge: the definition from the top of the hierarchy, the "official" point of view.

This outlook on knowledge is sometimes called "objective" or "the scientific outlook" of experts. In fact, it is absolutist, and when the definition of reality is given solely in terms of the tradition of the dominant in a dominant-subordinate structure, the outlook is, in fact, biased.

In part, Jane members were operating from the viewpoint of a subordinate group in our society: women. They were using this viewpoint to try to create new social structures which were not based on dominance and subordination and in which authority was natural authority—knowledge which suits the situation to the best degree that we know at the moment. When the woman I interviewed said that the members of Jane tried to show other women that they "have the power to learn to counsel and give a shot" and that they "have the power to change things and build alternatives," she is talking not only about the natural authority of knowledge but what we might call natural *moral* power, or *moral* authority.

In structuring the abortion service as they did, the members of Jane were developing an alternative to hierarchy, but they were also overcoming the vices of dependency and feelings of ignorance and impotence by showing women that they did have the power to learn and do things themselves. The Jane organization itself was built on nonauthoritarian, nonhierarchical principles, and Jane members tried to run it as a collective.

We tried to make it as nonauthoritarian as we could. We had rotating chairs. There wasn't a high value placed on one kind of work and a low value on another. Every position was so important to what we were doing, and it was treated as equally important, to the highest degree possible. This meant every one of us could do what she was best at. You didn't have people competing to do what was important, or feeling what they were doing wasn't valuable.

In April of 1973, the women of Jane asked themselves, "What next?" Whether abortion had been a good issue to move on or not, there was no place for an illegal abortion service now that abortions were legal. Some of the women went on to found a "well woman clinic," the Emma Goldman Clinic. They hoped to run the clinic on the nonauthoritarian, nonhierarchical model used by Jane. The clinic was organized around the concept of self-help, in which the "patients" are trained too in the kind of medical knowledge they need to understand and care for their own bodies for a large range of normal functions and slight disorders.

Bias in the World View

In my discussion here, both the Judith Thomson tradition and the Jane tradition were dealing with the problem of abortion. Neither would take it to be *the* problem. Abortion is a subsidiary problem chosen because of its connection with more central concerns. For Judith Thomson, it is a question of rights—we might even say a question of equal rights. But it cannot be described that way for the Jane tradition without begging questions.

Within the Jane tradition, the problem was taken to be one of meaningful lives for women, or of free choice among genuine alternatives for meaningful lives. Some phrasing of the general problem in these terms seems appropriate to both traditions. Let me quote Betty Friedan, an activist who stands within traditions associated with Judith Thomson's:

It is my thesis that the core of the problem for women today is not sexual but a problem of identity—a stunting or evasion of growth that is perpetuated by the feminine mystique. It is my thesis that as the Victorian culture did not permit women to accept or gratify their basic sexual needs, our culture does not permit women to accept or gratify their basic need to grow and fulfill their potentialities as human beings, a need which is not solely defined by their sexual roles.

The statement of purpose of the liberal feminist National Organization for Women (NOW) also concerns opportunities for a meaningful life and moral development as a human being: NOW pledges to "take action to bring women into full participation in the mainstream of American society now, exercising all the privileges and responsibilities thereof, in truly equal partnership with men." This makes it appear that for both traditions, the problem may be stated as one of equality, particularly equality so far as it relates to the moral questions of being a full human being and of having a meaningful (or good) life. I believe that this is a central concern of those within the Judith Thomson tradition. But it may be that the problem cannot be resolved under that tradition or its associated world view.

Concealing Data   . . . I [have] presented the moral activity of the organization Jane under one tradition. If we look at the Jane organization under the Judith Thomson tradition, we get a different selection of data. Here's a quotation from the newspaper article:

> From the beginning, we discussed the moral implications of abortion from all angles. We listened to right-to-lifers, Catholic clergy, population-control freaks and women's liberationists.
>
> We heard legislators and lobbyists and political commentators arguing fine points of "fetal viability." When does a fetus become a person? When it can survive outside the womb (after six months)? When it begins to move (after four months)? Or from the moment of conception?
>
> Many opponents of abortion called it "murder." We argued the logical counterarguments: If a fetus is a person, then why aren't abortionists and women who have abortions charged with murder?
>
> Or, if the fetus has the rights of a person, then does the woman who carries it become subject to its rights? What happens when the rights of the woman and those of the fetus come into conflict?
>
> All philosophical and legalistic positions lost relevance when we began doing and viewing abortions . . . we knew that we were grappling with matters of life and death and no philosophical arguments could alter that belief.

Judith Thomson, or someone from her tradition, would have been a great help to the Jane women in these early discussions on abortion. On the other hand, these early discussions had no clear relevance to the central moral activity the women of Jane were engaging in—*by their own judgment.* The terms in which they saw the problem were different. Their perception and their moral activity constitute data which are important to solving the problem of equality, but the Judith Thomson tradition not only

ignores those data: it makes them invisible. Let's look at some of the mechanisms by which the data are concealed.

One way a tradition conceals data is through the concepts and categories it uses. The Judith Thomson tradition would focus on the Jane discussions of rights. It would ignore the discussions of hierarchy, dominance, and subordination; and perhaps some within the tradition would not take these as morally relevant discussions at all. Any theory must use concepts. Through their very use, some data are selected and some ignored. Yet the question of whether the concepts properly capture the data, or of whether they are *appropriate,* is a central, critical question about the adequacy of any tradition.

In a similar way, the categories a tradition uses to organize data reveal some and conceal others. For example, the Judith Thomson tradition uses the categories of moral agent and of groups of moral agents as aggregates. The tradition also uses a division of moral phenomena into questions of individual conscience and those of public policy, where the latter is a matter of *official* public policy, made by those with legitimate authority. I don't want to argue that the tradition *rules out* other sorts of moral phenomena. But using those categories, it cannot capture the sort of moral phenomena Jane members took to be central: people in a subordinate position acting to create a set of social relations which are not structured by dominance and subordination, through the subordinates' coming to know their own power (as opposed to legitimate authority) through acting in collectives (not aggregates).

But am I being fair to the Judith Thomson tradition? After all, people within it don't claim to cover *all* moral phenomena. Few theories claim to cover everything within their purview, and even within chemistry there are divisions into organic and inorganic. Mightn't there be divisions within the field of moral phenomena so that another part of the tradition might deal with Jane's moral activity and thus reveal it?

Perhaps any new moral tradition we develop will have to have something to do with the concept of rights and associated concepts and deal in some way with groups as aggregates and with public policy as officially handed down. But that new tradition could not be the Judith Thomson tradition, for a revolutionary change in the methodology of her tradition is necessary to uncover data like Jane's.

The Judith Thomson tradition supposes that there exists a set of moral concepts embedded in moral principles which "we" all know and understand. In her paper, Judith Thomson herself is clarifying concepts "we" grasp by the standard method of the tradition: the use of hypothetical cases. This method presupposes a very mentalistic view of concepts and word meanings—mentalistic in the way philosophical empiricists are mentalistic in their views on meanings as "ideas." The concepts exist in the speaker's understanding. If someone understands the concept, he or she knows whether it applies in any given case. Considering hypothetical cases (in this view) points out cases the speaker might have overlooked; but once they are brought to his or her attention, the speaker allegedly knows whether the concepts apply or not, and so his or her explicit understanding of the concept is clarified. Similarly, one's explicit understanding of "our" moral principles is supposed to be clarified by considering hypothetical cases.

The most obvious thing to say about this method is that although bringing up hypothetical cases may clarify our understanding of concepts and principles, everyone knows that the selection of hypothetical cases also biases understanding. This bias may be (unintentionally) systematic. For example, Judith Thomson gives a case where Jones faces a frosty death because Smith owns the coat. Why not, instead, use a case where men, women, and children face poor diets, poor housing, and loss of dignity because the owner of a mill decides to move it out of one region into another having cheaper labor and lower tax rates? Philosophers may say the second example is too complicated, but the selection is not a trivial matter of simplicity. The coat example ignores an essential distinction in kinds of property ownership which the mill example reveals.

The method rules out empirical investigation to see what sorts of hypothetical cases might capture what is morally important to persons in a variety of circumstances in the United States. There seems to be no way whatsoever to insure that a fair consideration of hypothetical cases is made to reduce the bias. One can't develop a sampling procedure for hypothetical cases.

Worst of all, the method rules out empirical investigation to discover whether the moral concepts and principles the philosophers are dealing with are really the moral concepts which people use in the United States. It rules out empirical investigation to discover whether those concepts and those moral principles are relevant to the lives of people in different walks of life, investigation to discover whether they are relevant to solving those people's problems of human dignity and a meaningful life *as those people perceive* those problems.

The method itself has the mere appearance of being plausible only for ancient systems of concepts which are well worked out. It has not even the appearance of plausibility for a case like Jane's, in which people are in the process of creating new concepts through creating new social forms. The fundamental theory of meaning, of understanding, and of concept formation on which the method is based is not only inadequate: it is false.

All of this means that to encompass the Jane data, a revolutionary change is necessary in the methodology of the Judith Thomson tradition. Without it, the data remain concealed.

The data being concealed concern human moral activity and the possibilities of changing society. This constitutes a direct and very important value consequence. The Judith Thomson tradition dominates philosophy departments in the prestigious American universities, and even teachers in nonprestigious colleges are trained within it. This means that students are taught to see moral activity within that tradition. Activity requiring patterns of thinking and concepts and categories like Jane's is made invisible to them.

Official Points of View   From its beginnings, the tradition Judith Thomson works within has been centrally concerned with equality. People in this tradition have particularly been concerned that all human beings be equal under the moral law and under the positive law of the state. Equality before the moral or positive law means that the same laws and principles apply to all. Whether or not this is enlightened depends on which laws and principles one chooses and the society in which they apply.

The question of equality which those in the Jane tradition raise is one which takes dominant-subordinate structures in the society as *creators* of inequality. Their solution to the problem of equality is the use of the perception and power of the subordinate to eliminate dominant-subordinate structures through the creation of new social forms which do not have that structure. Those in the Judith Thomson tradition do not raise questions of dominance and subordination except in the moral, legal, and political spheres, where they are seen in terms of moral, legal, and political equality. Particularly, they do not raise the question of whether equality before the moral or positive law may not be rendered empty because of the dominant-subordinate structures in the economic or social (e.g., family) spheres.

It appears that there is a bias in our world view. It is a bias that allows moral problems to be defined from the top of various hierarchies of authority in such a way that the existence of the authority is concealed, and so the existence of alternative definitions that might challenge that authority and radically change our social organization is also concealed. But having acknowledged that, we must return to the question I asked at the beginning of the paper.

The Intellectual Pursuits

In this paper, I believe I uncovered a bias that requires a revolutionary change in ethics to remedy. But in the process of considering two approaches to the moral problem of abortion, it has become clear that there are serious questions to ask about the question with which I began the paper:

> Has a covert bias been introduced into our world view by the near exclusion of women from the domain of intellectual pursuits? If we ask about a bias in "our" world view, mustn't we ask who that "we" refers to? In fact, doesn't the question presuppose that "our" world view is constructed by people in the "intellectual pursuits"? That is, doesn't it presuppose a hierarchy of authority in which people in some occupations (academic humanists and scientists, professional writers, etc.) define a world view for everyone else? If so, then there is something further that the Jane case shows.

Judith Jarvis Thomson is a woman working in an established intellectual pursuit, and at the time she wrote her paper, she took a stand that amounted to criticizing certain ethical arguments for sex bias. She took her stand as an authority, she criticized other authorities, and her paper has been widely used by still other authorities who are certified to teach ethics classes. I have criticized her work in this paper, but I too write as an authority. This leads us to a certain conundrum—if I may call it that.

The women of Jane were certainly challenging the way men in important positions are certified to define the way we do things and, in fact, their authority to define "our" world view and say how things "really are." But some of the Jane members, at least, were not saying that we should remedy the problem by having women in important positions define the way we do things. They were saying that we should change the way we do things so that we do not have some important people giving the official world view for

everyone else. That change cannot be accomplished merely by hiring more women to work in the intellectual pursuits. It requires changing the intellectual pursuits themselves. If Jane shows that we need a revolutionary change from the old moral theory, it is a change in the status of the authorities as well as a change in what has been taken to be a moral theory. Unless we strive to find ways to do that, we violate the central moral and scientific injunction for respecting other human beings:

> . . . look upon human group life as chiefly a vast interpretive process in which people, singly and collectively *guide themselves* by *defining* the objects, events, and situations they encounter.

Writing and Discussion Topics

Questions 1–6 address content, critical analysis, personal choices, ethical options, specific discipline, and interdisciplinary alternatives, respectively.

1. Beyond providing illegal abortions, what was the major influence of "Jane" upon its members?
2. Why does Addelson want to distance herself from the "Thomson tradition"? What are the similarities and differences between the two?
3. If you were tormented with an unwanted pregnancy, and abortion was illegal, could you place yourself in the hands of a clinic where there was little formal medical training available? Did this article alter your views on the simplicity of an abortion? Explain.
4. What foundational ethicist from chapter one does Addelson follow? Are additional insights into the ethics of abortion brought out through case studies? Is her position strengthened through the use of case studies?
5. Is this article historically accurate? What other historical information could be used to add strength to this position?
6. Is this article stronger as a political statement or as a philosophical argument? What political structure is best developed through the "Jane" system?

Mary B. Mahowald

ABORTION AND EQUALITY

◆◆

M ary Mahowald is a widely published professor at the
University of Chicago. Her specialty is medical ethics, and her
scholarship includes several publications on the subject of abortion. She
is also interested in American philosophy and the philosophy of
women. ◆

Although views on abortion are typically treated as if there were only two opposing positions, "prochoice" and "prolife," these terms are often used uncritically and simplistically. The diversity of the contributions to this book attests to the inadequacy of such labels. Our subtle as well as obvious differences argue that there is actually a complicated continuum of positions stretching from total rejection to total support of abortion.

The complications derive from different conditions introduced as justificatory, for example, early stage of fetal development, fetal defect, danger to the health or life of the pregnant woman, economic or emotional hardship, and the unwanted nature of the pregnancy. They also derive from differing views about legality and morality: Some distinguish clearly between these, whereas others see them as integrally related. In the former group are those who approve of the legality but not the morality of abortion, as well as those who construe the moral dimensions of abortion as being irrelevant or nonexistent in a pluralistic society. The latter group includes those who seek to establish legal definitions of the morality or the immorality of abortion.

If the human fetus is to be respected, regardless of whether it counts as a fully human being or person, the claim that abortion decisions are morally neutral or irrelevant is clearly insupportable. Still, the history of the question, as well as current studies, provides convincing evidence that social disagreement on the morality of abortion will continue, and that laws will change because they reflect that disagreement.[1] Accordingly, I think it more useful to focus on the morality than on the legality of abortion. Insofar as the law coerces an individual to choose or to refuse abortion, the decision is amoral, even though the abortion itself has moral or an immoral character. Both the freedom to make moral decisions, and the likelihood that such decisions will be correct, can only be enhanced by a careful, rational analysis of the moral alternatives.

In this essay, I develop a position on the morality of abortion that falls somewhere between the extreme positions of total condemnation and total permissiveness. I regard this view as consistent with feminist and egalitarian principles, which are integrally related. In order to describe my position adequately, however, I need first to do "battle against the bewitchment of our intelligence by means of language," with which debate about abortion has been beset.[2]

Five Basic Affirmations

One way to reduce the bewitchment is to consider five basic affirmations embedded in the available arguments. Some are prochoice, others are prolife, and others still are proabortion, prowoman, or profetus. On analysis, each of these positions reveals implications that might startle their advocates. For example, a genuinely proabortion position emphasizes abortion itself as either morally neutral or positively recommended because the fetus is in reality an invasive growth, like a wart or a tumor, that may better (in some cases, at least) be expelled than preserved. Indeed, even without assuming that status for the fetus, one might argue that abortion is morally obligatory in some situations, for example, where world hunger and overpopulation threaten to deny the necessities of life to those already born. But a proabortion position could not logically argue the converse, namely, that in situations of depleted populations, abortions ought not to be permitted.

A genuinely prochoice position would impute to the pregnant woman the right to decide whether to terminate a pregnancy regardless of her reasons. If this position were consistent, however, it would also take account of the choices of others affected by abortion decisions, for example, the prospective father and health professionals who might assist in the procedure. It might further be argued that individuals whose taxes or insurance premiums contribute to the support of seriously defective newborns deserve to have their choices weighed in decisions regarding abortion. Needless to say, those popularly labeled as prochoice advocates are not usually concerned about the autonomy of others in addition to the pregnant woman.

A prowoman position would clearly stipulate that the interests of the pregnant woman are the exclusive determinant of whether her pregnancy should

This article is reprinted from Sidney Callahan and Daniel Callahan, *Abortion: Understanding Differences* (New York: Plenum Press, 1984), pp. 178–196. Used by permission.

[1]Cf. Kristin Luker Chapter 2, this volume; Daniel Callahn, *Abortion: Law, Choice and Morality* (New York: Macmillan, 1970); and John T. Noonan, *A Private Choice* (New York: Free Press, 1979).

[2]Ludwig Wittgenstein, *Philosophical Investigations*, trans. G. E. M. Anscombe (New York: Macmillan, 1968), p. 109.

be terminated or continued. Obviously, one need not be proabortion to be prowoman, as one may actually view abortion as morally wrong while endorsing the right of the pregnant woman to choose it. This position is more clearly related to a prochoice view because it affirms the right of the pregnant woman to choose her own interest over that of the fetus. However, in cases where those who are pregnant are children, or mentally retarded, or insane or comatose—that is, where the autonomy of the pregnant person is questionable or lacking—affirmation of her interests is obviously not equivalent to an affirmation of her choice.

A profetus position would stand at the opposite end of the spectrum from a proabortion view. It basically affirms that the interests of the fetus are the primary determinant of the morality of abortion decisions. Typically, this view entails a belief that the right of the fetus to continue developing *in utero* supersedes the rights and interests of all others affected by the decision—regardless of developmental immaturity, possible or actual defect, or threat to the life or health of the pregnant woman. If fetal life is to be preserved even at the cost of the pregnant woman's life, one might characterize this position as antiwoman. In some cases, however, a profetus position might entail the acceptability of abortion for severe fetal defect, justifying it in the name of fetal euthanasia.

In contrast to the popular view that is typically labeled prolife, a genuinely prolife position would reject all of the preceding views as unjustifiably limited in their affirmation of human life. The proabortion position negates the value of fetal life outright; the prochoice position makes life, at least fetal life, subordinate to liberty; and both the prowoman and the profetus positions ignore the relevance of other lives affected by abortion decisions. Because life is not lived by individuals in isolation from one another, but as an ongoing, complex system of interpersonal relationships, a really prolife position does not affirm the life of the fetus alone or the pregnant woman alone; it affirms the life of the community in which they both participate.

What has startled me in my own reexamination of the abortion issue is a recognition that arguments for all of the preceding affirmations have some validity. Because all five factors obviously cannot be affirmed simultaneously, some principle needs to be introduced as a criterion by which to order them. To that end, I propose a concept of equality, which I will subsequently describe and defend. In order to

represent that concept adequately, however, I first must explain the concepts of human nature and woman on which it rests.

Underlying Concepts of Woman and Human Nature

A further reason is pertinent to the discussion of these concepts, and it concerns the two individuals most affected by abortion decisions. Although the moral status of the fetus has remained a pivotal point of disagreement despite numerous attempts to clarify and justify its status, the status of the pregnant woman as a person is generally uncontested. If we assume that a valid argument concerning abortion entails a concept of woman consistent with a corresponding concept of human nature, then both of these concepts are crucial to understanding and assessing the argument. Yet, most of the leading arguments have either focused exclusively on the fetus, ignoring the concept of woman, or assumed a concept of woman that in my view is ultimately unacceptable.[3] Although I cannot here develop my criticisms of these two types of argument, I can at least avoid the points criticized by specifying and defending the concepts that underlie my alternative approach.

I shall begin, then, by defining woman as a biologically mature human being, typically capable during some portion of her life to conceiving, bearing, and nursing children. In contrast, man is a biologically mature human being, typically capable during part of his life of fertilizing human ova. Based on these definitions, the only significant difference between women and men is their distinctive biological capabilities.

Obviously, other male and female mammals have similar biological capabilities. What distinguishes human beings from other mammals, as Aristotle and Aquinas suggested, is a known capability for rationality and autonomy.[4] Thus, human beings are unique in that they are typically, during part of their lives, capable of exercising reason and choice. However,

---

[3]E.g., Baruch Brody, Michael Tooley, and Judith Thomson, in Joel Feinberg, ed., *The Problem of Abortion* (Belmont, Calif.: Wadsworth, 1973); Mary Anne Warren, "On the Moral and Legal Status of Abortion," *The Monist* 57 (1973), pp. 42–62; John T. Noonan, "An Almost Absolute Value in History," in John T. Noonan, ed. *The Morality of Abortion* (Cambridge: Harvard University Press, 1970).

[4]See Aristotle's *De Anima* and Thomas Aquinas on intellect and will, *Summa Theological* 1, Questions 75–83.

just as biological capabilities may not be exercised by specific members of a species, so the capability of reason and choice may never be exercised and may even be absent in some individuals. The specific meaning of human nature nonetheless depends on the presence of these developmental capacities in most members of the species.

Whether and when such capacities are present may be impossible to determine in some instances. Clearly, biological maturity is not compelling evidence of rational maturation. Nor is biological impairment or immaturity compelling evidence of its lack. The very meaning of *capacity* is controversial because it may or may not be identified with the potentiality of a healthy fetus or a newborn. But the certainty that such capacities are present in specific individuals is not crucial in determining whether they are human beings. A sufficient and necessary condition is that the individual belong to a class whose members typically possess those capabilities. Surely, one's womanhood (Freud to the contrary) is not negated by the fact that one has never become a mother, whether that "never" is determined by choice, by inability, or by circumstance. A similar point may be made about manhood and humanhood.

As they occur in individuals, capacities for reproduction, reason, and choice are developmental rather than sudden, all-or-nothing achievements. In other words, they develop (i.e., progress and/or regress) gradually from fertilization until death, whether these occur uterinely or extrauterinely. Such capacities vary within the same individual as well as among different individuals, and each is relative to some ideal of its complete fulfillment or realization.

Thus far, I have avoided the term *person* in characterizing human beings because it seems hopelessly controversial—and unnecessary. Its controversial quality is amply illustrated by popular as well as philosophical debate over the issue of criteria for personhood.[5] It is unnecessary because we can deal with the issue of whether it is moral to end a pregnancy or to terminate fetal life without settling the personhood question. Our household pets are not persons, but it is surely wrong to cut off their food supply or to poison them needlessly. Similarly, even if a human

fetus is not a person during any point in its development, deliberately expelling it from the uterus is not a morally indifferent matter. Neither is the deliberate continuation of a pregnancy a morally indifferent matter.

Because human life is a developmental continuum it is also morally relevant to advert to the level of development that an individual has reached or can reach, both physically and mentally, in determining the morality of that person's decisions.[6] Thus, just as the fact that a patient is near death is relevant to the morality of decisions regarding treatment, so the fact that a fetus is nearly viable, or seriously defective, is morally relevant to a decision regarding abortion.

Another morally relevant factor about human individuals is that they are interacting entities. Although their interactions may be minimal or inadvertent, they occur at every level of development. For example, a fetus interacts with a pregnant woman through biological and nutritional dependence on her, and many pregnant women (and others, sometimes) interact emotionally with fetuses, even before the final stages of pregnancy. Because human lives are inextricably related, these relationships are pertinent to moral decisions regarding individuals. Moreover, an analysis of such relationships provides the basis for determining how advantages and disadvantages are distributed among such individuals. That determination, in turn, constitutes an account of the meaning and the degree of equality that exists in the society. If equality is a good to be promoted, or even if it is simply an essential means to some good end, it represents a criterion by which to order the competing values relevant to abortion decisions.

The Concept of Equality

But the term *equality* is notorious for its diverse interpretations. Among its political and economic meanings, we might subscribe to a literal interpretation that entails a distribution of the identical share of resources available to every individual, regardless

---

[5]Cf. Tooley, Warren, and Noonan, *The Morality of Abortion;* Joseph Fletcher, "Humanness," in *Humanhood: Essays in Biomedical Ethics* (Buffalo, N.Y.: Prometheus Books, 1979).

[6]Noting the impact of such knowledge on actual abortion decisions, two physicians who have operated an abortion clinic in New York wrote the following: "About 25% of our patients decide not to have the procedure done when they learn that a formed fetus will be aborted." Selig Neubardt, M.D., and Harold Schulman, M.D., *Techniques of Abortion* (Boston: Little, Brown, 1977), p. 69.

of her or his different needs and capabilities. Alternatively, we might maintain a *laissez-faire* view by which equality is defined as leaving all individuals equally alone or "free" to pursue their own interests according to their different talents. Or, we might assume a Marxist notion, by which resources are to be equally distributed according to the distinctive traits of individuals, "from each according to ability, and to each according to need."[7] We will return to this point later.

Because none of these meanings defines the "individual" to whom equal shares (of material goods or liberty) are due, we might also distinguish concepts of equality on the basis of those defined as candidates for distribution. From a purely biological perspective, the term *equality* might apply to every living, distinct human organism, no matter what its level of development, functional capacity, or health status. From a psychological perspective, it might apply only to those who have achieved—or have the potential to achieve—consciousness, rationality, and/or autonomy. The key questions, then, for determining the meaning of equality that underlies various accounts of human relationships or interactions are: On what basis are individuals declared comparable, and how is that reflected in a policy of distribution?

Here, we are obviously dealing with the broader concept of justice. In effect, whenever we grapple with problems of fairness or equity, we argue on the basis of specific concepts of justice *and* equality, so that it seems impossible ever to speak of one without the other. This is particularly evident where distributive justice is the theme invoked, as in John Rawls's treatment of justice, which calls for equal liberty and a minimization of the inequities that arise because of that liberty (cf. "the difference principle").[8] It is also evident in the recent treatment of "distributive

equality" by Ronald Dworkin.[9] In such discussions, the terms *equality* and *justice* are often interchangeable, although the former may also be construed as a means to the latter.

Without attempting to explore further the conceptual and practical relations between equality and justice, I would like to suggest that either or both are means rather than ends in themselves. They are necessary means to the promotion of an ideal society, that is, a community in which the potentials of all individuals and their interrelations are maximally supported and supportive. Although such an ideal of community is unattainable, it remains approachable. As approachable, it represents a moral paradigm in light of which alternative decisions may be assessed by individuals. The ethical framework in which the ideal is embodied is one of virtue or invitation rather than an ethics of obligation.[10]

In contrast with an ethics of obligation, this framework does not provide—or attempt to establish—a clear line of demarcation between right and wrong. Rather, it allows that there are various paths to, and degrees of, achievement of a common moral ideal. Most of the moral decisions that human beings make, I believe, are of this type. In other words, we more often struggle to discern which is the better course of action among given alternatives, than we attempt to determine what is morally necessary or obligatory. This is particularly true with regard to abortion, where circumstances sometimes force an option among tragic alternatives, several of which may be moral. Accordingly, the notion of equality that I regard as most helpful in addressing the abortion issue is one that provides the possibility of applying a moral ideal to practical situations.

Consistent with the preceding account of human nature, I propose a concept of equality that respects both biological and psychological differences as these apply to human beings throughout their lives. Such a conception focuses primarily on individuals as such, insisting that advertence to the differences between them is the only possible way of establishing genuinely egalitarian relations among them. It is thus a

---

[7]Cf. Karl Marx, "Critique of the Gotha Program," *The Marx-Engels Reader*, ed. Robert C. Tucker (New York: Norton, 1972), p. 388. Although all of these concepts of equality have to do with treating people in the same way, their diversity shows that the "same way" may be interpreted quite differently in different political or economic contexts. Cf. R. Flathman, "Equality and Generalization: A Formal Analysis," *Nomos IX: Equality*, ed. J. R. Pennock and J. W. Chapman (New York: Atherton Press, 1967), p. 38.

[8]John Rawls, *A Theory of Justice* (Cambridge: Belknap Press of Harvard University Press, 1971), p. 60 ff.

[9]Ronald Dworkin, "What Is Equality?" *Philosophy and Public Affairs* 10, nos. 3, 4 (Summer and Fall 1981), pp. 185–246, 283–345.

[10]I am thinking here of an Aristotelian ethic of virtue such as that developed by Bernard Mayo in *Ethics and the Moral Life* (New York: St. Martin's Press, 1958).

conception that eschews generalizations based on sex or gender, or even on developmental stage, as adequately defining the moral status of individuals.

In this view of equality, each pregnant woman ought to be regarded not only as *a* pregnant woman, but as *this* pregnant woman, with such-and-such a set of abilities and desires regarding her pregnancy, her life, and so on; and every human fetus ought to be regarded not only as human and as *a* fetus, but as *this* fetus, with such-and-such a health status, potentiality, capability for pain, and so on. Moreover, where equality is invoked as a principle to be observed in an abortion decision, it entails regard for all the differences, present and anticipated, in those affected by the decision.

In his two-part article entitled "What is Equality?" Dworkin distinguished between equality and welfare and equality of resources, and he elaborated the difficulties involved in the former view. Although he did not advert to a biological view of equality, that notion generally represents a form of (his concept of) equality of welfare, one in which welfare is defined as biological fulfillment. The notion of psychological equality is clearly another form of equality of welfare, one that Dworkin usually identifies with the fulfillment of one's preferences. A useful and relevant vantage point from which to criticize both conceptions, as well as any other concept of equality of welfare, is Dworkin's proposed conception of *equality of resources*.

From that perspective, the unrestricted fulfillment of each one's preferences is an impossible and unjust goal. Not only are the resources inadequate, but individual and group interests are bound to clash, introducing new restrictions for some. As for the biological model, which proposes that all living human individuals ought to be supported without regard to limitations in social resources, it is unrealistic and possibly unjust. Surely, the quality as well as the quantity of human lives deserves to be considered in making decisions regarding human reproduction. However, despite these and other problems raised by an equality of welfare, the ideal need not and ought not to be dismissed entirely. A possible and desirable alternative is a notion of equality that determines the extent to which we can adhere to equality of welfare in the face of the limited resources available. In the next section, I describe such an alternative.

Toward an Egalitarian Ethic

The following principles are basic to the egalitarian ethic that I propose to apply to abortion[11]:

1. Individual lives should not be destroyed.
2. Those that can suffer should not be caused to suffer.
3. Those that can think and choose should not have their thoughts or choices ignored or impeded.
4. Individuals should not be misused or abused, that is, treated as other than who or what they are.

All but one (Number 3) of these principles are clearly applicable to others besides human beings, even (in Number 4) to nonliving individuals. I believe that all four principles are self-evident, as long as we acknowledge their status as *prima facie* rather than absolute responsibilities on the part of the moral agent. Any one principle may thus be subordinated to the others if adequate reasons are offered.

In order to resolve the conflicts that inevitably arise for moral agents who wish to pay due regard to all of these principles, a fifth principle is needed:

5. Equality demands that all individuals be given an equal share of the resources available, insofar as these are pertinent to their needs, desires, capabilities, and interests.

The obvious advantage of applying this principle is the avoidance of merely literal equality, that is, the distribution of the same resources to everyone, regardless of their relevance to the individual. Instead, the equal shares entail the equal distribution of the resources relevant to those among whom (which) they are distributed. Admittedly, the criteria of relevance are complicated and overlapping; for example, one might claim that a particular virgin forest should not be destroyed, but one may also claim that

---

[11]To provide a complete survey of plausible principles, I might have proposed the following, as preliminary even to the first: What already exists should not be destroyed. This principle would have extended my argument to nonliving entities, while suggesting that responsibilities to nonliving beings are less binding (in the application of conflicting principles) than those to living entities. For instance, I do believe that we have a *prima facie* responsibility not to deface a work of art or destroy natural resources.

a group of poor human beings who need its lumber for their homes may destroy it. It is therefore necessary to introduce a sixth principle that acknowledges a priority among different kinds of individuals. The sequence of Principles 1–3 already suggests that Principle 1 is subordinate to Principle 2, and Principle 2 to 3, so that Principle 6 may be described as follows:

> 6. Human beings have a primary responsibility to distribute equal shares of pertinent resources to human beings, a secondary responsibility to distribute equal shares of pertinent resources to other sentient beings, a tertiary responsibility to distribute equal shares of pertinent resources to other living beings, and a quartiary responsibility to distribute equal shares to nonliving beings.

Lest this principle evoke the charge of speciesism, I would respond to that anticipated objection by insisting that speciesism, like other chauvinisms, occurs only where irrelevant reasons are used as a basis for discriminatory behavior toward individuals of a particular group.[12] I believe that there are relevant reasons sufficient to justify the claim that human beings have a primary responsibility for distributing equal shares of pertinent resources to other human beings rather than to other members of other species. Among these are the following possibilities:

a. A natural, perhaps biologically rooted, inclination.
b. An *a priori* moral obligation toward one's kin.
c. Laws and customs.
d. Religious views.
e. Objective superiority of the species.

Regarding (a) we need not go as far as Edward O. Wilson's thesis that the members of every species are determined to preserve one another.[13] If a strong form of that thesis is true, then there is no question of moral obligation with regard to such behavior.

Short of sociobiological determinism, however, we can acknowledge what seems manifest: That human beings, like members of some other species, are naturally inclined to value members of their own species more highly than members of other species. Actually, there seems to be a natural inclination based on proximity of blood, cultural, and affective ties, so that one is most inclined to preserve one's own life, then the lives of one's closest kin, friends, less close kin or friends, neighbors, other citizens of one's own country, and so on. Concerning (b), the natural inclination of (a) suggests a basis for ordering one's responsibilities toward others: One does have a graver responsibility to one's children, spouse, friends, and so on, than one does toward those to whom one is totally unrelated by blood, affection, or acquaintance. Duties of fidelity are thus directly linked to kinship with one's family, race, species, and so on.

As for (c), clearly laws and customs support Principle 6. In our own country, as in others, legislation is not directed toward nonhumans, except insofar as its influence on them might affect human beings. Further, although those who live in modern cities may scarcely realize it, use of the environment to fill the needs of human beings has been generally sanctioned throughout history and prehistory. Regarding (d), religions and religious teachings have reinforced the notion that the world and everything in it (except other human beings) were created for the benefit of humankind.[14] But justification for the *use* of nonhuman by human creatures does not constitute justification for their abuse or misuse; accordingly, although raising or hunting and killing animals for necessary food is surely moral, it is probably wrong to kill or to inflict pain on them needlessly (cf. Principles 2 and 4). I shall return to this point later.

Perhaps the most convincing support for the claim that human beings have graver responsibilities to other human beings than to members of other species is the objective superiority of human over other species (e). Since we cannot preserve everything, surely we ought to focus our efforts on what is most worth preserving. In that context, it seems clear that no other species, on the whole, possesses worthier characteristics than our own. Some chimpanzees have been educated to a remarkable degree, and dolphins seem to have a rather impressive mode of communication, but human beings are generally not only educable but educated and educating to a high

---

[12]Radical proabortionists such as Tooley and Warren are likely to level the charge of speciesism, as they view membership in the human species as irrelevant to the morality of abortion decisions. A more recent attack on speciesism is in Peter Singer's *Practical Ethics* (New York: Cambridge University Press, 1979), pp. 48–69.

[13]Cf. Edward O. Wilson, *Sociobiology* (Cambridge: Harvard University Press, 1975); Edward O. Wilson, *On Human Nature* (Cambridge: Harvard University Press, 1978).

[14]E.g., cf. Genesis I.

degree of sophistication, and human beings have devised and practiced extremely advanced, complicated, and diverse modes of communication. This is not to say that an individual chimp or dolphin may not be more intelligent than a particular (say, profoundly retarded) human adult. The important point is that the average chimp or dolphin (and probably the most precocious or educated chimp or dolphin) is surely greatly inferior to the average human being in its ability to reason and communicate.

If we value such competencies as intelligence and speech, then we ought also to value—to a lesser degree of course—the probability of such competence that the average human fetus represents. I use the word *probability* here instead of *potentiality* to connote a stronger meaning than the latter. A potentiality may remain permanently unfulfilled unless certain steps are initiated in order to actualize it—for example, my potentiality for learning Russian, which I do not intend to actualize even though ability and opportunity for doing so are already present. A probability is likely to be actualized unless impeded from doing so. The application of this probability-potentiality distinction to the abortion issue is clear enough. Under normal circumstances, without the active intervention of abortion, a human zygote, embryo, or fetus will develop to term, will be born, and will eventually reach undisputable personhood. In contrast, human ova and spermatazoa may have the potentiality but not the probability of similar development. Although alive and human, germ cells do not develop into persons without the initiative of fertilization.

Another distinction between the human germ cell (egg or sperm) and a human zygote, embryo, or fetus is also relevant to the abortion issue: The former does not constitute *a* human life, whereas the latter does. (A fertilized ovum constitutes at least *a* human life; it may, of course, constitute more than one, as twinning remains possible until about two weeks after fertilization.) Of itself, a human germ cell is no more *a* human being than is any other human cell, such as skin or blood cells; in fact, we might say it is less human because it represents only half of the chromosomal endowment of normal human somatic cells. If human cloning from nongerm cells ever becomes feasible, then we might argue that every human cell represents a possible human life, but it would not constitute a probable human person until initiation of development in that direction through the technology of cloning, which is thus comparable to the initiative of fertilization.

Although it seems clear that a human life is of greater value than mere parts of a human life (e.g., blood or germ cells), this does not imply that every human life, at every stage of its development, is of greater value than the life of any or even every member of other species, at any point in their development. We might consider, for example, the way human beings treat other sentient animals as well as human fetuses in light of Principles 6 and 2. In Principle 6, we acknowledged a primary responsibility to distribute equal shares of pertinent resources to other human beings, and a secondary responsibility for doing so with regard to other sentient beings. Principle 2 implies a responsibility not to cause suffering to sentient beings. Our capability (resources) of reducing or eliminating pain is not pertinent to a zygote or an embryo as it is to later-stage fetuses and other sentient animals. Accordingly, an early abortion whose aim is to reduce or eliminate the pain or suffering (physical, mental, or both) of a pregnant woman may be justifiable, whereas a later abortion—that is, one that occurs after the fetal nervous system has developed to a degree sufficient for the experience of pain (surely during the third trimester, and possibly during the second trimester)—may be unjustifiable if the fetus's pain would be greater than that of the pregnant woman.

Just as a permissive view of capital punishment does not imply the moral acceptability of any means of inflicting that punishment (e.g., torture), so the fact that abortion is probably justified in certain cases does not imply that a specific abortive procedure is morally justified. Accordingly, the available techniques need to be assessed in light of Principle 2, as this principle applies to those affected by the procedure. Hysterotomy (removing the fetus intact from the uterus through surgery) is probably the least painful for the fetus, but the least safe for the woman. In contrast, dilatation and evacuation (D & E) involves mutilation and removal of the parts of the fetus by means of instruments inserted into the uterus through the vagina of the anesthetized woman. In addition to the obvious violence and probable pain inflicted on the fetus, assisting clinicians report that this is an anguishing experience for them; nonetheless, it is probably the safest among the available techniques for the pregnant woman. Saline infusion and prostaglandin injection are less extreme in their effects; both induce premature labor and the delivery of a nonviable fetus. Of the two, prostaglandin is probably both safer for the woman and less painful for the fetus (saline causes toxicity in utero).[15]

The moral relevance of these different techniques will probably be more fully appreciated as the understanding of fetal development increases, and as reproductive technology advances to the point at which artificial wombs are a reality. Even now, however, consideration of the moral justifications for alternative procedures is not only consistent with Principle 2 but also with the landmark U.S. Supreme Court decision of 1973 (Roe v. Wade) — which legalizes premature termination of pregnancy, but not necessarily the termination of fetal life.[16] If it were prevalently possible to end a pregnancy safely without seriously injuring the fetus, procedures such as D & E might well be outlawed.

Further Applications

Although I believe that the preceding account supports the claim that we have responsibilities toward human fetuses as (at least) probable persons and as sentient beings at some stage of their development, it does not constitute adequate justification for a profetus or an antiabortion position. It merely sets up the framework in which the principle of equality (whose meaning I have specified in Principles 5 and 6) may be applied to the controversy so as to provide a genuinely egalitarian solution.

In order to interpret that framework correctly, we need also to recall our concept of human beings as developing, psychosomatic entities. Typically, uterine development, as well as development during infancy and childhood, is almost exclusively progressive, consisting mainly of increments in one's physical and mental powers. After a certain point (the "prime of life"?), however, human development involves a larger component of regression or the deterioration

---

[15]Cf. CDC (Center for Disease Control) Abortion Surveillance Annual Summary 1978 (Washington: U.S. Department of Health and Human Services, 1980), p. 49. Table 23.

[16]This distinction is critically elaborated in my "Concepts of Abortion and Their Relevance to the Abortion Debate," Southern Journal of Philosophy 20, no. 2 (Summer 1982), pp. 195–207.

---

of one's powers. The life lost through an abortion is therefore likely to be a more progressive stretch of life than that lost in practicing euthanasia toward an elderly comatose patient. Nonetheless, there is more than individual development to be concerned about, because important interactions occur constantly among all developing individuals. In other words, human beings, like other species, are essentially social animals. One could further argue that the early, painless abortion of the healthy fetus of a woman whose pregnancy places her life or health in jeopardy is justified because the pregnancy also threatens the developing lives of those who depend on her.

Although both pregnant woman and fetus are developing, psychosomatic individuals, the responsibility of giving due regard to others' thoughts and choices (cf. Principle 3) is clearly applicable to the pregnant woman but not to the fetus. This, of course, is the point at which the debate over abortion often seems most heated, since woman's choice is pitted against fetus's life as irreconcilable values. One possible way of resolving the dilemma is through the egalitarian route of Principle 5, which maintains that equal shares of pertinent resources ought to be distributed to both fetus and pregnant woman. Health and life are pertinent resources to both fetus and pregnant woman, but autonomy is pertinent only to the pregnant woman. Hence, the woman's autonomy ought to be respected to the extent that this respect is compatible with her and the fetus's equal share of health and life. The autonomy of the woman in circumstances where both she and the fetus are at risk thus tips the scale in favor of the woman. If those circumstances are not present, however, the woman's autonomy alone does not seem to justify the termination of fetal life. In other words, abortion justified solely on the basis of the woman's choice at any stage of pregnancy cannot be defended on egalitarian grounds as long as we allow the reach of equality to include nonautonomous human individuals.

Other lives besides those of the pregnant woman and the fetus are obviously influenced by abortion decisions, as we all are affected by the lives and deaths of others. The prospective father, other family members, and close friends are often significantly affected by such decisions. Although it may be difficult to assess the impact, in some instances we can predict with a high degree of certitude that no one, including the fetus, will benefit by declining an abortion. Consider, for example, fetuses diagnosed through chromosomal or biochemical assays as having Tay-Sachs disease, trisomy–13, or trisomy–18.[17] In all of these cases, where the prognosis includes not only failure to survive infancy, but also a painful and painfully slow dying process, Principle 2 seems clearly applicable.

Beyond families and friends, clinicians are not only affected by, but at least partially responsible for, abortions or births in which they assist. And others who are totally uninvolved in specific cases are influenced by such decisions, for example, by contributing voluntarily or involuntarily to the support of some children who are not aborted, or through the enjoyment of the subsequent social contributions of those children. Nonetheless, the impact of abortion decisions on clinicians or other autonomous individuals is so much less than the impact on the pregnant woman herself that their contrary input could hardly justifiably override her choice. If we lived in an ideal world, where the responsibilities of pregnancy, abortion, childbirth, and child rearing were shared by all, the situation would be otherwise, because then the autonomy of everyone would be an equally pertinent resource.[18]

The fact that we live not in an ideal world—but in one in which the pregnant woman is overwhelmingly more affected by these events than anyone else (except the fetus)—is itself a gross affront to egalitarianism. And the affront is scarcely reduced by legalizing abortion. In fact, the law's insistence on the (practically) exclusive right of the pregnant woman to decide the fate of her fetus places a great and ultimately solitary burden on many women, some of whom are still children. For that right is not one that can be exercised or not; rather, as an unavoidable option, it also represents an unavoidable and absolute responsibility. To impute to the pregnant woman such exclusive responsibility is not sufficiently justified on the basis of her biological role—because there are surely social factors that greatly affect the decision and may severely limit the autonomy of the individual making it. If society were welcoming toward unwed mothers and defective infants as well as supportive of the option of abortion in certain

cases; if fathers and others really shared in child raising; if extrauterine means of reproduction were available; if overpopulation were not a matter of world concern—then we would have at least some of the conditions necessary for a genuinely egalitarian approach to the abortion issue.

We do not live in an egalitarian society, however, and therefore, we have to deal with the inequities that exist, while working toward an egalitarian, communal goal. Because that goal represents a moral ideal by which individuals may assess their own choices, a woman might decide whether to terminate her pregnancy (and how) by considering to what extent equal shares of pertinent resources will thereby be distributed to those affected. Or a couple might decide together whether, when, and how to have a child and to share in the responsibility for its rearing—in light of the same principle. Obviously, the more individuals and couples base their decisions on this egalitarian ideal, the more society in general will approximate the ideal, reflecting a recognition by others besides pregnant women and parents of the responsibility for uterine as well as extrauterine life.

Feminism and Egalitarianism

At the outset, I indicated that I regard the position developed here as consistent with feminist as well as egalitarian principles. As there are different concepts of equality, however, there are different versions of feminism. Accordingly, I would like to conclude my thoughts on abortion by briefly considering alternative versions of feminism, their corresponding views about sexual equality, and their implied or explicit positions on abortion.[19]

A liberal version of feminism is one that supports social structures that maximize individual liberty, and that criticizes the present system insofar as it fails to treat women on an equal basis with men. The notion of equality reflected here is essentially individualistic, where the main or the only benefit to be distributed equally in the name of justice is that of

[17]Cf. Richard M. Goodman and Arno G. Motulsky, eds., *Genetic Diseases among Ashkinazi Jews* (New York: River Press, 1969), pp. 217–231, 285–301; Jean de Grouchy, *Clinical Atlas of Human Chromosomes* (New York: Wiley Medical Publications, 1977), pp. 127–132, 160–164.

[18]An excellent elaboration of this argument is in Alison Jaggar, "Abortion and a Woman's Right to Decide," in Carol Gould and Marx Wartofsky, eds., *Women and Philosophy* (New York: Putnam 1976), pp. 347–360.

[19]These ideas are more fully developed in my "Feminism and Abortion Arguments," *Kinesis* 11, no. 2 (Spring 1982), pp. 57–68. Alison Jaggar discussed alternative theories of feminism, distinguishing between Marxist and socialist views, and between radical and lesbian separatist views, in her "Political Philosophies of Women's Liberation," in Sharon Bishop and Marjorie Weinzweig, eds., *Philosophy and Women* (Belmont, Calif.: Wadsworth, 1979), pp. 258–265.

liberty. Unfortunately, this view generally applied would serve to increase disparities other than liberty among individuals. Applied to abortion, it implies the absolute right of individual women to terminate pregnancy at any stage for any reason.

Some radical feminists view the relationship between the sexes as essentially unequal because women are superior to men. Lesbian separatism tends to endorse this approach, which represents a reversal of the traditional antifeminist view that women are naturally inferior and subservient to men. Applied to abortion, such a position would also support the absolute right of women to choose abortion at any stage of pregnancy for whatever reason. However, one would think that female fetuses have a counterclaim consistent with radical feminism, namely, that *they* have a right to survive, whereas male fetuses do not.

As readers may have surmised, the version of feminism to which I am ideologically committed is essentially socialistic, in the sense described by the young Marx in his "Critique of the Gotha Program." In that construal, equality between the sexes means that women and men have equal shares of pertinent rewards and social services. Those functions undertaken by women because they are able and choose to do so (e.g., pregnancy, childbirth, and lactation) are thus valued equally with other socially necessary or enriching functions—and are appropriately rewarded. Equality is thus an indispensable means to a communal ideal by which different needs and capabilities are equally respected, and social progress is maximized. The achievement of this ideal depends on the autonomy of individuals to build a society in which the benefits and deficits of its members are constantly adjusted so as to ensure as egalitarian a situation as possible. Autonomy is thus a crucial, yet not the only, factor to be considered in promoting equality among all individuals. Others' fundamental needs, such as life or health, may justify overriding individual autonomy. The liberation of women, then, like human liberation and equality generally, is not an end in itself, but a necessary means to the communal ideal in which the potentials of all individuals may be maximally, simultaneously fulfilled.

Applied to abortion, this version of feminism insists that the fetus is morally relevant to abortion decisions, but not exclusively determinative of their morality. At the same time, it insists that the mere assertion by law or social attitude that individual women are "free" to choose abortion does not mean that they are actually free to do so. In fact, until and unless men as well as women share equally in the responsibilities for children, there shall be no equality between the sexes, and no genuine liberation for women. Moreover, until and unless the fulfillment of those responsibilities is generally esteemed by others, and rewarded accordingly, the decisions of couples regarding the option of parenthood will be less than fully free. In general, under present circumstances, decisions to have children often place a greater burden on individuals than decisions not to have them—at least as far as the material situation is concerned. As feminist and egalitarian, I wish we might transform that situation into one where reproductive decisions were truly free, and so possibly moral, both subjectively and objectively.

Admittedly, such a transformation would constitute a radical shift in our way of viewing and valuing the "private" and the "public" spheres of life.[20] Minimally, it would require the dissolution of the prestige and power gap between the two. Those who are better at nurturing than others might continue to be women, but they would then not need to leave the workplace of their home to achieve equality with men. Some might combine roles of nurturing and material productivity; others would engage primarily or exclusively in the latter. And men might choose to be primary nurturers without suffering the disesteem of others. In such a turned-around world, feminism would no longer be necessary because sexual equality would be a reality. Abortions might still be moral in certain cases, but they would be an expression of, rather than a means of promoting, an egalitarian society. Moreover, because both men and women would take advantage of contraception or sterilization more consistently, and because the care of children would be more widely shared, there would actually be fewer abortions.

I would like to end by citing the suggestion of a daughter who recently learned that her favorite babysitter, an unmarried college coed, had just had a baby. When told that the new mother had quit school, needed financial assistance, and would now be less available to play with her, the little girl spurted out with enthusiasm, "I know what we should do. We should take the baby, because we have room, and could pay for what he needs, and could take care of

---

[20]Cf. Jean Bethke Elshtain's ideas in *Public Man, Private Woman* (Princeton, N.J.: Princeton University Press, 1981).

him. And his mom could go back to school and come here anytime." In terms of the egalitarian criterion that we have here elaborated, the child was surely on target. Unfortunately, none of those concerned were "free" or virtuous enough to implement her suggestion. So much for the gap between our own ideals and practices.

Writing and Discussion Topics

Questions 1–6 address content, critical analysis, personal choices, ethical options, specific discipline, and interdisciplinary alternatives, respectively.

1. Mahowald makes distinctions between being pro-woman, pro-choice, and pro-abortion. Compare and contrast these distinctions.
2. Mahowald believes men cannot fully understand the biological dimensions of abortion, nor do they appreciate adequately the legal and social differences between men and women. Explain the complexities surrounding the legal, social, and biological problems for women with an unwanted pregnancy. Would it be possible for a man to understand these conditions?
3. After reading this article, do you feel more compassion for a woman with an unwanted pregnancy who comes from a low socioeconomic status and cannot afford an abortion? Why or why not?
4. A contrast between a Marxist-based ethical system and duty-based ethical system is evident in this article. Cite examples of this contrast, and explain your views on the persuasiveness of each.
5. Mahowald constructs a utopian world that holds strictly to the ethical principles she develops. Is her world possible? Name some current laws that would conflict with her world.
6. As a Christian, Mahowald believes her philosophy meshes well with the teachings of her religion. Find a conflict with her ideal world and the way in which Christianity is practiced by churches today.

HUMANAE VITAE

◆◆◆

Pope Paul VI   Source: AP/
Wide World Photos.

P ope Paul VI was born Giovanni Battista Montini. He served as
262d pontiff of the Roman Catholic Church, from 1963 to 1978.
He demonstrated great concern for moral and social problems throughout
his papacy. ◆

Conjugal Love

Conjugal love reveals its true nature and nobility, when it is considered in its supreme origin, God, who is love, "the Father, from whom every family in heaven and on earth is named."

Marriage is not, then, the effect of chance or the product of evolution of unconscious natural forces; it is the wise institution of the Creator to realize in mankind His design of love. By means of the reciprocal personal gift of self, proper and exclusive to them, husband and wife tend towards the communion of their beings in view of mutual personal perfection, to collaborate with God in the generation and education of new lives.

For baptized persons, moreover, marriage invests the dignity of a sacramental sign of grace, inasmuch as it represents the union of Christ and of the Church.

Its Characteristics

Under this light, there clearly appear the characteristic marks and demands of conjugal love, and it is of supreme importance to have an exact idea of these.

This love is first of all fully human, that is to say, of the senses and of the spirit at the same time. It is not, then, a simple transport of instinct and sentiment, but also, and principally, an act of the free will, intended to endure and to grow by means of the joys and sorrows of daily life, in such a way that husband and wife become only one heart and only one soul, and together attain their human perfection.

Then, this love is total, that is to say, it is a very special form of personal friendship, in which husband and wife generously share everything, without undue reservations or selfish calculations. Whoever truly loves his marriage partner loves not only for what he receives, but for the partner's self, rejoicing that he can enrich his partner with the gift of himself.

Again, this love is faithful and exclusive until death. Thus in fact, do bride and groom conceive it to be on the day when they freely and in full awareness assume the duty of the marriage bond. A fidelity, this, which can sometimes be difficult, but is always possible, always noble and meritorious, as no one can deny. The example of so many married persons down through the centuries shows, not only that fidelity is according to the nature of marriage, but

also that it is a source of profound and lasting happiness and finally, this love is fecund for it is not exhausted by the communion between husband and wife, but is destined to continue, raising up new lives. "Marriage and conjugal love are by their nature ordained toward the begetting and educating of children. Children are really the supreme gift of marriage and contribute very substantially to the welfare of their parents.

Responsible Parenthood

Hence conjugal love requires in husband and wife an awareness of their mission of "responsible parenthood," which today is rightly much insisted upon, and which also must be exactly understood. Consequently it is to be considered under different aspects which are legitimate and connected with one another.

In relation to the biological processes, responsible parenthood means the knowledge and respect of their functions; human intellect discovers in the power of giving life biological laws which are part of the human person.

In relation to the tendencies of instinct or passion, responsible parenthood means that necessary dominion which reason and will must exercise over them.

In relation to physical, economic, psychological and social conditions, responsible parenthood is exercised, either by the deliberate and generous decision to raise a large family, or by the decision, made for grave motives and with due respect for the moral law, to avoid for the time being, or even for an indeterminate period, a new birth.

Responsible parenthood also and above all implies a more profound relationship to the objective moral order established by God, of which a right conscience is the faithful interpreter. The responsible exercise of parenthood implies, therefore, that husband and wife recognize fully their own duties towards God, towards themselves, towards the family and towards society, in a correct hierarchy of values.

In the task of transmitting life, therefore, they are not free to proceed completely at will, as if they could determine in a wholly autonomous way the honest path to follow; but they must conform their activity to the creative intention of God, expressed in the very nature of marriage and of its acts, and manifested by the constant teaching of the Church.

Source: *Humanae Vitae* "On the Regulation of Birth," originally issued by Pope Paul VI, July 25, 1968.

Respect for the Nature and Purpose of the Marriage Act

These acts, by which husband and wife are united in chaste intimacy, and by means of which human life is transmitted, are, as the council recalled, "noble and worthy," and they do not cease to be lawful if, for causes independent of the will of husband and wife, they are foreseen to be infecund, since they always remain ordained towards expressing and consolidating their union. In fact, as experience bears witness, not every conjugal act is followed by a new life. God has widely disposed natural laws and rhythms of fecundity which, of themselves, cause a separation in the succession of births. Nonetheless the Church, calling men back to the observance of the norms of the natural law, as interpreted by their constant doctrine, teaches that each and every marriage act (*quilibet matrimonii usus*) must remain open to the transmission of life.

Two Inseparable Aspects: Union and Procreation

That teaching, often set forth by the magisterium, is founded upon the inseparable connection, willed by God and unable to be broken by man on his own initiative, between the two meanings of the conjugal act: the unitive meaning and the procreative meaning. Indeed, by its intimate structure, the conjugal act, while most closely uniting husband and wife, empowers them to generate new lives, according to laws inscribed in the very being of man and of woman. By safeguarding both these essential aspects, unitive and procreative, the conjugal act preserves in its fullness the sense of true mutual love and its ordination towards man's most high calling to parenthood. We believe that the men of our day are particularly capable of seizing the deeply reasonable and human character of this fundamental principle.

Faithfulness to God's Design

It is in fact justly observed that a conjugal act imposed upon one's partner without regard for his or her condition and lawful desires is not a true act of love, and therefore denies an exigency of right moral order in the relationships between husband and wife. Hence, one who reflects well must also recognize that a reciprocal act of love, which jeopardizes the responsibility to transmit life which God the Creator, according to particular laws, inserted therein is in contradiction with the design constitutive of marriage, and with the will of the Author of life. To use this divine gift destroying, even if only partially, its meaning and its purpose is to contradict the nature both of man and of woman and of their most intimate relationship, and therefore, it is to contradict also the plan of God and His will. On the other hand, to make use of the gift of conjugal love while respecting the laws of the generative process means to acknowledge oneself not to be the arbiter of the sources of human life, but rather the minister of the design established by the Creator. In fact, just as man does not have unlimited dominion over his body in general, so also, with particular reason, he has no such dominion over his generative faculties as such, because of their intrinsic ordination towards raising up life, of which God is the principle. "Human life is sacred," Pope John XXIII recalled; "from its very inception it reveals the creating hand of God."

Illicit Ways of Regulating Birth

In conformity with these landmarks in the human and Christian vision of marriage, we must once again declare that the direct interruption of the generative process already begun, and, above all, directly willed and procured abortion, even if for therapeutic reason, are to be absolutely excluded as licit means of regulating birth.

Equally to be excluded, as the teaching authority of the Church has frequently declared, is direct sterilization, whether perpetual or temporary, whether of the man or of the woman. Similarly excluded is every action which, either in anticipation of the conjugal act, or in its accomplishment, or in the development of its natural consequences, proposes, whether as an end or as a means, to render procreation impossible.

To justify conjugal acts made intentionally infecund, one cannot invoke as valid reasons the lesser evil, or the fact that such acts would constitute a whole together with the fecund acts already performed or to follow later, and hence would share in one and the same moral goodness. In truth, if it is sometimes licit to tolerate a lesser evil in order to avoid a greater evil or to promote a greater good it is not licit, even for the gravest reasons, to do evil so that good may follow therefrom, that is, to make into the object of a positive act of the will something which is intrinsically disordered, and hence unworthy of the human person, even when the intention is to safeguard or promote individual, family, or social well-being. Consequently it is an error to think that a conjugal act which is deliberately made infecund and so is intrinsically dishonest could be made honest and right by the ensemble of a fecund conjugal life.

The Church, on the contrary, does not at all consider illicit the use of those therapeutic means truly necessary to cure diseases of the organism, even if an impediment to procreation, which may be foreseen, should result therefrom, provided such impediment is not, for whatever motive, directly willed.

Licitness of Recourse to Infecund Periods

To this teaching of the Church on conjugal morals, the objection is made today, as we observed earlier, that it is the prerogative of the human intellect to dominate the energies offered by irrational nature and to orientate them towards an end conformable to the good of man. Now, some may ask: in the present case, is it not reasonable in many circumstances to have recourse to artificial birth control if, thereby, we secure the harmony and peace of the family, and better conditions for the education of the children already born? To this question it is necessary to reply with clarity: the Church is the first to praise and recommend the intervention of intelligence in a function which so closely associates the rational creature with his Creator; but she affirms that this must be done with respect for the order established by God.

If, then, there are serious motives to space out births, which derive from the physical or psychological condition of husband and wife, or from external conditions, the Church teaches that it is then licit to take into account the natural rhythms immanent in the generative functions, for the use of marriage in the infecund periods only, and in this way to regulate birth without offending the moral principles which have been recalled earlier.

The Church is consistent with herself when she considers recourse to the infecund periods to be licit, while at the same time condemning, as being always illicit, the use of means directly contrary to fecundation, even if such use is inspired by reasons which may appear honest and serious. In reality, there are essential differences between the two cases; in the former, the married couple make legitimate use of a natural disposition; in the latter, they impede the development of natural processes. It is true that, in the one and the other case, the married couple are in agreement in the positive will of avoiding children for plausible reasons, seeking the certainty that offspring will not arrive; but it is also true that only in the former case are they able to renounce the use of marriage in the fecund periods when, for just motives, procreation is not desirable, while making use of it during infecund periods to manifest their affection and to safeguard their mutual fidelity. By so doing, they give proof of a truly and integrally honest love.

Grave Consequences of Methods of Artificial Birth Control

Upright men can even better convince themselves of the solid grounds on which the teaching of the Church in this field is based, if they care to reflect upon the consequences of methods of artificial birth control. Let them consider, first of all, how wide and easy a road would thus be opened up towards conjugal infidelity and the general lowering of morality. Not much experience is needed in order to know human weakness, and to understand that men—especially the young, who are so vulnerable on this point—have need of encouragement to be faithful to the moral law, so that they must not be offered some easy means of eluding its observance. It is also to be feared that the man, growing used to the employment of anticonceptive practices, may finally lose respect for the woman and, no longer caring for her physical and psychological equilibrium, may come to the point of considering her as a mere instrument of selfish enjoyment, and no longer as his respected and beloved companion.

Let it be considered also that a dangerous weapon would thus be placed in the hands of those public authorities who take no heed of moral exigencies. Who could blame a government for applying to the solution of the problems of the community those means acknowledged to be licit for married couples in the solution of a family problem? Who will stop rulers from favoring, from even imposing upon their peoples, if they were to consider it necessary, the method of contraception which they judge to be most efficacious? In such a way men, wishing to avoid individual, family, or social difficulties encountered in the observance of the divine law, would reach the point of placing at the mercy of the intervention of public authorities the most personal and most reserved sector of conjugal intimacy.

Consequently, if the mission of generating life is not to be exposed to the arbitrary will of men, one must necessarily recognize unsurmountable limits to the possibility of man's domination over his own body and its functions; limits which no man, whether a private individual or one invested with authority, may licitly surpass. And such limits cannot be determined otherwise than by the respect due to the integrity of the human organism and its functions, according to the principles recalled earlier, and also according to the correct understanding of the "principle of totality" illustrated by our predecessor Pope Pius XII.

The Church Guarantor of True Human Values

It can be foreseen that this teaching will perhaps not be easily received by all: Too numerous are those voices—amplified by the modern means of propaganda—which are contrary to the voice of the Church. To tell the truth, the Church is not surprised to be made, like her divine founder, a "sign of contradiction," yet she does not because of this cease to proclaim with humble firmness the entire moral law, both natural and evangelical. Of such laws the Church was not the author, nor consequently can she be their arbiter; she is only their depositary and their interpreter, without ever being able to declare to be licit that which is not so by reason of its intimate and unchangeable opposition to the true good of man.

In defending conjugal morals in their integral wholeness, the Church knows that she contributes towards the establishment of a truly human civilization; she engages man not to abdicate from his own responsibility in order to rely on technical means; by

that very face she defends the dignity of man and wife. Faithful to both the teaching and the example of the Saviour, she shows herself to be the sincere and disinterested friend of men, whom she wishes to help, even during their earthly sojourn, "to share as sons in the life of the living God, the Father of all men."

Writing and Discussion Topics

Questions 1–6 address content, critical analysis, personal choices, ethical options, specific discipline, and interdisciplinary alternatives, respectively.

1. Why is the use of birth control not in keeping with Roman Catholic doctrine? Why does Pope Paul VI believe abortion is a greater sin than the use of birth control?
2. Could there be circumstances inside and outside of marriage where avoidance of birth control is immoral? Cite Paul VI in your answer.
3. Do your views on abortion agree or conflict with those of your religion, family, or community? Examine and explain.
4. Would you blame the decline of marriage and the deterioration of society in general on the use of birth control and abortion? What ethical problems do birth control and abortion create in society?
5. Is it possible to know God's law with respect to abortion? If so, how and in what terms? If not, on what grounds do religious leaders influence their followers' stands on abortion?
6. Why do Mary Mahowald and Paul VI come up with different perspectives on abortion, particularly since they are both Roman Catholics? Compare and contrast the ideologies expressed in their articles.

Daniel C. Maguire

A CATHOLIC THEOLOGIAN AT AN
ABORTION CLINIC

———◆◆◆———

Daniel C. Maguire is a professor of theology at Marquette University. Prior to his work at Marquette, he taught at Villanova and Catholic University. His considerable research and publication focus on ethics in medicine, law, and politics. ◆

I should not have been nervous the first day I drove to the abortion clinic. After all, I wasn't pregnant. There would be no abortions done this day. I would see no patients and no picketers. And yet tremors from a Catholic boyhood wrenched my usually imperturbable stomach. I was filled with dread and foreboding.

What was it that brought this Philadelphia Irish-Catholic male moral theologian to the clinic door? Abortion has not been my academic obsession. My wife and I have had no personal experience with abortion, although it once loomed as a possible choice in our lives. Our first son, Danny, was diagnosed as terminally ill with Hunter's syndrome when Margie was three months pregnant with our second child. However, amniocentesis revealed that the fetus, now Tommy, was normal.

The stimulus for my visit was the woman who agonized with Margie and me over the decision she had rather conclusively made, and asked us, as ethicists, to ponder with her all the pro's and con's. She was almost six weeks pregnant. Her life situation was seriously incompatible with parenting and she could not bear the thought of adoption. After her abortion, she told us she had made the right decision, but she paid the price in tears and trauma.

More generally, I was drawn to this uneasy experience by women. I have often discussed abortion with women in recent years, been struck by how differently they viewed it. I experienced their sentiment at the treatment of the subject by the male club of moral theologians. One woman, an author and professor at a Chicago seminary, wrote me after reading my first article on abortion ("Abortion: A Question of Catholic Honesty," *The Christian Century*, September 14–21, 1983) thanking me and surprising me. She said she found it difficult to use the American bishop's pastoral letter on nuclear war because these *men* could agonize so long over the problems of *men* who might decide to end the world, but had not a sympathetic minute for the moral concerns of a woman who judges that she cannot bring her pregnancy to term.

I knew that my visit would not give me a woman's understanding of the abortion decision, but I hoped it might assist me, in the phrase of French novelist Jean Sulivan, to "lie less" when I write about this subject and to offend less those women who come this way in pain.

Those who write on liberation theology go to Latin America to learn; those who write on abortion stay at their desks. Until recently, all churchly writing on abortion has been done by desk-bound celibate males. If experience is the plasma of theory, the experience obtained in a clinic three blocks from Marquette, where I teach and have done research on abortion, could only enhance my theological ministry.

Meeting the Clinic Staff

One day last May, I called the Milwaukee Women's Health Organization and spoke to its director, Elinor Yeo, an ordained minister of the United Church of Christ. I was afraid she would find my request to spend time at her clinic unseemly and out of order. She said she would call back when she finished an interview with a patient and spoke to her staff. She called later to tell me that the staff was enthusiastic about my prospective visits, adding the ironic note that the patient she was interviewing when I first called was a Marquette University undergraduate.

The clinic door still had traces of red paint from a recent attack. The door was buzzed open only after I was identified. A sign inside read: PLEASE HELP OUR GUARD. WE MAY NEED WITNESSES IF THE PICKETS GET OUT OF CONTROL. YOU CAN HELP BY OBSERVING AND LETTING HIM/HER KNOW IF YOU SEE TROUBLE. I realized that these people live and work in fear of "pro-life" violence. In the first half of this year there have been 58 reported incidents of criminal violence at clinics, including bombing, arson, shootings, and vandalism.

Elinor Yeo sat with me for more than an hour describing the clinic's activities. Half of its patients are teenagers; half, Catholics, and 20 percent, black. Of the 14 patients seen on a single day the previous week, one was 13 years old; one, 14; and, one 15. Nationally, most abortions are performed within eight weeks of conception, at which point the *conceptus* is still properly called an embryo; 91 percent are within 12 weeks. At this clinic, too, most abortions are performed in the first two months. Most of the patients are poor; the clinic is busiest at the time when welfare checks come in. The normal cost for an abortion here is $185. For those on public assistance, it is $100.

I asked Elinor about the right-to-lifers' claim that most women who have abortions are rich. She replied: "The typical age of an abortion patient at this clinic is 19 years." In what sense is a 19–year-old woman with an unwanted pregnancy rich?

From Daniel C. Maguire, "A Catholic Theologian at an Abortion Clinic." Reprinted by permission of the author.

I asked about the charge that doing abortions makes doctors rich. She assured me that, given their budget, all the doctors who work for them would make more if they remained in their offices. These doctors are also sometimes subject to harassment and picketing at their homes. Their care of patients is excellent, and they often end up delivering babies for these same women at some later date.

Each patient is given private counseling. About half want their male partners with them for these sessions. If there is any indication that the man is more anxious for the abortion than the woman, private counseling is carefully arranged. Every interested woman is offered the opportunity to study charts on embryonic and fetal development, and all women are informed of alternatives to abortion. The consent form, to be signed at the end of the interview and counseling sessions, includes the words: "I have been informed of agencies and services available to assist me to carry my pregnancy to term should I desire. . . . The nature and purposes of an abortion, the alternatives to pregnancy termination, the risks involved, and the possibility of complications have been fully explained to me."

All counselors stress reproductive responsibility. Two of the counselors have worked with Elinor for 14 years. One is the mother of five children, the other, of three. Free follow-up advice on contraception is made available. It is the explicit goal of the counselors not to have the woman return for another abortion. According to Yeo, those most likely to have repeat abortions are women who reject contraceptive information and say they will never have sex again until they are married. It became ironically clear to me that the women working in this abortion clinic prevent more abortions than the zealous pickets demonstrating outside.

Yeo says that only 5 percent of the patients have ever seriously considered adoption as an alternative. *Abortion* or *keeping* are the two options considered by these young women. (Ninety-five percent of teenagers who deliver babies keep them, according to Elinor Yeo.)

Adoption is, of course, the facile recommendation of the bumper-sticker level of this debate. One patient I spoke to at a subsequent visit to the clinic told me how unbearable the prospect was of going to term and then giving up the born baby. For impressive reasons she found herself in no condition to have a baby. Yet she had begun to take vitamins to nourish the embryo in case she changed her mind.

"If I continued this nurture for nine months, how could I hand over to someone else what would then be my baby?" It struck me forcefully how aloof and misogynist it is not to see that the adoption path is full of pain. Here is one more instance of male moralists prescribing the heroic for women as though it were simply moral and mandatory.

The surgery lasts some 5 to 15 minutes. General anesthesia is not needed in these early abortions. Most women are in and out of the clinic in two and one half hours. They return in two weeks for a checkup. These early abortions are done by suction. I was shown the suction tube that is used and was surprised to find that it is only about twice the width of a drinking straw. This was early empirical information for me as to *what* it is that is aborted at this stage.

All patients are warned about pregnancy aftermath groups that advertise and offer support but actually attempt to play on guilt and recruit these women in their campaign to outlaw all abortions, even those performed for reasons of health. One fundamentalist Protestant group in Milwaukee advertises free pregnancy testing. When the woman arrives, they subject her to grisly slides on abortions of well-developed fetuses. They take the woman's address and phone number and tell her they will contact her in two weeks at home. The effects of this are intimidating and violative of privacy and often lead to delayed abortions of more developed fetuses.

Meeting the Women

My second visit was on a Saturday when the clinic was busy. I arrived at 8:30 in the morning. The picketers were already there, all men, except for one woman with a boy of 10. A patient was in the waiting room, alone. We greeted each other, and I sat down and busied myself with some papers, wondering what was going on in her mind. I was later to learn that she was five to six weeks pregnant. I was told that she was under psychiatric care for manic-depression, and receiving high doses of lithium to keep her mood swings under control. However, lithium in high doses may be injurious to the formation of the heart in embryos and early fetuses.

Pro-life? Pro-choice? How vacuous the slogans seemed in the face of this living dilemma. What life options were open to this woman? Only at the expense of her emotional well-being could a reasonably formed fetus come to term. This woman had driven alone a long distance that morning to get to the clinic and she would have to return home alone afterward. She had to walk to the door past demonstrators showing her pictures of fully formed fetuses and begging her: "Don't kill your baby! Don't do it." However well-intentioned they may be, in what meaningful moral sense were those picketers in this instance pro-life?

As I watched this woman I thought of one of my colleagues who had recently made a confident assertion that there could be no plausible reason for abortion except to save the physical life of the woman or if the fetus was anencephalic. This woman's physical life was not at risk and the embryo would develop a brain. But saving *life* involves more than cardiopulmonary continuity. How is it that in speaking of women we so easily reduce human life to physical life? What certitudes persuade theologians that there are only two marginal reasons to justify abortion? Why is the Vatican comparably sure that while there may be *just* wars with incredible slaughter, there can be no *just* abortions? Both need to listen to the woman on lithium as she testifies that life does not always confine itself within the ridges of our theories.

With permission I sat in on some of the initial interviews with patients. The first two were poor teenagers, each with an infant at home, and each trying to finish high school. One was out of work. Elinor Yeo let her know that they were now hiring at "Wendy's." I was impressed that the full human plight of the patients was of constant concern to the staff. The other young woman had just gotten a job after two years and would lose it through pregnancy. One woman counted out her $100 and said: "I hate to give this up; I need it so much."

The staff told me about the various causes of unwanted pregnancies. One staff member said that it would seem that most young men have "scorn for condoms." "Making love" does not describe those sexual invasions. For these hostile inseminators nothing is allowed to interfere with their pleasure. Often there is contraceptive failure. One recent case involved a failed vasectomy. Sometimes conception is admittedly alcohol- and drug-related. A few women concede that they were "testing the relationship." Often it is a case of a broken relationship where the woman, suddenly alone, feels unable to bring up a child. Economic causes were most common. Lack of job, lack of insurance, a desire to stay in school and break out of poverty.

I wondered how many "pro-lifers" voted for Ronald Reagan because of his antiabortion noises, even though Reaganomics decreased the income of the lowest fifth of society's families by 8 percent while increasing the income of the rich. More of this could only be more poverty, more ruin, more social chaos, more unwanted pregnancies, and more women at clinic doors.

Meeting the Picketers

The picketers are a scary lot. Because of them a guard has to be on duty to escort the patients from their cars. Before the clinic leased the adjacent parking lot—making it their private property—some picketers used to attack the cars of the women, screaming and shaking the car. The guard told me he was once knocked down by a picketer. Without the guard, some of the demonstrators surround an unescorted woman and force her to see and hear their message. Other picketers simply carry placards and pray. One day, 20 boys from Libertyville, Illinois, were bused in to picket. They were not passive. They had been taught to shout at the women as they arrived. One staff member commented: "Statistically, one quarter to one third of these boys will face abortion situations in their lives. I wonder how this experience will serve them then."

A reporter from the Milwaukee *Journal* arrived, and I followed her when she went out to interview the picketers. Two picketers recognized me. Since I have been quoted in the press in ways that did not please, I am a persona non grata to this group. I had a chance to feel what the women patients endure. "You're in the right place, Maguire. In there, where they murder the babies." I decided they were not ripe for dialogue, so I remained silent and listened in on the interview.

I learned that some of these men had been coming to demonstrate every Saturday for nine years. Their language was filled with allusions to the Nazi Holocaust. Clearly, they imagine themselves at the ovens of Auschwitz, standing in noble protest as innocent *persons* are led to their death. There could hardly be any higher drama in their lives. They seem not to know that the Nazis were antiabortion too—for Aryans. They miss the anti-Semitism and insult in this use of Holocaust imagery. The 6 million murdered Jews and more than 3 million Poles, Gypsies, and homosexuals were actual, not potential, persons who were killed. Comparing their human dignity to that of prepersonal embryos is no tribute to the Holocaust dead.

Sexism too is in bold relief among the picketers. Their references to "these women" coming here to "kill their babies" are dripping with hatred. It struck me that for all their avowed commitment to life, these are the successors of the witch-hunters.

Meeting the Embryos

On my third visit to the clinic, I made bold to ask to see the products of some abortions. I asked in such a way as to make refusal easy, but my request was granted. The aborted matter is placed in small cloth bags and put in jars awaiting disposal. I asked to see the contents of one of the bags of a typical abortion—a six- to nine-week pregnancy—and it was opened and placed in a small metal cup for examination. I held the cup in my hands and saw a small amount of unidentifiable fleshy matter in the bottom of the cup. The quantity was so little that I could have hidden it if I had taken it into my hand and made a fist.

It was impressive to realize that I was holding in the cup what many people think to be the legal and moral peer of a woman, if not, indeed, her superior. I thought too of the Human Life Amendment that would describe what I was seeing as a citizen of the United States with rights of preservation that would countermand the good of the woman bearer. I have held babies in my hands and now I held this embryo. I know the difference.

Conclusions

• My visits to the clinic made me more anxious to maintain the legality of abortions for women who judge they need them. There are no moral grounds for political consensus against this freedom on an issue where good experts and good people disagree. It also made me anxious to work to reduce the need for abortion by fighting the causes of unwanted pregnancies: *sexism* enforced by the institutions of church, synagogue, and state that diminishes a woman's sense of autonomy; *poverty* induced by skewed budgets; *antisexual* bias that leads to eruptive sex; and the other *macro* causes of these micro tragedies.

• I came to understand that abortion can be the *least* violent option facing a woman. It is brutally insensitive to pretend that for women who resort to abortion, death is the only extremity they face.

• I came away from the clinic with a new longing for a moratorium on self-righteousness and sanctimonious utterances from Catholic bishops on the subject of abortion. An adequate Catholic theology of abortion has not yet been written. But the bishops sally forth as though this complex topic were sealed in a simple negative. Bishops like New York's John O'Connor, who use tradition as though it were an oracle instead of an unfinished challenge, are not helping at all. A position like O'Connor's has two yields: (a) it insults the Catholic intellectual tradition by making it look simplistic, and (b) it makes the bishops the allies of a right wing that has been using its newfound love of embryos as an ideological hideaway for many who resist the bishops' call for peace and social justice.

• Finally, I come from the abortion clinic with an appeal to my colleagues in Catholic moral theology. Many theologians (especially clerics) avoid this issue or behave weirdly or skittishly when they touch it. How do Catholic theologians justify their grand silence when they are allowing physical, crude historical distortions, and fundamentalistic notions of "Church teaching" to parade as "the Catholic position"? Why are ethical errors that are thoroughly lambasted in the birth-control debate tolerated when the topic is abortion? Geraldine Ferraro and Governor Mario Cuomo of New York are taking the heat and trying to do the theology on this subject. Their debts to American Catholic theologians are minuscule. What service do we Church teachers give when errors, already corrected in theology, are allowed to roam unchallenged in the pastoral and political spheres? Why are nonexperts, church hierarchy or not, allowed to set the *theological* terms of this debate? What service is it to ecumenism to refuse serious dialogue not only with women but with main-line Jewish and Protestant theologians on this issue? Vatican II said the "ecumenical dialogue could start with discussions concerning the application of the gospel to moral questions." That dialogue has not happened on abortion, and our brothers and sisters from other communions are waiting for it.

I realize, as do my colleagues in Catholic ethics, that abortion is not a pleasant topic. At its best, abortion is a negative value, unlike the positive values of feeding the poor and working for civil rights. On top of that it has become the litmus test of orthodoxy, and that spells danger in the Catholic academe. But, beyond all this, we in the Catholic family have been conditioned against an objective and empathic understanding of abortion. We are more sensitized to embryos than to the women who bear them. I claim no infallibility on this subject, but I do insist that until we open our affections to enlightenment here, we will none of us be wise.

Writing and Discussion Topics

Questions 1–6 address content, critical analysis, personal choices, ethical options, specific discipline, and interdisciplinary alternatives, respectively.

1. Part of Maguire's article focuses on males making decisions for females. Why does he believe abortion should primarily be a woman's decision?

2. How does Maguire's definition of a human life differ from that of most Christian theologians? Does this detract or add to his credentials as an authority?

3. How do you feel about people who protest abortion clinics? Would your protest a clinic? Would you physically try to stop someone from getting an abortion? Would you destroy an abortion clinic? Explain the moral principles behind your answers.

4. Is adoption a necessary alternative to abortion? Maguire and Judith Jarvis Thomson both say that under various circumstances it is not necessary for a woman to go though an unwanted pregnancy for the sake of adoption. Examine their stands.

5. Compare Maguire's and Paul VI's views on human life beginning at conception.

6. Maguire visited abortion clinics hoping to gain a stronger female perspective on abortion. Would Kathryn Pyne Addelson or Mary Mahowald believe his perspectives are similar to those of women who terminate unwanted pregnancies?

Fred Rosner

THE JEWISH ATTITUDE TOWARD
ABORTION

◆◆◆

F red Rosner is a physician, assistant dean, and professor of
    medicine at Albert Einstein College of Medicine and director of
medicine at Long Island Jewish Medical Center Affiliation at Queens
Hospital Center. He was born in Germany and immigrated to the
United States where he attended Yeshiva University and Albert Einstein
College of Medicine. He is well known as an author, translator, and
editor in medicine, ethics, and Judaism. ◆

Jewish Legal Attitude Toward Abortion

An unborn fetus in Jewish law is not considered a person (Heb. *nefesh*, lit. "soul") until it has been born. The fetus is regarded as a part of the mother's body and not a separate being until it begins to egress from the womb during parturition. In fact, until forty days after conception, the fertilized egg is considered as "mere fluid." These facts form the basis for the Jewish legal view on abortion. Biblical, talmudic, and rabbinic support for these statements will now be presented.

Intentional abortion is not mentioned directly in the Bible, but a case of accidental abortion is discussed in Exodus 21:22–23, where Scripture states:

> When men fight and one of them pushes a pregnant woman and a miscarriage results, but no other misfortune ensues, the one responsible shall be fined as the woman's husband may exact from him, the payment to be based on judges' reckoning. But if other misfortune ensues, the penalty shall be life for life.

The famous biblical commentator Solomon ben Isaac, known as *Rashi*, interprets *no other misfortune* to mean no fatal injury to the woman following her miscarriage. In that case, the attacker pays only financial compensation for having unintentionally caused the miscarriage, no differently than if he had accidentally injured the woman elsewhere on her body. Most other Jewish Bible commentators, including Moses Nachmanides (*Ramban*), Abraham Ibn Ezra, Meir Leib ben Yechiel Michael (*Malbim*), Baruch Halevi Epstein (*Torah Temimah*), Samson Raphael Hirsch, Joseph Hertz, and others, agree with *Rashi's* interpretation. We can thus conclude that when the mother is otherwise unharmed following trauma to her abdomen during which the fetus is lost, the only rabbinic concern is to have the one responsible pay damages to the woman and her husband for the loss of the fetus. None of the rabbis raise the possibility of involuntary manslaughter being involved because the unborn fetus is not legally a person and, therefore, there is no question of murder involved when a fetus is aborted.

Based upon this biblical statement, Moses Maimonides asserts as follows: "If one assaults a woman, even unintentionally, and her child is born prematurely, he must pay the value of the child to the husband and the compensation for injury and pain to the woman.[1] Maimonides continues with statements regarding how these compensations are computed. A similar declaration is found in Joseph Karo's *Shulchan Aruch*.[2] No concern is expressed by either Maimonides or Karo regarding the status of the miscarried fetus. It is part of the mother and belongs jointly to her and her husband, and thus damages must be paid for its premature death. However, the one who was responsible is not culpable for murder, since the unborn fetus is not considered a person.

Murder in Jewish law is based upon Exodus 21:12, where it is written: *He that smiteth a man so that he dieth shall surely be put to death.* The word *man* is interpreted by the sages to mean a man but not a fetus.[3] Thus, the destruction of an unborn fetus is not considered murder.

Another pertinent scriptural passage is Leviticus 24:17, where it states: *And he that smiteth any person mortally shall surely be put to death.* However, an unborn fetus is not considered a person or *nefesh* and, therefore, its destruction does not incur the death penalty.

Turning to talmudic sources, the Mishnah asserts the following:[4] "If a woman is having difficulty in giving birth [and her life is in danger],[5] one cuts up the fetus within her womb and extracts it limb by limb, because her life takes precedence over that of the fetus. But if the greater part was already born, one may not touch it, for one may not set aside one person's life for that of another."

Rabbi Yom Tov Lippman Heller, known as *Tosafot Yom Tov*, in his commentary on this passage in the Mishnah, explains that the fetus is not considered a *nefesh* until it has egressed into the air of the world and, therefore, one is permitted to destroy it to save the mother's life. Similar reasoning is found in *Rashi's* commentary on the talmudic discussion of this mishnaic passage, where *Rashi* states that as long as the child has not come out into the world, it is not called a living being, i.e., *nefesh*.[6] Once the head of the child has come out, the child may not be harmed because it is considered as fully born, and one life may not be taken to save another.[7]

The Mishnah elsewhere states: "If a pregnant woman is taken out to be executed, one does not wait for her to give birth: but if her pains of parturition have already begun [lit. she has already sat on the birth stool], one waits for her until she gives birth."[8] One does not delay the execution of the

From Fred Rosner, M.D., *Modern Medicine and Jewish Ethics.* Copyright © 1986 KTAV Publishing House, Inc. and Yeshiva University Press. Reprinted by permission of the author.

mother in order to save the life of the fetus because the fetus is not yet a person (Heb. *nefesh*), and judgments in Judaism must be promptly implemented. The Talmud also explains that the embryo is part of the mother's body and has no identity of its own, since it is dependent for its life upon the body of the woman.[9] However, as soon as it starts to move from the womb, it is considered an autonomous being (*nefesh*) and thus unaffected by the mother's state. This concept of the embryo being considered part of the mother and not a separate being recurs throughout the Talmud and rabbinic writings.[10] The Talmud continues: "Rab Judah said in the name of Samuel: If a [pregnant] woman is about to be executed, one strikes her against her womb so that the child may die first, to avoid her being disgraced."[11] *Rashi* explains that if the child escaped death and came forth after the mother's execution, it might cause bleeding and thus expose the executed mother to disgrace. Thus, we have evidence that an unborn fetus does not have the status of a living being, and destroying it to save the mother embarrassment is not prohibited if it is going to die anyway.

The talmudic commentary known as *Tosafot* states that "it is permissible to kill an unborn fetus."[12] Some rabbinic authorities accept these words of *Tosafot* verbatim,[13] whereas others are of the opinion that *Tosafot* is not to be interpreted literally.[14] Yet others believe that *Tosafot* is in error.[15]

Prior to forty days after conception, the Talmud considers a fertilized egg nothing more than "mere fluid,"[16] and one "need not take into consideration the possibility of a valid childbirth."[17] However, after forty days have elapsed, fashioning, or formation of the fetus is deemed to have occurred. Laws of ritual uncleanliness must be observed for abortuses older than forty days.[18] This period of uncleanliness is similar to that prescribed following the birth of a child and is not the same as that for a menstruant woman. Furthermore, a woman who aborts after the fortieth day following conception is required to bring an offering just as if she had given birth to a live child.[19] These laws of ritual impurity and offerings apply even where the abortus "resembles cattle, a wild beast, or a bird" or a "shapeless piece of flesh." These rules imply that the unborn fetus, although not considered a living person (*nefesh*), still has some status. Nowhere in the Talmud, however, does it state that killing this fetus by premature artificial termination of pregnancy is considered murder.

Based upon these talmudic sources as well as the scriptural passages cited earlier, one may again ask why most rabbinic authorities prohibit abortion, except in certain situations, as a serious moral offense even though it is not considered legal murder. Distinguished Jewish physicians of ancient and more recent times also admonished against abortion. Denunciations of the practice of abortion are recorded in the medical oaths and prayers of Asaph Judaeus in the seventh century, Amatus Lusitanus in the sixteenth century, and Jacob Zahalon in the seventeenth century.[20] What are the objections to abortion in the opinion of these Jewish physicians in view of the fact that an unborn fetus does not have the status of a person (*nefesh*) in Jewish law? If abortion is not considered murder, on what legal basis is it prohibited?

Let us first establish the time that a fetus legally acquires the status equal to an adult human being. We have previously cited the main talmudic source upon which the Jewish legal attitude toward abortion is based.[21] The Talmud states in part that if the "greater part was already born, one may not touch it, for one may not set aside one person's life for that of another." Thus the act of birth changes the status of the fetus from a nonperson to a person (*nefesh*). Killing the newborn after this point is infanticide. Many talmudic sources and commentators on the Talmud substitute the word "head" for "greater part."[22] Others maintain the "greater part" verbatim.[23] Maimonides and Karo also consider the extrusion of the head to indicate birth.[24] They both further state that by rabbinic decree, even if only one limb of the fetus was extruded and then retracted, childbirth is considered to have occurred.[25]

Not only is the precise time of the birth of paramount importance in adjudicating whether aborting the fetus is permissible to save the mother's life, but the viability of the fetus must also be taken into account. The newborn child is not considered fully viable until it has survived thirty days following birth, as it is stated in the Talmud: "Rabban Simeon ben Gemliel said: Any human being who lives thirty days is not a *nephel* [abortus] because it is stated: *And those that are to be redeemed of them from a month old shalt thou redeem* [Num. 18:16], since prior to thirty days it is not certain that he will survive."[26] Further support for the necessity of a thirty-day postpartum viability period of adjudicating various Jewish legal matters pertaining to the newborn comes from Maimonides, who asserts: "Whether one kills an adult or a day-old child, a male or a female, he must be put to death if he kills deliberately . . . provided that the child is born after a full-term pregnancy. But, if it is born before the end of nine months, it is regarded as an abortion until it has lived for thirty days, and if one kills it during these thirty days, one is not put to death on its account."[27]

Thus, although the newborn infant reaches the status of a person or *nefesh*, which it didn't have prior to birth, it still does not enjoy all the legal rights of an adult until it has survived for thirty days post partum. The death penalty is not imposed if one kills such a child before it has established its viability, but killing it is certainly prohibited because "one may not set aside one person's life for that of another."[28]

The permissibility to kill the unborn fetus to save the mother's life rests upon the fact that such an embryo is not considered a person (*nefesh*) until it is born. Maimonides and Karo present a second reason for allowing abortion or embryotomy prior to birth where the mother's life is endangered, and that is the argument of "pursuit," whereby the fetus is "pursuing" the mother.[29] The argument of pursuit is based upon two passages in the Pentateuch.

> Deuteronomy 25:22–12. *When men strive together one with another, and the wife of one draws near to save her husband from the hands of the one that smiteth him, and she puts her hand and taketh hold of his genitals, then you shall cut off her hand, your eye shalt have no pity.*
> Leviticus 19:16. *Thou shalt not stand idly by the blood of thy neighbor.*

In the former case, the woman is pursuing the man by maiming him, and she should be stopped. The latter case is interpreted by *Rashi* and most other commentators to mean that one should not stand idly by without attempting to rescue one's fellowman whose life is threatened by robbers, drowning, or wild beasts. Based upon these biblical passages, the Mishnah states: "These may be delivered at the cost of their lives: he that pursues after his fellowman to kill him . . ."[30] The Talmud follows with a lengthy discussion asserting that it is one's duty to disable or even take the life of the assailant to protect the life of one's fellowman.[31]

This discussion prompted Maimonides to state: "Consequently, the sages have ruled that if a pregnant woman is having difficulty in giving birth, the child inside her may be excised, either by drugs or manually [i.e., surgery], because it is regarded as pursuing her in order to kill her. But if its head has

been born, it must not be touched, for one may not set aside one human life for that of another, and this happening is the course of nature [i.e., an act of God, that is, the mother is pursued by heaven, not the fetus]."[32] An identical statement is found in Karo's Code.[33]

Many rabbinic authorities pose the following question to Maimonides.[34] How can the argument of pursuit be invoked here, since if it were applicable, killing the fetus even after the head or greater part is born should be permissible? Rabbi Israel Lipshuetz, known as *Tiferet Israel*,[35] and others state that the argument of pursuit is totally inappropriate because the child's endangering of the mother's life is an act of God. The child does not intend to kill the mother. It is a case of heavenly pursuit. This concept of heavenly pursuit is discussed in the Talmud and mentioned by both Maimonides and Karo. Jakobovits amplifies the problem by stating that contradictory ruling seems to be emerging.[36] On the one hand, we invoke the argument of pursuit to allow therapeutic abortion, and on the other hand, the validity of this argument is dismissed because nature and not the child pursues the mother.

The problem is resolved by many rabbis who state that the nonperson status of the fetus prior to birth is not sufficient to warrant the embryo's destruction, since this would still constitute a serious moral offense, even if it is not a penal crime.[37] Thus one must invoke the additional argument of pursuit. After the baby's head has emerged, however, the fetus attains the status of a *nefesh*, even prior to proved thirty-day postpartum viability, and the "weak" argument of pursuit no longer justifies killing the child even if the mother's life is threatened, since it is a case of Heavenly pursuit. However, even after egress of the head, if both lives are threatened one may kill the fetus to save the mother.[38] The reason is that the mother's life is threatened, since it is a case of heavenly pursuit. Viability of the fetus is in doubt until thirty days have elapsed following birth. This viewpoint is also espoused by Rabbis Moses Schick and David Hoffman.[39] Others dispute this ruling.[40]

We now return to the original question. If the unborn child is not considered a *nefesh*, why should its destruction not be allowed under all circumstances? Why is only a threat to the mother's life or health an acceptable reason for therapeutic abortion?

One answer is given by Rabbi Ya'ir Bacharach, who, contrary to the Mishnah in Tractate Arachin 1:4, states that one waits for a condemned pregnant woman to give birth because a potential human being can arise from each drop of human seed (sperm). Interference with pregnancy would constitute expulsion of semen for naught, an act akin to *coitus interruptus* and strictly prohibited in Jewish law. This reason for prohibiting therapeutic abortion upon demand is also subscribed to by others.[41]

A second reason for not allowing abortion without specific indication is that the unborn fetus, although not a person, does have sufficient status, if it is aborted after forty days of conception, to require its mother to undergo the same ritual purification process as if she had given birth to a live child. The same process is also prescribed for a woman who has a spontaneous miscarriage. Thus, the fetus can be considered to be a "partial person."[42]

A third reason for prohibiting abortion on demand is that one is not permitted to wound oneself,[43] and a woman undergoing vaginal abortion by manipulative means is considered as intentionally wounding herself. At least two rabbinic authorities adhere to this viewpoint.[44]

A fourth reason for prohibiting abortion without maternal danger is that the operative intervention entails danger.[45] One is prohibited in Jewish law from intentionally placing oneself in danger, based upon Deuteronomy 4:15: *Take ye therefore good heed unto yourselves.*

Another reason for prohibiting therapeutic abortion in cases where no threat to the mother exists is offered by Rabbi Issur Yehuda Unterman, who states that one may desecrate the Sabbath to save the life or preserve the health of an unborn fetus in order that the child may observe many Sabbaths later.[46] As a result, destroying the fetus, although not legally murder, is nevertheless forbidden as an appurtenance to murder. Rabbi Bacharach, who permits abortion prior to forty days of pregnancy because the fetus has no status at all but is considered mere fluid, is taken to task by Rabbi Unterman, who states that even prior to forty days there is an appurtenance to murder.

Another argument of Rabbi Unterman is that a fetus, even less than forty days after conception, is considered a potential (lit. questionable) human being which, by nature alone, without interference, will become an actual human being. Thus a potential person (*sofek nefesh*) has enough status to prohibit its own destruction.

A final argument of Rabbi Unterman comes from the interpretation of Rabbi Ishmael of the scriptural verse: *Whoso sheddeth man's blood, by man shall his blood be shed, for in the image of God did He make man,*[47] which can be translated "whoso sheddeth the blood of man in man, his blood shall be shed." The "man in man" is interpreted to mean a fetus.[48] This Noachidic prohibition of killing a fetus applies also to Israelites, even though the Jewish legal consequences might differ.

The final reason and perhaps most important for prohibiting abortion on demand in Jewish law is suggested by Rabbi Immanuel Jakobovits and Rabbi Moshe Yonah Zweig among others.[49] They point to the Mishnah in Oholoth 7:6 which permits abortion prior to birth of the child only when the mother's life is endangered. The implication is that when the mother's life is not at stake, it would be prohibited to kill the unborn fetus.

Handicapped Babies and Defective Newborns

Treatment or nontreatment of a newborn with major medical or mental defects is the subject of considerable controversy. Numerous "Baby Doe" cases have been widely publicized in recent years, and the medical and lay literatures are replete with articles on the subject.

The Talmud quotes the following unusual birth: "In the case of a birth given to a creature which possesses a double back or a double spine, Rab said: If it was a woman [who miscarried], it is not regarded as an offspring,[50] that is, the laws concerning a birth are not observed. However, once this creature has been born, it has the status of a person, and killing it is considered infanticide, which is prohibited in Jewish law."

Rabbi Judah the Pious, author of the thirteenth-century work *Sefer Chasidim*, describes the case of a child born with grotesque teeth and a tail.[51] It was feared that people might consider the infant to be a fish and eat it. Rabbi Judah was asked whether it was permissible to kill it. His reply was that one should remove the teeth and the tail in spite of the risks and raise the child as an otherwise normal human being. This ruling clearly prohibits the killing of handicapped babies.

Another ruling related to a malformed child is that of nineteenth-century Rabbi Eleazar Fleckeles, who states that once a child is born it is a human being in all respects and may not be destroyed.[52] Starving it to death, as was suggested by the questioner, is considered infanticide and prohibited.

The problem of babies born without one or more limbs, technically known as phocomelia, to women who ingested the drug thalidomide early in pregnancy is discussed by Belgian Rabbi Zweig,[53] who condemns the killing of the thalidomide-deformed baby which resulted in the famous Liège trial involving parents, relatives and physician charged with murder.[54] Rabbi Zweig's lengthy dissertation, however, deals primarily with abortion (i.e., antenatal) and not infanticide (i.e., postnatal).

Although the subject of genetic screening and Tay-Sachs disease is discussed elsewhere in this book (see chap. 13), it seems pertinent to point out that Rabbi Eliezer Waldenberg allows abortion up to the seventh month of pregnancy if amniocentesis reveals that the mother is carrying a Tay-Sachs fetus.[55] His reason is the "great need" of the enormous mental anguish of the mother in knowing the fatal outcome that awaits her diseased child. On the other hand, Rabbi Moshe Feinstein states that every case must be individualized and that "routine" abortion for Tay-Sachs disease is not permissible.[56] In fact, the amniocentesis itself, if performed for no valid medical indication, may be prohibited because of the small but significant risk that this procedure entails. Rabbi Yitzchak Silberstein suggests that a couple both of whom are carriers of a genetic chromosomal defect and/or where one can anticipate the birth of a defective child, should be advised not to marry.[57] If they marry, they should be divorced unless divorce is very difficult and undesirable for them, in which case they should still have children and hope for the best. If they already have two children, they are not obligated to have more, concludes Silberstein.

Rabbi Jakobovits summarizes succinctly the Jewish view of the treatment of handicapped newborns as follows: A physically or mentally abnormal child has the same claim to life as a normal child because it is considered a person (*nefesh*). Furthermore, while only the killing of a born and viable child constitutes murder in Jewish law, the destruction of the fetus, too, is a moral offense and cannot be justified except out of consideration for the mother's life or health. Consequently, the fear that a child may or will be deformed is not in itself a legitimate indication for its abortion, particularly since there is usually a chance that the child might turn out to be quite normal. Killing a handicapped adult is similarly prohibited.[58]

Once a malformed child has been born, one cannot use the argument of euthanasia or mercy killing to sanction its destruction. This act is positively prohibited in Jewish law as nothing less than murder (infanticide) . . . .

Summary of Rabbinic Opinion on Abortion

Prior to forty days after conception, the fertilized egg is considered by some rabbinic authorities as mere fluid. Such an early zygote has no status at all, is not a person or *nefesh*, is regarded as part of the mother's flesh, and aborting it is not considered legal murder. According to this minority view, the slightest reason might be sufficient to allow abortion at this early stage.[59] Such a reason might be the fear that a deformed child may be born, due to exposure of the mother early in pregnancy to German measles or a teratogenic drug such a thalidomide or possibly even for socioeconomic reasons or family planning. A small minority of rabbis also allow abortion for reasons such as incest and rape.[60] Justification for this position rests on the grounds of concern for the mother, i.e., that such a birth would adversely affect her mental or physical health by causing her anguish, shame, or embarrassment.

Such permissive rulings are vigorously denounced by most rabbinic authorities who prohibit therapeutic abortion in cases such as exposure of the mother early in pregnancy to German measles[61] or to thalidomide.[62] Most rabbis permit and even mandate abortion where the health or life of the mother is threatened. Some authorities are stringent and require the mother's life to be in danger,[63] however remote that danger, whereas others permit abortion for a serious threat to the mother's health.[64] Such dangers to maternal health may include deafness,[65] cancer,[66] pain,[67] or psychiatric illness.[68] Psychiatric indication for abortion must be certified by competent medical opinion or by previous experiences of mental illness in the mother, such as a postpartum nervous breakdown.

If the mother becomes pregnant while nursing a child and the pregnancy changes her milk, so that the suckling's life is endangered, abortion is permitted.[69] Once the baby is in the process of being born, it becomes a person for Jewish legal purposes and may not be harmed. The only exception is if *both* the baby's and the mother's lives are threatened.

Then one may sacrifice the birthing child to save the mother because her life is a certainty without the fetal threat,[70] whereas the infant has not proved its viability until thirty days postpartum have elapsed. After thirty days of life, every human being, whether physically deformed, mentally deficient, or otherwise handicapped, is considered to be equal to every other human being and may not be harmed in any way.

For further discussion of the Jewish attitude toward abortion, the interested reader is referred to several recent reviews both in English and in Hebrew,[71] including one exhaustive review profusely annotated with 188 bibliographical citations.[72]

Since many important legal and moral considerations which cannot be spelled out in the presentation of general principles may weigh upon the verdict in any given case, it seems advisable to submit every individual case to rabbinic judgment in the light of the prevailing medical and other circumstances.

Jewish Moral Considerations on Abortion

The previous discussion has presented the Jewish legal principles relating to abortion. The destruction of the unborn fetus, although legally not considered murder, can be considered to constitute "moral murder." The unborn baby has a heartbeat, a brain, arms, legs, and nearly everything with which a healthy newborn baby is endowed. Thus, killing the unborn fetus, according to Rabbi Unterman, is an "appurtenance of murder" and strictly prohibited, although, because of a legal technicality, such an act is not considered murder for which the death penalty is imposed.

The major biblical citation dealing with abortion, Exodus 21:22–23, concerns accidental abortion, not intentional or induced abortion, a deed initiated at the outset (lechatchilah). Therefore, one can argue that premeditated interruption of pregnancy is not allowed except to save the life or preserve the health (mental or physical) of the mother. Though some maintain that in Jewish law the death penalty may not be imposed upon the mother or the person performing the abortion, the rabbinic concept of a non-penalized but prohibited act (patur aval assur) may prevail.

The concept of time seems all-important. If one destroys a baby five minutes after birth, it is considered murder in American and Jewish law; yet if one destroys the fetus five minutes before it is born, such

an act is not murder. Why not? What is the difference? Certainly it is moral murder, although not legal murder. The same principle applies if one destroys a baby five hours, five days, or five months before and after birth. To some people, abortion is acceptable if done prior to the time the fetus might be expected to live. How then is life defined? Must there be a heartbeat? Limbs? Is not the fertilized zygote already alive? Does life mean that which is able to duplicate itself in the biological sense? Does life refer to the stage of fetal development when physical movement is first detected? Or is life the "breath of life" instilled in a newborn infant immediately after the birth process?

The next moral issue is the question of potentiality. The unborn fetus, if left alone, may turn out to be a genius. Or he may just be a person of normal intelligence. Or, if physically deformed, he may still make a positive contribution to society. In the secular world, should we not cite the contributions made by such handicapped or deformed human beings as Helen Keller, Ludwig van Beethoven, and Henri de Toulouse-Lautrec? Or in our religious experience, should we not marvel at the learned and soul-rending contributions made by the blind talmudic scholars Rav Sheshes and Rav Yosef, the unsightly Rabbi Yehoshua ben Chananyah, and the limbless Rabbi Amnon of Mayence, author of the renowned Unethaneh Tokef prayer recited on the High Holy Days? The potential of an unborn infant is unknown. However, as Rabbi Unterman points out, the potential human being, i.e., the unborn fetus, if left alone, will develop into an actual human being. Hence, this potential person (sofek nefesh) has enough status to prohibit its destruction. Jewish law also allows, and in fact requires, that one desecrate the Sabbath to save the life or health of the unborn fetus in order that the fetus may observe many Sabbaths later, after it is born.

The Talmud compares the unborn fetus to an extra appendage of the mother (ubar yerech imo hu), destruction or damage to which requires that financial renumeration be paid to the mother for pain, shame, anguish, medical bills, inability to work, and the like. However, how can one compare the unborn fetus to a finger of the mother? If one destroys a finger, the woman has lost a finger, which would never have become anything other than a finger. The unborn fetus, if left alone, would have developed into a full and complete human being.

Philosophical-moral arguments against abortion are also very potent. If a woman becomes pregnant, almost certainly Almighty God so willed it. How dare we interfere? Even if the child might be born physically deformed, this too is the will of God. One is reminded of the encounter between King Hezekiah and the Prophet Isaiah as described in the Talmud.

> The Holy One, Blessed be He, brought sufferings upon Hezekiah and then said to Isaiah: Go visit the sick, for it is written: *In those days Hezekiah was sick unto death, and Isaiah the prophet, son of Amoz, came to him and said unto him, Thus saith the Lord, set your house in order, for you shall die and not live, etc.* [Isaiah 38:1]. What is the meaning of *you shall die and not live?* You shall die in this world and not live in the world-to-come. [Hezekiah] said to [Isaiah]: Why so bad? [Isaiah] replied: Because you did not try to have children. [Hezekiah] said: The reason was because I saw by the holy spirit that the children issuing from me would not be virtuous. [Isaiah] said to [Hezekiah]: What have you to do with the secrets of the All-Merciful? You should have done what you were commanded and let the Holy One, blessed be He, do that which pleases Him. [Although this defiance of God's will by Hezekiah was punished, the outcome of the story is a happy one: Hezekiah was healed and lived another fifteen years.][73]

King Hezekiah apparently knew that his children would be morally corrupt, so he put aside the "first" commandment of the Torah, *be fruitful and multiply,*[74] and did not take a wife. Isaiah charges him with lack of faith. In a similar vein, is not one's faith in the Almighty being challenged by the mother who requests abortion because she can see no way of solving her social or economic difficulty?

A further philosophical argument against abortion contends that throughout the ages, millions of Jews have perished at the hands of their enemies. Are we today to kill even more by performing indiscriminate abortion? Certainly not!

Let us turn to the possible consequences of legalized abortion. Will legal infanticide follow? Legal genocide? Legal extermination of social misfits, as Hitler proposed? Legal euthanasia? Where does the trend end? What about the psychological consequences to the mother? After the abortion, she cannot change her mind. The deed is done. Who decides whether an abortion is to be performed? Why only the mother? How about the father? Has he nothing to say? Why not? Why should not the boyfriend be consulted if an unwed pregnant girl seeks an abortion? How about the siblings of the unborn fetus? Should they have a say in this matter? Furthermore, who speaks for the fetus? We have a Society for the Prevention of Cruelty to Animals, a Society for the Prevention of Cruelty to Children, yet there is no Society for the Prevention of Cruelty to Fetuses. Theoretically, if we could communicate with the fetus and ask it whether it would choose life if it knew that it would be born without arms or legs, the answer would doubtless be a resounding yes. If the fetus were told he would be the twelfth child in a very poor family living in a very small apartment, it would still probably choose life. So who speaks for the fetus in the decision-making process concerning an abortion? Why is the mother the major, if not the only, determining factor? Why should we, society, not speak for the fetus? In divorce proceedings, the courts decide the disposition of the involved children, if any. Why should not the courts have a say about the continued life of the fetus?

Women, as human beings, were created in the image of God, and thus a woman is not the sole owner of her body and soul, to treat it as she pleases. A woman does not have the right to take her own life, i.e., to commit suicide. She is entrusted with her body and may use but not abuse it. She is commanded to care for her body and soul and do all that is necessary to protect and preserve both.

For an unwed girl who is pregnant, the dilemma is severe indeed. Which is better, to have the baby and give it away, or to destroy it before it is born? How would she feel in giving up her child for adoption to a foster mother? How would she feel in aborting the pregnancy? The argument that this unfortunate girl should not have become pregnant is no consolation to her in her present predicament. Should this mother-to-be be permitted to extinguish the life of what will probably be a healthy human being in order to avert her personal shame or a socially unpleasant situation?

What are the moral issues involved in the various social reasons proposed for liberalizing abortion? Practically everyone loyal to Jewish law would subscribe to the proposition that to sacrifice a potential life to save an actual living person is permissible, if there is danger to the latter. But even if abortion in thalidomide and German measles cases were allowed, should abortion for social reasons, or abortion on demand, be permitted? In such a situation (i.e., poverty, inadequate housing, accidental pregnancy, etc.), one is sacrificing a potential life solely for the convenience or happiness of an adult, either mother or father, or both.

If one is told to kill somebody or be killed oneself, one is not allowed to kill, because one may not set aside one person's life for that of another. True, the unborn fetus is only a potential life, but why should the mother be able to spill her unborn baby's blood? Why is her convenience more valuable than a potential life?

If a woman seeks an abortion for social reasons, might not the social conditions change? Perhaps the family's financial situation will improve. Perhaps larger living quarters will be provided to the family. Is not the abortion for social reasons a denial of one's faith in God and His ability to provide sustenance?

There are other reasons, moral and otherwise, which speak against legalized abortion. When a married woman or an unwed girl has an abortion, what guarantee does she have that she can ever become pregnant again? Is she so certain that the Divine mystery of conception will be hers again? Should she not pause and ask herself, "Will I ever regret denying myself this ultimate of feminine fulfillment, if I should never conceive again?"

Might it not happen that an abortion is contraindicated for medical or psychiatric reasons? If a physician can reject a woman for abortion because of such a contraindication, why should the abortion request not be rejected by the physician or society because of a moral contraindication? If induced abortion becomes commonplace, will there not be an undermining or subversion of the ethics of medical practice? Will there be a shift from the "healer" physician to the "exterminator" physician?

Another moral issue is the sale or use of aborted fetuses for medical research. Who should have the say regarding the disposal of the fetus? The woman? The father? The gynecologist? The pathologist? Society? Who? Jewish morality and law require burial not only for a dead body but for removed human organs (e.g., as a result of an operation or an accidental amputation) as well. Our sages refer to the human body and its parts as "vessels which contain the human soul." How coarse, therefore, are those who would deal with, and profit from, the sale of the fetus, this potential "soul container."

Concluding Note

The Jewish legal and moral aspects of abortion have been presented in great detail in this essay. More questions are posed than answers given. I would like to leave the reader with the ancient pronouncement:

"He who saves one life of the people of Israel is as if he had saved an entire world."[75] A single life, in Jewish teaching, is equivalent to a whole world. Furthermore, the fact that abortion on demand is legal in the United States and elsewhere does not mean that it is right. Legal permissibility is not synonymous with moral license.

Notes

1. Maimonides, *Mishneh Torah, Hilchot Chovel Umazik* 4:1.
2. Karo, *Shulchan Aruch, Choshen Mishpat* 423:1.
3. Sanhedrin 84b.
4. Oholot 7:6.
5. I. Lipschuetz, Commentary *Tiferet Yisroel* on *Oholot* 7:6.
6. Sanhedrin 72b.
7. Terumot 8:12.
8. Arachin 1:4.
9. Arachin 7a.
10. Talmud: Chullin 58a, Gittin 23b, Nazir 51a, Baba Kamma 88b, Temurah 31a, and elsewhere. Rabbinic writings: J. Trani, Responsa *Maharit*, pt. 1, nos. 97 and 99; Y. Bacharach, Responsa *Chavat Ya'ir*, no. 31; E. Landau, Responsa *Noda Biyehuda, Choshen Mishpat*, no. 59; Nachmanides, Novellae on Niddah 44b; J. Teomim, Commentary *Peri Megadim* on *Schulchan Aruch, Orach Chayim* 328:7:1; M. HaMeiri, Commentary *Beth Habechirah* on Sanhedrin 72b; Shneur Zalman of Lublin, Responsa *Torat Chesed, Even Haezer*, no. 42:32; Y. Emden, Responsa *She'elat Yavetz*, pt. 1, no. 43; S. Drimmer, Responsa *Bet Shlomo, Choshen Mishpat*, no. 132; E. Y. Waldenberg, Responsa *Tzitz Eliezer*, vol. 9, no. 5:3; and numerous others.
11. Arachin 7a.
12. Niddah 44b.
13. Waldenberg, Responsa *Tzitz Eliezer*, vol. 9, no. 51:3; and Bacharach, Responsa *Chavat Ya'ir*, no. 31.
14. I. Y. Unterman, in *Noam* 6 (1963): 1–11; and Emden, Responsa *She'elat Yavetz*, pt. 1, no. 43.
15. I. Schmelkes, Responsa *Bet Yitzchak, Yoreh Deah*, pt. 2, no. 162.
16. Yevamot 69b, Niddah 30b, and Keritot 1:3.
17. Niddah 3:7.
18. Niddah 3:2–6.
19. Keritot 1:3–6.
20. F. Rosner and S. Muntner, "The Oath of Asaph." *Annals of Internal Medicine* 63 (1965): 317–320; H. Friedenwald, "The Oath of Amatus," in *The Jews and Medicine* (Baltimore: Johns Hopkins Press, 1944), pp. 368–370; H. Savitz, "Jacob Zahalon and His book *The*

Treasure of Life," New England Journal of Medicine 213 (1935): 167–176; I. Simon, "La Prière des Medécins *Tephilat Harofim* de Jacob Zahalon, Médecin et Rabbin en italie (1630–1693)," *Revue d'Histoire de la Medécine Hebraique* 8 (1955): 38–51; H. Friedenwald, "The Physician's Prayer of Jacob Zahalon of Rome," in *The Jews and Medicine* (Baltimore: Johns Hopkins Press, 1944), pp. 273–279.

21. Oholot 7:6.
22. Talmud: Sanhedrin 72b, Niddah 3:5 and 29a, and *Tosefta* (additional Talmud) Yevamot 9:9. Commentaries of Ovadiah of Bertinoro, known as *Bertinoro*, Asher ben Yechiel, known as *Rosh*, and Isaiah Berlin, known as *Rishon Letzion*, on Oholot 7:6; commentaries of *Rashi* on Sanhedrin 72b and *Tosafot* on Sanhedrin 59a.
23. Jerusalem (Palestinian) Talumd, Shabbat 14:4 and Avodah Zarah 2:2.
24. Maimonides, *Mishneh Torah, Hilchot Issurey Biyah* 10:3; Karo, *Shulchan Aruch, Choshen Mishpat* 425:2.
25. Maimonides, loc. cit., and Karo, *Shulchan Aruch, Yoreh Deah* 194:10.
26. Shabbat 135b.
27. Maimonides, *Mishneh Torah, Hilchot Rotze'ach* 2:6.
28. Oholot 7:3.
29. Maimonides, *Mishneh Torah, Hilchot Rotze'ach* 1:9; Karo, *Shulchan Aruch, Choshen Mishpat* 425:2.
30. Sanhedrin 8:7.
31. Sanhedrin 72b–73a.
32. Maimonides, *Hilchot Rotze'ach* 1:9.
33. Karo, *Choshen Mishpat* 425:1.
34. M. Y. A. Zweig, in *Noam* 7 (1964): 36–56; A. Eger, *Tosafot R. Akiva Eger* on Oholot 7:6; E. Landau, Responsa *Noda Biyehudah, Choshen Mishpat*, pt. 2, no. 59; Waldenberg, Responsa *Tzitz Eliezer*, vol. 9, no. 51:3; Bacharach, Responsa *Chavat Ya'ir*, no. 31.
35. I. Lipschuetz, Commentary *Tiferet Yisrael* on Oholot 7:6.
36. I. Jakobovits, *Jewish Medical Ethics* (New York: Bloch, 1975), pp. 170–191.
37. Waldenberg, loc. cit.; Bacharach, loc. cit.; Unterman, loc. cit.; Emden, loc. cit.; Zweig, loc. cit.; Eger, loc. cit.; Landau, loc. cit.; Lipschuetz, loc. cit.
38. Eger, loc. cit.; Lipschuetz, loc. cit.; and others.
39. Schick, Responsa *Maharam Schick, Yoreh Deah*, no. 155; Hoffman, Responsa *Melamed Leho'il, Yoreh Deah*, no. 69.
40. Ch. Sofer, Responsa *Machanei Chayim, Choshen Mishpat*, no. 50; M. A. Eisenstadt, Responsa *Panim Me'irot*, pt. 3, no. 8.
41. B. T. Frankel, Responsa *Ateret Chachamim, Even Haezer*, no. 1; Emden, Responsa *She'elatz Yavetz*, pt. 1, no. 43.
42. J. Rosen, Responsa *Tzofnat Pane'ach*, pt. 1, no. 49.
43. Baba Kamma 91b; Maimonides, *Mishneh Torah, Hilchot Chovel Umazik* 5:1.

44. J. Trani, Responsa *Maharit*, pt. 1, no. 99; Zweig, in *Noam* 7 (1964): 36–56.
45. S. Drimmer, Responsa *Bet Shlomo, Choshen Mishpat*, no. 132.
46. Nachmanides, Commentary *Ramban* on Niddah 44b. See also M. Hershler, in *Halachah Urefuah* 2 (1981): 57–64.
47. Genesis 9:6.
48. Sanhedrin 57b.
49. I. Jakobovits, "Jewish Views on Abortion," in *Abortion and the Law*, ed. D. T. Smith (Cleveland: Western Reserve University Press, 1967), pp. 124–143; Zweig, in *Noam* 7 (1964); 36–56.
50. Bechorot 43b.
51. Judah ben Samuel the Pious , *Sefer Chasidim* no. 186.
52. Fleckeles, Responsa *Teshuva Me'Ahavah*, pt. 1, no. 53.
53. Zweig, loc. cit.
54. L. Colebrook, "The Liège Trial and the Problem of Voluntary Euthanasia," *Lancet* 2 (1962): 1225.
55. Waldenberg, Responsa *Tzitz Eliezer*, vol. 13, no. 102; also in *Assia* 2 (1981): 93–98.
56. M. Feinstein, in *Halachah Urefuah* 1 (1980): 304–306.
57. Y. Silberstein, in *Halachah Urefuah* 2 (1981): 106–113.
58. I. Jakobovits, in *The Jewish Review* (London), Nov. 14, 1962.
59. Schneur Zalman of Lublin, Responsa *Torat Chesed, Even Haezer*. no. 42:32.
60. Emden, Responsa *She'elatz Yavetz*, pt. 1, no. 43.
61. I. Y. Unterman, in *Noam* 6 (1963): 1–11.
62. I. Jakobovits, *Journal of a Rabbi* (New York: Living Books, 1966), pp. 262–266.
63. A. Lifschutz, Responsa *Aryeh Debei Ilay, Yoreh Deah*, no. 19; E. Deutsch, Responsa *Pri Hasadeh*, pt. 4, no. 50; S. Drimmer, Responsa *Bet Shlomo, Choshen Mishpat*, no. 132; D. Meislich, Responsa *Binyan David*, no. 47; M. Winkler, Responsa *Levushei Mordechai, Choshen Mishpat*, no. 39; I. Schorr, Responsa *Ko'ach Schor*, no. 21; A. J. Horowitz, Responsa *Tzur Yakov*, no. 141; Y. Teitelbaum, Responsa *Avnei Tzedek, Choshen Mishpat*, no. 19.
64. Yosef Chayim ben Eliyahu, Responsa *Rav Pa'alim, Even Haezer*, no. 4.
65. B. Z. Uziel, Responsa *Mishpetei Uziel, Choshen Mishpat*, pt. 3 no. 46.
66. G. Fiedler, Responsa *She'elatz Yeshurun*, pt. 1, no. 39.
67. I. M. Mizrachi, Responsa *Pri Ha'aretz, Yoreh Deah*, no. 21.
68. N. Z. Friedman, Responsa *Netzer Mata'ai*, pt. 1, no. 8.
69. Ch. Pallagi, Responsa *Chayim Veshalom*, pt. 1, no. 40; Y. Ayyas, Responsa *Bet Yehudah, Even Haezer*, no. 14; I. Oelbaum, Responsa *She'elat Yitzchak*, no. 69; Waldenberg, *Responsa Tzitz Eliezer*, vol. 9, no. 51:3.

70. Lipschuetz, Commentary *Tiferet Yisroel* on Oholot 7:6; A. Eger, Commentary *Tosefot Rabbi Akiba Eger* on Oholot 7:6.

71. D. M. Feldman, *Marital Relations, Birth Control and Abortion in Jewish Law* (New York: Schocken, 1975), pp. 251–294; J. D. Bleich, "Abortion in Halakhic Literature," in *Comtemporary Halakhic Problems* (New York: Ktav and Yeshiva University Press, 1977), pp. 325–371; I. Jakobovits, "Jewish Views on Abortion," in *Jewish Bioethics*, ed. F. Rosner and J. D. Bleich (New York: Hebrew Publishing Co., 1979), pp. 118–133; M. Stern, "Abortion," in *Harefuah Le'or HaHalachah* (Jerusalem, 1980), vol. 1, pt. 1, pp. 1–147; O. Yosef, "Interruption of Pregnancy According to Halachah," *Assia* 1 (1976): 78–94; S. Y. Cohen, "Abortion According to Halachah," *Halachah Urefuah* 3 (1983); 86–90; A. Steinberg, "Abortion According to Halachah," *Assia* 1 (1976): 107–124.

72. Stern, "Abortion."

73. Berachot 10a.

74. Genesis 1:28, 9:1 and 7, 35:11.

75. Sanhedrin 4:5.

Writing and Discussion Topics

Questions 1–6 address content, critical analysis, personal choices, ethical options, specific discipline, and interdisciplinary alternatives, respectively.

1. According to major Jewish writings, describe the four steps in the process of life.

2. Explain the difference between an abortion and a miscarriage according to Jewish texts.

3. Jewish laws seem to be more concerned about patriarchal interests and the male members of society than females and their interests. Does this perspective bother you? Why or why not?

4. Is the Jewish law on abortion based on rights or duty? What is the basis for your answer? Cite foundational authors from chapter one to support your answer.

5. Examine the major texts used for this writing. What is the background of each text? Is it confusing or helpful to have so many sources of "truth"?

6. Compare the perspectives on abortion expressed by Kathryn Pyne Addelson and those found in Jewish law. What religious advice is offered to single, Jewish women with unwanted pregnancies?

Basim F. Mussallam

WHY ISLAM PERMITTED CONTRACEPTION

◆◆◆

B asim F. Mussallam is a professor of history at the University of
Cambridge in Great Britain. He has published extensively in the
areas of Muslim society, law, and ethics. In this reading from his book,
Sex and Society in Islam, *he pulls together a wide range of viewpoints
on abortion from Muslim jurists.* ◆

1. Marriage was treated as polygamous.
2. Legitimate sexual intercourse was not confined to marriage, but extended also to the institution of concubinage.
3. Marriage was not viewed as a permanent relationship; easy divorce could end it at any time.
4. Marital intercourse needed no justification by procreative purpose, and was also based on the right to sexual fulfilment.
5. Contraception was permitted and abortion tolerated.

While Christianity confined legitimate sex to permanent monogamous marriage, Islam did not confine sex to marriage, and Islamic marriage was polygamous and subject to termination by easy divorce. The theoretical impermanence of marriage in Islam and the risk inherent in concubinage of fathering children who, following their mothers, could be slaves, were *prima facie* indications for the utility of birth control. One of the reasons for birth control cited by Muslim jurists was that a man might wish to divorce his wife in the foreseeable future,[1] and an argument most frequently used was the fear of begetting slave children.[2]

The Islamic attitude toward contraception consisted only of the opinions of Muslim jurists, both individually and in terms of the schools of legal interpretation to which they belonged (pp. 29ff.). Since the Quaran said nothing about contraception, and there was nothing like the Christian concept of the "Church" in Islam, there existed no "Islamic" attitude independent of or above that of the jurists.[3] The opinions of these private but specialized individual Muslims defined the attitude of Islam.

Who were the Muslim jurists? The jurists were 'ulama, learned specialists in the religion and traditions of Islam, a category of persons which was common to all historical Muslim societies. They were always one element of the population which specialized in studying Islam and strove to live the Islamic life. The 'ulama were the custodians of the community's traditions, keeping and passing on what in their judgment was worthy of historical record, and in this way deciding what was important to Islamic life. They were the authors of most of the written records of Muslim societies . . . .

One of the basic analytical principles of the classical theory of Islamic law was the *sunna*, that is, the example of the Prophet as incorporated in the recognized *hadith* (the reports of his words and actions). The classical theory of law was adopted by the majority of the Sunni Muslims by the tenth century, and will be stated below where it serves an important purpose in analyzing the Islamic doctrine on contraception . . . .

. . . the *hadith* embodied the earliest legal reasoning of Muslims on contraception. Secondly, the *hadith* were essential instruments of argument in later Islamic thought on contraception. Even in cases where it is clear that the jurist was exercising independent judgment, the relevant *hadith* were usually marshalled as additional evidence for his point of view. There is a large number of *hadith* on contraception (specifically on '*azl*: coitus interruptus);[4] the following are the ones which recurred most often in jurisprudence.

1. According to Jabir, "We used to practise coitus interruptus in the Prophet's lifetime while the Quran was being revealed." (There is another version of the same *hadith*, "We used to practise coitus interruptus during the Prophet's lifetime. News of this reached him and he did not forbid us.")
2. According to Jabir, "A man came to the Prophet and said, 'I have a slave-girl, and we need her as a servant and around the palm groves. I have sex with her, but I am afraid of her becoming pregnant.' The Prophet said, 'Practise coitus interruptus with her if you so wish, for she will receive what has been predestined for her.'"
3. According to Abu Sa'id, "We rode out with the Prophet to raid Banu al-Mustaliq and captured some female prisoners . . . We desired women, and abstinence became hard. [But] we wanted to practise coitus interruptus; and we asked the Prophet about it. He said, 'You do not have to hesitate, for God has predestined what is to be created until Judgement day.'"
4. According to Abus Sa'id, "The Jews say that coitus interruptus is minor infanticide, and the Prophet answered, 'The Jews lie, for if God wanted to create something, no one can avert it [or, divert Him].'"

From Basim F. Mussalam, "Why Islam Permitted Contraception," in *Sex and Society in Islam*. Copyright © Cambridge University Press, New York, NY. Reprinted by permission.

5. According to Judhama bint Wahb, "I was there when the Prophet was with a group saying, 'I was about to prohibit the *ghila*,[5] but I observed the Byzantines and the Persians, and saw them do it, and their children were not harmed.' They asked him about coitus interruptus, and the Prophet answered, 'It is hidden infanticide . . .'"

6. According to 'Umar Ibn al-Khattab, "The Prophet forbade the practice of coitus interruptus with a free woman except with her permission."

7. According to Anas, "A man asked the Prophet about coitus interruptus, and the Prophet said, 'Even if you spill seed from which a child was meant to be born on a rock, God will bring forth from that rock a child'". . . .

The most thorough statement of the Islamic permission of contraception was made by the great Shafi'i jurist Ghazali (1058–1111). In one of the most remarkable documents in the history of birth control, Ghazali stated explicitly the grounds of the permission that were mostly implied elsewhere.[6] In view of the absence of a religious text on contraception, he discussed it from premises rooted more in profane biology and economics than in the strictly religious sources of the law. He did employ the *hadith*, but only at the end, after he had completed his argument, and used it as supporting evidence . . . .

Ghazali supported contraceptive practice with one's wife or concubine to protect her from the dangers of childbirth, or simply to preserve her beauty. He especially favoured the economic motives for birth control. When practised with concubines, the intention was to safeguard one's property, for slave-women could not be sold after becoming mothers to their master's child. In this opinion, the taking of measures against alienating property was lawful.

A more general economic motive that he also supported was the wish to limit the family to a manageable size. He argued that the increase in the number of dependents multiplied material difficulties, led to extra toil in order to earn a living, and tempted men to engage in immoral or illegal transactions to meet their responsibilities. . . .

Ghazali strongly disapproved of people who practised contraception through fear of having daughters. He cautioned men not to express glee over the birth of sons, or show sadness over the birth of daughters: "there is no way of knowing who will prove to be good. There are many fathers of sons who wished they had daughters instead." He also disapproved of contraception by women for purely personal reasons. He reported that some women practised contraception because they disliked pregnancy, or because they had a fetish for absolute cleanliness, or simply because they did not want to bother with childbirth and nursing. To him these attitudes were an "innovation" (*bid'a*), alien to Muslim custom. Here, however, he was careful to add that it was the intent that was objectionable, not the actual prevention of pregnancy. It is difficult not to notice that Ghazali approved of a man's wish to preserve the physical appeal of the woman, but disapproved of a woman's wish to avoid pregnancy for her own personal convenience[7]. . . .

In the first half of the fifteenth century Ibn Hajar thought that people practised contraception for three reasons: in fear of fathering slave children, in fear of having a large number of dependents, and in fear of the ill-effects of pregnancy in the case of a nursing infant. This last was the only reason that met with Ibn Hajar's personal approval, for "experience" showed that "such pregnancies are generally harmful".[8] Another motive was the need to provide for the education and proper upbringing of children. Bujairimi maintained that "if contraception is practised for an excuse (*'udhr*), such as the raising (*tarbiya*) of a child, it is not even blameworthy (*lam yukrah*)". . . .[9]

Islamic Law and Abortion

Many regulations in Islamic law depended directly on the religious view of foetal development.[10] If someone hurt a pregnant woman and she aborted, the amount of blood money depended on whether the foetus was "formed" or "unformed"; if the aborted foetus showed any signs of volition the full *diya* had to be paid, just as in the case of an adult person; such a foetus also inherited (the importance of this regulation was that the foetus passed inheritance to its relatives); a slave woman, pregnant by her master, ultimately gained freedom if in the case of a spontaneous abortion the foetus was "formed"—she did not if it was an early embryo. Ceremonies of religious burial were permitted in the case of the "formed" foetus, and prohibited otherwise. The Muslim view of foetal development was also central to the Muslim arguments on abortion.

All Muslim jurists believed that the foetus became a human being after the fourth month of pregnancy (120 days). The majority of jurists, as a result, prohibited abortion after that stage. The Hanafi jurists, who comprised the majority of orthodox Muslims in later centuries, permitted abortion until the end of the fourth month. The Hanafis granted the pregnant woman the right to abort even without her husband's permission, but suggested that she should not do so without a reason.[11] One reason which was often mentioned was the existence of a nursing infant. A new pregnancy put an upper limit on lactation, and the jurists believed that if the mother could not be replaced by a wet-nurse, the infant would die.[12]

Most of the Maliki jurists prohibited abortion absolutely. They agreed with the others that the foetus was not a human being before ensoulment, but maintained that since the destiny of the semen, once it settles in the womb, is ensoulment, it should not be tampered with: "When the womb has retained the semen it is not permitted for the husband and wife, or one of them, or the master [of the slave wife] to induce an abortion. After ensoulment, however, abortion is prohibited absolutely and is akin to murder."[13] Evidently, the Malaki prohibition of abortion was stronger after ensoulment than before it, and a small minority of the Malikis permitted abortion of the young embryo of forty days or less.[14]

Compared to the remarkable agreement on the permission of contraception, on abortion there remained important differences between the jurists. Many Shafi'i and Hanbali jurists agreed with the Hanafis in their toleration of the practice, some putting an upper limit of forty days for a legal abortion, others eighty days or 120 days.[15] The variety of legal regulations blurred the exact religious attitude towards abortion. Not only that, but given the nature of Islamic law, both Hanafi opinion (permission) and Maliki opinion (prohibition) were deemed legitimate by all orthodox Muslims.

The Islamic discussion of abortion was related to that of contraception in two ways. In the first place, some jurists, to strengthen their argument for the permission of contraception, had maintained that it was preferable to abortion.[16] One Hanafi jurist put the case as follows: since a pregnant woman has the right to induce abortion before the foetus is 120 days old, she should also be given the right to use female contraceptives. By removing the necessity for abortion, contraceptives represent a better alternative.[17] Special pleading in this instance resulted from the fact that female contraceptives were only occasionally dealt with in jurisprudence, where the permission of contraception normally referred to withdrawal.

On the other hand, the general permission of contraception strengthened the tendency to legalize abortion. In Islam, conception was the beginning of a new living thing, but it was the separate act of ensoulment that created *human* life. In Judaism, Christianity, and Islam it is not the taking of "life" that is prohibited, for all three religions permit the slaughter of animals—that is, non-human life. Because murder was considered a crime against a human being, and not simply against any living thing, it was essential to decide at which moment the foetus became a person: was it at the moment of conception, of birth, or some point between? Christian theology recognized that the early embryo was not a true human being, and that it became one only when it was "ensouled" or "formed": "The dominant view in Christianity is that the foetus became a man only when 'formed'. The moment of formation appears to be the forty-day period set by Aristotle for males, and the eighty-day period suggested by Leviticus for females."[18] The Muslim view that the male semen was nothing until it united with the woman's to form an embryo was basic to the permission of contraception. If contraception is permitted because it does not tamper with human life, then abortion of the pre-ensoulment foetus can be permitted on the same grounds. Zaidi Islamic jurisprudence explicitly stated that since the "unformed" foetus, like the semen, had no human life, abortion, like contraception, was unconditionally permitted.[19]

Islamic legal attitudes toward abortion were not as consistent with those on contraception, and there was no simply Islamic religious position. But given the fact that prohibition was not the dominant view by any standard, given the fact that Muslims believed in ensoulment as the crucial event before which the foetus was not a person, and given the fact that the sanction of contraception strengthened the view that abortion should be legalized before ensoulment, perhaps we can say that, on the whole, abortion was religiously tolerated. This conclusion gains indirect support from the contemporary medieval Arabic secular literatures. Medicine, materia medica and popular literature all treated contraception and abortion as if they were two aspects of the same process: birth control.

Notes

1. Ibn 'Abidin, *Radd*, p. 622.
2. Ibn al-Najjar, *Muntaha*, vol. 2 p. 227; Ibn Abi Bakr, *Ghayat*, vol. 3, p. 91; Bahuti, *Kashshaf*, vol. 5, p. 189; Mardawi, *Taqih*, p. 230; Ruhaibani, *Matalib*, vol. 5, p. 263; and Ibn Qudama, *Mughni*, vol. 8, p. 134.
3. In studying the Christian attitude toward contraception, scholars face the problem of the position of the "Church", which can be seen as above and separate from the opinions of individual Christians, regardless of how prevalent, rooted in tradition, and continuous in history these opinions may be. All Christian theologians and thinkers could have been wrong or heretical: "Only the Church is free from errors." Noonan asks about his sources:

   Are these writers and legislative enactments to be equated with the Church? There is a tendency among some historians to make the identification, to say that the Catholic Church taught this or did that, when all that one can be certain of is that particular men, baptized Christians, occupying a particular role in the ecclesiastical system, did this or taught that . . . no great original theologian, not even an Augustine or a Thomas, has been able to write extensively on theology without writing what later has been determined to be heresy. Only the Church is free from error.

   (John T. Noonan, Jr., *Contraception, A History of Its Treatment by the Catholic Theologians and Canonists* [Harvard University Press, Cambridge, Mass., 1966]: pp. 4–5.)
4. For an index of these references see "Azl allowed", and "'Azl disapproved of" in A. J. Wensinck, *Handbook of Early Muhammadan Tradition* (E. J. Brill, Leiden, 1960), p. 112.
5. *Ghila* is the act of sexual intercourse with a woman in lactation.
6. Ghazali, *Ihya'*, vol. 2, pp. 41–2.
7. Ghazali, *Ihya'*, vol. 2, pp. 41–2.
8. Ibn Hajar, *Fath al-bari*, vol. 11, pp. 219–20.
9. Bujairimi, *Iqna'*, vol. 3, p. 40.
10. Muhammad Salam Madkur, *Al-Janin wa al-ahkam al-muta'alliqa bihi fi al-figh al-Islami* (Cairo, 1969).
11. Ibn Nujaim, *Bahr*, vol. 3, p. 214, Ibn 'Abidin, *Minhat*, vol. 3, p. 215; Ibn 'Abindin, *Hadiyya*, p. 246.
12. Ibn 'Abidin, *Minhat*, vol. 3, p. 215, and *Radd*, p. 622; and Ibn 'Abindin, *Hadiyya*, p. 246.
13. 'Ulaish, *Fath*, vol. 1, p. 398; Dardir, *Sharh*, vol. 2, p. 267; Kasadawi, *Badr*, pp. 263–4; Ibn Juzaiy, *Qawanin*, p. 212.
14. Dasuqi, *Hashiyat*, vol. 2, p. 267, says that it is only a *makruh* before forty days. They do not explain directly how they arrived at this figure of forty days, but it is obviously related to the medieval understanding of the first stage of foetal development, at the end of which an embryo begins to look human (above, pp. 53–5).
15. Hanafi: Ibn Nujaim, *Bahr*, vol. 3, p. 214; Ibn 'Abidin, *Minhat*, vol. 3, p. 215; *idem, Radd*, p. 622; Ibn al-Humam, *Sharh*, vol. 2, p. 495; *Fatawa al-'Alamgiriyya*, vol. 1, p. 335; Ibn 'Abidin, *Hadiyya*, p. 246. Hanbali: "It is permitted to induce abortion . . ., but Ibn al-Jawzi said in *Ahkam al-nisa'* that abortion is prohibited . . . [However] Ibn 'Aqil said . . . it is permitted before ensoulment" (Mardawi, *Insaf*, vol. 1, p. 386). Shafi'i: Ghazali, in discussing contraception (see Chapter 1 above), prohibited abortion, but in another context found room for permission before ensoulment. Some Shafi'is maintained that it was licit to abort the *nutfa* and *'alaqa* (the first two stages, eighty days or younger). See the article on *"Ijhad"*, *Mawsu'at Jamal 'Abd al-Nasir fi al-fiqh al-Islami* (Cairo, A. H. 1388), vol. 3, pp. 158–71.
16. For example, Ghazali, *Ihya'*, vol. 2, p. 41.
17. Ibn 'Abidin, *Minhat*, vol. 3, p. 215.
18. Noonan, *Contraception*, p. 90.
19. Murtada, *Al-Bahr al-zukhkhar*, vol. 3, p. 81.

Writing and Discussion Topics

Questions 1–6 address content, critical analysis, personal choices, ethical options, specific discipline, and interdisciplinary alternatives, respectively.

1. Why is the Islamic attitude on contraception important in the rulings on abortion?
2. Research the Islamic position on sexual relations, contraception, and marriage. From your studies, determine if the Islamic religion appears to be more or less tolerant of sexual relations and abortions than the Jewish or Roman Catholic traditions.
3. The Islamic religion accepts polygamy (up to four wives), sexual relations with concubines, and easy divorce. Compare and contrast this with your own views on marriage and sexual morality. Include the topic of abortion as part of your analysis.
4. Contraception and ensoulment are used in determining the ethical position on abortion by Roman Catholics. According to Mussallam, how are these two perspectives parts of the Islamic position on abortion?
5. Specify the different positions on abortion detailed by the jurists of the Maliki, Hanafi, Shafi'i, and Hanbali perspectives.
6. Does the Islamic religion engage in moral or immoral activity when predominantly men determine the use of contraception? When usually men approve abortion? Examine and explain your answers.

A. J. Cronin

"DOCTOR, I CAN'T . . . I WON'T HAVE A CHILD"

———◆◆◆———

A. J. Cronin (1896–1981) was born in Cardross, Scotland. He
practiced medicine from 1919 to 1930. He then turned his
attention to writing and became a very popular British novelist. He
wrote many short stories and books, including: Hatter's Castle, The
Stars Look Down, The Citadel, The Keys of the Kingdom, Two
Worlds, A Thing of Beauty, A Pocketful of Rye, and The Lady with
Carnations. Cronin is well-known for his critical study of the medical
profession. This short story offers an analytical look at a country doctor
faced with a demand from a wealthy patient. ◆

"Doctor, I can't . . . I won't have a child."

It was four o'clock in the afternoon, the hour of my "best" consultations, and the woman who spoke so vehemently was tall, distinguished, and handsome, fashionably dressed in a dark grey costume, with an expensive diamond clip in her smart black hat.

I had just examined her, and now, having dried my hands methodically, I put away the towel and turned toward her. "It's a little late to make that decision now. You should have thought of it two months ago. You are exactly nine weeks pregnant. Your baby will be born toward the middle of July."

"I won't have it . . . You've got to help me, Doctor. You simply must."

How often had I heard these words before. I had heard them from frightened little shopgirls in trouble; from a shamed spinster, aged thirty-five, who told me in a trembling voice, exactly like the heroine of the old-time melodrama, that she had been "betrayed"; from a famous film actress defiantly resolved that her career should not be ruined; above all had I heard them from selfish and neurotic wives, afraid of the pangs of childbirth, afraid of losing their figure, their health, their life, afraid—most specious pretext of all—of "losing their husband's love."

This case was somewhat different. I knew my patient, Beatrice Glendenning, socially; knew also her husband, Henry, and her two grown-up sons. They were wealthy people, with a town house in Knightsbridge and a large estate in Hampshire, where the pheasant shooting was excellent and where, indeed, I had spent several pleasant weekends.

"You understand . . . , it isn't just money, Doctor . . . I must get out of this business, and to do so I'll give anything." She looked me full in the face.

There was no mistaking her meaning. Indeed, that same offer, indescribable in its implications, had been made to me before, though perhaps never so blatantly. It had been made by a young French modiste, estranged from her husband, who had compromised herself with another man and who, slim, elegant, and bewitching, with affected tears in her beautiful eyes, leaned forward and tried to take my hands in hers.

Doctors are only human, they have the same difficulty in repressing their instincts as other men. Yet,

if not for moral reasons, from motives of sheer common sense, I had never lost my head. Once a doctor embarks upon a career as abortionist he is irretrievably lost.

There were, however, many such illicit practitioners in the vicinity, both men and women, plying their perilous undercover trade at exorbitant rates, until one day, inevitably, the death of some wretched girl brought them exposure, ruin, and a long term of imprisonment. Perhaps desperation blinded such patients as came to me, yet it always struck me as amazing how few of them were conscious of the infinite danger involved in illegal abortion. Under the best hospital conditions the operation holds a definite risk. Performed hastily in some backstairs room with a septic instrument by some brutal or unskilled practitioner, the result almost inevitably is severe hemorrhage, followed by infection and acute peritonitis.

There were others, too, among these women who believed it was within my power to relieve them of their incubus by such a simple expedient as an ergot pill or a mixture of jalap and senna. Others, too, who confessed to having tried the weirdest expedients, from boiling-hot baths to such eccentric gymnastics as descending the stairs backward, in a crouching position. Poor creatures, some were almost comic in their distress, and there were among them many who needed sympathy and comfort. This they got from me, with much good advice, but nothing more.

Beatrice Glendenning, however, was neither comic nor ignorant, but a strong-minded, intelligent woman of the world who moved with considerable éclat in the best society.

My only possible attitude was not to take her seriously. So I reasoned mildly:

"I daresay, it's rather inconvenient . . . , with these two grown-up sons of yours. And it'll spoil your London season. But Henry will be pleased."

"Don't be a fool, Doctor. Henry isn't the father."

Although I had half expected this, it silenced me.

During these country weekends I had met the inevitable family intimate, a close friend of Henry's, who went fishing and shooting with him, a sporting type, one of these "good fellows," whom I had disliked on sight and who obviously was on confidential terms with Henry's wife.

"Well," I said at last, "it's a bad business. But there's nothing I can do about it."

"You won't help me?"

"I can't."

There was a pause. The blood had risen to her cheeks and her eyes flashed fire at me. She drew on her gloves, took up her bag. A rejected woman is an enemy for life.

"Very well, Doctor, there's no more to be said."

"Just one thing before you go. . . . Don't put yourself in the hands of a quack. You may regret it."

She gave no sign of having heard, but swept out of the room without another word.

The interview left me not only with a bad taste in my mouth, but in a thoroughly bad mood. I felt that I had lost an excellent patient, an agreeable hostess, and the half dozen brace of admirable pheasants which I had come to regard as my annual autumnal perquisite. I never expected to see Mrs. Glendenning again. How wrong I was—how little I knew of that invincible woman's character!

About ten days later the telephone rang. It was Henry Glendenning himself. Beatrice, he told me, had a frightful cold, an attack of influenza, in fact. Would I be a dear chap and pop round to Knightsbridge as soon as convenient? Pleased by this *rapprochement*, I arrived within the hour at the Glendenning town house and was shown directly to Beatrice's room.

Attended by a nurse, a heavily built, middle-aged woman with a face like a trap, the patient was in bed. She appeared, at first sight, rather more ill than I had expected—fearfully blanched, with bloodless lips and every indication of a raging fever. Puzzled, I drew back the sheet . . . , and then the truth burst upon me. The thing had been done—botched and bungled—she was thoroughly septic and had been hemorrhaging for at least twelve hours.

"I have everything ready for you, Doctor." The nurse was addressing me in a toneless voice, proffering a container of swabs and gauze.

I drew back in cold fury. I wanted, there and then, to walk out of the room. But how could I? She was in *extremis*. I must do something for this damned woman, and at once. I was fairly trapped.

I began to work on her. My methods, I fear, were not especially merciful, but she offered no protest, suffered the severest pangs without a word. At last the bleeding was under control. I prepared to go.

All this time, as she lay there, Mrs. Glendenning's eyes had never left my face. And now, with an effort, she spoke:

"It's influenza, Doctor. Henry knows it's influenza. I shall expect you this evening."

Downstairs, in the library, Henry had a glass of sherry ready for me, concerned, naturally, about his wife, whom he adored, yet hospitable, as always. He was in stature quite a small man, shy and rather ineffectual in manner, who had inherited a fortune from his father and spent much of it in making others happy. As I gazed at his open, kindly face, all that I had meant to say died upon my tongue. I could not tell him. I could not.

"Nasty thing, this influenza, Doctor."

I took a quick breath.

"Yes, Henry."

"Quite a severe attack she has, too."

"I'm afraid so."

"You'll see her through, Doctor."

A pause.

"Yes, Henry. I'll see her through."

I called again that evening. I called twice a day for the next ten days. It was a thoroughly unpleasant case, demanding constant surgical attention. I suppose I did my part in maintaining the deception. But the real miracles of strategy were performed by Beatrice and the nurse. For Henry Glendenning, who lived all that time in the same house, who slept every night in the bedroom adjoining the sickroom, *never for a moment suspected the true state of affairs.* The thing sounds incredible, but it is true.

At the end of that month, I made my final visit. Mrs. Glendenning was up, reclining on the drawing-room sofa, looking ethereal and soulful in a rose-coloured tea gown with pure white lace at cuff and collar. Flowers were everywhere. Henry, delighted, still adoring, was dancing attendance. Tea was brought, served by a trim maid—the grim-visaged nurse had long since departed.

Toying with a slice of teacake, Beatrice gazed at me with wide and wistful eyes.

"Henry is taking me to Madeira next week, Doctor. He feels I need the change."

"You do indeed, darling."

"Thank you, sweetheart."

Oh God, the duplicity, the perfidy of woman . . . the calm, deep, premeditated, and infernal cunning!

"We'll be alone together for the first week," she concluded sweetly. "A second honeymoon. Then we expect George to join us. We're both very fond of George."

Her eyes sought mine, held it, and did not for an instant falter.

"More tea, Doctor, dear? You must come and shoot with us when we get back."

When I rose to go, Henry saw me to the door, shook my hand warmly.

"Thank you for all you've done, Doctor." And he added, "Confoundedly nasty thing, that influenza."

I walked all the way home across Kensington Gardens, gritting my teeth and muttering, "That creature, oh that damned, that most damnable creature!"

But in September I got my half-dozen brace of pheasants. They were nice, tender birds!

Writing and Discussion Topics

Questions 1–6 address content, critical analysis, personal choices, ethical options, specific discipline, and interdisciplinary alternatives, respectively.

1. How do we know that the doctor considers Beatrice a prime patient? Why would he like to keep her as a patient?

2. Analyze the doctor's behavior toward his patient. Is there a reason why he should treat her in a rough manner?

3. If you were this doctor's patient, what type of care would you expect from him?

4. Is the doctor obligated to tell the woman's husband about the abortion, or is this a confidential matter between the doctor and Beatrice? What other professional and ethical decisions are in this story?

5. This story has a strong element of irony. What is irony? What circumstances cause the irony to develop?

6. Would Beatrice have been a prime candidate for the "Jane" clinic? Compare and contrast the treatment she would have received at the clinic with the treatment she received from her abortionist and her doctor.

THE MOTHER

◆◆◆

Gwendolyn Brooks Source: AP/Wide World Photos.

Gwendolyn Brooks is an African-American poet, children's writer, and novelist. She has been awarded numerous distinctions including a Guggenheim Fellowship, a Pulitzer Prize, and was named Poet Laureate for the state of Illinois. Mademoiselle magazine has named her a "Woman of the Year." A native of Topeka, Kansas, Brooks is known for her bold, riveting style. ◆

Abortions will not let you forget.
You remember the children you got that you did not get,
The damp small pulps with a little or with no hair,
The singers and workers that never handled the air,
You will never neglect or beat
Them, or silence or buy with a sweet,
You will never wind up the sucking-thumb
Or scuttle off ghosts that come.
You will never leave them, controlling your luscious sigh,
Return for a snack of them, with gobbling mother-eye.

I have heard in the voices of the wind the voices of my dim killed children.
I have contracted. I have eased
My dim dears at the breasts they could never suck.
I have said, Sweets, if I sinned, if I seized
Your luck
And your lives from your unfinished reach,
If I stole your births and your names,
Your straight baby tears and your games,
Your stilted or lovely loves, your tumults, your marriages, aches, and your
    deaths,
If I poisoned the beginnings of your breaths,
Believe that even in my deliberateness I was not deliberate.
Though why should I whine,
Whine that the crime was other than mine?—
Since anyhow you are dead.
Or rather, or instead,
You were never made.
But that too, I am afraid,
Is faulty: oh, what shall I say, how is the truth to be said?
You were born, you had body, you died.
It is just that you never giggled or planned or cried.

Believe me, I loved you all.
Believe me, I knew you, though faintly, and I loved, I loved you,
All.

Writing and Discussion Topics

Questions 1–6 address content, critical analysis, personal choices, ethical options, specific discipline, and interdisciplinary alternatives, respectively.

1. What won't abortion let you forget, according to Brooks?
2. What does Brooks mean by "even in my deliberateness I was not deliberate"? Explain if this is a logical consistency or inconsistency.

3. Have you ever regretted anything in life to the extent indicated in Brook's writing? Would she live her life the same if she could live it over? Would you repeat your mistakes?
4. Examine the ethical approach based on relationships by Carol Gilligan in light of this poem. Do the two correspond?
5. Examine Brooks's poetic style. What figures of speech does she use to produce potent images?
6. How does Kant's ethical position compare with Brooks's?

HILLS LIKE WHITE ELEPHANTS

◆◆◆

Ernest Hemingway   Source:
UPI/Bettmann.

E rnest Hemingway was a popular and colorful American novelist. He won the Nobel Prize for Literature in 1954. His most famous works include The Sun Also Rises, A Farewell to Arms, and For Whom the Bell Tolls. In addition to his writing, Hemingway's active personal life was also notable. He was wounded in World War I and served in the Spanish Civil War. He loved bullfights in Spain and big-game safaris in Africa. ◆

The hills across the valley of the Ebro were long and white. On this side there was no shade and no trees and the station was between two lines of rails in the sun. Close against the side of the station there was the warm shadow of the building and a curtain, made of strings of bamboo beads, hung across the open door into the bar, to keep out flies. The American and the girl with him sat at a table in the shade, outside the building. It was very hot and the express from Barcelona would come in forty minutes. It stopped at this junction for two minutes and went on to Madrid.

"What should we drink?" the girl asked. She had taken off her hat and put it on the table.

"It's pretty hot," the man said.

"Let's drink beer."

"Dos cervezas," the man said into the curtain.

"Big ones?" a woman asked from the doorway.

"Yes. Two big ones."

The woman brought two glasses of beer, and two felt pads. She put the felt pads and the beer glasses on the table and looked at the man and the girl. The girl was looking off at the line of hills. They were white in the sun and the country was brown and dry.

"They look like white elephants," she said.

"I've never seen one," the man drank his beer.

"No, you wouldn't have."

"I might have," the man said. "Just because you say I wouldn't have doesn't prove anything."

The girl looked at the bead curtains. "They've painted something on it," she said. "What does it say?"

"Anis del Toro. It's a drink."

"Could we try it?"

The man called "Listen" through the curtain. The woman came out from the bar.

"Four reales."

"We want two Anis del Toro."

"With water?"

"Do you want it with water?"

"I don't know," the girl said. "Is it good with water?"

"It's all right."

"You want them with water?" asked the woman.

"Yes, with water."

"It tastes like licorice," the girl said and put the glass down.

"That's the way with everything."

"Yes," said the girl. "Everything tastes of licorice. Especially all the things you've waited so long for, like absinthe."

"Oh, cut it out."

"You started it," the girl said. "I was being amused. I was having a fine time."

"Well, let's try and have a fine time."

"All right. I was trying. I said the mountains looked like white elephants. Wasn't that bright?"

"That was bright."

"I wanted to try this new drink. That's all we do, isn't it—look at things and try new drinks?"

"I guess so."

The girl looked across at the hills.

"They're lovely hills," she said. "They don't really look like white elephants. I just meant the coloring of their skin through the trees."

"Should we have another drink?"

"All right."

The warm wind blew the bead curtain against the table.

"The beer's nice and cool," the man said.

"It's lovely," the girl said.

"It's really an awfully simple operation, Jig," the man said. "It's not really an operation at all."

The girl looked at the ground the table legs rested on.

"I know you wouldn't mind it, Jig. It's really not anything. It's just to let the air in."

The girl did not say anything.

"I'll go with you and I'll stay with you all the time. They just let the air in and then it's all perfectly natural."

"Then what will we do afterward?"

"We'll be fine afterward. Just like we were before."

"What makes you think so?"

"That's the only thing that bothers us. It's the only thing that's made us unhappy."

The girl looked at the bead curtain, put her hand out and took hold of two of the strings of beads.

"And you think then we'll be all right and be happy."

"I know we will. You don't have to be afraid. I've known lots of people that have done it."

"So have I," said the girl. "And afterward they were all so happy."

"Well," said the man, "if you don't want to you don't have to. I wouldn't have you do it if you didn't want to. But I know it's perfectly simple."

"And you really want to?"

"I think it's the best thing to do. But I don't want you to do it if you don't really want to."

"And if I do it you'll be happy and things will be like they were and you'll love me?"

"I love you now. You know I love you."

"I know. But if I do it, then it will be nice again if I say things are like white elephants, and you'll like it?"

"I'll love it. I love it now but I just can't think about it. You know how I get when I worry."

"If I do it you won't ever worry?"

"I won't worry about that because it's perfectly simple."

"Then I'll do it. Because I don't care about me."

"What do you mean?"

"I don't care about me."

"Well, I care about you."

"Oh, yes. But I don't care about me. And I'll do it and then everything will be fine."

"I don't want you to do it if you feel that way."

The girl stood up and walked to the end of the station. Across, on the other side, were fields of grain and trees along the banks of the Ebro. Far away, beyond the river, were mountains. The shadow of a cloud moved across the field of grain and she saw the river through the trees.

"And we could have all this," she said. "And we could have everything and every day we make it more impossible."

"What did you say?"

"I said we could have everything."

"We can have everything."

"No, we can't."

"We can have the whole world."

"No, we can't."

"We can go everywhere."

"No, we can't. It isn't ours any more."

"It's ours."

"No, it isn't. And once they take it away, you never get it back."

"But they haven't taken it away."

"We'll wait and see."

"Come on back in the shade," he said. "You mustn't feel that way."

"I don't feel any way," the girl said. "I just know things."

"I don't want you to do anything that you don't want to do—"

"Nor that isn't good for me," she said. "I know. Could we have another beer?"

"All right. But you've got to realize"

"I realize," the girl said. "Can't we maybe stop talking?"

They sat down at the table and the girl looked across at the hills on the dry side of the valley and the man looked at her and at the table.

"You've got to realize," he said, "that I don't want you to do it if you don't want to. I'm perfectly willing to go through with it if it means anything to you."

"Doesn't it mean anything to you? We could get along."

"Of course it does. But I don't want anybody but you. I don't want anyone else. And I know it's perfectly simple."

"Yes, you know it's perfectly simple."

"It's all right for you to say that, but I do know it."

"Would you do something for me now?"

"I'd do anything for you."

"Would you please please please please please please please stop talking?"

He did not say anything but looked at the bags against the wall of the station. There were labels on them from all the hotels where they had spent nights.

"But I don't want you to," he said. "I don't care anything about it."

"I'll scream," the girl said.

The woman came out through the curtains with two glasses of beer and put them down on the damp felt pads. "The train comes in five minutes," she said.

"What did she say?" asked the girl.

"That the train is coming in five minutes."

The girl smiled brightly at the woman, to thank her.

"I'd better take the bags over to the other side of the station," the man said. She smiled at him.

"All right. Then come back and we'll finish the beer."

He picked up the two heavy bags and carried them around the station to the other tracks. He looked up the tracks but could not see the train. Coming back, he walked through the barroom, where people waiting for the train were drinking. He drank an Anis at the bar and looked at the people. They were all waiting reasonably for the train. He went out through the bead curtain. She was sitting at the table and smiled at him.

"Do you feel better?" he asked.

"I feel fine," she said. "There's nothing wrong with me. I feel fine."

Writing and Discussion Topics

Questions 1–6 address content, critical analysis, personal choices, ethical options, specific discipline, and interdisciplinary alternatives, respectively.

1. How does the reader know this story is about an abortion? What is the woman's attitude toward the procedure? How does it differ from the man's?
2. What is the significance of "white elephants" in this piece?
3. Do you identify more with the man or the woman in this story? Who seems to be more reasonable in terms of lifestyle?
4. The woman says, "Then I'll do it. Because I don't care about me." How does this relate to the ethic based on care?
5. Cite several similes and metaphors in this piece. What meaning does each convey?
6. Compare and contrast this story with Linda Bird Francke's story.

Elaine Englehardt

THE SILENT PARTNER

◆◆◆

*E*laine Englehardt is an associate professor of humanities at Utah
Valley Community College. She works with the National
Endowment for the Humanities and the American Association for
Community and Junior Colleges as a consultant for two-year colleges.
She publishes in the area of ethics. ◆

It was 9:00 P.M. in the middle of January. Barbara was rushing home from work to her three children. Her husband of one month would be home in two days. In three days, she would have the abortion.

Barbara's thoughts were centered on her abdomen and the tiny being growing deep within her womb. The cold Chicago air ripped at her coat and burned her ears as she rested her head close to her chest and pulled her swollen feet the last block toward the metro. She felt an intense pain that began in her pelvis, stripped her heart, and shot daggers through her brain. The pain came from the "pea," her new silent partner.

The sudden gush of warm air in the train didn't change the problem or her thought process. "I feel you. I know what you can bring; I just can't see how I can fit you into my life. Why now? Can't you go to another family, a family where a mom needs and wants another child?"

Warmth began to permeate her legs, and the numbness from the cold wore off, but the aches and pains of her thirty-five years intensified. She pulled off the plaid scarf that hid her short blond hair. Her blue eyes surveyed the car. She felt self-conscious of her weight. She usually carried fifteen extra pounds of weight. Now that she was pregnant she carried an extra ten on top of that. She felt fat and swollen. She hoped her coat hid her bulges.

Her thoughts shifted to her job. The silent partner drained her energy and made her feel worthless at work. Some of her co-workers even complained to her about her performance. The work at the University of Chicago bookstore was interesting. She used to have a pleasant attitude toward the daily barrage of students, even when she was asked for the sixty-third time why the new physics 101 book cost forty-nine dollars for only 125 pages. Now she either ignored the students or asked them, "Do you want the book or not?" She saw their problems as trivial compared to her own.

The train continued its rhythmic movement. Barbara relaxed for the first time all day; her pulse slowed and her thoughts surveyed her adult past.

As a senior in high school, Barbara became pregnant three months before graduation. Hal was an admired, handsome athlete, and Barbara was a cute, chesty blonde. They were going to get married

anyway, so sooner would be better. The marriage gave Hal a great excuse to quit playing baseball, which had lost some of its appeal in the past year due to the pressure his dad put on him. His father and his grandfather firmly believed that athletic participation was the key to true manhood. But vicarious football and baseball play for relatives was secondary to Hal now. He no longer wanted to please them. He had to follow his heart in a different direction. Three years after Ellen was born, Kathi, their second child, was starting to take her first steps. On a sultry July night while Barbara was playing with her precious babies on her front porch, two policemen stepped out of a patrol car and approached her home. A ten-foot dike had collapsed while Hal was laying drainage pipe in it. He was dead.

There was no money. Hal and Barbara could barely make ends meet from month to month. They believed that Barbara should be home with the children. She really had no employable skills. Workman's compensation gave the family some subsistence but it was never enough.

Barbara found work at the bookstore, hired a baby-sitter for the girls, and tried to hide her grief. One evening after thirteen hours of stacking and ordering books, Steve, a co-worker, asked Barbara about her personal life. Steve was a senior majoring in zoology. He was handsome with a soothing smile, engaging brown eyes, and a warm personal charm. He had girlfriends, but he was obviously fascinated and enticed by Barbara's very ample chest. After they talked that first night, he listened to her life story every night for two weeks at his apartment. She would leave the girls with a sitter or sometimes steal away when they were fast asleep. After discovering almost everything about Barbara's body and life, he decided her life was too complicated, and he did not want to be part of it. In the meantime, a new girl, Amy, started work at the bookstore. Three weeks later, Steve was listening to Amy's stories with the same soulful brown eyes Barbara knew. But now Barbara was carrying his child. She wanted an abortion but her strong Christian faith kept telling her no. She would be murdering one of God's children—a special soul he had prepared for Barbara's life. After Randi was born, Barbara had an IUD inserted, and gave up the notion of childbearing.

There was never enough money or time. The clothes had to be *Esprit*, or *Guess?* or the week's most expensive brand name in jeans. Dance and piano lessons would be started only to be discontinued because of lack of funds. Even the cost for birthday parties and presents became overwhelming. Randi had trouble with math; Kathi was clumsy; Ellen had constant battles with peers.

Men came and came and came, and Barbara, who, prior to marriage, thought that commitment was a part of sex, became very cynical about relationships. Her professional life was now easy to manage. But her personal "woman" skills were a disaster. The rejection she felt when men tired of her was profound. She often asked herself, "Why even have a personal life? Why do I need men? Why do I need sex?" Her answer was that she felt the highest of highs and the lowest of lows when she was involved with a man. She knew she had low self-esteem, and that somehow attention from a man made her feel worthwhile. She would take the lows if only for the highs. She wanted to break from her horrible pattern, and she wanted relief from the financial and emotional responsibility of three children. In five years they would be out of the house and she would be alone. Yet, she grieved for the girls. Their complicated lives with sex, men, children, and work were only moments away.

It was then she met John. He was married. She was lonely. The stolen moments together became more frequent. There would be no commitment. John had a commitment and two children. He was safe. This time she would stay distant in the relationship. She wouldn't expect marriage. John would be like a toy she could take down from a shelf, play with, and then place back on the shelf when she was finished.

She met John for lunch on a Tuesday in early December at Muddy Waters coffeehouse located two blocks north of the campus. John was quiet at first, then a thin confident smile sliced his lips.

"My divorce will be final in three weeks," he said. Barbara sipped her coffee and returned his smile. A country man, a hardworking man, said he wanted Barbara forever. Barbara said yes. She felt a mix of relief and elation. They were married quietly in the middle of the month. Barbara felt a peace she hadn't felt since Hal.

She had no idea when she lost the IUD. She hadn't had a gynecological exam in two years. There had never been a problem with the "loop," so her self-examinations after each period had ended after the second year with the device. They didn't even know she was carrying a child when they married. But the taunt, swollen feeling in her breasts and a period six weeks behind schedule made Barbara's insides feel like a car wreck. Her suspicions couldn't be true. Her God and her body wouldn't do this to her.

Her most frequent thought was, "Just leave. Please just leave. Let's pretend you never were." But she couldn't pretend for long. The tests and her doctor confirmed that she was two-and-a-half months pregnant. John didn't want the abortion, but Barbara insisted.

"It's too late. You can't just kill the child. It will be our child. Maybe it's a son." John's words couldn't penetrate Barbara's firm hurt. She felt betrayed by God. She thought she let herself down; she should have been more conscientious with the IUD. But now she could right the wrong.

"I won't bear another child. I've done my time. I won't donate my next twenty years to another child," she mumbled. "The abortion will have to be at a hospital, and I want you with me. I promise life will be better for us without this unnecessary complication," Barbara said, tears dropping from her eyes.

The heater wouldn't work in the car until they arrived at the hospital. It was better to have teeth chatter than language bridge the impasse. They entered through automatic glass doors and measured their steps to the reception desk.

"Dr. Edmond is behind schedule, but if you'll take a seat we'll begin your prep in about an hour," the nurse, dressed in angelic white, informed them. The waiting room was rancid. It was too hot. Barbara's throat clogged. She couldn't breathe. Her spit was salty. Her head was spinning in the glare and buzz of the old florescent lights above. "Take me home. I can't do this today."

That was a week ago. Daily she brought up the topic of rescheduling the abortion. She could go to the hospital by herself now. She was prepared for the waiting room, the large nurse, the late doctor, and the procedure. But John had to go out of town on "business" and asked her to wait until he returned.

"Only three more days with my silent partner," she thought wearily. The subway train was nearing her stop. She winced as she rose from her seat. Her pelvis churned as she walked toward the door. Her thirty-five-year-old legs screamed in pain as she climbed the stairs to the street. The cold blasted at her as she shuffled home. The last block seemed like a mile. "Why can't you just leave?" her mind screamed to the partner inside of her. She opened the door, greeted her girls, and promptly went to bed.

At two in the morning she awakened. It was a usual bathroom time. Something felt strange. The night light revealed blood covering the sheets. She strained on the toilet for five minutes. A dead baby boy slipped from her womb. She cut the cord with fingernail clippers, made her way back to the bedroom, and called an ambulance. She wrapped her silent partner in a face towel and brought it with her to the hospital.

The next morning John was at her side. "I killed it, you know," she said. Trails of tears drained down her face. "The doctor said there was nothing wrong with the baby. He was a perfect boy. Our baby knew I didn't want him, and he left. Do you feel better it happened this way?" she whispered. She closed her eyes to rest for a moment. When she awoke, John was gone.

Writing and Discussion Topics

Questions 1–6 address content, critical analysis, personal choices, ethical options, specific discipline, and interdisciplinary alternatives, respectively.

1. Why does Barbara keep her third child and not opt for an abortion? Why does she now refuse to have another child? Construct her argument for an abortion.
2. Why is Barbara's personal life with men a "disaster" while her professional life is smooth? Can the two be separated?
3. Why is it important for a woman to have a support system when she goes through an abortion? Could you have an abortion in Barbara's situation, even if your husband were opposed to it?
4. Using Judith Jarvis Thomson's argument, would it be morally acceptable for Barbara to have an abortion? What type of Samaritan is Barbara at the end of this story?
5. Can a woman truly "wish" away a pregnancy? Is there a moral difference between an actual abortion and an intended abortion? What would Kant say?
6. According to *Roe v. Wade*, can Barbara have a legal abortion? Would Barbara be allowed to have an abortion in your state under the 1989 Webster decision? Should a state have the power to force a woman to finish an unwanted pregnancy?

Michael J. Gorman

THE PAGAN WORLD

◆◆◆

Michael J. Gorman is the Assistant Director of the Council for Religion in Independent Schools in Washington, D.C. and teaches early church history and moral theology in the Ecumenical Institute of Technology at St. Mary's Seminary and University in Baltimore, Maryland. He received his Ph.D. in New Testament from Princeton Theological Seminary. His publishing centers on Christian approaches to abortion and peace. ◆

Ancient Greece

Abortion was a subject of Greek legal, medical, philosophical and religious concern. Only a few of these writings remain, however, and some opinions are preserved only in the works of later authors; a precise understanding of Greek opinion and practice is consequently quite difficult. . . .

Since the exposure of newborns, however, was very common in Greece and not only went unpunished but was even expected in certain cases, it is highly unlikely that abortion of the unborn was punished.[1] If any laws against abortion did exist in classical Greece they were probably motivated out of concern for the safety of the woman or the right of the husband. . . .

The Oath of Hippocrates (460–357 B.C.), however, included a definite promise not to perform an abortion:

> I swear by Apollo Physician, by Asclepius, by Health, by Panacea, and by all the gods and goddesses, making them my witnesses, that I will carry out, according to my ability and judgment, this oath and this indenture . . . I will use treatment to help the sick according to my ability and judgment, but never with a view to injury and wrong-doing. Neither will I administer a poison to anybody when asked to do so, nor will I suggest such a course. Similarly, I will not give a woman a pessary to cause abortion.[2]

It is unclear to modern scholars where the Oath originated, who actually composed it and, most important, who subscribed to it. The last question is significant even if the text is by Hippocrates: the seriousness with which the Oath was written and taken has been questioned by some who find evidence that Hippocrates himself indicated means of abortion for those who wanted it.[3] Nevertheless, it is generally agreed that most Greek physicians opposed all nontherapeutic abortions.[4] An abortive pessary was seen as a poison and rejected as an attack not so much on the fetus as on the woman.

Whatever the source and integrity of the Oath, it won acceptance among Jews, Christians and Arabs; survived the Renaissance and Enlightenment with the approval of both ages; and stands as a testimony to the main, if not the only, Greek medical opinion.[5]

If medical ethics opposed abortion, social and philosophical ethics to some extent endorsed it. The "Greeks enjoy the dubious distinction of being the first [in the Ancient Near East or Western world] positively to advise and even demand abortion in certain cases."[6] In discussing the role of women in his ideal *Republic,* Plato (427–347 B.C.) commanded abortion for women who conceived after a proposed cutoff age of forty:

> A woman, I said, at twenty years of age may begin to bear children to the State, and continue to bear them until forty. . . . And we grant all this, accompanying the permission with strict orders to prevent any [subsequent] embryo which may come into being from seeing the light; and if any force a way to the birth, the parents must understand that the offspring of such an union can not be maintained, and arrange accordingly.[7]

Here Plato recommends both abortion and infanticide when "necessary." Although he believed that the fetus is a living being,[8] the state's ideals and needs take precedence over the life and rights of the unborn.[9]

Aristotle (384–322 B.C.) proposed a similar plan in his *Politics.* After introducing his subject (books 1–3) and discussing political realities (books 4–6), Aristotle revealed his "ideal" politics (books 7–8), "the most desirable form of life" for the individual and the state.[10] To produce the finest human material, the state must regulate marriage: marital age, number and spacing of children, physical conditions for procreation and pregnancy, and quality of children. In that context he writes:

> Let there be a law that no deformed child shall be reared; but on the ground of number of children, if the regular customs hinder any of those born being exposed, there must be a limit fixed to the procreation of offspring, and if any people have a child as a result of intercourse in contravention of these regulations, abortion must be practiced on it before it has developed sensation and life; for the line between lawful and unlawful abortion will be marked by the fact of having sensation and being alive.[11]

Aristotle calls for the accepted practice of infant exposure (abandonment to death) but realizes that others will not always agree; he nevertheless demands a limit to family size. Once the limit is potentially surpassed by a new pregnancy, however, abortion becomes compulsory in his ideal society.

Though Aristotle in the *Politics* did distinguish between "lawful and unlawful" abortions based on whether or not the fetus was alive, in that work he did not provide criteria for determining this. According to another of his works, life is present in a fetus when distinct organs have been formed: forty

---

From Michael J. Gorman, "The Pagan World," *Abortion and the Early Church.* Copyright © 1982 Inter-Varsity Press. Reprinted by permission of the author.

days after conception of males, ninety days for females.[12] His distinguishing between a fetus with sensation and life and one without finds parallels in other philosophers and in the Greek Septuagint version of Exodus 21:22–23, sources which influenced some later Christian writings. Aristotle's differentiation was made fundamentally from a legal perspective, however, not from a moral perspective as later occurred among the Christians he influenced.

Why did both Plato and Aristotle support abortion? It is highly unlikely that either philosopher condoned abortion generally or for personal convenience. Rather, each held a utilitarian view of the individual, born or unborn, seeing that individual as existing for the state. No rights granted to the individual were absolute. All rights—even the right to life—were subordinate to the welfare of the state (or the family, the religion or the race) and had to be sacrificed if the best interests of the state demanded it. Because territory was limited, one major concern for Greek city states was the problem of overpopulation and consequent poverty and weakness. This concern at least partially explains the philosopher's application of their utilitarian and subordinate view of the individual to the newborn or unborn, issuing in admonitions to expose or abort those that might be useless or damaging to the state.

Evidence for the positions of other Greek philosophical schools is slim. One important fact which is preserved is that the Stoics believed that the fetus is part of the mother and that life begins only with the fully developed infant's taking its first breath.[13] Given this viewpoint, one would expect the Stoics not to have opposed abortion, but if a first-century A.D. Stoic comment reflects earlier opinion, just the opposite was true. Musonius Rufus referred to abortion as "detrimental to the common good" and an act of impiety; he approved of the laws against it.[14] We know that Musonius and his predecessors supported large families, a fact which explains their opposition to abortion even though they believed the fetus is not a person. Although the Stoics differed from Plato and Aristotle, they all shared a common view of the welfare of the family and state—not the rights or life of the unborn—as the foremost consideration in the question of the propriety of abortion. Despite their antiabortion position, the Stoics' view of the beginning of human life, coupled with philosophical support for abortion, challenged Christian thinkers in later years.[15]

The later Stoics may have been influenced by the religious beliefs of the Orphics, who were the first Greeks to be concerned with the unborn's fate. This concern was prompted by an eschatology based on the idea that there is a normal cycle of life and death and a subsequent bodiless existence of the soul. People who die prematurely—such as those aborted—are doomed to an evil fate after death. This belief led to a condemnation of abortion, exposure and infanticide.[16]

Only one other Greek religious view of abortion is known. Several Greek inscriptions at public and private temples throughout the Mediterranean world mention birth, miscarriage and abortion as things which cause ritual, though not moral, impurity. After such events, a period of purification and abstinence from worship was required.[17] As in law and philosophy and probably also in medicine, no specific concern for the unborn is manifested.

The extent to which abortion was actually practiced in Greece is difficult to determine, but there are reasons to believe that it was not rare. The very fact of its being mentioned in a variety of contexts, the need to avoid overpopulation, and the frequency of infanticide and exposure (the latter with only rare condemnation) suggest that abortion was widely practiced. Though exposure may have been the preferred Greek method of controlling population quantity and quality, abortion was also useful. . . .

Writing and Discussion Topics

Questions 1–6 address content, critical analysis, personal choices, ethical options, specific discipline, and interdisciplinary alternatives, respectively.

1. Why might philosophers such as Plato and Aristotle favor abortion even against the advice of physicians?
2. What are the arguments, according to Gorman, made by Plato and Aristotle that placed the interests of society above those of the individual citizens?
3. Do you agree with the view that poverty and overcrowding make some abortions legal? Defend your answer.
4. Gorman says that Plato and Aristotle took a utilitarian approach to the abortion issue. Examine how they might also argue for abortion from an ethic of virtue.
5. We know the early Greeks supported abortion, but what direct evidence does Gorman have that Plato and Aristotle supported abortion?
6. Compare and contrast this historical writing with the Supreme Court opinion of Justice Blackmun.

Notes

1. On exposure in ancient Greece see Aristotle *Politics* 2. 6; 7. 16; Plato *Republic* 5; A. Cameron, "The Exposure of Children and Greek Ethics," *The Classical Review* 46, no. 3 (July 1932): 105–14.
2. Hippocrates, *Works,* 3 vols., Loeb Classical Library (London, 1923–27), 1: 291–92.
3. Huser, *Canon Law,* pp. 4–5, especially n. 12.
4. See Cameron, "Exposure," p. 110, and Waszink, "Abtreibung," 57.
5. Harold O. J. Brown, "What the Supreme Court Didn't Know," *Human Life Review* 1, no. 2 (Spring 1975): pp. 12–13.
6. Huser, *Canon Law,* pp. 4–5.
7. Plato *Republic* 5.9.
8. Plutarch *De placitis philosophorum* 5.15.
9. This point is made by Waszink, "Abtreibung," 56, and Crahay, "Les Moralistes," p. 23.
10. Aristotle *Politics* 7. 1. 1.
11. Aristotle *Politics* 7. 14. 10.
12. Aristotle *Historia animalium* 7. 3.
13. Hardon, "Euthanasia and Abortion," p. 93. See also Dölger, "Das Lebensrecht," p. 21.
14. Musonius Rufus *Discourse* 15.
15. Hardon, "Euthanasia and Abortion," p. 93.
16. Orphic concern for the unborn is noted by Waszink, "Abtreibung," col. 55. For Orphic influence on Stoicism, see Cameron, "Exposure," pp. 109–11.
17. Dölger, "Das Lebensrecht," pp. 15–20; Waszink, "Abtreibung," 56; Cameron, "Exposure," p. 108; Crahay, "Les Moralistes," pp. 16–17. These inscriptions date from several centuries before Christ to several centuries after.

Linda Gordon

THE PROHIBITION ON BIRTH CONTROL
and
THE CRIMINALS
◆◆◆

Linda Gordon Courtesy of
Linda Gordon.

*L*inda Gordon is the Florence Kelley Professor of History at the
University of Wisconsin in Madison. She is a graduate of
Swarthmore College and Yale University. Her scholarship and writing
are on the history of women, families, and the working class. "The
Prohibition on Birth Control" and "The Criminals" are chapters from
her book, Woman's Right, Woman's Body: A Social History of Birth
Control. ◆

The Prohibition on Birth Control

Although birth control is very old, the birth-control movement is young, with less than two centuries behind it. In the nineteenth century, when the movement began, birth control had become immoral and illegal with legal dangers so great that propaganda on the subject was written and distributed anonymously. Birth-control advocates were sentenced to jail terms for violation of obscenity laws. A campaign for freedom of speech and freedom of the press, therefore, became part of the modern birth-control movement. To understand these struggles we must first understand something about the nature and sources of censoring ideology.

Birth control* has always been socially regulated in some way. This is because birth control has consequences for two social issues crucial to overall social development: sexual activity and population size. Birth control bears, too, on a third social phenomenon: the role of women. Women's status cannot be correlated to a one-on-one basis with any particular system of regulation. But if the connections between social patterns of sexual activity and female activity are complex, they are nonetheless close. Systems of sexual control change as women's status changes; they both reflect and affect each other. There has been an especially strong causal connection between the subjection of women and the prohibition on birth control: the latter has been a means of enforcing the former. . . .

The prohibition of birth control required constant reinforcement because some women have always wished to limit and space their pregnancies, a motive at times overwhelming their understanding of the need for large families. Legal prohibitions and sanctions could suppress birth-control propaganda but could not stop birth-control use. Private practices could more effectively be altered by convincing the individuals themselves that birth control was immoral, and in this task religious ideologies played

the major role. The religious tradition dominant in the United States has been the Judeo-Christian tradition, and thus our focus here.

The ancient Jews had a somewhat mixed attitude toward birth control, which reflected, no doubt their nomadic origins. One method—*coitus interruptus*, or withdrawal—was condemned by the Talmud on the basis of a passage from Genesis:

> And Er, Judah's first-born was wicked in the sight of the Lord; and the Lord slew him. And Judah said unto Onan: "Go in unto they brother's wife, and perform the duty of a husband's brother unto her, and raise up seed to thy brother!" And Onan knew that the seed would not be his; and it came to pass, whenever he went in unto his brother's wife, that he used to spill it on the ground, lest he should give seed to his brother. And the thing which he did was evil in the sight of the Lord; and He slew him also.[1]

From the sin of Onan came the word "onanism," later applied by Christian theologians to both masturbation and all nonprocreative intercourse. The Talmudic tradition, however, interpreted it much more narrowly. Some scholars argue for a literal reading of the passage, in which Onan's crime consists specifically in refusing to perform the required levirate marriage† and impregnate his brother's wife. Most Talmudists hold that the passage forbade any form of "unnatural intercourse," their descriptions of that process mostly referring to ejaculation outside the vagina.[2] Contraception that did not interfere with "correct" heterosexual intercourse was, however, permitted in some cases in ancient Jewish law, and the Talmud itself prescribed two methods—a potion called the Cup of Roots‡ and a vaginal sponge.[3] Drinking the Cup of Roots was permitted to women and forbidden to men, because the responsibility for propagation was laid on men but not on women.[4] Thus ironically, in male supremacist law, women because of their very insignificance became free to practice birth control.

The permissibility of contraception in ancient Jewish law is part of a relatively relaxed attitude toward sexuality. For the ancient Jews, sexual abstinence was never a virtue. Marriage was not a necessary evil, but a *mitzvah*, a religious duty; and within

"The Prohibition on Birth Control" and "The Criminals" are from *Woman's Right, Woman's Body: A Social History of Birth Control in America*, 2d edition by Linda Gordon. Copyright © 1990 Viking-Penguin, New York. Reprinted by permission of the author.

*It bears repeating that birth control, in this book, means any kind of action taken to prevent having children, including not only abortion and infanticide but also periodic or even sustained sexual abstinence if it is done with that intent. Contraception, by contrast, will be used to refer to specific devices or chemicals or medicines used to prevent conception.

†Custom by which the brother or next of kin to a deceased man was bound to marry the widow.
‡According to the Talmud, the Cup of Roots was made of Alexandrian gum, liquid alum, and garden crocus, pulverized together.

marriage the husband had the duty not only to procreate but also to give his wife sexual satisfaction. At times when conception would be either impossible (as with a sterile woman) or dangerous, the Jewish husband nevertheless had the obligation to continue having sexual relations with his wife.[5] Indeed, the Talmud is somewhat egalitarian on sexual matters, treating men and women as having equal sexual needs, in contrast to its male-supremacist assumptions in most other areas. This may be connected to the fact that population expansion was neither a religious priority nor an economic necessity for the ancient Jews, since the sexual suppression of women had been partly a means of enforcing frequent motherhood upon them.

In contrast to the Jews, the Christians gradually evolved a total condemnation of birth control, a condemnation integral to the over-all Catholic attitude toward sexuality and women. The general hostility to women, sex, and birth control did not appear immediately, however. The Christianity of Jesus, in terms of the status of women in his historical period, was, to a revolutionary extent, pro-woman. Never before had a religion argued the universal equality of human beings. Jesus' respectful behavior toward women was often astonishing to contemporary others. Even the notorious anti-woman declarations of the Pauline tradition ("Let a woman learn in silence and with submissiveness. I permit no woman to teach . . .", "and Adam was not deceived, but the woman was deceived . . .," and so forth) are much worse as they have been used, out of context, by misogynistic churchmen; Paul himself was preoccupied with order and the good image of his new religion, and his pronouncements against women were conventional at worst.[6]

The early Christians developed an ascetic ideal that rejected sexual pleasure as the most evil of many evil pleasures, but at first it was not exclusively directed at the suppression of women. The Christian ascetics sought righteousness through mortifying themselves, not women. St. Paul's ideal was celibacy. When this was impracticable—"It is better to marry than to burn,"* after all—there was no condemnation of sexual enjoyment within marriage.

> Let the husband render to his wife what is due to her, and likewise the wife to her husband . . . You must not refuse each other, except perhaps by

consent, for a time, that you give yourselves to prayer, and return together again lest Satan tempt you because you lack self-control. But this I say by way of concession, not commandment.[7]

The Church Fathers developed these antisexual attitudes in new directions. In the first place, they had to be concerned with reproduction and with increasing the number of Christians. Paul had been able to recommend celibacy freely, since he expected the second coming imminently; Augustine, four centuries later, was more skeptical about the Messiah's imminent arrival and wanted to strengthen his religion. He distinguished for the first time in the Christian tradition between lust and procreation in order to condemn the former entirely, for married and unmarried people alike. Sexual intercourse, according to Augustinian thought, was inherently evil and could be justified only if procreation was its intent. The sexual drive itself was evil, laid as a burden upon man as a result of the Fall. Augustine's image of hell was "the burning of lust."[8] The pleasure of sex created a constant temptation to indulge in it for the wrong reasons. Best, perhaps, would have been to try to make the necessary procreative intercourse as pleasureless as possible. Couples that used an "evil appliance" to prevent propagation were not worthy of the name man and wife, were no longer covered by the license of matrimony, so to speak; they were in mortal sin. Augustine specifically condemned the "rhythm method" to avoid conception.[9]

In the thirteenth century Thomas Aquinas dogmatized and codified the idea that even within marriage sexual intercourse was justifiable only for procreation. Every act of intercourse was a sin unless performed with a reproductive intent.[10] That point of view was reaffirmed by Pope Pius XI in 1930 in the encyclical *Casti connubii*: the goods of marriage, it said, are offspring, fidelity, and sacrament, and offspring is the primary one[11]. . . .

Although individual women did use birth control despite this powerful prohibition, there was never an organized challenge to the ideology of motherhood until industrialization created a new economic system that did not require a high birthrate.

Several factors have made a lower birthrate economically advantageous in the more developed parts of the world in the last five centuries. They include improved diet and sanitation and thus a decline in the death rate, particularly the infant-mortality rate. Even before medical progress, however, mainly a

---

*That is, to burn with passion.

nineteenth- and twentieth-century phenomenon, social changes made smaller families more desirable. A money economy, high costs of living for city dwellers, and the decreasing relative economic contribution that children could make reversed the traditional family economy and made children cost more than they could contribute. Some social groups were affected by these changes before others, perhaps the earliest being professionals who had to live on salaries (in contrast to those who lived on the land, which could absorb children's labor power) and to cope with the high cost of education if their children were to inherit their status.[12] Gradually urbanization produced a decline in the birthrate among all classes. . . .

Greater public approval of birth control during the Renaissance was produced not by a smaller family ideal but by a higher valuation of extramarital sex. For this very reason the impact of the Renaissance in changing sexual values was probably confined to men of wealth and power. But since that group produced a significant literature about its new values, there is some evidence already (and undoubtedly much more to be found) about birth-control use. Pierre de Brantôme (1540–1614), a French courtier, chronicler, and abbé, in describing the sexual promiscuity of court life, wrote: "There are some who have no desire to receive the seed, like the noble lady who said to her lover, 'Do what you will, and give me delight, but on your life have a care to let no drop reach me.' Then the other must watch out for the right moment."[13] What is new in such expressions is not technique—withdrawal is as old as sexual intercourse itself, no doubt—but the proudly hedonistic attitude behind it. There were also new technological developments, however, as the rediscovery of pagan medical technology brought Arab and Persian contraceptive recipes to the attention of the educated.

During the Renaissance the men of new wealth—the bourgeoisie—tried to assimilate and even directly emulate the style of the aristocracy in the consumption of luxury goods and sexual pleasure. But as capitalists consolidated their economic dominance, most of them ceased imitating the nobility in favor of establishing new social standards more useful to their economic and political enterprises. These new social standards flowed from the need to develop and reinforce an individual character structure compatible with the new patterns of work and achievement possible under capitalism. Success in business came from willingness to take risks and to accept relative deprivation in the present in return for the hopes of long-range profits. The work of capitalist commerce and industry required discipline, the ability to resist temptations for immediate gratification, a mentality that valued saving and reinvestment, and competitiveness. Bourgeois culture honored the personalities that exemplified these so-called virtues.

These changes were far more profound than those of the Renaissance, for they were produced by an economic revolution that affected nearly the whole Western world and were carried within a mass ideological revolution—the Reformation. Through it new sexual values reached even the artisans and peasants not yet directly influenced by the capitalist mode of production. New Protestant religions supported the new values even among those who did not desert the Catholic Church, by breaking up the hegemony of certain Catholic traditions uncomfortable for capitalism, such as the ban on usury, the hierarchical integration of the Church with the aristocracy, and the monastic ideal. By abolishing confession and making the individual directly responsible to God, Protestantism helped create a new human character structure in which morality and sin were internalized values, enforced by the individual upon himself, a character structure capable of self-denial without external compulsion. . . .

If the confinement of sexuality within the family was more stringent during these early stages of capitalism, it was because the family was economically and socially more important than ever. As long as private property has existed, sex and reproduction have been controlled so as to regularize inheritance procedures. But in agricultural society, the family was less isolated from the larger community than it became under conditions of commerce and industry. For some time, historians accepted the generalization that in preindustrial Europe and America, the extended family was the dominant form—that is, that married children continued to live in the homes of one of their parental families, thus bringing children, grandchildren, cousins, aunts, and uncles under one roof. More recent empirical studies suggest that the nuclear family—only mother, father, and children under one roof—dominated even in many peasant communities. To measure family closeness only in terms of who lives under one roof is misleading; relationships of visiting, borrowing, sharing work, and giving emotional and financial support did not depend on living in one house.

Puritan attitudes toward birth control were more relaxed than those of the Catholic tradition. Whereas Luther held to an absolute opposition to birth control,[14] Calvin placed less emphasis on the child-bearing duty of women than Luther had and taught that procreation was not the primary purpose of marriage.[15] The later Protestant tradition did not include the constant attacks on these "unnatural practices" found in the Catholic Church. The reasons for the lack of vigilance against birth control are double: first, this was the period in which some communities of people developed, for the first time, an economic interest in smaller families; and second, the potential of birth control to promote sexual license was checked by more rigid enforcement of sexual chastity itself.

The process of industrialization that began in the eighteenth century set in motion several other social changes that ultimately weakened the Puritan family and sexual norm. Their immediate effect, however, was not to loosen the bonds on women and on human sexual expression but to secularize them and to apply them much more tightly to women than to men. The new cultural form of sexual repression is often called Victorian prudery, and it was the form of sexual repression that the birth-control campaigners had to contend with. . . .

As industrial production drew men out of their homes in socialized workplaces, the economic basis of family unity began to dissolve. In most working-class families, husbands and wives were separated for the greater part of their lives, so their attention was focused on rather different problems and they developed different skills and found different comrades. When women worked in factories, their jobs were almost always sexually segregated. All adult workers became individual employees, each with her or his separate wages. Wives became functionally independent of their husbands while remaining financially dependent. Furthermore, as industry began to produce outside the home what women had once manufactured for themselves, women's work at home became increasingly degraded to mere cleaning, repairing, consuming, and child-raising functions.[16]

Precisely because male authority was being weakened, the stability of the traditional family required the imposition of a repressive ideology. For women as for workers, internalized discipline was needed to supplement economic necessity. Victorian prudery was closely connected to the doctrine of a separate sphere of concerns for women. This notion that women were profoundly different from men—an idea newly emphasized after the late eighteenth century—was simultaneously a description of a new reality: a male-imposed doctrine to keep women from escaping from their homes and a women's adaptation to their new situation.

Because the rationale for Victorian prudery was the great difference between the sexes, its essential definition was the double standard. Seen as a system, Victorian sexual norms did not impose self-denial and chastity on all, but exclusively on women. Meanwhile men created the greatest prostitution industry in history. It is true, of course, that Victorian moralists continued some of the Puritan hostility to play, to spontaneous, unpredictable indulgence in pleasureful activity. Work had to be the first, and often the only, activity of most days; sex was reserved for bedtime, the hours of fatigue. Unlike their Puritan forebears, Victorian moralists argued that sex should be indulged in only for purposes of procreation. In response, men of all classes often patronized brothels rather than seek love with their wives. Sexual matters were slandered as dirty, immoral, and undignified and virtually removed from respectable discussion.

The very essence of Victorian respectability was hypocrisy. This hypocrisy accurately reflected the social function of prudery: an attempt to create in both working-class people and women of all classes a repression convenient for the new capitalist ruling class. (This attempt was complex as it required granting to working-class men some of the privileges of bourgeois men and to upper-class women some of the privileges of their husbands and fathers.) As it affected birth control, prudery was an obstacle partly because it defined any discussion of sexual matters as obscene. But as a system of sexual politics, prudery sought to hamper women's efforts to transcend their home-and-marriage prisons by keeping the burdens of motherhood upon them.

Thus Victorian prudery produced not only a prohibition on sexual discussion but also a cult of "motherhood." This romanticization of motherhood, like prudery itself, had many contributing factors. Partly it was a response of men and women alike to the decreasing permanence of families. New relations of production weakened ties between family members and undermined fathers' authority by making individuals economically independent. Simultaneously relationships outside the family for wage laborers and other big-city dwellers became less permanent and reliable, unlike the community patterns of mutual dependency that had prevailed in precapitalist society. All relationships, familial and otherwise, were increasingly composed of dependencies that were primarily psychological rather than material.* Furthermore, improved transportation and economic incentives to geographical mobility undermined close relationships with neighbors.

All these changes spelled greater freedom for individuals, especially those who had previously been subordinated to a master, such as children, unmarried women, apprentices. But these changes also carried the potential for loneliness and disorientation among individuals, and a resultant instability for the society as a whole which was quite alarming to many nineteenth-century working people, especially those who had recently migrated from nonindustrial areas.

The disintegration of the economic basis of family life in no way ended its necessity as a social institution. On the one hand, the family remained, at least throughout the nineteenth and first half of the twentieth centuries, the primary means of the socialization of children into adults with personalities appropriate to the demands of industrial capitalism . . . . On the other hand, the family was called upon to absorb the heavy strains that the economy placed upon individuals. . . .

Both these familial functions contributed to an intensification of the cult of motherhood, that is, the extension of motherliness to the very definition of femininity. In one function, maternal virtues justified and idealized the restriction of sex within marriage. In another function, the maternal tenderings of wives were now expected to extend beyond their children to their husbands, to turn their homes into soothing, comforting, challengeless escapes* for men returning from exhausting workdays of cut-throat competition and constant vigilance to buy cheap and sell dear, or of grinding physical labor and rigid external control. . . .

In justifying this further specialization of the sexes in the division of labor, nineteenth-century ideologists offered the view that the two sexes were not only different in all things but nearly opposite. It became unfashionable among the educated to say outright that women were inferior. (By contrast a forthright male-supremacist line had dominated most discussions of the sexes, both religious and secular, before the nineteenth century.) Victorian ideology about women included the pretense that the spheres of men and women were separate but equal. This belief, in turn, was part of a larger ideological system in which women, although considered inferior in intellectual, artistic, and physical potential, were told that they were morally superior and that their greater holiness came from their innate capacity for motherliness. Such a division of qualities was convenient for a ruling class that got its profits and achievements by means of which even its own religion disapproved. Only the female half of the population was really expected to act on Christian morality. . . .

The theory of the oppositeness of the sexes was particularly marked in matters of sex. Sex drive became exclusively a part of the masculine sphere of things, and some theories even denied that sex drives existed in women. Female chastity was no longer merely a man's right but now also a woman's destiny, as a naturally asexual being; men were asked merely to moderate the extremes of their powerful sexual urge. Although purity was raised to first place among women's desired virtues, a significant number of working-class women were sacrificed in a different way to the maintenance of male supremacy and the sexual character structure that industrial capitalism created. Prostitutes were available to men of all classes, providing a sop to working-class men similar in function to wives themselves.

The motherhood ideology also defined the extent that sexuality was allowable for women: the only justifiable purpose of sexual intercourse for "respectable" women was reproduction.* The choice for

---

*None of this should be taken to imply that family and community interdependencies vanished quickly or entirely. Many industrial workers to the present day continue to use patterns of sharing and mutual support which may be said to have originated in preindustrial communities but are now used in a fully proletarian manner to adapt to industrial conditions. My argument is only that a tendency toward increased individual independence was noticed and remarked upon by many people in the nineteenth century.

---

*By contrast with the typical workplace-home of the seventeenth century, crowded, hectic, and noisy.

*"Respectable" had originally meant not working with one's hands, which required, among other things, being able to keep servants. Thus originally working-class people were not "respectable" by definition, in the European usage of the term. In the United States, and in Europe in the nineteenth century, there emerged a new concept of respectability which included those of the working class who had adopted the social and moral standards of the bourgeoisie, such as refraining from drunkenness and requiring female virginity until marriage.

women became motherhood or prostitution, as the sexual standards became so rigid that all sexual activity outside of motherhood became identified with (and often in fact led to) prostitution. Supporting this view was the new theory that women had no sex drive (in contrast to the male view of women that had dominated for most of human history—that women had powerful lusts, and in equal contrast to the Puritan view which considered it an obligation of comparable difficulty for both sexes to control their sexual urges). This myth was accommodated to the cult of motherhood through emphasis on the virtue of purity for mothers, and literally identified with motherhood through the idea that the female analog to the male sex drive was the maternal instinct. The chastity and passionlessness of women was expected to prevail within marriage just as outside it. The desire for maternity was presumably the only selfish reason that women submitted, literally, to sexual intercourse; beyond the immediate desire for children their motivation should be to please their husbands.

In the nineteenth century this strange sexual morality was being defined not only by the clergy and the political philosophers, as in previous centuries, but also by the medical profession, a new and powerful source of control over women's lives. Many doctors wrote manuals of sexual conduct aimed at women. These doctors were far from unanimous in their views on female sexuality, and some argued merely for moderation of sexual appetites and practices. Even their moderation, however, served a repressive function: writing prescriptive manuals, attempting to establish moral norms for sexual behavior in as well as outside of marriage, most of the moderates as well as the extremists emphasized the debilitating effects of sexual indulgence, defined normal sexual intercourse as that leading most directly to male orgasm, and opposed contraception.

A more complex matter is the degree of success of the ideologues in making their proposed norms work in practice. After years of assuming that the ministers' and doctors' prescriptions were women's reality, a few historians have lately looked for and found evidence that women's minds and bodies were not mere clay in the hands of their moral censors but remained resistant to this indoctrination. Middle- and upper-middle-class women, the main audience for the prudish sex manuals, in small samples of letters, diaries, and at least one survey by a feminist gynecologist, said that they often enjoyed sex and

experienced orgasm.[17] Furthermore, the mask of prudery stimulated hypocrisy, and many men and women behaved and felt differently in private than in public, no doubt. Still, we know from our own experiences how helpless people can be, even in their own minds, against the norms of beauty, love, and propriety. The euphemistic avoidance of direct discussion of sexual matters made sex appear a dirty fact of life, unavoidable but unpleasant, like excretion. The moral guides urged excluding sex from consciousness as well as from behavior. Women were told that their purity of mind and body would determine not only their fate in the hereafter but also their marriage-ability on earth. Prudery was not merely an ideological system, for the sanctions on women who deviated were material and, often, permanent, such as spinsterhood, desertion, economic ruin, disease, and death. Physical though its basis may be, the sexual drive is susceptible to great variation and control from psychological pressures; and the anxieties attached to sex may well have produced many women who did not experience sexual drive, at least not in a form recognizable to them. Thus, however many individuals were able to resist it, Victorian sexual ideology produced, among the middle classes at least, many other women hostile to and fearful of sex.

The repression of female sexuality may have been accomplished through physical as well as psychological changes. Women learned to hate their own bodies. Many women never undressed, even when alone, and bathed under their shifts. When they submitted sexually to their husbands, they remained clothed; for many women sexual intercourse was reduced to such a quick act of penetration that they never had time to become aroused. People never exposed to sexual stimulation may indeed have had truncated, undeveloped sexual drives. Ill health also contributed to lessening sexual energy. Lack of exercise and confinement indoors made women even of the privileged classes physically weak; terrible working and living conditions made working-class women unhealthy in other, more serious ways. Among fashionable women, heavy corseting may have caused serious and permanent internal damage. The approach to pregnancy ("confinement" it was called and confinement it was, for a pregnant woman was considered indecent in "respectable" circles and was expected not to appear in public) prohibited exercise and weakened muscles, thus making pregnancy and parturition possibly more painful than earlier in history, and canceling out improvements gained through better sanitation and health care. Nothing can be more effective than the fear of painful and dangerous pregnancies and childbirths in depressing sexual interest.

Beyond these obstacles to sexual development, Victorian constraints on women created particular practical problems for birth control. The most effective traditional forms of birth control under women's control required handling one's genitals. The task of inserting a vaginal pessary may have been beyond the emotional capabilities of many nineteenth-century women. Prudery also interfered with the communication of traditional birth-control remedies from one generation to the next. And even the limited ingenuity and basic common sense required for developing home-remedy birth-control techniques may have been blocked by deep psychological fears of thinking about sexual matters.

The factors making birth control immoral were intensifying for the first three quarters of the nineteenth century. Although the rights of women were in many respects greater by the nineteenth century than they had been before in the Western world, the prohibition on birth control and on any open discussion of sexual matters had never been more severe. In 1873 in the United States, birth control was legally prohibited for the first time by the "Comstock law," which forbade the sending of obscene matter through the U.S. mail. Religious and political leaders denounced sexual immorality increasingly after midcentury. The greater sexual repression was primarily a response to growing rebellion against the Victorian sexual system. That rebellion, as we shall see, was closely connected to the feminist movement that arose in the 1840s—and the two rebellions had common causes. The two rebellions were related as the two forms of repression—the repression of sex and the subjugation of women—were related. . . .

Notes

1. Genesis, 38: 7–10.
2. Norman Himes, *Medical History of Contraception* ([1936] New York: Gamut Press, 1963), pp. 71–73; David M. Feldman, *Birth Control in Jewish Law* (New York: New York University Press, 1968), Chapter 8.
3. Feldman, *Birth Control*, pp. 169–70. Recipe and indications for the Cup of Roots are given in the *Babylonian Talmud, Tractate Shabbath*, trans. I. Epstein (London: Soncino Press, 1938), 109b–111a, II, pp. 532–39.
4. Feldman, *Birth Control,* Chapter 3 passim, p. 53 particularly. This is discussed in the *Babylonian Talmud, Seder Nashim, Tractate Yebamoth,* trans. Israel W. Slotki (London: Soncino Press, 1936), 65b–66a, I, pp. 436–40.
5. Feldman, *Birth Control*, pp. 297–98 and passim.
6. Mary Daly, *The Church and the Second Sex* ([1968] New York: Harper Torchbooks, 1975), pp. 79–82.
7. Quoted in John J. Noonan, Jr., *Contraception: A History of Its Treatment by Catholic Theologians and Canonists* (Cambridge: Harvard University Press, 1965), p. 42.
8. Quoted in Demosthenes Savramis, *The Satanizing of Woman*, trans. Martin Ebon (Garden City, New York: Doubleday, 1974), p. 51.
9. Ibid,., Chapter 7; Glanville Williams, *The Sanctity of Life and the Criminal Law* (New York: Knopf, 1957), pp. 51–57.
10. Savramis, *Satanizing of Woman*, Chapter 7; Williams, *Sanctity of Life,* p. 55; Noonan, *Contraception*, pp. 240 ff.
11. Noonan, *Contraception*, p. 426.
12. Joseph Ambrose Banks, *Prosperity and Parenthood: A Study of Family Planning among the Victorian Middle Classes* (London: Routledge & Kegan Paul, 1954).
13. Quoted in Himes, *Medical History of Contraception*, p. 190.
14. Noonan, *Contraception*, p. 353.
15. Vern Bullough, *The Subordinate Sex* (Urbana: University of Illinois Press, 1973), p. 199.
16. There have been no overall studies of the rise of industrial capitalism from the perspective of women, but my interpretation has been influenced by Alice Clark, *The Working Life of Women in the 17th Century* (London: Routledge, 1919).
17. For the findings of the survey and on the medical opposition to Victorian prudish extremism, see Carl N. Degler, "What Ought to Be and What Was: Women's Sexuality in the Nineteenth Century," *American Historical Review*, Winter 1974, pp. 1467–90. For other evidence of women's resistance to prudery, see Chapter 5.

The Criminals

The widespread popular knowledge of birth-control technique, combined with the inherently private nature of sexual intercourse, made birth control difficult to suppress. Long before the emergence of an organized, explicit social movement for birth control, individual women, groups of women friends, and couples defied the birth-control prohibition. The prohibition never did what it was intended to do. Rather it forced women underground in their search for reproductive control. It transformed traditional behavior into criminal behavior and thereby attached to birth control some of the characteristics of all criminal activity: it raised the cost and lowered the quality of birth-control practice. Before we can appreciate the significance of the birth-control movement we must take a look at the experience of ordinary women forced to become criminals as they practiced birth control. . . .

Abortion and Infanticide

Systematic study of women's diaries of the eighteenth and nineteenth centuries may reveal more evidence of birth-control practices. The evidence of abortion and infanticide is easier to get, because those practices were criminal and often prosecuted when discovered. This evidence still misses a great deal, since most abortions undoubtedly occurred safely and without detection. Still, the criminal evidence offers a reasonably representative suggestion of the motives and circumstances under which women used these destructive kinds of birth control.

The stigma on illegitimacy frequently drove unmarried women to commit infanticide. Julia Spruill, writing on women in the Southern colonies, found three cases of infanticide reported in the *Maryland Gazette* on one day in 1761. In two of the three cases the mother was identified and arrested, in a third the child's body remained unidentified. It was, of course, difficult to prove whether a child had been murdered or stillborn, and the legislation dealing with this problem—such as making it a crime to conceal a child's death—suggests that the problem was large. Women convicted were usually hanged.[1]. . .

Infanticide was still a regular occurrence in urban American society in the mid-nineteenth century.[2] Thomas Low Nichols, writing in the 1860s, speculated that the huge amounts of laudanum being sold were used not just to quiet crying children but also to kill infants painlessly.[3] Fifteen-year-old Mary Turtlot, for instance, working as a domestic for a well-to-do farm family in Warren County, New York, became pregnant by the son; her pregnancy discovered, she was discharged. The son gave her the address of a New York City abortionist, which he got from a cousin living in the city. Arriving there penniless, she persuaded the doctor to take her in as a domestic in return for his medical help; she remained in the doctor's house until arrested after the police found a seven-day-old child dead in the house.[4] Poor women like this, trapped by a double standard about sexual sin, became murderers.

Abortion was much more common than infanticide, however. This excerpt from a letter by an unmarried woman schoolteacher in South Hadley, Massachusetts, in 1859, to her parents in Derry, New Hampshire, suggests an acceptance of abortion as a common event: "Alphens' wife has been up here with her mother all summer. Poor Alphens he has got so poor that he cant keep house so he sent his wife to live on his father all winter—her poor health was caused by getting rid of a child as I suppose Alphens didn't feel able to maintain another one you must not say anything as I have only guessed it she was very large when she came here and in a short time she shrank to her normal size."[5] Elisa Adams, the author of this letter, was a rural, upper-middle-class, respectable young woman with strong family and community ties, not a poor, lonely immigrant girl in a big city. If Elisa Adams knew that women, married women, had abortions, one might suspect that the phenomenon was somewhat widespread. In 1871 Dr. Martin Luther Holbrook wrote that American women were "addicted" to the wicked practice, and that it was especially widespread in New England,[6] where the decline in the birthrate among Yankees was most pronounced. One antiabortion propagandist, in a style clearly intended to repel and frighten, wrote: "Nowadays, if a baby accidentally finds a lodgement in the uterus, it may perchance have a knitting-needle stuck in its eyes before it has any."[7] In 1871 *The New York Times* called abortion "The Evil of the Age."[8]

Part of the reason for the matter-of-factness of Elisa Adams's letter was that most abortions were safe and successful. This is one of the most important lessons both of anthropological studies and of recent studies of the contemporary illegal abortion industry. There is probably more misunderstanding about abortion safety today than earlier in history, because the campaign for legalized abortion has naturally tended to exaggerate the mortality rate from illegal abortion. In fact, illegal abortions in this country have an impressive safety record. The Kinsey investigators, for example, reported themselves impressed with the safety and skill of the abortionists they surveyed. Today more women die in childbirth than from abortions.[9] That was undoubtedly true in the mid-nineteenth century America also.

This does not mean that abortions were pleasant. They were usually quite painful, and they were sources of anxiety because they were gotten in sin, and, often, isolation. The physical risk was heightened by the illegality, just as it is today. Women facing childbirth also feared death, but the fear of dying alone, humiliated, unacknowledged in an abortion was a terrible ordeal. But if the risks were great, they were also calculated risks. Women knew them and still chose abortions in massive numbers. We must keep in mind that many nineteenth-century women and almost all women before that did not believe that abortion was a sin. Before the nineteenth century there were no laws against abortion done in the first few months of pregnancy. Until then the Protestant churches had gone along with the Catholic tradition that before "quickening"— the moment at which the fetus was believed to gain life—abortion was permissible.* The reversal of this tradition and the antiabortion legislation of the mid-nineteenth century did not immediately alter the customary belief that an early abortion was a woman's right.

In the 1870s, when a campaign of antiabortion propaganda had stimulated investigation, *The New York Times* estimated that there were two hundred full-time abortionists in New York City, not including doctors who sometimes did abortions.[11] It may be that tens of thousands of abortions were done in New York City alone in the 1870s, one judge estimating one hundred thousand a year in the 1890s.[12] In 1881 the Michigan Board of Health estimated one hundred thousand abortions a year in the United States, with six thousand deaths, or a 6 percent mortality rate.[13] In the 1890s doctors were estimating two million abortions a year.[14] In 1921, when statistics on these matters were more reliable, a Stanford University study estimated that one out of every 1.7 to 2.3 pregnancies ended in abortion of which at least 50 percent were criminal.[15] As better

and better statistics have been collected, they tend to suggest that earlier estimates of abortion frequency were far too low, and that the death rate estimate of 6 percent was far too high.

These two errors—underestimating abortions, overestimating deaths—are connected, since most illegal abortions were discovered only if they ended in disaster: if the aborted woman either died or became very ill. The mortality among women from abortions was high, even if small relative to the number of abortions. The most dangerous abortions were usually not the mechanical ones—those done with knitting needles as rudimentary catheters, or by scraping the uterus—but the chemical ones, for internal medicines can cause abortion only as a consequence of general harsh treatment of the body. Yet the advertisements for abortifacients were plentiful. Newspapers printed many ads like these: "Portuguese Female Pills, not to be used during pregnancy for they will cause miscarriage."[16] As the denomination "French" almost always indicated some contraceptive device (a "French letter," as mentioned before, was a condom), so "Portuguese" always referred to an abortifacient. Another standard euphemism for abortion was "relief" or "removing obstacles." "A Great and Sure Remedy for Married Ladies—The Portuguese Female Pills always give immediate relief . . . Price $5 . . ."[17] Many such ads were actually offering emmenagogues, medicines to stimulate menstruation when it was late or irregular. Thus they were often called "Female Regulators" and advertised without mentioning even the euphemisms for abortion.[18] In the 1830s one abortionist, known as Madame Restell, built herself fame and fortune through a veritable abortatorium in a Fifth Avenue brownstone. As she bragged, no doubt with at least some exaggeration, in her own advertisement, "Madame Restell, as is well known, was for thirty years Female Physician in the two principal female hospitals in Europe—those of Vienna and Paris—where, favored by her great experience and opportunities, she attained that celebrity in those great discoveries in medical science so specially adapted to the female frame. . . ."[19]

Abortions through internal medicine were not attempted only by professionals. Folk remedies for unwanted pregnancies were common. Even men knew them, or how to get them. Stories of men dosing their pregnant girlfriends with abortifacients came from all periods of American history. In Maryland in 1652, Susanna Warren, a single woman made pregnant by

---

*Quickening is not the same thing as viability, and most estimates of the time of quickening put it far earlier than the point when life outside the womb was possible. In accordance with general male-supremacist attitudes, the time of quickening was usually set earlier for males than for females, thus in theory giving an advantage to the male population: Aristotle computed it at about forty days after conception for the male, ninety days for the female; Hippocrates put the figures at thirty and forty-two days respectively; the later Roman view was forty and eighty days. How the pregnant woman was to know the sex of her fetus is, however, not explained. The Catholic Church, in accordance with its concerns, identified quickening with the acquisition of a soul, and most Protestant groups had gone along with that definition. Thus abortion before quickening was not only not a crime, but not even a sin.[10]

"prominent citizen" Captain Mitchell, said that he prepared for her a "'potion of Phisick,' put it in an egg, and forced her to take it. . . ." It didn't work and she brought charges against him![20] Slaves practiced abortion commonly. An antebellum doctor wrote that it was four times as frequent among blacks as among whites, and that "all country practitioners are aware of the frequent complaints of planters from this subject."[21] Though the doctor may have been underestimating the prevalence of abortion among whites, it seems at least possible that the rather exceptionally unpleasant conditions of child-raising for slave women might have made them reluctant to bear children.*

Abortions, then as now, were most common among the married and seemed frequent in all classes.[22] In 1862, when the wife of Confederate General William Dorsey Pender wrote him that unfortunately she was pregnant, he wrote her pious phrases about "God's will" but also sent her pills which his camp surgeon had thought might "relieve" her.[23]

One of the best ways to get a clear picture of a nineteenth-century abortion is to examine a particular case rather fully. The transcript of the trial of Dr. William Graves of Lowell, Massachusetts, in 1837, for the murder of Mary Anne Wilson of Greenfield, New Hampshire, offers us such a view.[24]

> *Testimony of Dr. James S. Burt:* Sometime in May latter part, 1837, I was in Greenfield and was called to see Mrs. Wilson. She said she was in a family way and wished to get relieved of her burden. I told her I had rather not give medicine for that purpose, that it would injure health or life. She said she had sent to Lowell for medicine and got a box of pills for that purpose . . . . she brought forward the box—I examined it—there were about two or three dozen common sized pills—she said it had been full. I told her she was injuring her health by doing so, and she had better not take any more of them—I also advised her to see the young man who had done it, tell him her situation and he would do the thing that was right. She said she had, but he seemed to be bashful or ugly and wouldn't do anything. I asked her how long she had been in this situation and she said about 4 months . . . . she said then she would go to Lowell, for she was informed there was a physician there who would perform this operation with safety.

---

*Indeed, if the doctor's figures are true, one would be practically forced to entertain the possibility that abortion among slaves was not only a tool of self-preservation, but also a form of resistance.

> I asked her how she came by her news or information and she said she heard it from good authority and that it could be performed without danger and that in 4 or 5 days, she could go about her daily employ. I then told her this is a folly—it will endanger your life, your health at any rate, and I advise you not to go—it may be done, but not without danger. I then said death is your portion if you do go, in my opinion, and you had better not go. . . .

> *Testimony of Elizabeth Bean:* I am a sister of Mary Anne Wilson . . . . I opened her trunk when it came back from Lowell—in it was a little slip of paper on which was written "Dr. Graves, Hurd street, No. 7." (The witness produces the paper.) It was folded together and fastened with a needle. . . .
>
> She had been married and was a widow. She had been a widow 4 years next January. . . . Mrs. Wallace her daughter and son lived in the house with my sister. In her own family lived Mr. Isaac Pollard and one child of her own, 3 years old last June. . . . It was understood in the family that Mrs. Wilson was courted by Mr. Pollard . . . for 2 years. . . .

> *Testimony of N. H. G. Welton* [stage-driver]: I left a lady at Dr. Graves's last summer. . . . I left her just at twilight. I rang the bell for Dr. Graves; he was not in; but just that moment he came up, and I said Dr, here is a lady to see you. . . . I heard the Dr. say as I left them, "well, well, walk in and I will see."

> *Testimony of Lucinda Sanborn:* I have lived at Dr. Graves's for nearly 1 1/2 years, and my business is to take charge of the house and doing the whole of the work. . . . The Monday before her death in the evening she was not so well, and Monday night she became very sick, and the abortion took place. She had severe pain in her back and bowels. . . . The abortion took place while she was in bed; we took her off, laid her onto another bed and removed the sheet. . . . We raked open the ashes in the fireplace and put the contents of the sheet into it and covered them up. . . . There was something that looked like a child which we found on the sheet. The after birth was with it. This was never removed from the fireplace; it was rather chilly, and I built up a small fire afterwards.

> *Testimony of Dr. Hanover Dickey, Jr.:* I lived at Dr. Graves's from June 17 to August 19, and boarded in the family. . . . I have previously studied with Dr. Graves. . . . I chose to go into that room from curiosity . . . I went in and found the . . . lady there on the bed. . . . She said she thought herself 3 months or more advanced in pregnancy. . . . She said she did not know but she should have

been freed the night before from her embarrassment. I don't know as she used the word embarrassment, but something referring to her pregnancy. . . . I saw her again Saturday, August 19 forenoon . . . —her hair was not adjusted—everything betokened suffering—her general appearance, dress and countenance—great suffering—mental and bodily. She made two statements to me—one was that she tho't should she would die—the other that she tho't her difficulties would subside, and that she should be well and be able to go home in a few days. . . .

Mary Anne Wilson died on August 24, after three weeks alone in Dr. Graves's house, without communication from her parents, sisters, child, or lover. At her death, Graves hired some Lowell men to bring her in her coffin to Greenfield and turn her over to Pollard. He told her family that she died in Boston of a "cholera morbus." But when her relatives initiated investigation, having found Graves's address—in Pollard's writing—in her trunk, Pollard disappeared.

Think of Mary Anne Wilson: widowed four years, supporting herself and child with millinery, "courted" by a boarder for two years but unable or unwilling to get his support for a child. Hardly a promiscuous woman, she paid very heavily for her "sin." Graves was convicted. It seemed he did a lot of business with people who lived "on the Appleton Corporation"—the Lowell mills. We do not know his sentence.

Although the notion of quickening was still popularly accepted during the first half of the nineteenth century, many states had already made abortion at any stage of fetal development a crime. This legislation was a severe blow to women, since abortions were usually performed in the early stages of pregnancy anyway. Indeed, next to the long tradition that abortion was a crime only after quickening, these laws appear as a repeal of a time-honored *right* of women.*

But despite the new laws, criminal abortionists were not only operating publicly, they were being acquitted by juries.[26] An antiabortion doctor complained in the 1860s: "In consequence of this

professional and most criminal apathy, public sentiment has become more and more blunted, until it is now given as a reason [of nonprosecution] by the public prosecuting officers that a jury could not be found in Boston to convict of this crime, even in the most flagrant and indisputable cases of maternal death."[27] In 1903 another doctor wrote that abortionists were everywhere "sheltered by the sympathy of the community."[28]

Increasing concern over the abortion "evil" beginning in mid-century led even *The New York Times* to consider this previously unmentionable problem now fit to print. It embarked on a series of investigative reports that reveal something of the workings of the abortion industry. The professional abortionists who advertised in the papers were often medical imposters—that is, they lacked medical degrees. On the other hand, diploma mills had been developed which sold fake degrees. Frequently the abortionists used many aliases, sometimes to avoid old prosecutions, sometimes to operate several establishments simultaneously under different names. Sometimes a woman would be named in the advertisement and might work with a male doctor, as women seeking help would be more likely to approach another woman. These two ads ran simultaneously in the *New York Herald:* "Madame Grindle, Female Physician, guaranteeing relief to all female complaints . . ." and "Ladies' Physician—Dr. H. D. Grindle, professor of midwifery . . . guarantees certain relief to ladies in trouble, with or without medicine; sure relief to the most anxious patient at one interview; elegant rooms for ladies requiring nursing. . . ."[29]

The Grindles, who catered to an upper-class clientele, asked $300 for an abortion.[30] But abortion transcended class distinctions. The abortion industry was highly stratified, and standards of cost and treatment varied enormously. Some advertisements offered medicines for five dollars. A Dr. Kemp, of Twenty-third St. at Seventh Avenue, just around the corner from the Grindles, charged ten dollars and promised to return half if the abortion wasn't successful; and indeed he did return five dollars to one patient, twenty-year-old Anna Livingston.[31] Some physicians kept an expensive office for rich ladies and a cheaper one for poor women. Much of the resentment against Madame Restell had a class basis. Once she was almost imprisoned, but "her lawyer stayed proceedings by a bill of exceptions, and now she rides over one of her judges, tosses up her beautiful head,

---

*The first legislation banning abortion altogether did not originate in Catholic canon law, as is widely believed, but in the secular law of England in 1803. The Catholic Church only legislated similarly in 1869, and in the United States most states had outlawed all abortions during the Civil War period.[25]

and says in effect, 'behold the triumph of virtue!' Instead of a linsey woolsey petticoat . . . she is gloriously attired in rich silks and laces, towers above her sex in a splendid carriage, snaps her fingers at the law and all its pains and penalties, and cries out for more victims and more gold. . . ."[32]

Not all abortionists were disreputable. Dr. Graves, of the 1837 Lowell trial, had the best credentials available at the time. A Dr. Cutter, tried for abortion in Newark in the 1870s, was "one of the best known of the younger physicians in the State."[33] Nearly every physician writing or speaking on the topic would admit to being frequently asked for abortions. Clearly not all refused—at least not all the time; even those who normally refused were undoubtedly sometimes prevailed upon by old patients and friends.

Such was the demand that not even occasional convictions suppressed abortionists' practices. Consider the case of Dr. Henry G. McGonegal. In 1888 he allegedly aborted Annie Goodwin, a young working woman living with her married sister on 126th Street in New York City. When she began to "see" a rich young man, Augustus Harrison, her sister kicked her out, and she went to live with another working girl, Sadie Traphagan. Later that year Annie moved to the boarding house of a Mrs. Collins on 127th Street, but was thrown out of there when discovered to be pregnant. She went to stay with a Mrs. Shaw, washerwoman, of 105th Street, and died there a few days later; her burial permit had been produced by Dr. McGonegal. Witnesses were able to place her in his office. An autopsy proved an abortion and McGonegal was convicted.[34] In that chronology lies the outlines of the fate of many young working women.

Four years later McGonegal, then seventy years old and free on appeal bail, was arrested again, and this time in association with quite a different social class. In this second trial he was alleged to have had the aid of Dr. Marian A. Dale, a graduate of the New York Women's Medical College, forty-four years old, who boarded with McGonegal and shared his practice. Together they called on Mrs. Louisa Webb, the daughter of an old and respected family of Ravenswood, Long Island, mother of one and temporarily staying with her parents. Shortly after their visit she gave birth to a stillborn child and became very ill; a doctor called in by her wealthy parents was able to save her life. They pressed charges against Mc-

Gonegal and Dale and also against her husband, Frank Webb, as accomplice. Frank Webb was of a lower social class than his wife, and worked as a Pinkerton at Homestead.[35]

When the medical establishment undertook a campaign against abortion in the second half of the nineteenth century, its stridence served as a further indication of the prevalence and tenacity of illegal abortions. The medical campaign was a response to several different factors: an increasingly prudish public moralism; higher health standards which made abortion-caused deaths less acceptable; and a desire to consolidate the official medical profession through attacks on unlicensed, quack and dissident physicians who were usually those more sympathetic to abortion. The medical doctors' offensive against abortion included both propaganda and lobbying for more rigorous prosecution of illegal abortionists. In 1857 the American Medical Association initiated a formal investigation of the frequency of abortion. Seven years later the American Medical Association offered a prize for the best popular antiabortion tract. Medical attacks on abortion grew in number and in the intensity of their moral condemnation until by the 1870s both professional and popular journals were virtually saturated with the issue. Physicians particularly bemoaned the widespread lay acceptance of abortion before quickening; in order to break that sympathy, they adopted a vocabulary that described abortion in terms designed to shock and repel.[36] As late as 1901 a doctor consistently referred to abortion as "antenatal infanticide."[37]

Physicians commonly attempted to frighten women away from abortion by emphasizing its dangers. Their common assertion that there was *no* safe abortion may have betrayed ignorance, but more likely it was exaggeration justified by what they believed was a higher moral purpose.[38] Yet occasionally even antiabortion doctors allowed the truth to slip out, revealing despite themselves why their campaign remained ineffective. "It is such a simple and comparatively safe matter for a skillful and aseptic operator to interrupt an undesirable pregnancy at an early date . . . ," wrote Dr. A. L. Benedict of Buffalo, an opponent of abortion, "that the natural temptation is to comply with the request."[39] . . .

When a birth-control *movement* began, the biological unity among women was left far behind. From the first attempts at arguing for the legalization of birth control, the birth-controllers sought reasons and justifications that expressed particular economic, social, ethnic, and even geographical identities as well as concern with the female sex. This difference between the orientation of an individual impulse and a social movement exists with every social issue. This is not only because all individuals are different and must seek their commonness from within many individualities when they choose to work together, but also because social issues are not seen in the same contexts by different persons. Birth control, a simple act of biological self-control for an individual, becomes involved with innumerable overlapping social factors when considered on a mass level. Factors such as ideal family size, wealth, cultural conditioning, religion, marital relations, child-raising arrangements, work necessities, physical space, geographical and climatic conditions mean that different social groups have different attitudes. Sharp and, for most, painful economic changes, increasing interpersonal harshness, new opportunities for women, the replacement of religion by technology—all these and many more things affected people's responses to the birth-control issue. Often, the birth-control campaigners thought they were conducting a universal movement, designed to benefit all women, but they were not, for other social factors overwhelmed women's personal desire for fewer conceptions and made them hostile to birth control. Often, too, the campaigners thought they were conducting a single-issue movement when in reality they were not, for their proposals carried implications for many other things. Perhaps every reform ultimately implies an entire political program. Certainly birth control had implications for sexual relations, for the family as an institution, for the status of women, and for the populations of continents which could not be disguised.

Notes

1. Julia Spruill, *Women's Life and Work in the Southern Colonies* (Chapel Hill: University of North Carolina Press, 1938), pp. 323–25.
2. Horatio Robinson Storer, *Why Not? A Book for Every Woman* (Boston: Lee and Shepard, 1868), pp. 16, 34–35. Also see, for example, *The Police Gazette*, May 28, 1892, for a story typical of its sensationalist reporting: Mary Wertheimer is indicted, along with her two boyfriends, for the death of her three-month-old baby.
3. Thomas Low Nichols, *Human Physiology: The Basis of Sanitary and Social Science* (London: Trübner, 1872), pp. 21–27.
4. *New York Times*, September 4, 1871, p. 8.
5. I am indebted to Joanne Preston for showing me this letter from her family collection.
6. Martin Luther Holbrook, *Parturition Without Pain: A Code of Directions for Escaping from the Primal Curse* (New York: Wood and Holbrook, 1871), p. 16.
7. Quoted in Horatio Robinson Storer, *Criminal Abortion: Its Nature, Its Evidence and Its Law* (Boston: Little, Brown, 1868), pp. 57–58.
8. *New York Times*, August 23, 1871, p. 6.
9. Edwin M. Schur, *Crimes Without Victims; Deviant Behavior and Public Policy: Abortion, Homosexuality, Drug Addiction* (Englewood Cliffs, New Jersey: Prentice-Hall, 1965), pp. 28–29.
10. Glanville Williams, *The Sanctity of Life and the Criminal Law* (New York: Knopf, 1957), pp. 148–52.
11. *New York Times*, August 23, 1871, p. 6.
12. Benjamin Grant Jefferis and J. L. Nichols, *Light on Dark Corners: A Complete Sexual and Science Guide to Purity* (New York, 1894, reprinted 1919 as *Search Lights on Health*), p. 138.
13. Quoted in V. F. Calverton, *The Bankruptcy of Marriage* (New York: Macauley, 1928), p. 187.
14. Jefferis and Nichols, *Light on Dark Corners*, p. 138; A. Lapthorn Smith, "Higher Education of Women and Race Suicide," *Popular Science Monthly*, March 1905, p. 470.
15. Arthur William Meyers, "The Frequency and Cause of Abortion," *American Journal of Obstetrics and Gynecology* 2, no. 2 (August 1921).
16. Quoted in Meade Minnigerode, *The Fabulous Forties* (New York: Putnam, 1924), pp. 101–102.
17. *New York Times*, August 23, 1871, p. 6.
18. For example in Adelaide Hechtlinger, *The Great Patent Medicine Era* (New York: Grosset & Dunlap, 1970), pp. 76 and 188.
19. Quoted in Minnigerode, *Fabulous Forties*, pp. 103–104.
20. Quoted by Spruill, *Women's Life and Work*, pp. 325–26.
21. Dr. E. N. Pendleton, "On the Susceptibility of the Caucasian and African Races to the Different Classes of Disease," in *Southern Medical Reports* 1 (1849): 338.
22. Storer, *Why Not?*, pp. 67–68; Storer, *Criminal Abortion*, p. 58; H. S. Pomeroy, *The Ethics of Marriage* (New York: Funk & Wagnalls, 1888), p. 57.
23. Quoted in Ann Scott, *The Southern Lady: From Pedestal to Politics, 1830–1930* (Chicago: University of Chicago Press, 1970), p. 38.
24. *Examination of Dr. William Graves before the Lowell Police Court from September 25 to September 29, 1837, for the Murder of Mary Anne Wilson . . .*, n.d., n.p.

25. Williams, *Sanctity of Life*, pp. 148–52.
26. Storer, *Criminal Abortion*, pp. 54–55. See also remarks of N.Y. District Attorney at trial of Dr. Michael A. Wolff, January 25–27, 1871, in *New York Times*, January 26, 1871, p. 3.
27. Quoted in M. S. Iseman, *Race Suicide* (New York: Cosmopolitan Press, 1912), p. 137.
28. George J. Engelmann, "Education Not the Cause of Race Decline," *Popular Science Monthly* 63, no. 2 (June 1903).
29. Augustus St. Clair, "The Evil of the Age," *New York Times*, August 23, 1871, p. 6.
30. Ibid.
31. Ibid., February 27, 1872, p. 6.
32. Orson Squire Fowler, *Love and Parentage* . . . (New York: Fowler and Wells, 1844), p. 69.
33. *New York Times*, May 6, 1871, p. 8.
34. Ibid., November 30, 1892, p. 10.
35. Ibid., July 28, 1892, p. 2.
36. Pomeroy, *Ethics of Marriage*, pp. 84–85.
37. Emma Frances Angell Drake, *What a Young Wife Ought to Know* (Philadelphia: Vir Publishing Co., 1901), p. 130.
38. For example, Mrs. R. B. Gleason, *Talks to My Patients* (New York: Wood and Holbrook, 1870).
39. *Medico-Pharmaceutical Critic and Guide* 9, no. 2 (June 1907): 59–63.

Writing and Discussion Topics

Questions 1–6 address content, critical analysis, personal choices, ethical options, specific discipline, and interdisciplinary alternatives, respectively.

1. Why has birth control always been a societal issue? Why did it intensify during the nineteenth century?

2. Trace the major historical developments in abortion. At what point is abortion acceptable? During what periods is it rejected? Use Gordon as a source in reviewing these developments.

3. Do you believe Gordon fairly represents the religious positions on abortion in these pieces?

4. Gordon says that most Christian denominations accepted abortion a century ago. What societal changes, including ethical changes, have occurred that caused some changes in this position?

5. Does Gordon's feminist leaning influence her writing? Using specific passages, explain your answer.

6. Compare and contrast Gordon's observations on abortion with those of Paul VI and Fred Rosner. Does her historical perspective clash with the writings of either of these theologians?

Recommended Readings

Callahan, Daniel. *Abortion: Law, Choice, and Morality*. New York: Macmillan, 1970.

Cohen, Marshall, Thomas Nagel, and Thomas Scanlon, eds. *The Rights and Wrongs of Abortion*. Princeton, N.J.: Princeton University Press, 1970.

Feinberg, Joel, ed. *The Problem of Abortion*, 2d ed. Belmont, Cal.: Wadsworth, 1984.

Grisez, Germain. *Abortion: the Myths, the Realities and the Arguments*. New York: Corpus, 1970.

Kluge Eike-Henner. *The Practice of Death*. New Haven: Yale University Press, 1984.

Noonan, John. *The Morality of Abortion*. Cambridge: Harvard University Press, 1970.

Perkins, Robert L., ed. *Abortion: Pro and Con*. Cambridge, Mass.: Schenkman, 1974.

Summer, L. W. *Abortion and Moral Theory*. Princeton: Princeton University Press, 1981.

Tooley, Michael. *Abortion and Infanticide*. New York: Oxford, 1983.

Recommended Periodical Readings

Armstrong, Robert L. "The Right to Life." *Journal of Social Philosophy* 8 (January 1977): 13–19.

Bok, Sissela. "Ethical Problems of Abortion." *Hastings Center Studies* 2 (January 1974): 33–52.

Englehardt, H. Tristram, Jr. "The Ontology of Abortion." *Ethics* 84 (April 1974): 217–234.

Hare, R. M. "Abortion and the Golden Rule." *Philosophy and Public Affairs* 4 (Spring 1975): 201–222.

Humber, James M. "Abortion: The Avoidable Moral Dilemma." *Journal of Value Inquiry* 9 (Winter 1975): 282–302.

Noonan, John. "Abortion and the Catholic Church: A Summary Theory." *Natural Law Forum*, 12 (1967): 125–131.

Warren, Mary Anne. "On the Moral and Legal Status of Abortion." *Monist* 57 (1973): 102–119.

Zaitchik, Alan. "Viability and the Morality of Abortion." *Philosophy and Public Affairs* 10, no. 1 (1981): 18–24.

chapter 3

WAR & NUCLEAR WAR

In the late 1930s atomic scientists were secretly stationed in the mountains of Los Alamos, New Mexico, under the direction of the United States government. They were assigned the task of employing nuclear fission to design a superior weapon. They were not asked to study the potential social or political problems, the ethical dilemmas, or the human suffering that might be connected with the use of the new weapon. They instead were directed to develop a sophisticated instrument capable of mass destruction. The weapon, as it turned out, was a scientific success. Major research and development of atomic and nuclear weapons has continued in earnest ever since. Today these weapons collectively could destroy human life on this planet several times over.

The prospect of war, and particularly nuclear war, is one of the most troubling ethical dilemmas of our time. The central moral question involved is whether nuclear weapons should ever be used in light of the large-scale and indiscriminate killing of innocent people that would result. What causes of war could ever justify such a virtually assured outcome? Is it likely that the devastation—to all forms of life—rendered by the use of thermonuclear weapons would be so massive that this very devastation is its own decisive objection? While the moral assessment of nuclear warfare covers a range of views, the fundamental issue involved is always the weight one gives to the

THE FAR SIDE By GARY LARSON

"Ooooooooooooooo!"

The Far Side cartoon by Gary Larson is reprinted by permission of Chronicle Features, San Francisco, CA.

extensive and inevitable destruction of life, both human and nonhuman, that would accompany such warfare.

The issues of war present fundamental ethical dilemmas. The disciplines of philosophy, religion, literature, and history can be used to expand our perspectives in the areas of war and nuclear war. Authors included in this chapter examine the issues and controversies, and they present a wide range of positions on war, nuclear war, and nuclear deterrence.

Most of the authors try to provide the best possible solutions for avoiding a nuclear conflict. However, their points of view can and often do conflict. Section one provides an overview of the nuclear disarmament issue. Soviet President Mikhail S. Gorbachev, in his sweeping peace proposal to the United States, offers a step-by-step process to rid the earth of nuclear weapons within the next fifteen years. This excerpt comes from a statement issued during the Reykjavik Summit. In this historically significant document, Gorbachev proposes on-site inspections of missile bases. Moreover, he asks Soviets and Americans to act as examples for the rest of the world with respect to nuclear disarmament. If disarmament and an end to all nuclear-explosion testing are to succeed, this process must be mandatory, he asserts, first for the two superpowers and then for all industrialized powers.

In September of 1991, George Bush, President of the United States, suggested and enacted several disarmament policies for the U.S. Mikhail Gorbachev has said he will implement these same policies and has suggested more moves in disarmament. Both leaders are making changes that could end some of the nuclear threat experienced since the 1940s. A synopsis of Bush's nuclear-policy changes follow Gorbachev's Reykjavik speech.

Carl Sagan's controversial classic, "The Nuclear Winter," predicts the devastation of this planet in the event of even a limited nuclear exchange. Sagan is an absolute pacifist and believes that it is impossible to justify any use of violence against people. He states that human life has absolute value and no other value can supersede it.

Colin S. Gray and Keith Payne emphasize the necessity of nuclear weapons in "Victory is Possible." As experienced military advisors, they argue that the United States can wage nuclear war and survive. They believe that "effective survival" during a nuclear war is possible through sound military planning. Philosophically, they follow the just-war doctrine, asking for counterforce targeting of military compounds. Minimal harm to noncombatants and quick victory are part of their recommended strategy.

Among the philosophy readings, Burton M. Leiser examines the foundations of the just-war concept. This concept has a long and honorable history, dating back to the Middle Ages and late Hellenistic times, and beyond that to biblical ideas. Christian love, for example, may require resisting invading forces in order to protect the innocent. Leiser's discussion of just-war principles includes a corollary, the concept of the unjust war. In addition, he notes the important development of the "laws of war" or rules concerning the conduct of war.

Douglas P. Lackey sets forth a utilitarian view of nuclear arms. He examines three prominent nuclear strategies, concluding that unilateral disarmament is not only the most rational choice but also the moral one. Through utilitarian principles, he argues that the harm and destruction caused by nuclear war is such an immense evil that no good consequences could possibly outweigh it.

James P. Sterba, another philosopher, defends the possession of nuclear weapons. He examines the pacifist, conventionalist, collectivist, and feminist challenges to nuclear deterrence in the light of just-war theory. Sterba holds that it is moral for the United States to possess nuclear weapons, but he does not condone their use.

Some religious writers believe that nuclear weapons make the just-war theory obsolete. The National Conference of Catholic Bishops believes that nuclear war is never morally justified. They state that the resultant massive killings of innocent noncombatants rule out defensive as well as offensive nuclear fighting. The bishops insist that a nuclear war would fail a "just conduct in war" test on two counts: (1) the level of force employed would not be proportional to the good that the action is intended to achieve; and (2) force could not be used in a way that respects the distinction between combatants and noncombatants.

A group of Roman Catholic scientists from Los Alamos, New Mexico, disagrees with the bishops' position. D. E. Carrol and other scientists have been involved in the development of nuclear weapons. They reject both the first strike option and unilateral disarmament, but they encourage the negotiated reduction of nuclear arms. They believe nuclear arms are necessary for three reasons: (1) society requires governments to defend the common good; (2) within limits, self-defense is a moral use of deadly force; and (3) Christian motivation is to establish peace and justice quickly and with minimal force. They state that for the past forty years nuclear weapons themselves have been the strongest deterrent to nuclear war.

David Novak, in examining Jewish perspectives, concludes that nuclear war is immoral. He argues from biblical passages that God will not allow the destruction of the earth again, as is reflected in the story of Noah and the flood. Novak believes that the Divine promise (the covenant between God and Noah) prevents a second global destruction. He does not dismiss, however, the possibility of nuclear war. He urges disarmament among the leaders of the nations of the world. He believes that the money spent on arms could be better spent on humanitarian needs.

Victor Danner explains the Islamic tradition of war. He states that warfare is not a matter of choice for Muslims; it is a necessary part of carrying its religious message to the non-Arab world. A holy war (jihad) has a prescribed set of rules with peace as the eventual goal. The greater jihad is a war in the name of the religion. The lesser jihad is a war for political and protective reasons. A writing by Ayatollah Ruhollah Khomeini adds to this view. To Khomeini, war is meant to promote spiritual values. He points out that Islamic nations historically have had the need to protect their culture, heritage, homes, and religion. Some of the reasoning behind the Islamic religious position is explained by Gholam-Reza Fada'i Araqi. "Islam's objective from war is the establishment of the government of Allah and thus the completion of the process of evolution," says Araqi. Neither Araqi nor Khomeini express views on nuclear arms; they only state the necessity of arms in general. Their firm position comes from passages in the Qur'an, which establish that those who suffer from tyranny possess every right to have the recourse of war. The Qur'an also permits the killing of idolaters and unbelievers who reject Islam and wage war on Islam.

Subjective enactments of war through the eyes of great writers can be found in the discipline of literature. Of course, classic literature on war does not mention the problems of thermonuclear war, but stories, poems, and essays show the trauma found in most war conditions. The heroics, honors, and devastations of war have also been recurring themes. Czeslaw Milosz, a Nobel Prize winner from Poland, examines the naive attitudes of many Americans toward invasion and war. Milosz believes that because Americans have not experienced "world war" invasions on their soil, they do not readily understand what it means to have lost their freedom. Milosz is critical of the moral thinking of Americans, wondering if they even care to understand the ethical consequences of weapons testing, nuclear weapons storage, and actual combat.

In the story "War" by Luigi Pirandello, passengers on a train understand the brutalities and atrocities of war all too well. While comparing notes on the war, they discover that each has suffered a severe loss. The glamour of a war won in the hope of a better life is gone, and the heartbreak of sacrificed life is present.

Richard Lovelace sincerely represents the honor of war in "To Lucasta, Going to the Wars." Pride in the defense of principles, morals, and country seems secondary to the hero's ability to win personal acclaim through battle. Even our hero's lover is replaced by the mistress war.

Mark Twain's "War Prayer" is a poignant comparison between two prayers on war. The first prayer asks the Lord for help in battle and glory for the brave soldiers. The pastor proclaims that there is a duty to go to battle to preserve life. The second prayer is offered by a stranger who says he has a message from God. In typical Twain sarcasm, the stranger prays to the Lord to destroy and to lay waste to the enemy. The second prayer presents the human side of the enemy: the blood to be spilt, the hearts to be broken, the homes to be divided. When the prayer is concluded, the people determine the stranger is crazy.

Isaac Asimov's character, Naron, believes earthlings must be insane to allow nuclear weapons and testing of weapons on their planet. In "Silly Asses," aliens scoff at Earth's ultimate suicide. Asimov's writing demonstrates in a basic way the ultimate danger of nuclear arms.

In a short excerpt from *Late Night Thoughts on Listening to Mahler's Ninth Symphony*, Lewis Thomas expresses his horror at the consequences and destruction caused by nuclear war. He cannot listen to Mahler's piece without feeling the explosion and the resultant suffering of a global, nuclear exchange. His overall theme is that we have many wonders of existence that should be combined with a duty to preserve the planet and human life.

The discipline of history adds different perspectives to nuclear war. In *Children of Hiroshima*, Arata Osada has collected narratives of school children who experienced the day of the atomic explosion in Japan. The children give eyewitness accounts of the blast, and also of the tragedy and destruction that followed. Exposure to the bomb's burning radiation left hundreds of thousands of individuals injured with little prospect for treatment.

Hiroshima, by Marion Yass, details the events that led up to the detonation of the atomic bomb in Japan. In the selection entitled "The Decision to Bomb Japan," Yass links the decision to use the atomic bomb with defective judgments made by American and European leaders. This analysis of the alternatives was far removed from the potential reality of the bomb on human lives. Yass's historical excerpt faults politicians because their desire to avoid loss of human life was merely abstract and consequently counted for little in the decision-making process.

Mikhail S. Gorbachev

NUCLEAR DISARMAMENT BY THE YEAR 2000

◆◆◆

Mikhail Gorbachev   Source: J. Scott Applewhite/Associated Press Photo.

M ikhail Sergeyevich Gorbachev became the youngest president in the history of Communist rule in the Soviet Union. He joined the Communist Party in 1952 and quickly advanced to the ranks of regional positions. In 1971 he became a member of the central committee as secretary for agriculture. In 1985, he became general secretary of the Communist Party's Central Committee. ♦

The Soviet Union proposes that a step-by-step, consistent process of ridding the earth of nuclear weapons be implemented and completed within the next 15 years, before the end of this century. . . .

How does the Soviet Union envisage today in practical terms the process of reducing nuclear weapons, both delivery vehicles and warheads, up to their complete elimination? Our proposals on this subject can be summarized as follows.

Stage One. Within the next 5 to 8 years the USSR and USA will reduce by one half the nuclear weapons that can reach each other's territory. As for the remaining delivery vehicles of this kind, each side will retain no more than 6,000 warheads.

It stands to reason that such a reduction is possible only if both the USSR and the USA renounce the development, testing and deployment of space-strike weapons. As the Soviet Union has repeatedly warned, the development of space-strike weapons will dash the hopes for a reduction of nuclear armaments on earth.

The first stage will include the adoption and implementation of a decision on the complete elimination of medium-range missiles of the USSR and the USA in the European zone—both ballistic and cruise missiles—as a first step towards ridding the European continent of nuclear weapons.

At the same time the United States should undertake not to transfer its strategic and medium-range missiles to other countries, while Britain and France should pledge not to build up their respective nuclear arsenals.

The USSR and the USA should from the very beginning agree to stop all nuclear explosions and call upon other states to join in such a moratorium as soon as possible.

The reason why the first stage of nuclear disarmament should concern the Soviet Union and the United States is that it is they who should set an example for the other nuclear powers. We said that very frankly to President Reagan of the United States during our meeting in Geneva.

Stage Two. At this stage, which should start no later than 1990 and last for 5 to 7 years, the other nuclear powers will begin to join the process of nuclear disarmament. To start with, they would pledge to freeze all their nuclear arms and not to have them on the territories of other countries.

In this period the USSR and the USA will continue to carry out the reductions agreed upon during the first stage and also implement further measures aimed at eliminating their medium-range nuclear weapons and freezing their tactical nuclear systems.

Following the completion by the USSR and the USA of a 50–percent reduction of their respective armaments at the second stage, another radical step will be taken: all nuclear powers will eliminate their tactical nuclear weapons, i.e. weapons having a range (or radius of action) of up to 1,000 kilometers.

At this stage the Soviet–US accord on the prohibition of space-strike weapons would become multilateral, with the mandatory participation in it of major industrial powers.

All nuclear powers would top nuclear weapon tests.

There would be a ban on the development of non-nuclear weapons based on new physical principles, whose destructive power is close to that of nuclear arms or other weapons of mass destruction.

Stage Three will begin no later than 1995. At this stage the elimination of all remaining nuclear weapons will be completed. By the end of 1999 there will be no nuclear weapons on earth. A universal accord will be drawn up that such weapons should never again come into being.

We envisage that special procedures will be worked out for the destruction of nuclear weapons as well as for the dismantling, reequipment or scrapping of delivery vehicles. In the process, agreement will be reached on the number of weapons to be scrapped at each stage, the sites of their destruction and so on.

Verification of the destruction or limitation of arms should be carried out both by national technical means and through on-site inspections. The USSR is ready to reach agreement on any other additional verification measures.

Adoption of the nuclear disarmament programme that we are proposing would unquestionably have a favourable impact on the negotiations conducted at bilateral and multilateral forums. The programme would envisage clearly-defined routes and reference points, establish a specific time-table for achieving agreements and implementing them and would make the negotiations purposeful and task-oriented. This would stop the dangerous trend whereby the momentum of the arms race is greater than the progress of negotiations.

Thus, we propose that we should enter the third millennium without nuclear weapons, on the basis

From Mikhail S. Gorbachev, statement as General Secretary of the CPSU Central Committee, January 15, 1986. Reprinted by permission of Novosti Information Agency.

of mutually acceptable and strictly verifiable agreements. If the United States Administration is indeed committed to the goal of the complete elimination of nuclear weapons everywhere, as it has repeatedly stated, it now has a practical opportunity to carry it out in practice. Instead of spending the next 10 to 15 years in developing new space weapons, which are extremely dangerous for mankind, weapons, allegedly designed to make nuclear arms unnecessary, would it not be more sensible to start eliminating those weapons and finally doing away with them altogether? The Soviet Union, I repeat, proposes precisely that.

The Soviet Union calls upon all peoples and states, and, naturally, above all nuclear states, to support the programme of eliminating nuclear weapons before the year 2000. It is absolutely clear to any unbiased person that if such a programme is implemented, nobody would lose and all stand to gain. This is a problem common to all mankind and it can and must be solved only through joint efforts. And the sooner this programme is translated into practical deeds, the safer life on our planet will be . . . .

George Bush's 1991 Disarmament Proposal

George Bush was elected 41st president of the United States in 1988. He served as vice-president under Ronald Reagan for two terms. His other political capacities include two terms in the House of Representatives, U.S. ambassador to the United Nations, and director of the Central Intelligence Agency. Before entering politics Bush was successful in the oil industry. The following are short excerpts from his September 1991 speech, and a summary of his disarmament proposal:

"I have asked the Soviets to go down this road with us—to destroy their entire inventory of ground-launched theater nuclear weapons. . . .

The prospect of a Soviet invasion into Western Europe, launched with little or no warning, is no longer a realistic threat. The Warsaw Pact has crumbled. In the Soviet Union, the advocates of democracy triumphed over a coup that would have restored the old system of repression. . . . We can now take steps to make the world a less-dangerous place than ever before in the nuclear age. . . . The Joint Chiefs of Staff support this measure. . . .

Leaders in the Kremlin and the republics are questioning their need for a huge nuclear arsenal. As a result we now have an unparalleled opportunity to change the nuclear posture of both the United States and the Soviet Union. . . . Let no one doubt we will still retain the necessary strength to protect our security and that of our allies. . . ."

Summary of Bush's Initiative

- Eliminate all ground-launched short-range nuclear weapons.
- Move all sea-based short-range nuclear weapons off ships and destroy "many."
- Keep air-delivered nuclear weapons.
- No longer keep strategic bombers on permanent alert.
- Speed up destruction of some long-range missile warheads as soon as the START treaty is ratified and immediately put out of active service those slated for destruction.
- Stop developing mobile missiles.
- Continue developing a single-warhead ICBM (land-based, long-range missile).
- Combine control of strategic nuclear weapons under a new U.S. Strategic Command, with Navy and Air Force participants.
- Ask the Soviet Union to make similar arms cuts and improvements in controls over their nuclear arsenals.
- Negotiate a new U.S.–Soviet pact to eliminate all ICBMs with multiple warheads.
- Ask the Soviets to allow the deployment of the Strategic Defense Initiative's non-nuclear "Star Wars" defenses against missile attacks.
- Seek technical cooperation with the Soviets on preventing accidental use of nuclear weapons.

Writing and Discussion Topics

Questions 1–6 address content, critical analysis, personal choices, ethical options, specific discipline, and interdisciplinary alternatives, respectively.

1. Describe in detail the three stages of disarmament that Gorbachev proposes. How does Bush's new policy match this proposal? Do both leaders seem sincere in

their efforts regarding nuclear weapons, or are these merely surface changes?

2. Is Gorbachev writing for an American audience or an international audience? Is this a peace proposal or is it an argument that favors Soviet views? Explain.

3. Do you believe that we should ban all nuclear weapons? Why or why not? If nuclear weapons are banned, should nuclear power also be banned?

4. If nuclear weapons are banned, but a terrorist group builds a nuclear bomb, how should governments respond to such a threat? What ethical system would you draw on in this situation?

5. Examine the political ramifications of Gorbachev's message. Then examine the politics involved in Bush's policy. Which leader is taking the greater risk? Are these suggested changes prudent? What global changes do you predict in the next two years as a result of the new U.S./Soviet nuclear policy? The next five years?

6. Historically, can the United States trust treaties with the Soviet Union? Why should the United States believe that the Soviets will follow this step-by-step disarmament plan? How might the recent, improved relations between the United States and the Soviet Union bear on nuclear disarmament?

THE NUCLEAR WINTER

Carl Sagan   Source: UPI/
Bettmann.

*T*he Nuclear Winter," by Carl Sagan, has become a controversial
classic in the nuclear arms debate. Sagan has established an
international reputation in astronomy, biology, and physics. He is a
professor of astronomy and space sciences at Cornell University. As a
member of the Union of Concerned Scientists, Sagan coauthored a
petition calling for an international treaty to ban all nuclear weapons
from space. He has been awarded numerous literary and scientific
awards, including the Pulitzer Prize. "The Nuclear Winter" examines
not only the short-term, but also the long-range effects of a
thermonuclear exchange. ♦

"Into the eternal darkness, into fire, into ice."
—DANTE, *The Inferno*

Except for fools and madmen, everyone knows that nuclear war would be an unprecedented human catastrophe. A more or less typical strategic warhead has a yield of 2 megatons, the explosive equivalent of 2 million tons of TNT. But 2 million tons of TNT is about the same as all the bombs exploded in World War II—a single bomb with the explosive power of the entire Second World War but compressed into a few seconds of time and an area 30 or 40 miles across . . .

In a 2-megaton explosion over a fairly large city, buildings would be vaporized, people reduced to atoms and shadows, outlying structures blown down like matchsticks and raging fires ignited. And if the bomb were exploded on the ground, an enormous crater, like those that can be seen through a telescope on the surface of the Moon, would be all that remained where midtown once had been. There are now more than 50,000 nuclear weapons, more than 13,000 megatons of yield, deployed in the arsenals of the United States and the Soviet Union—enough to obliterate a million Hiroshimas.

But there are fewer than 3000 cities on the Earth with populations of 100,000 or more. You cannot find anything like a million Hiroshimas to obliterate. Prime military and industrial targets that are far from cities are comparatively rare. Thus, there are vastly more nuclear weapons than are needed for any plausible deterrence of a potential adversary.

Nobody knows, of course, how many megatons would be exploded in a real nuclear war. There are some who think that a nuclear war can be "contained," bottled up before it runs away to involve much of the world's arsenals. But a number of detailed analyses, war games run by the U.S. Department of Defense, and official Soviet pronouncements all indicate that this containment may be too much to hope for: Once the bombs begin exploding, communications failures, disorganization, fear, the necessity of making in minutes decisions affecting the fates of millions, and the immense psychological burden of knowing that your own loved ones may already have been destroyed are likely to result in a nuclear paroxysm. Many investigations, including a number of studies for the U.S. government, envision the explosion of 5000 to 10,000 megatons—the detonation of tens of thousands of nuclear weapons

that now sit quietly, inconspicuously, in missile silos, submarines and long-range bombers, faithful servants awaiting orders.

The World Health Organization, in a recent detailed study chaired by Sune K. Bergstrom (the 1982 Nobel Laureate in physiology and medicine), concludes that 1.1 billion people would be killed outright in such a nuclear war, mainly in the United States, the Soviet Union, Europe, China and Japan. An additional 1.1 billion people would suffer serious injuries and radiation sickness, for which medical help would be unavailable. It thus seems possible that more than 2 billion people—almost half of all the humans on Earth—would be destroyed in the immediate aftermath of a global thermonuclear war. This would represent by far the greatest disaster in the history of the human species and, with no other adverse effects, would probably be enough to reduce at least the Northern Hemisphere to a state of prolonged agony and barbarism. Unfortunately, the real situation would be much worse.

In technical studies of the consequences of nuclear weapons explosions, there has been a dangerous tendency to underestimate the results. This is partly due to a tradition of conservatism which generally works well in science but which is of more dubious applicability when the lives of billions of people are at stake. In the Bravo test of March 1, 1954, a 15-megaton thermonuclear bomb was exploded on Bikini Atoll. It had about double the yield expected; and there was an unanticipated last-minute shift in the wind direction. As a result, deadly radioactive fallout came down on Rongelap in the Marshall Islands, more than 200 kilometers away. Almost all the children on Rongelap subsequently developed thyroid nodules and lesions, and other long-term medical problems, due to the radioactive fallout.

Likewise, in 1973, it was discovered that high-yield airbursts will chemically burn the nitrogen in the upper air, converting it into oxides of nitrogen; these, in turn, combine with and destroy the protective ozone in the Earth's stratosphere. The surface of the Earth is shielded from deadly solar ultraviolet radiation by a layer of ozone so tenuous that, were it brought down to sea level, it would be only 3 millimeters thick. Partial destruction of this ozone layer can have serious consequences for the biology of the entire planet.

These discoveries, and others like them, were made by chance. They were largely unexpected. And now another consequence—by far the most dire—has been uncovered, again more or less by accident.

The U.S. Mariner 9 spacecraft, the first vehicle to orbit another planet, arrived at Mars in late 1971. The planet was enveloped in a global dust storm. As the fine particles slowly fell out, we were able to measure temperature changes in the atmosphere and on the surface. Soon it became clear what had happened.

The dust, lofted by high winds off the desert into the upper Martian atmosphere, had absorbed the incoming sunlight and prevented much of it from reaching the ground. Heated by the sunlight, the dust warmed the adjacent air. But the surface, enveloped in partial darkness, became much chillier than usual. Months later, after the dust fell out of the atmosphere, the upper air cooled and the surface warmed, both returning to their normal conditions. We were able to calculate accurately, from how much dust there was in the atmosphere, how cool the Martian surface ought to have been.

Afterwards, I and my colleagues, James B. Pollack and Brian Toon of NASA's Ames Research Center, were eager to apply these insights to the Earth. In a volcanic explosion, dust aerosols are lofted into the high atmosphere. We calculated by how much the Earth's global temperature should decline after a major volcanic explosion and found that our results (generally a fraction of a degree) were in good accord with actual measurements. Joining forces with Richard Turco, who has studied the effects of nuclear weapons for many years, we then began to turn our attention to the climatic effects of nuclear war. [The scientific paper, "Global Atmospheric Consequences of Nuclear War," is written by R. P. Turco, O. B. Toon, T. P. Ackerman, J. B. Pollack and Carl Sagan. From the last names of the authors, this work is generally refered to as "TTAPS."]

We knew that nuclear explosions, particularly groundbursts, would lift an enormous quantity of fine soil particles into the atmosphere (more than 100,000 tons of fine dust for every megaton exploded in a surface burst). Our work was further spurred by Paul Crutzen of the Max Planck Institute for Chemistry in Mainz, West Germany, and by John Birks of the University of Colorado, who pointed out that huge quantities of smoke would be generated in the burning of cities and forests following a nuclear war.

Groundbursts—at hardened missile silos, for example—generate fine dust. Airbursts—over cities and unhardened military installations—make fires and therefore smoke. The amount of dust and soot generated depends on the conduct of the war, the yields of the weapons employed and the ratio of groundbursts to airbursts. So we ran computer models for several dozen different nuclear war scenarios. Our baseline case, as in many other studies, was a 5000-megaton war with only a modest fraction of the yield (20 percent) expended on urban or industrial targets. Our job, for each case, was to follow the dust and smoke generated, see how much sunlight was absorbed and by how much the temperatures changed, figure out how the particles spread in longitude and latitude, and calculate how long before it all fell out of the air back onto the surface. Since the radioactivity would be attached to these same fine particles, our calculations also revealed the extent and timing of the subsequent radioactive fallout.

Some of what I am about to describe is horrifying. I know, because it horrifies me. There is a tendency—psychiatrists call it "denial"—to put it out of our minds, not think about it. But if we are to deal intelligently, wisely, with the nuclear arms race, then we must steel ourselves to contemplate the horrors of nuclear war.

The results of our calculations astonished us. In the baseline case, the amount of sunlight at the ground was reduced to a few percent of normal—much darker, in daylight, than in a heavy overcast and too dark for plants to make a living from photosynthesis. At least in the Northern Hemisphere, where the great preponderance of strategic targets lies, an unbroken and deadly gloom would persist for weeks.

Even more unexpected were the temperatures calculated. In the baseline case, land temperatures, except for narrow strips of coastline, dropped to minus 25° Celsius (minus 13° Fahrenheit) and stayed below freezing for months—even for a summer war. (Because the atmospheric structure becomes much more stable as the upper atmosphere is heated and the lower air is cooled, we may have severely *under*estimated how long the cold and the dark would last.) The oceans, a significant heat reservoir, would not freeze, however, and a major ice age would probably not be triggered. But because the temperatures would drop so catastrophically, virtually all crops and farm animals, at least in the Northern Hemisphere, would be destroyed, as would most varieties of uncultivated or domesticated food supplies. Most of the human survivors would starve.

In addition, the amount of radioactive fallout is much more than expected. Many previous calculations simply ignored the intermediate time-scale fallout. That is, calculations were made for the prompt fallout—the plumes of radioactive debris blown downwind from each target—and for the long-term fallout, the fine radioactive particles lofted into the stratosphere that would descent about a year later, after most of the radioactivity had decayed. However, the radioactivity carried into the upper atmosphere (but not as high as the stratosphere) seems to have been largely forgotten. We found for the baseline case that roughly 30 percent of the land at northern midlatitudes could receive a radioactive dose greater than 250 rads, and that about 50 percent of northern midlatitudes could receive a dose greater than 100 rads. A 100-rad dose is the equivalent of about 1000 medical X-rays. A 400-rad dose will, more likely than not, kill you.

The cold, the dark and the intense radioactivity, together lasting for months, represent a severe assault on our civilization and our species. Civil and sanitary services would be wiped out. Medical facilities, drugs, the most rudimentary means for relieving the vast human suffering, would be unavailable. Any but the most elaborate shelters would be useless, quite apart from the question of what good it might be to emerge a few months later. Synthetics burned in the destruction of the cities would produce a wide variety of toxic gases, including carbon monoxide, cyanides, dioxins and furans. After the dust and soot settled out, the solar ultraviolet flux would be much larger than its present value. Immunity to disease would decline. Epidemics and pandemics would be rampant, especially after the billion or so unburied bodies began to thaw. Moreover, the combined influence of these severe and simultaneous stresses on life are likely to produce even more adverse consequences—biologists call them synergisms—that we are not yet wise enough to foresee.

So far, we have talked only of the Northern Hemisphere. But it now seems—unlike the case of a single nuclear weapons test—that in a real nuclear war, the heating of the vast quantities of atmospheric dust and soot in northern midlatitudes will transport these fine particles toward and across the Equator. We see just this happening in Martian dust storms. The Southern Hemisphere would experience effects that, while less severe than in the Northern Hemisphere, are nevertheless extremely ominous. The illusion with which some people in the Northern Hemisphere reassure themselves—catching an Air New Zealand flight in a time of serious international crisis, or the like—is now much less tenable, even on the narrow issue of personal survival for those with the price of a ticket.

But what if nuclear wars *can* be contained, and much less than 5000 megatons is detonated? Perhaps the greatest surprise in our work was that even small nuclear wars can have devastating climatic effects. We considered a war in which a mere 100 megatons were exploded, less than one percent of the world arsenals, and only in low-yield airbursts over cities. This scenario, we found, would ignite thousands of fires, and the smoke from these fires alone would be enough to generate an epoch of cold and dark almost as severe as in the 5000-megaton case. The threshold for what Richard Turco has called The Nuclear Winter is very low.

Could we have overlooked some important effect? The carrying of dust and soot from the Northern to the Southern Hemisphere (as well as more local atmospheric circulation) will certainly thin the clouds out over the Northern Hemisphere. But, in many cases, this thinning would be insufficient to render the climatic consequences tolerable—and every time it got better in the Northern Hemisphere, it would get worse in the Southern.

Our results have been carefully scrutinized by more than 100 scientists in the United States, Europe and the Soviet Union. There are still arguments on points of detail. But the overall conclusion seems to be agreed upon: There are severe and previously unanticipated global consequences of nuclear war—subfreezing temperatures in a twilit radioactive gloom lasting for months or longer.

Scientists initially underestimated the effects of fallout, were amazed that nuclear explosions in space disabled distant satellites, had no idea that the fireballs from high-yield thermonuclear explosions could deplete the ozone layer and missed altogether the possible climatic effects of nuclear dust and smoke. What else have we overlooked?

Nuclear war is a problem that can be treated only theoretically. It is not amenable to experimentation. Conceivably, we have left something important out of our analysis, and the effects are more modest than we calculate. On the other hand, it is also possible—and, from previous experience, even likely—that there are further adverse effects that no one has yet been wise enough to recognize. With billions of lives at stake, where does conservatism lie—in assuming that the results will be better than we calculate, or worse?

Many biologists, considering the nuclear winter that these calculations describe, believe they carry somber implications for life on Earth. Many species of plants and animals would become extinct. Vast numbers of surviving humans would starve to death. The delicate ecological relations that bind together organisms on Earth in a fabric of mutual dependency would be torn, perhaps irreparably. There is little question that our global civilization would be destroyed. The human population would be reduced to prehistoric levels, or less. Life for any survivors would be extremely hard. And there seems to be a real possibility of the extinction of the human species.

It is now almost 40 years since the invention of nuclear weapons. We have not yet experienced a global thermonuclear war—although on more than one occasion we have come tremulously close. I do not think our luck can hold forever. Men and machines are fallible, as recent events remind us. Fools and madmen do exist, and sometimes rise to power. Concentrating always on the near future, we have ignored the long-term consequences of our actions. We have placed our civilization and our species in jeopardy.

Fortunately, it is not yet too late. We can safeguard the planetary civilization and the human family if we so choose. There is no more important or more urgent issue.

Writing and Discussion Topics

Questions 1–6 address content, critical analysis, personal choices, ethical options, specific discipline, and interdisciplinary alternatives, respectively.

1. What is the explosive power of a typical nuclear weapon? What is the chain of events that could happen after an explosion? Why are Sagan's findings so controversial regarding these two questions?
2. Opponents of Sagan argue that we must have deterrence in order to keep international peace. How does he counteract the deterrence argument?
3. Some Americans are willing to be arrested at nuclear testing sites as a protest. Would you protest at a site? To the point of being arrested? Why or why not?
4. Are American government leaders opposed to disarmament because the making of weapons is big business and employs a great many Americans? What ethical systems collide when money becomes the focus of nuclear arms?
5. Much debate and discussion have centered around "The Nuclear Winter." How does Sagan assure us that his findings are accurate? Review the flaws his critics most often cite, and discuss their validity.
6. Thomas Hobbes believed we must use all means to protect our lives. In light of the vast destructiveness of nuclear weapons, do you believe that Hobbes would temper his statement were he living today?

Colin S. Gray and Keith Payne

VICTORY IS POSSIBLE

◆◆◆

C olin S. Gray works as an analyst at the National Institute for Policy in McLean, Virginia. He has been a consultant with the Department of Defense on the MX missile project and has served on the General Advisory Committee, which advises the Pentagon. Keith Payne worked as a strategic analyst with Gray at the Hudson Institute, a conservative "think tank." In this essay, Gray and Payne give several alternatives for nuclear strategy. ◆

Nuclear war is possible. But unlike Armageddon, the apocalyptic war prophesied to end history, nuclear war can have a wide range of possible outcomes. Many commentators and senior U.S. government officials consider it a nonsurvivable event. The popularity of this view in Washington has such a pervasive and malign effect upon American defense planning that it is rapidly becoming a self-fulfilling prophecy for the United States.

Recognition that war at any level can be won or lost, and that the distinction between winning and losing would not be trivial, is essential for intelligent defense planning. Moreover, nuclear war can occur regardless of the quality of U.S. military posture and the content of American strategic theory. If it does, deterrence, crisis management, and escalation control might play a negligible role. Through an inability to communicate or through Soviet disinterest in receiving and acting upon American messages, the United States might not even have the option to surrender and thus might have to fight the war as best it can. Furthermore, the West needs to devise ways in which it can employ strategic nuclear forces coercively, while minimizing the potentially paralyzing impact of self-deterrence.

If American nuclear power is to support U.S. foreign policy objectives, the United States must possess the ability to wage nuclear war rationally. This requirement is inherent in the geography of East-West relations, in the persisting deficiencies in Western conventional and theater nuclear forces, and in the distinction between the objectives of a revolutionary and status quo power.

U.S. strategic planning should exploit Soviet fears insofar as is feasible from the Soviet perspective; take full account of likely Soviet responses and the willingness of Americans to accept those responses; and provide for the protection of American territory. Such planning would enhance the prospect for effective deterrence and survival during a war. Only recently has U.S. nuclear targeting policy been based on careful study of the Soviet Union as a distinct political culture, but the U.S. defense community continues to resist many of the policy implications of Soviet responses to U.S. weapons programs. In addition, the U.S. government simply does not recognize the validity of attempting to relate its freedom

Reprinted with permission from *Foreign Policy* 39 (Summer 1980). Copyright © 1980 by the Carnegie Endowment for International Peace.

of offensive nuclear action and the credibility of its offensive nuclear threat to the protection of American territory.

Critics of such strategic planning are vulnerable in two crucial respects: They do not, and cannot, offer policy prescriptions that will insure that the United States is never confronted with the stark choice between fighting a nuclear war or surrendering, and they do not offer a concept of deterrence that meets the extended responsibilities of U.S. strategic nuclear forces. No matter how elegant the deterrence theory, a question that cannot be avoided is what happens if deterrence mechanisms fail? Theorists whose concept of deterrence is limited to massive retaliation after Soviet attack would have nothing of interest to say to a president facing conventional defeat in the Persian Gulf or in Western Europe. Their strategic environment exists only in peacetime. They can recommend very limited, symbolic options but have no theory of how a large-scale Soviet response is to be deterred.

Because many believe that homeland defense will lead to a steeper arms race and destabilize the strategic balance, the U.S. defense community has endorsed a posture that maximizes the prospect for self-deterrence. Yet the credibility of the extended U.S. deterrent depends on the Soviet belief that a U.S. president would risk nuclear escalation on behalf of foreign commitments.

In the late 1960s the United States endorsed the concept of strategic parity without thinking through what that would mean for the credibility of America's nuclear umbrella. A condition of parity or essential equivalence is incompatible with extended deterrent duties because of the self-deterrence inherent in such a strategic context. However, the practical implications of parity may be less dire in some areas of U.S. vital interest. Western Europe, for example, is so important an American interest that Soviet leaders could be more impressed by the character and duration of the U.S. commitment than by the details of the strategic balance.

A Threat to Commit Suicide

Ironically, it is commonplace to assert that war-survival theories affront the crucial test of political and moral acceptability. Surely no one can be comfortable with the claim that a strategy that would kill millions of Soviet citizens and would invite a strategic response that could kill tens of millions of U.S.

citizens would be politically and morally acceptable. However, it is worth recalling the six guidelines for the use of force provided by the "just war" doctrine of the Catholic Church: Force can be used in a just cause; with a right intent; with a reasonable chance of success; in order that, if successful, its use offers a better future than would have been the case had it not been employed; to a degree proportional to the goals sought, or to the evil combated; and with the determination to spare noncombatants, when there is a reasonable chance of doing so.

These guidelines carry a message for U.S. policy. Specifically, as long as nuclear threat is a part of the U.S. diplomatic arsenal and provided that threat reflects real operational intentions—it is not a total bluff—U.S. defense planners are obliged to think through the probable course of a nuclear war. They must also have at least some idea of the intended relationship between force applied and the likelihood that political goals will be achieved—that is, a strategy.

Current American strategic policy is not compatible with at least three of the six just-war guidelines. The policy contains no definition of success aside from denying victory to the enemy, no promise that the successful use of nuclear power would insure a better future than surrender, and no sense of proportion because central war strategy in operational terms is not guided by political goals. In short, U.S. nuclear strategy is immoral.

Those who believe that a central nuclear war cannot be waged for political purposes because the destruction inflicted and suffered would dwarf the importance of any political goals can construct a coherent and logical policy position. They argue that nuclear war will be the end of history for the states involved, and that a threat to initiate nuclear war is a threat to commit suicide and thus lacks credibility. However, they acknowledge that nuclear weapons cannot be abolished. They maintain that even incredible threats may deter, provided the affront in question is sufficiently serious, because miscalculation by an adversary could have terminal consequences; because genuinely irrational behavior is always possible; and because the conflict could become uncontrollable.

In the 1970s the U.S. defense community rejected this theory of deterrence. Successive strategic targeting reviews appeared to move U.S. policy further and further from the declaratory doctrine of mutual assured destruction adopted by former Secretary of Defense Robert S. McNamara. Yet U.S. defense planners have not thoroughly studied the problems of nuclear war nor thought through the meaning of strategy in relation to nuclear war. The

U.S. defense community has always tended to regard strategic nuclear war not as war but as a holocaust. Former Secretary of Defense James R. Schlesinger apparently adopted limited nuclear options (LNOs)—strikes employing anywhere from a handful of several dozen warheads—as a compromise between the optimists of the minimum deterrence school and the pessimists of the so-called warfighting persuasion. By definition, LNOs apply only to the initial stages of a war. But what happens once LNOs have been exhausted? If the Soviets retaliated after U.S. LNOs, the United States would face the dilemma of escalating further or conciliating.

Deterrence may fail to be restored during war for several reasons: The enemy may not grant, in operational practice, the concept of intrawar deterrence and simply wage the war as it is able; and command, control, and communications may be degraded so rapidly that strategic decisions are precluded and both sides execute their war plans. Somewhat belatedly, the U.S. defense community has come to understand that flexibility in targeting the LNOs do not constitute a strategy and cannot compensate for inadequate strategic nuclear forces.

LNOs are the tactics of the strong, not of a country entering a period of strategic inferiority, as the United States is now. LNOs would be operationally viable only if the United States had a plausible theory of how it could control and dominate later escalation.

The fundamental inadequacy of flexible targeting, as presented in the 1970s, is that it neglected to take proper account of the fact that the United States would be initiating a process of competitive escalation that it had no basis for assuming could be concluded on satisfactory terms. Flexible targeting was an adjunct to plans that had no persuasive vision of how the application of force would promote the attainment of political objectives.

War Aims

U.S. strategic targeting doctrine must have a unity of political purpose from the first to the last strikes. Strategic flexibility, unless wedded to a plausible theory of how to win a war or at least insure an acceptable end to a war, does not offer the United States an adequate bargaining position before or during a conflict and is an invitation to defeat. Small, preplanned strikes can only be of use if the United States enjoys strategic superiority—the ability to wage a nuclear war at any level of violence with a reasonable prospect of defeating the Soviet Union and of recovering sufficiently to insure a satisfactory postwar world order.

However, the U.S. government does not yet appear ready to plan seriously for the actual conduct of nuclear war should deterrence fail, in spite of the fact that such a policy should strengthen deterrence. Assured-destruction reasoning is proclaimed officially to be insufficient in itself as a strategic doctrine. However, a Soviet assured-destruction capability continues to exist as a result of the enduring official U.S. disinterest in strategic defense, with potentially paralyzing implications for the United States. No matter how well designed and articulated, targeting plans that allow an enemy to inflict in retaliation whatever damage it wishes on American society are likely to prove unusable.

Four interdependent areas of strategic policy—strategy, weapons development and procurement, arms control, and defense doctrine—are currently treated separately. Theoretically, strategy should determine the evolution of the other three areas. In practice, it never has. Most of what has been portrayed as war-fighting strategy is nothing of the kind. Instead, it is an extension of the American theory of deterrence into war itself. To advocate LNOs and targeting flexibility and selectivity is not the same as to advocate a war-fighting, war-survival strategy.

Strategists do not find the idea of nuclear war fighting attractive. Instead, they believe that an ability to wage and survive war is vital for the effectiveness of deterrence; there can be no such thing as an adequate deterrent posture unrelated to probable wartime effectiveness; victory or defeat in nuclear war is possible, and such a war may have to be waged to that point; and, the clearer the vision of successful war termination, the more likely war can be waged intelligently at earlier stages.

There should be no misunderstanding the fact that the primary interest of U.S. strategy is deterrence. However, American strategic forces do not exist solely for the purpose of deterring a Soviet nuclear threat or attack against the United States itself. Instead, they are intended to support U.S. foreign policy, as reflected, for example, in the commitment to preserve Western Europe against aggression. Such a function requires American strategic forces that would enable a president to initiate strategic nuclear use for coercive, though politically defensive, purposes.

U.S. strategy, typically, has proceeded from the bottom up. Such targeting does not involve any conception of the war as a whole, nor of how the war might be concluded on favorable terms. The U.S. defense community cannot plan intelligently for lower levels of combat, unless it has an acceptable idea of where they might lead.

Most analyses of flexible targeting options assume virtually perfect stability at the highest levels of conflict. Advocates of flexible targeting assert that a U.S. LNO would signal the beginning of an escalation process that the Soviets would wish to avoid in light of the American threat to Soviet urban-industrial areas. Yet it seems inconsistent to argue that the U.S. threat of assured destruction would deter the Soviets from engaging in escalation following an LNO but that U.S. leaders could initiate the process despite the Soviet threat. What could be the basis of such relative U.S. resolve and Soviet vacillation in the face of strategic parity or Soviet superiority?

Moreover, the desired deterrent effect would probably depend upon the Soviet analysis of the entire nuclear campaign. In other words, Soviet leaders would be less impressed by American willingness to launch an LNO than they would be by a plausible American victory strategy. Such a theory would have to envisage the demise of the Soviet state. The United States should plan to defeat the Soviet Union and to do so at a cost that would not prohibit U.S. recovery. Washington should identify war aims that in the last resort would contemplate the destruction of Soviet political authority and the emergence of a postwar world order compatible with Western values.

The most frightening threat to the Soviet Union would be the destruction or serious impairment of its political system. Thus, the United States should be able to destroy key leadership cadres, their means of communication, and some of the instruments of domestic control. The USSR, with its gross overcentralization of authority, epitomized by its vast bureaucracy in Moscow, should be highly vulnerable to such an attack. The Soviet Union might cease to function if its security agency, the KGB, were severely crippled. If the Moscow bureaucracy could be eliminated, damaged, or isolated, the USSR might disintegrate into anarchy, hence the extensive civil defense preparations intended to insure the survival of the Soviet leadership. Judicious U.S. targeting and weapon procurement policies might be able to deny the USSR the assurance of political survival.

Once the defeat of the Soviet state is established as a war aim, defense professionals should attempt to identify an optimum targeting plan for the accomplishment of that goal. For example, Soviet political control of its territory in Central Asia and in the Far East could be weakened by discriminate nuclear targeting. The same applies to Transcaucasia and Eastern Europe.

The Ultimate Penalty

Despite a succession of U.S. targeting reviews, Soviet leaders, looking to the mid-1980s, may well anticipate the ability to wage World War III successfully. The continuing trend in the East-West military balance allows Soviet military planners to design a theory of military victory that is not implausible and that may stir hopes among Soviet political leaders that they might reap many of the rewards of military success even without having to fight. The Soviets may anticipate that U.S. self-deterrence could discourage Washington from punishing Soviet society. Even if the United States were to launch a large-scale second strike against Soviet military and economic targets, the resulting damage should be bearable to the Soviet Union given the stakes of the conflict and the fact that the Soviets would control regions abroad that could contribute to its recovery.

In the late 1960s the United States identified the destruction of 20–25 percent of the population and 50–75 percent of industrial capacity as the ultimate penalty it had to be able to inflict on the USSR. In the 1970s the United States shifted its attention to the Soviet recovery economy. The Soviet theory of victory depends on the requirement that the Soviet Union survive and recover rapidly from a nuclear conflict. However, the U.S. government does not completely understand the details of the Soviet recovery economy, and the concept has lost popularity as a result. Highly complex modeling of the Soviet economy cannot disguise the fact that the available evidence is too rudimentary to permit any confidence in the analysis. With an inadequate data base it should require little imagination to foresee how difficult it is to determine targeting priorities in relation to the importance of different economic targets for recovery.

Schlesinger's advocacy of essential equivalence called for a U.S. ability to match military damage for military damage. But American strategic development since the early 1970s has not been sufficient to maintain the American end of that balance. Because the U.S. defense community has refused to recognize the importance of the possibility that a nuclear war could be won or lost, it has neglected to think beyond a punitive sequence of targeting options.

American nuclear strategy is not intended to defeat the Soviet Union or insure the survival of the United States in any carefully calculated manner. Instead, it is intended to insure that the Soviet Union is punished increasingly severely. American targeting philosophy today is only a superficial improvement over that prevalent in the late 1960s, primarily because U.S. defense planners do not consider anticipated damage to the United States to be relevant to the integrity of their offense war plans. The strategic case for ballistic missile defense and civil defense has not been considered on its merits for a decade.

In the late 1970s the United States targeted a range of Soviet economic entities that were important either to war-supporting industry or to economic recovery. The rationale for this targeting scheme was, and remains, fragile. War-supporting industry is important only for a war of considerable duration or for a period of post-war defense mobilization. Moreover, although recovery from war is an integral part of a Soviet theory of victory, it is less important than the achievement of military success. If the USSR is able to win the war, it should have sufficient military force in reserve to compel the surviving world economy to contribute to Soviet recovery. Thus, the current trend is to move away from targeting the recovery economy.

To date, the U.S. government has declined to transcend what amounts to a deterrence-through-punishment approach to strategic war planning. Moreover, the strategic targeting reviews of the 1970s did not address the question of self-deterrence adequately. The United States has no ballistic missile defense and effectively no civil defense, while U.S. air defense is capable of guarding American air space only in peacetime. The Pentagon has sought to compensate for a lack of relative military muscle through more imaginative strategic targeting. Review after review has attempted to identify more effective ways in which the USSR could be hurt. Schlesinger above all sought essential equivalence through a more flexible set of targeting options without calling for extensive new U.S. strategic capabilities. Indeed, he went to some pains to separate the question of targeting design from procurement issues.

The United States should identify nuclear targeting options that could help restore deterrence, yet would destroy the Soviet state and enhance the likelihood of U.S. survival if fully implemented. The first priority of such a targeting scheme would be Soviet military power of all kinds, and the second would be the political, military, and economic control structure of the USSR. Successful strikes against military and political control targets would reduce the Soviet ability to project military power abroad and to sustain political authority at home. However, it would not be in the interest of the United States actually to implement an offensive nuclear strategy no matter how frightening in Soviet perspective, if the U.S. homeland were totally naked to Soviet retaliation.

Striking the USSR should entail targeting the relocation bunkers of the top political and bureaucratic leadership, including those of the KGB; key communication centers of the Communist party, the military, and the government; and many of the economic, political, and military records. Even limited destruction of some of these targets and substantial isolation of many of the key personnel who survive could have revolutionary consequences for the country.

The Armageddon Syndrome

The strategic questions that remain incompletely answered are in some ways more difficult than the practical problems of targeting the political control structure. Is it sensible to destroy the government of the enemy, thus eliminating the option of negotiating an end to the war? In the unlikely event that the United States identifies all of the key relocation bunkers for the central political leadership, who would then conduct the Soviet war effort and to what ends? Since after a large-scale counter-control strike the surviving Soviet leadership would have little else to fear, could this targeting option be anything other than a threat?

The U.S. defense community today believes that the political control structure of the USSR is among the most important targets for U.S. strategic forces. However, just how important such targeting might be for deterrence or damage limitation has not been determined. Current American understanding of exactly how the control structure functions is less than perfect. But that is a technical matter that can in principle be solved through more research. The issue of whether the Soviet control structure should actually be struck is more problematic.

Strategists cannot offer painless conflicts or guarantee that their preferred posture and doctrine promise a greatly superior deterrence posture to current American schemes. But, they can claim that an intelligent U.S. offensive strategy, wedded to homeland defenses, should reduce U.S. casualties to approximately 20 million, which should render U.S. strategic threats more credible. If the United States developed the targeting plans and procured the weapons necessary to hold the Soviet political, bureaucratic, and military leadership at risk, that should serve as the functional equivalent in Soviet perspec-

tive of the assured-destruction effect of the late 1960s. However, the U.S. targeting community has not determined how it would organize this targeting option.

A combination of counterforce offensive targeting, civil defense, and ballistic missile and air defense should hold U.S. casualties down to a level compatible with national survival and recovery. The actual number would depend on several factors, some of which the United States could control (the level of U.S. homeland defenses); some of which it could influence (the weight and character of the Soviet attack); and some of which might evade anybody's ability to control or influence (for example, the weather). What can be assured is a choice between a defense program that insures the survival of the vast majority of Americans with relative confidence and one that deliberately permits the Soviet Union to wreak whatever level of damage it chooses.

No matter how grave the Soviet offense, a U.S. president cannot credibly threaten and should not launch a strategic nuclear strike if expected U.S. casualties are likely to involve 100 million or more American citizens. There is a difference between a doctrine that can offer little rational guidance should deterrence fail and a doctrine that a president might employ responsibly for identified political purposes. Existing evidence on the probable consequences of nuclear exchanges suggests that there should be a role for strategy in nuclear war. To ignore the possibility that strategy can be applied to nuclear war is to insure by choice a nuclear apocalypse if deterrence fails. The current U.S. deterrence posture is fundamentally flawed because it does not provide for the protection of American territory.

Nuclear war is unlikely to be an essentially meaningless, terminal event. Instead it is likely to be waged to coerce the Soviet Union to give up some recent gain. Thus, a president must have the ability, not merely to end a war, but to end it favorably. The United States would need to be able to persuade desperate and determined Soviet leaders that it has the capability, and the determination, to wage nuclear war at ever higher levels of violence until an acceptable outcome is achieved. For deterrence to function during a war each side would have to calculate whether an improved outcome is possible through further escalation.

An adequate U.S. deterrent posture is one that denies the Soviet Union any plausible hope of success at any level of strategic conflict; offers a likely prospect of Soviet defeat; and offers a reasonable chance of limiting damage to the United States. Such a deterrence posture is often criticized as contributing to the arms race and causing strategic instability, because it would stimulate new Soviet deployments. However, during the 1970s the Soviet Union showed that its weapon development and deployment decisions are not dictated by American actions. Western understanding of what determines Soviet defense procurement is less than perfect, but it is now obvious that Soviet weapon decisions cannot be explained with reference to any simple action-reaction model of arms-race dynamics. In addition, highly survivable U.S. strategic forces should insure strategic stability by denying the Soviets an atractive first-strike target set.

An Armageddon syndrome lurks behind most concepts of nuclear strategy. It amounts either to the belief that because the United States could lose as many as 20 million people, it should not save the 80 million or more who otherwise would be at risk, or to a disbelief in the serious possibility that 200 million Americans could survive a nuclear war.

There is little satisfaction in advocating an operational nuclear doctrine that could result in the deaths of 20 million or more people in an unconstrained nuclear war. However, as long as the United States relies on nuclear threats to deter an increasingly powerful Soviet Union, it is inconceivable that the U.S. defense community can continue to divorce its thinking on deterrence from its planning for the efficient conduct of war and defense of the country. Prudence in the latter should enhance the former.

Writing and Discussion Topics

Questions 1–6 address content, critical analysis, personal choices, ethical options, specific discipline, and interdisciplinary alternatives, respectively.

1. What do Gray and Payne mean when they say that "nuclear war is unlikely to be an essentially meaningless, terminal event"? Why do they believe that a plan for the actual conduct of nuclear war should strengthen deterrence?

2. Examine the strengths and weaknesses of the arguments in this essay in light of events currently happening with respect to war and nuclear arms. Would it be best to follow the advice in this article or the advice of today's politicians?

3. Assume you are a top-level Pentagon official. You are seated at a summit table and have just been given Gray and Payne's nuclear warfare strategies. Would you argue that these can be effective? Write a proposal for an upcoming summit meeting. This proposal should be your strategy for strengthening world peace. You may use any of the writers in this section as sources for your proposal.

4. Gray and Payne are policy analysts and not ethicists. Do you find any ethical problems in their policy analysis? For example, is any type of nuclear exchange immoral? Are nuclear weapons in themselves immoral? Explain.

5. How would Gray and Payne respond to Gorbachev's proposal? What do the authors specifically suggest be done in a war with the Soviet Union? Is this an obsolete notion considering the current relationship between the United States and the Soviet Union?

6. From a biblical standpoint, what is Armageddon? How do the authors define the Armageddon Syndrome? Why do they object to the "syndrome" type of thinking?

Burton M. Leiser

WAR CRIMES AND CRIMES AGAINST HUMANITY

———◆◆◆———

*B*urton M. Leiser is professor of philosophy at Pace University. He received his Ph.D. from Brown University and his J.D. from Drake University. He is the recipient of numerous awards including the American Jurisprudence Award. He is the author of several books, including Liberty, Justice, and Morals: Contemporary Value Conflicts, from which this writing is taken. ◆

Divine Right and Sovereign Immunity

Those who are familiar with the course of events that usually follows a charge of police brutality or the abuse of official powers know how difficult it is to make such a charge stick. Ancient doctrines that can be traced far beyond the medieval theory of the divine right of kings interpose nearly insurmountable obstacles between the citizen who believes that he has been injured (that is, unjustly or illegally harmed) by an officer of the state and the satisfaction of any claim that he may make for reparation of the injury or retribution against the wrongdoer. The officer is surrounded by immunities, for the state does not look kindly upon the suggestion that it has done wrong. The officer, being a part of the state's apparatus, enjoys many of the immunities that the state itself enjoys against its citizens. No one could prosecute the king, for who would hear the case, who would serve as the judge, and who would declare the law? The king was himself the supreme judge and the supreme legislator. How, then, could one ask the king to judge himself? If one complained against one of the king's officers, it was, in a sense, a complaint against the king himself. The king would act upon the complaint only at his pleasure. Officers of the law, then, and judges, governors, presidents, members of Congress and the Senate, and ministers of government enjoy many immunities that ordinary citizens, and even those same persons, in their private capacities, do not have.

If it is difficult to get satisfaction in a claim for damages against an officer of the law, or to convict a public official of a criminal charge with regard to an action that he took in his official capacity, it is *virtually impossible* to get such a judgment against the highest officials of a national state; for, with a few extraordinary exceptions, there is no one to prefer the charges, no one to hear the cases, no one to execute the judgments but these very persons themselves. And even if they are no longer in office, they can claim that when they were, they merely carried out their duties and responsibilities as they saw them and understood them at the time. How can the very state in whose service they performed the acts about which the complaint is being laid now prosecute them and possibly punish them for doing what they did?

Even more difficult, however, is the problem of the aggrieved party who considers himself a victim of unjustified aggression on the part of a foreign state. To whom shall he turn for relief? What court will hear his argument and pass judgment against a sovereign nation? And even if there were such a court, what sovereign nation would submit to its judgment or acquiesce in its demands? If such a hypothetical court rendered judgment against the nation, decreed that it had indeed engaged in a wrongful act of hostility, and ordered it to pay compensation to the aggrieved party, who would enforce the court's order?

Finally, by what rule of law would any court presume to convict him or anyone who had followed his orders? An ancient and respected rule of justice decrees that no one should be convicted or punished for any act that was not forbidden by the law at the time that he committed it. The sovereign may rightly point out that the law under which he performed his allegedly criminal acts was the law of the land at the time. Who would know better than he, after all, for he had signed it himself? He was the sovereign and he made the laws. His subordinates followed the laws, as they and every proper citizen were supposed to do. Therefore, no law was broken by him or any of his subordinates during the time in question. If it be claimed that the law broken was the law of some other state, he can rightly reply that he is not subject to the law of any other state. He is subject only to the law of *his* state. If some foreign state wishes to convict him of a violation of *its* laws, let it do so; but it will be powerless to do more than pronounce words, without laying itself open to a charge of aggression and the strong possibility of reprisals, including the ultimate reprisal of war.

The Just-War Concept

The concept of the just war extends back through the Middle Ages into late Hellenistic times, and beyond that even into Biblical times. It has been said that the concept of Christian charity is itself one of the foundations of the just-war idea. As Paul Ramsey has put it,

> The justification of warfare and of Christian participation in it was not actually an exception (certainly not an arbitrary one, or a compromise from the purity of Christian ethics), but instead an *expression* of the Christian understanding of moral and political responsibility . . . . In the ancient theory of just war, Christian conscience took the

form of allowing any killing at all of men for whom Christ died only because military personnel were judged to stand, factually and objectively, at the point where, as combatants, resistance to them was judged to be necessary in responsibility to many other neighbors.[1]

He explains that though Jesus advocated turning the other cheek, he did not tell his disciples to raise the head of another oppressed man so that his tormentor could strike him again. For the sake of love itself, he says, Christianity taught that violence could be used, if necessary, to repel invading forces in order to protect the innocent against harm to which they might otherwise have been subjected. Or, to put it another way, it may be a work of charity to resist by force of arms an act of aggression against the forces that enable the citizens of a state or its institutions to carry out their work of healing the sick, educating the young, and feeding the poor.[2]

These principles have their corollaries, of course. If it is meaningful to talk of just wars, then the concept of unjust war must be meaningful as well. Advocates of the just-war theory have, in fact, developed elaborate accounts of the distinctions between just and unjust wars. Grotius, in introducing his discussion of just wars, distinguishes them from the wars of savages, which are fought out of the sheer love of slaughtering and butchering men or facing dangerous situations; and there are also wars of robbers—those who, in the words of Augustine, "from the mere lust of ruling . . . crush peoples who have not troubled [them]." And Philo, too, described those "who have acquired the strength of robbers [and] lay waste whole cities, taking no thought of punishments, because they appear to be stronger than the laws. These are men whose nature is unsuited to civil life, who seek after tyrannies and despotisms, who carry out plundering on a large scale, concealing under the respected names of government and authority what is more correctly called robbery."[3]

Some wars, according to Grotius, merely present an appearance of justice—but the appearance is a false one. Unjust wars are those that are fought for expansionistic purposes or, as the Germans called it, Lebensraum. Paternalistic colonialism—the desire to rule others against their will on the pretext that it is for their welfare—is another unjust cause of war. Still another is the war that is fought on the ground that a certain emperor or church has the self-proclaimed right or authority to universal dominion. There are others, but these examples are sufficient.

These principles and guidelines were of great interest to legal and moral scholars and were the occasion for many hours of fascinating discussion. But as one of the great modern authorities in the field of international law has commented, "So long as war was a recognized instrument of national policy, both for giving effect to existing rights and for changing the law, the justice or otherwise of the causes of war was not of legal relevance. The right of war, for whatever purposes, was a prerogative of national sovereignty. Thus conceived, *every war was just.*"[4] Until the present century, whatever moralists and writers might have said, war was primarily a means of self-help utilized by nations whenever they felt the need to enforce what they conceived to be their rights under the law. In fact, it mattered little what the law was, for each state decided that issue for itself. States rejected the distinction between just and unjust wars, insisting that international law was itself determined by the actions of states. In the absence of an international legislature, war was one way of changing the law and of "rectifying" or at least altering the rights of states relative to one another. So long as this state of affairs endured, the law of the jungle—might makes right—prevailed, and no war was unjust. As Hobbes wrote in 1651:

> In all times kings and persons of sovereign authority, because of their independency, are in continual jealousies and in the state and posture of gladiators, having their weapons pointing and their eyes fixed on one another—that is, their forts, garrisons, and guns upon the frontiers of their kingdoms, and continual spies upon their neighbors—which is a posture of war . . . . [When there is a state of war—as there is in the relations of one nation to another,] nothing can be unjust. The notions of right and wrong, justice and injustice, have there no place. Where there is no common power, there is no law; where no law, no injustice.[5]

Laws that cannot be enforced are no laws at all. Where there are no enforceable laws, every man is in practice (if not in conscience) free to do what he considers right or what he considers to be in his own interest. Where no enforceable laws exist, nations are in fact governed only by the limits of their own power.

In the relations among the nations of the world, no enforceable laws regarding warfare existed prior to this century, though there were many moral pronouncements as to what nations should do and what they should refrain from doing. Where anarchy reigns, Mao's principle, that right is to be found at the end of a gun, holds true. Therefore, so long as the state of anarchy described so graphically by Hobbes prevailed among the nations of the world, there was no measure of justice and right except that which emerged from the barrels of guns. But in civilized society, justice and right—though they may ultimately have to be enforced by physical power—are not measured in those terms, but are determined, so far as possible, by reasoned responses to the needs, desires, and aspirations of the people. The gun may loom in the background as an ultimate threat, but justice and right are better conceived of as the results of voluntary commitments and concessions made by each man to every other as a means of achieving a degree of mutual security and freedom from the fear of aggression. Similarly, among the nations of the world, law may be regarded, in part, at least, as commitments and concessions made by each nation to the others, one concession being an agreement that each nation sacrifices its prior right to make war against the others in return for a guarantee that they will not make war against it.

First Steps Toward a Law of War

Writing more than three and a half centuries ago Hugo Grotius, the father of modern international law, said, "Throughout the Christian world I observed a lack of restraint in relation to war, such as even barbarous races should be ashamed of; I observed that men rush to arms for slight causes, or no cause at all, and that when arms have once been taken up there is no longer any respect for law, divine or human; it is as if, in accordance with a general decree, frenzy had openly been let loose for the committing of all crimes."[6] It is not true, he declared, that in war, all laws are in abeyance. "On the contrary, war ought not to be undertaken except for the enforcement of rights; when once undertaken, it should be carried on only within the bounds of law and good faith."[7] The laws of the state may be silent as regards the conduct of war, but certain unwritten laws remain in force, even as regards the conduct of hostile nations. Quoting an ancient author, he declared, "War has its laws no less than peace." The Greeks, the Romans, and others recognized the importance of adhering to just and reasonable policies in war as in peace and often felt that their defeats

were due retribution for their failure to settle disputes by arbitration, their hasty decisions to enter into war, their cruel treatment of the enemy or of prisoners, and other wicked deeds. "We try to restrain murders and the killing of individuals," said Seneca. "Why are wars and the crime of slaughtering nations full of glory? Avarice and cruelty know no bounds. In accordance with decrees of the Senate and orders of the people atrocities are committed, and actions forbidden to private citizens are commanded in the name of the state."[8] More than once in ancient times, it was said that those who committed petty crimes were looked upon as villains and scoundrels, whereas those who murdered men by the thousands, plundered great cities, and kidnapped and enslaved whole populations were hailed as great heroes and military geniuses. A pirate was once talking about Alexander the Great, conqueror of the world and hero of an entire age. "Alexander," he said, "is a pirate, too, just like me. The difference between the two of us is simply this: I sink only one ship at a time, while he sinks whole fleets of them."

The view that military leaders are all criminals on a grand scale cannot be seriously maintained. To be sure, their profession sometimes requires the killing of other men; the burning of homes, farms, and sometimes entire cities; and the subjugation of whole populations. But not all killing is murder, not all burning is arson, and some instances of the deprivation of civil rights and civil liberties are neither wrong nor unjustified. Charles J. Whitman, an honor student at the University of Texas, was shot to death by the police after he had shot a total of forty-four persons, killing fourteen of them, from a tower on the university campus. He had earlier slain two relatives at home. The police, who clearly had no alternative but to shoot Whitman in order to bring his sniping to an end, could hardly be called murderers. On the contrary, their behavior was courageous and heroic, and was deserving of commendation. The officers and men of the military are often put into a similar situation, but on a far grander scale; for sometimes not only the students, the faculty, and the staff of a university are threatened, but the entire population of a nation. The military are called in, at great risk to themselves, to stave off the aggression and to protect the civilian population. Where there is a clear and immediate danger of overt aggression by one state against another, the threatened state's forces may properly bomb and burn the aggressor's tanks and planes; immobilize his troops; and occupy and subdue areas that are strategically located. If one can see the justification for such acts on the small scale represented by the Whitman case, then it is difficult to see why analogous acts on the larger scale represented by the relationships of nations to one another should not also be justifiable.

But this is not to say that pretense, misrepresentation, the fabrication of evidence or excuses, fraud, or lies would suffice in either case to justify such violent actions. If police fire upon a man or a group of persons on the *pretext* that they or innocent civilians were attacked by them with deadly weapons, then that police action is nothing more nor less than murder, or attempted murder, and a conspiracy to deprive innocent persons of their rights. Similarly, if a nation sends its army onto foreign territory on the *pretext* that the actions that they are to carry out there are necessary for the security of its own people, or through a fraudulent misrepresentation of facts which, if true, would justify such actions under treaties or other binding international agreements, then it would seem that that nation and its leaders are guilty of a crime against the people of the state whose territory they invaded, or whose cities and factories they bombarded, or whose military personnel they wounded, maimed, and killed.

But no behavior is criminal unless it is forbidden by law. No prohibition has anything more than moral or hortatory force unless it is backed up by sanctions, the threat of penalties. Where there is no law, Hobbes once said, all things are permitted to all men. Though men may preach against practices that they consider to be evil, their exhortations ordinarily have no permanent or lasting effect upon human behavior unless they are reinforced by the sanctions of the state. There is no absolute guarantee that men will behave in such a way as to minimize the harm that they do to one another. The law and the sanctions that it brings to bear upon its violators tend, however, to render such harmful behavior less likely than it might be in the absence of such regulation. Law, then, is the handmaiden of morals. It offers some assurance that that which is forbidden by morals—but which moral feelings and beliefs alone are powerless to prevent—will not occur. It is the instrument through which the ideals of justice are realized in this world. In its absence men must look to self-help to right the wrongs inflicted upon them by others, or else they must helplessly suffer them.

The frontier of law and morals in our generation is in the realm of international law. The law of nations is still in a primitive and rudimentary state. Many of its principles remain pious hopes rather than solid achievements. Nowhere is this more evident than in the laws of war, which have been applied to concrete situations for the first time in this half century. Here it is possible, perhaps as nowhere else, to observe a new system of law in the making, the first tentative steps toward the construction of a new international society, the first painful and frustrating efforts of men to reduce their moral ideals and their dreams of a just society to concrete terms that will have a real and noticeable effect upon the lives of the people who inhabit this planet.

War crimes and crimes against humanity are not merely moral problems; they are legal problems as well. But the law governing war crimes and crimes against humanity is not so well developed as that which governs other areas of human concern. In such other areas as torts, contracts, property, and the criminal law of a particular state, the problem is often a matter of conflict of rights and duties, of efforts to reform laws that may have been on the books for many years and that have had a long history. Here the situation is radically different, for it is said by some that there is no law to reform. Even those who concede that there *is* a law agree that it is rudimentary and that nations must learn how to apply it—to make the terms *war crime* and *crime against humanity* as meaningful in the society of nations as *murder* and *larceny* are in a civil society.

The worthy sentiments of Grotius, of Seneca, and of all the learned writers who denounced the lawlessness and the cruelties of men and nations at war had little practical effect upon the actual conduct of states or their citizens, for there was no sanction that could meaningfully be applied against those who violated the so-called unwritten laws of war, even after those laws had been reduced to writing by Grotius and those who came after him. Not until the twentieth century, when tormented mankind suffered through the most barbarous wars ever waged, did the international community finally take its first halting steps toward making the concepts of war crimes and crimes against humanity meaningful and operative in the lives of nations. . . .

Writing and Discussion Topics

Questions 1–6 address content, critical analysis, personal choices, ethical options, specific discipline, and interdisciplinary alternatives, respectively.

1. What is one Christian justification of warfare and participation in warfare?
2. What is the difference between a just war and an unjust war?
3. Jesus taught that his followers should love one another. He included in this to love your enemy, do good to those who would use you, and to "turn the other cheek." By going to war or declaring war, are Jesus' followers saying they don't believe in his doctrine?
4. Ethically, can we rationalize that every war is just? Can laws be a part of war to make it more just? Could laws in war ever be enforced?
5. Seneca questions why we glorify war. He says that in war avarice and cruelty know no bounds. Is it true that wars are usually exceptionally decadent? Explain your answer.
6. War often involves crimes against humanity. Are these crimes merely moral problems, or are they also legal problems? Could they involve religious problems as well?

Notes

1. Paul Ramsey, "The Case for Making a 'Just War' possible," in *The Just War* (New York: Scribner, 1968), p. 150.
2. Paul Ramsey, "Justice in War," in *The Just War*, pp. 142 F. For more Christian justifications for war, see, for example, Hugo Grotius, *De Jure Belli Ac Pacis, Libri Tres*, tr. by F. W. Kelsey, first published by Carnegie Endowment for International Peace in the "Classics of International Law" series in 1925. Reprinted by Oceana Publications, New York, 1964.
3. Philo Judaeus, *On the Ten Commandments*, 26. Cf. Grotius, op. cit., Vol. II, Chap. 22, Sec. 4 (p. 548, no. 3). Also cf. Augustine, *City of God*, Vol. IV, Chap. 6, cited in Grotius, p. 548.
4. H. Lauterpacht, *Oppenheim's International Law*, 7th ed. (London: Longmans, 1952), Vol. II, Section 63. My emphasis.
5. Hobbes, *Leviathan*, Library of Liberal Arts edition, p. 108.
6. Grotius, op. cit. Prolegomenon, 28.
7. Ibid., 25.
8. Cf. Grotius, op. cit., Vol. II, Chap. 1, 1.

Douglas P. Lackey

MISSILES AND MORALS: A UTILITARIAN LOOK AT NUCLEAR DETERRENCE

D ouglas P. Lackey is a professor of philosophy at Baruch College
of the City University of New York. He is considered an expert
on nuclear disarmament, and many of his views coincide with the
Catholic bishops' statement on arms. His scholarly articles have
appeared in numerous publications. He is the author of "The Moral
Case for Unilateral Nuclear Disarmament," "Ethics and Nuclear
Deterrence," and Moral Principles and Nuclear Weapons. In this
article, Lackey discusses the greatest happiness principle in terms of
nuclear war and determines that the most ethical global policy is to
disarm. ♦

Though there are many strategies for nuclear armament, these three have been at the center of the strategic debate at least since the late 1950s:

S: Maintain second strike capacity; seek first strike capacity; threaten first and second strikes ("Superiority").

E: Maintain second strike capacity; do not seek first strike capacity; threaten second strikes only ("Equivalence").

ND: Do not seek to maintain second strike capacity ("Nuclear Disarmament").

In the statement of these strategies the terminology standard: Nation A is presumed to have *first-strike capacity* against B if A can launch a nuclear attack on B without fear of suffering unacceptable damage from B's subsequent counterstrike; nation A is said to have *second-strike capacity* against B if A is capable of inflicting unacceptable damage on B after having suffered a nuclear first strike by B.

Strategy S has been the favored strategy of hardline anticommunists ever since the early 1950s. In its original form, as we find it in John Foster Dulles, the Superiority Strategy called for threats of American first strikes against Russian cities in retaliation for what American policy defined as Soviet acts of aggression. In its present form, as it is developed by Paul Nitze, Colin Gray, and others, the Superiority Strategy calls for threats, or implied threats, of American first strikes against Soviet military forces, combined with large-scale increases in American strategic arms.[1]

The Superiority Strategy, however, is not the exclusive property of doctrinaire anticommunists or hard-line "forward" strategists. Since aiming one's missiles at enemy missiles implies a desire to destroy those missiles before they are launched, that is, a desire to launch a first strike, all retargeting of American missiles from Soviet cities to Soviet missiles, up to and including President Carter's Directive 59 in the summer of 1980, imply partial endorsement of Strategy S. Such "counterforce" as opposed to "countervalue" targetings are entailed by Strategy S even if they do not in fact bring first strike capacity; Strategy S as defined implies that the United States will *seek* first strike capacity, not that it will in fact obtain it. Strategy S advocates steps which will produce first strike capacity unless new countermeasures are developed by the Soviet Union to cancel them out.

Strategy E, the "equivalence" strategy, enshrines Robert McNamara's doctrine of Assured Destruction, and includes both massive retaliations against massive strikes and flexible responses against lesser strikes.[2] The possibility and permanence of Strategy E seemed assured by SALT 1 in 1972, since negotiated restrictions on the deployment of antiballistic missiles seemed to guarantee permanent second-strike capacity to both sides. Unfortunately, SALT 1 did not limit the development and deployment of MIRVs (multiple independently targeted reentry vehicles), and the deployment of MIRVs through the 1970s has led to cries on both sides that mutual second-strike capacity is dissolving and mutual first-strike capacity is emerging.

Notice that although Strategy E permits bilateral arms control, it actually prohibits substantial reductions in nuclear arms. The delicate balance of mutual second-strike capacity becomes increasingly unstable as arms levels are lowered, and sooner or later, mutual disarmament brings a loss of second-strike capacity on one side and the emergence of first-strike capacity on the other, contrary to E.

Strategy ND calls for a unilateral halt in the development of American nuclear weapons and delivery systems, even if such a halt eventuates in Soviet first strike capacity. Strategy ND is a policy of *nuclear* disarmament; it does *not* call for the abandonment of conventional weapons and should not be equated with pacifism or confused with general and complete disarmament. In fact, increases in conventional weapons levels are compatible with Strategy ND. . . .

From Douglas P. Lackey, "Missiles and Morals: A Utilitarian Look at Nuclear Deterence," *Philosophy & Public Affairs*, Vol. II, No. 3 (Summer 1982). Copyright © 1982 Princeton University Press. Reprinted by permission of Princeton University Press.

[1]On "massive retaliation" see John Foster Dulles, Dept. of State Bulletin 30, 791, 25 Jan. 1954. For Superiority policy in the 1960s see, for example, Barry Goldwater, *Why Not Victory?* (New York: McGraw-Hill, 1962), p. 162 . . . .

For a recent interpretation of Superiority see Colin Gray and Keith Payne, "Victory Is Possible," *Foreign Policy* 39 (Summer 1980): 14–27, and Colin Gray, "Nuclear Strategy: The Case for a Theory of Victory," *International Security* 4 (Summer 1979): 54–87.

[2]Robert MacNamara, *The Essence of Security* (London: Hodder and Stoughton, 1968).

TABLE 1

	ONE-SIDED STRIKE*	ALL-OUT NUCLEAR WAR	SOVIET AGGRESSION	VERY HIGH MILITARY SPENDING
Superiority	Fifty-fifty [a]	Fifty-fifty [b]	Small [c]	Certain [d]
Equivalence	Small [e]	Small [f]	Small [g]	Fifty-fifty [h]
Nuclear Disarmament	Small [i]	Zero [j]	Small [k]	Small [l]

*A "one-sided strike" is a first strike that may or may not be answered by a second strike. A comparison of the probability of one-sided strikes and two-sided strikes in a given row indicates that a first strike will lead to an all-out nuclear war.

Expected Value

Perhaps the most natural of all responses to the problem of uncertainty is to discount the weight of consequences by whatever chance there is that they will not occur. To compute the "expected value" of a policy, then, we should consider each possible outcome of the policy, multiply the utility of that outcome by the probability that it will occur, and take the sum of all these products. In the area of nuclear strategy we cannot supply precise numbers for the probabilities of the outcomes, nor can we attempt to supply precise figures for the corresponding utilities. Nevertheless, we *do* have much more information about these subjects than [an ordering] of probabilities . . . and what imprecision there is in our information can be respected by stating the information in the form of approximations. For example, we can classify the probability of outcomes as "negligible," "small but substantial," "fifty-fifty," "very likely," and "almost certain," and we can classify outcomes as "extremely bad," "bad," "neutral," and so forth. In considering the products of utilities and outcomes, we can neglect all outcomes of negligible probability, and all outcomes of small but substantial probability *except* those classified as extremely good or extremely bad. In many cases, use of such estimates will yield surprisingly definite results.

Now, what are the "outcomes" the probabilities of which we ought to consider? Given the traditionally assumed goals of deterrence, we should certainly consider the effects of each policy on the probability of nuclear war, the probability of Soviet nonnuclear aggression, and the probability of Soviet nuclear blackmail . . . . In considering the probability of nuclear war, it is essential to distinguish the probability of a one-sided nuclear strike from the probability of all-out nuclear war. Among other outcomes, we will consider only the effects of nuclear strategies on military spending, since the impact of policies on spending can be determined with little controversy. Since we have four outcomes and three policies to consider, the probabilities can be represented on a three-by-four grid (see table 1). Each probability assessment will be defended in turn.

Value of the Superiority Strategy   [a] Strategists disagree about the probability of Soviet or American first strike under the Superiority Strategy. All students of the subject rate it as having at least a small but substantial probability. I believe that it is more reasonable to rate the probability as fifty-fifty within a time frame of about fifty years, since (1) every real or presumed step towards first strike capacity by either side raises the chance of a preemptive first strike by the side falling behind; (2) the concentration on technological development prompted by the Superiority Strategy raises that chance of a technological breakthrough that might destabilize the balance of power; (3) the increasing technological complexity of weapons required by the Superiority Strategy raises the chance of a first strike as a result of accident or mistake; (4) the constant changes of weaponry required by the Superiority Strategy creates pressure for proliferation, either because obsolete weapons are constantly disposed of on the international arms market or because wealthy developing countries, dazzled by new weapons, make buys to keep up with appearances.

[b] Under Superiority, the chance of an American second strike—given a Soviet first strike—is practically the same as the chance of a Soviet first strike. Though it is always possible that the President or his survivor will not respond to a Soviet first strike, the military and technological systems installed under the Superiority Strategy are geared for belligerence. Accordingly the chance of an American failure to respond is negligible.

[c] Even in the face of the Superiority Strategy, the chance of Soviet nonnuclear aggression (an invasion of West Germany or Iran, for example) must be rated as small but not negligible. The prospect of an American first strike in response to a Soviet conventional attack may not be taken seriously by the Soviets, especially if Soviet military personnel think that they can deter any American first strike with the prospect of a mass Soviet second strike.

[d] The sums of money required to sustain the Superiority Strategy are staggering. The Reagan administration's rejection of SALT and its apparent acceptance of the Superiority Strategy will produce an increase in the fraction of the American gross national product devoted to defense from five to six and one-half percent: an increase of over $150 billion per year over the Carter projections, which were largely keyed to the Equivalence Strategy.

Value of the Equivalence Strategy

[e] Most students of strategy agree that the chance of an American or Soviet first strike under the Equivalence Strategy is small but substantial. The peculiar pressures for a first strike listed under the Superiority Strategy are absent, but there is still the chance of a first strike through accident, mistake, human folly, or a suicidal leadership.

[f] Since the chance of a first strike is less under Equivalence than under Superiority, there is less chance of an all-out nuclear war under Equivalence than under Superiority. The chance of a first strike under Equivalence is small, and the chance of all-out war following a first strike is smaller still. Since the primary aim of the Equivalence Strategy is not to "defeat" the Soviet Union or to develop a first-strike capacity, but to deter a Soviet first strike, it may be obvious to the President or his survivor that once a Soviet first strike is actually launched, there is no point whatsoever in proceeding with an American second strike. If the chance that the President

will fail to respond is substantial, the chance of an all-out war under Equivalence is considerably less than the chance of a first strike under Equivalence. On the other hand, the credibility of the American deterrent to a first strike depends on the perception by Soviet planners that an American second strike is inevitable once a Soviet first strike is launched, and the President and his defense strategists may decide that the only convincing way to create this perception is to make the American second strike a *semi-automatic* response. Thus it might be difficult to stop an American second strike even if the President wished to forgo it. On balance, it seems reasonable to rate the chance of the second strike as greater than one-half the chance that the Soviet first strike will be launched. This would make the chance small but still substantial.

[g] Over the years two arguments have been proposed to show that Superiority provides a more effective deterrent against Soviet aggression than does Equivalence.

(1) The Superiority Strategy requires constant technological innovation, and technological innovation is an area in which the United States possesses a relative advantage. If the United States presses forward with strategic weapons development, the Soviet Union will be so exhausted from the strain of keeping up with the United States that it will have little money or energy left over for nonnuclear aggression. In the end, the strain such competition will exert on the Soviet economy might produce food riots like those in Poland in 1970, and might even bring down the Soviet socioeconomic system.

But since "the strain of keeping up" did not stop the Soviets from invading Hungary, Czechoslovakia, and Afghanistan, the level of expenditure needed to produce truly effective strain is unknown. Furthermore, the assumption of *relative* economic stress is undemonstrated: at least one economist who has seriously studied the subject has argued on various grounds that a unit of military spending by the United States disrupts the American economy far more than the equivalent military spending by the Soviet Union.[3]

(2) It is occasionally argued that the Soviets will take the possibility of an American second strike more seriously under the Superiority Strategy than

---

[3]See Seymour Melman, *Our Depleted Society* (New York: Holt, Rinehart & Winston, 1965), and *Pentagon Capitalism* (New York: McGraw-Hill, 1970).

under the Equivalence Strategy, since the Superiority Strategy gives the United States something closer to first-strike capacity and therefore something less to fear from a Soviet second strike.

But in the game of nuclear strategy one cannot "almost" have first strike capacity; one either has it or one doesn't. There is no reason to think that the Superiority Strategy will ever yield first-strike capacity, since the Soviet Union will feel forced to match the United States step for step. The Soviets know that the President will never be confident enough in American striking capacity to risk the survival of the United States on a nuclear response to Soviet nonnuclear aggression. Consequently, there is no reason to think that Superiority provides a better deterrent against Soviet aggression than does Equivalence. The chance of serious nonnuclear Soviet aggression under Equivalence is small.

[h] In the presence of serious efforts at arms control, expenditures for strategic weapons will be much less under Equivalence than under Superiority. If efforts at arms control fail, then expenditures will remain very high. The chance of very high expenditures under Equivalence would best be put at about fifty-fifty.

Value of the Nuclear Disarmament Strategy

[i] Most strategists are agreed that the chance of a Soviet first strike under the Equivalence Strategy is small. I believe that the chance of a Soviet first strike is small even under the strategy of Nuclear Disarmament.

(1) Since under Nuclear Disarmament at most one side retains nuclear arms, the chance of nuclear war occurring by accident is reduced at least by one half, relative to the Equivalence Strategy. Since only half the technology is deployed, there is only half the chance of a mechanical malfunction leading to war.

(2) Since at most one side remains armed, there is considerably less chance under Nuclear Disarmament that a nuclear war will occur by mistake. The principal mistake that might cause a nuclear war is the mistake of erroneously thinking that the other side is about to launch a nuclear attack. Such mistakes create enormous pressure for the launching of preemptive strikes, in order to get one's weapons in the air before they are destroyed on the ground. There is no chance that this mistake can occur under Nuclear Disarmament. The side that remains armed (if any) need not fear that the other side will launch a nuclear attack. The side that chooses to disarm cannot be tempted to launch a preemptive strike no

matter what it believes the other side is doing, since it has no weapons with which to launch the strike.

(3) Even the opponents of Nuclear Disarmament describe the main peril of nuclear disarmament as nuclear blackmail by the Soviet Union. Opponents of disarmament apparently feel that after nuclear disarmament, nuclear threats are far more probable than nuclear disasters.

(4) Though nuclear weapons are not inherently more destructive than other sorts of weapons, conceived or actual (the napalm raids on Tokyo in March 1945 caused more deaths than Hiroshima or Nagasaki), nuclear weapons are universally *perceived* as different in kind from nonnuclear weapons. The diplomatic losses a nation would incur upon using even tactical nuclear weapons would be immense.

(5) A large scale nuclear attack by the Soviet Union against the United States might contaminate the American and Canadian Great Plains, a major source of Soviet grain imports. The Soviets could still turn to Argentina, but the price of grain after the attack would skyrocket, and no combination of Argentinean, Australian, or other grain sources could possibly compensate for American or Canadian losses.

(6) The Soviets will find it difficult to find actual military situations in which it will be practical to use atomic weapons against the United States, or against anyone else. Nuclear weapons proved superfluous in the Soviet invasions of Hungary and Czechoslovakia, and they do not seem to be practicable in Afghanistan, where the human costs of the Soviet attempt to regain control are high. If the Soviets did not use nuclear weapons against China between 1960 and 1964 in order to prevent the development of Chinese nuclear capacity, it is hardly likely that they could use them against a nonnuclear United States. Of course it is always *possible* that the Soviet Union might launch a nuclear attack against a nonnuclear United States, perhaps as an escalatory step in a conventional conflict, but it is also *possible* that the Soviet Union will launch a nuclear attack on the United States *right now*, despite the present situation of Equivalence. The point is that there is no such thing as a guarantee against nuclear attack, but the probability of an actual attack is small under either strategy.

[j] The chance of all-out nuclear war under the Equivalence Strategy is slight, but the chance of all-out nuclear war under Nuclear Disarmament is zero. There cannot be a two-sided nuclear war if only one side possesses nuclear arms.

[k] In considering the threat of Soviet nonnuclear aggression under Nuclear Disarmament, we must consider Soviet nuclear threats—usually called "nuclear blackmail"—as well as possible uses of conventional arms by the Soviets.

(1) Suppose that the United States unilaterally gives up second-strike capacity. What are the odds that the Soviet Union would attempt to influence American behavior through nuclear threats? Obviously, one's views about the chances for successful nuclear blackmail depend on one's views about the chances of a Soviet first strike against a nonnuclear United States. If the chances of a Soviet first strike are slight, then the chances of successful blackmail will also be slight. We have already argued on a variety of grounds that chances of a Soviet first strike under ND are small. I would suggest that the ability of the Soviet Union to manipulate a nonnuclear United States would be the same as the ability of the United States to manipulate the Soviet Union from 1945 to 1949, when strategic conditions were reversed. Anyone who reflects on events from 1945 to 1949 will conclude that nuclear threats have little effect on nations capable of acting with resolve.

There is always the chance that the Soviet Union will carry out its nuclear threats, but there is always the chance that the Soviet Union will carry out its threats even if the United States retains nuclear weapons. There is no device that provides a guarantee against nuclear blackmail. Consequently it cannot be argued that Equivalence provides a guarantee against blackmail that Nuclear Disarmament does not.

The foregoing dismissal of nuclear blackmail violates conventional strategic wisdom, which is concerned with nuclear blackmail almost to obsession. Numerous authors, for example, cite the swift fall of Japan after Hiroshima as evidence of the strategic usefulness of nuclear weapons and nuclear threats. The case of Japan is worth considering. Contrary to the canonical view certified by Secretary Stimson in his famous (and self-serving) *Harper's* article in 1947,[4] I believe that the bombings of Hiroshima and Nagasaki had almost no effect on events leading to

the surrender of Japan. If so, the force of the Japanese precedent, which still influences strategic thought, is greatly attenuated.

Obviously the bombings of Hiroshima and Nagasaki had no effect on the popular desire for peace in Japan, since the Japanese public did not know of the atomic bombings until the war was over. What is more surprising is that the bombings do not seem to have influenced either the Emperor or the military command in making the decision to sue for peace. The Emperor, as is now well known , had decided for peace as early as January 1945, and if he was set on peace in January, he did not need the bombings of August to make up his mind. The military, on the other hand, do not seem to have desired peace even after the bombs were dropped; the record shows that the military (a) correctly surmised that the United States had a small supply of these bombs, (b) debated improved antiaircraft measures to prevent any further bombs from being delivered, and (c) correctly inferred that bombs of this type could not be used to support a ground invasion, which they felt they could repulse with sufficient success to secure a conditional surrender. What tipped the political scales so that the Emperor could find his way to peace was not the bombing of Nagasaki on 9 August, but the Russian declaration of war on 8 August. Unaware of Stalin's commitment at Yalta to enter the war against Japan, the Japanese had hoped through the spring and summer of 1945 that the Soviets would mediate a negotiated settlement between the United States and Japan rather than send the Red Army into a new theater of war. When the Russians invaded Manchuria on 9 August, Premier Suzuki, according to reports, cried, "The game is over," and when the Emperor demanded surrender from the Council of Elders on 10 August, he never mentioned atomic bombs as the occasion of his demand for peace.[5] Little can be inferred from such evidence about the effectiveness of nuclear threats.

(2) The strategy of Nuclear Disarmament does not forbid uses of conventional arms in response to acts of aggression. Since there is no reason to believe that

---

[4]Stimson's "The Decision to Use the Atomic Bomb" appeared in the February 1947 *Harper's Magazine*, pp. 97–107. Typical of Stimson's *post hoc ergo propter hoc* is: We believed that our attacks struck cities which must certainly be important to the Japanese military leaders, both Army and Navy, and we waited for a result. We waited one day.

[5]For the Emperor's active attempts to obtain peace see Herbert Feis, *The Atomic Bomb and the End of World War II* (Princeton: Princeton University Press, 1966), p. 66. For the military response to the atomic bombings see Hanson Baldwin, *Great Mistakes of the War* (New York: Collins-Knowlton-Wing, 1950), pp. 87–107. For Suzuki's remark that "The game is over" see W. Craig, *The Fall of Japan* (New York: Dial, 1967), p. 107 . . . .

adoption of the strategy of Nuclear Disarmament by the United States will make acts of Soviet aggression any more palatable than they are at present, in all probability the American government under ND will appropriate funds for conventional arms sufficient to provide a deterrent to Soviet aggression roughly comparable to the deterrent provided by nuclear arms under S and E. This argument assumes that the deterrent effects of the American strategic nuclear arsenal (whatever they are) can be obtained with a developed arsenal of modern conventional weapons. A review of the difficulties involved in the use of strategic nuclear weapons in concrete situations may convince the reader that conventional weapons can match the deterrent effect of nuclear weapons. Indeed, the whole development of "flexible response" systems during the McNamara era testifies to the widespread recognition that strategic nuclear weapons provide little leverage to nations who would seek to control the flow of world events.

[I] Since it is impossible to predict how much money must be spent on conventional forces in order to supply a deterrent equal to the present (nuclear) deterrent against Soviet nonnuclear aggression, it is possible that levels of military spending under ND will be greater than levels under E. But it is also possible that the levels of spending will be much less. The technical equipment needed to maintain E is fantastically expensive, but the labor costs of training and improving conventional forces can also be staggering. All things considered, it is still likely that spending will be less under ND than under E, especially if the draft is revived.

Comparison of Superiority and Equivalence

The chance of a Soviet first strike is greater under Superiority than under Equivalence, and the chance of all-out nuclear war is greater under Superiority than under Equivalence. The ability of Equivalence to deter Soviet nonnuclear aggression is equal to the ability of Superiority to deter such aggression, and the Equivalence strategy costs less. Thus Equivalence is preferable to Superiority from both the prudential and the moral point of view.

Comparison of Equivalence and Nuclear Disarmament

We have argued that Nuclear Disarmament and Equivalence are equal in their ability to deter Soviet nonnuclear aggression. In the category of military spending Nuclear Disarmament is preferable to Equivalence. In the category of "all-out war" ND is clearly superior to E, and in the category of "first strikes," ND seems to be about equal to E. Thus we have what seems to be a decisive prudential and moral argument in favor of Nuclear Disarmament: in every category, ND is either equal to or superior to E . . . . Furthermore, since there is the possibility of *two* first strikes under E and *at most* the possibility of one first strike under ND, there is considerable reason to conclude that the probability of a first strike under ND is less than the probability of a first strike under E.

On the other hand, the chance that the Soviet Union will start a nuclear war through calculation of presumed advantage is greater under ND than under E. Certainly the fact that the Soviet Union could use nuclear weapons against the United States without fear of American nuclear reprisal might tempt them to use these weapons, especially if the United States and the Soviet Union were involved in a large-scale war using conventional weapons. After all, that was the way nuclear weapons came to be used the first time around. But such a strike would have difficulties and costs, which we have already enumerated, and in general the Soviet Union might be disinclined to use nuclear weapons against a nation it does not perceive as a source of nuclear threats. Though aggression studies have been among the most lavishly funded of recent psychological projects, we still do not have anything like a set of rules which tell us whether aggression is more or less likely between two parties who fear each other than it is between two parties, one of whom has nothing to fear from the other.

Considering the military awkwardness and diplomatic costs of using nuclear weapons, I find it quite incredible that the majority of official statements on this subject consider the chance of a calculated Soviet attack on a nonnuclear United States as greater than the chance under Equivalence of a Soviet attack by accident *or* a Soviet attack by mistake *or* an American attack by accident *or* an American attack by mistake . . . .

From Morals to Politics

Nuclear Disarmament, Superiority, and Equivalence are the nuclear strategies most discussed by theorists, and other strategies are largely variants or specifications of these three. If utilitarianism favors

Nuclear Disarmament over Superiority and Equivalence, it favors Nuclear Disarmament *tout court*. For utilitarians, ND is morally right, and ought to be adopted.

It remains to consider whether it is also morally right to *advocate* or *support* Nuclear Disarmament. Support is logically distinct from adoption, and acts of support have their own sets of consequences. It is possible, and by no means paradoxical, that within the utilitarian framework support for the morally right policy may be morally wrong.

The commonest situation where support for the right leads to the wrong is a three-way election in which support for the best candidate will elect the worst, while support for the second best outcome will defeat the worst. Moderate liberals whose support for Charles Goodell over Richard Ottinger led to the election of James Buckley in 1972 and whose support for Jacob Javits over Elizabeth Holtzman led to the election of Al d'Amato in 1980 found themselves in each case with their least preferred candidate. In such situations utilitarianism joins hands with a Weberian ethic of responsibility and calls on moral agents to support the second best.

It is often alleged that the competition between S, E, and ND is rather like the Senate race in New York in 1972 and 1980, and many who agree that ND is morally superior to E fear that open advocacy of ND will drain support from E and lead to victory for the Superiority Strategy. The flaw in this reasoning is to compare a three-way election with winners determined by votes to a three-way policy choice with winners determined by the ultimate vector of political pressure. With candidates and votes, support for the extreme steals votes from the center. With policies and pressures, pressure from one extreme helps support the center against pressure from the other. In choosing platforms and policies, Americans have traditionally shied away from extremes, and a three-way race between S, E, and ND places E in the central position historically favored by the American people. A two-way race, which places the "center" between Equivalence and Superiority, allows the supporters of Superiority to argue that their strategy is no more extreme than Equivalence. If the moral principle which evaluates support of strategic policies (as opposed to the policies themselves) determines that support should be exercised in the way most likely to defeat Superiority, there is as much a case for public support of Nuclear Disarmament as there is for Nuclear Disarmament itself.

Writing and Discussion Topics

Questions 1–6 address content, critical analysis, personal choices, ethical options, specific discipline, and interdisciplinary alternatives, respectively.

1. According to Lackey, what is the value of a nuclear disarmament strategy? Is there a prudential value and a moral value?
2. Does Lackey believe that utilitarian thinkers can make any difference in policy decisions regarding nuclear weapons? Does he have a strategy for action? Examine and explain his logic.
3. What is the difference between a first strike and a second strike in a nuclear confrontation? Do you believe it is moral to retaliate after a first strike? Does Lackey?
4. In an international conflict, a utilitarian would accept the policy that would tend to produce the best consequences when the interests of everyone affected are counted equally. Explain Lackey's international, utilitarian position on nuclear arms.
5. Is the massive use of conventional bombs that destroy a city or industry morally less objectionable than the use of nuclear weapons? Examine this view from a utilitarian perspective.
6. If Lackey, Gorbachev, and Sagan could work out an international peace proposal, what would each of them include in the document? Write your version of this document.

James P. Sterba

JUST WAR THEORY AND NUCLEAR STRATEGY

◆◆◆

*J*ames P. Sterba is a professor of philosophy at the University of
Notre Dame. He has authored numerous articles on ethics and has
written and edited several college textbooks. Sterba discusses concepts of
nuclear warfare from the perspective of just war theory. He defines the
pacifist, conventionalist, collectivist, and feminist challenges and argues
why the possession of nuclear weapons is ethically justified. ◆

In traditional just war theory, there are two basic components: a set of criteria which establish a right to go to war (jus ad bellum) and a set of criteria which determine legitimate conduct in war (jus in bello). The first set of criteria can be grouped under the label "just cause," the second under the label "just means." In recent years, the just cause component of just war theory has been subjected to a pacifist challenge, the just means component has been subjected to conventionalist and collectivist challenges and both components have been subject to a feminist challenge. In this paper, I will attempt to respond to each of these challenges in turn and then go on to determine the practical implications of just war theory for nuclear strategy.

The Pacifist Challenge to Just Cause

In traditional just war theory, just cause is usually specified as follows:

Just Cause There must be substantial aggression and nonbelligerent correctives must be hopeless or too costly.

Needless to say, the notion of substantial aggression is a bit fuzzy, but it is generally understood to be the type of aggression that violates people's most fundamental rights. To suggest some specific examples of what is and what is not substantial aggression, usually nationalization of particular firms owned by foreigners is not regarded as substantial aggression while the taking of hostages is so regarded. But even when substantial aggression occurs, frequently nonbelligerent correctives are neither hopeless nor too costly.

However, according to the pacifist challenge to just war theory nonbelligerent correctives, or at least nonlethal correctives, are never hopeless or too costly. Thus, for pacifists there aren't any just causes.

But this pacifist challenge to just war theory is sometimes claimed to be incoherent. In a well-known article, Jan Narveson rejects pacifism as incoherent because it recognizes a right to life yet rules out any use of force in defense of that right.[1] The view is incoherent, Narveson claims, because having a right

entails the legitimacy of using force in defense of that right at least on some occasions. But as Cheyney Ryan has pointed out Narveson's argument only works against the following extreme form of pacifism:

Pacifism I Any use of force is morally prohibited.

It doesn't touch the form of pacifism that Ryan thinks is most defensible, which is the following:

Pacifism II Any lethal use of force is morally prohibited.[2]

This form of pacifism only prohibits the use of lethal force in defense of people's rights.

Ryan goes on to argue that there is a substantial issue between the pacifist and the nonpacifist concerning whether we can or should create the necessary distance between ourselves and other human beings in order to make the act of killing possible. To illustrate, Ryan cites George Orwell's reluctance to shoot at an enemy soldier who jumped out of a trench and ran along the top of a parapet half-dressed and holding up his trousers with both hands. Ryan contends that what kept Orwell from shooting was that he couldn't think of the soldier as a thing rather than a fellow human being.

But do we have to objectify other human beings in order to kill them? If we do, this would seem to tell in favor of the form of pacifism Ryan defends. However, it is not clear that Orwell's encounter supports such a view. For it may be that what kept Orwell from shooting the enemy soldier was not his inability to think of the soldier as a thing rather than a fellow human being but rather his inability to think of the soldier who was holding up his trousers with both hands as a threat or a combatant. Under this interpretation, Orwell's decision not to shoot would accord well with the requirements of just war theory.

Let us suppose, however, that someone is attempting to take your life. Why does that permit you, the pacifist might ask, to kill the person making the attempt? Isn't such killing prohibited by the principle that one should never intentionally do evil that good may come of it? Of course, someone might not want to endorse this principle as an absolute requirement, but surely it cannot be reasonable to regard all cases of justified killing in self-defense as exceptions to this principle.

One response to this pacifist objection is to allow that killing in self-defense can be morally justified provided that the killing is the foreseen consequence of an action whose intended consequence is

From James P. Sterba, "Just War Theory and Nuclear Strategy," *Analyse & Kritik*, (Special Issue), pp. 427–437. Copyright © 1987 Westdeutscher Verlag GmbH, Wiesbaden, Germany. Reprinted with permission of author and publisher.

the stopping of the attempt upon one's life. Another response is to allow that intentional killing in self-defense can be morally justified provided that you are reasonably certain that your attacker is wrongfully engaged in an attempt upon your life. It is claimed that in such a case the intentional killing is not evil, or at least not morally evil, because anyone who is wrongfully engaged in an attempt upon your life has already forfeited her or his right to life by engaging in such aggression.

Taken together, these two responses seem to constitute an adequate reply to the pacifist challenge. The first response is theoretically closer to the pacifist's own position since it rules out all intentional killing, but the second response is also needed when it does not seem possible to stop a threat to one's life without intentionally killing one's attacker.

The Conventionalist Challenge to Just Means

Now the just means component of just war theory can be specified as follows:

Just Means

1. The harm resulting from the belligerent means employed should not be disproportionate to the military objective to be attained.
2. Harm to innocents should not be directly intended as an end or a means.
3. Harm to innocents should be minimized by accepting risks (costs) to oneself that would not render it impossible to attain the military objective.

Obviously, the notion of what is disproportionate is a bit fuzzy in (1), but the underlying idea is that the harm resulting from the belligerent corrective should not outweigh the benefit to be achieved from attaining the military objective. By contrast, (2) is a relatively precise requirement. Where it was obviously violated was in the antimorale terror bombing of Dresden and Hamburg and in the use of atomic bombs against Hiroshima and Nagasaki in World War II.[3]

Some people think that (1) and (2) capture the essential requirements of just means. Others maintain that something like (3) is also required. Michael Walzer provides an example from Frank Richard's memoir of World War I which shows the attractiveness of (3).

When bombing dug-outs or cellars, it was always wise to throw the bombs into them first and have a look around after. But we had to be very careful in this village as there were civilians in some of the cellars. We shouted down to them to make sure. Another man and I shouted down one cellar twice and receiving no reply were just about to pull the pins out of our bomb when we heard a woman's voice and a young lady came up the cellar steps. . . . She and the members of her family . . . had not left (the cellar) for some days. They guessed an attack was being made and when we first shouted down had been too frightened to answer. If the young lady had not cried out when she did we would have innocently murdered them all.[4]

Many restrictions on the operation of police forces also seem to derive from a requirement like (3).

As one would expect, these criteria of just means have been incorporated to some degree in the military codes of different nations and adopted as international law. Yet rarely has anyone contended that the criteria ought to be met simply because they have been incorporated into military codes or adopted as international law. Recently, however, George Mavrodes has defended just such a conventionalist view.[5] Mavrodes arrives at this conclusion largely because he finds the standard attempts to specify the convention-independent basis for (2) and (3) to be so totally unsuccessful. All such attempts, Mavrodes claims, are based on an identification of innocents with noncombatants. But by any plausible standard of guilt and innocence that has moral content, Mavrodes contends, noncombatants can be guilty and combatants innocent. For example, noncombatants who are doing everything in their power to financially support an unjust war would be morally guilty, and combatants who were forced into military service and intended never to fire their weapons at anyone would be morally innocent. Consequently, the guilt/innocence distinction will not support the combatant/noncombatant distinction.

Hoping to still support the combatant/noncombatant distinction, Mavrodes suggests that the distinction might be grounded on a convention to observe it. This would mean that our obligation to morally abide by (2) and (3) would be a convention-dependent obligation. Nevertheless, Mavrodes does not deny that we have some convention-independent obligation. Our obligation to refrain from wantonly murdering our neighbors is given as an example of a convention-independent obligation, as is our obligation to reduce the pain and death involved in combat. But to refrain from harming noncombatants when harming them would be the most effective way of pursuing a just cause is not included among our convention-independent obligations.

Yet Mavrodes does not claim that our obligation to refrain from harming noncombatants is *purely* convention-dependent. He allows that, in circumstances in which the convention of refraining from harming noncombatants does not exist, we might still have an obligation to unilaterally refrain from harming noncombatants provided that our action will help give rise to a convention prohibiting such harm with its associated good consequences. According to Mavrodes, our primary obligation is to maximize good consequences, and this obligation requires that we refrain from harming noncombatants when that will help bring about a convention prohibiting such harm. By contrast, someone who held that our obligation to refrain from harming noncombatants was purely convention-dependent, would never recognize an obligation to unilaterally refrain from harming noncombatants. On a purely convention-dependent account, obligations can only be derived from existing conventions; the expected consequences from establishing a particular convention could never ground a purely convention-dependent obligation. But while Mavrodes does not claim that our obligation to refrain from harming noncombatants is purely convention-dependent, he does claim that this obligation generally arises only when there exists a convention prohibiting such harm. According to Mavrodes, the reason for this is that generally only when there exists a convention prohibiting harm to noncombatants will our refraining from harming them, while pursuing a just cause, actually maximize good consequences.

But is there no other way to support our obligation to refrain from harming noncombatants? Mavrodes would deny that there is. Consider, however, Mavrodes's own example of the convention-independent obligation not to wantonly kill our neighbors. There are at least two ways to understand how this obligation is supported. Some would claim that we ought not to wantonly kill our neighbors because this would not maximize good consequences. This appears to be Mavrodes's view. Others would claim that we ought not to wantonly kill our neighbors, even if doing so would maximize good consequences, simply because it is not reasonable to believe that our neighbors are engaged in an attempt upon our lives. Both these ways of understanding how the obligation is supported account for the convention-independent character of the obligation,

but the second approach can also be used to show how our obligation to refrain from harming noncombatants is convention-independent. According to this approach since it is not reasonable to believe that noncombatants are engaged in an attempt upon our lives, we have an obligation to refrain from harming them. So interpreted, our obligation to refrain from harming noncombatants is itself convention-independent, although it will certainly give rise to conventions.

Of course, some may argue that whenever it is not reasonable to believe that persons are engaged in an attempt upon our lives, an obligation to refrain from harming such persons will also be supported by the maximization of good consequences. Yet even if this were true, which seems doubtful, all it would show is that there exists a utilitarian or forward-looking justification for a convention-independent obligation to refrain from harming noncombatants; it would not show that such an obligation is a convention-dependent obligation, as Mavrodes claims.

The Collectivist Challenge to Just Means

Now according to the collectivist challenge to just means, more people should be included under the category of combatants than the standard interpretation of (2) allows. The reason for this is that the standard interpretation of (2) does not assume, as the advocates of the collectivist challenge do, that the members of a society are collectively responsible for the actions of their leaders unless they have taken radical steps to oppose or disassociate themselves from those actions, e.g., by engaging in civil disobedience or emigration. Of course, those who are unable to take such steps, particularly children, would not be responsible in any case, but, for the rest, advocates of the collectivist challenge contend that failure to take the necessary radical steps, when one's leaders are acting aggressively, has the consequence that one is no longer entitled to full protection as a noncombatant. Some of those who press this objection against the just means component of just war theory, like Gregory Kavka, contend that the members of a society can be directly threatened with nuclear attack to secure deterrence but then deny that carrying out such an attack could ever be morally justified.[6] Others, like James Child, contend that the members of a society who fail to take the necessary radical steps can be both indirectly threatened and indirectly attacked with what would otherwise be a disproportionate attack.[7]

In response to this collectivist challenge, the first thing to note is that people are more responsible for disassociating themselves from the unjust acts of their leaders than they are for opposing those same acts. For there is no general obligation to oppose all unjust acts, even all unjust acts of one's leaders. Nevertheless, there is a general obligation to disassociate oneself from unjust acts and to minimize one's contribution to them. Of course, how much one is required to disassociate oneself from the unjust acts of one's leaders depends upon how much one is contributing to those actions. If one's contribution is insignificant, as presumably a farmer's or a teacher's would be, only a minimal effort to disassociate oneself would be required, unless one's action could somehow be reasonably expected, in cooperation with the actions of others, to put a stop to the unjust actions of one's leaders. However, if one's contribution is significant, as presumably a soldier's or a munitions worker's would be, a maximal effort at disassociating oneself would be immediately required, unless by delaying, one could reasonably expect to put a stop to the unjust actions of one's leaders.

In support of the collectivist challenge, James Child offers the following example:

> A company is considering engaging in some massively immoral and illegal activity—pouring large quantities of arsenic into the public water supply as a matter of ongoing operations, let us say. A member of the board of directors of the company, when the policy is before the board, votes no but does nothing else. Later, when sued in tort (or charged in crime) with these transgressions of duty, she pleads that she voted no. What would our reaction be? The answer is obvious! We would say, you are responsible as much, or nearly as much, as your fellow board members who voted yes. You should have blown the whistle, gone public or to regulatory authorities, or at the very least, resigned from the board of so despicable a company. Mere formal dissent in this case does almost nothing to relieve her liability, legal or moral.[8]

But while one might agree with Child that in this case the member of the board of directors has at least the responsibility to disassociate herself from the actions of the board by resigning, this does not show that farmers and teachers are similarly responsible for disassociating themselves from the unjust actions of their leaders either by engaging in civil disobedience or by emigration. This is because neither

their contributions to the unjust actions of their leaders nor the effect of their disassociation on those unjust actions would typically be significant enough to require such a response.

This is not to deny that some other response (e.g. political protest or remunerations at the end of the war) would not be morally required. However, to meet the collectivist challenge, it suffices to show that not just any contribution to the unjust actions of one's leaders renders the contributor subject to attack or threat of attack; one's contribution must be significant enough to morally justify such a response.

The Feminist Challenge to Just Cause and Just Means

According to the feminist challenge to both components of just war theory, sexism and militarism are inextricably linked in society. They are linked, according to Betty Reardon, because sexism is essentially a prejudice against all manifestations of the feminine, and militarism is a policy of excessive military preparedness and eagerness to go to war that is rooted in a view of human nature as limited to masculine characteristics.[9] Seen from a militarist perspective, other nations are competitive, aggressive and adverse to cooperation, the same traits that tend to be fostered exclusively in men in a sexist society. By contrast, the traits of openness, cooperativeness and nurturance which promote peaceful solutions to conflicts tend to be fostered exclusively in women who are then effectively excluded from positions of power and decision-making in a sexist society. Consequently, if we are to rid society of militarism, Reardon argues, we need to rid society of sexism as well.

But even granting that sexism and militarism are inextricably linked in society in just the way Reardon maintains, how does this effect the validity of just war theory? Since just war theory expresses the values of proportionality and respect for the rights of innocents, how could it be linked to militarism and sexism? The answer is that the linkage is practical rather than theoretical. It is because the leaders in a militarist/sexist society have been socialized to be competitive, aggressive and adverse to cooperation that they will tend to misapply just war theory when making military decisions. This represents an important practical challenge to just war theory. And, the only way of meeting this challenge, as far as I can tell, is to rid society of its sexist and militarist attitudes and practices so as to increase the chances that just war theory will be correctly applied in the future.

Practical Implications for the Use of Nuclear Weapons

The requirements for just war theory that have been defended so far are directly applicable to the question of the morality of nuclear war. In particular, requirements (2) and (3) on just means would prohibit any counter-city or counter-population use of nuclear weapons. While this prohibition need not be interpreted as absolute, it is simply not foreseeable that any use of nuclear weapons could ever be a morally justified exception to this prohibition.

But what about a counter-force use of nuclear weapons? Consider the massive use of nuclear weapons by the United States or the Soviet Union against industrial and economic centers. Such a strike, involving three to five thousand warheads, could destroy between 70–80% of each nation's industry and result in the immediate death of as many as 165 million Americans and 100 million Russians respectively, in addition to running a considerable risk of a retaliatory nuclear strike by the opposing superpower.[10] It has also been estimated by Carl Sagan and others that such a strike is very likely to generate firestorms which would cover much of the earth with sooty smoke for months, creating a "nuclear winter" that would threaten the very survival of the human species.[11] Applying requirement (1) on just means, there simply is no foreseeable military objective which could justify such morally horrendous consequences.

The same holds true for a massive use of nuclear weapons against tactical and strategic targets. Such a strike, involving two to three thousand warheads, directed against only ICBMs and submarine and bomber bases could wipe out as many as 20 million Americans and 28 million Russians respectively, in addition to running a considerable risk of a retaliatory nuclear strike by the opposing superpower.[12] Here too there is a considerable risk of a "nuclear winter" occurring. This being the case, what military objective might foreseeably justify such a use of nuclear weapons?

Of course, it should be pointed out that the above argument does not rule out a limited use of nuclear weapons at least against tactical and strategic targets. Such a use is still possible. Yet practically it would be quite difficult for either superpower to distinguish between a limited and a massive use of nuclear weapons, especially if a full-scale conventional war is raging. In such circumstances, any use of nuclear weapons is likely to be viewed as part of a massive use of such weapons, thus increasing the risk of a massive nuclear retaliatory strike.[13] In addition, war games have shown that if enough tactical nuclear weapons are employed over time in a limited area, such as Germany, the effect on noncombatants in that area would be much the same as in a massive nuclear attack.[14] As Bundy, Kennan, McNamara and Smith put the point in their recent endorsement of a doctrine of no first use of nuclear weapons:

> Every serious analysis and every military exercise, for over 25 years, has demonstrated that even the most restrained battlefield use would be enormously destructive to civilian life and property. There is no way for anyone to have any confidence that such a nuclear action will not lead to further and more devastating exchanges. Any use of nuclear weapons in Europe, by the Alliance or against it, carries with it a high and inescapable risk of escalation into the general nuclear war which would bring ruin to all and victory to none.[15]

For these reasons, even a limited use of nuclear weapons generally would not meet requirement (1) on just means.

Nevertheless, there are some circumstances in which a limited use of nuclear weapons would meet all the requirements on just means. For example, suppose that a nation was attacked with a massive nuclear counterforce strike and it was likely that, if the nation did not retaliate with a limited nuclear strike on tactical and strategic targets, a massive attack on its industrial and population centers would follow. Under such circumstances, it can be argued, a limited nuclear retaliatory strike would satisfy all the requirements on just means. Of course, the justification for such a strike would depend on what foreseen effect the strike would have on innocent lives and how likely it was that the strike would succeed in deterring a massive attack on the nation's industrial and population centers. But assuming a limited nuclear retaliatory strike on tactical and strategic targets was the best way of avoiding a significantly greater evil, it would be morally justified according to the requirements on just means.

Practical Implications for the Threat to Use Nuclear Weapons

Yet what about the morality of threatening to use nuclear weapons to achieve nuclear deterrence? Obviously, the basic requirements of just war theory are not directly applicable to threats to use nuclear weapons. Nevertheless, it seems clear that the just war theory would support the following analogous requirements of what we could call "just threat theory."

Just Cause   There must be a substantial threat or the likelihood of such a threat and nonthreatening correctives must be hopeless or too costly.

Just Means

1. The risk of harm resulting from the use of threats (or bluffs) should not be disproportionate to the military objective to be attained.
2. Actions that are prohibited by just war theory cannot be threatened as an end or a means.
3. The risk of harm to innocents from the use of threats (bluffs) should be minimized by accepting risks (costs) to oneself that would not render it impossible to attain the military objective.

Now if we assume that the requirement of just cause is met, the crucial restriction of just threat theory is requirement (2) on just means. This requirement puts a severe restriction on what we can legitimately threaten to do, assuming, that is, that threatening implies an intention to carry out under appropriate conditions what one has threatened to do. In fact, since, as we have seen, only a limited use of nuclear weapons could ever foreseeably be morally justified, it follows from requirement (2) that only such a use can be legitimately threatened. Obviously, this constitutes a severe limit on the use of threats to achieve nuclear deterrence.

Nevertheless, it may be possible to achieve nuclear deterrence by other means, for example, by bluffing. Now there are two ways that one can be bluffing while proclaiming that one will do actions that are prohibited by just war theory. One way is *by not being committed to doing* what one proclaims one will do should deterrence fail. The other is *by being committed not to do* what one proclaims one would do should deterrence fail. Of course, the first form of bluffing is more morally problematic than the

second since it is less of a barrier to the subsequent formation of a commitment to do what would be prohibited by just war theory, but since it lacks a present commitment to carry out actions prohibited by just war theory should deterrence fail, it still has the form of a bluff rather than a threat.[16]

The possibility of achieving nuclear deterrence by bluffing, however, has not been sufficiently explored because it is generally not thought to be possible to institutionalize bluffing. But suppose we imagine bluffing to include deploying a survivable nuclear force and preparing that force for possible use in such a way that leaders who are bluffing a morally prohibited form of nuclear retaliation need outwardly distinguish themselves from those who are threatening such retaliation only in their strong moral condemnation of this use of nuclear weapons. Surely this form of bluffing is capable of being institutionalized.

This form of bluffing can also be effective in achieving deterrence because it is subject to at least two interpretations. One interpretation is that the leaders of a nation are actually bluffing because while the leaders do deploy nuclear weapons and do appear to threaten to use them in certain ways, they also morally condemn those uses of nuclear weapons, so they can't really be intending to so use them. The other interpretation is that the leaders are not bluffing but are in fact immoral agents intentionally committed to doing what they regard as a grossly immoral course of action. But since the leaders of other nations can never be reasonably sure which interpretation is correct, a nation's leaders can effectively bluff under these conditions.

Moreover, citizens who think that only a bluffing strategy with respect to certain forms of nuclear retaliation can ever be morally justified would look for leaders who express their own views on this issue in just this ambiguous manner. It is also appropriate for those who are in places of high command within a nation's nuclear forces to express the same ambiguous views; only those low in the command structure of a nation's nuclear forces need not express the same ambiguous views about the course of action they would be carrying out, assuming they can see themselves as carrying out only (part of) a limited nuclear retaliatory strike. This is because, as we noted earlier, such a strike would be morally justified under certain conceivable but unlikely conditions.

Yet even granting that a threat of limited nuclear retaliation and a bluff of massive nuclear retaliation can be justified by the requirements of just means, it would not follow that we are presently justified in so threatening or bluffing unless there presently exists a just cause for threatening or bluffing. Of course, it is generally assumed that such a cause does presently exist. That is, it is generally assumed that both superpowers have a just cause to maintain a state of nuclear deterrence vis-á-vis each other by means of threats and bluffs of nuclear retaliation.

But to determine whether this assumption is correct, let us consider two possible stances a nation's leaders might take with respect to nuclear weapons:

1. A nation's leaders might be willing to carry out a nuclear strike *only* in response to either a nuclear first strike or a massive conventional first strike on itself or its principal allies.

2. A nation's leaders might be willing to carry out a massive conventional strike *only* in response to either a nuclear first strike or a massive conventional first strike on itself or its principal allies.

Now assuming that a nation's leaders were to adopt (1) and (2) then threats or bluffs of nuclear retaliation could not in fact be made against them! For a threat or bluff must render less eligible something an agent might otherwise want to do, and leaders of nations who adopt (1) and (2) have a preference structure that would not be affected by any attempt to threaten or bluff nuclear retaliation. Hence, such threats or bluffs could not be made against them either explicitly or implicitly.

Of course, a nation's leaders could try to threaten or bluff nuclear retaliation against another nation but if the intentions of the leaders of that other nation are purely defensive then although they may succeed in restricting the liberty of the leaders of that other nation by denying them a possible option, they would not have succeeded in threatening them for that would require that they render less eligible something those leaders might otherwise want to do.[17]

Now if we take them at their word, the leaders of both superpowers seem to have adopted (1) and (2). As Casper Weinberger recently characterized U.S. policy:

> Our strategy is a defensive one, designed to prevent attack, particularly nuclear attack, against us or our allies.[18]

And a similar statement of Soviet policy can be found in Mikhail Gorbachev's recent appeal for a return to a new era of detente.[19] Moreover, since 1982 Soviet leaders appear to have gone beyond simply endorsing (1) and (2) and have ruled out the use of a nuclear first strike under any circumstances.[20]

Assuming the truth of these statements, it follows that the present leaders of the U.S. and the Soviet Union could not be threatening or bluffing each other with nuclear retaliation despite their apparent attempts to do so. This is because a commitment to (1) and (2) rules out the necessary aggressive intentions that it is the purpose of such threats or bluffs to deter. Leaders of nations whose strategy is a purely defensive one would be immune from threats or bluffs of nuclear retaliation. In fact, leaders of nations who claim their strategy is purely defensive yet persist in attempting to threaten or bluff nuclear retaliation against nations whose proclaimed strategy is also purely defensive eventually throw into doubt their own commitment to a purely defensive strategy. It is for these reasons, that a just cause for threatening or bluffing nuclear retaliation does not exist under present conditions.

Of course, the leaders of a superpower might claim that threatening or bluffing nuclear retaliation would be morally justified under present conditions on the grounds that the proclaimed defensive strategy of the other superpower is not believable. Surely this stance would be reasonable if the other superpower had launched an aggressive attack against the superpower or its principal allies. But neither U.S. intervention in Nicaragua nor Soviet intervention in Afghanistan nor other military actions taken by either superpower are directed against even a principal ally of the other superpower. Consequently, in the absence of an aggressive attack of the appropriate sort and in the absence of an opposing military force that could be used without risking unacceptable losses from retaliatory strikes, each superpower is morally required to provisionally place some trust in the proclaimed defensive strategy of the other superpower.

Nevertheless, it would still be morally legitimate for both superpowers to retain a retaliatory nuclear force so as to be able to threaten or bluff nuclear retaliation in the future should conditions change for the worse. For as long as nations possess nuclear weapons, such a change could occur simply with a change of leadership bringing to power leaders who can only be deterred by a threat or bluff of nuclear retaliation.

For example, suppose a nation possesses a survivable nuclear force capable of inflicting unacceptable damage upon its adversary, yet possession of such a force alone would not suffice to deter an adversary from carrying out a nuclear first strike unless that possession were combined with a threat of limited nuclear retaliation or a bluff of massive nuclear retaliation. (With respect to massive nuclear retaliation, bluffing would be required here since leaders who recognize and respect the above just war constraints on the use of nuclear weapons could not in fact threaten such retaliation.) Under these circumstances, I think the required threat or bluff would be morally justified. But I also think that there is ample evidence today to indicate that neither the leadership of the United States nor that of the Soviet Union requires such a threat or bluff to deter them from carrying out a nuclear first strike.[21] Consequently, under present conditions, such a threat or bluff would not be morally justified.

Nevertheless, under present conditions it would be legitimate for a nation to maintain a survivable nuclear force in order to be able to deal effectively with a change of policy in the future. Moreover, if either superpower does in fact harbor any undetected aggressive intentions against the other, the possession of a survivable nuclear force by the other superpower should suffice to deter a first strike since neither superpower could be sure whether in response to such strike the other superpower would follow its moral principles or its national interest.[22]

Of course, if nuclear forces were only used to retain the capacity for threatening or bluffing in the future should conditions change for the worse then surely at some point this use of nuclear weapons could also be eliminated. But its elimination would require the establishment of extensive political, economic and cultural ties between the superpowers so as to reduce the present uncertainty about the future direction of policy, and obviously the establishment of such ties, even when it is given the highest priority, which it frequently is not, requires time to develop.

In the meantime a nuclear force deployed for the purpose of being capable of threatening or bluffing in the future should conditions change for the worse, should be capable of surviving a first strike and then inflicting either limited or massive nuclear retaliation on an aggressor. During the Kennedy-Johnson years, Robert McNamara estimated that massive nuclear retaliation required a nuclear force capable of destroying one-half of a nation's industrial capacity along with one-quarter of its population, and comparable figures have been suggested by others.

Clearly, ensuring a loss in this neighborhood should constitute unacceptable damage from the perspective of any would-be aggressor.

Notice, however, that in order for a nation to maintain a nuclear force capable of inflicting such damage, it is not necessary that components of its land-, its air- and its sea-based strategic forces all be survivable. Accordingly, even if all of the land-based ICBMs in the United States were totally destroyed in a first strike, surviving elements of the U.S. air and submarine forces could easily inflict the required degree of damage and more. In fact, any one of the 37 nuclear submarines maintained by the United States, each with up to 192 warheads, could almost single-handedly inflict the required degree of damage. Consequently, the U.S. submarine force alone should suffice as a force capable of massive nuclear retaliation.

But what about a nuclear force capable of limited nuclear retaliation? At least with respect to U.S. nuclear forces, it would seem that as Trident I missiles replace less accurate Poseidon missiles, and especially when Trident II missiles come on line in the next few years, the U.S. submarine force will have the capacity for both limited and massive nuclear retaliation. However, until this modernization is complete, the U.S. will still have to rely, in part, on survivable elements of its air- and land-based strategic forces for its capacity to inflict limited nuclear retaliation. And it would seem that the Soviet Union is also in a comparable situation.[23]

To sum up, I have argued for the following practical implications of just war theory and just threat theory for nuclear strategy:

1. Under present conditions, it is morally justified to possess a survivable nuclear force in order to be able to quickly threaten or bluff nuclear retaliation should conditions change for the worse.
2. If conditions do change for the worse, it would be morally justified at some point to threaten a form of limited nuclear retaliation.
3. If conditions worsen further so that a massive nuclear first strike can only be deterred by the bluff or threat of a massive nuclear retaliation, it would be morally justified to bluff but not threaten massive nuclear retaliation.

4. Under certain conceivable but unlikely conditions, a limited retaliatory use of nuclear weapons against tactical and strategic targets would be morally justified in order to restore deterrence.

Yet isn't there something better than the practical implications of just war theory and just threat theory that I have just proposed? What about President Reagan's Strategic Defense Initiative or "Star Wars" defense? Admittedly, this strategy is presently only at the research and development stage, but couldn't such a strategy turn out to be morally preferable to the one I have proposed? Not as far as I can tell, for the following reasons.

Strategic Defense Initiative or SDI is sometimes represented as an umbrella defense and sometimes as a point or limited defense. As an umbrella defense, SDI is pure fantasy. Given the variety of countermeasures either superpower might employ, such as shortening the booster phase of their rockets so as to make them less of a target for lasers and dispersing various types of decoys, no defensive system could track and destroy all the land- and sea-based warheads either superpower could use in an all out attack.[24] Estimates by supporters of SDI have put the effectiveness of such a defensive system at 30%.[25] This means that SDI could reduce by 30% the effective nuclear force either superpower might use against the other.

But a similar or greater reduction of nuclear forces could more easily be achieved by bilateral negotiations if a reduction of nuclear forces is what both superpowers want. Moreover, a unilateral attempt to get such a reduction though SDI is not likely to succeed. Either superpower only needs to increase their nuclear forces by 30% to offset the effect of SDI. And this is what either superpower might do if they thought that an SDI program was part of a general defensive and offensive nuclear buildup.

In addition, the cost of SDI is astronomical. President Reagan wants a research and development budget for SDI of over $30 billion for the next five years. For comparison that is more than the total research and development and *production* costs for the B1 bomber or for the MX missile system. And estimates for the total cost of SDI are in the neighborhood of 1 trillion dollars.[26] For comparison the total federal budget for 1985 was only 1.8 trillion dollars. Now what kind of a nation would spend 1 trillion dollars for an SDI that gave it a 30% reduction of the nuclear forces that could be used against

it—a reduction that could have been achieved by bilateral negotiations and would most likely be negated in the absence of such negotiations? Certainly not a nation that is known for the wisdom of its leaders or its citizenry. For these and other reasons, I think that SDI is certainly not morally preferable to those practical implications of just war theory and just threat theory for nuclear strategy that I have been defending.

Notes

1. Jan Narveson, "Pacifism: A Philosophical Analysis," *Ethics* Vol. 75 (1965).
2. Cheyney Ryan, "Self-Defense and Pacifism," in *The Ethics of War and Nuclear Deterrence*, edited by James P. Sterba (Belmont, Wadsworth Publishing Co. 1985).
3. Even if these bombings did help shorten World War II, and there is considerable evidence that they did not, they would have still been in violation of requirement (2) on just means.
4. See Michael Walzer, *Just and Unjust Wars* (New York, 1977) p. 152.
5. George Mavrodes, "Conventions and the Morality of War," in *Morality in Practice*, 1st ed., edited by James P. Sterba, (Belmont, 1983) pp. 302–310.
6. Gregory Kavka, "Nuclear Deterrence: Some Moral Perplexities," in *The Ethics of War and Nuclear Deterrence*, edited by James P. Sterba (Belmont, 1985) pp. 127–138.
7. James Child, *Nuclear War: The Moral Dimension*, (Bowling Green, 1986) especially pp. 140–149.
8. Child, p. 142.
9. Betty Reardon, *Sexism and the War System* (New York, 1985) especially Chapter 3.
10. *The Effects of Nuclear War*, Office of Technology Assessment (Washington, D.C., U.S. Government Printing Office 1979), pp. 94, 100; Nigel Calder, *Nuclear Nightmare* (New York, Viking 1979), p. 150; Sidney Lens, *The Day Before Doomsday* (Boston, Beacon Press 1977), p. 102.
11. Carl Sagan, "Nuclear War and Climate Catastrophe: Some Policy Implications," *Foreign Affairs* Vol 62 (1983) pp. 257–292.
12. *The Effects of Nuclear War*, pp. 83, 91; Jerome Kahan, *Security in the Nuclear Age* (Washington, D.C., The Brookings Institution, p. 202; Lens, pp. 98, 99, 102.
13. Lens, pp. 78–79; Spurgeon Keeny and Wolfgang Panofksy "MAD verse NUTS" *Foreign Affairs* Vol 60 (1981–2), pp. 297–298; Ian Clark, *Limited Nuclear War*, (Princeton, Princeton University Press 1982) p. 242.

14. Lens, p. 73.

15. McGeorge Bundy, George F. Kennan, Robert S. McNamara and Gerald Smith, "Nuclear Weapons and the Atlantic Alliance," *Foreign Affairs* Vol 61 (1982), p. 757. It should be noted that Bundy, Kennan, McNamara and Smith believed that their endorsement of a doctrine of no first use of nuclear weapons *may* involve increased spending for conventional forces in Europe. Others, however, have found NATO's existing conventional strength to be adequate to meet a Soviet attack. See David Barash and Judith Lipton, *Stop Nuclear War* (New York, Gwne Press 1982), pp. 138–140; Harold Brown, *Department of Defense, Annual Report* (1981).

16. For a defense of this second form of bluffing although mistakenly classified as a form of threatening, see Kenneth Kemp, "Nuclear Deterrence and the Morality of Intentions" *The Monist* (1987).

17. On my view to succeed in threatening two conditions must be met:
    1. One must have the intention to carry out the action one is purporting to threaten under the stated conditions, that is, one must expect that if the stated conditions do obtain then one will carry out that action.
    2. The preference structure of the party that one is trying to threaten must be so affected that something the party might otherwise have wanted to do is rendered less eligible.

18. Caspar Weinberger, "Why We Must Have Nuclear Deterrence," *Defense* (March 1983) p. 3.

19. *The New York Times*, May 9, 1985.

20. See Leonid Brezhnev's message to the U.N. General Assembly on June 2, 1982.

21. See Kahan, *Security in the Nuclear Age*; Lens, *The Day Before Doomsday*; Henry Kendall and others, *Beyond the Freeze* (Boston, Beacon Press 1982); George Kistiakowsky, "False Alarm: The Story Behind Salt II," *The New York Review of Books* (April 1, 1979); Les Aspin, "How to Look at the Soviet-American Balance" *Foreign Policy* Vol 22 (1976); Gordon Adams, "The Iron Triangle," *The Nation* (October, 1981), pp. 425, 441–444. Much of this evidence is reviewed in my paper "How to Achieve Nuclear Deterrence Without Threatening Nuclear Destruction," included in *The Ethics of War and Nuclear Deterrence*.

22. It might be objected that this proposed policy is hypocritical because it allows a nation following it to benefit from an adversary's uncertainty as to whether that nation would follow its moral principles or its national interest. But it seems odd to deny a nation such a benefit. For we all know that moral people can lose out in so many ways to those who are immoral. Occasionally, however, being immoral does have its liabilities and one such liability is that it is hard for immoral people to believe that others will not act in just the way they themselves do, especially when the benefits from doing so are quite substantial. Why then should not moral people be allowed to extract some benefit from the inability of immoral people to believe that moral people are as good as they say they are. After all, it is not the fault of moral people that immoral people are blinded in their judgment in this regard. Consequently, I see no reason to allow a nation to benefit from its adversary's uncertainty as to whether it will follow the requirements of morality or those of national interest.

23. *Soviet Military Power*, U.S. Department of Defense (Washington, D.C., U.S. Government Printing Office, 1983); David Holloway, *The Soviet Union and the Arms Race* (New Haven, Yale University Press 1983); Andrew Cockburn, *The Threat* (New York, Random House 1983) Chapter 12.

24. U.S. Office of Technology Assessment, *Ballistic Missile Defense Technologies* (Washington D.C., U.S. Government Printing Office 1985); Union of Concerned Scientists, "Ballistic Missile Defense: A Dangerous Dream" in *Braking Point* Vol 2 (1984).

25. See Colin Campbell, "At Columbia, 3 Days of Arms Talks," *New York Times*, February 11, 1985 and "Star Wars Chief Takes Aim at Critics," *Science*, August 10, 1984.

26. Union of Concerned Scientists, "Boosting Star Wars," *Nucleus* Vol 6 (1985), pp. 2, 4.

Writing and Discussion Topics

Questions 1–6 address content, critical analysis, personal choices, ethical options, specific discipline, and interdisciplinary alternatives, respectively.

1. Sterba makes a distinction in his just-war explanation between the possession of nuclear weapons and the threat to use nuclear weapons. Explain this distinction.
2. Does Sterba support current government strategies on nuclear defense? Explain how Sterba's arguments coincide or differ from these strategies.
3. According to the collectivist challenge, we are all combatants in modern warfare because, as members of a society, we are collectively responsible for the actions of our leaders. Would you take radical steps to disassociate yourself from aggressive steps your leaders might take in a war you believe to be unjust? Would you emigrate or participate in civil disobedience?

4. Are the practical implications Sterba claims for nuclear weapons ethical in your judgment? Evaluate your response using Kant's system of ethics.

5. Sterba defends the just war theory against feminist challenges. What connections do you see between those challenges and the ethic of care? How might Gilligan respond?

6. Using Sterba's point of view, compare and contrast the style of a philosopher with the satirical style of Mark Twain or the dramatic effects of Luigi Pirandello on the subject of war. (Twain and Pirandello are authors in the literature section of this chapter.)

The National Conference of Catholic Bishops

NUCLEAR WEAPONS AND NUCLEAR DETERRENCE

◆◆◆

D uring a general meeting of the National Conference of Catholic Bishops in 1980, a committee of bishops was appointed to study nuclear deterrence and draft a pastoral letter on war and peace. In 1983 the body of bishops approved the letter, The Challenge of Peace: God's Promise and Our Response, in the plenary assembly. The following is an excerpt from this letter. ◆

The Use of Nuclear Weapons

Establishing moral guidelines in the nuclear debate means addressing first the question of the use of nuclear weapons. That question has several dimensions.

It is clear that those in the Church who interpret the gospel teaching as forbidding all use of violence would oppose any use of nuclear weapons under any conditions. In a sense the existence of these weapons simply confirms and reinforces one of the initial insights of the non-violent position, namely, that Christians should not use lethal force since the hope of using it selectively and restrictively is so often an illusion. Nuclear weapons seem to prove this point in a way heretofore unknown.

For the tradition which acknowledges some legitimate use of force, some important elements of contemporary nuclear strategies move beyond the limits of moral justification. A justifiable use of force must be both discriminatory and proportionate. Certain aspects of both U.S. and Soviet strategies fail both tests as we shall discuss below. The technical literature and the personal testimony of public officials who have been closely associated with U.S. nuclear strategy have both convinced us of the overwhelming probability that major nuclear exchange would have no limits.

On the more complicated issue of "limited" nuclear war, we are aware of the extensive literature and discussion which this topic has generated. As a general statement, it seems to us that public officials would be unable to refute the following conclusion of the study made by the Pontifical Academy of Sciences:

> Even a nuclear attack directed only at military facilities would be devastating to the country as a whole. This is because military facilities are widespread rather than concentrated at only a few points. Thus, many nuclear weapons would be exploded.
>
> Furthermore, the spread of radiation due to the natural winds and atmospheric mixing would kill vast numbers of people and contaminate large areas. The medical facilities of any nation would be inadequate to care for the survivors. An objective examination of the medical situation that would follow a nuclear war leads to but one conclusion: prevention is our only recourse.[1]

Moral Principles and Policy Choices

In light of these perspectives we address three questions more explicitly: (1) counter population warfare; (2) initiation of nuclear war; and (3) limited nuclear war.

1 Counter Population Warfare   Under no circumstances may nuclear weapons or other instruments of mass slaughter be used for the purpose of destroying population centers or other predominantly civilian targets. Popes have repeatedly condemned "total war" which implies such use. For example, as early as 1954 Pope Pius XII condemned nuclear warfare "when it entirely escapes the control of man," and results in "the pure and simple annihilation of all human life within the radius of action."[2] The condemnation was repeated by he Second Vatican Council:

> Any act of war aimed indiscriminately at the destruction of entire cities or of extensive areas along with their population is a crime against God and man itself. It merits unequivocal and unhesitating condemnation.[3]

Retaliatory action whether nuclear or conventional which would indiscriminately take many wholly innocent lives, lives of people who are in no way responsible for reckless actions of their government, must also be condemned. This condemnation, in our judgment, applies even to the retaliatory use of weapons striking enemy cities after our own have already been struck. No Christian can rightfully carry out orders or policies deliberately aimed at killing non-combatants.[4]

---

[1] Pontifical Academy of Sciences, "Statement on the Consequences of the Use of Nuclear Weapons," in *Peace and Disarmament: Documents of the World Council of Churches and the Roman Catholic Church* (Geneva and Rome: 1982), p. 243.

[2] Pius XII, "Address to the VIII Congress of the World Medical Association," ibid., p. 131.

[3] Vatican II, the *Pastoral Constitution on the Church in the Modern World* (hereafter cited: *Pastoral Constitution*), #80. Papal and conciliar texts will be referred to by title with paragraph number.

[4] Ibid.

We make this judgment at the beginning of our treatment of nuclear strategy precisely because the defense of the principle of noncombatant immunity is so important for an ethic of war and because the nuclear age has posed such extreme problems for the principle. Later in this letter we shall discuss specific aspects of U.S. policy in light of this principle and in light of recent U.S. policy statements stressing the determination not to target directly or strike directly against civilian populations. Our concern about protecting the moral value of noncombatant immunity, however, requires that we make a clear reassertion of the principle our first word on this matter.

2 The Initiation of Nuclear War

We do not perceive any situation in which the deliberate initiation of nuclear warfare, on however restricted a scale, can be morally justified. Non-nuclear attacks by another state must be resisted by other than nuclear means. Therefore, a serious moral obligation exists to develop non-nuclear defensive strategies as rapidly as possible. . . .

At the same time we recognize the responsibility the United States has had and continues to have in assisting allied nations in their defense against either a conventional or a nuclear attack. Especially in the European theater, the deterrence of a *nuclear* attack may require nuclear weapons for a time, even though their possession and deployment must be subject to rigid restrictions.

The need to defend against a conventional attack in Europe imposes the political and moral burden of developing adequate, alternative modes of defense to present reliance on nuclear weapons. Even with the best coordinated effort—hardly likely in view of contemporary political division on this question—development of an alternative defense position will still take time.

In the interim, deterrence against a conventional attack relies upon two factors: the not inconsiderable conventional forces at the disposal of NATO and the recognition by a potential attacker that the outbreak of large scale conventional war could escalate to the nuclear level through accident or miscalculation by either side. We are aware that NATO's refusal to adopt a "no first use" pledge is to some extent linked to the deterrent effect of this inherent ambiguity. Nonetheless, in light of the probable effects of initiating nuclear war, we urge NATO to move rapidly toward the adoption of a "no first use" policy, but doing so in tandem with development of an adequate alternative defense posture.

3 Limited Nuclear War

It would be possible to agree with our first two conclusions and still not be sure about retaliatory use of nuclear weapons in what is called a "limited exchange." The issue at stake is the *real* as opposed to the *theoretical* possibility of a "limited nuclear exchange."

We recognize that the policy debate on this question is inconclusive and that all participants are left with hypothetical projections about probable reactions in a nuclear exchange. While not trying to adjudicate the technical debate, we are aware of it and wish to raise a series of questions which challenge the actual meaning of "limited" in this discussion.

- Would leaders have sufficient information to know what is happening in a nuclear exchange?
- Would they be able under the conditions of stress, time pressures, and fragmentary information to make the extraordinarily precise decision needed to keep the exchange limited if this were technically possible?
- Would military commanders be able, in the midst of the destruction and confusion of a nuclear exchange, to maintain a policy of "discriminate targeting"? Can this be done in modern warfare, waged across great distances by aircraft and missiles?
- Given the accidents we know about in peacetime conditions, what assurances are there that computer errors could be avoided in the midst of a nuclear exchange?
- Would not the casualties, even in a war defined as limited by strategists, still run in the millions?
- How "limited" would be the long-term effects of radiation, famine, social fragmentation, and economic dislocation?

Unless these questions can be answered satisfactorily, we will continue to be highly skeptical about the real meaning of "limited." One of the criteria of the just-war tradition is a reasonable hope of success in bringing about justice and peace. We must ask whether such a reasonable hope can exist once nuclear weapons have been exchanged. The burden of proof remains on those who assert that meaningful limitation is possible.

A nuclear response to either conventional or nuclear attack can cause destruction which goes far beyond "legitimate defense." Such use of nuclear weapons would not be justified.

In the face of this frightening and highly speculative debate on a matter involving millions of human lives, we believe the most effective contribution or moral judgment is to introduce perspectives by which we can assess the empirical debate. Moral perspective should be sensitive not only to the quantitative dimensions of a question but to its psychological, human, and religious characteristics as well. The issue of limited war is not simply the size of weapons contemplated or the strategies projected. The debate should include the psychological and political significance of crossing the boundary from the conventional to the nuclear arena in any form. To cross this divide is to enter a world where we have no experience of control, much testimony against its possibility, and therefore no moral justification for submitting the human community to this risk. We therefore express our view that the first imperative is to prevent any use of nuclear weapons and our hope that leaders will resist the notion that nuclear conflict can be limited, contained, or won in any traditional sense.

Deterrence in Principle and Practice

The moral challenge posed by nuclear weapons is not exhausted by an analysis of their possible uses. Much of the political and moral debate of the nuclear age has concerned the strategy of deterrence. Deterrence is at the heart of the U.S.-Soviet relationship, currently the most dangerous dimension of the nuclear arms race. . . .

1 The Moral Assessment of Deterrence
The distinctively new dimensions of nuclear deterrence were recognized by policy-makers and strategists only after much reflection. Similarly, the moral challenge posed by nuclear deterrence was grasped only after careful deliberation. The moral and political paradox posed by deterrence was concisely stated by Vatican II:

> Undoubtedly, armaments are not amassed merely for use in wartime. Since the defensive strength of any nation is thought to depend on its capacity for immediate retaliation, the stockpiling of arms which grows from year to year serves, in a way hitherto unthought of, as a deterrent to potential

attackers. Many people look upon this as the most effective way known at the present time for maintaining some sort of peace among nations. Whatever one may think of this form of deterrent, people are convinced that the arms race, which quite a few countries have entered, is no infallible way of maintaining real peace and that the resulting so-called balance of power is no sure genuine path to achieving it. Rather than eliminate the causes of war, the arms race serves only to aggravate the position. As long as extravagant sums of money are poured into the development of new weapons, it is impossible to devote adequate aid in tackling the misery which prevails at the present day in the world. Instead of eradicating international conflict once and for all, the contagion is spreading to other parts of the world. New approaches, based on reformed attitudes, will have to be chosen in order to remove this stumbling block, to free the earth from its pressing anxieties, and give back to the world a genuine peace.[5]

Without making a specific moral judgment on deterrence, the council clearly designated the elements of the arms race: the tension between "peace of a sort" preserved by deterrence and "genuine peace" required for a stable international life, the contradiction between what is spent for destructive capacity and what is needed for constructive development.

In the post-conciliar assessment of war and peace, and specifically of deterrence, different parties to the political-moral debate within the Church and in civil society have focused on one aspect or another of the problem. For some, the fact that nuclear weapons have not been used since 1945 means that deterrence has worked, and this fact satisfies the demands of both the political and the moral order. Others contest this assessment by highlighting the risk of failure involved in continued reliance on deterrence and pointing out how politically and morally catastrophic even a single failure would be. Still others note that the absence of nuclear war is not necessarily proof that the policy of deterrence has prevented it. Indeed, some would find in the policy of deterrence the driving force in the superpower arms race. Still other observers, many of them Catholic moralists, have stressed that deterrence may not morally include the intention of deliberately attacking civilian populations or noncombatants. . . .

---

[5]*Pastoral Constitution*, #81.

In June 1982, Pope John Paul II provided new impetus and insight to the moral analysis with his statement to the United Nations Second Special Session on Disarmament. The pope first situated the problem of deterrence within the context of world politics. No power, he observes, will admit to wishing to start a war, but each distrusts others and considers it necessary to mount a strong defense against attack. He then discusses the notion of deterrence:

> Many even think that such preparations constitute the way—even the only way—to safeguard peace in some fashion or at least to impede to the utmost in an efficacious way the outbreak of wars, especially major conflicts which might lead to the ultimate holocaust of humanity and the destruction of the civilization that man has constructed so laboriously over the centuries.
>
> In this approach one can see the "philosophy of peace" which was proclaimed in the ancient Roman principle: *Si vis pacem, para bellum.* Put in modern terms, the "philosophy" has the label of "deterrence" and one can find it in various guises of the search for a "balance of forces" which sometimes has been called, and not without reason, the "balance of terror."[6]

Having offered this analysis of the general concept of deterrence, the Holy Father introduces his considerations on disarmament, especially, but not only, nuclear disarmament. Pope John Paul II makes this statement about the morality of deterrence:

> In current conditions "deterrence" based on balance, certainly not as an end in itself but as a step on the way toward a progressive disarmament, may still be judged morally acceptable. Nonetheless in order to ensure peace, it is indispensable not to be satisfied with this minimum which is always susceptible to the real danger of explosion.[7]

In Pope John Paul II's assessment we perceive two dimensions of the contemporary dilemma of deterrence. One dimension is the danger of nuclear war, with its human and moral costs. The possession of nuclear weapons, the continuing quantitative growth of the arms race, and the danger of nuclear proliferation all point to the grave danger of basing "peace of a sort" on deterrence. The other dimension is the independence and freedom of nations and entire peoples, including the need to protect smaller nations from threats to their independence and integrity. Deterrence reflects the radical distrust which marks international politics, a condition identified as a major problem by Pope John XIII in *Peace on Earth* and reaffirmed by Pope Paul VI and Pope John Paul II. Thus a balance of forces, preventing either side from achieving superiority, can be seen as a means of safeguarding both dimensions.

The moral duty today is to prevent nuclear war from ever occurring *and* to protect and preserve those key values of justice, freedom and independence which are necessary for personal dignity and national integrity. In reference to these issues, Pope John Paul II judges that deterrence may still be judged morally acceptable, "certainly not as an end in itself but as a step on the way toward a progressive disarmament." . . .

In preparing this letter we have tried, through a number of sources, to determine as precisely as possible the factual character of U.S. deterrence strategy. Two questions have particularly concerned us: (1) the targeting doctrine and strategic plans for the use of the deterrent, particularly their impact on civilian casualties; and (2) the relationship of deterrence strategy and nuclear war-fighting capability to the likelihood that war will in fact be prevented.

Moral Principles and Policy Choices

Targeting doctrine raises significant moral questions because it is a significant determinant of what would occur if nuclear weapons were ever to be used. Although we acknowledge the need for deterrent, not all forms of deterrence are morally acceptable. There are moral limits to deterrence policy as well as to policy regarding use. Specifically, it is not morally acceptable to intend to kill the innocent as part of a strategy of deterring nuclear war. The question of whether U.S. policy involves an intention to strike civilian centers (directly targeting civilian populations) has been one of our factual concerns.

This complex question has always produced a variety of responses, official and unofficial in character. The NCCB Committee has received a series of statements of clarification of policy from U.S. government officials. Essentially these statements declare that it is not U.S. strategic policy to target the Soviet civilian population as such or to use nuclear weapons deliberately for the purpose of destroying population centers. These statements respond, in principle at least, to one moral criterion

[6]John Paul II, "Message to the Second Special Session of the United Nations General Assembly Devoted to Disarmament" (June 1982) thereafter cited: ("Message U.N. Special Session 1982"), #3.

[7]Ibid., #8.

for assessing deterrence policy: the immunity of non-combatants from direct attack either by conventional or nuclear weapons.

These statements do not address or resolve another very troublesome moral problem, namely, that an attack on military targets or militarily significant industrial targets could involve "indirect" (i.e., unintended) but massive civilian casualties. We are advised, for example, that the United States strategic nuclear targeting plan (SIOP—Single Integrated Operational Plan) has identified 60 "military" targets within the city of Moscow alone, and that 40,000 "military" targets for nuclear weapons have been identified in the whole of the Soviet Union. It is important to recognize that Soviet policy is subject to the same moral judgment; attacks on several "industrial targets" or politically significant targets in the United States could produce massive civilian casualties. The number of civilians who would necessarily be killed by such strikes is horrendous. This problem is unavoidable because of the way modern military facilities and production centers are so thoroughly interspersed with civilian living and working areas. It is aggravated if one side deliberately positions military targets in the midst of a civilian population. In our consultations, administration officials readily admitted that, while they hoped any nuclear exchange could be kept limited, they were prepared to retaliate in a massive way if necessary. They also agreed that once any substantial numbers of weapons were used, the civilian casualty levels would quickly become truly catastrophic, and that even with attacks limited to "military" targets, the number of deaths in a substantial exchange would be almost indistinguishable from what might occur if civilian centers had been deliberately and directly struck. These possibilities pose a different moral question and are to be judged by a different moral criterion: the principle of proportionality.

While any judgment of proportionality is always open to differing evaluations, there are actions which can be decisively judged to be disproportionate. A narrow adherence exclusively to the principle of noncombatant immunity as a criterion for policy is an inadequate moral posture for it ignores some evil and unacceptable consequences. Hence, we cannot be satisfied that the assertion of an intention not to strike civilians directly, or even the most honest effort to implement that intention, by itself constitutes a "moral policy" for the use of nuclear weapons.

The location of industrial or militarily significant economic targets within heavily populated areas or in those areas affected by radioactive fallout could well involve such massive civilian casualites that, in our judgment, such a strike would be deemed morally disproportionate, even though not intentionally indiscriminate.

The problem is not simply one of producing highly accurate weapons that might minimize civilian casualties in any single explosion, but one of increasing the likelihood of escalation at a level where many, even "discriminating," weapons would cumulatively kill very large numbers of civilians. Those civilian deaths would occur both immediately and from the long-term effects of social and economic devastation.

A second issue of concern to us is the relationship of deterrence doctrine to war-fighting strategies. We are aware of the argument that war-fighting capabilities enhance the credibility of the deterrent, particularly the strategy of extended deterrence. But the development of such capabilities raises other strategic and moral questions. The relationship of war-fighting capabilities and targeting doctrine exemplifies the difficult choices in this area of policy. Targeting civilian populations would violate the principle of discrimination—one of the central moral principles of a Christian ethic of war. But "counterforce targeting," while preferable from the perspective of protecting civilians, is often joined with a declaratory policy which conveys the notion that nuclear war is subject to precise rational and moral limits. We have already expressed our severe doubts about such a concept. Furthermore, a purely counterforce strategy may seem to threaten the viability of other nations' retaliatory forces making deterrence unstable in a crisis and war more likely.

While we welcome any effort to protect civilian populations, we do not want to legitimize or encourage moves which extend deterrence beyond the specific objective of preventing the use of nuclear weapons or other actions which could lead directly to a nuclear exchange.

These considerations of concrete elements of nuclear deterrence policy, made in light of John Paul II's evaluation, but applying it through our own prudential judgments, lead us to a strictly conditioned moral acceptance of nuclear deterrence. We cannot consider it adequate as a long-term basis for peace.

This strictly conditioned judgment yields *criteria* for morally assessing the elements of deterrence strategy. Clearly, these criteria demonstrate that we cannot approve of every weapons system, strategic doctrine, or policy initiative advanced in the name of strengthening deterrence. On the contrary, these criteria require continual public scrutiny of what our government proposes to do with the deterrent.

On the basis of these criteria we wish now to make some specific evaluations:

1. If nuclear deterrence exists only to prevent the *use* of nuclear weapons by others, then proposals to go beyond this to planning for prolonged periods of repeated nuclear strikes and counterstrikes, or "prevailing" in nuclear war, are not acceptable. They encourage notions that nuclear war can be engaged in with tolerable human and moral consequences. Rather, we must continually say "no" to the idea of nuclear war.

2. If nuclear deterrence is our goal, "sufficiency" to deter is an adequate strategy; the quest for nuclear superiority must be rejected.

3. Nuclear deterrence should be used as a step on the way toward progressive disarmament. Each proposed addition to our strategic system or change in strategic doctrine must be assessed precisely in light of whether it will render steps toward "progressive disarmament" more or less likely.

Moreover, these criteria provide us with the means to make some judgments and recommendations about the present direction of U.S. strategic policy. Progress toward a world freed of dependence on nuclear deterrence must be carefully carried out. But it must not be delayed. There is an urgent moral and political responsibility to use the "peace of a sort" we have as a framework to move toward authentic peace through nuclear arms control, reductions, and disarmament. Of primary importance in this process is the need to prevent the development and deployment of destabilizing weapons systems on either side; a second requirement is to insure that the more sophisticated command and control systems do not become mere hair triggers for automatic launch on warning; a third is the need to prevent the proliferation of nuclear weapons in the international system.

In light of these general judgments *we oppose* some specific proposals in respect to our present deterrence posture:

1. The addition of weapons which are likely to be vulnerable to attack, yet also possess a "prompt hard-target kill" capability that threatens to make the other side's retaliatory forces vulnerable. Such weapons may seem to be useful primarily in a first strike; we resist such weapons for this reason and we oppose Soviet deployment of such weapons which generate fear of a first strike against U.S. forces.

2. The willingness to foster strategic planning which seeks a nuclear war-fighting capability that goes beyond the limited function of deterrence outlined in this letter.

3. Proposals which have the effect of lowering the nuclear threshold and blurring the difference between nuclear and conventional weapons.

In support of the concept of "sufficiency" as an adequate deterrent, and in light of the present size and composition of both the U.S. and Soviet strategic arsenals, *we recommend:*

1. Support for immediate, bilateral, verifiable agreements to halt the testing, production, and deployment of new nuclear weapons systems.

2. Support for negotiated bilateral deep cuts in the arsenals of both superpowers, particularly those weapons systems which have destabilizing characteristics; U.S. proposals like those for START (Strategic Arms Reduction Talks) and INF (Intermediate-range Nuclear Forces) negotiations in Geneva are said to be designed to achieve deep cuts; our hope is that they will be pursued in a manner which will realize these goals.

3. Support for early and successful conclusion of negotiations of a comprehensive test ban treaty.

4. Removal by all parties of short-range nuclear weapons which multiply dangers disproportionate to their deterrent value.

5. Removal by all parties of nuclear weapons from areas where they are likely to be overrun in the early stages of war, thus

forcing rapid and uncontrollable decisions on their use.

6. Strengthening of command and control over nuclear weapons to prevent inadvertent and unauthorized use.

These judgments are meant to exemplify how a lack of unequivocal condemnation of deterrence is meant only to be an attempt to acknowledge the role attributed to deterrence, but not to support its extension beyond the limited purpose discussed above. Some have urged us to condemn all aspects of nuclear deterrence. This urging has been based on a variety of reasons, but has emphasized particularly the high and terrible risks that either deliberate use or accidental detonation of nuclear weapons could quickly escalate to something utterly disproportionate to any acceptable moral purpose. That determination requires highly technical judgments about hypothetical events. Although reasons exist which move some to condemn reliance on nuclear weapons for deterrence, we have not reached this conclusion for the reasons outlined in this letter.

Nevertheless, there must be no misunderstanding of our profound skepticism about the moral acceptability of any use of nuclear weapons. It is obvious that the use of any weapons which violate the principle of discrimination merits unequivocal condemnation. We are told that some weapons are designed for purely "counterforce" use against military forces and targets. The moral issue, however, is not resolved by the design of weapons or the planned intention for use; there are also consequences which must be assessed. It would be a perverted political policy or moral casuistry which tried to justify using a weapon which "indirectly" or "unintentionally" killed a million innocent people because they happened to live near a "militarily significant target."

Even the "indirect effects" of initiating nuclear war are sufficient to make it an unjustifiable moral risk in any form. It is not sufficient, for example, to contend that "our" side has plans for "limited" or "discriminate" use. Modern warfare is not readily contained by good intentions of technological designs. The psychological climate of the world is such that mention of the term "nuclear" generates uneasiness. Many contend that the use of one tactical nuclear weapon could produce panic, with completely unpredictable consequences. It is precisely this mix of political, psychological, and technological uncertainty which has moved us in this letter to reinforce with moral prohibitions and prescriptions the prevailing political barrier against resort to nuclear weapons. Our support for enhanced command and control facilities, for major reductions in strategic and tactical nuclear forces, and for a "no first use" policy (as set forth in this letter) is meant to be seen as a complement to our desire to draw a moral line against nuclear war.

Any claim by any government that it is pursuing a morally acceptable policy of deterrence must be scrutinized with the greatest care. We are prepared and eager to participate in our country in the ongoing public debate on moral grounds.

The need to rethink the deterrence policy of our nation, to make the revisions necessary to reduce the possibility of nuclear war, and to move toward a more stable system of national and international security will demand a substantial intellectual, political and moral effort. It also will require, we believe, the willingness to open ourselves to the providential care, power and word of God, which call us to recognize our common humanity and the bonds of mutual responsibility which exist in the international community in spite of political differences and nuclear arsenals. . . .

Writing and Discussion Topics

Questions 1–6 address content, critical analysis, personal choices, ethical options, specific discipline, and interdisciplinary alternatives, respectively.

1. The bishops place two limits on the just use of force. What are they? Do the bishops see a moral difference between conventional warfare and nuclear warfare? Examine the differences.

2. Take a stand on the issue of separation of church and state. Should the state be totally independent of official religious beliefs concerning nuclear arms? Should religious concerns influence funding for nuclear experimentation? Should religious leaders be invited to meet with world leaders of state to discuss nuclear arms?

3. If you were a soldier and Roman Catholic, would you carry out orders aimed at killing noncombatants? Why or why not? Would

the bishops want you to carry out these orders? What if you came across an enemy soldier who had been shot? What if examining his belongings you found he was of the same faith as you. What would you do?

4. The bishops do not think that a limited nuclear exchange can ever be ethically justified. Why do they take such a firm stand? Explain their position and compare or contrast it with yours. What ethical system do you use to support your views?

5. The bishops have a "strictly conditional" acceptance of nuclear deterrence policies. Compare their moral views with Lackey's.

6. Compare the bishops' position with the Sermon on the Mount. Do you think the bishops follow Jesus' teachings on turning the other cheek and loving your enemy? Why is religion an important discipline in the study of war? Are there different reasons for theologians and philosophers to study war?

Daniel E. Carrol, Albert W. Charmatz, James W. Gordon,
Raymond J. Juzaitis, Morris B. Pongratz, Henry L. Rutkowski.

RESPONSE TO THE U.S. BISHOPS' SECOND DRAFT OF A PROPOSED PASTORAL LETTER ON WAR, ARMAMENTS, AND PEACE

—◆◆◆—

T*his excerpt is taken from a book written by a group of scientists, all of whom are Roman Catholics, who develop and test nuclear weapons at the Los Alamos Scientific National Laboratory. This is their response to the Catholic bishops' letter. This excerpt defends the need for nuclear arms as a strong deterrence factor.* ◆

Introduction

We welcome the second draft prepared by the US bishops' ad hoc committee on war and peace. It is a thoughtful, sober, and comprehensive effort to articulate the Spirit of Christ in regard to this important issue of nuclear weapons and their use. In a world in which unspiritual forces such as greed, lust for power, and de facto atheism are so prevalent, it is essential that the spiritual leaders of the Church speak out forcefully and lead the faithful in God's direction as the world tries so insistently to drive them in the other direction.

There are many areas of agreement between our group and the authors of the bishops' letter, not the least of which is the horror of nuclear war. We wish to emphasize that we also recognize the dangers of nuclear weapons and the importance of preventing nuclear war. We also recognize, with the bishops, the importance of true peace which comes only from and through God. We agree that this peace can only be achieved by the turning of people's hearts toward Christ so that they may receive the unity which is His gift to His people. A consequence of this repentance is an awareness of the sanctity of human life that is derived from God Himself. This awareness makes the taking of human life on any scale a very grave matter indeed. Unfortunately the fullness of this peace is not to be seen by us before the triumph of Christ's kingdom over the world, a triumph which already has existed in potency since Jesus' sacrifice on the Cross. We agree that the threat of nuclear war is the result of sin in the world and that only when sin is obliterated will the full and true peace that we all desire be actualized in the world.

We also agree that the wanton destruction of helpless people in the pursuit of military ends is an evil and we condemn it as such. The bishops are correct in stating that modern conventional weapons are also capable of being used in immoral ways and must be controlled. Because Christianity is a religion of intentions, the intentions of the user of modern weapons are of almost decisive importance in defining the morality of his actions.

Finally, we welcome the bishops' letter as an invitation to evaluate the situation of nuclear weapons as they affect the morality of our own country's actions. The bishops are to be commended on their openness on the pacifism-just war debate and on their insistence that disarmament be multilateral and verifiable.

The Nature and Attainment of Peace in the World

A definition of peace that Christians would accept is that of a right relationship with God. This relationship is attained through His Son, Jesus Christ, and is attained in day to day life through the action of the Holy Spirit. If this peace is our goal, and it certainly must be, then how does the existence of nuclear weapons bear on its attainment? The bishops quote St. Paul in Ephesians 2:14–16 to say that Christ is our peace. This is certainly true; but who are the recipients of this peace and under what conditions do they receive it? This section of Scripture, taken in context, discusses the problem of disunity between converted Jews and converted uncircumsized Gentiles in the early church. Paul is saying that there is to be no disunity in the Christian community as a result of this rite of physical circumcision because Jesus has made them one in spirit. Plainly only through the action of Jesus and the acceptance of Jesus by these people was such unity to be achieved according to Paul. This unity allowed the Ephesians to have complete communion together in Christ, regardless of whether they were circumcised or not. Neither side had anything to fear for Jesus presided over both sides. It was not enough for them to simply agree to get along in some superficial way without Jesus' involvement. The fundamental division had to be healed. If we place the nations in analogy to the Ephesians we must realize that true accord will not occur if we simply abolish nuclear weapons. The Ephesians probably had weapons of their own; nevertheless it was not weapons but Christ that made the difference.

Thus both we and the bishops must admit that we are not making proposals for peace in the full Christian sense but rather for a kind of survival or absence of conflict. Hatred, malice, and greed exist in the heart and no treaty can touch them.

In the first sentence of their letter, the bishops refer to the current situation involving nuclear weapons, as a "moment of supreme crisis" as the human race advances toward maturity. In what sense is the term "supreme crisis" valid and in what sense can mankind be said to be advancing toward maturity? The supreme crisis for a Christian is the crisis of salvation. The only ultimate evil that can befall a Christian is permanent separation from God. All other

From Daniel E. Carroll, et al., *Nuclear Weapons and Morality: a View from Los Alamos.* Copyright © 1983 Immaculate Heart of Mary Catholic Church, Los Alamos, New Mexico. Reprinted by permission.

evils pale into insignificance by comparison. The supreme crisis the world faces is not that of nuclear weapons which can only cause physical destruction but rather the crisis of choice for or against God. As Jesus said in Matthew 10:28, "Do not be afraid of those who kill the body but cannot kill the soul; fear him rather who can destroy both body and soul in hell."

Man can advance toward maturity, but how? Spiritual progress is not an inevitable journey toward an ideal, regardless of the attitudes of men. Spiritual progress is achieved when individual men choose to cooperate with the grace of the Holy Spirit who gives them the wisdom to make the right choice and who gives them the strength to persist in those right choices in spite of temptation. St. Paul clearly understood this as we can see from the beginning of I Corinthians, Chapter 3. The Corinthians needed to progress from being infants in Christ, not yet ready for solid spiritual food, with the help of the Holy Spirit. One need only look at the state of our society with its divorce rate, pornography, drug addiction, materialism, violence and de facto atheism to see that it is not marching toward a secular paradise. On the Soviet side there is official atheism, total disregard for man's spiritual needs, persecution of their own and other peoples, and conquest of other nations. Abolishing nuclear weapons will neither resolve the supreme crisis nor put man back on the road to spiritual progress.

The true achievement of peace will come only from the eschatological fulfillment of Christ's kingdom. We cannot through our own efforts bring about this fulfillment. What we can do is to live ourselves as closely to God's will as possible and to try to bring more people to the kind of relationship with God that gives them true peace.

We agree with the bishops' 1980 pastoral letter on Marxism, which addressed the need for states with different political systems to live together in an interdependent world. However, although the church recognized the ideological differences, the bishops allege the differences are *overruled* by the practical need for cooperative efforts in the human interest. We feel, however, that the bishops severely underestimate the extent and consequences of the basic ideological differences dividing our societies. We believe that temporary cooperation for the sake of expediency is tolerable and in order, but the success of long term cooperation and collaboration is highly unlikely because the goals of totalitarian states are incompatible with human rights and dignity. We agree with Pope John Paul II:

> " . . . a political society can really collaborate in building international peace only if it itself is peaceful, that is to say it takes seriously the advancement of human rights at home."[1]

This is an area in which the bishops together with the faithful can do the greatest good possible. Their's is the essential work that must be done if men's hearts are to be changed. However, it must be done without cutting corners and without using stop-gap measures, i.e., remove weapons rather than changing attitudes. The bishops must realize that there is, and always has been, a fundamental dichotomy between Christ's kingdom and the world's philosophy. Peace is not to be found in accommodation, especially with powers that are manifestly hostile to God and His purposes.

Christian Values

How then are we to live in this environment? Jesus did not command us to achieve worldly peace at any cost. He did command us to love one another. We believe that this love is at the foundation of the just-war theory. If one of us were to see another in danger of being killed by a third person, we believe that Christian love would require us to intervene and use lethal force if necessary to save the innocent person's life. We believe that it is precisely the God-derived value of the individual human which makes it necessary to intervene so radically.

This regard for human life and the command to love is the reason why governments have the authority from God that they do. It is not simply the fact that they are a corporate entity that gives them power but this caring for one another. Thus in Romans 13:1–7, Paul legitimizes governmental use of force for the common good and enjoins us to respect the one who bears the sword for the state. St. Augustine and St. Thomas Aquinas recognized the legitimate use of lethal force by governments, as indeed does God in the Old Testament.

The modern equivalent of the sword in international affairs is a nuclear weapon. Like it or not, technological development has made it so. Our duty as Christians is to use these weapons out of love and respect for human life in the protection of basic human rights and the lives of others. The question of the likely consequences on Europe, and on ourselves, of unilaterally abolishing our nuclear weapons is not dealt with in the bishops' letter. There is ample empirical evidence to indicate that great spiritual and physical suffering would result. We do not believe that we have the right to purchase a form of moral rectitude by surrendering others to domination by a godless and inhuman political force.

What seems to be ignored in the pacifist position is the question of why Jesus did not defend himself physically. He was here to die for our sins, a necessary sacrifice. We are not in that situation. The death of any one of us would not expiate the single sin of one man. In the Gospel of John 2:13–17 we see Jesus violently casting the money changers out of the Temple because of zeal for His Father's house. This episode is recorded by an apostle who was very close to Jesus and who wrote many accounts emphasizing Jesus' loving approach to men. In addition, we have the warlike pictures of Jesus in the apocalypse of John, and Eusebius sees Him as a warrior in the theophany of Josh. 5:13–15. We also have God sanctioning the violent wars of Israel when they are against sinful nations. In the pacifist-just war debate, the conclusion that imitation of Christ requires pacifism is unsupported. A sentimental approach to Christ's example is no better guarantee of a moral stand than is harsh, narrow legalism.

Rejecting pacifism does not imply that we take violence and death as routine policy. Indeed it is precisely real for God's truth and the value of his creation, Man, that causes us to say that violence and death can be invoked. Neither do we say that the United States is a new Israel, chosen by God. However, there is clear distinction between the Soviet Union's philosophy of man and that of the US, in spite of all the corruption that exists in the US. It is worth risking and exercising violence to preserve religious liberty and to prevent human degradation. The defense of right is important and of consequence to God.

As Christians we must recognize that man is both a physical being and a spiritual being, destined for union with God. If we restrict the use of force to the preservation of man's physical survival we deny the importance of the spiritual well being. Man's spiritual health is just as proper to his nature as is physical health. We easily see the duty of Christians to relieve physical suffering endured by our neighbor.

Why then is it so hard for us to see the need to protect ourselves and others from spiritual enslavement to a totalitarian state?

Nuclear War

So far we have said that true peace is not fully achievable by man alone in this fallen world or before the second coming of Christ, but that it must be pursued through individual repentance. Only if this route of conversion is followed will the necessary trust ever exist. We have also seen that there is theological evidence to accept the use of force, including lethal force, to protect the basic rights and lives of others. Indeed in this world, marred by sin and its consequent disunity before God, it may be necessary to use it.

The bishops think that the poor will benefit from abolition of nuclear weapons. The US spends about six billion dollars on nuclear weapons each year. This sum is miniscule compared to the national budget. If the necesssary conventional forces are built up this money would vanish quickly or the money would be spent on other projects.

The question remains of whether or not nuclear arms fit into a Christian framework. Can they be held and used within the constraint of Christ's command to love? We are required to love those we protect and those who are our enemies. Can we do this and still possess and possibly use nuclear weapons? To love someone is to wish for them the greatest good and to provide it to them within our own abilities. Therefore we must decide whether it is best for both our friends and enemies to keep these weapons or to abolish them.

As the bishops' letter states, Pope John Paul II has determined that deterrence is a morally acceptable holding action on the way to disarmament. The bishops also recognized in the letter that the US would not be bound in any disarmament process if the Soviets showed bad faith.

If we unilaterally disarm (not called for by the bishops) the result would be very unpleasant for all of us. The Soviets do not recognize morality as we do.[2] They could be expected to treat us as their satellite countries. This course cannot be characterized as love of friend or enemy. We must ask if we do our enemies the greatest good by allowing them to perpetrate a great evil? Just as one does no good for an unruly child by not disciplining him, so one does not do good to an evil man by not restraining him. Mere restraint is not enough. We must also seek conversion and this is where the bishops and the faithful under their leadership have the only solution and hope that can be offered. This idea of restraint of an enemy also applies to the nuclear deterrence case. Even a pacifist might accept the idea of restraining an enemy from evil.

An experiment in unilateral arms reduction has already been conducted. From the time of the Cuban missile crisis to the late seventies the US dropped its spending on nuclear arms in terms of percentage of the national budget and reduced the rate of arms development. The Soviets responded by the massive arms buildup that all now acknowledge to be real. Henry Kissinger has stated that an important reason for the Nixon Administration's pursuit of SALT was that it offered an opportunity to temporarily delay the Soviet buildup. He also describes the Soviets negotiating position, which was hardly one of humanitarian concern but rather one of trying to obtain advantage in the negotiations to improve their strategic position.[3] The Soviets went beyond their defensive needs in taking advantage of this situation.

From the Baruch Proposal (a 1946 US initiative for UN control of all nuclear weapons declined by the Soviets) to the present, the US has demonstrated a great reluctance to use nuclear weapons to coerce other nations. The US has sought no territorial gain in the post-war-period while the Soviets have acquired a large empire. Soviet intentions are clear. They routinely use force and subjugate peoples, unlike the US. Where, then, can be the basis for any real peace between the US and USSR? The idea that the Soviets have increased their arms out of a fear of US aggression is unjustified.

The main objection of the bishops to deterrence is that it risks tremendous destruction. The bishops consider this destruction to be immoral because of its allegedly indiscriminate nature. If the bishops wish to object to the absolute level of casualties they must define the level at which casualties become unacceptable. We believe such a definition would violate the Christian view of the value of human life. Thus, the main objections are the lack of control of weapons, their potential for collateral damage, and the risk of "cosmic" destruction. We think the term cosmic is an exaggeration as is the allegation that we are on the verge of threatening God's sovereignty. Such a threat is impossible.

From their discussion in the letter we believe the bishops have an inadequate understanding of modern nuclear strategy. As long as the doctrine of deterrence only risks great destruction there must logically be a chance for success. We believe that the magnitude of destruction will in fact deter. We do not have the view mentioned by the bishops that Soviet leaders are "irrational leaders striving insanely for world conquest at any cost." On the contrary, we believe they are very shrewd, careful, calculating leaders who are bent on world conquest at the least cost. One of the means available to them is the pressure of nuclear forces, that is, thermonuclear blackmail. We are convinced that this sober, conservative leadership will not risk a nuclear war if they are afraid they will not succeed. Therefore, we do not consider the risk to be irresponsible but rather a necessary price to pay for the preservation of human rights. The problem of collateral damage is real. We question the real validity of the combatant-noncombatant distinction in modern society. If we all don't share in weapon building and use, we all do share in being causes of war. The economic reasons and political pressures that cause nations to fight are generated by all of us. When indiscriminate weapons were the only thing available they were acceptable because they were the only reasonable course open. Nothing deters a nuclear power but another nuclear power. However, we agree that "massive retaliation" is an immoral course if a less destructive course is open and we find it difficult to understand why the bishops condemn a war-fighting strategy.

In the January 1956 issue of Foreign Affairs, Paul Nitze published an article in which he urged using small warheads in restricted target areas and argued against bombing cities or factories. US presidents have been dissatisfied with the idea of being reduced, in a nuclear war in which a first strike disabled our land based missiles and bombers, to using submarine based missiles which are less capable against military targets because of their limited accuracy. Many people, notably Soviet propagandists, have said that the nuclear war fighting strategy was born in Presidential Directive 59 issued by President Carter when in fact Soviet strategic literature was full of such thinking while the US was still operating under MAD.[4]

The result is that we are faced with an adversary that rejects MAD and is building a war fighting force, its propaganda not withstanding. At the same time technology is making nuclear war fighting more feasible, in that the weapons are becoming more discriminate and controllable. Modern weapons development and strategy are moving in precisely the direction of answering the bishops' objections of riskiness and lack of discrimination toward military targets.

Nuclear war-fighting capability provides two advantages. First, it deters, and even more, it is the only adequate deterrent against a foe who does not accept MAD as a viable strategy. Second, if deterrence fails it provides protection, while there is none with a MAD position. This mitigates the risk involved in deterrence. The problem is, that the same objection is being raised that was raised in 1962 when then-Secretary of Defense Robert McNamara first said that we should treat nuclear war in the same way as conventional war. People said then that talking about nuclear war would make it happen. We cannot afford such an ostrich approach to defense policy. At that time this attitude resulted in the transfer of US strategy from massive retaliation to MAD. A freeze at this time would simply freeze in deterrence imbalances.

In regard to first use, we think this is the only available deterrence at the present time in central Europe. The Soviets do not view nuclear weapons as "magical" or qualitatively different from conventional weapons. Therefore, use of tactical nuclear weapons in Europe by no means guarantees a strategic response. We agree with the bishops that building up conventional forces to reduce the threshold for a nuclear encounter is a necessary course.

We think that the position we have outlined above is morally acceptable because it allows us to achieve a number of objectives that we are required to achieve. First, it enables us to discharge our obligations to Christian love and justice as discussed earlier. Second, it creates an environment that is more hopeful for arms reductions because this environment does not allow either side to anticipate capitulation by the other. Therefore, both sides have an interest in concluding agreements. Third, in the event of nuclear war, a development of war-fighting capability will reduce the collateral damage. This third point is vital because a government's prime duty is to defend its own people, not to destroy other people.

The disadvantage to this position is, of course, that it is fraught with pressure and danger. However, national states are extremely jealous of their sovereignty and reserve the right, when pressed, to do almost anything. This makes a viable benign world government very unlikely. Our best hope, then, is to increase the chances for preventing nuclear war through arms reduction. Because nations act the way they do, only a coincidence between self-interest and moral behavior will allow progress. We must, therefore, maintain an atmosphere where it is in everyone's interest to reduce nuclear arms, while not abrogating our obligations to defend our own freedoms and those of our allies.

We join the bishops in a call for prayerful thought and mature deliberations, striving with God's help to achieve true peace. We hope that our discussions will have contributed in a positive sense to the goal we all seek. . . .

Conclusions and Recommendations

We are Americans and as Americans our societal goals include the preservation of life, liberty and the pursuit of happiness. Our Bill of Rights guarantees vital freedoms. We are also Catholics. Richard P. McBrien describes the Church's goals:

> "The mission of the Church is unintelligible apart from the Kingdom of God. The Church is called, first, to proclaim in word and in sacrament the definitive arrival of the Kingdom in Jesus of Nazareth; secondly, to offer itself as a test-case or sign of its own proclamation—i.e., to be a people transformed by the Spirit into a community of faith, hope, love, freedom, and truthfulness; and thirdly, to enable and facilitate the coming of the reign of God through service within the community of faith and in the world at large."[5]

We believe that the goals of the American and Catholic societies are complementary. We also believe these goals to be contrary to those of totalitarian societies.

A serious ideological conflict exists between the United States and the Soviet Union. It has as its basis the incompatibility between the values of freedom and totalitarianism. This conflict is pursued in every quarter, not only in the arms race. Examples are "wars of liberation", clandestine operations and orchestrated propaganda campaigns. As demonstrated by the Soviets' massive buildup of conventional and nuclear forces during the past decade, they have no higher priority than victory in their struggle for world domination. The proponents of freedom must face the conflict just as seriously. However, resorting to the use of nuclear weapons to resolve this struggle will not be to either side's advantage.

An examination of the morality of involvement with nuclear weapons cannot be honestly done without taking this conflict into account. Thus it is important for us to state our position on the struggle between freedom and totalitarianism.

We do not wish to present issues in black-and-white. Evils have been committed in the name of both sides. However, at the heart of the Soviet philosophy there is an untenable premise, one that no lover of individual liberty can abide. This is the assumption that the rights of the individual are of no importance when compared to the historical destiny of man as a species. We believe that democratic societies generally recognize moral principles that are consistent with a Christian outlook, i.e., that government exists to benefit the common good and to ensure individual rights of self-determination. In contrast, the Marxist-Leninist view of morality is summed up in a 1970 statement by Brezhnev:

> "Our morality is completely subordinated to the interests of the class struggle of the proletariat . . . Morality is that which serves to destroy the old exploiting society . . . We deny all morality that is drawn from some conception beyond class."[6]

This belief that all methods that lead to the triumph of communism are justified has led to innumerable atrocities and a flagrant disregard for human rights on the part of communist governments.

We believe that totalitarianism is a force of evil in the world. By this we include any system of government or society that imposes its will by force, that believes that might makes right. In particular, we believe that we have a Christian duty to resist Soviet totalitarianism, to preserve freedoms where they exist in the world, and to offer a hope to hundreds of millions of citizens who are prisoners of their own governments.

As an example, Nobel Peace Prize winner Andrei Sakharov, inventor of the Soviet H-bomb, finds his own society unacceptable. He says that his government fails the test of democracy by not allowing its citizens essential freedoms, including permission to emigrate. He also says that, after strategic parity in conventional arms has been achieved, and if totalitarian expansion is brought to an end, then agreements should be reached prohibiting first use of nuclear weapons and later, agreements should be reached banning nuclear weapons. Note the implied sequence of steps toward disarmament, and the implications of allowing a disparity in conventional arms.[7]

The threat of nuclear war is not the only threat we must take into account. We can and must protect our freedoms by means other than nuclear weapons, but in considering potential uses of these weapons we must not lose sight of the threat posed by Soviet imperialism. We conclude that not only is possession and deployment of nuclear weapons consistent with Christian morality, but also that such weapons can be used morally in certain circumstances. We strongly disagree with the claim that US policy is that of MAD (mutually assured destruction) with an alleged goal of murdering noncombatants. Deliberate attack of civilians is not US policy. We are surprised that some proponents of a nuclear weapon development freeze base their arguments on the observation that the West already has enough nuclear firepower to destroy every Russian many times over. Such a policy, which our government did at one time espouse, is now morally questionable because technological advances have allowed us to progress away from such a strategy. The development of small, low-yield, high-accuracy weapons provides the US with the ability to attack Soviet military and related targets while minimizing the danger to civilians.

Under the Following Circumstances We Believe that Nuclear Weapons Can Be Used Morally:

A. *Strategic and Tactical Deterrence.* The possession, deployment and possible use of nuclear weapons should assist in preventing general war. This deterrence requires credible, survivable nuclear forces and the will to use them.

B. *Tactical Defense.* The presence of nuclear weapons in a defensive role on allied territory presents no threat to a non-aggressive adversary. However, their use does present a danger of escalation to large-scale nuclear war and therefore should be avoided. Reliance on the use of tactical nuclear forces in Europe to respond to a non-nuclear, conventional attack by Warsaw Pact countries is morally questionable if the motivation is that of economic expediency.

C. *Ballistic Missile Defense.* Moral considerations dictate that we take positive actions to defend our home country against nuclear attack. These might include the use of nuclear weapons as part of a BMD system.

D. *General Nuclear War.* The consequences of a large-scale nuclear war cannot be predicted by anyone. However, we have a responsibility to ourselves and to the rest of the world not to allow victory to totalitarianism and abandon the world to hostile domination. An abrogation of this responsibility would rob mankind of freedom as surely as if we had used our own forces for subjugation. Methods of control that avoid indiscriminate attacks can limit damage and appropriate civil defense measures can save millions of lives.

We recommend the following:

A. *Education.* We stress the need for all people to become better informed. Educational efforts should be directed toward an understanding of nuclear weapons and their effects, with an emphasis on how these weapons influence national strategic policy. We also recognize the need to foster an awareness of the differences between US and Soviet foreign, domestic and military policies.

B. *Arms Reduction and Control.* We believe in sincere negotiations and agreements. However, we cannot assume success, and we caution against an optimism that might foster actions which result in unbalanced or unverifiable reductions in force levels. We believe that:

1. Verification has limits. It would be impossible to ensure that all existing nuclear weapons were destroyed, or that new ones were not produced clandestinely. Therefore, we can never guarantee a nuclear-weapon-free world, and we must concentrate our efforts on controlling and reducing the verifiable entities.

2. On-site verification and inspection are critical. The hazards are too great to rely on questionable and inadequate means of detection, such as satellite reconnaissance and seismic sensing.

3. Reduction and controls must be multilateral rather than bilateral. Proliferation of knowledge, hardware and production methods enlarges the number of potential nuclear weapon states, and those states must be included in discussions.

4. Verification committees, which may be international, must examine the facts of possible violations objectively and bring them to the attention of elected public officials and to the general public as well. These facts should include original or raw data, to allow an objective evaluation. Suppression of facts and conclusions indicates a mistrust of the common sense of the general public, or even a fear to admit errors.

C. *Technology Base.* The US must maintain a technology base to avoid surprises or a sudden weakening of our deterrent due to technological breakthrough by other nations, and to allow production of weapon systems essential to national defense. A nuclear freeze would solidify significant advantages in favor of the Soviets. "Heavy" ICBMs with large-yield weapons to attack land-based missiles constitute an example of such a current imbalance. The nuclear weapon design laboratories develop safer, more efficient weapons, certify their performance, and maintain design and production capability. A freeze would result in the erosion of US nuclear capability, solidify Soviet advantages, and offer great opportunities for unilateral advantage to the cheater.

D. *Conventional Forces.* NATO must strengthen theater conventional forces to provide a credible alternative to the use of nuclear weapons to defend against a conventional attack. Continued reliance on weapons merely because they are less expensive than an adequate conventional force is difficult to justify. However, NATO must maintain a nuclear theater capability both to act as a deterrent against first use by the Soviets and to act as a nuclear response if the Soviets employ nuclear weapons first. To increase the number of options in the use of these weapons and to minimize the danger to noncombatants, development and deployment of limited collateral-damage weapons should be accelerated.

E. *Defense.* The US needs both active defense (against ballistic missiles, cruise missiles, and aircraft) and passive defense (civil defense). Leaving the US civilian population to the mercies of the Soviet leadership is not consistent with the Christian obligation to avoid suicide. We believe the US government has a moral obligation to save lives.

F.   *Continue the Dialogue.*   Those involved in national security activities must continue to examine the morality of their work and to speak out. Conscience formation requires consideration of all aspects of the problem. Everyone is encouraged to participate in this ongoing discussion in a responsible manner, including those who have been associated with the nuclear weapons program for decades and who have considered these issues for many years. We repeat Cardinal Cooke's words:

> "Every individual in uniform and every civilian directly involved in national defense, particularly in defense industry, must be conscious of the many needs of the nation, especially the needs of the poor, and use the nation's resources responsibly, with meticulous honesty and care."[8]

G.   *Prayer.*   We ask our bishops to lead us in praying that governments will respect human dignity, the cornerstone for peace on earth. We pray that governments protect and promote the values of justice, truth, freedom and love. Although at present our nuclear weapons are vital in preserving the values indispensable to human dignity, they are not effective in gaining those values for our brothers persecuted by totalitarian governments. For the achievement of world peace such governments must change. The value of prayer in this regard can not be overestimated.

Notes

1. Pope John Paul II, "1982 World Day of Peace Message," *Origins*, Jan. 7, 1982, p. 477.
2. Leonid Brezhnev, "Guiding Principles for Communists," *Pravda*, Nov. 25, 1970.
3. Henry Kissinger, *The White House Years* (Boston: Little, Brown and Co., 1979), p. 550.
4. *Ibid.*, pp. 534–551.
5. Richard P. McBrien, *Catholicism* (Minneapolis, Minn.: Winston Press, 1981), p. 716.
6. Brezhnev, "Guiding Principles for Communists."
7. Andrei Sakharov, "The Social Responsibility of Scientists," *Physics Today*, June 1981, pp. 25–30.
8. Cardinal Terrence Cooke, "The Church, Military Service, and Nuclear Weapons," *Origins*, Jan. 7, 1982, p. 472.

Writing and Discussion Topics

Questions 1–6 address content, critical analysis, personal choices, ethical options, specific discipline, and interdisciplinary alternatives, respectively.

1. Why do the scientists contend that society requires governments to defend the common good? What is the common good?
2. Does the scientific community encourage its members to take moral stands on nuclear arms? Find proof of such encouragement. What kinds of reinforcements for morality are available in the scientific community?
3. If someone were going to use deadly force to kill you, would you protect yourself? Do you believe that self-defense is a moral use of deadly or near-deadly force? What limits would you set for yourself? How does this position tie in with the scientists continuing their research?
4. The scientists believe that true Christian motivation is to establish peace and justice quickly with minimal force. Explain the ethical perspective involved in this position.
5. These authors reject a "first strike" and would like to see a negotiated reduction of nuclear arms. Evaluate this position in light of their employment and the current political situation in the United States. Do the president and Congress of the United States agree with the scientists?
6. The option of unilateral disarmament is rejected by the scientists. Compare their view with that of the Catholic bishops. How does their position differ with that of Thomas Hobbes?

David Novak

THE THREAT OF NUCLEAR WAR: JEWISH PERSPECTIVES

———◆◆◆———

*D*avid Novak is a professor in the Department of Social Sciences at Lansing Community College in Lansing, Michigan. He is an authority on Jewish customs. In this article Novak explains why, in his judgment, a nuclear war will never occur. ◆

1. Introduction

For the past thirty-nine years, since we have been aware of the threat of nuclear war, an enormous body of diverse opinion has emerged concerning this question. It would seem that this diverse body of opinion, however, can now be reduced to two basic viewpoints. (1) Nuclear war would necessarily involve the extinction of human civilization, if not all life on this planet. (2) Nuclear war, while undoubtedly more destructive than any other war heretofore in human history, would not necessarily involve the destruction of human civilization or the destruction of all life on this planet. For the first point of view nuclear war is truly eschatological, that is, it marks the absolute end of human existence, no future beyond it being conceivable. For the second point of view, on the other hand, the difference between nuclear war and conventional war is one of degree—even vast degree—but not one of kind. Wars have been a continual part of human history, but they have not transcended human history by providing it with an absolute limit.—So these people say.[1]

It would seem, then, that this dispute is in essence empirical, and that it can be ultimately resolved on the basis of enough evidence and the testimony of enough expert specialists. If this is the case, it is becoming more and more plausible to agree with the viewpoint which holds that there is a fundamental difference in kind between nuclear war and conventional war, that nuclear war would most certainly entail the end of the world as we humans now know it. This point of view is presented in the pastoral letter, "The Challenge of Peace: God's Promise and Our Response," drawn up by the National Conference of Catholic Bishops in 1982. My references are to the first draft of October, 1982, but the points I discuss are reiterated in the final version as well.

2. The Theology of the Pastoral Letter

I would like to examine some of the presuppositions of the document, which is an articulate expression of one major viewpoint in the debate over nuclear war. These presuppositions, being in essence theological, involve questions which are far deeper than the empirical question about the probable effects of nuclear war on our life and civilization in this world. As such, it will be even more difficult to address these questions than the already difficult empirical question I have just mentioned. In the context of this theological reflection on a major social and political question—if not *the* major social and political question—of our age, I hope to bring some small light from the insights of Jewish tradition.

If I have read the pastoral letter correctly, it presupposes two points. (1) Although man is not the creator of his world, man has the power to totally destroy it. (2) The affirmation of the absolute value of human life is a rationally self-evident principle. Despite the erudite citations from Scripture and Roman Catholic tradition, both of these points are presented in such a way as to be within the discipline known as "natural theology," a discipline which for many Catholics found its most profound expression in the writings of St. Thomas Aquinas. These points are presented as principles which, using a Talmudic expression, "if they had not been written, they should have been written."[2]

Nevertheless, these two points raise important theological problems, which indicate that they might not be so indisputable after all.

I was amazed that the pastoral letter, which is an essentially theological document, and which refers to "God's Promise", never once mentions that Divine promise to Noah after the Flood, namely, "I will uphold my covenant with you, and all flesh will never again be cut off by the waters of the flood; there will be no flood again to destroy (*leshahet*) the earth." (Genesis 9:11)

Now one could of course argue two exegetical points which would evade this problem. (1) The text only speaks about a flood *of water*. Perhaps other forms of destruction are excluded. (2) The text only speaks about God's restraint of his destructive potential, not man's restraint of his own. However, neither of these evasions is very convincing.

Even though there is one rabbinic opinion which holds that the Divine promise does not preclude "a destruction (*mabul*) of fire and sulphur", most rabbinic treatments of this text see it as the manifestation of God's first promise to humankind. This promise, then, is the paradigm for all subsequent Divine promises. Thus Isaiah states, "for this which I have promised is like the waters of Noah to me" (Isaiah 54:9).[3] God's first promise would not have been very heartening if it implied that some form of destruction other than a flood was not included in it. Surely God was addressing a more widespread human fear than hydrophobia! Global destruction is global destruction, and the fear of global destruction is the fear of global destruction, irrespective of the means of global destruction.

From David Novak, "Halakhah in a Theological Dimension," *The Threat of Nuclear War: Jewish Prspectives*, Brown Judaic Studies No. 68. Copyright © 1968 Brown University, Providence, RI.

Concerning the attempted distinction between God's promise not to destroy the earth again and man's ability to do so, one must remember that the first destruction of the earth, the Flood, was seen by Scripture as the direct consequence of human sinfulness. Thus the very verb used in the Divine promise not to destroy the earth again—*shahet*—is used to describe the very state of affairs which led to the first destruction. "And God saw that the earth was indeed corrupt (*nishhatah*), for all flesh had corrupted (*hishheet*) its way on earth." (Genesis 6:12) And the preceding verse (6:11) tells us what that corruption was, namely, "the earth was filled with violence."

Therefore, it would seem that careful exegesis surely indicates that it is Scriptural doctrine that man's sinfulness can never again cause global destruction. Surely the counterpoint offered by this recurrent Scriptural doctrine must be taken with utmost seriousness by Jewish and Christian theologians who look to the Hebrew Bible as the word of God, however we might use the secular tools of philology, archaeology and history to aid us in our sacred exegetical tasks.

The second presupposition of the pastoral letter is that the affirmation of the absolute value of human life is a rationally self-evident principle. However, this too is open to theological criticism.

Scripture states the following about the affirmation of human life. "See I place before you today life and good, death and evil . . . the blessing and the curse. You shall choose life that you and your progeny will live" (Deuteronomy 30:15, 19). Note that a choice between good and evil, blessing and curse, is not presented. It seems practically impossible that one would affirm anything other than what he or she believed to be good and blessed, at least for him or herself, no matter how misguided the subsequent choice of means might be. Aristotle was right when he said that such affirmation is presupposed by any choice.[4] The choice between life and death, however, is not self-evident in this sense. Many people have chosen death believing it to be both good and blessed. Did not Jonah beg God to die saying, "My death is better (*tob*) than my life" (Jonah 4:8)? Did not Socrates argue that:

> The state of death (*to thethnanai*) is one of two things: either it is virtual nothingness . . . or a change and migration of the soul from this to another place. And if it is unconsciousness (*mēdemia aisthēsis*) . . . death would be a wonderful (*thaumasion*) gain.[5]

Did not Freud argue that:

> The attributes of life were at some time evoked in inanimate matter . . . The tension which then arose in what hitherto been an inanimate substance endeavored to cancel itself out. In this way the first instinct came into being: the instinct to return to the inanimate state.[6]

Therefore, it seems as though the categorical identification of human life with good is not something which comes from reason and experience but, rather, from revelation. If human life as the *imago Dei* is sacred and thus intrinsically good, it is because of its capacity for a relationship with God, not because of such inherent properties as intellect and will, which can easily be shown to be non-existent when inoperative.[7] Indeed, in the creation account in Scripture the goodness of the whole created order is not declared by creation itself about itself but, rather, it is declared by God about *His* creation. "And God saw all that he made and it was indeed very good" (Genesis 1:31).

Nevertheless, no matter how correct my Scriptural exegesis and theology might be, it would seem as though it leads to some rather unacceptable moral conclusions. (1) If God will never again allow man's sinfulness to destroy life on earth, then it would seem that nuclear war and conventional war are in essence the same. Thus all the old rules about "just war," rules which assumed that human history always transcends wars, are as operative as they ever were.[8] All the attempts to see nuclear war as something *sui generis* are thereby rejected by this theology. (2) If the rule to always choose life as good is revealed rather than rational, then how can people of faith convince those of no faith, or of faiths not based on Scriptural revelation—the majority of the people of the earth—that nuclear war is inherently evil because it threatens all of human life? Jewish tradition was wary of even the most cogent exegesis if it led to results unacceptable to the moral consensus of the community.[9] Surely there is an international consensus, a *consensus gentium*, that nuclear war is evil and that everyone should affirm the goodness, if not the sanctity, of all human life.

3.   Warning About Imminent Destruction and Human Responsibility

At this point in our reflection we must examine what the threat of global destruction, or any mass destruction, means in theological terms.

It seems to be the purpose of that growing number of people, who advocate that nuclear war would quickly end in global destruction, to warn everyone else about these dire consequences. Hopefully, this warning will inspire masses of people to force those to whom they have given political power to reverse the nuclear arms race and eventually ban nuclear weapons altogether. The rabbis saw Noah's purpose in taking a long time to build the Ark in public as being similar, namely, to warn his fellow humans about the coming disaster.[10] *Nihil volitum nisi praecognitum,* that is, one cannot will what he does not know. Only true information will lead to correct choice.[11] This presupposes, then, that such knowledge will heighten the sense of human moral power to affect a clear change in the course of historical events. However, I seriously question whether our experience corroborates this judgment. Since the nuclear destruction of Hiroshima and Nagasaki in 1945, the obvious consequences of nuclear war have become evident to almost everyone. Yet has this led to a feeling of moral power, or a feeling of moral impotence? Do we now feel more in control of historical destiny or less in control of it? It seems to me that the latter is the case, that the more we talk of the imminence of nuclear war and holocaust the more we impress on ourselves how little power we really do have over the course of human events. After all, nuclear holocaust could come as the result of mechanical failure in a computer! This is the effect of becoming preoccupied with doom.

Come and see how Scripture judges the effects of such thinking and talk.

> My Lord God of hosts summoned on that day weeping and mourning, baldness and the wearing of sackcloth. But instead there was joy and gladness, the killing of cattle and the slaughter of sheep. "Eat meat and drink wine! Eat, drink for tomorrow we die!" (Isaiah 22:12–13)

In other words, the threat of imminent destruction does not necessarily lead to greater social responsibility and personal care for the genuine needs of others. Rather, more often than not it leads to the very opposite, to greater narcissistic preoccupation with immediate self-gratification and raw hedonism. Surely our own experience these past thirty-nine years confirms the truth of Scripture's description of the attitude of the people of ancient Jerusalem on the eve of their doom. Have we not seen an unending emphasis on narcissistic self-indulgence, on individual pleasure?

Now why do I cite this fact as a disturbing one? It is not because I adhere to any Manichean or quasi-Manichean notion that the body is evil and its pleasures sinful per se. How could I as a theologian rooted in the Hebrew Scriptures adhere to such a notion when the chief expression of God's love for his people is seen through the intense eroticism of Song of Songs?[12] Furthermore, a prominent rabbinic tradition regarded the Nazarite's vow of abstinence from the legitimate pleasure of wine, for example, as being itself sinful.[13] Asceticism per se found few adherents in my tradition.[14]—No, it is not any such dualistic metaphysics which causes my discomfort and concern. Rather, it is the fact that the emphasis on pleasure as an end to itself too often diverts human attention from the real needs of others, attention which requires sacrifice and at times suffering for the sake of what is good for all. Along these lines I would like to share with you a rabbinic treatment of the "eat, drink and be merry" passage we just saw in Isaiah.

> At a time when the community is in a state of sorrow one should not say, 'I will go to my house to eat and drink and it will be well with my life! Concerning such a person Scripture states, 'But instead there was joy and gladness . . . and what is written thereafter? There was revealed in my ears the Lord of Hosts saying that this iniquity will not be atoned even until they die.' (Isaiah 22:14) This is the quality of ordinary people (*midat baynonim*—people who fear death [Rashi]). But concerning the quality of the wicked it is written, 'Come I will buy wine. Let us get drunk together with liquor. And tomorrow will be the same as today.' (Isaiah 56:12) And what is written after that? 'The righteous one perishes and no one considers that because of evil the righteous one was taken away.' (57:1)—But let one be in sorrow with the community.[15]

Here we see a prophecy that well describes what two generations living with the imminent threat of nuclear war have experienced. The belief that the end of the world is not only possible but highly probable has not engendered a greater sense of human community. Rather, by emphasizing that there is no secure future it has enabled many to conclude that any sacrifice for the future is an exercise in futility, that the only security is the enclosed present of the physical senses. Is it not the hope for a future which enables community to develop toward the common horizon of what is yet to come out of a shared present? "Thus says the Lord, 'stop your voice from weeping and your eyes from tears, for there is reward for your effort . . . and there is hope for your future,' says the Lord." (Jeremiah 31:15–16) Indeed, after the cessation of the flood the new humanity emerging from the sons of Noah had to hear the following before they could be given law and thereby be required to act responsibly again.

> And the Lord said to himself, 'I will not ever again curse the earth because of man, for the inclination of man's heart is bad from his youth, and I will not smite all life which I have made. Furthermore, all the seasons of the earth: planting and harvest, cold and heat, summer and winter, shall not cease.' (Genesis 8:21–22)

Or, as one of the most astute students of politics in recent times, the late Professor Hans J. Morgenthau, wrote conversely, over twenty years ago,

> The significance of the possibility of nuclear death is that it radically affects the meaning of death, of immortality. It affects that meaning by destroying most of it . . . Thus nuclear destruction destroys the meaning of death by depriving it of its individuality. It destroys the meaning of immortality by making both society and history impossible.[16]

Is it not this despair of the future, with its narcissistic implications, which diverts so much of the time, energy and money, especially of our youth, away from the building of true community into such things as drugs, games, and depersonalized, irresponsible, sex?[17] I raise all of these points because it does not seem to me that the affirmation of the probability of nuclear destruction leads to a sense of personal and social power and freedom needed to radically change the course of human events. Rather, it seems more often than not to lead to the sense of powerlessness and meaninglessness about which T.S. Eliot wrote over fifty years ago in "The Hollow Men,"

> This is the way the world ends. This is the way the world ends. This is the way the world ends. Not with a bang but a whimper.[18]

Furthermore, no matter how much we may protest to the contrary, the emphasis on nuclear destruction has actually stimulated the development of the so-called "conventional" weapons. For no one can argue that they would lead to global destruction. All they can do is destroy part of our world. After all the talk about the global destruction of nuclear war, the old-time conventional weapons sound better and better. It is here where the danger lies, it seems to me. By making nuclear weapons and the probability of nuclear war something *sui generis,* we have accomplished two rather dubious results. (1) We have increased the sense of international despair, which mitigates against reasoned and free responsibility. (2) We have diverted instead of confronted the perpetual problem of human sinfulness and

aggression by concentrating on only one symptom of it—albeit a terrifying symptom–instead of dealing with the many symptoms of it, let alone the deeper causes.

The belief that man can indeed destroy his world is emphasized by the pastoral letter in these words.

> We can threaten the created order. For people of faith this means we read the Book of Genesis with a new awareness; the moral issue at stake in nuclear war involves the meaning of sin in its most graphic dimensions. Every sinful act is a confrontation of the creature and the Creator. Today the destructive potential of the nuclear powers threatens the sovereignty of God over the world he has brought into being. We could destroy his work. (312)

While I am sympathetic with the moral concern that inspired such a statement, I cannot accept its theology. I do not believe, basing myself on Scriptural revelation, that man has the power to so threaten the sovereignty of God. In fact, I believe that the Divine promise to never again permit global destruction mitigates against such arrogant delusion, delusion which lies at the heart of sin. For the moral task of Scripturally based theology today should be to convince humankind that its desire to engage in nuclear war is futile because of our creaturely limits. All such attempts to magnify the human power to wage war against God have had the results of increasing, not decreasing, sin and its destructive manifestations. Did not the very first rejection of God's sovereignty and authority begin when the first woman, and then the first man with her, believed that they could "be like God" (Genesis 3:5), thereby replacing his sovereignty and authority with a new equality between heaven and earth? Furthermore, rabbinic tradition saw that one of the motivations of the builders of the Tower of Babel was to wage war against God. And it was precisely this group, seeking as they did international unity based on delusion of their own power, who experienced disunity, dispersion, and the loss of the power of effective communication.[19]

I am at least as desirous that the threat of nuclear war be ended as those with whose theology I cannot agree. However, I believe that we should not be emphasizing the power of the war-makers to destroy the entire planet and with its God's kingship. Rather, I believe we should emphasize that they only have the power to destroy themselves, that in truth "the victory is the Lord's" (I Chronicles 29:11)—with or without them. It is more frightening for people to believe that their destructive power will destroy themselves but that the world will go on without them, than to believe that they can bring the whole world down with them as Samson said, "let my life die with the Philistines" (Judges 16:30). This theological point comes out in the rabbinic treatment of the scriptural verse uttered by King David, "were it that I believed that I will see the goodness of the Lord in the land of the living" (Psalms 27:13). The rabbis were surprised that pious King David was so lacking in faith that he seemed to deny belief in God's ultimate sovereignty and providence. However, they put the following in his mouth as a means of explanation. "Master of the universe! I am certain that You indeed recompense the righteous in the future, but I do not know whether my portion is among them, lest my sin prevent it."[20] In other words, the sinner is more likely to change when he is told by the people of faith of the ultimate futility not the ultimate efficacy of his sinful power. I think that this is both better theology and better psychology.

4.   Halakhah and Social Priorities

Heretofore the insights from Jewish tradition I have attempted to show you have all been from that tradition in its aggadic manifestation, that is, that aspect of our tradition which deals with attitudes and suggestions about attitudes, rather than with specific norms. For Halakhah which does deal with such specific normative questions, cannot be invoked when dealing with the question of global destruction, because this theme is one with which the human imagination alone has dealt, but it is not within the realm of actual human experience. We have no specific normative precedents for dealing with the question of global destruction. Where there are no precedents there is no Halakhah.[21] Nevertheless, if we are not to believe that God will break his promise and permit global destruction, then we do have normative precedents for dealing with the question of how to control human aggression and where the priorities of society are to lie.

The Talmud presents the following example of a halakhic treatment of social priorities.

> In Ammon and Moab the tithe for the poor is to be given even during the Sabbatical year, as an earlier authority indicated: Many towns were captured by those who left Egypt but were not captured by those who left Babylonia. For the sanctification of the land in the first instance was only established for that time (*le-shaàtah*) but not for the future. They excluded these towns from the latter conquest in order that the poor might rely on them during the Sabbatical year.[22]

To see the relevance of this passage we must explain it. During the Sabbatical year, when the land was to lie fallow, the people were to basically live off of produce they had already accumulated during the previous six years (Leviticus 25:3). Now all of this was well and good if one had sufficient means to do such long-term planning. The poor, on the other hand, might more often than not be in great difficulty, especially if there was not enough food around. Therefore, the rabbis reasoned that Jewish society limited its own sovereignty and limited the results of its military power. In other words, it decided that the needs of the most helpless, the most vulnerable people in its population, took priority over the fruits of military success and the ultimate concerns of territorial integrity and political security.

The historical background of this type of legal enactment can be seen in the differing approaches to national destruction taken by the Zealots and the Pharisees, respectively, in the first century of this era.

The Zealots chose national sovereign pride over national life without it. At least according to Josephus, they chose suicide at Masada as their only option. Josephus put the following soliloquy in the mouth of their leader, Eleazar ben Jair.

> Let our wives thus die not dishonoured, our children unacquainted with slavery; and when they are gone, let us render a generous service to each other . . . in keeping with our initial resolve, we preferred death to slavery (*thanaton thelomenoi pro douleias*).[23]

The Pharisees, conversely, chose national life over national pride. Thus the Talmud notes that when Jerusalem was to be destroyed the Pharisee leader, Rabban Johanan ben Zakkai, bargained with the Roman commander, Vespasian, asking for "Yavneh and its sages."[24] By so doing he saved at least a remnant of Jewish life and community rather than opting for more death and destruction. And, indeed, subsequent Jewish tradition attempted to mitigate as much as possible against heroic martyrdom.[25] The lives of the people were to take precedence over their pride and even their full national political sovereignty.

The lesson to be learned from this normative precedent and the historical situation of the first century Jewish community should be clear by now. The nuclear arms race has not only threatened us with great destruction in the future, it has already led in the present to the neglect of the immediate human needs of all the nations in the world. For the more we spend in time, money and energy on the arms race, the less we spend in dealing with poverty, crime, alienation and all of the human ills which plague us more and more. Instead of making all of our arguments for arms freezes, arms reduction, and preventing nuclear war hang on the question of future nuclear holocaust, let them hang on the more immediate question of where do our present priorities lie, and where should they lie.[26]

Along these lines I find the attitude of the current Reagan administration to be morally wrong because the needs of the insatiable military establishment are seen as prior and immediate, whereas the truly wretched in this land are told to wait and be patient and ask for less. Indeed, the prophet Samuel warned the people of Israel, who wanted a king so as to achieve military superiority, that in the end "you will be his slaves" (I Samuel 8:17).[27] Our current government policies of giving more and more to the military and less and less to the needy are morally wrong and based on theological error, for they assume that our security lies "in chariots and horses" (Psalms 20:8) instead of in the righteousness of God which bids us "to loosen the bands of wickedness and untie the cords of the yoke; to free the oppressed; to share your bread with the hungry, and to take the suffering poor into your home . . ." (Isaiah 58:6-7). If we demand that the social and political priorities in this nation be changed, we will then see an automatic decrease in the arms race and a lessening of the threat of nuclear war. There is just so much money we can spend. The question is where it is spent first. We have erred in being more concerned with our future safety than with our present needs. "The secret things belong to the Lord our God, but what has been revealed is for we and our children to do now, all the words of this Torah." (Deuteronomy 29:28)

5.   Conclusion

The last issue I would like to consider is the assumption that it is self-evident that human life is absolutely good and, therefore, always to be affirmed. Earlier I questioned that assumption. For whereas we are not commanded by God to choose good, inasmuch as we could not choose what seemed to us to be bad, we are commanded by God to choose life. The problem that this presents is that it seems to limit absolute concern with the sanctity of human life to those who base their faith on Scriptural revelation. As we all know, the majority of the people of the world either base their moral choices on totally secular realities, or on sacred realities which are not those of Scriptural revelation. In other words, does not our theology limit our moral effectiveness

in an international world, in this "global village."[28] This is certainly an important problem for people of faith who wish to address issues which are not formally religious.

Nevertheless, I believe it is more humanly realistic, as well as more theologically correct, to assume that the absolute sanctity of human life is by no means self-evident. If it were, it would be hard to accept the miserable and dangerous situation human beings find themselves in this last part of the twentieth century, a situation epitomized by the threat of nuclear war. When we assume that it is self-evident that all human life is sacred, we are actually engaging in a very dangerous type of Utopian thinking. Utopian thinking assumes that if only humankind would acknowledge the obvious, the human condition would be quickly and radically improved. Utopianism is dangerous because it totally underestimates the obstinancy of the human heart, the difficulty of the human condition, and the complexity of human history. All three of these factors work against the sanctity of human life.

The obstinancy of the human heart is its pride. "The heart is most devious; who can know it?" (Jeremiah 17:9) This pride all too frequently prefers the works of human hands to the existence of human life itself. For humankind's propensity for idolatry is precisely its preference for its own works over those of God, of which human life is in His image and likeness. "Their idols of silver and gold are the works of human hands . . . . All who make them will be like them; all who trust in them." (Psalms 115:4, 8) Indeed, the Talmud queries that if one is to love God "with all your life (be-khol nafshekha)" (Deuteronomy 6:5), is it not obvious that one should love God "with all your possessions (be-khol me'odekha)?" Why does the obvious inference have to be specifically mentioned in Scripture? The answer is that some people, maybe most people, prefer their possessions to their own life, and certainly to the lives of others.[29] In ancient Jewish legend one of the sins of the builders of the Tower of Babel was that they were more upset over the loss of a brick than over the death of a worker.[30]

The difficulty of the human condition is seen in the fact that no one moral issue is ever isolated from a plethora of related issues. The attempt to see the threat of nuclear war as something sui generis is a simplistic avoidance of the true complexity of the human condition. It is becoming one more example of "one issue politics" which in our day so quickly retreats into fanatical sectarianism. The threat of nuclear war is related to many other issues and cannot be adequately addressed without dealing with them as well. It is related to the whole question of technology. What is man's proper relation to the works of his hands? Is man the master or the steward of the earth? It is related to the whole question of man's relation to his own body. Does man look to his own progeny or to the work of his hands for his authentic future? If we are concerned about there being no future for this generation of the earth's children, what have we been doing or not doing to provide them with an authentic present? Rabbinic tradition states that the sin of the two and one half tribes who did not want to go into the Promised Land with the rest of the people of Israel was that they stated "we will build sheep-pens for our flocks and, then, cities for our children" (Numbers 32:16).[31] Their priorities were out of order and, indeed, they were a society far more violent than that of the rest of the people.[32] The problem of nuclear war is connected with the whole difficulty of the human condition and its propensity for violence and destruction. Thus our efforts can never be total solutions for "the work is not for you to finish, but you are not free to neglect it either."[33]

The complexity of human history indicates that whatever problems we are indeed able to even somewhat alleviate are more than a simple matter of making a reasonable decision. Human beings have a history of self-destructiveness going back to the first event outside of the Garden of Eden, the fratricide of Abel by Cain. Now according to one rabbinic comment they fought over the love of a woman.[34] This is an extraordinary insight, for it focuses the whole history of human aggression and destructiveness on our inescapable feeling of being unloved, or not being loved enough. In modern times W. H. Auden stated it powerfully in his great poem, "September 1, 1939."

> The windiest militant trash important persons shout
> It is not so crude as our wish: What mad Nijinsky
> wrote about Diaghelev is true of the normal heart;
> For the error bread in the bone of each woman and
> of each man craves what it cannot have,
> Not universal love but to be loved alone.

And Auden goes on to say,

> There is no such thing as the State and no one exists
> alone; Hunger allows no choice to the citizen or the
> police
> We must love one another or die.[35]

Yes, we must love one another or die. But the people of faith know that "you shall love your neighbor as yourself" is an imperative only because "I am the Lord" (Leviticus 19:18).[36] There is nothing more unnatural than being required to love

our neighbor whom we more often fear than love. *Bellum omnium contra omnes* in Hobbes' words, universal conflict, is the true "state of nature."[37] It is a matter of grace over nature. Unlike the Utopian who simply assumes universal love and goodwill as facts, people of faith regard them as messianic desiderata, something for which we can hope and even work, but not something we can truly accomplish ourselves, something we must pray that God will 'write on their heart' (Jeremiah 31:32). By affirming our messianic hope for the coming of God's kingdom of peace we work to prepare our own hearts at least as much as we work to change the world. We resist the simple solution of Utopianism and thereby save ourselves from the despair which overcomes the idealists when they realize that their dreams are only dreams. We believe human history has a goal and is not an endless trail of disappointments.

> Happy is the person whose strength is in You,
> with the highways in his heart.
> Passing through the vale of tears, they are
> watered with blessings by the early rain.
> They go from strength to strength until appearing
> before God in Zion. (Psalms 84:6-8)

To do our best to limit the threat of nuclear war, or any war, is one of the tasks we must do on the highway. It cannot be avoided by any one of the travellers of Zion. God requires as much—no more, but no less.

Notes

1. For a critical discussion of these views, see Reinhold Niebuhr, *The Structure of Nations and Empires* (New York, 1959), 267ff.
2. B. *Yoma* 67b.
3. T. *Ta'aniyot* 2.13; *Mekhilta:* Yitro, beg., ed. Horovitz Rabin, 188; *Zebahim* 116a (cf. B. *Shebu'ot* 36a); Philo, *De Vita Mosis*, 2.53ff. Also, see L. Ginzberg, *The Legends of the Jews* (Philadelphia, 1925), 5:149, n. 53; S. Lieberman, *Tosefta Kifshuta: Moed* (New York, 1962), 1097.
4. *Nicomachean Ethics*, 1112b12ff. See Plato, *Protagoras*, 357D-358D; Thomas Aquinas, *Summa Theologiae*, 1-2, q. 94, a. 2 and German G. Grisez, "The First Principle of Practical Reason," *Natural Law Forum*, 10 (1965), 168ff.
5. Plato, *Apology*, 40C, trans. H. N. Fowler (Cambridge, MA, 1914), 40-41. See D. Novak, *Suicide and Morality* (New York, 1975), 7ff.
6. *Beyond the Pleasure Principle*, trans. J. Strachey (New York, 1959), 71.

7. See D. Novak, *Law and Theology in Judaism*, 2:108ff.; *supra.*, 99ff.

8. For the Jewish concept of "just war," see, e.g., *Sotah* 8.7; B. *Sotah* 44b; *Sotah* 8/23a; Maimonides, *Hilkhot Melakhim*, 6.1–7.15.

9. Thus the great 2nd century C.E. sage, R. Akibah, who was famous for his great exegetical acumen, was, nevertheless, criticized more than once by colleagues for interpretations which, although quite clever, were, however, contrary to accepted Jewish ruling and opinion. See B. *Sanhedrin* 51b; *Menahot* 89a; cf. P. *Pesahim* 6.1/33a.

10. See B. *Sanhedrin* 108a–108b; *Beresheet Rabbah* 30.7.

11. Thus in ancient Jewish law a criminal had to be forewarned (*hatra'ah*) of his act as a crime and its punishment before being prosecutable. See B. *Sanhedrin* 40b–41a.

12. Song of Songs is called "holy of holies." See M. *Yadayim* 3.5.

13. B. *Nedarim* 10a and parallels. See *supra.*, 73–74.

14. The great exceptions, of course, were the Essenes. See Josephus, *Bellum Judaicum*, 2.133, 138; Philo, *Vita Contemplativa*, 73–74; also, B. *Yebamot* 20a and Nahamanides on Lev. 19:2.

15. B. *Ta'anit* 11a.

16. "Death in the Nuclear Age," quoted in *Jewish Reflections on Death*, ed. J. Riemer (New York, 1974), 44. For a philosophical analysis of how one's view of death affects his being in the present, see M. Heidegger, *Sein und Zeit*, 8th ed. (Tuebingen, 1957), 251ff.

17. One rabbinic source interprets the incest of Lot's daughters with him, after the destruction of Sodom by fire and sulphur, as having been motivated by their fear that the whole world was once again to be destroyed. See *Beresheet Rabbah* 51.8. Cf. Josephus, *Antiquities*, 1.205.

18. *Collected Poems: 1909–1935* (New York, 1936), 105.

19. See B. *Sanhedrin* 109a.

20. B. *Berakhot* 4a. See, also, B. *Sotah* 11a re Is. 54:9.

21. Thus the Talmud views *halakhah* never practiced and never to be practiced as it does *aggadah*. See B. *Sanhedrin* 71a.

22. B. *Yebamot* 16a. Rabbinic legislation on behalf of the poor applied to the gentile poor as well as to the Jewish poor. See *Gittin* 5.8–9 and B. *Gittin* 61a.

23. *Bellum Judaicum*, 7.334–336, trans. H. St. John Thackeray, *Josephus* (Cambridge, MA, 1928), 3:598–599.

24. B. *Gittin* 56b.

25. See D. Novak, *Law and Theology in Judaism*, 1:80ff.

26. The Talmud (B. *Ta'anit* 21a) reports that the sage, Nahum of Gimzo, was punished by God because he hesitated too long in attending to the needs of a poor man.

27. In the Talmud the rabbis debated whether Samuel's warning was just a warning or the actual right of kings (B. *Sanhedrin* 20b).

28. The term is Marshall McLuhan's. See *War and Peace in the Global Village* (New York, 1968).

29. B. *Berakhot* 61b. See B. *Sanhedrin* 72a.

30. See Ginzberg, *The Legends of the Jews* 1:179 and 5:201ff., n. 88.

31. *Tanhuma: Mattot*, sec. 7.

32. See B. *Makkot* 9b–10a re Hos. 6:8.

33. M. *Abot* 2.16.

34. *Beresheet Rabbah* 22.7.

35. Quoted in *Seven Centuries of Verse: English and American*, 2nd rev. ed., A. J. M. Smith (New York, 1957), 687. See Ginzberg, *op. cit.*, 5:138–139, n. 17.

36. This is the view of Nahmanides in his commentary thereon. Maimonides, on the other hand, seems to have regarded this love as more natural. See *Sefer Ha-Mitzvot*, pos. no. 206 (Cf. *Targum Pseudo-Jonathan* on Lev. 19:18). This contrast is made by Dr. C. B. Chavel in his edition of Nahmanides' commentary (Jerusalem, 1963), 119.

37. See *Leviathan*, chap. 13.

Writing and Discussion Topics

Questions 1–6 address content, critical analysis, personal choices, ethical options, specific discipline, and interdisciplinary alternatives, respectively.

1. Does Novak believe that nuclear war could be a reality? How does Novak dismiss global destruction? What can be done by all people, according to Novak, to prevent a nuclear war?

2. Did Novak write this essay for a general audience or primarily for a Jewish audience? Defend your answer with specific examples from this essay.

3. Talk to a Jewish family or friend or to a rabbi concerning views on war. Are their views on conventional warfare different from their views on nuclear warfare? Examine your own views. Is one form of warfare any more moral or immoral than the other?

4. Explain the concept of the sanctity of human life from a Jewish viewpoint. What ethical concepts are involved in the issue of the sanctity of human life?

5. Why does Novak use the pastoral letter as a basis for explaining Jewish perspectives on nuclear war? What are some of the basic differences regarding nuclear arms and nuclear war between Novak and the pastoral letter?

6. Compare Islamic religious views on war and death with those of Novak.

Victor Danner

THE HOLY WAR

—◆◆◆—

V ictor Danner is a professor at Indiana University in the
Department of Near East Language and Religion. Danner
explains the tradition of the Islamic jihad and the religious need for a
war waged in the name of God. ◆

We may return now to the *shari'ah* itself to consider the question of Holy War (*jihād*), which is sometimes construed as the sixth Pillar of the religion. Unlike Christianity, which spread throughout the Roman Empire under the cover of its far-flung legal, administrative, and military system, and had only to move along the byways and highways of the excellent Roman road network in order to preach the Word, Islam had to unsheathe its sword from the very beginning to establish itself in Arabia and to carry its message to the non-Arab world. Warfare was not a matter of choice for the Muslims. They were enjoined to fight by both the Qur'ān and the Sunnah, so that the *jihād* has a binding quality to it, in the eyes of the Law, whenever the integrity of *dar al-islam,* or parts of it, is menaced, or whenever there is felt the need to spread the faith through the force of arms. The fighting prescribed by the *shari'ah* is not an end in itself, for the goal of warfare is eventual peace through treaty arrangements, and not perpetual warfare. Nor is the *jihād* to be conducted outside the framework of rules and conditions established by the Law, which restricts the amplitude of the fighting and seeks to protect the noncombatants. But this is not to say that all wars in the history of Islam between Muslims and non-Muslims have been fought in conformity with the rules set down in the Law and interpreted by the religious authorities. There have been many wars that were in violation of these rules. Such infringements or violations of the rules of Holy War were more or less inevitable, since Muslims have never had any qualms about engaging in warfare and Islam has tended to create a combative disposition that is all the more explosive and unbridled in that the Qur'ān itself sanctions fighting and even urges the believers to draw the sword against disbelief.

The revelation took the ancient Arabs as they were, an extremely volatile and warlike people with a certain chivalric and magnanimous character. Without changing the positive traits of their impulsivity and passional nature, Islam sublimated their warring instinct by incorporating them into the structure of the Law. The Arabs embodied the characteristic combativity of Islam and even transmitted something of its igneous psychism to the other people who joined the religion. Warfare, in those days, was not peculiar to Islam alone: the Christian Byzantine Empire and the Persian Zoroastrian Empire had been locked in battle for some time before Islam appeared on the scene. Like all religious civilizations, Christianity, once it became the religion of the State after the fourth century A.D., did not hesitate to use the sword.

Islam was born as a combative faith in the midst of a Mediterranean world that was torn by strife and warfare. But its combativity is for the sake of an eventual equilibrium and peace, or for the integration of a community of disbelievers into its message. Nevertheless, it can be said that, while the religion has indeed spread by the sword, it has mostly spread by persuasion and example, and continues in this latter fashion to gain converts to the present day. Although the notion of warfare sanctioned by revelation might seem strange to the outsider, one has to remember that Islam takes human nature as it is, with all of its passional attachments, and seeks to penetrate it with the idea of the Divine Unity as much as possible. It seeks to convert the warring instincts into a spiritual force that is compatible with the Islamic message. It is better to control the fighting instincts with religious injunctions which keep them within the pale of the Law and in view of man's last ends than it is to give vent to them without restraint and with purely worldly goals in view. At least that is one way of looking at the Qur'ānic sanctioning of warfare on behalf of Islam.

We should also recall here the distinction made by the Prophet between the "lesser *jihād*", or military warfare, and the "greater *jihād*", or spiritual warfare. The latter pits the virtues in man's soul against the vices and passions with a view to the ultimate triumph of the Spirit within man over its interior enemies. The peace of soul that follows the round of spiritual battles in the "greater *jihād*" is the contemplative prototype of the peace that should follow the military warfare of the "lesser *jihād*." The Qur'ānic view of *jihād* permits of its interpretation in a military as well as in a purely spiritual case. While a Muslim may be prevented from engaging in the "lesser *jihād*", no one is really exempt from the "greater *jihād*", for the whole question of salvation revolves around the successful outcome of the inner warfare in man's soul, right up to the hour of death. It is perhaps for this reason that Sūfism has quite a bit to say about the spiritual warfare that must take place within man's soul to undo the effects of forgetfulness and ignorance and to permit the luminous raying-out of the victorious Spirit. . . .

Source: "The Holy War" from *The Islamic Tradition* by Victor Danner. Copyright © The Amity House, Rockport, MA.

Writing and Discussion Topics

Questions 1–6 address content, critical analysis, personal choices, ethical options, specific discipline, and interdisciplinary alternatives, respectively.

1. Why does the Islamic tradition give war a "holy" connotation? Under what conditions is war acceptable? Why do the Muslims believe it is necessary to have holy wars?

2. Is this piece designed to convince readers who have no political opinions, or to rally the men and women who are already committed to the religion? Support your answer with passages from the three Islamic writings.

3. Imagine you are a member of the Islamic religion. You believe in the Qur'ān and the traditions of your forefathers. You and your fourteen-year-old son have been called to a jihād. Will you both go? Why or why not?

4. Do Muslims live according to an ethic of duty? If so, to whom is the duty directed?

5. Explain the religious difference between the "lesser jihād" and the "greater jihād." Why would a religion favor warfare? How might a Christian differ on the "righteous defense of the truth"?

6. Compare war for Muslims with war for Americans or Russians. What political or religious perspectives would compel each of these peoples into a first strike? Would the concept of war with nuclear weapons, as compared to conventional warfare, change the opinions of the Muslims toward war and types of war?

Ayatollah Ruhollah Khomeini
and
Gholam-Reza Fada'i Araqi

ISLAM IS NOT A RELIGION OF PACIFISTS
and
DEATH IS NOT AN END BUT A CONTINUATION
◆◆◆

Ayatollah Khomeini Source: AP/Wide World Photos.

Ayatollah Ruhollah Khoemeini was an Iranian religious leader who governed Iran fom 1979 until his death in 1989. His most notorious offense was the taking of hostages from the United States Embassy in Iran. Prior to this, he was a religious teacher in Qom. Khomeini was arrested after riots over the Shah of Iran's land reforms and was exiled in Turkey, Iraq, and France for sixteen years. While in exile, he aimed to create an Islamic Republic. From France he was the most powerful influence on the revolution that toppled Shah Mohammed Riza Pahlavij. Khomeini explains some of the nature of the Islamic religion in this essay. Gholam-Reza Fada'i Araqi continues by explaining the Islamic views on death. ♦

Islam Is Not a Religion of Pacifists

There are two kinds of war in Islam: one is called [Holy War], which means the conquest of [other] countries in accordance with certain conditions. The other [type] is war to preserve the independence of the [Muslim] country and the repulsion of foreigners. Jihad or Holy War, which is for the conquest of [other] countries and kingdoms, becomes incumbent after the formation of the Islamic state in the presence of the Imam or in accordance with his command. Then Islam makes it incumbent on all adult males, provided they are not disabled and incapacitated, to prepare themselves for the conquest of [other] countries so that the writ of Islam is obeyed in every country in the world.

But world public opinion should know that Islamic conquest is not the same as conquests made by other rulers of the world. The latter want to conquer the world for their own personal profit, whereas Islam's conquest is aimed at serving the interests of the inhabitants of the globe as a whole. [Non-Islamic] conquerors want to rule the world so that they can spread through it every injustice and sexual indecency, whereas Islam wants to conquer the world in order to promote spiritual values, and to prepare mankind for justice and divine rule. [Non-Islamic] conquerors sacrifice the lives and possessions of the people to their own leisure and pleasure. But Islam does not allow its leaders and generals to enjoy themselves or to have a moment's leisure; in this way the lives and property of people can be protected and the bases of injustice destroyed in the world.

Islam's Holy War is a struggle against idolatry, sexual deviation, plunder, repression and cruelty. The war waged by [non-Islamic] conquerors, however, aims at promoting lust and animal pleasures. They care not if whole countries are wiped out and many families left homeless. But those who study Islamic Holy War will understand why Islam wants to conquer the whole world. All the countries conquered by Islam or to be conquered in the future will be marked for everlasting salvation. For they shall live under Light Celestial Law. . . .

Those who know nothing of Islam pretend that Islam counsels against war. Those [who say this] are witless. Islam says: Kill all the unbelievers just as they

would kill you all! Does this mean that Muslims should sit back until they are devoured by [the unbelievers]? Islam says: Kill them [the non-Muslims], put them to the sword and scatter [their armies]. Does this mean sitting back until [non-Muslims] overcome us? Islam says: Kill in the service of Allah those who may want to kill you! Does this mean that we should surrender [to the enemy]? Islam says: Whatever good there is exists thanks to the sword and in the shadow of the sword! People cannot be made obedient except with the sword! The sword is the key to Paradise, which can be opened only for Holy Warriors!

There are hundreds of other [Qur'anic] psalms and Hadiths [sayings of the Prophet] urging Muslims to value war and to fight. Does all that mean that Islam is a religion that prevents men from waging war? I spit upon those foolish souls who make such a claim.

Death Is Not an End but a Continuation

Unlike those [other religions] which consider death to be the end of man's life, in the vision of the Qur'an death is not the end of life but its continuation in another form. Man's evolutionary movement towards infinity, towards the full accomplishment of life, continues after death. Thus death is no more than a hyphen between two parts of man's existence. . . .

In the Qur'an's vision chaos and sedition are but two instruments, two means of measurement for the individual as well as for society as a whole. . . . Through chaos, sedition and other forms of hardship, the individual is tested; his purity, the depth of his faith and his commitment [to the cause] are measured so that he can have his just reward. . . .

The Qur'an rejects the [Marxist] idea of many classes in society. Basing itself on true historical realities, the Qur'an recognizes only two classes in society: the rulers, who are tyrants, exploiters and members of the party of Satan, form one of the two classes. They are always in a minority. The other class, according to the Qur'an, is that of the ruled, the vast majority of people who are dispossessed, exploited and subjected to injustice—the members of the Party of Allah. The whole history of mankind consists of the struggle between these two mutually exclusive classes. The rulers, with Satan in their command, have always fought those who have

"Islam is Not a Religion of Pacifists," by Ayatollah Khomeini, and "Death is Not an End but a Continuation," by Gholam-Reza Fada'i Araqi; both from Amir Taheri, *Holy Terror*, Bethesda, MD: Adler & Adler © 1987 by Amir Taheri. Reprinted by permission.

upheld mankind's objectives: Abel against Cain, Nimrod against Abraham, the Pharaoh against Moses, Abu-Sufyan, Abu-Jahl and Abu-Lahab against Muhammad, Muawyyah against Ali, Yazid against Hussein and the present-day heirs to the government of Satan against us—members of the Party of Allah. . . .

The ideal society of Islam and the Qur'ān is one [that is] for justice and against tyranny. In it all signs of idolatry and whatever else is considered by the Qur'ān to be invalid have disappeared. As far as Islam is concerned, there are no basic differences between the slave-owning society, the feudal society, capitalism and communism. All 'isms'—fascism, Marxism, liberalism, racism, socialism, existentialism, capitalism etc. are against Islam. Why? Simply because all of them have one thing in common: they are not based on the vision of the Qur'ān. . . .

One [social] group that is the enemy of the Qur'ān by definition is known under the name of *muturaffin* or those who want to have a good time in this world. Their presence is deadly both before and after the establishment of the Qur'ānic rule under the Party of Allah. They usually stay out of politics, but even when they participate in political life their basic aim does not change. That aim is to satisfy their animal lust, to enjoy themselves and indulge their base desires. Their opposition to the new Islamic revolutionary system is motivated by the fact that [the new government] is opposed to their levity and debauchery. These [elements] know how to make a lot of money and get rich, so that they can finance the good time they constantly seek. . . . These [elements] will never reconcile themselves to the idea of an [austere] life in accordance with the strictures of the Faith. . . .

Struggle and Holy War are essential characteristics of an Islamic community that has attained self-awareness and is dynamic. The Islamic community, in accordance with the laws of creation that stipulate movement as the sole guarantee for survival, cannot stand still. It knows that a single moment of inaction might spell its perdition. . . . Peace and quiet have no meaning for the members of the party of God. They do not waste a single second and constantly fight to uproot the rule of tyranny and crime. . . . The divine society does not allow its members to sit back and enjoy themselves in the belief that everything is now properly arranged. We cannot and must not think that we can go on holiday, enjoy ourselves, or even devote ourselves entirely to prayer. . . . The Islamic man must be constantly on the watch to prevent the commission of sin and to rectify every wrong. . . .

Tyrants and members of the party of Satan often use armed violence in order to suppress the movement of the Partisans of Allah. Thus war becomes inevitable. It is the duty of Muslims to take up arms in support of the oppressed, especially if the oppressed in question have converted to Islam. Islam does not recognize earthly frontiers [between countries]; what matters to Islam are the frontiers of Faith. . . . Islamic wars have always been the continuation of Islamic ideological struggle. . . . The Qur'ān teaches that those who suffer from tyranny possess every right to have recourse to war. It also teaches us to kill the idolaters and the unbelievers who reject Islam and wage war on us. Islam's objective from war is the establishment of the government of Allah and thus the completion of the process of evolution. . . .

The Qur'ān teaches us to kill those who make trouble, but it also insists that we should not overdo it. The Qur'ān forbids excess in killing and emphasizes the fact that the aim of the duty of *qital* [killing] is not to kill everyone but to eliminate only the ringleaders and some of their agents. . . . Islam recognizes revenge as an authorized value, but insists that we should not go too far. . . . The Qur'ān invites us to kill until troublemakers are eliminated. What is meant by trouble is the oppression imposed on Muslims by non-Muslim governments or governments that are Islamic in appearance only. To end that we are allowed to take up arms and to kill. . . . War and bloody revolution are necessary to preserve the Faith, otherwise Muslims suffering oppression may give up their beliefs. . . . But it is equally important to wage an ideological struggle, to take the message of Islam everywhere and to show the whole of mankind that only Islam can save it from annihilation. . . . Revolution is like a match put to the harvest of tyranny so that a huge fire can be lit. But to keep this fire alive and ever glowing one needs the fuel of doctrine that must be propagated with true zeal. . . .

Only Islam can offer the possibility of [making] a genuine revolution. We have all seen what has happened to the Chinese revolution which once made so much noise about its defence of Marxism but is now moving in the opposite ideological direction, so as to resemble an imperialist [society]. As for the Soviet Union, which claims to be the cradle of communism, nothing has really changed and exploitation continues as before. . . .

Writing and Discussion Topics

Questions 1–6 address content, critical analysis, personal choices, ethical options, specific discipline, and interdisciplinary alternatives, respectively.

1. Outline Khomeini's major points concerning the Islamic view on war. Why can't Islam be a religion of pacifists, according to Khomeini?
2. What was Khomeini trying to accomplish in his essay? Does he make any concessions to the men and women who oppose Islam?
3. Pretend you had one hour to talk with the deceased Ayatollah Khomeini. What questions would you ask him? On what issues would you debate?
4. Ponder Khomeini's statement, "Kill in the service of Allah those who may want to kill you! . . . Whatever good there is exists thanks to the sword and in the shadow of the sword!" With which ethical systems does this viewpoint conflict? How and why?
5. Muslims see death as no more than a hyphen between two parts of human existence; they believe that people continue to exist and evolve throughout eternity. Explain why you agree or disagree with the Islamic views.
6. Compare Islamic views on war with those of the scientists from New Mexico in their statement, "Response to the Bishops' . . ." Are the two similar in seeking to preserve a system of ideologies? If so, how? How are the two different?

Czeslaw Milosz

AMERICAN IGNORANCE OF WAR

◆◆◆

C zeslaw Milosz is recognized as one of Poland's greatest authors. He won the Nobel Prize in literature in 1980, yet his poetry and prose were banned in Poland from 1936 until 1980. Milosz was born in 1911 in Lithuania. He now lives in Berkeley, California, where he continues to write. In this essay, he shows why it is important for Americans to understand the many tragedies of war, because no world war has been fought on American soil. ◆

"Are Americans *really* stupid?" I was asked in Warsaw. In the voice of the man who posed the question, there was despair, as well as the hope that I would contradict him. This question reveals the attitude of the average person in the people's democracies toward the West: it is despair mixed with a residue of hope.

During the last few years, the West has given these people a number of reasons to despair politically. In the case of the intellectual, other, more complicated reasons come into play. Before the countries of Central and Eastern Europe entered the sphere of the Imperium, they lived through the Second World War. That war was much more devastating there than in the countries of Western Europe. It destroyed not only their economies, but also a great many values which had seemed till then unshakable.

Man tends to regard the order he lives in as *natural*. The houses he passes on his way to work seem more like rocks rising out of the earth than like products of human hands. He considers the work he does in his office or factory as essential to the harmonious functioning of the world. The clothes he wears are exactly what they should be, and he laughs at the idea that he might equally well be wearing a Roman toga or medieval armor. He respects and envies a minister of state or a bank director, and regards the possession of a considerable amount of money as the main guarantee of peace and security. He cannot believe that one day a rider may appear on a street he knows well, where cats sleep and children play, and start catching passersby with his lasso. He is accustomed to satisfying those of his physiological needs which are considered private as discreetly as possible, without realizing that such a pattern of behavior is not common to all human societies. In a word, he behaves a little like Charlie Chaplin in *The Gold Rush*, bustling about in a shack poised precariously on the edge of a cliff.

His first stroll along a street littered with glass from bomb-shattered windows shakes his faith in the "naturalness" of his world. The wind scatters papers from hastily evacuated offices, papers labeled "Confidential" or "Top Secret" that evoke visions of safes, keys, conferences, couriers, and secretaries. Now the wind blows them through the street for anyone to read; yet no one does, for each man is more urgently concerned with finding a loaf of bread. Strangely enough, the world goes on even though the offices and secret files have lost all meaning. Farther down the street, he stops before a house split in half by a bomb, the privacy of people's homes—the family smells, the warmth of the beehive life, the furniture preserving the memory of loves and hatreds—cut open to public view. The house itself, no longer a rock, but a scaffolding of plaster, concrete, and brick; and on the third floor, a solitary white bathtub, rain-rinsed of all recollection of those who once bathed in it. Its formerly influential and respected owners, now destitute, walk the fields in search of stray potatoes. Thus overnight money loses its value and becomes a meaningless mass of printed paper. His walk takes him past a little boy poking a stick into a heap of smoking ruins and whistling a song about the great leader who will preserve the nation against all enemies. The song remains, but the leader of yesterday is already part of an extinct past.

He finds he acquires new habits quickly. Once, had he stumbled upon a corpse on the street, he would have called the police. A crowd would have gathered, and much talk and comment would have ensued. Now he knows he must avoid the dark body lying in the gutter, and refrain from asking unnecessary questions. The man who fired the gun must have had his reasons; he might well have been executing an Underground sentence.

Nor is the average European accustomed to thinking of his native city as divided into segregated living areas, but a single decree can force him to this new pattern of life and thought. Quarter A may suddenly be designated for one race; B, for a second; C, for a third. As the resettlement deadline approaches, the streets become filled with long lines of wagons, carts, wheelbarrows, and people carrying bundles, beds, chests, caldrons, and bird cages. When all the moves are effected, 2,000 people may find themselves in a building that once housed 200, but each man is at last in the proper area. Then high walls are erected around quarter C, and daily a given lot of men, women, and children are loaded into wagons that take them off to specially constructed factories where they are scientifically slaughtered and their bodies burned.

And even the rider with the lasso appears, in the form of a military van waiting at the corner of a street. A man passing that corner meets a leveled rifle, raises his hands, is pushed into the van, and from that moment is lost to his family and friends. He may be sent to a concentration camp, or he may face a firing squad, his lips sealed with plaster lest he cry out against the state; but, in any case, he serves as a warning to his fellow men. Perhaps one might escape such a fate by remaining at home. But the father of a family must go out in order to provide bread and soup for his wife and children; and every night they worry about whether or not he will return. Since these conditions last for years, everyone gradually comes to look upon the city as a jungle, and upon the fate of twentieth-century man as identical with that of a caveman living in the midst of powerful monsters.

It was once thought obvious that a man bears the same name and surname throughout his entire life; now it proves wiser for many reasons to change them and to memorize a new and fabricated biography. As a result, the records of the civilian state become completely confused. Everyone ceases to care about formalities, so that marriage, for example, comes to mean little more than living together.

Respectable citizens used to regard banditry as a crime. Today, bank robbers are heroes because the money they steal is destined for the Underground. Usually they are young boys, mothers' boys, but their appearance is deceiving. The killing of a man presents no great moral problem to them.

The nearness of death destroys shame. Men and women change as soon as they know that the date of their execution has been fixed by a fat little man with shiny boots and a riding crop. They copulate in public, on the small bit of ground surrounded by barbed wire—their last home on earth. Boys and girls in their teens, about to go off to the barricades to fight against tanks with pistols and bottles of gasoline, want to enjoy their youth and lose their respect for standards of decency.

Which world is "natural"? That which existed before, or the world of war? Both are natural, if both are within the realm of one's experience. All the concepts men live by are a product of the historic formation in which they find themselves. Fluidity and constant change are the characteristics of phenomena. And man is so plastic a being that one can even conceive the day when a thoroughly self-respecting citizen will crawl on all fours, sporting a tail of brightly colored feathers as a sign of conformity to the order he lives in.

The man of the East cannot take Americans seriously because they have never undergone the experiences that teach men how relative their judgements and thinking habits are. Their resultant lack of imagination is appalling. Because they were born and raised in a given social order and in a given system of values, they believe that any other order must be "unnatural," and that it cannot last because it is incompatible with human nature. But even they may one day know fire, hunger, and the sword. In all probability this is what will occur; for it is hard to believe that when one half of the world is living through terrible disasters, the other half can continue a nineteenth-century mode of life, learning about the distress of its distant fellow men only from movies and newspapers. Recent examples teach us that this cannot be. An inhabitant of Warsaw or Budapest once looked at newsreels of bombed Spain or burning Shanghai, but in the end he learned how these and many other catastrophes appear in actuality. He read gloomy tales of the NKVD[1] until one day he found he himself had to deal with it. *If something exists in one place, it will exist everywhere.* This is the conclusion he draws from his observations, and so he has no particular faith in the momentary prosperity of America. He suspects that the years 1933–1945 in Europe[2] prefigure what will occur elsewhere. A hard school, where ignorance was punished not by bad marks but by death, has taught him to think sociologically and historically. But it has not freed him from irrational feelings. He is apt to believe in theories that foresee violent changes in the countries of the West, for he finds it unjust that they should escape the hardships he had to undergo.

Writing and Discussion Topics

Questions 1–6 address content, critical analysis, personal choices, ethical options, specific discipline, and interdisciplinary alternatives, respectively.

1. Milosz makes the statement, "The man of the East cannot take Americans seriously because they have never undergone the experiences that teach men how relative their judgements and thinking habits are." According to Milosz, what are the reasons for Americans lacking these experiences? Are they valid reasons for "despair"?

---

[1]The Soviet secret police, 1935–1943.—ED.
[2]Hitler's takeover of Germany through World War II.—ED.

2. Discuss in depth if this essay is an argument or simply a report. What is the major premise? What are the supporting factors? What is Milosz's conclusion?

3. Write an essay entitled "What Americans Know About War." Summarize in the essay your response to an invasion of the United States by a foreign country.

4. Milosz says that the nearness of death destroys shame. Explain the ethical problems in this statement. Are America's youth plagued by the nearness of death? How?

5. Write a critical analysis of this essay. Is the writing symbolic and poetic? Cite some examples. Could this piece be more persuasive? If so, how?

6. This essay was written in approximately 1953. Explain the historical events that have happened since 1953 that could validate or invalidate Milosz's argument. Have the attitudes of Americans changed regarding the preservation of peace? If so how? If not, why not?

Luigi Pirandello

WAR

◆◆◆

L uigi Pirandello (1867–1936) was an Italian dramatist and novelist. He won the 1934 Nobel Prize in literature. He was educated in Rome and at the University of Bonn. He was a professor of Italian literature at the Normal College for Women in Rome. He wrote over three hundred stories and about fifty plays. In this story, passengers on a train swap accounts of the personal heartbreaks of war. ◆

The passengers who had left Rome by the night express had had to stop until dawn at the small station of Fabriano in order to continue their journey by the small old-fashioned "local" joining the main line with Sulmona.

At dawn, in a stuffy and smoky second-class carriage in which five people had already spent the night, a bulky woman in deep mourning, was hoisted in—almost like a shapeless bundle. Behind her—puffing and moaning, followed her husband—a tiny man, thin and weakly, his face death-white, his eyes small and bright and looking shy and uneasy.

Having at last taken a seat he politely thanked the passengers who had helped his wife and who had made room for her; then he turned round to the woman trying to pull down the collar of her coat and politely enquired:

"Are you all right, dear?"

The wife, instead of answering, pulled up her collar again to her eyes, so as to hide her face.

"Nasty world," mutter the husband with a sad smile.

And he felt it his duty to explain to his travelling companions that the poor woman was to be pitied for the war was taking away from her only son, a boy of twenty to whom both had devoted their entire life, even breaking up up their home at Sulmona to follow him to Rome where he had to go as a student, then allowing him to volunteer for war with an assurance, however, that at least for six months he would not be sent to the front and now, all of a sudden, receiving a wire saying that he was due to leave in three days' time and asking them to go and see him off.

The woman under the big coat was twisting and wriggling, at times growling like a wild animal, feeling certain that all those explanations would not have aroused even a shadow of sympathy from those people who—most likely—were in the same plight as herself. One of them, who had been listening with particular attention, said:

"You should thank God that your son is only leaving now for the front. Mine has been sent there the first day of the war. He has already come back twice wounded and been sent back again to the front."

"What about me? I have two sons and three nephews at the front," said another passenger.

"Maybe, but in our case it is our *only* son," ventured the husband.

"What difference can it make? You may spoil your only son with excessive attentions, but you cannot love him more than you would all your other children if you had any. Paternal love is not like bread that can be broken into pieces and split amongst the children in equal shares. A father gives *all* his love to each one of his children without discrimination, whether it be one or ten, and if I am suffering now for my two sons, I am not suffering half for each of them but double . . . ."

"True . . . true . . ." sighed the embarrassed husband, "but suppose (of course we all hope it will never be your case) a father has two sons at the front and he loses one of them, there is still one left to console him . . . while . . ."

"Yes," answered the other, getting cross, " a son left to console him but also a son left for whom he must survive, while in the case of the father of an only son if the son dies the father can die too and put an end to his distress. Which of the two positions is the worse? Don't you see how my case would be worse than yours?"

"Nonsense," interrupted another traveller, a fat, red-faced man with blood-shot eyes of the palest grey.

He was panting. From his bulging eyes seemed to spurt inner violence of an uncontrolled vitality which his weakened body could hardly contain.

"Nonsense," he repeated, trying to cover his mouth with his hand so as to hide the two missing front teeth. "Nonsense. Do we give life to our children for our own benefit?"

The other travellers stared at him in distress. The one who had had his son at the front since the first day of the war sighed: "You are right. Our children do not belong to us, they belong to the Country . . . ."

"Bosh," retorted the fat traveller. "Do we think of the Country when we give life to our children? Our sons are born because . . . well, because they must be born and when they come to life they take our own life with them. This is the truth. We belong to them but they never belong to us. And when they reach twenty they are exactly what we were at their age. We too had a father and mother, but there were so many other things as well . . . girls, cigarettes, illusions, new ties . . . and the Country, of course, whose call we would have answered—when we were twenty—even if father and mother had said no. Now, at our age, the love of our Country is still great, of course, but stronger than it is the love for our children. Is there any one of us here who wouldn't gladly take his son's place at the front if he could?"

There was a silence all round, everybody nodding as to approve.

"Why then," continued the fat man, "shouldn't we consider the feelings of our children when they are twenty? Isn't it *natural* that at their age they should consider the love for their Country (I am speaking of decent boys, of course) even greater than the love for us? Isn't it *natural* that it should be so, as after all they must look upon us as upon old boys who cannot move any more and must stay at home? If Country exists, if Country is a natural necessity like bread, of which each of us must eat in order not to die of hunger, somebody must go to defend it. And our sons go, when they are twenty, and they don't want tears, because if they die, they die inflamed and happy (I am speaking, of course, of decent boys). Now, if one dies young and happy, without having the ugly sides of life, the boredom of it, the pettiness, the bitterness of disillusion . . . what more can we ask for him? Everyone should stop crying: everyone should laugh, as I do . . . or at least thank God—as I do—because my son, before dying, sent me a message saying that he was dying satisfied at having ended his life in the best way he could have wished. That is why, as you see, I do not even wear mourning . . . ."

He shook his light fawn coat as to show it; his livid lip over his missing teeth was trembling, his eyes were watery and motionless and soon after he ended with a shrill laugh which might well have been a sob.

"Quite so . . . quite so . . ." agreed the others.

The woman who, bundled in a corner under her coat, had been sitting and listening had—for the last three months—tried to find in the words of her husband and her friends something to console her in her deep sorrow, something that might show her how a mother should resign herself to send her son not even to death but to a probable danger of life. Yet not a word had she found amongst the many which had been said . . . and her grief had been greater in seeing that nobody—as she thought—could share her feelings.

But now the words of the traveller amazed and almost stunned her. She suddenly realized that it wasn't the others who were wrong and could not understand her but herself who could not rise up to the same height of those fathers and mothers willing to resign themselves, without crying, not only to the departure of their sons but even to their death.

She lifted her head, she bent over from her corner trying to listen with great attention to the details which the fat man was giving to his companions about the way his son had fallen as a hero, for his King and his Country, happy and without regrets. It seemed to her that she had stumbled into a world she had never dreamt of, a world so far unknown to her and she was so pleased to hear everyone joining in congratulating that brave father who could so stoically speak of his child's death.

Then suddenly, just as if she had heard nothing of what had been said and almost as if waking up from a dream, she turned to the old man, asking him:

"Then . . . is your son really dead?"

Everybody stared at her. The old man, too, turned to look at her, fixing his great, bulging, horribly watery light grey eyes, deep in her face. For some little time he tried to answer, but words failed him. He looked and looked at her, almost as if only then—at that silly, incongruous question—he had suddenly realized at last that his son was really dead . . . gone for ever . . . for ever. His face contracted, became horribly distorted, then he snatched in haste a handkerchief from his pocket and, to the amazement of everyone, broke into harrowing, heart-rending, uncontrollable sobs.

Writing and Discussion Topics

Questions 1–6 address content, critical analysis, personal choices, ethical options, specific discipline, and interdisciplinary alternatives, respectively.

1. Why does the portly traveler end up sobbing after arguing that sons should go to war?
2. What, if anything, does Pirandello expect his audience to do about war? What specific parts of this story support this argument?

3. Explain the character of the old woman. Is her character believable? How would you react in her circumstances?

4. What does this story say about the morality and consequences of war? Do our ethics and values, in general, change in times of war?

5. Do you believe Pirandello captures realistic emotion, or is this a satire?

6. Pirandello refers to a war that was fought over seventy years ago. How would he have written a different story, had a nuclear winter been the possible outcome?

Richard Lovelace

TO LUCASTA, GOING TO THE WARS

◆◆◆

R ichard Lovelace (1618–1657) was a wealthy English poet. Educated at Oxford, he was briefly imprisoned when he presented a controversial Kentish petition to the Commons. In 1648 he was again imprisoned by the Commonwealth. After he lost his fortune he published his first book of poetry. He was recognized as one of the English Cavalier Poets. He is well known for the line "I could not love thee, dear, so much, loved I not honor more," that is found in this poem. ◆

Tell me not, sweet, I am unkind
That from the nunnery
Of thy chaste breast and quiet mind,
To war and arms I fly.

True, a new mistress now I chase,
The first foe in the field;
And with a stronger faith embrace
A sword, a horse, a shield.

Yet this inconstancy is such
As you too shall adore;
I could not love thee, dear, so much,
Loved I not honor more.

Writing and Discussion Topics

Questions 1–6 address content, critical analysis, personal choices, ethical options, specific discipline, and interdisciplinary alternatives, respectively.

1. Why does our hero run from one set of arms into another? What is the purpose of the famous line, "I could not love thee, dear, so much, loved I not honor more"?
2. Writers sometimes present self-portraits by showing themselves in action in a moral dilemma. What portrait or sketch do you see in Lovelace that presents a moral dilemma?
3. Do you believe that honor is more important than love or family? Why should a woman be jealous of the "mistress" war? Why is war sometimes seen as tantalizing?
4. Is it ethical to make profits in war, whether they be economic or in personal esteem?
5. Which words of the poem convey a religious tone? Examine the connotation and denotation of these words.
6. How would the Catholic bishops view this poem? Interpret this poem in relation to the Crusades.

Mark Twain

THE WAR PRAYER
◆◆◆

M ark Twain is the pen name of Samuel Longhorne Clemens
(1835–1910). His formal education ended in his teens, yet
his shrewd eye provided him with an education of people, places, and
politics. He is one of the major authors of American fiction and is also
considered the greatest humorist in American literature. His works
include novels, short stories, essays, sketches, and travel narratives.
"War Prayer" is a short satire probing both sides of war. ◆

It was a time of great and exalting excitement. The country was up in arms, the war was on, in every breast burned the holy fire of patriotism; the drums were beating, the bands playing, the toy pistols popping, the bunched firecrackers hissing and spluttering; on every hand and far down the receding and fading spread of roofs and balconies a fluttering wilderness of flags flashed in the sun; daily the young volunteers marched down the wide avenue gay and fine in their new uniforms, the proud fathers and mothers and sisters and sweethearts cheering them with voices choked with happy emotion as they swing by; nightly the packed mass meetings listened, panting, to patriot oratory which stirred the deepest deeps of their hearts, and which they interrupted at briefest intervals with cyclones of applause, the tears running down their cheeks the while; in the churches the pastors preached devotion to flag and country, and invoked the God of Battles, beseeching His aid in our good cause in outpourings of fervid eloquence which moved every listener. It was indeed a glad and gracious time, and the half dozen rash spirits that ventured to disapprove of the war and cast a doubt upon its righteousness straight way got such a stern and angry warning that for their personal safety's sake they quickly shrank out of sight and offended no more in that way.

Sunday morning came—next day the battalions would leave for the front; the church was filled; the volunteers were there, their young faces alight with martial dreams—visions of the stern advance, the gathering momentum, the rushing charge, the flashing sabers, the flight of the foe, the tumult, the enveloping smoke, the fierce pursuit, the surrender!—then home from the war, bronzed heroes, welcomed, adored, submerged in golden seas of glory! With the volunteers sat their dear ones, proud, happy, and envied by the neighbors and friends who had no sons and brothers to send forth to the field of honor, there to win for the flag, or failing, die the noblest of noble deaths. The service proceeded; a war chapter from the Old Testament was read; the first prayer was said; it was followed by an organ burst that shook the building, and with one impulse the house rose, with glowing eyes and beating hearts, and poured out that tremendous invocation—

"God the all-terrible! Thou who ordainest,
  Thunder thy clarion and lightning thy sword!"

Then came the "long" prayer. None could remember the like of it for passionate pleading and moving and beautiful language. The burden of its supplication was, that an ever-merciful and benignant Father of us all would watch over our noble young soldiers, and aid, comfort, and encourage them in their patriotic work; bless them, shield them in the day of battle and the hour of peril, beat them in His mighty hand, make them strong and confident, invincible in the bloody onset; help them to crush the foe, grant to them and to their flag and country imperishable honor and glory—

An aged stranger entered and moved with slow and noiseless step up the main aisle, his eyes fixed upon the minister, his long body clothed in a robe that reached to his feet, his head bare, his white hair descending in a frothy cataract to his shoulders, his seamy face unnaturally pale, pale even to ghastliness. With all eyes following him and wondering, he made his silent way; without pausing, he ascended to the preacher's side and stood there, waiting. With shut lids the preacher, unconscious of this presence, continued his moving prayer, and at last finished it with the words uttered in fervent appeal, "Bless our arms, grant us the victory, O Lord our God, Father and Protector of our land and flag!"

The stranger touched his arm, motioned him to step aside—which the startled minister did—and took his place. During some moments he surveyed the spellbound audience with solemn eyes, in which burned an uncanny light; then in a deep voice he said:

"I come from the Throne—bearing a message from Almighty God!" The words smote the house with a shock; if the stranger perceived it he gave no attention. "He has heard the prayer of His servant your shepherd, and will grant it if such shall be your desire after I, His messenger, shall have explained to you its import—that is to say, its full import. For it is like unto many of the prayers of men, in that it asks for more than he who utters it is aware of—except he pause and think.

"God's servant and yours has prayed his prayer. Has he paused and taken thought? Is it one prayer? No, it is two—one uttered, the other not. Both have reached the ear of Him Who heareth all supplications, the spoken and the unspoken. Ponder this—

keep it in mind. If you would beseech a blessing upon yourself, beware! lest without intent you invoke a curse upon a neighbor at the same time. If you pray for the blessing of rain upon your crop which needs it, by that act you are possibly praying for a curse upon some neighbor's crop which may not need rain and can be injured by it.

"You have heard your servant's prayer—the uttered part of it. I am commissioned of God to put into words the other part of it—that part which the pastor—and also you in your hearts—fervently prayed silently. And ignorantly and unthinkingly? God grant that it was so! You heard these words: 'Grant us the victory, O Lord our God!' This is sufficient. The *whole* of the uttered prayer is compact into those pregnant words. Elaborations were not necessary. When you have prayed for victory you have prayed for many unmentioned results which follow victory—*must* follow it, cannot help but follow it. Upon the listening spirit of God the Father fell also the unspoken part of the prayer. He commandeth me to put it into words. Listen!

"O Lord our Father, our young patriots, idols of our hearts, go forth to battle—be Thou near them! With them—in spirit—we also go forth from the sweet peace of our beloved firesides to smite the foe. O Lord our God, help us to tear their soldiers to bloody shreds with our shells; help us to cover their smiling fields with the pale forms of their patriot dead; help us to drown the thunder of the guns with the shrieks of their wounded, writhing in pain; help us to lay waste their humble homes with a hurricane of fire; help us to wring the hearts of their unoffending widows with unavailing grief; help us to turn them out roofless with their little children to wander unfriended the wastes of their desolated land in rags and hunger and thirst, sports of the sun flames of summer and the icy winds of winter, broken in spirit, worn with travail, imploring Thee for the refuge of the grave and denied it—for our sakes who adore Thee, Lord, blast their hopes, blight their lives, protract their bitter pilgrimage, make heavy their steps, water their way with their tears, stain the white snow with the blood of their wounded feet! We ask it, in the spirit of love, of Him Who is the Source of Love,

and Who is the ever-faithful refuge and friend of all that are sore beset and seek His aid with humble and contrite hearts. Amen."

(*After a pause.*) "Ye have prayed it; if ye still desire it, speak! The messenger of the Most High waits."

It was believed afterward that the man was a lunatic, because there was no sense in what he said.

Writing and Discussion Topics

Questions 1–6 address content, critical analysis, personal choices, ethical options, specific discipline, and interdisciplinary alternatives, respectively.

1. What is the essential meaning of the second prayer? Critically analyze the role of the stranger.
2. Twain uses a style of comparison and contrast in "The War Prayer." What is the argument in the first prayer? What is the argument in the second prayer? Why did Twain say the people were not persuaded by the second prayer?
3. How would you view and feel about the noncombatants of war if you were on the winning side? When your country appears to be losing a war, how would you view and feel about the noncombatants? Explain and defend your answers.
4. What happens when a few people question the noble purpose of war? Ethically, do you believe it is your duty today to voice your views about a dispute between your country and another? Why? Are you morally responsible for your leaders' choices?
5. What is the essential theme and tone of the first prayer? What was its purpose? Critically analyze the first preacher in comparison to Richard Lovelace's hero.
6. Compare "The War Prayer" with the writing by the Catholic bishops. Which preacher seems more in line with Roman Catholic doctrine as expressed in the bishops' letter.

SILLY ASSES

————◆◆————

I saac Asimov is one of the most prolific authors in American history. He started writing at age eleven, had his first story published at eighteen, and has written more than 340 books since then. He has won science fiction's highest award, the Hugo, five times. He has also published books in virtually every field of science and humanities. His works have been translated into more than forty languages. This science fiction story symbolically portrays the effects of nuclear weapons. ◆

Naron of the long-lived Rigellian race was the fourth of his line to keep the galactic records.

He had the large book which contained the list of the numerous races throughout the galaxies that had developed intelligence, and the much smaller book that listed those races that had reached maturity and had qualified for the Galactic Federation. In the first book, a number of those listed were crossed out; those that, for one reason or another, had failed. Misfortune, biochemical or biophysical shortcomings, social maladjustment took their toll. In the smaller book, however, no member listed had yet blanked out.

And now Naron, large and incredibly ancient, looked up as a messenger approached.

"Naron," said the messenger. "Great One!"

"Well, well, what is it? Less ceremony."

"Another group of organisms has attained maturity."

"Excellent. Excellent. They are coming up quickly now. Scarcely a year passes without a new one. And who are these?"

The messenger gave the code number of the galaxy and the coordinates of the world within it.

"Ah, yes," said Naron. "I know the world." And in flowing script he noted it in the first book and transferred its name into the second, using, as was customary, the name by which the planet was known to the largest fraction of its populace. He wrote: Earth.

He said, "These new creatures have set a record. No other group has passed from intelligence to maturity so quickly. No mistake, I hope."

"None, sir," said the messenger.

"They have attained to thermonuclear power, have they?"

"Yes, sir."

"Well, that's the criterion." Naron chuckled. "And soon their ships will probe out and contact the Federation."

"Actually, Great One," said the messenger, reluctantly, "the Observers tell us they have not yet penetrated space."

Naron was astonished. "Not at all? Not even a space station?"

"Not yet, sir."

"But if they have thermonuclear power, where then do they conduct their tests and detonations?"

"On their own planet, sir."

Naron rose to his full twenty feet of height and thundered, "On their own planet?"

"Yes, sir."

Slowly Naron drew out his stylus and passed a line through the latest addition in the smaller book. It was an unprecedented act, but, then, Naron was very wise and could see the inevitable as well as anyone in the galaxy.

"Silly asses," he muttered.

Writing and Discussion Topics

Questions 1–6 address content, critical analysis, personal choices, ethical options, specific discipline, and interdisciplinary alternatives, respectively.

1. What is the message Naron delivers in this short story?
2. Could the conclusion of this short story become the premise for another essay? List the major points that should be developed.
3. You have just been elected supreme commander of one of the largest galaxies in the universe. What policies will you establish regarding the use of nuclear weapons? How will you enforce these policies?
4. Why is Naron so shocked about the use of thermonuclear power? Ethically, explain whether or not the people on Earth are making a bad choice in their use and testing of nuclear power.
5. Isaac Asimov is highly recognized for his authenticity in science fiction writing. Do any parts of this story seem inconceivable? If so, which ones? If not, explain your response.
6. Compare the theme in Asimov's story with Douglas P. Lackey's view in "Missiles and Morals: A Utilitarian Look at Nuclear Deterrence." What are the similarities? What are the differences?

Lewis Thomas

LATE NIGHT THOUGHTS ON LISTENING TO MAHLER'S NINTH SYMPHONY

◆◆◆

*L*ewis Thomas was born in Flushing, New York, in 1913. He is a distinguished medical researcher. He has taught at Cornell, Johns Hopkins, Tulane, the University of Minnesota, New York University, and Yale. Since 1973, Thomas has been president and chief executive officer of the Memorial Sloan-Kettering Cancer Center in New York City. He is the author of over two hundred highly specialized papers in the fields of immunology and pathology. In 1971, he began writing a column for the New England Journal of Medicine, *which became very popular. In 1974, he published his columns in a book entitled* The Lives of a Cell. *This selection is an excerpt from Thomas' book,* Late Night Thoughts on Listening to Mahler's Ninth Symphony. ◆

I cannot listen to Mahler's Ninth Symphony with anything like the old melancholy mixed with the high pleasure I used to take from this music. There was a time, not long ago, when what I heard, especially in the final movement, was an open acknowledgement of death and at the same time a quiet celebration of the tranquility connected to the process. I took this music as a metaphor for reassurance, confirming my own strong hunch that the dying of every living creature, the most natural of all experiences, has to be a peaceful experience. I rely on nature. The long passages on all the strings at the end, as close as music can come to expressing silence itself, I used to hear as Mahler's idea of leave-taking at its best. But always, I have heard this music as a solitary, private listener, thinking about death.

Now I hear it differently. I cannot listen to the last movement of the Mahler Ninth without the door-smashing intrusion of a huge new thought: death everywhere, the dying of everything, the end of humanity. The easy sadness expressed with such gentleness and delicacy by that repeated phrase on faded strings, over and over again, no longer comes to me as old, familiar news of the cycle of living and dying. All through the last notes my mind swarms with images of a world in which the thermonuclear bombs have begun to explode, in New York and San Francisco, in Moscow and Leningrad, in Paris, in Paris, in Paris. In Oxford and Cambridge, in Edinburgh. I cannot push away the thought of a cloud of radioactivity drifting along the Engadin, from the Moloja Pass to Ftan, killing off the part of the earth I love more than any other part.

I am old enough by this time to be used to the notion of dying, saddened by the glimpse when it has occurred but only transiently knocked down, able to regain my feet quickly at the thought of continuity, any day. I have acquired and held in affection until very recently another sideline of an idea which serves me well at dark times: the life of the earth is the same as the life of an organism: the great round being possesses a mind: the mind contains an infinite number of thoughts and memories: when I reach my time I may find myself still hanging around in some sort of midair, one of those small thoughts, drawn back into the memory of the earth: in that peculiar sense I will be alive.

Now all that has changed. I cannot think that way any more. Not while those things are still in place, aimed everywhere, ready for launching.

This is a bad enough thing for the people in my generation. We can put up with it, I suppose, since we must. We are moving along anyway, like it or not. I can even set aside my private fancy about hanging around, in midair.

What I cannot imagine, what I cannot put up with, the thought that keeps grinding its way into my mind, making the Mahler into a hideous noise close to killing me, is what it would be like to be young. How do the young stand it? How can they keep their sanity? If I were very young, sixteen or seventeen years old, I think I would begin, perhaps very slowly and imperceptibly, to go crazy.

There is a short passage near the very end of the Mahler in which the almost vanishing violins, all engaged in a sustained backward glance, are edged aside for a few bars by the cellos. Those lower notes pick up fragments from the first movement, as though prepared to begin everything all over again, and then the cellos subside and disappear, like an exhalation. I used to hear this as a wonderful few seconds of encouragement: we'll be back, we're still here, keep going, keep going.

Now, with a pamphlet in front of me on a corner of my desk, published by the Congressional Office of Technology Assessment, entitled *MX Basing,* an analysis of all the alternative strategies for placement and protection of hundreds of these missiles, each capable of creating artificial suns to vaporize a hundred Hiroshimas, collectively capable of destroying the life of any continent, I cannot hear the same Mahler. Now, those cellos sound in my mind like the opening of all the hatches and the instant before ignition.

If I were sixteen or seventeen years old, I would not feel the cracking of my own brain, but I would know for sure that the whole world was coming unhinged. I can remember with some clarity what it was like to be sixteen. I had discovered the Brahms symphonies. I knew that there was something going on in the late Beethoven quartets that I would have to figure out, and I knew that there was plenty of time ahead for all the figuring I would ever have to do. I had never heard of Mahler. I was in no hurry. I was a college sophomore and had decided that Wallace Stevens and I possessed a comprehensive understanding of everything needed for a life. The years stretched away forever ahead, forever. My great-great grandfather had come from Wales, leaving his signature in the family Bible on the same page that carried, a century later, my father's signature. It never crossed my mind to wonder about the twenty-first century; it was just there, given, somewhere in the sure distance.

The man on television, Sunday midday, middle-aged and solid, nice-looking chap, all the facts at his fingertips, more dependable looking than most high-school principals, is talking about civilian defense, his responsibility in Washington. It can make an enormous difference, he is saying. Instead of the outright death of eighty million American citizens in twenty minutes, he says, we can, by careful planning and practice, get that number down to only forty million, maybe even twenty. The thing to do, he says, is to evacuate the cities quickly and have everyone get under shelter in the countryside. That way we can recover, and meanwhile we will have retaliated, incinerating all of Soviet society, he says. What about radioactive fallout? he is asked. Well, he says. Anyway, he says, if the Russians know they can only destroy forty million of us instead of eighty million, this will deter them. Of course, he adds, they have the capacity to kill all two hundred and twenty million of us if they were to try real hard, but they know we can do the same to them. If the figure is only forty million this will deter them, not worth the trouble, not worth the risk. Eighty million would be another matter, we should guard ourselves against losing that many all at once, he says.

If I were sixteen or seventeen years old and had to listen to that, or read things like that, I would want to give up listening and reading. I would begin thinking up new kinds of sounds, different from any music heard before, and I would be twisting and turning to rid myself of human language.

Writing and Discussion Topics

Questions 1–6 address content, critical analysis, personal choices, ethical options, specific discipline, and interdisciplinary alternatives, respectively.

1. What are Thomas's thoughts about nuclear war? Why does he bring in the "middle-aged and solid, nice-looking chap" to discuss nuclear war? Would someone view nuclear arms differently at ages eighteen and forty-five? What point is Thomas making?
2. What parts of this essay are the strongest? Where does this essay use emotion and where does it use science as argumentation strategies?
3. Place yourself in a quiet, peaceful environment and reflect on the outcome of a nuclear exchange. Interpret, explain, and define your reflections. Paint a picture with words of the situation the way your mind sees the events unfolding.
4. Which philosophers from chapter one and this chapter seem most in line with Thomas's thoughts in this essay? Are the ideas contained in this essay rational and logical, or do you see them as fictional?
5. What is the overall theme of this selection? Select your favorite passage from this excerpt and examine what words and phrases in it portray the horrors of nuclear war.
6. How is the utilitarian perspective similar to Thomas's? Compare Thomas's ethical perspective with the ethical positions of Douglas Lackey and John Stuart Mill.

Arata Osada

CHILDREN OF HIROSHIMA
◆◆◆

A rata Osada was appointed president of Hiroshima University of Humanities and Science shortly after surviving the bombing of Japan in August, 1945. A strong advocate for peace, Osada collected 105 essays from school children who survived the blast and suffered through its aftereffects in the hopes that the children might convince us that destructive wars are a foolish way to try to gain world peace. ◆

Tomoyuki Satoh
4th grade boy (4 years old at the time)

I hadn't started school yet. On August 6, I was playing in front of a public bathhouse in our neighborhood. Sei-chan asked me to go to the fields and bring her some flowers so I was on my way there. Then it suddenly got very bright. I was very surprised, so I thought I would go into the house, but suddenly it seemed like dozens of needles were stuck in my eyes and I didn't know who I was or where I was going. I struggled toward the house and ran into the front door. When I opened my eyes, it was dim and gloomy. Then I saw my grandma running away as fast as she could with Keika-chan (my younger brother) on her back. I went with her. We went to the air-raid shelter. One of my big sisters was already inside so the four of us all huddled together. Then another big sister came running in and joined us. She was working at the Mitsuboshi Bakery making cakes. My mother had already got sick and died.

My father had gone to work as a volunteer and he came back looking for us. My oldest sister heard him calling and she took my father's hand and led him to our air-raid shelter. My father was burned everywhere above his waist. Both of my older sisters and the other people were scared, when they saw the burns. A stranger put some oil on my father's burns. I said thank you to him in my heart.

After that, we went to a hill in Fuchu. We put up a mosquito net in the ruins of a temple and slept inside. We lived there a long time. Then some of the other people began to return to their homes, so we did, too. When we got back, we saw all the glass broken, our cupboards all knocked over, our Buddhist altar all upset, the outer screens of the rooms destroyed, the roof tiles broken and the walls broken. We cleaned everything up and put Father to bed.

About sixty days later, Father called Grandma in the middle of the night and said he wanted to eat a sweet potato. "Very well," replied Grandma and cooked one for him.

"It's ready," she said, but he didn't answer and I touched him to see what the matter was. He felt cold and I knew he had died. Goodbye, dear Mummy and Daddy! . . .

Source: *Children of Hiroshima*, edited by Arata Osada. Copyright © 1982 Harper and Row.

Hiroaki Ichikawa
5th grade boy (5 years old at the time)

It is already six years since the atom bomb was dropped on Hiroshima. At that time, I was only five years old, and now I am already in fifth grade. "You will never forget those terrible things as long as you live, will you?" My mother has said these words again and again. The anniversary of the dropping of the atom bomb on the sixth of August will soon be here again. It makes me sad just to think what things would be like now if my father and mother had died then and I feel sorry for my many friends who did lose their parents.

That morning just as I was going outdoors, I was trapped under the house as it fell on top of me. I wriggled with all my might. Even now, I cannot forget how frightened I felt when I crawled out crying, "Mother! Mother!" and how happy I was when I heard my Mother's reply, "Mother's coming, so don't cry." At first, it was so dark that I could hardly see people's faces. Then it grew terribly hot and everything brightened all at once. When I asked why it got so dark like that, Mother told me that it was because all the houses in Hiroshima had collapsed at once. My whole family was inside the house so nobody was burned. I alone was pinned under the house and hurt my finger. When Mother saw my finger, she said, "I'm glad it wasn't your face, but it hurts, doesn't it?"

We lived in a shack for a while and then went to live where my father was born in Shiga Prefecture. Every year on the sixth of August, we remember what happened on that day in 1945. When the crape myrtles in our country garden were in bloom, my mother would say, "Don't they remind you of the red ones that used to grow by our hut in town?" And she would continue, "When the atom bomb fell, there were people who said that nothing would grow for about twenty years, but that wasn't true, was it? On the vacant lot by our shack, pumpkins and flowers and other things used to grow."

On the day after the bomb, we started toward the country and when we came to Hijiyama Bridge, we saw naked people with their burned skin hanging from them like rags. We saw others covered with blood, being carried to safer places in trucks. In the tobacco factory about a mile and a half from the bomb center were many people crying from the pain of their burns. Both Mother and Father often tell us that it was like hell.

After five years, our whole family was able to return to Hiroshima. After so many years, Hiroshima had changed completely. I was surprised to see what a beautiful town it had become. I pray that Hiroshima, where I was born, will become a splendid City of Peace. I also pray that peace will last forever. . . .

Shizuo Sumi
7th grade boy (1st grade at the time)

When the atom bomb was dropped on Hiroshima City at about 8:15 on August 6, I was playing outside with my sister. I saw a flash but I had no idea what it was. Mother ran out and picked up my sister so she didn't get burned. Mother was burned on the arms and I was burned on the face, neck and hands.

I was lying on the ground. I could see but I couldn't talk. Mother was hurrying to get our things out of the house. I seethed with anger. I closed my eyes but couldn't go to sleep because my burns smarted. After a while, I could see something red through my closed eyelids and I opened my eyes. Fire was spreading from house to house. I gritted my teeth as I watched our house burn down. It was a sea of fire spreading in every direction without the slightest sign of dying down. Mother was speaking with the neighbors, and I kept on crying all the time.

Night came. Miraculously, the main shop was saved. I think this was because Mother and the others had kept throwing water on this building only. We slept there. I cried and cried and mother did all she could to make me feel better but I couldn't sleep all night. I was still crying the next morning. Mother said the fire was still raging in the western part of the city. The day passed and night came again but I was still crying. The man lying next to me told me to shut up.

The next morning, Mother put some medicine on my burns. This hurt terribly and I cried some more. There was a doctor who passed our house every now and then and when he did he dropped in to see me. After about twenty days, the burns on my hands were a little better but those on my face and around my neck still smarted. I hoped I would get better soon and expected the doctor to come to see me but he stopped coming, and I had only Mother to take care of me. I couldn't eat anything but soup. At night, mosquitoes and fleas bit me so hard that I sometimes cried. After a couple of months, I could open my mouth wide enough to eat boiled rice by myself.

One night, there was a terrible storm and the wind howled and made a racket as it tore the tin off the roof. My sister and I were so scared that we cried. The water rose to just beneath the floor. The wind died down by morning but we couldn't leave the house because of the water. Two or three days later, the flood receded. Mother and the others got up on the roof and put back the tin that had been blown off so that it wouldn't leak.

I got very tired of staying in the house and got Mother to put me in a cart and take me to my school. The school I had attended was gone and there were only piles of debris there. Many columns of smoke were rising from the military parade ground and the air smelled bad because they were cremating bodies. I felt sorry for those who were killed and it came to me how lucky I was to survive the blast. I went home and lay in bed with a slight headache. In the evening, my head began to ache terribly. Mother told me that the headache came from my being exposed to the sun during the daytime. I stopped going out. The headache continued for four or five days. Mother cooled my head with cold towels and this made me feel better.

About a year passed and most of the burns healed except those on my neck and cheeks. By that time, I could go out by myself. Houses were being built one after another. But the electric lights weren't back on yet so it was pitch dark at night. During the day, everyone in the house worked at cleaning up the debris. Eventually, my burns completely healed and I joined the others. The burned light and telephone poles were taken away and roads were cleared of debris.

At last, the school was reopened. Mother took me to the opening ceremony. But there were no schoolrooms and we had to study outside in vacant lots or on the side of the hill. It was very inconvenient. After I went into the second grade, they put up some temporary buildings. How happy we were! After that, I studied all the harder. Rain or shine, I always went to school. Now, there are a lot of houses all over town. Our middle school has many new buildings, too.

I will never forget that day. I want to repay Mother for everything she did for me. Six years have passed since the bomb was dropped on Hiroshima. How fast time flies! Our new constitution renounces war and I think we must keep the promise of the constitution and love peace above all. . . .

Yoshihiro Kimura
9th grade boy (3rd grade at the time)

Every day at that time, I had to heat the bath. After that, I used to go back to my homework. About five, I would go to the streetcar stop to meet Father and my big sister, and we'd go back home and have supper together. That was what we did every day then.

On the morning of August 6, Father was in bed because he had a slight fever. My big brother was cooking some cuttlefish to eat at work. After everyone had gone, there were four of us, me, Mother and Father and my sister. Then my sister and I got ready for school. My sister went to the main school and I to the branch school. It was a temple, really. Me and my friends were talking about the war. Then we heard an air-raid warning. I ran home and was playing there for a while. I was used to all this. Then the all-clear was given and I went to school again. Our teacher had not come yet, so we were just talking. About then, we heard the sound of an airplane and we could see it, very small, in the southeastern sky. It got bigger and bigger and soon was over our heads. I was looking at it all the time, I didn't know whether it was an American plane or ours. All of a sudden, something white like a parachute fell out from the plane. Five or six seconds later, everything turned yellow. It was like I'd looked right at the sun. Then there was a big sound a second or two later and everything went dark. Stones and tiles fell on my head and I was knocked out for a bit. Then I woke up because heavy pieces of wood fell on me and hurt my back. I crawled out into the open. There I saw lots of people lying on the ground. Most of them were burned, and their faces had gone black. I felt better when I got out on the road and then suddenly felt my right arm hurting. The skin from the elbow to the fingers had peeled off. I began to walk toward where I thought my home was.

"Sumi-chan," cried a voice. I turned around and saw my sister. Her dress was torn to rags and her face completely different. The two of us went home, but our house had crumbled down and no one was there. We looked around nearby. When we got back, we found Father, who was trying to get something out from under the fallen roof. He gave up and walked up to us.

"Where is Mother?" I said.

"She is dead," he replied weakly.

When I heard that, I felt as if I had been hit on the head. I couldn't think. After a while, Father said, "What's the matter with your head?"

I felt the back of my head. It felt rough and was soaked with blood. A nail five inches long had stuck into Mother's head, and she died instantly.

It began to rain. The raindrops looked like muddy water. We took shelter under a railway bridge which was smoldering. Soon, the rain stopped. We felt cold and went near some burning houses to get warm. There were a lot of people there. There were almost no ordinary-looking people there. They had swollen faces and black lips. A man was waving the Japanese flag as if he was mad, shouting, "Banzai, banzai!" Another was swaggering around and saying, "I am a general." I felt very thirsty and went to the river to drink some water. Many blackened dead bodies were floating down the stream. I had to keep pushing them away while I drank. Along the edge of the water were lots of dead people. Some were still alive. A child was crying, "Mother, mother." Already, when I saw dead bodies, I didn't think much about it. Some people came staggering up and fell into the river and died. Sis fell down on the road maybe because she was badly hurt. Father carried her on his back and laid her on some ground cleared by the flames. Toward evening, my brother came back.

That night, we made a shed and slept in it. But cries for help and moans of pain were heard all the night through, and continually interrupted our sleep. I kept dozing and waking. The dawn came. My brother went to our relatives in the country to borrow a cart and came back about three in the afternoon. Then my sister and I were put on the cart and all of us started out. When we got to our relatives' home, Father almost just fell down, maybe because he didn't have to worry about keeping going any more. When night came, I felt lonely. 'About this time last night,' I said to my self, 'Mom was quite well, but now she's gone!' Two of my sisters were still missing. Father, one brother, one sister, and I were now all there were in my family. We couldn't say anything, we just looked emptily into space. When I went to the toilet, I cried out, "Mother." But Mother was not there any more. When I realized she was really dead, the loneliness and sadness were painful. I cried my heart out. But no matter how hard I cry, she won't come back. When I thought that, the sadness came again. The thought that I could never see her gentle face seemed to suffocate me and my head swam. I cried a lot. Then Grandmother said, "Now Mother is a Buddha, so if you want to see her, ask him." Although Father saw her die with his own eyes, I could not believe she was dead.

Then we had another misfortune. About three in the morning on the fifteenth, my sister died. By the time I was awoke, she was dead. It must have been a hard death, for her eyes were open. Her eyes seemed to be staring at me. I shouted "Sister," and shook her, but she had become a Buddha, too. That day, the war came to an end.

Some people who had been missing began to come back. I felt that Mother, too, might come back. But although I waited, of course there was no hope of her return. I hoped that at least my eldest sister would come home. In the meantime, my eldest brother had been discharged from the army. Every day was full of loneliness. Gradually, I was able to face the fact that both my mother and sister were dead. I began to be able to resign myself to the fact. My oldest sister's remains were never found, but Father got some ashes from a mass-cremation. But no matter how hard I tried, I couldn't forget my mother. The gentlest, kindest person. Two sisters were also very kind. Mother used to make cakes and give them to me every day when I came back from school. Oh, kind Mother; good Mother! Where are you now? I am sure that she has gone to a better place. I often picture to myself Mother living in Heaven and beautifully dressed, like a goddess. She always used to say, "Children, be good to each other."

Later, we moved back to Hiroshima City again, and now I have a second mother. But whenever I have something that is hard to talk to other people about, I miss my real mother so badly.

I hate war now from the bottom of my heart. It is entirely due to the war that my kind mother and sisters were killed. I don't hate anybody because Mother is dead, but I hate war. I don't want hateful war to happen again. War is everyone's enemy. Mother's soul in heaven will be happy if we stop wars and peace comes to the world. . . .

Susumu Kimura
11th grade boy (5th grade at the time)

It must have been about ten minutes before eight when the ominous sound of the siren rang through the air. I switched on the radio and heard, "Enemy aircraft are proceeding north from the Bungo Straits. . . ."

My father had already left for the office, but we, my mother, my sister (a seventh-grade student of the Hiroshima Prefectural First Girls' High School at the

time) and I (a fifth-grader) had lifted up a *tatami* mat to get into the shelter. Outside, people were rushing to and fro.

My sister was scheduled to take part in the building clearance project near Dobashi on that day. The tension lasted about ten minutes and then the all-clear was sounded. It was in fact this all-clear signal which killed most of the people in Hiroshima.

My sister left the house to go to work. I can still recall how she looked then. She had on a pair of tennis shoes and was carrying her packed lunch and her air-raid hood.

After my sister had gone, we were getting ready to go to the station to buy train tickets so that my sister and I could visit the country. I was in the kitchen and my mother in the next room in front of the mirror. It was at that moment that the atom bomb which took a toll of 300,000 lives was exploded over Hiroshima.

An intense light flashed through the window and hit my eyes. It flashed from red to yellow, just like fireworks. For a moment everything went black, I could not see an inch. "Mother," I shouted, and rushed over. We spent that dreadful moment holding each other. That moment was a very long one, it seemed as if ten years went by. Maybe two or three minutes later I started to be able to see again. The house was wrecked, the walls knocked down, doors splintered. My mother silently looked around and then said, "It's dangerous here. Let's get out."

We crawled out of the house. Outside was a world I had never seen or heard of. I saw raw flesh, people who no longer looked like human beings. My mother put her hands over my eyes saying, "Don't look." But I pushed my mother's hands away and fearfully looked around. On the street were a lot of people lying dead, and others with fatal injuries. I suddenly thought of myself and discovered that I had escaped without a scratch. My mother was not injured either. I stood blankly by the gate for a while. A lady, bleeding badly, ran by, shouting her child's name. Her voice made me think of my sister. 'My sister might be hurt, too.'

My mother was helping a neighbor and here and there cries for help could be heard. I even felt ashamed because I had escaped unhurt. Many people were rushing to escape toward Ujina. In the sky, black smoke was rising more thickly and the flames were getting nearer. Someone called my name, and I ran to the back of the house and found it was my father, who had come back from the office. He told me that he had been blown five or six yards by the blast. Three of us were safe and together, but what had happened to my sister? We left for Ujina, taking with us the left-overs from breakfast and leaving a message on the gate of our house: "Keiko, we are going to Ujina."

Night came and we decided to sleep in a field. More and more fires broke out. The night dragged on. I woke several times. Morning finally came. My father went to the city to find my sister, while my mother and I left for our relatives'. Their home was also wrecked, but after working for half a day we were able to make a place to sleep. I was so tired from what happened the previous day that I lay down and didn't wake up till evening. I looked around hoping to see my sister, but she was not there. My father had come back. He told us that he was unable to get into the Dobashi area because of the fires. Another sleepless night came. I would doze, the alert would be sounded. The flames made the sky crimson like the glow of a sunset.

On the following day, my father and mother both went out to look for my sister, but couldn't find her. I went with my father during the afternoon and found the streets were quite dangerous, what with tangled and broken streetcar wires. We went along the bank of the river and saw school boys and girls of my sister's age lying in groups, already dying in agony. They pleaded for water from anyone who walked by. My father said, "Your father or mother is sure to come looking for you soon, so take heart and don't give up."

They said nothing, but their swollen and burned faces smiled painfully at us. We could not do anything for them. They must have come here looking for somewhere cool. What they had been wearing was burned, and they had nothing on. Their skin was slimy from burns and already infested with maggots. Was my sister in the same state? We went along this road to Dobashi. There was even a horse, burned to death, beside the road. We asked a man looking among the dead bodies, "Do you happen to know anything about the students of the Prefectural Girls' High School?"

He answered that he had seen some at Koi. We pedaled our bicycles as fast as we could, but we were so anxious to get there it seemed as slow as walking. At the top of the hill near Koi, we did see some of the girls of my sister's school, but she was not among them.

We also spent the next day searching like that. The students on the river bank who had been livelier the day before now could not speak, and were looking wistfully at us. Many that had been alive yesterday were now dead. As we started to move past them, a frail, soft voice said, "Goodbye."

It was hard for us to leave them. When we went there the following day, all those students were dead.

We couldn't find my sister, though we searched every day for five days. I thought she had returned each time I heard footsteps at the door. We had left the door open so that she could come in, but it was useless. I had to go back to where I'd been evacuated, in the country.

Days passed and on August 15 Japan surrendered. War, war. Each time I see this word, I remember my sister's words. It was a letter she had written me when I was evacuated out of the city.

"Dear Susumu,

"You must be very lonely there, all by yourself. We are lonely too, without you. But when the war ends, we'll all live together again. . . ."

I returned to Hiroshima, but I no longer saw my sister who always greeted me with "Is that you, Susumu?" when I came in the front door.

My father was at the office and my mother was by herself at home, thinking of my sister, when I came back. She was very happy, but in her happiness I felt there was also some sadness.

The greatest sacrifice I suffered in the atom bombing was the loss of my sweet, innocent sister. I take out and read my sister's letter whenever I feel lonely.

This letter is to me the main force that keeps me on the right path. . . .

Tetsuo Miyata
University student

I

Eight o'clock on the morning of August 6, 1945. I was serving as an assistant teacher in Kakogawa Village Primary School in Hiroshima Prefecture's Asa County, although I had only just left middle school; I lodged in the school. I was conscious of the fatigue caused by the long periods of air-raid alerts the previous night, but as I stood in the school playground I felt relieved that Hiroshima had not been attacked.

With the increasingly heavy incendiary bombings by the B-29s since March, Japan's cities, first one, then the next, were being reduced to ashes. How many times it happened that halfway through the night the warning would be given, and as we tightened our leggings and helmets we would think: Tonight it will be Hiroshima. At that time, Hiroshima was Japan's seventh largest city with a population of 400,000, and even amidst the tense atmosphere it was bustling and lively. With smaller cities being hit one after the other, why had Hiroshima been spared? This question that came to the mind of everyone living there appeared together with a kind of desperate irritation, a feeling of 'If it's going to happen, let it come quickly'; or there were the wishful rumors it gave rise to that Hiroshima would absolutely not be attacked by the ravages of war because its gods were giving it special protection. But when one's dreams were shattered in the night by the chill sound of the air-raid siren and we stared up into the black sky, such feelings of irritation and complacent credulity dwindled and disappeared.

The start of morning roll-call. The summer sun was already burning down, and the white-shirted figures of the lines of children dazzled the eye. The number of children evacuated to this village since spring had passed two hundred. It was certain that they and local children seated beside them had a nameless sense of foreboding. And in addition to that, what were the feelings of the children who'd been evacuated? It was already three months since they had streamed off the train at the village station, rucksack on back, holding their small roll of bedding bound with reeds, looking around at everything, as if it were all so strange to them. Even they, who during the day played happily, gathering herbs, would all gaze toward the southern sky, toward where their parents lived, as twilight came over the mountains and fields and lamps flickered on in the farm houses. The child who slipped away in the night and ran twelve miles over mountain roads back to his parents stands here today; and with their feet in sandals and burned black by the sun, the town children cannot be distinguished from the country children.

Suddenly far overhead in the sky, the roar of B-29 engines! Probably just one, or maybe two. The alarm hasn't sounded; no need to worry. It had probably just come to check on the effect of last night's air-raid. Thus were we so used to B-29 reconnaissance flights that we didn't think much about it at first. Suddenly, though, the roar changed to a high howl and we looked up without thinking. A single B-29, its huge fuselage gleaming in the direct rays of the midsummer sun, was turning sharply and tearing up into the blue, leaving a trail of vapor in the sky. Thinking about it now, everything was already over at that instant. It was at that time. A flash like lightning—no, a much more intense flash. I covered my eyes and dived onto the ground. And how much time passed then? An immense, earth-shaking, thunderous explosion. "We've been hit! This village, this school is done for! The white shirts were too noticeable!'

"Escape!"

The children fled into the bamboo groves, scattering like so many young spiders.

It was only when I saw the bright red mushroom-shaped cloud billowing up into the azure sky way off to the south that I became conscious that we were safe. Beneath that red cloud was Hiroshima. Hiroshima had already had it. But what had been dropped? Ordinary bombs, or incendiaries? But no, it seems to have been something bigger than that. And what had happened to my sister, Fusae, under that red cloud? Had my father already reached his office? And what of my brother and his wife? My mother was supposed to be on a trip to Shikoku, so she at least was all right, but . . . I stood there alone on the exercise ground, absent-mindedly thinking all this.

II

It was in the evening of that day that the first train carrying people from Hiroshima arrived. The figure of a woman, dressed in a tattered utility suit and with a nominal strip of blood-stained bandage, trudging along wearily on bare feet, but still firmly holding the hand of a wailing child. A man limping along, wounds all over his body and carrying on his back a child whose whole face was so blistered from burns that it could not see. An old woman came by, a small parcel cradled in one arm and using a hand to keep wiping away the sweat, stained brown from the blood and dust, that threatened to enter her eyes. She was wearing odd clogs she must have found somewhere and was mumbling something as she walked along, but suddenly she staggered and sat down heavily on the ground, clawed at the earth, looked up at the sky and started crying noisily, like a baby. The parcel, covered with a gray *furoshiki* cloth, was dropped and went rolling along the ground. A man, arm in a sling and looking like a laborer; inside a haversack hung carelessly from a shoulder, some rags could be seen: he was behind the old woman but went on, stepping around her and her parcel with nothing more than a quick glance.

The pitiful line of victims continued to stream toward the school. It was an eerily silent procession, a scene of wretched humanity, people who, even while in pain and trembling before a callous fate, were trying to somehow carry on living. They had no objective; all they could think of was to automatically keep following the person in front. As to where the resting place was that would receive them, or what kind of place they were heading for—such things probably never entered their mind. Even if one of those at the front had made a mistake and lost his way on a mountain road, the others would probably just have followed along without a word, gasping for breath.

The victims the school accommodated that day numbered several hundreds. It was made into a temporary first-aid station, with thin mats spread over the classroom floors. There were some—though very few—uninjured people who, with blood-shot eyes and a high, excited color to their faces, bustled back and forth along the corridors, giving shrill shouts and cries. A girl student, her face so swollen by burns it looked like she had mumps, came in, her mother leading her by the hand. When I asked them, it turned out that she'd been in school when the bomb fell, and although she'd been caught in the flames she's walked the two miles to her home barefooted. As she lay on the matting, gripping her mother's hand, she asked in a faint voice where she was. The poor girl couldn't see. Suddenly I thought of Fusae— I hoped that she was safe somewhere. . . .

"This is the Kako River."

"I see. What's-her-name at school comes from here."

The girl, breathing so feebly, was yet in full command of her senses. Her mother just kept gripping her hand tightly. With burns over half of her body and no medicine, what could be done? To leave her fate to heaven? Was this a time to pray only to God? No, perhaps it was more true to say that no urge to pray to God arose. From the figure of the mother, who was dithering around as if possessed, no attitude of piety could be discerned.

By next morning the girl was a corpse. Except that there was a white cloth over her face, she seemed the same as before, lying there beside the other wounded and injured.

"The tears won't come. It's strange," was all her mother said.

III

I set out on foot for Hiroshima, holding a bag of rice-balls. The weather was very fine that day, too. Along the way I got a lift from a passing truck. As the truck rolled along the road to Hiroshima, raising a trail of white dust, what was I thinking and worrying about? Oddly enough, I can't recall how I felt at that time. All I can remember is that as I felt the blood racing around my body and a stifling pressure in my chest, the blood in my head would be sucked away somewhere, and this kept on happening.

There were lines of injured people along both sides of the road, and they kept on wearily trudging north, always to the north. Old people being moved on carts; children being led by the hand; a soldier hunched in the shade of a tree. The eyes of all were blank and vacant. They were like people who were not seeking anything, or who were filled with limitless desires.

Kitayama was still burning and we circled it to the right, whereupon before our eyes we saw Hiroshima—but how changed it was! In the midst of a plain of rubble stood trees and power poles, charred black by the flames; the skeletons of concrete buildings burning here and there presented a lurid spectacle. Overhead, a lone B-29 was circling, but soon after disappeared toward the south. Oh, B-29! What did you find? This field of rubble? That scorched mountain? Were you able to see the figure of the young girl near me, her whole body burned and swollen, lying as if dead, with no protection from the sizzling heat of the sun? Were you able to hear her call faintly yet clearly for her mother, her dying cry?

The unpleasant odor of bodies being burned filled my nostrils.

Picking my way between piles of rubble and dangling electricity wires, using Hijiyama Hill to orient myself, I reached home about midday. Luckily, my house was in the shadow of Hijiyama so it hadn't been burned, but it seemed so badly damaged it didn't look like somewhere you could live. My brother and his wife had just come back from one of the designated safe areas, but there was no sign of my father or Fusae.

I said the first thing that came to mind: "Father and Fusae have probably had it," though in my heart I hoped, no, I was certain, that they were all right.

We quickly left the house and went back along the road to search for the two who had not come home.

The men and women who were lying by the side of the road were so burned and injured that it was hard to tell them apart. I searched among them, peering into each face. I tried enquiring at two or three schools on the outskirts. They were all packed full of the injured, who overflowed into the exercise ground; but we couldn't see anyone among them who looked like the two we were looking for.

Where were Father and Fusae? Had they really had it? Or were they in some safe area somewhere we hadn't thought of. I forced myself to hang on to this vague hope; driving away the despair that threatened to overcome me, I took another mouthful of food.

When I arrived at the school the sun had already set.

IV

The second time I visited Hiroshima was on August 13, six days later. What had I been doing at the school for five whole days? And if I was looking for Father and Fusae, why hadn't I even tried to tread the soil of Hiroshima? It was a state of mind hard even for me myself to understand, now. But anyway, in the end there was nothing to do but shake off any weakness. While I was taking care of people in the school, if the two of them were alive they would probably have returned home within four or five days; if they were not back yet, I decided it meant there was no hope. Until the door of fate opened for me of its own accord, on 'life' or 'death' as the case might be, I wanted to leave it untouched. I remember the day the middle school entrance exam results were announced and I deliberately came an hour late, sneaking in to see by myself, trying to control the pounding of my heart. But while this kind of individual characteristic of mine is a thing of the past, it is a fact that my thinking at that time regarding people's deaths was different from what it is now. Of the disaster victims who had brought themselves to this school, five died yesterday and ten today. I just watched them, as if emptied of feeling. It is the evanescence of inanimate nature, as seen in the red-ripe wild persimmons which, as if drawn by something, drop one by one, in the autumn, to the earth. What a miserable death for a human being.

As I stepped inside the half-wrecked house that smelled peculiar to burns came to my nostrils. I went through into the living room with a foreboding of something bad. There was my father lying down, breathing painfully, completely transformed by the burns which covered half his face and his limbs.

The first words to leave my lips were, "What about Fusae?" "Look, over there," my mother said, then broke down crying. A single small urn wrapped in a white cloth was standing there.

"Oh, I see," I said, pretending as hard as possible to be calm, and I moved shakily into the next room, as I couldn't bear to stay there any more. Fusae's desk was there. Two or three of the girls' novels she used to like reading were scattered carelessly around. Inside a drawer were her notebooks and school texts and her diary, containing the dreams of a sweet, innocent girl, all just as she left them. It was then, for the first time, that it came home to me that I'd lost someone. My choking gasps changed to wracking sobs.

"Fusae, Fusae; you're not here any more. No matter where I go in the world, I can never meet you again."

She was a thin, sickly girl, always catching colds and having to miss school. And she was nervous, too, susceptible, but she also had a wild side. It may have been because she was the youngest. My next brother was a full six years older than me, and when I was in the fourth grade of primary school he went to school in Tokyo, so after that it was just the two of us, Fusae and myself. We used to play a lot, but we also used to fight a lot. She liked to win, and seldom screamed about a little hit, but when she did cry it was in such a loud voice that I'd shut up. After she entered girls' school, she suddenly became a bit precocious; but even then, in those pure eyes there was always a touch of playfulness, and that never changed. One day, I remember, we went to Grandmother's place to play. I was a rather bashful boy and was somehow embarrassed walking together with her, so I couldn't help issuing a 'categorical imperative'—"You must walk five yards behind me." Commendably, perhaps because she understood the feelings of this poor middle-school student, she followed along disconsolately, never saying anything about it being unfair.

When she became a third-year student this spring, she was drafted under the Student Mobilization Program to work on the communications staff of the Hiroshima division general headquarters.

Fusae had died. Her life had ended when she was fourteen years and some months old. Thinking about it, the last time we'd met was August 4. That was a

Saturday so I'd returned home for the first time in some days. She was wearing her work trousers and busily helping with the dinner.

"Oh, welcome home, Tetsuo," she said, turning around, with that special smile of hers. Her black hair round her shoulders and neatly tied looked so adult.

"Got my salary. I'll give you ten yen." I drew a ten-yen note from my forty-five yen pay packet and thrust it in front of her eyes. She protested that she didn't need it, but I forced it into her pocket. That ten-yen note probably stayed in her pocket right to the end. On Sunday, the next day, while I was still in bed, she went out in high spirits for a 24-hour work stint. Behind her, she left the home she could never return to. It was while she was on standby in the underground communications room that she was bathed in that attack. Fortunately, she did not receive any injury and she quickly tried to crawl out of the underground room through the escape hatch, but the flames were already everywhere. As the flames came nearer, she and her friends were forced to jump into the river at the back, but she was a sickly girl and didn't know how to swim. Somewhere, though, she'd picked up a wooden bucket and was clutching it. But how cruel fate is, for she let go of that bucket which meant life to her. She called frantically for help, but there was no one to extend a helping hand.

Thus it was that she drowned.

On the morning of the eighth, a first-aid worker recovered her body downstream, where it had fetched up against a support of Yanagi Bridge; she was promptly cremated.

My mother came back to Hiroshima that day and without pausing for rest wandered aimlessly through the scorched plain, calling Fusae's name. And, perhaps through her determination, she discovered Fusae's remains just after cremation was completed. The only clue was the name, Miyata Fusae, written on some underwear.

V

On that day, Father breathed his last, watched over by everyone in the house. After the hardships he'd had as the father of seven children, he'd entered the peaceful life of old age only to suddenly have to finish his life at the age of sixty. He was moved in a coffin made of boards from the collapsed ceiling.

"Please put up with this." My mother's words were heart-breaking, spoken as if to a living person. On Hijiyama, it seemed that many cremations had already taken place, with here and there dug-out depressions in which scattered wooden embers disturbed the white ash.

The coffin flared into flame; inside it my father was stretched out quietly, hands pressed together. The kind, gentle father of bygone days. My brother and I, gripping the wooden pokers, dazedly sat down on a rock. The purple smoke swirled around two or three times, then was lifted into the sky by a wind from somewhere.

VI

Already six years have passed since then. The atomic desert, on which it is said nothing would grow for seventy years, was quickly cleared up, and the shacks with their rusting tin roofs were replaced by new homes smelling of fresh wood, and by reinforced concrete apartments. Where immediately after the war tents were set up on the rubble and a few objects arranged to sell to the people passing by, now there are shopping streets lit by neon lamps, with young men and women jostling after the latest fashions.

Just as weeds send forth shoots no matter how much they are trampled or kicked, so the savage desire to live can never be removed as long as it is rooted in man's true nature.

There is no sign now of that memorable place where my father was cremated; now there is only thick green grass everywhere.

On the clear waters of the Ohta, boats now float, and as I idly gaze up at the white clouds in the blue sky, I cannot believe that this was the stream which swallowed up that poor young girl, as she gave her death cries. But if I stare at the blue waters I feel that her figure is going to appear, rising up from the depths, smiling. And isn't the gentle sound of the waves lapping against the side of the boat the soft murmur of her voice?

Day by day, such sad recollections fade from a person's memory. However, maybe even the power of time cannot heal such blows that have pierced to the marrow of our being. In the blood that flows through me there is a black undercurrent that ebbs and flows, sometimes with great pressure, sometimes gougingly, but never can I control it. Rather, as time passes, it becomes more distinct, more intense. . . .

Writing and Discussion Topics

Questions 1–6 address content, critical analysis, personal choices, ethical options, specific discipline, and interdisciplinary alternatives, respectively.

1. Does age make any difference when looking at the atom bomb's effects on the children of Hiroshima? Explain your answer.

2. Is this history tainted because the responses are from youths under age twenty-one? Are these stories too emotional to be historically valid? Comment in depth on your answers.

3. What images and feelings linger in your mind from these essays? What might you learn from these images and feelings that you do not know already about the human effects of nuclear war? These essays were written by students brought up in a culture that is quite different from American culture. If the bomb had fallen on your city in the United States, how do you think your essay might differ from those in the *Children of Hiroshima?*

4. Using James Sterba's article as a comparison, explain which ethical system(s) would give the strongest insights into the nuclear war revealed by these essays. Which arguments of Sterba would discount or ignore the children's messages?

5. It is easy to see that the next selection by Marion Yass is the work of a historian. Would you want to call Osada's book of essays a history, a historical document, or both? If it is a history, who is the historian? If it is a historical document, how does it differ from the documents Yass used? What can be learned from these firsthand accounts that cannot be learned from the accounts of President Truman or Arthur Compton recorded by Marion Yass in the following selection, "The Decision to Bomb Japan"?

6. These essays read much like a work of literature. Is there any difference between what we learn from them about nuclear war and what we learn from Pirandello or Lovelace? Osada hoped these essays would convince people that war is a foolish route to peace. Would they convince Gray and Payne?

Marion Yass

THE DECISION TO BOMB JAPAN
◆◆◆

M arion Yass is a historian and author whose specialty is Pacific Rim areas. This excerpt from Yass's book exposed problems of communication between world leaders prior to dropping the atomic bomb on Japan. Yass would like to understand the workings of President Harry S. Truman's mind prior to authorizing the bombings. ◆

COLONEL PASH and his Alsos secret agents did much to reassure the Manhattan District. There seemed little doubt that Hitler had fallen behind in the race to build an atomic weapon. But a new fear overtook the scientists. Leo Szilard remembered: "During 1943 and part of 1944 our greatest worry was the possibility that Germany would perfect an atomic bomb before the invasion of Europe. . . . In 1945 when we ceased worrying about what the Germans might do to us, we began to worry about what the government of the United States might do to other countries."[1]

The first scientist to be worried was the Dane, Niels Bohr. He saw that the atomic bomb would create new world problems. As the war progressed, suspicion of Joseph Stalin's Russian dictatorship grew. Bohr knew that tension between Russia and her Western Allies would probably develop after the war—the more so if Russia was left to find out about the bomb for herself. The secret must be shared. Bohr talked to Roosevelt's advisors and wrote to Sir John Anderson in London. Anderson, much impressed, contacted Winston Churchill in March, 1944, echoing his friend's sentiments: "No plans for world organization which ignore the potentialities of Tube Alloys can be worth the paper on which they are written. Indeed, it may well be that our thinking on these matters must now be on an entirely new plane."[2]

Churchill merely scribbled—"I do not agree"—on Anderson's note. He granted Bohr an interview when he arrived in England the following month. But he was distracted by plans for the D-Day landings. He was unimpressed by the scientist's low voiced circumlocutions. On returning to the United States, Bohr in desperation wrote a long memorandum to President Roosevelt: "A weapon of unparalleled power is being created. . . . Quite apart from the question of how soon the weapon will be ready for use and what role it may play in the present war, this situation raises a number of problems which call for most urgent attention. Unless, indeed, some agreement about the control of the use of the new active materials can be obtained, any temporary advantage, however great, may be outweighed by a perpetual menace to human security."[3]

Reprinted by permission of the Putnam Publishing Group from *Hiroshima* by Marion Yass. Copyright © 1972 by G. P. Putnam's Sons.

Roosevelt and Churchill met at Hyde Park, Washington, in September, 1944. Neither was moved by Bohr's plea for caution. The two leaders had the first formal, if tentative, talks on what to do with the bomb: "The suggestion that the world should be informed regarding Tube Alloys, with a view to an international agreement regarding its control and use, is not accepted. The matter should continue to be regarded as of the utmost secrecy; but when a 'bomb' is finally available, it might perhaps, after mature consideration, be used against the Japanese." Also, "enquiries should be made regarding the activities of Professor Bohr, and steps taken to ensure that he is responsible for no leakage of information—particularly to the Russians."[4]

These Hyde Park talks were not made public. Bohr was, as usual, discreet about his political campaigning. Nevertheless most of the physicists agreed that the politicians were unwise to keep the atomic weapon secret from their Allies. One of them dramatically took things into his own hands. In February, Klaus Fuchs, working with Peierls at Los Alamos, passed on information about the new weapon to a Russian spy, Harry Gold. Whatever his motives, Fuchs—like Bruno Pontecorvo at the Canadian atomic plant who also turned spy—had access to atomic secrets valuable to the Russians.

Other physicists worried about the bomb took a less extreme course. A group at the Metallurgical Laboratory in Chicago, including Leo Szilard and James Franck, had also grown disturbed about the future of the bomb. The first meeting of the United Nations Assembly was planned for April, 1945, in San Francisco. How could the powers decide the future of the world if not all of them knew about the bomb? Leo Szilard once again approached the great Einstein. He asked him to sign a petition to the President cautioning him about the use of the bomb. While the petition lay on his desk in April, Roosevelt died.

Harry S. Truman, the new President, knew no more about the bomb than he had done when asked to call off his investigations at Oak Ridge and Hanford. He now received a note from Stimson: "I think it is very important that I should have a talk with you as soon as possible on a highly secret matter. It has such a bearing on our present foreign relations . . . that I think you ought to know about it without much further delay."[5]

In his memoirs, Truman wrote under the dateline April 25th: "At noon I saw Secretary of War Stimson in connection with the urgent letter he had written. . . . I listened with absorbed interest, for Stimson was a man of great wisdom and foresight. He went into considerable detail in describing the nature and the power of the projected weapon. If expectations were to be realized, he told me, the atomic bomb would be certain to have a decisive influence. . . . And if it worked, the bomb in all probability would shorten the war. . . . The Secretary appeared confident of the outcome and told me that in all probability success would be attained within the next few months. He also suggested that I designate a committee to study and advise me of the implications of this new force."[6]

Truman took Stimson's advice. He set up the Interim Committee. This included Stimson and his deputy George Harrison, James Byrnes the President's new Secretary of State, Ralph Bard the Under-Secretary of the Navy, Karl Compton President of the Massachusetts Institute of Technology, and Dr. Vannevar Bush. An advisory panel of four scientists was attached to the new Committee: Robert Oppenheimer, Enrico Fermi, Ernest Lawrence and Arthur Compton. The scientists were brought nearer the political arena.

The European war was over before the Interim Committee met. Germany surrendered unconditionally in 1945. Hitler committed suicide in Berlin. Truman announced the Allied victory on May 9th, and then "called on Japan to surrender unconditionally, and urged the Japanese to do so by stating that, otherwise, utter destruction awaited them. . . . Mr. Truman warned the American people . . . to 'work, work, work . . . the West is free but the East is still in bondage to the treacherous tyranny of the Japanese. When the last Japanese division has surrendered unconditionally, then only will our fighting job be done' "[7] The Burmese and Far Eastern campaigns had been the toughest of the war. The bitter, barbarous fights at Bataan and Corregidor in 1942 were as fresh in American minds as the attack on Pearl Harbor. Such memories gave force to the agreement of Churchill and Roosevelt at Casablanca that the Allied war aim should be the unconditional surrender of each enemy.

Secretary of War Stimson urged the new Interim Committee "to recommend action that may turn the course of civilization. In our hands we expect soon to have a weapon of wholly unprecedented destructive power. Today's prime fact is war. Our great task is to bring this war to a prompt and successful conclusion. We may assume that our new weapon puts in our hands overwhelming power. It is our obligation to use this power with the best wisdom we can command."[8]

Arthur Compton recalled: "Throughout the morning's discussions it seemed a foregone conclusion that the bomb would be used. . . . At the luncheon following the morning meeting I was seated at Mr. Stimson's left. In the course of the conversation I asked whether it might not be possible to arrange a non-military demonstration of the bomb in such a manner that the Japanese would be so impressed that they would see the uselessness of continuing the war. The Secretary opened this question for general discussion by those at the table.

"Various possibilities were brought forward. One after the other it seemed necessary that they should be discarded. If a bomb were exploded in Japan with previous notice, the Japanese air power was still adequate to give serious interference. . . . If during the final adjustments of the bomb the Japanese defenders should attack, a faulty move might easily result in some kind of failure. Such an end to an advertised demonstration of power would be much worse than if the attempt had not been made.

"It was now evident that when the time came for bombs to be used we should have only one of them available, followed afterwards by others at long intervals. We could not afford the chance that one of them might be a dud. If the test were made on some neutral territory, it was hard to believe that Japan's determined and fanatical military men would be impressed. If such an open test were made first, and failed to bring surrender, the chance would be gone to give the shock of surprise. Though the possibility of a demonstration that would not destroy human life was attractive, no one could suggest a way in which it could be made so convincing that it would be likely to stop the war."[9]

James Byrnes also explained: "We feared that, if the Japanese were told that the bomb would be used on a given locality, they might bring our boys who were prisoners of war to that area."[10]

So the Interim Committee wanted the atomic bomb to hit Japan without warning. Further, it should be dropped on a combined military and residential target to produce the maximum psychological shock. The decision was unanimous, though Bard later changed his mind and thought that some warning should be given. Oppenheimer now invited the scientific advisory panel to meet informally at Los Alamos. On June 9th they concluded: "We can propose no technical demonstration likely to bring an end to the war; we can see no acceptable alternative to direct military use."[11]

Arthur Compton wrote later: "Our hearts were heavy as on June 16th we turned in this report to the Interim Committee."[12] The four scientists were fully aware of the doubts of some of their colleagues. They did not actually see the memorandum which James Franck and Leo Szilard were drafting early in June; but they knew of their increasing doubts about the use of the bomb.

The memorandum declared: "Nuclear bombs cannot possibly remain a 'secret weapon' at the exclusive disposal of this country for more than a few years . . . the United States, with its agglomeration of population and industry in comparatively few metropolitan districts, will be at a disadvantage compared to nations whose populations are scattered over large areas. We believe that these considerations make the use of nuclear bombs for an early unannounced attack against Japan inadvisable. If the United States were to be the first to release this new means of indiscriminate destruction upon mankind, we would sacrifice public support throughout the world, precipitate the race for armaments, and prejudice the possibility of reaching an international agreement on the future control of such weapons. Much more favourable conditions for the eventual achievement of such an agreement could be created if nuclear bombs were first to be revealed to the world by a demonstration in an appropriately selected and uninhabited area."[13]

The Franck Report was handed to Stimson on June 11th. The Interim Committee was not given a chance to study it. However, by the time the scientific advisory panel had reported, Karl Compton had gone over it with Franck. Thus the advice of the two groups of scientists were known to the Committee when they came to their conclusion: "The opinions of our scientific colleagues on the initial use of these weapons are not unanimous. They range from the proposal of a purely technical demonstration to that of the military application best designed to induce surrender. . . . We find ourselves closer to these latter views."[14]

Oppenheimer wrote: "We didn't know beans about the military situation in Japan. We didn't know whether they could be caused to surrender by other means or whether the invasion was really inevitable. . . . We thought the two overriding considerations were the saving of lives in the war and the effect of our actions on the stability of the postwar world. We did say that we did not think exploding one of these things as a firecracker over a desert was likely to be very impressive. This was before we had actually done that."[15]

The New Mexico test showed that such a demonstration could in fact be very impressive. True, the crater in the desert gave little idea of what the blast and radiation might do to a living city. Yet all who watched the test had been amazed. At this point the four scientists might have reconsidered their advice, and opted merely for a demonstration.

They might also have noted a poll which Compton took among his Chicago scientists. This poll offered a choice between five ways of using the bomb. Most of the Chicago men called for a military target, choosing "a military demonstration in Japan to be followed by renewed opportunity for surrender before full use of the weapon is employed."[16] But neither this poll, nor the test, made Oppenheimer and his three colleagues change their minds. In any case, it was too late for them to alter the Interim Committee's advice to the President. The decision in principle to use the bomb without warning had been taken.

At this point, formal British agreement was needed under the Quebec Agreement. Sir John Anderson had been told two months ago: "The Americans propose to drop a bomb. . . . Do we agree that the weapon should be used against the Japanese? If for any reason we did not, the matter would presumably have to be raised by the Prime Minister with the President. If we do agree, various points still arise on which it would be desirable to have consultation with the Americans . . . whether any warning should be given to the Japanese."[17]

But Churchill never raised these questions with President Truman. He accepted that the decision would really belong to America. The Pacific, where the bomb would be used, was the American field of action; and the Americans, despite the Maud Report and the presence of British scientists at Los Alamos, had taken over the whole project. Churchill agreed with Anderson to note the decision at the next meeting of the Combined Policy Committee. On July 4th, "The Committee took note that the governments of the United Kingdom and the United States had agreed that Tube Alloy weapons should be used by the United States against Japan.[18]

The long term arguments of the Franck-Szilard report—and its moral implications—were of slight interest to the politicians. Nor, as some people have claimed, were the politicians under financial pressure. They would certainly have liked to justify the two billion dollars spent on the Manhattan project by the time Truman became President. At Los Alamos it was believed that Congress would hold an enquiry if the project should fail. When General Groves told his assistants that he hoped to make a bomb by August, 1945, he added: "If this weapon fizzles, each of you can look forward to a lifetime of testifying before congressional investigating committees."[19] But the Interim Committee was not responsible for Manhattan, and so was under no financial pressure.

Nor were the scientists on the advisory panel influenced by budgeting. They naturally wanted to prove the success of their work. As Robert Oppenheimer said, "When you see something that is technically sweet you go ahead and do it, and you argue about what to do about it only after you have had your technical success. That is the way it was with the atomic bomb."[20] Admiral Leahy remarked that "the scientists and others wanted to make this test because of the vast sums that had been spent on the project."[21] But their success had already been proved in New Mexico. A repetition in Japan was unnecessary.

The decision recorded on July 4th was strategic. Secretary of War Stimson had told the Interim Committee that their great task was to secure victory. The "objective of the United States in the summer of 1945 was the prompt and complete surrender of Japan. . . . There was as yet no indication of any weakening in the Japanese determination to fight rather than accept unconditional surrender. If she could persist in her fight to the end, she still had a great military force. As we understood it in July, there was a very strong possibility that the Japanese government might determine upon resistance to the end."[22]

How could Japan be defeated? General ("Hap") Arnold was convinced that conventional bombing, plus a naval blockade, would win the day. The Japanese surely could not endure more great "fire raids" such as Tokyo had suffered at the end of May? On the other hand, an intelligence report told Stimson early in July that, while "the Japanese economic position has deteriorated greatly, increasingly heavy air attacks, supplementing continued and intensified blockade, are seriously reducing Japan's produc-

tion. . . . The Japanese believe that unconditional surrender would be the equivalent of national extinction. There are as yet no indications that the Japanese are ready to accept such terms."[23] The report advocated that heavy bombing should be followed by an invasion of the Japanese mainland.

General Marshall believed that an invasion would succeed if Russia helped with an attack launched from Siberia. He told President Truman that "it might cost one half million lives to force the enemy's surrender on his home grounds."[24] Secretary Stimson thought the figure over-optimistic and the price too high. He advised Truman: "There is reason to believe that the operation for the occupation of Japan following the landing may be a very long, costly and arduous struggle on our part. The terrain . . . would be susceptible to a last ditch defence such as has been made on Iwo Jima and Okinawa. . . . If we once land on one of the main islands and begin a forceful occupation of Japan we shall probably have cast the die of last ditch resistance. The Japanese are highly patriotic, and certainly susceptible to calls for fanatical resistance to repel an invasion."[25] But contingency plans were still made for a landing in the south in November and on the Tokyo plain next spring.

Stimson had talked of "fanatical resistance." The bravery of the Japanese suicide pilots in their Kamikaze planes had already caused heavy losses of American men and ships. In the Okinawa campaign they had sunk 16 ships and damaged 185 more. They would have made invasion terribly costly. A journalist wrote that, "Although 2,500 Kamikaze planes had been expended, there were 5,350 of them still left and 7,000 under repair or in storage; and 5,000 young men were training for the Kamikaze corps."[26]

Neither bombing nor invasion, it seemed, would end the war swiftly. Might the Japanese agree to negotiate? It was known that a peace party led by the Foreign Minister, Togo, existed within the Tokyo government. The Emperor lent his ear to this party. Its members decided at a meeting in June: "Although we have no choice but to continue the war so long as the enemy insists upon unconditional surrender, we deem it advisable while we still possess considerable power of resistance, to propose peace through neutral powers."[27] The Japanese approached the Russians—still ostensibly neutral—and asked them to act as intermediaries with the Allies.

The Japanese peace party was offering talks, not surrender. Japan had five million men in the field, a mainland free of enemy troops, and a fanatic patriotism. She was unlikely to accept the forcible occupation, change of government and disarmament implied by unconditional surrender.

Perhaps she would heed a powerful warning. Stimson told Truman: "I am inclined to think that there is enough such chance to make it well worth while our giving them a warning of what is to come and a definite opportunity to capitulate. . . . Japan is not a nation composed wholly of mad fanatics. . . . I think the Japanese nation has the mental intelligence to recognize the folly of a fight to the finish and to accept the proffer of what will amount to an unconditional surrender. It is therefore my conclusion that a carefully timed warning be given to Japan. . .

"Success of course will depend on the potency of the warning which we give her. This warning should contain . . . the varied and overwhelming character of the force we are about to bring to bear on the islands, the inevitability and completeness of the destruction which the full application of this force will entail. . . . I personally think that if in saying this . . . we do not exclude a constitutional monarchy under her present dynasty, it would substantially add to the chance of acceptance."[28] In adding this rider, Stimson recognized the intensely loyal and semi-religious attachment of the Japanese to their Emperor.

Within a week of receiving this note from his Secretary for War, Truman left for the victory conference of the Allied powers at Potsdam. There he received a telegram telling him of the successful New Mexico test: "Operated on this morning. Diagnosis not yet complete but results seem satisfactory and already exceeding expectations." The next day came another: "Dr. Groves has just returned most enthusiastic and confident that the little boy is as husky as his big brother."[29]

Churchill was at once told about the New Mexico test. He recalled: "In the afternoon Stimson called at my abode and laid before me a sheet of paper on which was written 'Babies satisfactorily born'."[30] An official present at the meeting reported Churchill's reaction: "Stimson, what was gunpowder? Trivial. What was electricity? Meaningless. The atomic bomb is the second coming in wrath."[31] Churchill himself described his feelings, and his dread of the necessary invasion of Japan: ". . . for we were resolved to share

the agony. Now all this nightmare had vanished. In its place was the vision—fair and bright it seemed—of the end of the whole war in one or two violent shocks. . . . Moreover, we should not need the Russians."[32]

In Potsdam on 23rd July General Sir Alan Brooke lunched with Churchill: "He had seen the American reports of results of the new Tube Alloys secret explosive. He was completely carried away. It was no longer necessary for the Russians to come into the Japanese war; the new explosive alone was enough to settle the matter."[33]

Relations with the Russians had grown worse. Stalin had failed to help the Polish resistance in Warsaw, and had aroused suspicions at the Allied conference at Yalta in February. The invasion of Japan would require the help of Russian troops from the east, as General Marshall had made clear. Russia had promised to enter the war within three months of Germany's surrender. If she did, she would no doubt lay claim after the victory to Manchuria and extend her influence in eastern Europe. Byrnes spoke for many Americans when he wrote: "I must frankly admit that, in view of what we knew of Soviet actions in eastern Germany and the violations of the Yalta agreements. . . . I would have been satisfied had the Russians determined *not* to enter the war."[34]

If the war could be ended swiftly other than by invasion, Russia's chance would be lost. But neither Churchill nor Truman wanted to use the bomb primarily to keep Russia out of the war. Russian neutrality would just be an added bonus.

The question now facing America and Britain was how much—if anything—to tell Stalin about the bomb? Churchill reported to his Cabinet: "The President . . . asked what I thought should be done about telling the Russians. He seemed determined to do this, but asked about the timing, and said he thought that the end of the Conference would be best. I replied that if he were resolved to tell, it might well be better to hang it on the experiment, which was a new fact on which he had only just had knowledge. . . ."[35]

A few days later Truman accosted Stalin at the end of a meeting: "On July 24th I casually mentioned to Stalin that we had a new weapon of special destructive force. The Russian Premier showed no unusual interest. All he said was that he was glad to hear it and hoped we would make 'good use of it against the Japanese'."[36] Churchill who watched

Stalin's face across the room, wrote a more vivid account of the exchange: "He seemed to be delighted. A new bomb! Of extraordinary power! Probably decisive in the whole Japanese war! What a bit of luck! This was my impression of the moment, and I was sure that he had no idea of the significance of what he was being told."[37]

Churchill's impression was probably wrong. Since the spring, Communist agents had been giving Moscow reports of the Manhattan project slipped to them by Klaus Fuchs in Los Alamos, and by Pontecorvo and Nunn May in Canada. We do not know how seriously the Russian scientists took these reports, or to whom they had passed them. But perhaps they explained Stalin's indifference on hearing President Truman's news.

Truman wrote in his memoirs that after hearing of the Mexico test, "I then agreed to the use of the atomic bomb if Japan did not yield."[38] The Japanese war party seemed to be in the ascendant. James Byrnes recalled: "We faced a terrible decision. We could not rely on Japan's inquiries to the Soviet Union about a negotiated peace as proof that Japan would surrender unconditionally without the use of the bomb. In fact, Stalin stated the last message to him had said that Japan would 'fight to the death rather than accept unconditional surrender.' Under these circumstances, agreement to negotiate could only arouse false hopes. Instead, we relied upon the Potsdam Declaration."[39]

America decided to warn Japan rather as suggested by Stimson. The Japanese were told that the leaders of the United States, Great Britain and China "have conferred and agreed that Japan shall be given an opportunity to end the war. . . . The following are our terms. We shall not deviate from them. There are no alternatives. We shall brook no delay. . . . Japanese sovereignty shall be limited to the islands of Honshu, Hokkaido, Kyushu, Shikoku and such minor islands as we determine. The Japanese military forces, after being completely disarmed, shall be permitted to return to their homes. . . . We do not intend that the Japanese shall be enslaved as a race nor destroyed as a nation. . . . The occupying forces of the Allies shall be withdrawn as soon as . . . there has been established, in accordance with the freely expressed will of the Japanese people, a peacefully inclined and responsible government. We call upon the Government of Japan to proclaim now the unconditional surrender of all the Japanese armed forces. . . . The alternative for Japan is complete and utter destruction."[40]

This was a milder version of the warning advocated by Stimson. Stimson had stressed that the success of any warning would depend on its potency. The vague threat of "complete and utter destruction" hardly matched the "overwhelming character of the force" about to be unleashed. Also, the declaration was ambiguous as to the future of the Emperor. The "peacefully inclined and responsible government" was hardly the "present dynasty" which Stimson had in mind. Admiral Leahy commented later: "It was noteworthy that the message contained no hint of the projected employment against the Japanese of our recently completed atom bomb."[41]

The peace party in the Japanese War Council was still trying to negotiate through the Russians. But Truman's ultimatum ended their hope that any talks might be acceptable. The war party persuaded the aged Prime Minister Suzuki to reject the ultimatum. Byrnes wrote: "We devoutly hoped that the Japanese would heed our warning that, unless they surrendered unconditionally, the destruction of their armed forces and the devastation of their homeland was inevitable. But, on July 28th, the Japanese Premier issued a statement saying the declaration was unworthy of notice. That was disheartening. There was nothing left to do but use the bomb."[42]

A week earlier Truman had received more cables from home: "Patient progressing rapidly and will be ready for final operation first good break August." And then, "Operation may be possible any time from August 1st depending on state of preparation of patient and conditions of atmosphere."[43] He then told the War Department to order the Commanding General of the United States Army, General Spaatz, to drop the bomb as soon as possible after August 3rd.

Truman was later asked why he had given this order *before* the ultimatum had been sent to Japan. He replied: "I ordered atomic bombs dropped on the two cities named on the way back from Potsdam when we were in the middle of the Atlantic Ocean. In your letter, you raise the fact that the directive to General Spaatz to prepare for delivering the bomb is dated July 25th. It was, of course, necessary to set the military wheels in motion, as these orders did, but the final decision was in my hands and was not made until I was returning from Potsdam."[44]

Aboard the *Augusta*, in mid-Atlantic, Truman confirmed the order to Spaatz.

Notes

1. Leo Szilard to Robert Jungk. Quoted Robert Jungk, *Brighter than a Thousand Suns* (1956)
2. John Anderson's memorandum to Winston Churchill, March, 1944
3. Niels Bohr's memorandum to President Roosevelt, 3rd July, 1944
4. Aide-memoire of Hyde Park Conversation, 19th September, 1944
5. Henry L. Stimson to President Truman, 24th April, 1945
6. Harry S. Truman, *Year of Decisions* (1955). Entry 25th April, 1945
7. *New York Times*, 4th May, 1944
8. Interim Committee Meeting minutes, 31st May, 1944
9. Arthur Compton, *Atomic Quest* (1956)
10. James Byrnes, *Speaking Frankly* (1947)
11. Report of the Scientific Advisory Panel of Interim Committee, 9th June, 1945
12. Arthur Compton, *Atomic Quest* (1956)
13. Franck Report, 11th June, 1945
14. Interim Committee Report, 16th June, 1945
15. J. R. Oppenheimer to General Nichols, 4th May, 1954. Transcript of hearings before Personnel Security Board of U.S.A.E.C., April–May, 1954
16. Poll of scientists, 12th July, 1945. Quoted Knebel & Bailey, *No High Ground* (1960)
17. Field-Marshall Wilson to Sir John Anderson, 30th April, 1945
18. Minutes of Combined Policy Committee meeting, 4th July, 1945
19. Leslie R. Groves address to Los Alamos scientists, 24th December, 1944
20. J. R. Oppenheimer to General Nichols, 4th May, 1954. Transcript of hearings before Personnel Security Board of U.S.A.E.C., April–May, 1954
21. William D. Leahy, *I Was There* (1950)
22. *Harpers Magazine*, February, 1947. Henry L. Stimson, "Decision to use the Atom Bomb"
23. Combined Intelligence Committee Report, July, 1945
24. Harry S. Truman, *Year of Decisions* (1955)
25. Henry L. Stimson's memorandum to President Truman, 2nd July, 1945
26. *Atlantic Monthly*, October, 1960. Samuel E. Morison, "Why Japan Surrendered"
27. Report of 18th June meeting of Peace Party, quoted by Toshikasu Kase, *Eclipse of the Rising Sun* (1951)
28. Henry L. Stimson's memorandum to President Truman, 2nd July, 1945
29. George Harrison cables to President Truman, 17th/18th July, 1945
30. Winston Churchill, *History of the Second World War*, Vol. VI, *Triumph and Tragedy* (1953)
31. *Atlantic Monthly*, March, 1957. Article by Harvey H. Bundy
32. Winston Churchill, *History of the Second World War*, Vol. VI, *Triumph and Tragedy*
33. Sir Alan Brooke's diary. Entry of 23rd July, 1945. Arthur Bryant, *The Turn of the Tide* (1957)
34. James Byrnes, *Speaking Frankly* (1947)
35. Winston Churchill's note to Cabinet, 18th July, 1945
36. Harry S. Truman, *Year of Decisions* (1955)
37. Winston Churchill, *History of the Second World War*, Vol. VI, *Triumph and Tragedy*
38. Harry S. Truman, *Year of Decisions* (1955)
39. James Byrnes, *Speaking Frankly* (1947)
40. Potsdam Declaration, 26th July, 1945
41. William D. Leahy, *I Was There* (1950)
42. James Byrnes, *Speaking Frankly* (1947)
43. George Harrison cables to President Truman, 21st/23rd July, 1945
44. President Truman to Professor Cate, 12th January, 1953. Professor Cate, *United States Army Air Forces in World War Two* (1948)

Writing and Discussion Topics

Questions 1–6 address content, critical analysis, personal choices, ethical options, specific discipline, and interdisciplinary alternatives, respectively.

1. What issues did the Interim Committee take into account as they prepared their report? What additional concerns did President Truman have? How much consideration did either give to the long-term consequences of the decision to bomb Japan?

2. What arguments against the use of nuclear weapons are presented in this essay? Does fear play a role in any of these arguments?

3. Suppose you were advising the president of the United States on whether or not to demonstrate the power of the new atomic weapon by using it against troops from an unfriendly nation who have invaded a country friendly and strategically important to the United States. Explain what you have learned from the decision to bomb Hiroshima and Nagasaki and how this will impact your recommendation. How important are the factual details of the situation? Could you make up your mind largely on the basis of the ethical issues involved?

4. From which ethical tradition(s) from chapter one were Truman and the committee apparently drawing as they

thought through the issues? What other considerations might they have taken into account had they used another ethical tradition? Would they have come out with a different conclusion?

5. How can a historian claim to know what was going on in Truman's mind as he moved toward his decision? On what different kinds of sources does Yass depend in this case? Can you think of any other kind of source, which might still exist, that would strengthen Yass's case?

6. Should Carl Sagan's argument against the deployment of nuclear weapons be modified in light of the issues raised by Truman and the Interim Committee? How do you think the committee or Truman might have decided if they had known then what Sagan claims to know now about the consequences of nuclear explosions?

Recommended Readings

Bryerton, G. *The Nuclear Dilemma.* New York: Ballantine, 1970.

Cohen, A. and S. Lee. *Nuclear Weapons and the Future of Humanity.* Totowa: Rowman and Littlefield, 1986.

Cohen, Marshall, Thomas Nagle, and Thomas Scanlon, eds. *War and Moral Responsibility.* Princeton, N.J.: Princeton University Press, 1974.

Goodwin, G., eds. *Ethics and Nuclear Deterrence.* New York: St. Martin's, 1982.

Gordon, Peter. *Dr. Strangelove.*

Harvard Nuclear Study Group. *Living with Nuclear Weapons.* Cambridge, Mass.: Harvard University Press, 1983.

Hershey, J. *Hiroshima.* New York: Bantam, 1966.

Kennan, G. *The Nuclear Delusion.* New York: Pantheon, 1982.

Kissinger, Henry. *Nuclear Weapons and Foreign Policy.* New York: Harper and Row, 1958.

Lindburg, Charles. *Banana River.*

Maclean, Douglas, ed. *The Security Gamble: Deterrence Dilemmas in the Nuclear Age.* Totowa, N.J.: Rowman & Allanheld, 1984.

Mailor, Norman. *The Naked and the Dead.*

Mills, W. *An End to Arms.* New York: Athenaeum, 1965.

Panofsky, W. K. *Arms Control and Salt II.* Seattle, Wash.: University of Washington Press, 1979.

Pauling, Linus. *No More War!* New York: Dodd-Mead, 1958.

Sakharov, A. *My Country and the World.* Translated by G. Daniels, New York: Knopf, 1975.

Schell, Jonathan. *The Abolition.* New York: Knopf, 1984.

Stein, W. *Nuclear Weapons, Catholic Response.* New York: Sheed & Ward, 1961.

Tolstoy, Leo. *War and Peace.* New York: Bantam.

U.S. Department of Defense. *Soviet Military Power.* Washington, D.C.: GPO, 1983.

Vonnegut, Kurt. *Slaughterhouse Five.*

Recommended Periodical Readings

Ethics 95 (April 1985).

Gay, William, ed. "Philosophy and the Debate on Nuclear Weapons Systems and Policies." *Philosophy and Social Criticism* 10 (Winter 1984).

Hardin, Russell: "Unilateral Versus Mutual Disarmament." *Philosophy and Public Affairs* 12 (1983) 236–254.

Kavka, Gregory S. "Doubts About Unilateral Nuclear Disarmament." *Philosophy and Public Affairs* 12 (Summer 1983): 255–265.

Kavka, Gregory S. "Some Paradoxes of Deterrence." *The Journal of Philosophy* 75 no. 6 (June 1978): 285–302.

Krauthammer, Charles. "On Nuclear Morality." *Commentary* (October 1983).

Lackey, Douglas P. "Moral Principles and Strategic Defense." *The Philosophical Forum* 18, no. 1 (Fall 1986): 1–7.

O'Brien, William V. "Just-War Doctrine in a Nuclear Context." *Theological Studies* 44 (1983): 191–220.

Wasserstrom, Richard. "Noncombatants, Indiscriminate Killing and the Immorality of Nuclear War." *In Nuclear War: Philosophical Perspectives,* edited by M. A. Fox and L. Groarke. New York: Peter Lang Publishing, 1985.

chapter 4

CORPORATE RESPONSIBILITY

In the spring of 1989, the Exxon Tanker, *Valdez,* carrying hundreds of thousands of tons of oil, ran aground in Prince William Sound, Alaska, spilling much of its cargo over protected wetlands, animal habitats, and aquatic culture. The damage to the environment was seen as almost irreparable, as crews of workers tried to contain the spill and mop up pools of oil by almost any method possible, even by hand. Exxon Corporation's reputation was also damaged as details of the incident focused on an irresponsible crew and slow-reacting corporate officers. Individuals and corporations alike chastised Exxon officials for their lack of social responsibility in the *Valdez* matter. After spending millions of dollars trying to restore the shoreline, Exxon said it had done enough. Scientists and other environmental experts countered that years of cleanup in the sound were still necessary. Exxon then shifted its main focus to public relations by donating considerable money to the Alaskan tourism industry. Advertisements in the media invited the public to see the restored environment.

Exxon is the largest petroleum company in the world. It operates in nearly one hundred countries and has more than three hundred subsidiaries. Its profit statements show it could continue to pay millions of dollars to clean

Drawing by Modell; © 1985
   The New Yorker Magazine,
   Inc.

"*Obviously, some people here do not appreciate the gravity of our situation.*"

up the damage in Prince William Sound. Indeed, the state of Alaska and the United States government have forced Exxon to do just that. In March 1991, Exxon agreed to plead guilty to four misdemeanor environmental crimes and pay a record fine of one hundred million dollars as part of a 1.1 billion dollar settlement from the *Valdez* oil spill. However, judges have determined this amount is not sufficient and at this writing the court battle continues. It appears there will be litigation against Exxon from various groups, including native Alaskans, fishermen, and environmentalists.

Is it important for a corporation to exhibit social responsibility? This is a question of business ethics. In studying business ethics, we examine moral issues in business institutions, policies, and behavior. Sometimes this examination focuses largely on the application of ethical norms of individuals to business activity (e.g., one should be honest in business dealings just as one should be honest in personal relationships). At other times, the discussion is directed more toward business as a corporate member of society—a "guest," as it were—whose purposes, actions, and obligations should be measured, in part at least, by moral standards. This view of business ethics may be seen as a study of "corporate responsibility" or the social responsibility of business. In this section, we will address some of the many regulated and unregulated social responsibilities of business, whether to employees, consumers, stockholders, the public, or to the environment.

In Adam Smith's day (the eighteenth century), hard work and high profits were the recognized standards for business activity. Indeed, Smith's philosophy of "economic self-interest" provided the ideological formula for business growth and profit maximization. Moreover, most business owners came to believe that hard work, accumulated profits, and wealth were morally connected. Little thought, on the other hand, was given to fair labor practices, worker safety, or affirmative action. Businesses often polluted drinking water, spoiled natural resources, damaged the air, or manufactured unsafe products. Accumulating capital for the corporation, its shareholders, and themselves was the primary responsibility of business owners. What these individuals, as private citizens, did with their wealth was certainly of moral interest, as is evidenced by the enormous philanthropy of some industrialists in the late nineteenth and early twentieth centuries; but, in the end, morality was basically an individual matter.

Today, many businesses take the trust of social responsibilities seriously. Legislation at all levels has contributed to this development. In addition, the American public has demanded greater social responsibility from the business community because of the hardships and deaths that have been caused by unsound business practices. The safety flaws in the Ford Pinto, the fatal design of an IUD birth control device by A. H. Robins Corporation, and the defective "o-rings" produced by Morton-Thycol in the destroyed space shuttle *Challenger* are just a few of the well-known examples of corporate irresponsibility within the recent past. More significant, perhaps, are the many lives that have been lost or harmed due to defects in manufactured products, factory conditions, and other workplace circumstances.

There is a growing expectation today that corporations, even at a temporary loss of profit, should behave in a responsible manner. An example of responsible action was Johnson and Johnson's response, in 1982, to the cyanide poisoning of Tylenol pain-relief capsules. The corporation conducted a full recall of the product at a loss of approximately $100 million. The corporation redesigned the capsule and the container before wide-scale marketing began again. No more human life was lost and Johnson and Johnson has now far exceeded in profit the original loss. The government did not ask Johnson and Johnson to conduct the recall. The corporation decided it was important for the safety of consumers and for future profits. Fortunately, more and more businesses today are taking it upon themselves to be "good neighbors" within their communities, locally, nationally, and even internationally.

The authors in this section will address the issues surrounding corporate social responsibility. Milton Friedman begins the chapter with a declaration for profits over ethics. Corporations, according to Friedman, meet their responsibility to society when they make a profit. The officers of the corporation have the responsibility to make money for their stockholders. The officers' concern is not for the social good in any other way. Friedman stipulates, however, that at all times the officers must behave honestly and comply with governmental regulations.

John DeLorean examines his years with General Motors and says that individual honesty does not make a corporation socially responsible. He watched honest officers, working together for faceless stockholders, making decisions that cost human life, polluted air, wasted valuable resources, and harmed the public. DeLorean describes a "group think" culture that clouds the judgment of decision-makers. Executives feel protected by the corporate shell, yet they perceive an intense pressure to make a profit and to never lose money. He believes that there is often no one person to blame for unethical corporate decisions. Rather, such decisions are the result of an irresponsible, unethical management perspective that pervades the corporate climate.

Robert Hay and Edmund Gray believe that the Friedman perspective produces harmful consequences for society, and they suggest that his philosophy is of a bygone era in business practices. Business owners have learned they must make decisions that serve the interests of the general public, their customers, and their employees, as well as the stockholders. According to Hay and Gray, this expanded sense of responsibility has been achieved largely through governmental regulations, although part of this change is due to a heightened consciousness within the business community for improving the quality of life. Hay and Gray question the wisdom of reverting back to corporate advantage and free-market capitalism, as Friedman urges. They further wonder if the gaining of profit at a high cost to society and to the environment is an indictment of the free-enterprise system.

Kenneth Goodpaster and John Matthews also disagree with Friedman. They assert that corporations do have a conscience; corporations are not artificial "persons" with little or no moral accountability. Individuals and corporations have similar obligations in the areas of social responsibility and ethical behavior.

Melvin Anshen does not believe that social responsibility needs to come at a great cost to corporate profits. He stresses that as society has prospered, social responsibility, along with profits, has been demanded of corporations. Anshen does not want to replace free-market capitalism, but he believes corporate America can find ways to enlarge its responsibility.

John Simon, Charles Powers, and Jon Gunnemann argue that ethical individuals in corporations will act in a socially responsible manner. Their essay suggests that while it is difficult to determine the specific social responsibilities that corporations should accept, they believe that corporations should adopt the principles of correcting any social injury they cause and of avoiding harm to society. The conditions needed for initiating socially responsible actions and the extent these actions should be allowed to affect profits are major issues the authors believe should be addressed.

Religious perspectives on corporate ethics often revolve around the theme of corporate aid to society. The Catholic bishops, in their official pastoral letter, ask for a partnership between governments and corporations to help with problems in society such as poverty, quality of human life, and pollution. The economic system of a country, they conclude, should help maintain the dignity of human life by supplying "food, clothing, shelter, rest, medical care, education and employment" for all citizens.

The Protestant scholar Robert Benne criticizes the bishops on the ground of promoting socialism. He states that their proposal ignores the initiative and efficiency inherent in most existing societies. Benne stresses the Protestant work ethic more than any other writer in this section. He does, however, join with the bishops in pressing for relief from the widespread poverty in American society.

Ronald Green, a Jewish scholar, contends that "work, however menial is superior to dependency." While Green agrees with many points found in the bishops' proposal, he says that the Jewish tradition insists it is important for the sake of dignity that people work for and take care of their lives and possessions. He realizes that poverty-stricken people in some societies do not have belongings and need aid. This plight is uncharacteristic in Jewish cultures, but a problem Jews must address, nevertheless.

Yusuf Al-Qaradawi explains business practices under Islamic law. Free-market competition as well as individual freedom are esteemed. "Allah has directed people toward exchanging goods and utilities through buying and selling because such transactions make social and economic life function smoothly and encourage people to be productive." He also indicates that Islamic law prohibits business practices that would harm Islamic society in any way, particularly spiritually. The charging of interest when lending money is viewed as immoral in Islam.

Moving from religion to literature, Machiavelli encourages his prince to practice miserliness over generosity, cruelty over mercy, deceit over integrity. The prince is told how to gain power and how to stay in power. In spite of the increased interest in and the demand for corporate responsibility today, Machiavelli's principles continue to be practiced by some in business, as well as elsewhere.

The corporate lifestyle may bring in wealth but perhaps not happiness. This idea is examined in Edwin Arlington Robinson's poem, "Richard Cory." Howard Fast's "The Cold, Cold Box" is a short story that explores a utilitarian concept of social good. Should a majority of society benefit at the expense of one individual? A board of trustees must make this determination in Fast's story.

The final literary selection, *An Enemy of the People,* is by Henrik Ibsen. In the excerpt from this play, a physician discovers that the main industry in the town is causing disease and death. The town chooses to ignore the findings of the physician in favor of continuing jobs and profits. In the excerpt, Ibsen dramatizes the human inclination toward greed and social irresponsibility.

Historical accounts offer a diverse look at the evolution of American business practices and profits and the inflictions resulting from past mistakes. Robert Almeder questions the pursuit of profits at any cost. Using the utilitarian perspective as a standard, he believes the greatest happiness for society is not to create great wealth for a few. Almeder cites the Robber Baron epic of American history to show that corporations need to be regulated. He accepts Friedman's point that it is impossible to agree on a "priority ranking of major social needs." However, he says we can at least agree it is wrong to kill for profit. He believes that some corporations have killed for profit.

Neil Chamberlain gives an account of the establishment of the corporation in the nineteenth century and its role in serving the public welfare. During the Industrial Revolution, corporations were given the challenge to promote economic development. Often there was no obligation to be socially responsible. Single-minded pursuit of wealth was acceptable until the realization that natural resources were limited and that such an aggressive pursuit brought permanent damage to the work force and to the environment. Chamberlain says, as do most of our authors in this section, that we need to rethink absolute corporate autonomy if corporations do not voluntarily take on more social responsibility.

Milton Friedman

THE SOCIAL RESPONSIBILITY OF BUSINESS
IS TO INCREASE ITS PROFITS

◆◆◆

M ilton Friedman is senior research fellow at the Hoover
Institution at Stanford University. He was an economics
professor at the University of Chicago for over thirty-five years. He was
the winner of the 1976 Nobel Prize in economics for his work in
monetary theory, price theory, and the role of government. ◆

When I hear businessmen speak eloquently about the "social responsibilities of business in a free-enterprise system," I am reminded of the wonderful line about the Frenchman who discovered at the age of 70 that he had been speaking prose all his life. The businessmen believe that they are defending free enterprise when they declaim that business is not concerned "merely" with profit but also with promoting desirable "social" ends; that business has a "social conscience" and takes seriously its responsibilities for providing employment, eliminating discrimination, avoiding pollution and whatever else may be the catchwords of the contemporary crop of reformers. In fact they are—or would be if they or anyone else took them seriously—preaching pure and unadulterated socialism. Businessmen who talk this way are unwitting puppets of the intellectual forces that have been undermining the basis of a free society these past decades.

The discussion of the "social responsibilities of business" are notable for their analytical looseness and lack of rigor. What does it mean to say that "business" has responsibilities? Only people can have responsibilities. A corporation is an artificial person and in this sense may have artificial responsibilities, but "business" as a whole cannot be said to have responsibilities, even in this vague sense. The first step toward clarity to examining the doctrine of the social responsibility of business is to ask precisely what it implies for whom.

Presumably, the individuals who are to be responsible are businessmen, which means individual proprietors or corporate executives. Most of the discussion of social responsibility is directed at corporations, so in what follows I shall mostly neglect the individual proprietors and speak of corporate executives.

In a free-enterprise, private-property system, a corporate executive is an employee of the owners of the business. He has direct responsibility to his employers. That responsibility is to conduct the business in accordance with their desires, which generally will be to make as much money as possible while conforming to the basic rules of the society, both those embodied in law and those embodied in ethical custom. Of course, in some cases his employers

may have a different objective. A group of persons might establish a corporation for an eleemosynary purpose—for example, a hospital or a school. The manager of such a corporation will not have money profit as his objectives but the rendering of certain services.

In either case, the key point is that, in his capacity as a corporate executive, the manager is the agent of the individuals who own the corporation or establish the eleemosynary institution, and his primary responsibility is to them.

Needless to say, this does not mean that it is easy to judge how well he is performing his task. But at least the criterion of performance is straightforward, and the persons among whom a voluntary contractual arrangement exists are clearly defined.

Of course, the corporate executive is also a person in his own right. As a person, he may have many other responsibilities that he recognizes or assumes voluntarily—to his family, his conscience, his feelings of charity, his church, his clubs, his city, his country. He may feel impelled by these responsibilities to devote part of his income to causes he regards as worthy, to refuse to work for particular corporations, even to leave his job, for example, to join his country's armed forces. If we wish, we may refer to some of these responsibilities as "social responsibilities." But in these respects he is acting as a principal, not an agent; he is spending his own money or time or energy, not the money of his employers or the time or energy he has contracted to devote to their purposes. If these are "social responsibilities," they are the social responsibilities of individuals, not of business.

What does it mean to say that the corporate executive has a "social responsibility" in his capacity as businessman? If this statement is not pure rhetoric, it must mean that he is to act in some way that is not in the interest of his employers. For example, that he is to refrain from increasing the price of the product in order to contribute to the social objective of preventing inflation, even though a price increase would be in the best interests of the corporation. Or that he is to make expenditures on reducing pollution beyond the amount that is in the best interests of the corporation or that is required by law in order to contribute to the social objective of improving the environment. Or that, at the expense of corporate profits, he is to hire "hardcore" unemployed instead of better qualified available workmen to contribute to the social objective of reducing poverty.

In each of these cases, the corporate executive would be spending someone else's money for a general social interest. Insofar as his actions in accord with his "social responsibility" reduce returns to stockholders, he is spending their money. Insofar as his actions raise the price to customers, he is spending the customers' money. Insofar as his actions raise the price to customers, he is spending the customer's money. Insofar as his actions lower the wages of some employees, he is spending their money.

The stockholders or the customers or the employees could separately spend their own money on the particular action if they wished to do so. The executive is exercising a distinct "social responsibility," rather than serving as an agent of the stockholders or the customers or the employees, only if he spends the money in a different way than they would have spent it.

But if he does this, he is in effect imposing taxes, on the one hand, and deciding how the tax proceeds shall be spent, on the other.

This process raises political questions on two levels: principle and consequences. On the level of political principle, the imposition of taxes and the expenditure of tax proceeds are governmental functions. We have established elaborate constitutional, parliamentary and judicial provisions to control these functions, to assure that taxes are imposed so far as possible in accordance with the preferences and desires of the public—after all, "taxation without representation" was one of the battle cries of the American Revolution. We have a system of checks and balances to separate the legislative function of imposing taxes and enacting expenditures from the executive function of collecting taxes and administering expenditure programs and from the judicial function of mediating disputes and interpreting the law.

Here the businessman—self-selected or appointed directly or indirectly by stockholders—is to be simultaneously legislator, executive and jurist. He is to decide whom to tax by how much and for what purpose, and he is to spend the proceeds—all this guided only by general exhortations from on high to restrain inflation, improve the environment, fight poverty and so on and on.

The whole justification for permitting the corporate executive to be selected by the stockholders is that the executive is an agent serving the interests of his principal. This justification disappears when the corporate executive imposes taxes and spends the proceeds for "social" purposes. He becomes in effect a public employee, a civil servant, even though he remains in name an employee of a private enterprise. On grounds of political principle, it is intolerable that such civil servants—insofar as their actions in the name of social responsibility are real and not just window-dressing—should be selected as they are now. If they are to be civil servants, then they must be elected through a political process. If they are to impose taxes and make expenditures to foster "social" objectives, then political machinery must be set up to make the assessment of taxes and to determine through a political process the objectives to be served.

This is the basic reason why the doctrine of "social responsibility" involves the acceptance of the socialist view that political mechanisms, not market mechanisms, are the appropriate way to determine the allocation of scarce resources to alternative uses.

On the grounds of consequences, can the corporate executive in fact discharge his alleged "social responsibilities"? On the one hand, suppose he could get away with spending the stockholders' or customers' or employees' money. How is he to know how to spend it? He is told that he must contribute to fighting inflation. How is he to know what action of his will contribute to that end? He is presumably an expert in running his company—in producing a product or selling it or financing it. But nothing about his selection makes him an expert on inflation. Will his holding down the price of his product reduce inflationary pressure? Or, by leaving more spending power in the hands of his customers, simply divert it elsewhere? Or, by forcing him to produce less because of the lower price, will it simply contribute to shortages? Even if he could answer these questions, how much cost is he justified in imposing on his stockholders, customers and employees for this social purpose? What is his appropriate share and what is the appropriate share of others?

And, whether he wants to or not, can he get away with spending his stockholders', customers' or employees' money? Will not the stockholders fire him? (Either the present ones or those who take over when his actions in the name of social responsibility have reduced the corporation's profits and the price of its stock.) His customers and employees can desert him for other producers and employers less scrupulous in exercising their social responsibilities.

This facet of "social responsibility" doctrine is brought into sharp relief when the doctrine is used to justify wage restraint by trade unions. The conflict of interest is naked and clear when union officials are asked to subordinate the interest of their members to some more general purpose. If the union officials try to enforce wage restraint, the consequence is likely to be wildcat strikes, rank-and-file revolts and the emergence of strong competitors for their jobs. We thus have the ironic phenomenon that union leaders—at least in the U.S.—have objected to Government interference with the market far more consistently and courageously than have business leaders.

The difficulty of exercising "social responsibility" illustrates, of course, the great virtue of private competitive enterprise—it forces people to be responsible for their own actions and makes it difficult for them to "exploit" other people for either selfish or unselfish purposes. They can do good—but only at their own expense.

Many a reader who has followed the argument this far may be tempted to remonstrate that it is all well and good to speak of Government's having the responsibility to impose taxes and determine expenditures for such "social" purposes as controlling pollution or training the hard-core unemployed, but that the problems are too urgent to wait on the slow course of political processes, that the exercise of social responsibility by businessmen is a quicker and surer way to solve pressing current problems.

Aside from the question of fact—I share Adam Smith's skepticism about the benefits that can be expected from "those who affected to trade for the public good"—this argument must be rejected on grounds of principle. What it amounts to is an assertion that those who favor the taxes and expenditures in question have failed to persuade a majority of their fellow citizens to be of like mind and that they are seeking to attain by undemocratic procedures what they cannot attain by democratic procedures. In a free society, it is hard for "evil" people to do "evil," especially since one man's good is another's evil.

I have, for simplicity, concentrated on the special case of the corporate executive, except only for the brief digression on trade unions. But precisely the same argument applies to the newer phenomenon of calling upon stockholders to require corporations to exercise social responsibility (the recent G.M. crusade for example). In most of these cases, what is in effect involved is some stockholders trying to get

other stockholders (or customers or employees) to contribute against their will to "social" causes favored by the activists. Insofar as they succeed, they are again imposing taxes and spending the proceeds.

The situation of the individual proprietor is somewhat different. If he acts to reduce the returns of his enterprise in order to exercise his "social responsibility," he is spending his own money, not someone else's. If he wishes to spend his money on such purposes, that is his right, and I cannot see that there is any objection to his doing so. In the process, he, too, may impose costs on employees and customers. However, because he is far less likely than a large corporation or union to have monopolistic power, any such side effects will tend to be minor.

Of course, in practice the doctrine of social responsibility is frequently a cloak for actions that are justified on other grounds rather than a reason for those actions.

To illustrate, it may well be in the long-run interest of a corporation that is a major employer in a small community to devote resources to providing amenities to that community or to improving its government. That may make it easier to attract desirable employees, it may reduce the wage bill or lessen losses from pilferage and sabotage or have other worthwhile effects. Or it may be that, given the laws about the deductibility of corporate charitable contributions, the stockholders can contribute more to charities they favor by having the corporation make the gift than by doing it themselves, since they can in that way contribute an amount that would otherwise have been paid as corporate taxes.

In each of these—and many similar—cases, there is a strong temptation to rationalize these actions as an exercise of "social responsibility." In the present climate of opinion, with its widespread aversion to "capitalism," "profits," the "soulless corporation" and so on, this is one way for a corporation to generate goodwill as a by-product of expenditures that are entirely justified in its own self-interest.

It would be inconsistent of me to call on corporate executives to refrain from this hypocritical window-dressing because it harms the foundations of a free society. That would be to call on them to exercise a "social responsibility"! If our institutions, and the attitudes of the public make it in their self-interest to cloak their actions in this way, I cannot summon much indignation to denounce them. At the same time, I can express admiration for those individual proprietors or owners of closely held corporations or stockholders of more broadly held corporations who disdain such tactics as approaching fraud.

Whether blameworthy or not, the use of the cloak of social responsibility, and the nonsense spoken in its name by influential and prestigious businessmen, does clearly harm the foundations of a free society. I have been impressed time and again by the schizophrenic character of many businessmen. They are capable of being extremely far-sighted and clear-headed in matters that are internal to their businesses. They are incredibly short-sighted and muddle-headed in matters that are outside their businesses but affect the possible survival of business in general. This short-sightedness is strikingly exemplified in the calls from many businessmen for wage and price guidelines or controls or income policies. There is nothing that could do more in a brief period to destroy a market system and replace it by a centrally controlled system than effective governmental control of prices and wages.

The short-sightedness is also exemplified in speeches by businessmen on social responsibility. This may gain them kudos in the short run. But it helps to strengthen the already too prevalent view that the pursuit of profits is wicked and immoral and must be curbed and controlled by external forces. Once this view is adopted, the external forces that curb the market will not be the social consciences, however highly developed, of the pontificating executives; it will be the iron fist of Government bureaucrats. Here, as with price and wage controls, businessmen seem to me to reveal a suicidal impulse.

The political principle that underlies the market mechanism is unanimity. In an ideal free market resting on private property, no individual can coerce any other, all cooperation is voluntary, all parties to such cooperation benefit or they need not participate. There are no values, no "social" responsibilities in any sense other than the shared values and responsibilities of individuals. Society is a collection of individuals and of the various groups they voluntarily form.

The political principle that underlies the political mechanism is conformity. The individual must serve a more general social interest—whether that be determined by a church or a dictator or a majority. The individual may have a vote and say in what is to be done, but if he is overruled, he must conform. It is appropriate for some to require others to contribute to a general social purpose whether they wish to or not.

Unfortunately, unanimity is not always feasible. There are some respects in which conformity appears unavoidable, so I do not see how one can avoid the use of the political mechanism altogether.

But the doctrine of "social responsibility" taken seriously would extend the scope of the political mechanism to every human activity. It does not differ in philosophy from the most explicitly collectivist doctrine. If differs only by professing to believe that collectivist ends can be attained without collectivist means. That is why, in my book "Capitalism and Freedom," I have called it a "fundamentally subversive doctrine" in a free society, and have said that in such a society, "there is one and only one social responsibility of business—to use its resources and engage in activities designed to increase its profits so long as it stays within the rules of the game, which is to say, engages in open and free competition without deception or fraud."

Writing and Discussion Topics

Questions 1–6 address content, critical analysis, personal choices, ethical options, specific discipline, and interdisciplinary alternatives, respectively.

1. Friedman says that business people who hide under a cloak of social responsibility affect the possible survival of business in general. What specific actions, according to Friedman, cause this potential harm?
2. What does eleemosynary mean? What point is Friedman making with respect to this concept?
3. You have stock with a corporation that made a major contribution to a charity this year. The stock has now gone down in value for the past three months. Are the two related? Will you keep your stock?
4. If individuals have ethical responsibilities, and corporations are made up of individuals, do corporations have ethical responsibilities? Why or why not? What problems may be created by allowing a

large number of people in a corporation to be devoid of social and ethical responsibility?

5. Is the government's imposition of taxes a necessary condition for taking care of social ills? Is it an evil akin to taxation without representation for business to enter into the domain of the "social good"?

6. Throughout this article, Friedman uses the terms "he" and "businessman." Are these terms generic, meaning both sexes, or does this type of reference harm women in the business world by contributing to an environment of discrimination?

HOW MORAL MEN MAKE IMMORAL DECISIONS

◆◆◆

John DeLorean Source: AP/
Wide World Photos.

J ohn DeLorean has been an automotive engineer and an executive
with both General Motors and his own DeLorean Corporation. He
has served for one year, unpaid, as president of the National Alliance of
Businessmen. In this position, he helped the unemployed and ex-convicts
and American Indians who needed assistance. In this piece from his
book, On a Clear Day You Can See General Motors, *he speaks*
through a ghostwriter, J. Patrick Wright. ◆

"We feel that 1972 can be one of Chevrolet's great years . . . . Most of the improvements this year are to engines and chassis components aimed at giving a customer a better car for the money . . . . I want to reiterate our pledge that the 1972 Chevrolets will be the best in Chevrolet history . . . . We recognize that providing good dealer service is the surest way to keep quality-built Chevrolets for 1972 in top quality condition . . . . This is the lineup of cars for every type of buyer that we offer for 1972. Cars that are the best built in Chevrolet history . . . ."

The words seemed to fall out of my mouth like stones from an open hand. Effortlessly. Almost meaninglessly. It was August 31, 1971. I was powergliding through the National Press Preview of 1972 Chevrolet cars and trucks at the Raleigh House, a mock-Tudor restaurant-banquet hall complex in suburban Detroit. The audience was filled with reporters from all over the country. In their midst was a plentiful sprinkling of Chevrolet managers. The new product presentation and question-answer session went smoothly, and I was stepping down from the podium and receiving the usual handshakes and compliments from some of the sales guys and a few of the members of the press when a strange feeling hit me:

"My God! I've been through all this before."

It was a strange feeling because somehow I was detached from it all. Looking down on myself in the banquet hall surrounded by executives, newsmen and glittering Chevrolets. And I was questioning why I was there and what I was doing. The answers were not satisfactory.

"This whole show is nothing but a replay of last year's show, and the year before that and the year before that. The speech I just gave was the same speech I gave last year, written by the same guy in public relations about the same superficial product improvements as the previous years. And the same questions were being asked by the same newsmen I've seen for years. Almost nothing has changed."

I looked around the room for a brief moment searching for something, anything that could show me that there was real meaning in the exercises we were going through, that the national press conference and the tens of similar dealer product an-

nouncements I conducted across the country were something more than just new product sales hypes. But I found nothing.

Instead, I got the empty feeling that "what I am doing here may be nothing more than perpetuating a gigantic fraud," a fraud on the American consumer by promising him something new but giving him only surface alterations—"tortured sheet metal" as former chairman Frederic G. Donner used to say—or a couple of extra horsepower and an annual price increase. A fraud on the American economy, because I always had a vague suspicion that the annual model change may be good for the auto business in the short term but that it wasn't good for the economy and the country. Couldn't the money we spent on annual, superficial styling changes be better spent in reducing prices or in improving service and reliability? Or seeking solutions to the sociological problems which our products were creating in areas of pollution, energy consumption, safety and congestion?

And a fraud on our own company because, when General Motors began to grow on the principle of annual model changes and the promotion of something new and different, cars were almost all alike with the same basic color—black. There was room for cosmetic changes as well as substantial advancement in technology with new and better engines, more sophisticated transmissions, improved performance and comfort characteristics.

But now there was nothing new and revolutionary in car development and there hadn't been for years. As a company, we were kidding ourselves that these slight alterations were innovative. They were not. We were living off the gullibility of the consumer combined with the fantastic growth of the American economy in the 1960s. Salting away billions of dollars of profits in the process and telling ourselves we were great managers because of these profits. This bubble was surely going to break, I thought. The consumer is going to get wise to us, and when he does we will have to fight for a long time to get back into his favor.

Those feelings during the preview led me to tell newsmen during lunch that I would probably leave the auto industry when I was age 55 or so, to get involved in helping find answers to America's problems. There was skepticism and disbelief in their voices as we talked about this subject. They didn't know that I had petitioned management to let me resign from the corporation to take a dealership in

From *On a Clear Day You Can See General Motors* by J. Patrick Wright. Copyright © 1979 J. Patrick Wright. Available in paperback from Avon Books. Reprinted by permission.

San Jose, California. Nevertheless, the newsmen wrote about my lunchtime revelation.

The Fourteenth Floor went through the ceiling when the stories appeared the next day saying I was going to forsake General Motors in eight or nine years. It looked to them as if I was trying to force their hand by saying: "Make me President by then or I will quit."

To anyone in the corporation who asked about them, I explained that my luncheon comments, though not irrevocable, were sincerely motivated and that I was having some internal conflicts about my job. My doubts about the worth of the annual model change were just a part of a growing concern I had about the general level of morality practiced in General Motors, in particular, and parts of American business in general.

It seemed to me, and still does, that the system of American business often produces wrong, immoral and irresponsible decisions, even though the personal morality of the people running the businesses is often above reproach. The system has a different morality as a group than the people do as individuals, which permits it to willfully produce ineffective or dangerous products, deal dictatorially and often unfairly with suppliers, pay bribes for business, abrogate the rights of employees by demanding blind loyalty to management or tamper with the democratic process of government through illegal political contributions.

I am not a psychologist, so I can't offer a professional opinion on what happens to the freedom of individual minds when they are blended into the group management thought process of business. But my private analysis is this: Morality has to do with people. If an action is viewed primarily from the perspective of its effect on people, it is put into the moral realm.

Business in America, however, is impersonal. This is particularly true of large American multi-national corporations. They are viewed by their employees and publics as faceless. They have no personality. The ultimate measure of success and failure of these businesses is not their effect on people but rather their earnings per share of stock. If earnings are high, the business is considered good. If they are low or in the red ink, it is considered a failure. The first question to greet any business proposal is how will it affect profits? *People* do not enter the equation of a business decision except to the extent that the effect on

them will hurt or enhance earnings per share. In such a completely impersonal context, business decisions of questionable personal morality are easily justified. The unwavering devotion to the bottom line brings this about, and the American public until now has been more than willing to accept this. When someone is forced into early retirement in a management power-play or a supplier is cheated out of a sale by under-the-table dealings, the public reaction is generally, "Oh, well. That's business." And management's reaction is often, "It's what's on the bottom line that counts." A person who shoots and kills another is sentenced to life in prison. A businessman who makes a defective product which kills people may get a nominal fine or a verbal slap on the hands, if he is ever brought to trial at all.

The impersonal process of business decision-making is reinforced by a sort of mob psychology that results from group management and the support of a specific system of management. *Watergate* certainly proved what can happen when blind devotion to a system or a process of thought moves unchecked. Members of the Nixon Administration never raised any real questions about the morality of the break-in and the coverup. The only concern was for the expedient method to save the system. So too in business. Too often the only questions asked are: What is the expedient thing to do to save the system? How can we increase profits per share?

Never once while I was in General Motors management did I hear substantial social concern raised about the impact of our business on America, its consumers or the economy. When we should have been planning switches to smaller, more fuel-efficient, lighter cars in the late 1960s in response to a growing demand in the marketplace, GM management refused because "we make more money on big cars." It mattered not that customers wanted the smaller cars or that a national balance-of payments deficit was being built in large part because of the burgeoning sales of foreign cars in the American market.

Refusal to enter the smaller car market when the profits were better on bigger cars, despite the needs of the public and the national economy, was not an isolated case of corporate insensitivity. It was typical. And what disturbed me is that it was indicative of fundamental problems with the system.

General Motors certainly was no more irresponsible than many American businesses. But the fact that the "prototype" of the well-run American business engaged in questionable business practices and delivered decisions which I felt were sometimes illegal, immoral or irresponsible is an indictment of the American business system.

Earlier in my career, I accepted these decisions at GM without question. But as I was exposed to more facets of the business, I came to a realization of the responsibilities we had in managing a giant corporation and making a product which substantially affected people and national commerce. It bothered me how cavalierly these responsibilities were often regarded.

The whole Corvair case is a first-class example of a basically irresponsible and immoral business decision which was made by men of generally high personal moral standards. When Nader's book threatened the Corvair's sales and profits, he became an enemy of the system. Instead of trying to attack his credentials or the factual basis of his arguments, the company sought to attack him personally. This move failed, but, in the process, GM's blundering "made" Ralph Nader.

When the fact that GM hired detectives to follow and discredit Nader was exposed, the system was once again threatened. Top management, instead of questioning the system which would permit such an horrendous mistake as tailing Nader, simply sought to preserve the system by sacrificing the heads of several executives who were blamed for the incident. Were the atmosphere at GM not one emphasizing profits and preservation of the system above all else, I am sure the acts against Nader would never have been perpetrated.

Those who were fired no doubt thought they were loyal employees. And, ironically, had they succeeded in devastating the image of Ralph Nader, they would have been corporate heroes and rewarded substantially. I find it difficult to believe that knowledge of these activities did not reach into the upper reaches of GM's management. But, assuming that it didn't, top management should have been held responsible for permitting the conditions to exist which would spawn such actions. If top management takes credit for a company's successes, it must also bear the brunt of the responsibility for its failures.

Furthermore, the Corvair was unsafe as it was originally designed. It was conceived along the lines of the foreign-built Porsche. These cars were powered by engines placed in the rear and supported by an independent, swing-axle suspension system. In the Corvair's case, the engine was all-aluminum and air-cooled (compared to the standard water-cooled iron engines). This, plus the rear placement of the engine, made the car new and somewhat different to the American market.

However, there are several bad engineering characteristics inherent in rear-engine cars which use a swing-axle suspension. In turns at high speeds they tend to become directionally unstable and, therefore, difficult to control. The rear of the car lifts or "jacks" and the rear wheels tend to tuck under the car, which encourages the car to flip over. In the high-performance Corvair, the car conveyed a false sense of control to the driver, when in fact he may have been very close to losing control of the vehicle. The result of these characteristics can be fatal.

These problems with the Corvair were well documented inside GM's Engineering Staff long before the Corvair ever was offered for sale. Frank Winchell, now vice-president of Engineering, but then a engineer at Chevy, flipped over one of the first prototypes on the GM test track in Milford, Michigan. Others followed.

The questionable safety of the car caused a massive internal fight among GM's engineers over whether the car should be built with another form of suspension. On one side of the argument was Chevrolet's then General Manager, Ed Cole, an engineer and product innovator. He and some of his engineering colleagues were enthralled with the idea of building the first modern, rear-engine, American car. And I am convinced they felt the safety risks of the swing-axle suspension were minimal. On the other side was a wide assortment of top-flight engineers, including Charles Chayne, then vice-president of Engineering; Von D. Polhemus, engineer in charge of Chassis Development on GM's Engineering Staff, and others.

These men collectively and individually made vigorous attempts inside GM to keep the Corvair, as designed, out of production or to change the suspension system to make the car safer. One top corporate engineer told me that he showed his test results to Cole but by then, he said, "Cole's mind was made up."

Albert Roller, who worked for me in Pontiac's Advanced Engineering section, tested the car and pleaded with me not to use it at Pontiac. Roller had been an engineer with Mercedes-Benz before joining

GM, and he said that Mercedes had tested similarly designed rear-engine, swing-axle cars and had found them far too unsafe to build.

At the very least, then, within General Motors in the late 1950s, serious questions were raised about the Corvair's safety. At the very most, there was a mountain of documented evidence that the car should not be built as it was then designed.

However, Cole was a strong product voice and a top salesman in company affairs. In addition, the car, as he proposed it, would cost less to build than the same car with a conventional rear suspension. Management not only went along with Cole, it also told the dissenters in effect to "stop these objections. Get on the team, or you can find someplace else to work." The ill-fated Corvair was launched in the fall of 1959.

The results were disastrous. I don't think any one car before or since produced as gruesome a record on the highway as the Corvair. It was designed and promoted to appeal to the spirit and flair of young people. It was sold in part as a sports car. Young Corvair owners, therefore, were trying to bend their car around curves at high speeds and were killing themselves in alarming numbers.

It was only a couple of years or so before GM's legal department was inundated with lawsuits over the car. And the fatal swath that this car cut through the automobile industry touched the lives of many General Motors executives, employees and dealers in an ironic and tragic twist of fate.

The son of Cal Werner, general manager of the Cadillac Division, was killed in a Corvair. Werner was absolutely convinced that the design defect in the car was responsible. He said so many times. The son of Cy Osborne, an executive vice-president in the 1960s, was critically injured in a Corvair and suffered irreparable brain damage. Bunkie Knudsen's niece was brutally injured in a Corvair. And the son of an Indianapolis Chevrolet dealer also was killed in the car. Ernie Kovacs, my favorite comedian, was killed in a Corvair.

While the car was being developed at Chevrolet, we at Pontiac were spending $1.3 million on a project to adapt the Corvair to our division. The corporation had given us the go-ahead to work with the car to give it a Pontiac flavor. Our target for introduction was the fall of 1960, a year after Chevy introduced the car.

As we worked on the project, I became absolutely convinced by Chayne, Polhemus and Roller that the car was unsafe. So I conducted a three-month campaign, with Knudsen's support, to keep the car out of the Pontiac lineup. Fortunately, Buick and Oldsmobile at the time were tooling up their own compact cars, the Special and F-85, respectively, which featured conventional front-engine designs.

We talked the corporation into letting Pontiac switch from a Corvair derivative to a version of the Buick-Oldsmobile car. We called it the Tempest and introduced it in the fall of 1960 with a four-cylinder engine as standard equipment and a V-8 engine as an option.

When Knudsen took over the reins of Chevrolet in 1961, he insisted that he be given corporate authorization to install a stabilizing bar in the rear to counteract the natural tendencies of the Corvair to flip off the road. The cost of the change would be about $15 a car. But his request was refused by The Fourteenth Floor as "too expensive."

Bunkie was livid. As I understood it, he went to the Executive Committee and told the top officers of the corporation that, if they didn't reappraise his request and give him permission to make the Corvair safe, he was going to resign from General Motors. This threat and the fear of the bad publicity that surely would result from Knudsen's resignation forced management's hand. They relented. Bunkie put a stabilizing bar on the Corvair in the 1964 models. The next year a completely new and safer independent suspension designed by Frank Winchell was put on the Corvair. And it became one of the safest cars on the road. But the damage done to the car's reputation by then was irreparable. Corvair sales began to decline precipitously after the waves of unfavorable publicity following Nader's book and the many lawsuits being filed across the country. Production of the Corvair was halted in 1969, four years after it was made a safe and viable car.

To date, millions of dollars have been spent in legal expenses and out-of-court settlements in compensation for those killed or maimed in the Corvair. The corporation steadfastly defends the car's safety, despite the internal engineering records which indicated it was not safe, and the ghastly toll in deaths and injury it recorded.

There wasn't a man in top GM management who had anything to do with the Corvair who would purposely build a car that he knew would hurt or kill people. But, as part of a management team pushing for increased sales and profits, each gave his individual approval in a group to decisions which produced the car in the face of the serious doubts that were raised about its safety, and then later sought to squelch information which might prove the car's deficiencies.

The corporation became almost paranoid about the leaking of inside information we had on the car. In April of 1971, 19 boxes of microfilmed Corvair owner complaints, which had been ordered destroyed by upper management, turned up in the possession of two suburban Detroit junk dealers. When The Fourteenth Floor found this out, it went into panic and we at Chevrolet were ordered to buy the microfilm back and have it destroyed.

I refused, saying that a public company had no right to destroy documents of its business and that GM's furtive purchase would surely surface. Besides, the $20,000 asking price was outright blackmail.

When some consumer groups showed an interest in getting the films, the customer relations department was ordered to buy the film, which it did. To prevent similar slip-ups in the future, the corporation tightened its scrapping procedures.

Chevrolet products were involved in the largest product recall in automotive history when, in 1971, the corporation called back 6.7 million 1965–69 Chevrolet cars to repair defective motor mounts. The rubber mounts, which anchor the engine to the car, were breaking apart and causing the engine to lunge out of place. This action often locked the accelerator into an open position at the speed of about 25 miles per hour. Cars were smashing up all across the country when panicky drivers couldn't stop them or jumped out of them in fright. The defect need never have been.

At Pontiac, when I was chief engineer, we developed a safety-interlock motor mount which we put on our 1965 car line. It was developed because we discovered that the mounts we were using were defective. We made our findings and the design of the new motor mount available to the rest of the car divisions. None of them opted for it.

However, reports started drifting in from the field in 1966 that the Chevrolet mounts were breaking apart after extensive use. The division did nothing. Dealers replaced the mounts and charged the customers for the parts and labor.

When I got to Chevrolet in 1969, the reports about motor mount failures were reaching crisis proportions. When a motor mount failure was blamed for a fatal accident involving an elderly woman in Florida, I asked Kyes, my boss, to let me quietly recall all the cars with these problem mounts and repair

them, at GM's expense. He refused on the ground that it would cost too much money. By 1971, however, the motor mount trouble was becoming widely known outside of the corporation because unsatisfied owners were complaining to local newspapers, the National Highway Traffic Safety Administration and several consumer groups.

The pressure began to build on GM to recall the cars with these mounts. Soon GM began to repair these cars at company expense, but it refused to recall all the cars, preferring to wait until the mounts broke in use before doing anything. Bob Irvin, of the Detroit *News*, who was receiving huge numbers of complaints, began to write almost daily stories about the mount trouble and GM's steadfast refusal to recall all the cars.

The fires of discontent were further fanned when Ed Cole, who was opposing the recall internally, was asked by a reporter why GM continued to refuse to recall the cars. He replied that the mounts were not a problem and that anyone who "can't manage a car at 25 miles per hour shouldn't be driving." It was an unfortunately callous remark, for which I am sure Cole was later sorry. But he became more rigid in his stance against a recall campaign. So I wrote a memo to my immediate boss in 1971, Tom Murphy, and it said in part:

> At this point in time, it seems to me that we have no alternative (but to recall the Chevrolets). Certainly if GM can spend over $200,000,000 a year on advertising, the $30 or $40,000,000 this campaign would cost is not a valid reason for delaying. Certainly, it would be worth the cost to stop the negative publicity, even if management cannot agree to campaign these cars on moral grounds.

Murphy received the memo and returned it to me, refusing to accept it.

Finally, about a month or so later, under the weight of government, consumer group and newspaper pressure, GM recalled the 6.7 million cars with defective engine mounts. The price was about $40 million to recall the cars and wire the engines to the car so they wouldn't slip out of place when the mounts broke.

But the cost was much greater in the incredibly bad publicity GM received because of its unwillingness to admit its responsibility for the defect and to repair the cars on its own. It was really a case of the corporation taking an attitude of "the owners be damned" when it came to spending the money it needed to fix the engine mount problem.

The motor mount affair reflected a general corporate attitude toward the consumer movement, an attitude shared by some American businesses in a wide variety of industries. The reason that consumer advocates, such as Ralph Nader, have emerged as public champions, and that city, state and national governments have set up offices to look after consumer affairs, is that people have legitimate beefs about the quality and safety of the products they are buying. If almost everybody who bought products was happy with them, there would be no Naders at the local, state or national level. And even if there were, their cries would fall on deaf ears.

Car service is an example of an area of wide consumer displeasure today. At best, automotive service is poor. Car owners are suspicious of their dealers' service. More and more people are turning to the corner gasoline station mechanic for service, even though the nearby dealer is supposedly the specialist at fixing their car. The reason is that the auto companies, especially GM, have never committed themselves to improving the serviceability of the dealership.

A car dealer is judged by how many new cars he pushes out of the showroom doors in the front and not how he services them in the back. Dealers are graded primarily on their sales results, because this puts money into the corporate bank account and profit on the financial sheet. A big-volume dealer with a poor service operation is handled very gingerly by the manufacturer. Unfortunately, he often gets better treatment from the company than the dedicated, conscientious dealer with lower volume who invests heavily in a proper service facility.

The relationship between the company and its retail dealer body is a study in paradox. The corporation depends on its dealers to market its cars and trucks. Without the dealer body, GM or its competitors could not stay in business. Dealers and their businesses represent about half the total investment in General Motors.

The local Chevrolet or Buick dealer often is the only personal contact a customer has with General Motors. His perceptions of GM and its car divisions come from the way he is treated at the retail sales level. Such interlocking needs between the dealers and the company would seem to dictate a close and friendly relationship between the two.

In some cases, most often with high-volume dealers, this is the case. More often, behind the smiles, handshakes and backslapping of dealer-company sales meetings, there is an adversary relationship which is contrary to the practical dictates of business. Dealers often don't trust the company and vice-versa.

I found the majority of car dealers I worked with to be hard-working, sound and honest businessmen. In their struggles with the corporation, the dealers received the short straw more times than not.

There were some bad and dishonest dealers as well as good ones. Some, for instance, were notorious for cheating on warranty claims.

Chevrolet division in late 1974 purged practically two entire zone sales offices when it uncovered a dealer warranty fraud scheme which was working with the help of the zone officials. This scandal was more than a routine case of fraud, however. The Chevrolet service manager for the Boston Zone was murdered in the scheme.

Conversely, in many instances, dealers performing legitimate warranty repairs to customers' cars had their claims for restitution disallowed on a purely capricious basis, a practice I fought against.

The tone for an adversary relationship between company and dealers has been set, I think, by shoddy treatment of the dealer body. While General Motors owes its very existence today to its dealers, the manner in which GM has manipulated and browbeaten them falls into the area of questionable ethics.

When I got to Chevrolet, the dealer body as a whole was very distrustful of divisional and corporate management because it had been left with a string of broken promises about new product developments and the exclusivity of its markets. In one instance, Bob Lund, Chevy's general sales manager, and I were asked to attend a Fourteenth Floor meeting to report on how Chevrolet dealers would react if Pontiac dealers were given a version of the compact Nova. At the time, our dealers were selling every Nova they could get into their dealerships. They also had been promised by corporate management that they would have this compact car market all to themselves among GM's divisions.

Before the meeting "upstairs," I was called into a small top management conference by Kyes and told that if I opposed a decision to give a Nova derivative to Pontiac, the small-car program I was pushing (the K-car project) would be taken from Chevrolet.

Nevertheless, in the meeting I opposed the move, along with Lund, on the ground that our dealers couldn't get enough Novas as it was and that we had to keep our promise of exclusivity to them.

Lund and I were wasting our breath; the corporation gave Pontiac a version of the Nova called the Ventura. As it turned out, Pontiac dealers had trouble selling their compact cars while Chevrolet dealers lost sales that they practically had in the bag. They were livid at the double-talk they had been given by The Fourteenth Floor. And my small-car program was never approved.

This was not an isolated case. The dealers are often bounced around at the whim of corporate management. And it is a wonder that car dealers have not formed an organization like the National Football League Players Association to represent their consolidated interests before the manufacturer. In the past, when GM effected a price cut to meet its competition or improve the sales of a particular car line, the cut often came out of the dealer's markup.

In other words, hypothetically assuming that GM announced a four percent price reduction on a $3,000 car, this would be a drop of $120 on the sticker price of the car. The public would praise the corporation's move, but what it wouldn't know was that the price of that car to the dealer from the company hadn't changed one bit. The company had lowered the manufacturer's suggested retail price by $120 by narrowing the profit spread between that price and the price of the car to the dealer. If the spread was 21 percent, it fell to 17 percent. The price reduction came out of the dealer's potential profit.

The company often leans on its dealers to maintain or increase its own profit levels, with little regard to the dealer's business climate. After the Arab oil embargo there was a sharp drop in big car sales. GM's big car divisions watched their business drop 50 percent or more. The plight was the same for the dealers, yet GM continued to force big cars on dealers with no relaxation in the payment schedules.

I thought that GM should give its dealers 90 days free interest, and I told people so, even though by now I was out of management. Instead, management maintained its standard billing program—payment in full 20 days after the cars are received. When the corporation provided General Motors Acceptance Corporation (GMAC), which finances dealer inventories and retail purchases, with a $500–million interest-free loan during the crunch, none of the interest break was passed on to the dealers. GM dealers didn't get a one-tenth of one percent reduction in their loan rates because of the free loan to GMAC. So GMAC made money at the dealers' expense, and that compounded the business troubles for the dealers during the auto recession.

A practice which I opposed in GM was the constant pressuring of dealers to buy their service and aftermarket parts from the General Motors Parts Division (GMPD), when they could get some of the same parts cheaper from the warehouse distributors of the AC Spark Plug and Delco Products Division.

The situation was complicated. GMPD was a business of $400 million a year or so, primarily set up to give GM car and truck dealers a single source for the parts they need to repair vehicles or sell over-the-counter. The parts they offered included spark plugs, condensers, oil filters and shock absorbers made by other GM divisions such as AC and Delco products.

These divisions, however, also had their own network of warehouse distributors, which sold primarily to non-GM dealers, repair shops and gasoline stations. Both the GM car dealers and the warehouse distributors bought their parts at similar discounts, in some cases 25 percent. The dealers got this discount from GMPD, and the warehouse got them from their home division.

There was some overlapping of business, however, a problem which no one ever sought to straighten out. The distributor could also sell to the GM dealers. When they did, they received an additional discount from the divisions to make the sale profitable. Otherwise, they could offer the dealer no better deal than he could get from GMPD. Whatever this additional discount was, the distributor often offered to split it with the dealer. When this happened, the dealer could get the part cheaper at the distributor level than he could from GMPD.

Nevertheless, to keep GMPD viable, pressure was constantly applied to the dealers to buy parts from GMPD at a higher price. When GMPD held a big sales push, a car division sales or service representative would be given a quota of say 25,000 spark plugs to sell.

He'd walk into a GM car dealer and say, "Your quota is 1,000 spark plugs." If the dealer balked, he was badgered and browbeaten by the sales representatives of his own car division to meet his quota. In the end, a balking dealer knew that the company held the upper hand because it could get even in many different ways, one of which was to slow up deliveries to him of hot-selling cars. Sometimes, large-volume dealers who were important to the corporation could fend off this pressure without fear of reprisal. But, more often than not, dealers had to knuckle under and buy the parts from GMPD at a higher price than they could get elsewhere.

During one dealer service meeting at Great Gorge, New Jersey, an east coast dealer complained about being badgered into buying GMPD parts. He said he had just weathered a couple of bad business years and added:

"I couldn't get anybody to come out and help me save my dealership, or help me with my business problems. But I had seven different people call on me, including the regional manager (of the division), about taking my quota of these goddamn spark plugs from GMPD that I could buy cheaper somewhere else. It cost me a lot of extra money (thousands of dollars) each year to buy parts from the GMPD." There were other such cases.

In a somewhat different situation, there was a Chevy dealer in Florida who was the low bidder on the sale of a large fleet of cars. To win the bid he had to price the cars very close to his own cost. So, to save about $35 a car, his bid included Motorola radios instead of the GM-built Delco units. This $35 represented most of the profit for him per car. When the dealer ordered the cars from Chevrolet, sans Delco radios, the company representative contacted him and made it clear that, unless he bought Delco radios for the cars, his order would be delayed three to four months. Such a delay would bring the cars to the dealer much later than the delivery date promised to the fleet consumer. The Florida dealer was forced to buy Delco radios, and he made very little profit on the sale of these cars, while GM made thousands of dollars on the Delco radios alone. Later, I ran into a divisional guy who was gleeful in his replay of this case, crowing about how he forced this dealer to take company radios.

In many respects, I felt that the dealers had carried the division and the corporation through rough sales periods. Chevy's dealers kept the division afloat during the mid-1960s. Our thanks for their help was to constantly put the squeeze on them for every last nickel of corporate profit. Our policies with dealers were shoddy. What we were doing was often a blatant violation of our own precepts of free enterprise.

When we were called down before Congressional hearings to explain our side of the growing problem of governmental control of the industry, a frequent defense of our business was that we needed to preserve the free enterprise system. "In a free market, the customer is the winner. And the true principles of business prevail because the customer decides which businesses are successful and which are not," the corporation would tell any willing ear.

Yet, within our corporate walls, we engaged in business practices which were not only monopolistic, but sometimes were downright violations of the free-enterprise system. We stifled competition. Our dealers weren't always free to run their businesses as they saw fit. We were forcing them at times to buy our parts and products at inflated prices.

We certainly could not tolerate the use of inferior parts by our dealers in repairing General Motors vehicles. But we sure as hell shouldn't have forced them to pay higher prices for our own parts that they could get elsewhere in the company. And, in situations where they had the choice of choosing our product, such as Delco radios or a competitor's product of similar quality, we should have had to sell the dealers on the merits of the GM product over the competition. That is what free enterprise is all about. We shouldn't have forced our dealers to take the GM product. If General Motors was buying a product from one company, it would buy it the cheapest way. That is just good business. Therefore, I felt what we were doing with our dealers was immoral and probably illegal.

So I told the Chevrolet sales executives, who were our dealer contact people, that we were never again going to force our dealers to pay more for a product they could get cheaper elsewhere. That was an order. There would be no more intimidation of Chevrolet dealers by the field sales force about buying spark plugs from GMPD. Our dealers could get GM parts where they got the best price.

Word quickly got to The Fourteenth Floor about this directive (I think it took less than an hour). I got a call that Mr. Kyes wanted to see me in his office immediately. When I got there, he was red-faced and mad. He launched a 15-minute, blistering attack on me as a person, citizen, employee and businessman. I was verbally raked up one end of executive row and down the other. I thought he was going to fire me on the spot. His diatribe ended on a typically low note:

"You don't know how business is done. You're a goddamn amateur, De Lorean."

"That's just the way I feel. You don't solve the problem of an unequal discount structure on our parts by intimidating the dealers into paying a higher price. What you should do is look for a way to fix the problem," I responded.

I left his office. My order stuck. Chevrolet people stopped pressuring our dealers to take parts from GMPD.

Not all GM dealers fared poorly in their association with the company. Some profited quite well by their friendships with top executives. Hanley Dawson, a big company dealer in the Midwest was one who profited exceptionally well from his corporate friendships, especially with Ed Cole.

On one occasion, Cadillac decided to sell all its "company stores," which is an inside term for retail dealerships which are owned by a division of the corporation. One of these was the Rush Street "store" in downtown Chicago, which is a prime location for a Cadillac dealership. The property and building were leased on a long-term agreement with Prudential Life Insurance, as I recall.

So valuable was the land that Prudential wanted to buy the lease back from Cadillac for a price that was in the millions. But the division wanted the valuable location, Harry Hollywood, an assistant sales manager at Cadillac, said he wanted to buy the Rush Street Store. He had been a general manager of this dealership prior to coming into Cadillac management in 1967. And it was well known in the corporation that he was brought into GM then by Chairman Roche with the promise that when he wanted to go back into the retail business, he would get a Cadillac dealership. So Hollywood was exercising this option when he bid for the Chicago dealership.

The company told him the selling price would require Hollywood to come up with something like $500,000 to $800,000 of his own money. This was a staggering sum for Hollywood. He couldn't afford it and had to turn the deal down.

Shortly thereafter Cole set up an arrangement which permitted Hanley Dawson to buy the same dealership with only about $350,000 or less of his own money. It was blatantly unfair to Hollywood, who might have been able to raise $350,000 or less but had no chance of coming up with $150,000 to $450,000 more. For him the selling price was as

much as half-a-million more than it was for Cole's friend Dawson. I don't think it was anything personal against Hollywood. It was a "business decision," not a personal decision.

There are scores of Harry Hollywoods (he has a Cadillac dealership in Florida now, fortunately) in every American industry, who are run over by the system. General Motors, I think, probably treats its employees as well as any American company. But the treatment of its employees is financially oriented, not personally oriented.

When a hard-working executive slips up along the way, or finds himself on the wrong side of a corporate argument, or grows too old in his job, having given his best years to the company, he is eased into early retirement. The corporate rationale is very simple. The executive is given severance pay and a retirement pension that should keep him comfortable for the rest of his life. With that, the corporation management feels that it has discharged its obligations to the executive.

The corporate obligation is considered purely in financial terms. No one considers the effect on the executive's life and pride. After years of service, he is suddenly jobless, no longer a part of the corporate fraternity to which he has given his life's blood.

Suppliers often feel the brunt of corporate power, pressure and influence. A GM decision to stop buying one part from a particular company can send that firm into bankruptcy. GM and its auto company cohorts hold the power of life and death over many of their suppliers. In most cases that power is exercised responsibly. In some cases it is not.

During the development and introduction of the subcompact Vega, a problem arose in controlling emissions on the engines with two-barrel carburetors. We asked GM's Rochester Products Division to help us work on this problem. Its executives refused. We had to add a $25 air pump to these engines to burn exhaust gases more effectively. It was a costly and unsatisfactory remedy to the problem.

Holly Carburetor Co., an independent supplier, however, gladly worked with us on the problem. It developed a different type of two-barrel carburetor which promoted better combustion of the fuel in the engine. We were able to meet the pollution standards with this new carburetor. We could get rid of the expensive air pump and improve engine performance. This saved Chevrolet about $3 million per year.

Now, development of such a new product by an outside supplier carries with it an implicit gentleman's promise by the company that the supplier will get some of the business. Suppliers sometimes do not take out patents on such work, or if they do, they give their client free access to the design. In this case, when Rochester Products Division found out about the Holly breakthrough, it got panicky that it was going to lose the Vega business. The corporate management came to Rochester's aid and threw out Holly as a possible supplier on the carburetor it designed, and it gave the job to Rochester. Chevrolet's Director of Purchasing, George Ford, a tremendous man of sound integrity, brought the problem to my attention. We found our way to the top of the corporation. Holly was finally allowed to keep a little piece of the business.

GM management did a similar "number" on the Kelsey-Hayes Company, which developed a single piston disc brake only to have General Motors appropriate the design and build most of the parts internally.

The morality of such arbitrary action compelled me to write a memo to my superior, Tom Murphy, after the Holly incident in August of 1971, and send a copy to Ed Cole. It said in part:

> Obviously, Holly will never help us again—and Rochester will never again heed one of our threats to go outside—so that the next time the $3,000,0000 a year (cost savings) will go down the drain. Needless to say, the impact on our technical and purchasing people has been great—because we have made them a party to a questionable, shabby business practice against their will.
>
> I have instructed our people to stop getting outside quotations in competition with Allied Division, since it is unfair to ask a firm to spend time and money preparing a quote when they have no chance at the business. I should point out that outside quotes have enabled Chevrolet and GM to reduce our product costs by over $30,000,000 per year, over the past two years.
>
> In my opinion, this decision was shortsighted—and is one of the main reasons that General Motors has not led in a significant technical innovation since the automatic transmission. Power steering, reheat air conditioning, power brakes, power windows, disc brakes, the alternator and the two-way tail gate all originated with our competitors.

The memo concluded:

> To my mind, a supplier who makes a significant contribution earns some business—to use our suppliers otherwise is immoral. To use the size and might of General Motors in this way borders on illegality and invites antitrust action.

I never got a reply to this memo, but my dwindling stock as a team player fell a few extra points.

GM's dearth of product innovations, which I felt would be prolonged by its shoddy dealings with suppliers, produced an unquenchable thirst for information on what the competition was doing in product areas. This thirst led the company into areas which I felt were of questionable legality. So concerned was management with the plans of the competition, especially Ford, that the final okay on product programs was often delayed until we received the latest up-to-date intelligence on Ford's product programs.

I was told by Lou Bauer, once Chevrolet Division's comptroller, that, when Bunkie Knudsen took over Chevrolet in 1961, he was shocked to find on Chevy's payroll two men who worked for and spied on Ford. They worked in Ford's product planning area and passed on new product information to Chevrolet for a price. Knudsen, I was told, fired the spies the day he confirmed their existence.

Later, when I was at Chevy, an executive walked into my office one day with a copy of Ford's complete marketing program for the coming model year. He said that copies were being distributed all over the corporation. I was surprised but later I learned that it was corporate practice to maneuver such information out of the competition. When Ross Malone, corporate counsel at the time, learned of this, he severely admonished the entire Administration Committee for this action. I was proud of him.

This practice reached a height of sorts when several of us walked into a meeting of the Administration Committee, sometime after 1971, and found the top corporate officers poring over a very confidential "spread sheet," that listed all of Ford's product costs. This report gave the definitive breakdown, product-by-product, of what it cost Ford to build and sell its cars. It was the kind of information which, for our products, never got off The Fourteenth Floor. GM top management wouldn't even let the divisional management in on all the corporate costs, let alone the competition. But somehow, top management had gotten this information about Ford and they were studying it with deep concentration when again General Counsel Malone was incensed. He snapped, "Goddamnit! You guys shouldn't be doing this."

His voice was at once angry and pleading. It was obvious to me that Malone thought that what was taking place had serious legal overtones.

After he spoke, someone scooped up the Ford cost reports and hustled them off to one of the front offices. None of us at the divisional level ever heard about the report again. Now, I am sure that the men studying these confidential cost sheets and giving their approval to a system which procured them would be outraged at the suggestion of similar conduct in their personal lives. Like most Americans, they were probably angered by the disclosures in the wake of *Watergate* that the CIA, U.S. Army, FBI and other governmental agencies spied and gathered intelligence on unsuspective citizens. And yet, in business, they were justifying the very same sort of conduct on the grounds that "this is business."

General Motors took its place in the line with scores of other American businesses in promoting what I think are, at the very least, improper political campaign contributions from its top executives. The system was complicated and far more secretive than the outright corporate political gifts for which a number of major corporations have paid fines and their top executives have been fined or sentenced to jail.

Nevertheless, General Motors solicited from its executives substantial political contributions which most likely totalled in the hundreds of thousands of dollars during a national presidential campaign. Off-year campaigns, state and local contests, produced proportionately lower amounts.

The contributions program was operated, as I understood it, by the financial side of the business with assistance from some people on the public relations staff. The finance staff apparently collected the money and a few PR people distributed it with guidance from The Fourteenth Floor.

There were two tiers to the system. Middle and upper middle management were generally allowed to contribute a sum of money to the party of their choice. However, once an executive reached upper management levels (divisional or corporate), it was decided for him how much he would contribute and to whom it would go. As a general manager, I can

remember the divisional controller walking into my office with a sheet of paper that apparently had been given to him by the corporate finance staff. On the sheet was written my name and the amount I was to donate to that year's election campaigns—national, state or local. I was told to make a check out to "cash" for the amount assigned to me and give it to the controller who returned it to the corporation. Once the check was made out, an executive did not know to whom or for whom the political contribution was made, or in the manner it was made: whether it was an anonymous cash contribution, one that was made in his name or a corporate gift. All the executive knew was that he wrote out a check to "cash" for the predetermined amount.

The sums were big. For a GM vice president, it was maybe as much as $3,000 in a presidential campaign, less for an off-year congressional election and so on down to a few hundred dollars for a city election.

I participated in the system several times at Pontiac. I cannot recall whether I made the donations myself or wrote a check to "cash." But finally, I just couldn't accept the practice, and I refused to participate. The whole thing seemed wholly improper. Whether the money was donated in my name or not, it was still a corporate gift over which I had no control. What's more, my franchise to vote and donate as I saw fit was too important to me as a citizen to delegate it to management or some guy on one of the corporate staffs. The corporation has no right to tell any executive how to vote, or to know how he votes.

After I refused to participate in the contribution program at GM on several different occasions, top management hit the roof. As in the past, the chore of trying to bring me in line fell to Kyes. When I entered his office at his request, he was ready for battle.

"John, you'd better damn well play this game," he said. "If you don't, you are telling us you aren't on the team. We don't think highly of guys who aren't on the team at GM."

Then he sought to reduce the questions and doubts in my mind to merely a matter of money, the common rationalization in business.

"We take care of you at bonus time. When you make this contribution you get that back as part of your bonus. And if you don't make it, then you aren't going to get that much bonus."

The meeting ended angrily, as usual, with neither of us giving an inch. I continued to boycott the political contribution system at GM, and instead made personal donations to candidates I thought were worthy. And I must admit I never noticed an inexplicable drop in the bonus I received for my work at GM thereafter.

While these business practices, to which I and a number of other GM executives at varying levels objected, involved questionable ethics exercised for the good of the business, there were disturbing activities in upper management in which executives used their positions of power and knowledge to profit *personally* in corporate business. These were by no means widespread and perhaps confined to only a few individuals. My contact with them came often in a tangential or strange way. In one instance, when I was directing Pontiac, several GM dealers were purchasing the troubled National Car Rental Co. for almost nothing—less than $4 million. The price, as I remember, was 2 or 3 dollars per share.

While they were doing this, they also worked a deal with upper corporate management for GM to provide $22 million in advertising assistance, because National was going to emphasize GM cars in its business and promotion. The confirmation of this arrangement was known only to a few people. But once it became public the stock of the company would surely jump in value. One day one of the participants in the purchase of National came to me and said, "You've got to get some of this stock. We're buying it at $2 to $3 a share." I said, "That's an obvious conflict of interest. I can't do it."

He said, "Hell, I'll buy it for you and keep it in my name. Tell me how much you want." I refused his second offer because it was wrong and what's more, once you let a guy do something like that, he owns you forever. You're his puppet. He was irritated by my refusal and said, "Hell, we're doing it for—" and he named a high-ranking GM official. It was quite a surprise. I never personally verified whether the guy this dealer named was in on the deal or not, which is why I am not disclosing the names involved. But I do know that word was rife through the corporation that officers were making bundles from insider information on National Car Rental Company stock. So well-known was this rumor in the company, that management conducted an investigation and demanded to examine National's stockholder list to see if any GM executives were on it. There were none. But then there wouldn't be if the stock was held in someone else's name.

On yet another occasion when I was at Chevrolet, word got around that company and divisional executives were speculating on land around the Lordstown assembly plant in Ohio. Since these people would be privy to our plans for the Lordstown area, they could buy the land and sell when its value rose as GM increased its activity in the plant area. I wasn't aware which executives were supposedly involved.

Again the corporation conducted an investigation and apparently fingered several people, including one of our Chevy managers. Word was that the culprits were going to be fired. One day, the Chevy executive in question walked into my office obviously nervous and excited, and snapped: "If you guys make something out of this, I'm going to blow the lid off this goddamn thing."

"What the hell do you mean?" I asked.

He replied by telling me the name of a real estate man in the Lordstown area who he said was acting as the agent in these land transactions and who was willing to implicate top corporate managers in the speculating venture. Some of the executives the Chevy man mentioned to me were the same ones who were trying to have him fired in the brewing scandal. I told the guy I knew nothing about the matter and was not a part of the firing action. But he must have put the same threat to his prosecutors in the corporation because it wasn't too long before this executive who was on the verge of being fired was plucked from Chevy management, promoted to a corporate job and given a $5,000 raise.

Writing and Discussion Topics

Questions 1–6 address content, critical analysis, personal choices, ethical options, specific discipline, and interdisciplinary alternatives, respectively.

1. Why do you believe that the "fourteenth floor" rejected minor safety improvements on the Corvair?
2. Other than the problems associated with the Corvair, what unethical corporate decisions did DeLorean say GM management made? Did these situations deal with issues of social responsibility or with honesty?
3. If your corporation asked you to do something that you truly believed was socially irresponsible, would you refuse to

do it? If refusal placed your job in jeopardy, how much of a difference would this make in your decision?

4. DeLorean believes that corporate executives are far removed from people who are affected by management decisions. This often allows the executives to make collective immoral decisions with impunity. How does Hobbes's philosophy apply to this situation? Are there checks and balances for an "immoral corporation"?

5. Compare and contrast DeLorean's argument with Friedman's. Cite specific examples where they concur and differ.

6. What is the definition of propaganda? Explain how DeLorean's speech on the first page of this excerpt could fit the definition.

Robert D. Hay and Edmund R. Gray

INTRODUCTION TO SOCIAL
RESPONSIBILITY

◆◆◆

Robert D. Hay is a professor of management at the University of Arkansas. He is widely published in the field of management, having authored nine books. He is a graduate of the University of Oklahoma and Ohio State University.

Edmund R. Gray is professor and chair of the Department of Management at Loyola Marymount University. He is the author of several management textbooks and is a recognized scholar on the subject of management. ◆

It was Jeremy Bentham, late eighteenth century English philosopher, who espoused the social, political, and economic goal of society to be "the greatest happiness for the greatest number." His cardinal principle was written into the Declaration of Independence as "the pursuit of happiness," which became a societal goal of the American colonists. Bentham's principle was also incorporated into the Constitution of the United States in the preamble where the goal was stated "to promote the general welfare."

The economic-political system through which we in America strive to achieve this societal goal emphasizes the economic and political freedom to pursue individual interests. Adam Smith, another English political economist of the late eighteenth century, stated that the best way to achieve social goals was as follows:

> Every individual is continually exerting himself to find out the most advantageous employment for whatever capital he can command. It is his own advantage, indeed, and not that of the society, which he has in view. But the study of his own advantage, naturally, or rather necessarily, leads him to prefer that employment which is most advantageous to the society . . . .
>
> As every individual, therefore, endeavors as much as he can both to employ his capital in the support of domestic industry, and so to direct that industry that its produce may be of the greatest value, every individual necessarily labours to render the annual revenue of the society as great as he can. He generally, indeed, neither intends to promote the public interest, nor knows how much he is promoting it. By preferring the support of domestic to that of foreign industry, he intends only his own security; and by directing that industry in such a manner as its produce may be of the greatest value, he intends only his own gain, and he is in this, as in many other cases, led by an invisible hand to promote an end which was not part of his intention. Nor is it always the worse for the society that it was no part of it. By pursuing his own interest he frequently promotes that of the society more effectually than when he really intends to promote it. I have never known much good done by those who affected to trade for the public good. It

is an affectation, indeed, not very common among merchants, and very few words need be employed in dissuading them from it.[1]

Adam Smith's economic values have had an important influence on American business thinking. As a result, most business people for the first hundred and fifty years of our history embraced the theory that social goals could be achieved by pursuing individual interests.

By 1930 American values were beginning to change from that of the individual owner ethic to that of the group or social ethic. As part of this changing mood, it was felt that Smith's emphasis on owner's interests was too predominant at the expense of other contributors to a business organization. Consequently, a new philosophy of management took shape which stated that the social goals could be achieved by balancing the interests of several groups of people who had an interest in a business. It was stated by Charles H. Percy, then president of Bell and Howell, in the 1950s as follows:

> There are over 64 million gainfully employed people in the United States. One half of these work directly for American corporations, and the other half are vitally affected by business directly or indirectly. Our entire economy, therefore, is dependent upon the type of business management we have. Business management is therefore in many respects a public trust charged with the responsibility of keeping America economically sound. We at Bell & Howell can best do this by keeping our own company's program on a firm foundation and by having a growing group of management leaders to direct the activities of the company.
>
> Management's role in a free society is, among other things, to prove that the real principles of a free society can work within a business organization.
>
> Our basic objective is the development of individuals. In our own present program we are doing everything conceivable to encourage, guide, and assist, and provide an opportunity to everyone to improve their abilities and skills, thus becoming more valuable to the company and enabling the company to improve the rewards paid to the individual for such additional efforts.

[1] Adam Smith, *Wealth of Nations*, Book IV, Chapter 2 (1776), as quoted in E. Bakke et al., *Unions, Management and the Public* (3d ed; New York: Harcourt, Brace & World, Inc., 1967), p. 22.

Our company has based its entire program for the future on the development of the individual and also upon the building of an outstanding management group. This is why we have emphasized so strongly the supervisory training program recently completed by all Bell & Howell supervisors, and why we are now offering this program to others in the organization training for future management responsibilities.

But a company must also have a creed to which its management is dedicated. I hope that we can all agree to the following:

We believe that our company must develop and produce outstanding products that will perform a great service or fill a need for our customers.

We believe that our business must be run at an adequate profit and that the services and products that we offer must be better than those offered by competitors.

We believe that management must serve employees, stockholders, and customers, but that we cannot serve the interests of any one group at the undue expense of the other two. A proper and fair balance must be preserved.

We believe that our business must provide stability of employment and job security for all those who depend on our company for their livelihood.

We believe that we are failing in our responsibility if our wages are not sufficiently high to not only meet the necessities of life but provide some of the luxuries as well. Wherever possible, we also believe that bonus earning should be paid for performance and output "beyond the call of duty."

We believe that every individual in the company should have an opportunity for advancement and growth with the organization. There should be no dead-end streets any place in an organization.

We believe in the necessity for constantly increasing productivity and output. Higher wages and greater benefits can never be "given" by management. Management can only see that they are paid out when "earned."

We believe in labor-saving machinery. We do not think human beings should perform operations that can be done by mechanical or electronic means. We believe in this because we believe in the human dignity and creative ability of the individual. We are more interested in the intellect, goodwill, initiative, enthusiasm, and cooperativeness of the individual than we are in his muscular energy.

We believe that every person in the company has a right to be treated with the respect and courtesy that is due a human being. It is for this reason that we have individual merit ratings, individual pay increases, job evaluation, and incentive pay; and it is why we keep every individual fully informed—through The Finder, through our annual report, through Family Night, and through individual letters—about the present program of the company and also about our future objectives.

We believe that our business must be conducted with the utmost integrity. We may fight the principle of confiscatory taxation, but we will pay our full share. We will observe every governmental law and regulation, local, state, and national. We will deal fairly with our customers, we will advertise our product truthfully, and we will make every attempt to maintain a friendly relationship with our competitors while at the same time waging the battle of free competition.

Some business leaders, on the one hand, preach the virtues of the free enterprise, democratic system and, on the other hand, run their own business in accordance with autocratic principles—all authority stemming from the top with little delegation of responsibility to individuals within the organization. We believe in democracy—in government and in our business.

We hope that every principle we believe in is right and is actually being practiced throughout the company as it affects every individual.[2]

Then in the late 1960s American business leaders began to take another look at the problems of society in light of the goal of "the greatest happiness for the greatest number." How could people be happy if they have to breathe foul air, drink polluted water, live in crowded cities, use very unsafe products, be misled by untruthful advertising, be deprived of a job because of race, and face many other problems? Thus, another philosophy of management emerged. It was voiced by several American business leaders:

Business must learn to loop upon its social responsibilities as inseparable from its economic function. If it fails to do so, it leaves a void that will quickly be filled by others—usually by the

---

[2]"Management Creeds and Philosophies," *American Management Association Research Report No. 32.*

government. (George Champion, Chase National Bank, 1966.)

I believe there is one basic principle that needs to be emphasized more than ever before. It is the recognition that business is successful in the long term only when it is directed toward the needs of the society. (Robert F. Hansberger, Boise Cascade, 1971.)

The actions of the great corporations have so profound an influence that the public has come to judge them not only by their profit-making record, but by the contribution of their work to society as a whole. Under a political democracy such as ours, if the corporation fails to perceive itself and govern its action in essentially the same manner as the public at large, it may find itself in serious trouble. (Louis B. Lundborg, Bank of America, 1971.)

With these remarks we can see that there has been a shift in managerial emphasis from owners' interests to group interests, and finally, to society's interests. Managers of some American businesses have come to recognize that they have a social responsibility.

Historical Perspective of Social Responsibility

The concept of the social responsibility of business managers has in recent years become a popular subject of discussion and debate within both business and academic circles. Although the term itself is of relatively recent origin, the underlying concept has existed as long as there have been business organizations. It rests on the logical assumption that because the firm is a creation of society, it has a responsibility to aid in the accomplishment of society's goals. In the United States concepts of social responsibility have moved from three distinct phases which may be labeled Phases I, II, and III.[3]

Phase I—Profit Maximizing Management
The Phase I concept was based on the belief that business managers have but one single objective—to maximize profits. The only constraint on this pursuit was the legal framework within which the firm operated. The origin of this view may be found in Adam Smith's *Wealth of Nations*. As previously noted, Smith believed that individual business people

acting in their own selfish interest would be guided by an "invisible hand" to promote the public good. In other words, the individual's drive for maximum profits and the regulation of the competitive marketplace would interact to create the greatest aggregate wealth for a nation and therefore the maximum public good. In the United States this view was universally accepted throughout the nineteenth century and the early part of the twentieth century. Its acceptance rested not only on economic logic but also on the goals and values of society.

America in the nineteenth and first half of the twentieth centuries was a society of economic scarcity; therefore, economic growth and the accumulation of aggregate wealth were primary goals. The business system with its emphasis on maximum profit was seen as a vehicle for eliminating economic scarcity. In the process employee abuses such as child labor, starvation wages, and unsafe working conditions could be tolerated. No questions were raised with regard to using up the natural resources and polluting streams and land. Nor was anyone really concerned about urban problems, unethical advertising, unsafe products, and poverty problems of minority groups.

The profit maximization view of social responsibility also complemented the Calvinistic philosophy which pervaded nineteenth and twentieth century American thinking. Calvinism stressed that the road to salvation was through hard work and the accumulation of wealth. It then logically followed that a business person could demonstrate diligence (and thus godliness) and accumulate a maximum amount of wealth by adhering to the discipline of profit maximization.

Phase II—Trusteeship Management
Phase II, which may be labeled the "trusteeship" concept, emerged in the 1920s and 30s. It resulted from structural changes in both business institutions and in society. According to this concept, corporate managers were responsible not simply for maximizing the stockholders' wealth but rather for maintaining an equitable balance among the competing claims of customers, employees, suppliers, creditors, and the community. In this view the manager was seen as a "trustee" for the various contributor groups to the firm rather than simply an agent of the owners.[4]

---

[3]A great portion of the discussion which follows is drawn from Robert D. Hay and Edmund R. Gray, "Social Responsibilities of Business Managers," *Academy of Management Journal* (March, 1974).

---

[4]Howard R. Bowen and William T. Greenwood, "Business Management: A Profession," *Issues in Business and Society* (2d ed.; Boston: Houghton-Mifflin, 1971).

The two structural trends largely responsible for the emergence of this newer view of social responsibility were: (1) the increasing diffusion of ownership of the shares of American corporations, and (2) the development of a pluralistic society. The extent of the diffusion of stock ownership may be highlighted by the fact that by the early 1930s the largest stockholders in corporations such as American Telephone and Telegraph, United States Steel, and the Pennsylvania Railroad owned less than one percent of the total shares outstanding of these companies.[5] Similar dispersion of stock ownership existed in most other large corporations. In such situations management typically was firmly in control of the corporation. Except in rare circumstances, the top executives were able to perpetuate themselves in office through the proxy mechanism. If an individual shareholder was not satisfied with the performance of the firm, there was little recourse other than to sell the stock. Hence, although the stockholder's legal position was that of an owner—and thus a principal-agent relationship existed between the stockholder and the managers—the stockholder's actual position was more akin to bondholders and other creditors of the firm. Given such a situation it was only natural to ask, "To whom is management responsible?" The "trusteeship" concept provided an answer. Management was responsible to all the contributors to the firm—that is, stockholders, workers, customers, suppliers, creditors, and the community.

The emergence of a largely pluralistic society reinforced the logic of the "trusteeship" concept. A pluralistic society has been defined as "one which has many semi-autonomous and autonomous groups through which power is diffused. No one group has overwhelming power over all others, and each has direct or indirect impact on all others."[6] From the perspective of business firms this translated into the fact that exogenous groups had considerable impact upon and influence over them. In the 1930s the major groups exerting significant pressure on business were labor unions and the federal government. Today the list has grown to include numerous minority, environmental, and consumer groups among

others. Clearly, one logical approach to such a situation is to consider that the firm has a responsibility to each interested group and that management's task is to reconcile and balance the claims of the various groups.

Phase III—"Quality of Life" Management

Phase III, which may be called the "quality of life" concept of social responsibility, has become popular in recent years.[7] The primary reason for the emergence of this concept is the very significant metamorphosis in societal goals which this nation is experiencing. Up to the middle part of this century, society's principal goal was to raise the standard of living of the American people, which could be achieved by producing more goods and services. The fact that the U.S. had become the wealthiest nation in the world was testimony to the success of business in meeting this expectation.

In this process, however, the U.S. has become what John Kenneth Galbraith calls an "affluent society" in which the aggregate scarcity of basic goods and services is no longer the fundamental problem.[8] Other social problems have developed as direct and indirect results of economic success. Thus, there are pockets of poverty in a nation of plenty, deteriorating cities, air and water pollution, defacement of the landscape, and a disregard for consumers to mention only a few of the prominent social problems. The mood of the country seems to be that things have gotten out of balance—the economic abundance in the midst of a declining social and physical environment does not make sense. As a result, a new set of national priorities which stress the "Quality of life" appear to be emerging.

Concomitant with the new priorities, societal consensus seems to be demanding that business, with its technological and managerial skills and its financial resources, assume broader responsibilities—responsibilities that extend beyond the traditional economic realm of the Phase I concept or the mere balancing of the competing demands of the sundry

---

[5]Adolph A. Berle and Gardiner C. Means, *The Modern Corporation and Private Property* (New York: Macmillan, 1932), p. 47.

[6]George A. Steiner, *Business and Society* (New York: Random House, 1971), pp. 70–71.

[7]Committee for Economic Development, *Social Responsibilities of Business Corporations* (New York: Research and Business Policy Committee, CED, June, 1971).

[8]John K. Galbraith, *The Affluent Society* (Boston: Houghton Mifflin Company, 1958), Chapter 1. With emerging energy and raw material shortages we may be once again in the process of a fundamental economic change.

contributors and pressure groups of the Phase II concept. The socially responsible firm under Phase III reasoning is one that becomes deeply involved in the solution of society's major problems.

Personal Values of the Three Styles of Managers

Values are the beliefs and attitudes which form one's frame of reference and help to determine the behavior which an individual displays. All managers have a set of values which affect their decisions, but the values are not the same for each manager; however, once values are ingrained in a manager, they do not change except over a period of time. It is possible to group these values into a general pattern of behavior which characterizes three styles of managers—the profit-maximizing style, the trusteeship style, and the "quality of life" style of management.

Phase I Managers

Phase I, profit-maximizing managers have a personal set of values which reflects their economic thinking. They believe that raw self-interest should prevail in society, and their values dictate that "What's good for me is good for my country." Therefore, Phase I managers rationalize that making as much profit as is possible would be good for society. They make every effort to become as efficient as possible and to make as much money as they can. To them money and wealth are the most important goals of their lives.

In the pursuit of maximum profit the actions of Phase I managers toward customers are reflected in a caveat emptor philosophy. "Let the buyer beware" characterizes decisions and actions in dealing with customers. They are not necessarily concerned with product quality or safety, or with sufficient and/or truthful information about products and services. A profit-maximizing manager's view toward employees can be stated as, "Labor is a commodity to be bought and sold in the marketplace." Thus, chief accountability lies with the owners of the business, and usually the Phase I manager is the owner or part owner of the organization.

To profit maximizers technology is very important. Machines and equipment rank high on their scale of values. Therefore, materialism characterizes their philosophy.

Social values do not predominate the thinking of Phase I managers. In fact, they believe that employee problems should be left at home. Economics should be separate from societal or family concerns. A Phase I manager's leadership style is one of the rugged individualist—"I'm my own boss, and I'll manage my business as I please." Values about minority groups dictate that such groups are inferior, so they must be treated accordingly.

Political values are based on the doctrine of laissez-faire. "That government is best which governs the least" characterizes the thinking of Phase I managers. As a result, anything dealing with politicians and governments is foreign and distasteful to them.

Their beliefs about the environment can be stated, "The natural environment controls one's destiny; therefore, use it to protect your interests before it destroys you. Don't worry about the physical environment because there are plenty of natural resources which you can use."

Aesthetic values to the profit maximizer are minimal. In fact, Phase I managers would say, "Aesthetic values? What are they?" They have very little concern for the arts and cultural aspects of life. They hold musicians, artists, entertainers, and social scientists in low regard.

The values that a profit-maximizing manager holds were commonly accepted in the economic textbooks of the 1800s and early 1900s although they obviously did not apply to all managers of those times. It is easy to see how they conflict with the values of the other two styles of management.

Phase II Managers

Phase II, trusteeship managers have a somewhat different set of values. They recognize that self-interest plays a large role in their actions, but they also recognize the interests of those people who contribute to the organization—the customers, employees, suppliers, owners, creditors, government, and community. In other words, they operate with self-interest plus the interests of other groups. They believe that "What is good for my company is good for the country." They balance profits of the owners and the organization with wages for employees, taxes for the government, interest for the creditors, and so forth. Money is important to them but so are people, because their values tell them that satisfying people's needs is a better goal than just making money.

In balancing the needs of the various contributors to the organization, Phase II managers deal with customers as the chief providers of revenue to the firm. Their values tell them not to cheat the customers because cheating is not good for the firm.

They are concerned with providing sufficient quantities of goods as well as sufficient quality for customer satisfaction. They view employees as having certain rights which must be recognized and that employees are more than mere commodities to be traded in the marketplace. Their accountability as managers is to owners as well as to customers, employees, suppliers, creditors, government, and the community.

To the trusteeship-style manager, technology is important, but so are people. Innovation of technology is to be commended because new machines, equipment, and products are useful to people to create a high standard of living. Materialism is important, but so is humanism.

The social values held by trusteeship managers are more liberal than those held by profit maximizers. They recognize that employees have several needs beyond their economic needs. Employees have a desire for security and a sense of belonging as well as recognition. Phase II managers see themselves as individualists, but they also appreciate the value of group participation in managing the business. They view minority groups as having their place in society. But, a trusteeship manager would add: "Their place is usually inferior to mine; they are usually not qualified to hold their jobs but that's not my fault."

The political values of Phase II managers are reflected in recognizing that government and politics are important, but they view government and politics as necessary evils. They distrust both, recognizing that government serves as a threat to their existence if their firms do not live up to the laws passed since the 1930s.

The environmental beliefs of trusteeship managers are stated as follows: "People can control and manipulate their environment. Therefore, let them do it for their own benefit and incidentally for society's benefit."

Aesthetic values are all right to the trusteeship manager, but "they are not for our firm although someone has to support the arts and cultural values."

Phase III Managers

In contrast to profit maximizers and trustee managers, "quality of life" managers believe in enlightened self-interest. They agree that selfishness and group interests are important, but that society's interests are also important in making decisions. "What's good for society is good for our company"

is their opinion. They agree that profit is essential for the firm, but that profit in and of itself is not the end objective of the firm. As far as money and wealth are concerned, their set of values tell them that money is important but people are more important than money.

In sharp contrast to *caveat emptor* in dealings with customers, the philosophy of Phase III managers is *caveat venditor*, that is, let the seller beware. The company should bear the responsibility for producing and distributing products and services in sufficient quantities at the right time and place with the necessary quality, information, and services necessary to satisfy customers' needs. Their views about employees are to recognize the dignity of each, not treating them as a commodity to be bought and sold. Their accountability as managers is to the owners, to the other contributors of the business, and to society in general.

Technological values are important but people are held in higher esteem than machines, equipment, computers, and esoteric products. A "quality of life" manager is a humanist rather than a materialist.

The social values of "quality of life" managers dictate that a person cannot be separated into an economic being or family being. Their philosophy is, "We hire the whole person including any problems that person might have." Phase III managers recognize that group participation rather than rugged individualism is a determining factor in an organization's success. Their values about minority groups are different from the other managers. Their view is that "A member of a minority group needs support and guidance like any other person."

The political values of "quality of life" managers dictate that government and politicians are necessary contributors to a quality of life. Rather than resisting government, they believe that business and government must cooperate to solve society's problems.

Their environmental beliefs are stated as, "A person must preserve the environment, not for the environment's sake alone, but for the benefit of people who want to lead a quality life."

As far as aesthetic values are concerned, Phase III managers recognize that the arts and cultural values reflect the lives of people whom they hold in high regard. Their actions support aesthetic values by committing resources to their preservation and presentation.

FIGURE **1**   *Comparison of Managerial Values*

Phase I Profit Maximizing Management	Phase II Trusteeship Management	Phase III "Quality of Life" Management
	Economic Values	
1) Raw self-interest	1) Self-interest 2) Contributor's interests	1) Enlightened self-interest 2) Contributor's interests 3) Society's interests
"What's good for me is good for my country."	"What's good for my company is good for our country."	"What's good for society is good for our company."
Profit maximizer	Profit satisfier	Profit is necessary, but . . .
Money and wealth are most important.	Money is important but so are people.	People are more important than money.
"Let the buyer beware." *(caveat emptor)*	"Let's not cheat the customer."	"Let the seller beware." *(caveat venditor)*
"Labor is a commodity to be bought and sold."	"Labor has certain rights which must be recognized."	"Employee dignity must be satisfied."
Accountability of management is to the owners.	Accountability of management is to the owners *and* customers, employees, suppliers, and other contributors.	Accountability of management is to the owners, contributors, and society.
	Technological Values	
Technology is very important.	Technology is important but so are people.	People are more important than technology.
	Social Values	
"Employee personal problems must be left at home."	"We recognize that employees have needs beyond their economic needs."	"We hire the whole person."
"I'm a rugged individualist, and I'll manage the business as I please."	"I am an individualist, but I recognize the value of group participation."	"Group participation is fundamental to our success."
"Minority groups are inferior. They must be treated accordingly."	"Minority groups have their place in society but their place is inferior to mine."	"Minority groups are people like you and I are."
	Environmental Values	
"The natural environment controls one's destiny."	"One can control and manipulate one's environment."	"One must preserve the environment."
	Political Values	
"That government is best which governs least."	"Government is a necessary evil."	"Business and government must cooperate to solve society's problems."
	Aesthetic Values	
"Aesthetic values? What are they?"	"Aesthetic values are okay, but not for us."	"We must preserve our aesthetic values and we'll do our part."

Comparison of Managerial Values

The contrast among the three sets of values creates an awareness of the differing ideologies of each managerial decision maker (see Figure 1). A managerial set of values is important because it determines what decisions are made. These values are the norms for managerial statements of an organization's objectives. They determine the managerial policies that an organization follows in trying to accomplish these objectives. They determine the strategies and tactics which are used. Values become the standards upon which a manager judges whether some action is right or wrong. They are the filters which a manager unconsciously uses to sort out one alternative versus another. And finally, values determine the tones of a manager's action.

Enlightened Self-Interest

It was stated that enlightened self-interest is an important value held by the Phase III, "quality of life" manager. Beyond this, it is the major intellectual concept for convincing managers who lean toward profit-maximizing values that they must be aware of and consider the needs and goals of society in their internal decision processes. *Enlightened self-interest* may be broadly described as an action by a firm which cannot be clearly justified on the basis of cost and revenue projections but is taken because it is believed to be in the best interests of the firm in the long run. It has both positive and negative dimensions.

On the positive side one can reason that anything a firm does to produce a better environment for the society will be of at least long-range benefit to it. This proposition was established in the famous 1953 A. P. Smith case in which the New Jersey Superior Court upheld the right of a company to contribute funds to a university. Since industry gets the bulk of its executive and technical talent from American universities, contributing funds to universities represents a wise investment policy. Analogous reasoning can be applied to expenditures for urban rehabilitation, health care, vocational training, cultural facilities, and many other problem areas.[9] The

---

[9]It should be noted that the federal corporation income tax law encourages corporate giving for educational, charitable, scientific, and religious purposes by allowing corporations to deduct contributions up to 5 percent of their taxable income. Gifts by partnerships and proprietorships are governed by individual income tax laws.

improvement of internal opportunities and the job environment represents a more traditional expression of this philosophy.

Publicized social investments, moreover, tend to improve the firm's public image, which may result in direct but difficult-to-measure economic benefits in several ways. First, social investments can be viewed as a form of institutional advertising to get the firm's name known to the public and thereby to improve its long-run sales potential. Second, since so many of today's college students are strongly idealistic and looking for opportunities to make social contributions, a firm with a known social action program will have an advantage in attracting the best young talent. Finally, these investments tend to give the company's employees a pride in the company and a feeling that it is doing something worthwhile. Hopefully, this will result in higher morale and greater efficiency.

Where governmental incentives apply, the possibilities for enlightened self-interest become even clearer. For example, private enterprise has become involved in ghetto rehabilitation programs through incentives of low-interest rate loans from the Federal Housing Authority and government-guaranteed rent supplements. Some business firms have participated in the federal JOBS (Job Opportunities in the Business Sector) program because the government will reimburse them for the extraordinary costs involved in training disadvantaged persons.

Finally, it should be noted that interest in solving social problems may lead to profitable market opportunities. The growing market for pollution abatement equipment is an obvious example of this. The development of new types of low-income housing represents another potentially rich market.

Ignoring the doctrine of enlightened self-interest may result in negative repercussions. Insensitivity to social needs sooner or later leads to additional governmental regulation of business. For example, in the early part of this century, worker's compensation laws were enacted as a direct result of employers' indifference to worker safety. A current illustration is the stringent antipollution measures which have come about because of industry's reluctance or inability to clean up the environment.

Social involvement programs may also avert harassment by social action groups and other critics. The Wonder Bread Bakery plant in Boston, for example, became much more sensitive to minority employment problems as a result of a threatened boycott of its products in minority areas. At a less dramatic level, harassment can be expensive in terms of an executive's time. One executive has been quoted as saying, "I can think of few more foolish expenditures of salary dollars than having the corporate secretary or public relations officer, not to mention the chairman of the board, spending hours debating a second-year law student who owns three shares."[10]

It is also conceivable that social insensitivity may result in lower stock prices for the firm. In recent years several investment funds have been formed which have the express policy of not investing in companies which have poor records in the social area (in other words, they blacklist firms considered socially irresponsible). Moreover, churches, universities, and charitable foundations are increasingly examining the social performance of the firms in which they invest. The potential of lower stock prices may provide a powerful negative incentive to corporate managers in two ways: (1) lower stock prices increase the cost of raising capital—a principal economic need of the firm; and (2) if managers own stock in the firm, its lower price will result in a reduction in their personal wealth.

The Current State of Social Responsibility of Management

The concept of social responsibility has gone through the three distinct phases described above—each corresponding to a descriptive set of managerial values. Each new phase has not merely replaced the earlier phase but rather has been superimposed on it. Thus, a modern view of social responsibility would to some degree incorporate essential parts of all three phases of the concept. It would encompass not only a deep commitment to social problems, but also an understanding of the firm's responsibility to its contributors and, most importantly, a realistic comprehension of the need for profit as an essential prerequisite for operating at higher levels of social responsibility.

In today's business world and academic community there are people who ascribe to all three phases of the social responsibility concept. One rather vocal group follows the logic of Milton Friedman who believes that Phase I logic still prevails.[11] He feels that

a corporate manager is an agent of the stockholders and any diversion of resources from the task of maximizing stockholder wealth amounts to spending the stockholders' money without their consent. Moreover, he argues that government, not business, is the institution best suited for solving social problems. Although this position is vigorously supported by its proponents, in practice it often breaks down because of the extreme difficulty in drawing a line between spending the stockholders' money for charity and spending it in the "enlightened self-interest" of the firm.

Probably the majority of business managers today adhere to a Phase II concept of social responsibility. These individuals understand the pluralistic nature of our society and are generally committed to being equitable in dealing with the various contributors to the firm and concerned outside pressure groups. Such business people emphasize good wages, good working conditions, and fairness and forthrightness in dealing with their customers and suppliers.

A growing number of academicians and business executives, however, appear to be accepting the Phase III concept of social responsibility. As a result, we have witnessed a number of our largest corporations such as IBM, Chase Manhattan Bank, Xerox, Eli Lilly, and Coca Cola becoming involved in major social action programs.

It must not be forgotten, however, that managers are constrained in their actions by the economic needs of their companies. Profit and positive cash flow are still the *sine qua non* for all firms. Thus, the top management of a large profitable corporation has much greater latitude in the social area than does the manager of a small marginal operation. Small firms can make a contribution to a better quality of life through social action programs also, but it should be stressed that no executive can afford to jeopardize a firm's financial position in the name of social involvement.

Boise Cascade Corporation, for example, promoted a minority enterprise in the heavy construction industry. The venture resulted in a pretax loss of approximately $40 million to Boise Cascade. As a result, the corporation's stock price plummeted 60 points and, undoubtedly, there was much serious soul searching within the organization.

The point we are trying to emphasize here is that a business firm is still fundamentally an economic entity and must be concerned first with its own economic well-being. It is true that the public does expect business to become socially involved but not

---

[10]"The First Attempts at a Corporate 'Social Audit'," *Business Week* (September 23, 1972), pp. 88–92.

[11] Milton Friedman, "The Social Responsibility of Business Is to Increase Its Profits," *The New York Times Magazine* (September 13, 1970), pp. 122–126.

at the expense of its primary mission—making a profit and thereby contributing to a healthy and vigorous economy.

A Socially Responsible Business Organization

What is meant by a socially responsible management of a business organization? The managers of such an organization have to agree to three actions. First, they must have an awareness of the firm's obligations to solve some of the problems facing society. This awareness of social problems must exist in the firm's relationships with its customers, owners, employees, suppliers, creditors, management, government, community, and society in general. Second, there must be a willingness on the part of the firm to help solve some of these social problems. Obviously, not all the problems of society can be solved by business organizations, but the firm must be willing to tackle some of society's problems. Third, and more specifically, it must attempt to make decisions and actually commit resources of various kinds in some of the following problem areas:

1. Pollution problems—air, water, solid waste, land, noise.
2. Poverty and discrimination problems— minority groups and women, black capitalism, urban problems.
3. Consumerism—product safety, misleading advertising, consumer complaints.
4. Other social problem areas.

Conclusion

Currently there are three concepts in business and academic circles concerning business management's social responsibility—profit maximization, trusteeship, and the "quality of life" concepts. Disagreement among those who study, teach, and practice business has contributed greatly to public confusion and disenchantment concerning the role of business in today's society. Despite the confusion and disenchantment concerning the role of business, the public views business as the most productive and efficient institution in society and therefore regards business as a major resource in the struggle to solve our great social problems. Since business as an institution exists only because it is sanctioned by society, it is inevitable that business managers will come

in line with society's expectations. Hence, the modern concept (Phase III) of the social responsibility of business will become more and more accepted by business people in the future.

In conclusion it should be reemphasized that the United States has entered a new era where business is faced with a new and more complex set of public expectations. In terms of enlightened self-interest the responsible manager must be sensitive to society's needs in making business decisions; at the same time the responsibility for making profit has not been reduced correspondingly. As a result, the manager's job has become exceedingly more difficult. However, it must be done, and done well, if the U.S. business system is to survive.

Writing and Discussion Topics

Questions 1–6 address content, critical analysis, personal choices, ethical options, specific discipline, and interdisciplinary alternatives, respectively.

1. Review briefly the theme of corporate responsibility in American economic history over the past two centuries. At what times in this history were profits more important than ethics?
2. Should corporate executives, as agents of stockholders, consider the interests of customers and employees when making decisions? What is the historical pattern on this issue?
3. What are the most impressive historical changes in the capitalistic system? Why are these changes meaningful?
4. What ethical perspective seemed to dominate business at the turn of the century? How has this changed today?
5. Hay and Gray use a systematic method of dividing history into stages. What benefits does this procedure have over an elementary chronology of historical circumstances? What dangers may be intrinsic to this system?
6. Using examples from history, Hay and Gray charge that Friedman's view of business is old-fashioned. How do you respond to this charge? How would Friedman answer their assessment?

Kenneth E. Goodpaster and John B. Matthews, Jr.

CAN A CORPORATION HAVE A
CONSCIENCE?

◆◆◆

K enneth Edwin Goodpaster is a lecturer in philosophy at the
University of St. Thomas in St. Paul, Minnesota. He is a widely
published scholar on the topic of corporate values and ethics. He has
served as a consultant to the National Conference of Catholic Bishops.
   John Bowers Matthews, Jr. is the Joseph C. Wilson Professor in the
Harvard Graduate School of Business Administration. He is a graduate
of Bowdoin College and Harvard University. He has published
extensively in the area of corporate ethics. ◆

During the severe racial tensions of the 1960s, Southern Steel Company (actual case, disguised name) faced considerable pressure from government and the press to explain and modify its policies regarding discrimination both within its plants and in the major city where it was located. SSC was the largest employer in the area (it had nearly 15,000 workers, one-third of whom were black) and had made great strides toward removing barriers to equal job opportunity in its several plants. In addition, its top executives (especially its chief executive officer, James Weston) had distinguished themselves as private citizens for years in community programs for black housing, education, and small business as well as in attempts at desegregating all-white police and local government organizations.

SSC drew the line, however, at using its substantial economic influence in the local area to advance the cause of the civil rights movement by pressuring banks, suppliers, and the local government:

"As individuals we can exercise what influence we may have as citizens," James Weston said, "but for a corporation to attempt to exert any kind of economic compulsion to achieve a particular end in a social area seems to me to be quite beyond what a corporation should do and quite beyond what a corporation can do. I believe that while government may seek to compel social reforms, any attempt by a private organization like SSC to impose its views, its beliefs, and its will upon the community would be repugnant to our American constitutional concepts and that appropriate steps to correct this abuse of corporate power would be universally demanded by public opinion."

Weston could have been speaking in the early 1980s on any issue that corporations around the United States now face. Instead of social justice, his theme might be environmental protection, product safety, marketing practice, or international bribery. His statement for SSC raises the important issue of corporate responsibility. Can a corporation have a conscience?

Weston apparently felt comfortable saying it need not. The responsibilities of ordinary persons and of "artificial persons" like corporations are, in his view, separate. Persons' responsibilities go beyond those of corporations. Persons, he seems to have believed, ought to care not only about themselves but also about the dignity and well-being of those around

them—ought not only to care but also to act. Organizations, he evidently thought, are creatures of, and to a degree prisoners of, the systems of economic incentive and political sanction that give them reality and therefore should not be expected to display the same moral attributes that we expect of persons.

Others inside business as well as outside share Weston's perception. One influential philosopher—John Ladd—carries Weston's view a step further:

"It is improper to expect organizational conduct to conform to the ordinary principles of morality," he says. "We cannot and must not expect formal organizations, or their representatives acting in their official capacities, to be honest, courageous, considerate, sympathetic, or to have any kind of moral integrity. Such concepts are not in the vocabulary, so to speak, of the organizational language game."[1]

In our opinion, this line of thought represents a tremendous barrier to the development of business ethics both as a field of inquiry and as a practical force in managerial decision making. This is a matter about which executives must be philosophical and philosophers must be practical. A corporation can and should have a conscience. The language of ethics does have a place in the vocabulary of an organization. There need not be and there should not be a disjunction of the sort attributed to SSC's James Weston. Organizational agents such as corporations should be no more and no less morally responsible (rational, self-interested, altruistic) than ordinary persons.

We take this position because we think an analogy holds between the individual and the corporation. If we analyze the concept of moral responsibility as it applies to persons, we find that projecting it to corporations as agents in society is possible.

We maintain that the processes underlying moral responsibility can be defined and are not themselves vague, even though gaining consensus on specific moral norms and decisions is not always easy.

What, then, characterizes the processes underlying the judgment of a person we call morally responsible? Philosopher William K. Frankena offers the following answer:

"A morality is a normative system in which judgments are made, more or less consciously, [out of a] consideration of the effects of actions . . . on the

Reprinted by permission of *Harvard Business Review,* "Corporate Responsibility" by Kenneth E. Goodpaster and John B. Matthews, Jr., January–February 1982. Copyright © 1982 by the President and Fellows of Harvard College; all rights reserved.

[1] See John Ladd, "Morality and the Ideal of Rationality in Formal Organizations," *The Monist,* October 1970, p. 499.

lives of persons . . . including the lives of others besides the person acting. . . . David Hume took a similar position when he argued that what speaks in a moral judgment is a kind of sympathy. . . . A little later, . . . Kant put the matter somewhat better by characterizing morality as the business of respecting persons as ends and not as means or as things. . . ."[2]

Frankena is pointing to two traits, both rooted in a long and diverse philosophical tradition:

1. **Rationality.** Taking a moral point of view includes the features we usually attribute to rational decision making, that is, lack of impulsiveness, care in mapping out alternatives and consequences, clarity about goals and purposes, attention to details of implementation.

2. **Respect.** The moral point of view also includes a special awareness of and concern for the effects of one's decisions and policies on others, special in the sense that it goes beyond the kind of awareness and concern that would ordinarily be part of rationality, that is, beyond seeing others merely as instrumental to accomplishing one's own purposes. This is respect for the lives of others and involves taking their needs and interests seriously, not simply as resources in one's own decision making but as limiting conditions which change the very definition of one's habitat from a self-centered to a shared environment. It is what philosopher Immanuel Kant meant by the "categorical imperative" to treat others as valuable in and for themselves.

It is this feature that permits us to trust the morally responsible person. We know that such a person takes our point of view into account not merely as a useful precaution (as in "honesty is the best policy") but as important in its own right.

These components of moral responsibility are not too vague to be useful. Rationality and respect affect the manner in which a person approaches practical decision making: they affect the way in which the individual processes information and makes choices. A rational but not respectful Bill Jones will not lie to his friends *unless* he is reasonably sure he will not be found out. A rational but not respectful Mary Smith will defend an unjustly treated party *unless* she thinks it may be too costly to herself. A rational *and* respectful decision maker, however, notices—and cares—whether the consequences of his or her conduct lead to injuries or indignities to others.

Two individuals who take "the moral point of view" will not of course always agree on ethical matters, but they do at least have a basis for dialogue.

Projecting Responsibility to Corporations

Now that we have removed some of the vagueness from the notion of moral responsibility as it applies to persons, we can search for a frame of reference in which, by analogy with Bill Jones and Mary Smith, we can meaningfully and appropriately say that corporations are morally responsible. This is the issue reflected in the SSC case.

To deal with it, we must ask two questions: Is it meaningful to apply moral concepts to actors who are not persons but who are instead made up of persons? And even if meaningful, is it advisable to do so?

If a group can act like a person in some ways, then we can expect it to behave like a person in other ways. For one thing, we know that people organized into a group can act as a unit. As business people well know, legally a corporation is considered a unit. To approach unity, a group usually has some sort of internal decision structure, a system of rules that spell out authority relationships and specify the conditions under which certain individuals' actions become official actions of the group.[3]

If we can say that persons act responsibly only if they gather information about the impact of their actions on others and use it in making decisions, we can reasonably do the same for organizations. Our proposed frame of reference for thinking about and implementing corporate responsibility aims at spelling out the processes associated with the moral responsibility of individuals and projecting them to the level of organizations. This is similar to, though an inversion of, Plato's famous method in the *Republic*, in which justice in the community is used as a model for justice in the individual.

Hence, corporations that monitor their employment practices and the effects of their production processes and products on the environment and human health show the same kind of rationality and respect that morally responsible individuals do. Thus, attributing actions, strategies, decisions, and moral

[2] See William K. Frankena, *Thinking About Morality* (Ann Arbor: University of Michigan Press, 1980), p. 26.

[3] See Peter French, "The Corporation as a Moral Person," *American Philosophical Quarterly*, July 1979, p. 207.

responsibilities to corporations as entities distinguishable from those who hold offices in them poses no problem.

And when we look about us, we can readily see differences in moral responsibility among corporations in much the same way that we see differences among persons. Some corporations have built features into their management incentive systems, board structures, internal control systems, and research agendas that in a person we would call self-control, integrity, and conscientiousness. Some have institutionalized awareness and concern for consumers, employees, and the rest of the public in ways that others clearly have not.

Evaluating the Idea of Moral Projection

Concepts like moral responsibility not only make sense when applied to organizations but also provide touchstones for designing more effective models than we now have for guiding corporate policy.

Now we can understand what it means to invite SSC as a corporation to be morally responsible both in-house and in its community, but *should* we issue the invitation? Here we turn to the question of advisability. Should we require the organizational agents in our society to have the same moral attributes we require of ourselves?

Our proposal to spell out the processes associated with moral responsibility for individuals and then to project them to their organizational counterparts takes on added meaning when we examine alternative frames of reference for corporate responsibility.

Two frames of reference that compete for the allegiance of people who ponder the question of corporate responsibility are emphatically opposed to this principle of moral projection—what we might refer to as the "invisible hand" view and the "hand of government" view.

The Invisible Hand

The most eloquent spokesman of the first view is Milton Friedman (echoing many philosophers and economists since Adam Smith). According to this pattern of thought, the true and only social responsibilities of business organizations are to make profits and obey the laws. The workings of the free and competitive marketplace will "moralize" corporate behavior quite independently of any attempts to expand or transform decision making via moral projection.

A deliberate amorality in the executive suite is encouraged in the name of systemic morality: the common good is best served when each of us and our economic institutions pursue not the common good or moral purpose, advocates say, but competitive advantage. Morality, responsibility, and conscience reside in the invisible hand of the free market system, not in the hands of the organizations within the system, much less the managers within the organizations.

To be sure, people of this opinion admit, there is a sense in which social or ethical issues can and should enter the corporate mind, but the filtering of such issues is thorough: they go through the screens of custom, public opinion, public relations, and the law. And in any case, self-interest maintains primacy as an objective and a guiding star.

The reaction from this frame of reference to the suggestion that moral judgment be integrated with corporate strategy is clearly negative. Such an integration is seen as inefficient and arrogant, and in the end both an illegitimate use of corporate power and an abuse of the manager's fiduciary role. With respect to our SSC case, advocates of the invisible hand model would vigorously resist efforts, beyond legal requirements, to make SSC right the wrongs of racial injustice. SSC's responsibility would be to make steel of high quality at least cost, to deliver it on time, and to satisfy its customers and stockholders. Justice would not be part of SSC's corporate mandate.

The Hand of Government

Advocates of the second dissenting frame of reference abound, but John Kenneth Galbraith's work has counterpointed Milton Friedman's with insight and style. Under this view of corporate responsibility, corporations are to pursue objectives that are rational and purely economic. The regulatory hands of the law and the political process rather than the invisible hand of the marketplace turns these objectives to the common good.

Again, in this view, it is a system that provides the moral direction for corporate decision making—a system, though, that is guided by political managers, the custodians of the public purpose. In the case of SSC, proponents of this view would look to the state for moral direction and responsible management, both within SSC and in the community. The corporation would have no moral responsibility beyond political and legal obedience.

EXHIBIT   *Three Uses of the Term* Responsible

THE CAUSAL SENSE	"He is responsible for this." Emphasis on holding to account for past actions, causality.
THE RULE-FOLLOWING SENSE	"As a lawyer, he is responsible for defending that client." Emphasis on following social and legal norms.
THE DECISION-MAKING SENSE	"He is a responsible person." Emphasis on an individual's independent judgment."

What is striking is not so much the radical difference between the economic and social philosophies that underlie these two views of the source of corporate responsibility but the conceptual similarities. Both views locate morality, ethics, responsibility, and conscience in the systems of rules and incentives in which the modern corporation finds itself embedded. Both views reject the exercise of independent moral judgment by corporations as actors in society.

Neither view trusts corporate leaders with stewardship over what are often called non-economic values. Both require corporate responsibility to march to the beat of drums outside. In the jargon of moral philosophy, both views press for a rule-centered or a system-centered ethics instead of an agent-centered ethics. In terms of the *Exhibit,* these frames of reference countenance corporate rule-following responsibility for corporations but not corporate decision-making responsibility.

The Hand of Management   To be sure, the two views under discussion differ in that one looks to an invisible moral force in the market while the other looks to a visible moral force in government. But both would advise against a principle of moral projection that permits or encourages corporations to exercise independent, non-economic judgment over matters that face them in their short- and long-term plans and operations.

Accordingly, both would reject a third view of corporate responsibility that seeks to affect the thought processes of the organization itself—a sort of "hand of management" view—since neither seems willing or able to see the engines of profit regulate themselves to the degree that would be implied by taking the principle of moral projection seriously. Cries of

inefficiency and moral imperialism from the right would be matched by cries of insensitivity and illegitimacy from the left, all in the name of preserving us from corporations and managers run morally amok.

Better, critics would say, that moral philosophy be left to philosophers, philanthropists, and politicians than to business leaders. Better that corporate morality be kept to glossy annual reports, where it is safely insulated from policy and performance.

The two conventional frames of reference locate moral restraint in forces external to the person and the corporation. They deny moral reasoning and intent to the corporation in the name of either market competition or society's system of explicit legal constraints and presume that these have a better moral effect than that of rationality and respect.

Although the principle of moral projection, which underwrites the idea of a corporate conscience and patterns it on the thought and feeling processes of the person, is in our view compelling, we must acknowledge that it is neither part of the received wisdom, nor is its advisability beyond question or objection. Indeed, attributing the role of conscience to the corporation seems to carry with it new and disturbing implications for our usual ways of thinking about ethics and business.

Perhaps the best way to clarify and defend this frame of reference is to address the objections to the principle found in the ruled insert. . . . There we see a summary of the criticisms and counterarguments we have heard during hours of discussion with business executives and business school students. We believe that the replies to the objections about a corporation having a conscience are convincing.

Leaving the Double Standard Behind

We have come some distance from our opening reflection on Southern Steel Company and its role in its community. Our proposal—clarified, we hope, through these objections and replies—suggests that it is not sufficient to draw a sharp line between individual's private ideas and efforts and a corporation's institutional efforts but that the latter can and should be built upon the former.

Does this frame of reference give us an unequivocal prescription for the behavior of SSC in its circumstances? No, it does not. Persuasive arguments might be made now and might have been made then that SSC should not have used its considerable economic clout to threaten the community into desegregation. A careful analysis of the realities of the environment might have disclosed that such a course would have been counterproductive, leading to more injustice than it would have alleviated.

The point is that some of the arguments and some of the analyses are or would have been moral arguments, and thereby the ultimate decision that of an ethically responsible organization. The significance of this point can hardly be overstated, for it represents the adoption of a new perspective on corporate policy and a new way of thinking about business ethics. We agree with one authority, who writes that "the business firm, as an organic entity intricately affected by and affecting its environment, is as appropriately adaptive . . . to demands for responsible behavior as for economic service."[4]

The frame of reference here developed does not offer a decision procedure for corporate managers. That has not been our purpose. It does, however, shed light on the conceptual foundations of business ethics by training attention on the corporation as a moral agent in society. Legal systems of rules and incentives are insufficient, even though they may be necessary, as frameworks for corporate responsibility. Taking conceptual cues from the features of moral responsibility normally expected of the person in our opinion deserves practicing managers' serious consideration.

The lack of congruence that James Weston saw between individual and corporate moral responsibility can be, and we think should be, overcome. In this process, what a number of writers have characterized as a double standard—a discrepancy between our personal lives and our lives in organizational settings—might be dampened. The principle of moral projection not only helps us to conceptualize the kinds of demands that we might make of corporations and other organizations but also offers the prospect of harmonizing those demands with the demands that we make of ourselves.

Is a Corporation a Morally Responsible 'Person'?

Objection 1 to the Analogy: Corporations are not persons. They are artificial legal constructions, machines for mobilizing economic investments toward the efficient production of goods and services. We cannot hold a corporation responsible. We can only hold individuals responsible.

Reply: Our frame of reference does not imply that corporations are persons in a literal sense. It simply means that in certain respects concepts and functions normally attributed to persons can also be attributed to organizations made up of persons. Goals, economic values, strategies, and other such personal attributes are often usefully projected to the corporate level by managers and researchers. Why should we not project the functions of conscience in the same way? As for holding corporations responsible, recent criminal prosecutions such as the case of Ford Motor Company and its Pinto gas tanks suggest that society finds the idea both intelligible and useful.

Objection 2:   A corporation cannot be held responsible at the sacrifice of profit. Profitability and financial health have always been and should continue to be the "categorical imperatives" of a business operation.

Reply: We must of course acknowledge the imperatives of survival, stability, and growth when we discuss corporations, as indeed we must acknowledge them when we discuss the life of an individual. Self-sacrifice has been identified with moral responsibility in only the most extreme cases. The pursuit of profit and self-interest need not be pitted against

---

4 See Kenneth R. Andrews, *The Concept of Corporate Strategy*, revised edition (Homewood, Ill.: Dow Jones-Irwin, 1980), p. 99.

the demands of moral responsibility. Moral demands are best viewed as containments—not replacements—for self-interest.

This is not to say that profit maximization never conflicts with morality. But profit maximization conflicts with other managerial values as well. The point is to coordinate imperatives, not deny their validity.

Objection 3:   Corporate executives are not elected representatives of the people, nor are they anointed or appointed as social guardians. They therefore lack the social mandate that a democratic society rightly demands of those who would pursue ethically or socially motivated policies. By keeping corporate policies confined to economic motivations, we keep the power of corporate executives in its proper place.

Reply: The objection betrays an oversimplified view of the relationship between the public and the private sector. Neither private individuals nor private corporations that guide their conduct by ethical or social values beyond the demands of law should be constrained merely because they are not elected to do so. The demands of moral responsibility are independent of the demands of political legitimacy and are in fact presupposed by them.

To be sure, the state and the political process will and must remain the primary mechanisms for protecting the public interest, but one might be forgiven the hope that the political process will not substitute for the moral judgment of the citizenry or other components of society such as corporations.

Objection 4:   Our system of law carefully defines the role of agent or fiduciary and makes corporate managers accountable to shareholders and investors for the use of their assets. Management cannot, in the name of corporate moral responsibility, arrogate to itself the right to manage those assets by partially noneconomic criteria.

Reply: First, it is not so clear that investors insist on purely economic criteria in the management of their assets, especially if some of the shareholders' resolutions and board reforms of the last decade are any indication. For instance, companies doing business in South Africa have had stockholders question their activities, other companies

have instituted audit committees for their boards before such auditing was mandated, and mutual funds for which "socially responsible behavior" is a major investment criterion now exist.

Second, the categories of "shareholder" and "investor" connote wider time spans than do immediate or short-term returns. As a practical matter, considerations of stability and long-term return on investment enlarge the class of principals to which managers bear a fiduciary relationship.

Third, the trust that managers hold does not and never has extended to "any means available" to advance the interests of the principals. Both legal and moral constraints must be understood to qualify that trust—even, perhaps, in the name of a larger trust and a more basic fiduciary relationship to the members of society at large.

Objection 5:   The power, size, and scale of the modern corporation—domestic as well as international—are awesome. To unleash, even partially, such power from the discipline of the marketplace and the narrow or possibly nonexistent moral purpose implicit in that discipline would be socially dangerous. Had SSC acted in the community to further racial justice, its purposes might have been admirable, but those purposes could have led to a kind of moral imperialism or worse. Suppose SSC had thrown its power behind the Ku Klux Klan.

Reply: This is a very real and important objection. What seems not to be appreciated is the fact that power affects when it is used as well as when it is not used. A decision by SSC not to exercise its economic influence according to "non-economic" criteria is inevitably a moral decision and just as inevitably affects the community. The issue in the end is not whether corporations (and other organizations) should be "unleashed" to exert moral force in our society but rather how critically and self-consciously they should choose to do so.

The degree of influence enjoyed by an agent, whether a person or an organization, is not so much a factor recommending moral disengagement as a factor demanding a high level of moral awareness. Imperialism is more to be feared when moral reasoning is absent than when it is present. Nor do we suggest that the "discipline of the marketplace" be diluted; rather, we call for it to be supplemented with the discipline of moral reflection.

Objection 6: The idea of moral projection is a useful device for structuring corporate responsibility only if our understanding of moral responsibility at the level of the person is in some sense richer than our understanding of moral responsibility on the level of the organization as a whole. If we are not clear about individual responsibility, the projection is fruitless.

Reply: The objection is well taken. The challenge offered by the idea of moral projection lies in our capacity to articulate criteria or frameworks of reasoning for the morally responsible person. And though such a challenge is formidable, it is not clear that it cannot be met, at least with sufficient consensus to be useful.

For centuries, the study and criticism of frameworks have gone on, carried forward by many disciplines, including psychology, the social sciences, and philosophy. And though it would be a mistake to suggest that any single framework (much less a decision mechanism) has emerged as the right one, it is true that recurrent patterns are discernible and well enough defined to structure moral discussion.

In the body of the article, we spoke of rationality and respect as components of individual responsibility. Further analysis of these components would translate them into social costs and benefits, justice in the distribution of goods and services, basic rights and duties, and fidelity to contracts. The view that pluralism in our society has undercut all possibility of moral agreement is anything but self-evident. Sincere moral disagreement is, of course, inevitable and not clearly lamentable. But a process and a vocabulary for articulating such values as we share is no small step forward when compared with the alternatives. Perhaps in our exploration of the moral projection we might make some surprising and even reassuring discoveries about ourselves.

Objection 7: Why is it necessary to project moral responsibility to the level of the organization? Isn't the task of defining corporate responsibility and business ethics sufficiently discharged if we clarify the responsibilities of men and women in business as individuals? Doesn't ethics finally rest on the honesty and integrity of the individuals in the business world?

Reply: Yes and no. Yes, in the sense that the control of large organizations does finally rest in the hands of managers, of men and women. No, in the sense that what is being controlled is a cooperative system for a cooperative purpose. The projection of responsibility to the organization is simply an acknowledgment of the fact that the whole is more than the sum of its parts. Many intelligent people do not an intelligent organization make. Intelligence needs to be structured, organized, divided, and recombined in complex processes for complex purposes.

Studies of management have long shown that the attributes, successes, and failures of organizations are phenomena that emerge from the coordination of person's attributes and that explanations of such phenomena require categories of analysis and description beyond the level of the individual. Moral responsibility is an attribute that can manifest itself in organizations as surely as competence or efficiency.

Objection 8: Is the frame of reference here proposed intended to replace or undercut the relevance of the "invisible hand" and the "government hand" views, which depend on external controls?

Reply: No. Just as regulation and economic competition are not substitutes for corporate responsibility, so corporate responsibility is not a substitute for law and the market. The imperatives of ethics cannot be relied on—nor have they ever been relied on—without a context of external sanctions. And this is true as much for individuals as for organizations.

This frame of reference takes us beneath, but not beyond, the realm of external systems of rules and incentives and into the thought processes that interpret and respond to the corporation's environment. Morality is more than merely part of that environment. It aims at the projection of conscience, not the enthronement of it in either the state or the competitive process.

The rise of the modern large corporation and the concomitant rise of the professional manager demand a conceptual framework in which these phenomena can be accommodated to moral thought. The principle of moral projection furthers such accommodation by recognizing a new level of agency in society and thus a new level of responsibility.

Objection 9: Corporations have always taken the interests of those outside the corporation into account in the sense that customer relations and public relations generally are an integral part of rational economic decision making. Market signals and social signals that filter through the market mechanism inevitably represent the interests of parties affected by the behavior of the company. What, then, is the point of adding respect to rationality?

Reply: Representing the affected parties solely as economic variables in the environment of the company is treating them as means or resources and not as ends in themselves. It implies that the only voice which affected parties should have in organizational decision making is that of potential buyers, sellers, regulators, or boycotters. Besides, many affected parties may not occupy such roles, and those who do may not be able to signal the organization with messages that effectively represent their stakes in its actions.

To be sure, classical economic theory would have us believe that perfect competition in free markets (with modest adjustments from the state) will result in all relevant signals being "heard," but the abstractions from reality implicit in such theory make it insufficient as a frame of reference for moral responsibility. In a world in which strict self-interest was congruent with the common good, moral responsibility might be unnecessary. We do not, alas, live in such a world.

The element of respect in our analysis of responsibility plays an essential role in ensuring the recognition of unrepresented or under-represented voices in the decision making of organizations as agents. Showing respect for persons as ends and not mere means to organizational purposes is central to the concept of corporate moral responsibility.

Writing and Discussion Topics

Questions 1–6 address content, critical analysis, personal choices, ethical options, specific discipline, and interdisciplinary alternatives, respectively.

1. How does a conscience reside in an organization, according to Goodpaster and Matthews?
2. How do these authors define corporate responsibility and social responsibility?
3. Southern Steel Company executives were criticized for not promoting the social good of their community even though as individuals they were praised for their gifts to society. Do you agree with SSC's behavior? How would you act in a similar situation?
4. What does the term "moral projection" mean? What part of the authors' argument is based on this term?
5. What are some moral differences between corporations and individual human beings? Is it feasible to discern logical problems in the authors' analogy and still accept it?
6. This article refers to a "double standard." What is it and how do the authors believe it can be corrected? How would this reform undermine Friedman's philosophy?

Melvin Anshen

CHANGING THE SOCIAL CONTRACT:
A ROLE FOR BUSINESS
◆◆◆

M*elvin Anshen is professor emeritus of the Graduate School of Business at Columbia University. Before coming to Columbia, he taught business at Indiana University, Carnegie Institute of Technology, and worked on wartime production controls in the Franklin D. Roosevelt administration. Two of his books are* Managing the Socially Responsible Corporation *and* Corporate Strategies for Social Performance. ◆

Among the problems confronting top corporate officers none is more disturbing than the demand that they modify or abandon their traditional responsibility to devote their best talent and energy to the management of resources with the goal of maximizing the return of the owners' investment.

This demand takes many forms. It may appear as pressure:

> to withhold price increases to cover rising costs;
> to give special financial support to black ghetto properties and businesses;
> to provide special training and jobs for the hard-core unemployed;
> to invest in equipment designed to minimize environmental contamination by controlling, scrubbing or eliminating industrial process discharges into air or water;
> to contribute generously to the support of charitable, educational and artistic organizations and activities;
> to refuse to solicit or accept defense and defense-related contracts;
> to avoid or dispose of investments in countries where racial or political policies and practices offend elements of the citizenry;
> to provide for "public" or "consumer" representation on boards of directors;
> to make executives available to serve without compensation on public boards or other non-business assignments.

The common element in all these pressures is their departure from, even contradiction of, the economic considerations which have been regarded as appropriate criteria for determining the allocation and use of private resources. They challenge the thesis that decisions taken with a view to maximizing private profit also maximize public benefits. They deny the working of Adam Smith's "invisible hand."

This cluster of pressures is not limited to alleged deficiencies in the traditional elements of management decision making. It also raises fundamental questions about the intellectual ability of business managers—reflecting their education, experience and norms of behavior—to respond adaptively and creatively to new goals, new criteria for administering resources, new measures of performance. . . .

From Melvin Ashen, "Changing the Social Contract: A Role for Business," *Columbia Journal of World Business,* Vol. 5, No. 6. Reprinted with the permission of the *Columbia Journal of World Business,* copyright 1970.

One way of comprehending the whole development is to view it as an emerging demand for a new set of relationships among business, government, non-economic organizations and individuals. Some such set of relationships, of changing character and composition, has existed throughout recorded history. Without some implicit and broadly accepted design for living together, man's existence with his fellow men would be chaotic beyond endurance.

Philosophers and political theorists have observed the persistence and the necessity of this organizing concept. They have even coined a useful descriptive phrase for it: "the social contract." . . .

The ultimate determinant of the structure and performance of any society is a set of reciprocal, institutionalized duties and obligations which are broadly accepted by its citizens. The acceptance may be described as an implicit social contract. Without such a contract, not less real or powerful for being implicit, a society would lack cohesiveness, order and continuity. Individuals would be confused about their own behavior and commitments as well as about their appropriate expectations with respect to the behavior and commitments of the private and public institutions which employ them, service them and govern them. . . .

The concept of the implied social contract is an old one in Western civilization. It found early expression in the writings of the Greek philosopher Epictetus. It was central to the intellectual system developed by Thomas Hobbes in the first half of the seventeenth century. Without such an implicit contract, he observed, man faces the terror of anarchy, for the natural condition of man is "solitary, short, brutish and nasty." Hobbes used his concept to rationalize the power of the state to compel obedience to the terms of the implied contract. A few decades later, John Locke converted this view of compulsion as the lever to the view of consent as the lever—the consent of the citizens to a relationship of reciprocal duties and obligations.

In the next century, Jean Jacques Rousseau expanded the idea into an intellectual system in which each member of society entered into an implicit contract with every other member, a contract that defined the norms of human behavior and the terms of exchanges and trade-offs among individuals and organizations, private and public. His view even provided for handling disagreements about ends and means. The implied social contract, he wrote, stipulated that the minority would accept the decisions of the majority, would express its opposition through legitimate channels of dissent, and would yield before proceeding to rebellion. To Rousseau, therefore, the act of rebellion signified not what it appeared to be on the surface—a rebellion against the ends and means favored by the majority—but rather a rejection of the very terms of the contract itself.

Most recently, the fundamental thrust of such a book as John Kenneth Galbraith's *The New Industrial State* challenges the terms of the implicit social contract that defines, among other things, the function and role of private enterprise in today's society, the popular view of the responsibilities and performance of private corporations and the network of reciprocal relationships among corporations, government, and citizens. Galbraith's description of the enterprise system is distorted and incomplete, but his perception of the fundamental contract and its pervasive influence is accurate.

The terms of the historic social contract for private business, now coming under critical attack, are brilliantly clear. They existed for more than a hundred years with only minor modifications. Indeed, they acquired a popular, almost mythic, concept which purported to define a set of institutional arrangements uniquely advantageous for the national well-being, superior to all alternatives. . . .

These contractual terms were an outgrowth of interlaced economic, social and technological considerations in which the economic issues were overwhelmingly dominant. Economic growth, summed in the grand measure of gross national product, was viewed as the source of all progress. The clear assumption was that social progress (including those benefits associated with ideas about the quality of life) was a by-product of economic progress and impossible to achieve without it. Technological advance both fueled economic progress and was fueled by it in a closed, self-generating system.

The engine of economic growth was identified as the drive for profits by unfettered, competitive, private enterprise. Natural and human resources were bought in an open market and were administered in the interest of profit maximization. Constraints were applied only at the margins and were designed either to assure the continuance of the system (as in antitrust legislation and administration) or to protect those who could not protect themselves in the open market (as in legislation prohibiting child labor, assuring labor's right to organize or restraining deliberate injury to consumers). These and similar constraints were "the rules of the game," a suggestive term. The rules protected the game and assured its continuance as a constructive activity.

The implicit social contract stipulated that business could operate freely within the rules. Subject only to the constraints on conduct imposed by the rules, the responsibility of business was to search for and produce profits. In doing this competitively, business yielded benefits for society in the form of products and services wanted by consumers who earned the purchasing power to supply their wants by working at jobs created by business. . . .

The most dramatic element for business in the emerging new contract is a shift in the conceptual relation between economic progress and social progress. Until recently, the primacy of economic growth as the chief engine of civilization was generally not seriously questioned. Some of its unpleasant or wounding by-products were, to be sure, superficially deplored from time to time. But they were accepted by most people as fundamentally inevitable and were appraised as a reasonable price to pay for the benefits of a steadily rising gross national product. As a result, the by-products were rarely studied in depth, their economic and social costs were not measured—indeed, little was done even to develop accounting techniques for tooling such measurement.

Michael Harrington's book, *The Other America,* with its quantitative documentation of the existence of an unacknowledged poor nation within a rich nation, could strike with genuine shock on the mind and conscience of many professional and managerial leaders in public and private organizations. The facts of urban decay and the implications of trends projected into the future were not analyzed and reported in terms that would permit a realistic assessment of their present and future costs. Nor, certainly until the outbreak of mass riots in minority ghettos, was there penetrating consideration of the relation of social disturbance to continued economic progress.

While much remains to be done in scientific research and analysis of the side effects of economic progress, the accumulating formal and informal documentation has begun to influence the set of general ideas that constitute the terms of the contract for business. The clause in the contract that stipulated the primacy of economic growth, and thereby gave a charter to free enterprise within broad rules of competitive economic behavior, is now widely challenged. It is becoming clear that in the emerging new contract, social progress (the quality of life) will weigh equally in the balance with economic progress. . . .

Such equality foreshadows some drastic revisions in the rules of the game. As one example, it will no longer be acceptable for corporations to manage their affairs solely in terms of the traditional internal costs of doing business, while thrusting external costs on the public. Since the 1930s, of course, some external costs have been partially returned to business firms, as in the case of unemployment compensation. But most have not, and this situation is on the edge of revision. This means, as is even now beginning to occur, that the costs associated with environmental contamination will be transferred from the public sector to the business firms which generate the contamination. It also means that corporations whose economic activities are judged to create safety hazards (from automobiles to atomic power plants) will be compelled to internalize the costs of minimizing these hazards by conforming with stipulated levels of acceptable risk or of mandatory manufacturing and performance specifications.

To be rigorously correct, it should be noted that industry's new cost structure will be reflected in its prices. Purchasers of goods and services will be the ultimate underwriters of the increased expenses. But a moment's reflection on the supply-demand charts that sprinkle the pages of economics texts will demonstrate that a new schedule of supply prices will intersect demand curves at different points than formerly. This may lead to a changed set of customer purchase preferences among the total assortment of goods and services. What is implied is not a simple pass-through of newly internalized social costs. The ultimate results will alter relative market positions among whole industries and, within industries, among firms. Choices from available options in short-term technological adjustments to the new contamination and safety requirements and in long-term pricing strategies to reflect higher costs will, in the familiar competitive way, determine success or failure for a number of companies. Some interesting management decisions lie ahead.

The internalization of traditional social costs of private operations is the most obvious of the changes that will follow on striking a new balance between economic and social progress. More subtle, and eventually more radical, relocations of responsibility can be foreseen. The complex cluster of socio-

economic problems associated with urbanization, population shifts and the needs of disadvantaged minorities are already overwhelming the administrative capacities, probably also the resources, of city, county and state governments. Evidence is accumulating that the public expects private business to contribute brains and resources to the amelioration and resolution of these massive strains. History suggests that such expectations will be transformed into demands. . . .

If the thrust of this analysis is generally on target, the principal lesson for private management is clear. It must participate actively in the redesign of the social contract. There can be no greater danger than to permit the new rules to be formulated by either the small group of critics armed only with malevolence toward the existing system or the much larger group sincerely motivated by concern for ameliorating social ills but grossly handicapped by their ignorance of the techniques and dynamism of private enterprise. . . .

A good place to begin would be the uncharted jungle of cost estimates. We need concepts and techniques for measuring and accounting for the real costs of environmental contamination. We need to build a body of reliable information about what the costs are in all their complexity, where they originate, where they impact. We also need to evaluate present and potential technologies for suppressing or removing contaminants, along both engineering and economic parameters. Using history, experimentation and game theory, we need to study the relative effectiveness of all types of cost transfer instruments, both inducements and penalties. One might speculate that the conclusion will be in favor of applying a variety of devices, each fitted to a specific set of technical and economic circumstances, rather than a single instrument. But this is a foresighted guess, not a basis for public policy determination.

A second area where business competence can make a contribution is the cluster of problems associated with poverty in the midst of plenty, unemployed or underemployed minorities, and urban decay. Less clearly defined than the contamination issue, this area possesses much greater potential for violent disruption that could mortally shred the fabric of our society. If this occurs (and there are too many recent examples of limited local disruptions to be comfortably skeptical about the possibilities ahead), many of the environmental conditions essential for the private enterprise system will disappear. There can be little doubt that what would follow would be an authoritarian, social-service, rigid society in which the conditions of production and distribution would be severely controlled. In such a setting, the dynamism, creativeness and flexibility of the economy would disappear, together with all the incentives for individual achievement in any arena other than, possibly, the political.

It is not easy to project with confidence how private business might move effectively into this area while retaining its fundamental profit orientation. One interesting possibility is to transfer the concept of the defense contractor to the non-defense sector. The brute economics of low-cost urban housing, for example, may rule out unsubsidized, business-initiated investment. Not ruled out, however, is business as contractor, remodeler and operator under negotiated or competitive-bid contracts. There has been limited experimentation in arrangements of this type, in housing, education, urban systems analysis and planning, and other fields. Freer exploration in diverse circumstances and in public-private relationships might discover an attractive potential for alleviating and removing major causes of gross social discontent while retaining a large degree of private initiative and the familiar web of revenue-cost relationships. The true social costs remaining, representing the layer of subsidies that may be found necessary to absorb the remaining expenses of an acceptable ground level of general welfare, could then be allocated through the tax system.

This is obviously not the only possibility in sight. Business has made only a few limited experiments in the application of incentives. More extensive analysis and trial might suggest at least the special circumstances in which this tool could effectively supplement or supplant the public contractor device. A third possibility is suggested by the concept embodied in Comsat—the mixed public-private corporation. Other options, including combinations of the foregoing, await imaginative creation.

The incentive for business management to enroll as a participant in the general exploration of ways and means for removing the cancerous growth in the vitals of society is classically selfish. Somehow, this cancer will be removed. The recognition is spreading rapidly that its continuance is intolerable. Some of the proposed or still-to-be-proposed lines of attack may be destructive of other elements in society, including the private enterprise system. Management is in a position to contribute rational analysis, technical competence and imaginative innovations. The interests served by continuing the enterprise system coincide here with other social interests.

These and comparable innovations imply for private managers a willingness to think about new economic roles and social relationships that many will see as dangerous cracks in the wall of custom. It is not unreasonable, however, to suggest that we are considering nothing more adventurous than the explorations and commitments that managers have long been accustomed to underwrite in administering resources. The only significant difference is that the stakes are higher. In place of the marginal calculus of profit and loss, what may be involved is the preservation of the civilization that has created such an unparalleled record of wealth and growth.

Writing and Discussion Topics

Questions 1–6 address content, critical analysis, personal choices, ethical options, specific discipline, and interdisciplinary alternatives, respectively.

1. Explain the historical underpinnings of ethical systems based on social contract.
2. Is it reasonable for corporate social policy to be blamed for the homelessness and poverty existing in America today? Anshen points out these conditions were even worse in the nineteenth century. Examine these conditions with respect to corporate social policy.
3. Do you believe that the consumer picks up the tab through higher prices when businesses enact social responsibility policies? Explain your answer.
4. Why does Anshen believe that business competence needs to be applied to the problems of poverty, unemployment, and urban decay? Explain why you agree or disagree with this stand.
5. Detail which of Anshen's business innovations for economic and social responsibility seems workable.
6. Compare and contrast Anshen's environmental suggestions with those of the philosophers in this section. What do they each say about projecting the costs of future damage and about accounting for real damage to the environment by business and society?

John G. Simon, Charles W. Powers, and Jon P. Gunnemann

THE RESPONSIBILITIES OF CORPORATIONS
AND THEIR OWNERS

◆◆◆

J ohn G. Simon is a professor of law at Yale University. His
scholarship and publications are centered in the law of public
education, families, housing, and non-profit institutions. He is president
of the Taconic Foundation.

Charles W. Powers is a founding partner of Resources for Responsible
Management and is also a consultant on ethics and public policy to
business and government. He previously taught social ethics at Yale
University. His experience in business has been extensive, as vice
president of Cummins Engine Company, president of Clean Sites, Inc.,
and director of the Health Effects Institute.

Jon P. Gunnemann is a professor at Emory University in social ethics.
He is a graduate of Harvard College and Yale University. He is a widely
published author in the areas of business ethics, justice, and Christian
morality. ◆

For better or worse, the modern American business corporation is increasingly being asked to assume more responsibility for social problems and the public welfare. How corporate responsibility is understood, and whether it is perceived to be for better or worse, may depend in the last analysis on the beholder's emotional reaction to the corporation itself: one either extols the corporation as part of the creative process or condemns it as the work of the Devil. Thus, almost four centuries ago the English jurist Sir Edward Coke wrote of corporations that "they cannot commit treason nor be outlawed nor excommunicated for they have no souls," while more recently Justice Louis D. Brandeis characterized the corporation as the "master instrument of civilized life. . . ."[1]

Our analysis of the controversies surrounding the notion of corporate responsibility—and the suggestion that the university as an investor should be concerned with corporate responsibility—proceeds in large part from our approach to certain issues in the area of social responsibility and public morals. In particular, we (1) make a distinction between negative injunctions and affirmative duties; (2) assert that all men have the "moral minimum" obligation not to impose social injury; (3) delineate those conditions under which one is held responsible for social injury, even where it is not clear that the injury was self-caused; and (4) take a position in the argument between those who strive for moral purity and those who strive for moral effectiveness.

Negative Injunctions and Affirmative Duties

A distinction which informs much of our discussion differentiates between injunctions against activities that injure others and duties which require the affirmative pursuit of some good. The failure to make this distinction in debate on public ethics often results in false dichotomies, a point illustrated by an article which appeared just over a decade ago in the *Harvard Business Review*. In that article, which provoked considerable debate in the business community, Theodore Levitt argued against corporate social responsibility both because it was dangerous for society and because it detracted from the primary goal of business, the making of profit. We deal with the merits of these arguments later; what is important for our immediate purpose, however, is Levitt's designation of those activities and concerns which constitute social responsibility. He notes that the corporation has become "more concerned about the needs of its employees, about schools, hospitals, welfare agencies and even aesthetics," and that it is "fashionable . . . for the corporation to show that it is a great innovator; more specifically, a great public benefactor; and, very particularly, that it exists 'to serve the public.' "[2] Having so delimited the notion of corporate responsibility, Levitt presents the reader with a choice between, on the one hand, getting involved in the management of society, "creating munificence for one and all," and, on the other hand, fulfilling the profit-making function. But such a choice excludes another meaning of corporate responsibility: the making of profits in such a way as to minimize social injury. Levitt at no point considers the possibility that business activity may at times injure others and that it may be necessary to regulate the social consequences of one's business activities accordingly. . . .

Our public discourse abounds with similar failures to distinguish between positive and perhaps lofty ideals and minimal requirements of social organization. During the election campaigns of the 1950's and the civil rights movement of the early 1960's, the slogan, "You can't legislate morality," was a popular cry on many fronts. Obviously, we have not succeeded in devising laws that create within our citizens a predisposition to love and kindness; but we can devise laws which will minimize the injury that one citizen must suffer at the hands of another. Although the virtue of love may be the possession of a few, justice—in the minimal sense of not injuring others—can be required of all.

The distinction between negative injunctions and affirmative duties is old, having roots in common law and equity jurisprudence.[3] Here it is based on the premise that it is easier to specify and enjoin a civil wrong than to state what should be done. In the Ten Commandments, affirmative duties are spelled out only for one's relations with God and parents; for the more public relationships, we are given only the negative injunction: "Thou shalt not. . . ." Similarly, the Bill of Rights contains only negative injunctions.

Avoidance and Correction of Social Injury as a "Moral Minimum"

We do not mean to distinguish between negative injunctions and affirmative duties solely in the interests of analytical precision. The negative injunction to avoid and correct social injury threads its way through all morality. We call it a "moral minimum," implying that however one may choose to limit the concept of social responsibility, one cannot exclude this negative injunction. Although reasons may exist why certain persons or institutions cannot or should not be required to pursue moral or social good in all situations, there are many fewer reasons why one should be excused from the injunction against injuring others. Any citizen, individual or institutional, may have competing obligations which could, under some circumstances, override this negative injunction. But these special circumstances do not wipe away the prima facie obligation to avoid harming others.

In emphasizing the central role of the negative injunction, we do not suggest that affirmative duties are never important. A society where citizens go well beyond the requirement to avoid damage to others will surely be a better community. But we do recognize that individuals exhibit varying degrees of commitment to promote affirmatively the public welfare, whereas we expect everyone equally to refrain from injuring others.

The view that all citizens are equally obligated to avoid or correct any social injury which is self-caused finds support in our legal as well as our moral tradition. H. L. A. Hart and A. M. Honoré have written:

> In the moral judgments of ordinary life, we have occasion to blame people because they have caused harm to others, and also, if less frequently, to insist that morally they are bound to compensate those to whom they have caused harm. These are the moral analogues of more precise legal conceptions: for, in all legal systems liability to be punished or to make compensation frequently depends on whether actions (or omissions) have caused harm. Moral blame is not of course confined to such cases of causing harm.[4]

We know of no societies, from the literature of anthropology or comparative ethics, whose moral codes do not contain some injunction against harming others. The specific notion of *harm* or *social injury* may vary, as well as the mode of correction and restitution, but the injunctions are present.

In using the term *moral minimum* to describe this obligation, we mean to avoid any suggestion that the injunction against doing injury to others can serve as the basis for deriving the full content of morality. Moreover, we have used an expression which does not imply that the injunction is in any way dependent upon a natural law point of view. A person who subscribed to some form of natural law theory might indeed agree with our position, but so could someone who maintained that all morality is based on convention, agreement, or contract. Social contract theorists have generally maintained that the granting of rights to individuals by mutual consent involves some limitation on the actions of all individuals in the contract: to guarantee the liberty of all members, it is essential that each be enjoined against violating the rights of others.[5]

We asserted earlier that it is easier to enjoin and correct a wrong than it is to prescribe affirmatively what is good for society and what ought to be done. Notions of the public good and the values that men actively seek to implement are subjects of intense disagreement. In this realm, pluralism is almost inevitable, and some would argue that it is healthy. Yet there can also be disagreement about what constitutes social injury or harm. What some people think are affirmative duties may be seen by others as correction of social injury. For example, the notion that business corporations should make special effort to train and employ members of minority groups could be understood by some to fulfill an affirmative duty on the part of corporations to meet society's problems; but it could be interpreted by others as the correction of a social injury caused by years of institutional racism. As a more extreme example, a Marxist would in all probability contend that *all* corporate activity is socially injurious and that therefore all social pursuits by corporations are corrective responses rather than affirmative actions.[6]

Although the notion of *social injury* is imprecise and although many hard cases will be encountered in applying it, we think that it is a helpful designation and that cases can be decided on the basis of it. In the law, many notions (such as *negligence* in the law of torts or *consideration* in the law of contracts) are equally vague but have received content from repeated decision making over time. We would hope that under our proposed Guidelines similar "case law" would develop. Moreover, our Guidelines attempt to give some content to the notion of *social injury* by referring to external norms: *social injury* is defined as "particulary including activities which violate, or frustrate the enforcement of, rules of domestic or international law intended to protect individuals against deprivation of health, safety or basic freedoms."[7]

In sum, we would affirm the prima facie obligation of all citizens, both individual and institutional, to avoid and correct self-caused social injury. Much more in the way of affirmative acts may be expected of certain kinds of citizens, but none is exempt from this "moral minimum."

In some cases it may not be true—or at least it may not be clear—that one has caused or helped to cause social injury, and yet one may bear responsibility for correcting or averting the injury. We consider next the circumstances under which this responsibility may arise.

Need, Proximity, Capability, and Last Resort (The Kew Gardens Principle)

Several years ago the public was shocked by the news accounts of the stabbing and agonizingly slow death of Kitty Genovese in the Kew Gardens section of New York City while thirty-eight people watched or heard and did nothing.[8] What so deeply disturbed the public's moral sensibilities was that in the face of a critical human need, people who were close to that need and had the power to do something about it failed to act.

The public's reaction suggests that, no matter how narrowly one may conceive of social responsibility, there are some situations in which a combination of circumstances thrusts upon us an obligation to respond. Life is fraught with emergency situations in which a failure to respond is a special form of violation of the negative injunction against causing social injury: a sin of omission becomes a sin of commission.

Legal responsibility for aiding someone in cases of grave distress or injury, even when caused by another, is recognized by many European civil codes and by the criminal laws of one of our states:

A. A person who knows that another is exposed to grave physical harm shall, to the extent that the same can be rendered without danger or peril to himself or without interference with important duties owed to others, give reasonable assistance to the exposed person unless that assistance or care is being provided by others. . . .

C. A person who willfully violates subsection (A) of this section shall be fined not more than $100.00.[9]

This Vermont statute recognizes that it is not reasonable in all cases to require a person to give assistance to someone who is endangered. If such aid imperils himself, or interferes with duties owed to others, or if there are others providing the aid, the person is excepted from the obligation. These conditions of responsibility give some shape to difficult cases and are in striking parallel with the conditions which existed at Kew Gardens. The salient features of the Kitty Genovese case are (1) critical need; (2) the proximity of the thirty-eight spectators; (3) the capability of the spectators to act helpfully (at least to telephone the police); and (4) the absence of other (including official) help; i.e., the thirty-eight were the last resort. There would, we believe, be widespread agreement that a moral obligation to aid another arises when these four features are present. What we have called the "moral minimum" (the duty to avoid and correct self-caused social injury) is an obvious and easy example of fulfillment of these criteria—so obvious that there is little need to go through step-by-step analysis of these factors. Where the injury is not clearly self-caused, the application of these criteria aids in deciding responsibility. We have called this combination of features governing difficult cases the "Kew Gardens Principle." There follows a more detailed examination of each of the features:

Need. In cases where the other three criteria are constant, increased need increases responsibility. Just as there is no precise definition of social injury (one kind of need), there is no precise definition of need or way of measuring its extent.

Proximity. The thirty-eight witnesses of the Genovese slaying were geographically close to the deed. But proximity to a situation of need is not necessarily spatial. Proximity is largely a function of notice: we hold a person blameworthy if he knows of imperilment and does not do what he reasonably can do to remedy the situation. Thus, the thirty-eight at Kew Gardens were delinquent not because they were near but because nearness enabled them to know that someone was in need. A deaf person who could not hear the cries for help would not be considered blameworthy even if he were closer than those who could hear. So also, a man in Afghanistan is uniquely responsible for the serious illness of a man in Peoria, Illinois, if he has knowledge of the man's illness, if he can telephone a doctor about it, and if he alone has that notice. When we become aware of a wrongdoing or a social injury, we take on obligations that we did not have while ignorant.

Notice does not exhaust the meaning of proximity, however. It is reasonable to maintain that the sick man's neighbors in Peoria were to some extent blameworthy if they made no effort to inquire into the man's welfare. Ignorance cannot always be helped, but we do expect certain persons and perhaps institutions to look harder for information about critical need.[10] In this sense, proximity has to do with the network of social expectations that flow from notions of civic duty, duties to one's family, and so on. Thus, we expect a man to be more alert to the plight of his next-door neighbor than to the needs of a child in East Pakistan, just as we expect a man to be more alert to the situation of his own children than to the problems of the family down the block. The failure of the man to act in conformance with this expectation does not give him actual notice of need, but it creates what the law would call *constructive notice*. Both factors—actual notice and constructive notice growing out of social expectation—enter into the determination of responsibility and blame.

Capability. Even if there is a need to which a person has proximity, that person is not usually held responsible unless there is something he can reasonably be expected to do to meet the need. To follow Immanuel Kant, *ought* assumes *can*. What one is reasonably capable of doing, of course, admits to some variety of interpretation. In the Kew Gardens incident, it might not have been reasonable to expect someone to place his body between the girl and the knife. It was surely reasonable to expect someone to call the police. So also it would not seem to be within the canons of reasonability for a university to sacrifice education for charity. . . . But if the university is able, by non-self-sacrificial means, to mitigate injury caused by a company of which it is an owner, it would not seem unreasonable to ask it to do so.

Last Resort. In the emergency situations we have been describing, one becomes more responsible the less likely it is that someone else will be able to aid. Physical proximity is a factor here, as is time. If the knife is drawn, one cannot wait for the policeman. It is important to note here that determination of last resort becomes more difficult the more complex the social situation or organization. The man on the road to Jericho, in spite of the presence of a few other travelers, probably had a fairly good notion that he was the only person who could help the man attacked by thieves. But on a street in New York City, there is always the hope that someone else will step forward to give aid. Surely this rationalization entered into the silence of each of the thirty-eight: there were, after all, thirty-seven others. Similarly, within large corporations it is difficult to know not only whether one alone has notice of a wrongdoing, but also whether there is anyone else who is able to respond. Because of this diffusion of responsibility in complex organizations and societies, the notion of last resort is less useful than the other Kew Gardens criteria in determining whether one ought to act in aid of someone in need or to avert or correct social injury. Failure to act because one hopes someone else will act—or because one is trying to find out who is the last resort—may frequently lead to a situation in which no one acts at all.[11] This fact, we think, places more weight on the first three features of the Kew Gardens Principle in determining responsibility, and it creates a presumption in favor of taking action when those three conditions are present.[12]

Notes

1. We are indebted for the juxtaposition of these two quotes to Harris Wofford, president of Bryn Mawr College. From some points of view, of course, being the "master instrument of civilized life" is to be convicted of soullessness.

    Debate about the corporation in American society and about its desirability in a democratic nation goes back at least to the writers of the American Constitution: Hamilton wanted to give the federal government the power to issue corporate charters for the purpose of promoting trade and industry; Madison felt that corporations would prevent men from participating in public action and were thus a threat to freedom. The debate was resolved in Madison's favor—although in later years some federal charters were issued.

    For a brief discussion of the early debates between the Jeffersonians and the Hamiltonians, see Harvey C. Bunke, *A Primer on American Economic History* (New York, 1969), Ch. 3, and Edwin M. Epstein, *The Corporation in American Politics* (Englewood Cliffs, N.J., 1969). For fuller discussion, see Oscar and Mary Handlin, "Origins of the American Business Corporation," *Journal of Economic History* 5 (May 1945), and Joseph S. David, *Essays in the Earlier History of American Corporations* vol. 2 (Cambridge, Mass., 1917).

2. Theodore Levitt, "The Dangers of Social Responsibility," in Marshall, ed., *Business and Government*, pp. 22–23.
3. We are grateful to President Edward Bloustein of Rutgers University for suggesting this terminology and for inviting our attention to its historical antecedents. Further analysis of the distinction between *negative injunctions* and *affirmative duties* is given in the following sections of this chapter.
4. H. L. A. Hart and A. M. Honoré, *Causation in the Law* (Oxford, 1959), p. 59.
5. Jeremy Bentham wrote that " . . . [A]ll rights are made at the expense of liberty. . . . [There is] no right without a correspondent obligation. . . . All coercive law, therefore . . . and in particular all laws creative of liberty, are, as far as they go, abrogative of liberty." "Anarchical Fallacies," in *Society, Law and Morality*, ed. F. A. Olafsson (Englewood Cliffs, N.J., 1961), p. 350. Clearly, Bentham understood that any creation of rights or liberties under the law entailed recognition of an injunction against violating the rights of others.
6. The notion of social injury may also change over time. External norms in the form of government regulations now provide that failure to actively recruit minority group members constitutes discrimination, i.e., is a matter of social injury. See the "affirmative action" requirements, including recruiting measures, imposed on all federal contractors by the federal "contract compliance" regulations. 41 *Code of Federal Regulations*, Section 60–62. At one time, such recruitment was not subject to a negative injunction.
7. We do not suggest that social injury is identical to violation of the legal norms to which we are referring. (In other words, we recognize that some laws themselves cause social injury in the eyes of many persons, and also that not all social injury is prohibited by law.) We are only saying that reference to legal norms will help individuals and institutions to make their own judgments about social injury.
8. See A. M. Rosenthal, *Thirty-Eight Witnesses* (New York, 1964).
9. "Duty to Aid the Endangered Act," *Vt. Stat. Ann.*, Ch. 12, § 519 (Supp. 1968). See G. Hughes, "Criminal Omissions," 67 *Yale L. J.* 590 (1958).
10. See, for example, Albert Speer's reflection on his role during the Hitler regime: "For being in a position to know and nevertheless shunning knowledge creates direct responsibility for the consequences—from the very beginning." *Inside the Third Reich* (New York, 1970), p. 19.
11. Failure to respond to need in social situations may also have another effect, equally detrimental to public morality: it suggests to others who might have stepped forward that the situation is really not serious. Thus, two psychologists, John M. Darley and Bibb Latané, after conducting experiments on social reaction to simulated emergencies, concluded that "it is possible for a state of 'pluralistic ignorance' to develop, in which each bystander is led by the apparent lack of concern of the others to interpret the situation as being less serious than he would if alone. To the extent that he does not feel the situation is an emergency, he will be unlikely to take any helpful action." Darley and Latané, *The Unresponsive Bystander: Why Doesn't He Help?* (New York, 1970), cited by Israel Shenker, *New York Times*, 10 April 1971, p. 25. The latter article was based on a separate experiment conducted by Prof. Darley and Dr. C. Daniel Batson at Princeton Theological Seminar designed to determine why people do not help. A group of students were given biblical texts to record, then given individual directions to the recording studio that required them to pass a writhing, gasping student lying in a doorway. It was found that the only significant differentiating factor in determining whether a student stopped to aid was the amount of time he thought he had; those who were told that they were late for the recording session stopped to help much less often (10 per cent) than those who were told that they had sufficient time (63 per cent). It made no statistical difference that half of the seminary students had been given the Parable of the Good Samaritan to record.
12. We do not invoke the Kew Gardens Principle to establish corporate responsibility for clearly self-caused social harm, but rather to demonstrate how shareholders—who may not appear to be directly involved in corporate-caused injury—are obligated to attempt to avert or avoid such injury.

Writing and Discussion Topics

Questions 1–6 address content, critical analysis, personal choices, ethical options, specific discipline, and interdisciplinary alternatives, respectively.

1. What is the definition of corporate social responsibility, according to these authors?
2. Should a corporation meet a moral minimum by merely avoiding social injury? What is the authors' definition of a moral minimum?
3. Invent a society in which everyone meets a moral minimum. What would be the benefits and problems in such a society? Use this article as one of your sources.
4. A corporation has been doing business in a small midwestern city for the past fifty years. Market analysis shows the

corporation could make a larger profit by moving to Korea. A large part of the town is employed by this corporation. What is the moral minimum for the executives in this situation? If the corporation decided to stay because of responsibilities to the work force, would this be going beyond the moral minimum?

5. Compare and contrast the virtue-based ethics of Aristotle with the moral minimum of these authors. Examine three points of comparison.
6. Each of the philosophers in this section has a definition of social responsibility. Briefly parallel each of the authors' views.

The National Conference of Catholic Bishops

ECONOMIC JUSTICE FOR ALL:
A PASTORAL MESSAGE

◆◆◆

*I*ssues of social importance have often been the impetus for the
Roman Catholic Church to submit statements declaring its views on
these issues. After much study and worldwide deliberation, a message is
released to the Church and to the world, as was the case in this pastoral
letter. The bishops' economic message in its entirety is lengthy.
Significant points have been excerpted that apply to the moral and social
responsibilities of business. The reading begins with the Introduction and
uses portions of chapters one and four. The original numbering of the
bishops has been retained. ◆

Principal Themes of the Pastoral Letter

12. The pastoral letter is not a blueprint for the American economy. It does not embrace any particular theory of how the economy works, nor does it attempt to resolve the disputes between different schools of economic thought. Instead, our letter turns to Scripture and to the social teachings of the Church. There, we discover what our economic life must serve, what standards it must meet. Let us examine some of these basic moral principles.

13. *Every economic decision and institution must be judged in light of whether it protects or undermines the dignity of the human person.* The pastoral letter begins with the human person. We believe the person is sacred—the clearest reflection of God among us. Human dignity comes from God, not from nationality, race, sex, economic status, or any human accomplishment. We judge any economic system by what it does *for* and *to* people and by how it permits all to *participate* in it. The economy should serve people, not the other way around.

14. *Human dignity can be realized and protected only in community.* In our teaching, the human person is not only sacred but also social. How we organize our society—in economics and politics, in law and policy—directly affects human dignity and the capacity of individuals to grow in community. The obligation to "love our neighbor" has an individual dimension, but it also requires a broader social commitment to the common good. We have many partial ways to measure and debate the health of our economy: Gross National Product, per capita income, stock market prices, and so forth. The Christian vision of economic life looks beyond them all and asks, Does economic life enhance or threaten our life together as a community?

15. *All people have a right to participate in the economic life of society.* Basic justice demands that people be assured a minimum level of participation in the economy. It is wrong for a person or group to be excluded unfairly or to be unable to participate or contribute to the economy. For example, people who are both able and willing, but cannot get a job are deprived of the participation that is so vital to human development. For, it is through employment that most individuals and families meet their material needs, exercise their talents, and have an opportunity to contribute to the larger community. Such participation has a special significance in our tradition because we believe that it is a means by which we join in carrying forward God's creative activity.

16. *All members of society have a special obligation to the poor and vulnerable.* From the Scriptures and church teaching, we learn that the justice of a society is tested by the treatment of the poor. The justice that was the sign of God's covenant with Israel was measured by how the poor and unprotected—the widow, the orphan, and the stranger—were treated. The kingdom that Jesus proclaimed in his word and ministry excludes no one. Throughout Israel's history and in early Christianity, the poor are agents of God's transforming power. "The Spirit of the Lord is upon me, therefore he has anointed me. He has sent me to bring glad tidings to the poor" (Lk 4:18). This was Jesus' first public utterance. Jesus takes the side of those most in need. In the Last Judgment, so dramatically described in St. Matthew's Gospel, we are told that we will be judged according to how we respond to the hungry, the thirsty, the naked, the stranger. As followers of Christ, we are challenged to make a fundamental "option for the poor"—to speak for the voiceless, to defend the defenseless, to assess life styles, policies, and social institutions in terms of their impact on the poor. This "option for the poor" does not mean pitting one group against another, but rather, strengthening the

whole community by assisting those who are most vulnerable. As Christians, we are called to respond to the needs of *all* our brothers and sisters, but those with the greatest needs require the greatest response.

17. *Human rights are the minimum conditions for life in community.* In Catholic teaching, human rights include not only civil and political rights but also economic rights. As Pope John XXIII declared, "all people have a right to life, food, clothing, shelter, rest, medical care, education, and employment." This means that when people are without a chance to earn a living, and must go hungry and homeless, they are being denied basic rights. Society must ensure that these rights are protected. In this way, we will ensure that the minimum conditions of economic justice are met for all our sisters and brothers.

18. *Society as a whole, acting through public and private institutions, has the moral responsibility to enhance human dignity and protect human rights.* In addition to the clear responsibility of private institutions, government has an essential responsibility in this area. This does not mean that government has the primary or exclusive role, but it does have a positive moral responsibility in safeguarding human rights and ensuring that the minimum conditions of human dignity are met for all. In a democracy, government is a means by which we can act together to protect what is important to us and to promote our common values.

19. These six moral principles are not the only ones presented in the pastoral letter, but they give an overview of the moral vision that we are trying to share. This vision of economic life cannot exist in a vacuum; it must be translated into concrete measures. Our pastoral letter spells out some specific applications of Catholic moral principles. We call for a new national commitment to full employment. We say it is a social and moral scandal that one of every seven Americans is poor, and we call for concerted efforts to eradicate poverty. The fulfillment of the basic needs of the poor is of the highest priority. We urge that all economic policies be evaluated in light of their impact on the life and stability of the family. We support measures to halt the loss of family farms and to resist the growing concentration in the ownership of agricultural resources. We specify ways in which the United States can do far more to relieve the plight of poor nations and assist in their development. We also reaffirm church teaching on the rights of workers, collective bargaining, private property, subsidiary, and equal opportunity. . . .

Chapter I
The Church and the Future
of the U.S. Economy

B. Urgent Problems of Today

10. The preeminent role of the United States in an increasingly interdependent global economy is a central sign of our times.[6] The United States is still the world's economic giant. Decisions made here have immediate effects in other countries; decisions made abroad have immediate consequences for steelworkers in Pittsburgh, oil company employees in Houston, and farmers in Iowa. U.S. economic growth is vitally dependent on resources from other countries and on their purchases of our goods and services. Many jobs in U.S. industry and agriculture depend on our ability to export manufactured goods and food.

11. In some industries the mobility of capital and technology makes wages the main variable in the cost of production. Overseas competitors with the same technology but with wage rates as low as one-tenth of ours put enormous pressure on U.S. firms to cut wages, relocate abroad, or close. U.S. workers and their communities should not be expected to bear these burdens alone.

12. All people on this globe share a common ecological environment that is under increasing pressure. Depletion of soil,

water, and other natural resources endangers the future. Pollution of air and water threatens the delicate balance of the biosphere on which future generations will depend.[7] The resources of the earth have been created by God for the benefit of all, and we who are alive today hold them in trust. This is a challenge to develop a new ecological ethic that will help shape a future that is both just and sustainable.

13. In short, nations separated by geography, culture, and ideology are linked in a complex commercial, financial, technological, and environmental network. These links have two direct consequences. First, they create hope for a new form of community among all peoples, one built on dignity, solidarity, and justice. Second, this rising global awareness calls for greater attention to the stark inequities across countries in the standards of living and control of resources. We must not look at the welfare of U.S. citizens as the only good to be sought. Nor may we overlook the disparities of power in the relationships between this nation and the developing countries. The United States is the major supplier of food to other countries, a major source of arms sales to developing nations, and a powerful influence in multilateral institutions such as the International Monetary Fund, the World Bank, and the United Nations. What Americans see as a growing interdependence is regarded by many in the less developed countries as a pattern of domination and dependence.

14. Within this larger international setting, there are also a number of challenges to the domestic economy that call for creativity and courage. The promise of the "American dream"—freedom for all persons to develop their God-given talents to the full—remains unfulfilled for millions in the United States today.

15. Several areas of U.S. economic life demand special attention. Unemployment is the most basic. Despite the large number of new jobs the U.S. economy has generated in the past decade, approximately 8 million people seeking work in this country are unable to find it, and many more are so discouraged they have stopped looking.[8] Over the past two decades the nation has come to tolerate an increasing level of unemployment. The 6 to 7 percent rate deemed acceptable today would have been intolerable twenty years ago. Among the unemployed are a disproportionate number of blacks, Hispanics, young people, or women who are the sole support of their families.[9] Some cities and states have many more unemployed persons than others as a result of economic forces that have little to do with people's desire to work. Unemployment is a tragedy no matter whom it strikes, but the tragedy is compounded by the unequal and unfair way it is distributed in our society.

16. Harsh poverty plagues our country despite its great wealth. More than 33 million Americans are poor, by any reasonable standard another 20 to 30 million are needy. Poverty is increasing in the United States, not decreasing.[10] For a people who believe in "progress," this should be cause for alarm. These burdens fall most heavily on blacks, Hispanics, and Native Americans. Even more disturbing is the large increase in the number of women and children living in poverty. Today children are the largest single group among the poor. This tragic fact seriously threatens the nation's future. That so many people are poor in a nation as rich as ours is a social and moral scandal that we cannot ignore.

17. Many working people and middle-class Americans live dangerously close to poverty. A rising number of families must rely on the wages of two or even three members just to get by. From 1968 to 1978 nearly a quarter of the U.S. population was in poverty part of the time and received welfare benefits in at least one year.[11] The loss of a job, illness, or the breakup of a marriage may be all it takes to push people into poverty.

18. The lack of a mutually supportive relation between family life and economic life is one of the most serious problems facing the United States today.[12] The economic

and cultural strength of the nation is directly linked to the stability and health of its families.[13] When families thrive, spouses contribute to the common good through their work at home, in the community, and in their jobs; and children develop a sense of their own worth and of their responsibility to serve others. When families are weak or break down entirely, the dignity of parents and children is threatened. High cultural and economic costs are inflicted on society at large.

19. The precarious economic situation of so many people and so many families calls for examination of U.S. economic arrangements. Christian conviction and the American promise of liberty and justice for all give the poor and the vulnerable a special claim on the nation's concern. They also challenge all members of the Church to help build a more just society.

20. The investment of human creativity and material resources in the production of the weapons of war makes these economic problems even more difficult to solve. Defense Department expenditures in the United States are almost $300 billion per year. The rivalry and mutual fear between superpowers divert into projects that threaten death, minds and money that could better human life. Developing countries engage in arms races they can ill afford, often with the encouragement of the superpowers. Some of the poorest countries of the world use scarce resources to buy planes, guns, and other weapons when they lack the food, education, and health care their people need. Defense policies must be evaluated and assessed in light of their real contribution to freedom, justice, and peace for the citizens of our own and other nations. We have developed a perspective on these multiple moral concerns in our 1983 pastoral letter, *The Challenge of Peace: God's Promise and Our Response*.[14] When weapons or strategies make questionable contributions to security, peace, and justice and will also be very expensive, spending priorities should be redirected to more pressing social needs.[15]

21. Many other social and economic challenges require careful analysis: the movement of many industries from the Snowbelt to the Sunbelt, the federal deficit and interest rates, corporate mergers and takeovers, the effects of new technologies such as robotics and information systems in U.S. industry, immigration policy, growing international traffic in drugs, and the trade imbalance. All of these issues do not provide a complete portrait of the economy. Rather they are symptoms of more fundamental currents shaping U.S. economic life today: the struggle to find meaning and value in human work, efforts to support individual freedom in the context of renewed social cooperation, the urgent need to create equitable forms of global interdependence in a world now marked by extreme inequality. These deeper currents are cultural and moral in content. They show that the long-range challenges facing the nation call for sustained reflection on the values that guide economic choices and are embodied in economic institutions. Such explicit reflection on the ethical content of economic choices and policies must become an integral part of the way Christians relate religious belief to the realities of everyday life. In this way, the "split between the faith which many profess and their daily lives,"[16] which Vatican II counted among the more serious errors of the modern age, will begin to be bridged. . . .

Chapter IV
A New American Experiment: Partnership for the Public Good

295. For over two hundred years the United States has been engaged in a bold experiment in democracy. The founders of the nation set out to establish justice, promote the general welfare, and secure the blessings of liberty for themselves and their posterity. Those who live in this land today are the beneficiaries of this great venture. Our review of some of the most pressing problems in economic life today

shows, however, that this undertaking is not yet complete. Justice for all remains an aspiration; a fair share in the general welfare is denied to many. In addition to the particular policy recommendations made above, a long-term and more fundamental response is needed. This will call for an imaginative vision of the future that can help shape economic arrangements in creative new ways. We now want to propose some elements of such a vision and several innovations in economic structures that can contribute to making this vision a reality.

296. Completing the unfinished business of the American experiment will call for new forms of cooperation and partnership among those whose daily work is the source of the prosperity and justice of the nation. The United States prides itself on both its competitive sense of initiative and its spirit of teamwork. Today a greater spirit of partnership and teamwork is needed; competition alone will not do the job. It has too many negative consequences for family life, the economically vulnerable, and the environment. Only a renewed commitment by all to the common good can deal creatively with the realities of international interdependence and economic dislocations in the domestic economy. The virtues of good citizenship require a lively sense of participation in the commonwealth and of having obligations as well as rights within it.[1] The nation's economic health depends on strengthening these virtues among all its people, and on the development of institutional arrangements supportive of these virtues.[2]

297. The nation's founders took daring steps to create structures of participation, mutual accountability, and widely distributed power to ensure the political rights and freedoms of all. We believe that similar steps are needed today to expand economic participation, broaden the sharing of economic power, and make economic decisions more accountable to the common good. As noted above, the principle of subsidiary states that the pursuit of economic justice must occur on all levels of society. It makes demands on communities as small as the family, as large as the global society and on all levels in between. There are a number of ways to enhance the cooperative participation of these many groups in the task of creating this future. Since there is no single innovation that will solve all problems, we recommend careful experimentation with several possibilities that hold considerable hope for increasing partnership and strengthening mutual responsibility for economic justice.

A. Cooperation Within Firms and Industries

298. A new experiment in bringing democratic ideals to economic life calls for serious exploration of ways to develop new patterns of partnership among those working in individual firms and industries.[3] Every business, from the smallest to the largest, including farms and ranches, depends on many different persons and groups for its success: workers, managers, owners or shareholders, suppliers, customers, creditors, the local community, and the wider society. Each makes a contribution to the enterprise, and each has a stake in its growth or decline. Present structures of accountability, however, do not acknowledge all these contributions or protect these stakes. A major challenge in today's economy is the development of new institutional mechanisms for accountability that also preserve the flexibility needed to respond quickly to a rapidly changing business environment.[4]

299. New forms of partnership between workers and managers are one means for developing greater participation and accountability within firms.[5] Recent experience has shown that both labor and management suffer when the adversarial relationship between them becomes extreme. As Pope Leo XIII stated, "Each needs the other completely: capital cannot do without labor, nor labor without capital."[6] The organization of firms should reflect and enhance this mutual partnership. In particular, the development of work patterns for men

and women that are more supportive of family life will benefit both employees and the enterprises they work for.

300. Workers in firms and on farms are especially in need of stronger institutional protection, for their jobs and livelihood are particularly vulnerable to the decisions of others in today's highly competitive labor market. Several arrangements are gaining increasing support in the United States: profit sharing by the workers in a firm; enabling employees to become company stockholders; granting employees greater participation in determining the conditions of work; cooperative ownership of the firm by all who work within it; and programs for enabling a much larger number of Americans, regardless of their employment status, to become shareholders in successful corporations. Initiatives of this sort can enhance productivity, increase the profitability of firms, provide greater job security and work satisfaction for employees, and reduce adversarial relations.[7] In our 1919 Program of Social Reconstruction, we observed "the full possibilities of increased production will not be realized so long as the majority of workers remain mere wage earners. The majority must somehow become owners, at least in part, of the instruments of production."[8] We believe this judgment remains generally valid today.

301. None of these approaches provides a panacea, and all have certain drawbacks. Nevertheless we believe that continued research and experimentation with these approaches will be of benefit. Catholic social teaching has endorsed on many occasions innovative methods for increasing worker participation within firms.[9] The appropriateness of these methods will depend on the circumstances of the company or industry in question and on their effectiveness in actually increasing a genuinely cooperative approach to shaping decisions. The most highly publicized examples of such efforts have been in large firms facing serious

financial crises. If increased participation and collaboration can help a firm avoid collapse, why should it not give added strength to healthy businesses? Cooperative ownership is particularly worthy of consideration in new entrepreneurial enterprises.[10]

302. Partnerships between labor and management are possible only when both groups possess real freedom and power to influence decisions. This means that unions ought to continue to play an important role in moving toward greater economic participation within firms and industries. Workers rightly reject calls for less adversarial relations when they are a smokescreen for demands that labor make all the concessions. For partnership to be genuine it must be a two-way street, with creative initiative and a willingness to cooperate on all sides.

303. When companies are considering plant closures or the movement of capital, it is patently unjust to deny workers any role in shaping the outcome of these difficult choices.[11] In the heavy manufacturing sector today, technological change and international competition can be the occasion of painful decisions leading to the loss of jobs or wage reductions. While such decisions may sometimes be necessary, a collaborative and mutually accountable model of industrial organization would mean that workers not be expected to carry all the burdens of an economy in transition. Management and investors must also accept their share of sacrifices, especially when management is thinking of closing a plant or transferring capital to a seemingly more lucrative or competitive activity. The capital at the disposal of management is in part the product of the labor of those who have toiled in the company over the years, including currently employed workers.[12] As a minimum, workers have a right to be informed in advance when such decisions are under consideration, a right to negotiate with management about possible alternatives, and a right to fair compensation and assistance with

retraining and relocation expenses should these be necessary. Since even these minimal rights are jeopardized without collective negotiation, industrial cooperation requires a strong role for labor unions in our changing economy.

304. Labor unions themselves are challenged by the present economic environment to seek new ways of doing business. The purpose of unions is not simply to defend the existing wages and prerogatives of the fraction of workers who belong to them, but also to enable workers to make positive and creative contributions to the firm, the community, and the larger society in an organized and cooperative way.[13] Such contributions call for experiments with new directions in the U.S. labor movement.

305. The parts played by managers and shareholders in U.S. corporations also need careful examination. In U.S. law, the primary responsibility of managers is to exercise prudent business judgment in the interest of a profitable return to investors. But morally this legal responsibility may be exercised only within the bounds of justice to employees, customers, suppliers, and the local community. Corporate mergers and hostile takeovers may bring greater benefits to shareholders, but they often lead to decreased concern for the well-being of local communities and make towns and cities more vulnerable to decisions made from afar.

306. Most shareholders today exercise relatively little power in corporate governance.[14] Although shareholders can and should vote on the selection of corporate directors and on investment questions and other policy matters, it appears that return on investment is the governing criterion in the relation between them and management. We do not believe this is an adequate rationale for shareholder decisions. The question of how to relate the rights and responsibilities of shareholders to those of the other people and communities affected by corporate decisions is complex and insufficiently understood. We,

therefore, urge serious, long-term research and experimentation in this area. More effective ways of dealing with these questions are essential to enable firms to serve the common good.

B. Local and Regional Cooperation

307. The context within which U.S. firms do business has direct influence on their ability to contribute to the common good. Companies and indeed whole industries are not sole masters of their own fate. Increased cooperative efforts are needed to make local, regional, national, and international conditions more supportive of the pursuit of economic justice.

308. In the principle of subsidiarity, Catholic social teaching has long stressed the importance of small- and intermediate-sized communities or institutions in exercising moral responsibility. These mediating structures link the individual to society as a whole in a way that gives people greater freedom and power to act.[15] Such groups include families, neighborhoods, church congregations, community organizations, civic and business associations, public interest and advocacy groups, community development corporations, and many other bodies. All these groups can play a crucial role in generating creative partnerships for the pursuit of the public good on the local and regional level.

309. The value of partnership is illustrated by considering how new jobs are created. The development of new businesses to serve the local community is key to revitalizing areas hit hard by unemployment.[16] The cities and regions in greatest needs of these new jobs face serious obstacles in attracting enterprises that can provide them. Lack of financial resources, limited entrepreneurial skill, blighted and unsafe environments, and a deteriorating infrastructure create a vicious cycle that makes new investment in these areas more risky and therefore less likely.

310. Breaking out of this cycle will require a cooperative approach that draws on all

the resources of the community.[17] Community development corporations can keep efforts focused on assisting those most in need. Existing business, labor, financial, and academic institutions can provide expertise in partnership with innovative entrepreneurs. New cooperative structures of local ownership will give the community or region an added stake in businesses and even more importantly give these businesses a greater stake in the community.[18] Government on the local, state, and national levels must play a significant role, especially through tax structures that encourage investment in hard hit areas and through funding aimed at conservation and basic infrastructure needs. Initiatives like these can contribute to a multilevel response to the needs of the community.

311. The Church itself can work as an effective partner on the local and regional level. First-hand knowledge of community needs and commitment to the protection of the dignity of all should put Church leaders in the forefront of efforts to encourage a community-wide cooperative strategy. Because churches include members from many different parts of the community, they can often serve as mediator between groups who might otherwise regard each other with suspicion. We urge local church groups to work creatively and in partnership with other private and public groups in responding to local and regional problems.

C. Partnership in the Development of National Policies

312. The causes of our national economic problems and their possible solutions are the subject of vigorous debate today. The discussion often turns on the role the national government has played in creating these problems and could play in remedying them. We want to point to several considerations that could help build new forms of effective citizenship and cooperation in shaping the economic life of our country.

313. First, while economic freedom and personal initiative are deservedly esteemed in our society, we have increasingly come to recognize the inescapably social and political nature of the economy. The market is always embedded in a specific social and political context. The tax system affects consumption, saving, and investment. National monetary policy, domestic and defense programs, protection of the environment and worker safety, and regulation of international trade all shape the economy as a whole. These policies influence domestic investment, unemployment rates, foreign exchange, and the health of the entire world economy.

314. The principle of subsidiarity calls for government intervention when small or intermediate groups in society are unable or unwilling to take the steps needed to promote basic justice. Pope John XXIII observed that the growth of more complex relations of interdependence among citizens has led to an increased role for government in modern societies.[19] This role is to work in *partnership with* the many other groups in society, helping them fulfill their tasks and responsibilities more effectively, not replacing or destroying them. The challenge of today is to move beyond abstract disputes about whether more or less government intervention is needed, to consideration of creative ways of enabling government and private groups to work together effectively.

315. It is in this light that we understand Pope John Paul II's recommendation that "society make provision for overall planning" in the economic domain.[20] Planning must occur on various levels, with the government ensuring that basic justice is protected and also protecting the rights and freedoms of all other agents. In the Pope's words:

In the final analysis this overall concern weighs on the shoulders of the state, but it cannot mean one-sided centralization by the public authorities. Instead what is in question is a just and rational coordination within the framework of which the initiative of individuals, free groups, and local work centers and complexes must be safeguarded.[21]

316. We are well aware that the mere mention of economic planning is likely to produce a strong negative reaction in U.S. society. It conjures up images of centralized planning boards, command economies, inefficient bureaucracies, and mountains of government paperwork. It is also clear that the meaning of "planning" is open to a wide variety of interpretations and takes very different forms in various nations.[22] The Pope's words should not be construed as an endorsement of a highly centralized form of economic planning, much less a totalitarian one. His call for a "just and rational coordination" of the endeavors of the many economic actors is a call to seek creative new partnership and forms of participation in shaping national policies.

317. There are already many forms of economic planning going on within the U.S. economy today. Individuals and families plan for their economic future. Management and labor unions regularly develop both long- and short-term plans. Towns, cities, and regions frequently have planning agencies concerned with their social and economic future. When state legislatures and the U.S. Congress vote on budgets or on almost any other bill that comes before them, they are engaged in a form of public planning. Catholic social teaching does not propose a single model for political and economic life by which these levels are to be institutionally related to each other. It does insist that reasonable coordination among the different parts of the body politic is an essential condition for achieving justice. This is a moral precondition of good citizenship that applies to both individual and institutional actors. In its absence no political structure can guarantee justice in society or the economy. Effective decisions in these matters will demand greater cooperation among all citizens. To encourage our fellow citizens to consider more carefully the appropriate balance of private and local initiative with national economic policy, we make several recommendations.

318. *First, in an advanced industrial economy like ours, all parts of society, including government, must cooperate in forming national economic policies.* Taxation, monetary policy, high levels of government spending, and many other forms of governmental regulation are here to stay. A modern economy without governmental interventions of the sort we have alluded to is inconceivable. These interventions, however, should help, not replace, the contributions of other economic actors and institutions and should direct them to the common good. The development of effective new forms of partnership between private and public agencies will be difficult in a situation as immensely complex as that of the United States in which various aspects of national policy seem to contradict one another.[23] On the theoretical level, achieving greater coordination will make demands on those with the technical competence to analyze the relationship among different parts of the economy. More practically, it will require the various subgroups within our society to sharpen their concern for the common good and moderate their efforts to protect their own short-term interests.

319. *Second, the impact of national economic policies on the poor and the vulnerable is the primary criterion for judging their moral value.* Throughout this letter we have stressed the special place of the poor and the vulnerable in any ethical analysis of the U.S. economy. National economic policies that contribute to building a true commonwealth should reflect this by standing firmly for the rights of those who fall through the cracks of our economy: the poor, the unemployed, the homeless, the displaced. Being a citizen of this land means sharing in the responsibility for shaping and implementing such policies.

320. *Third, the serious distortion of national economic priorities produced by massive national spending on defense must be remedied.* Clear-sighted consideration of the role of government shows that government and the economy are already closely intertwined through military research and defense contracts. Defense-related industries make up a major part of the U.S. economy and have intimate links with both the military and civilian government, they often depart from the competitive model of free-market capitalism. Moreover, the dedication of so much of the national budget to military purposes has been disastrous for the poor and vulnerable members of our own and other nations. The nation's spending priorities need to be revised in the interests of both justice and peace.[24]

321. We recognize that these proposals do not provide a detailed agenda. We are also aware that there is a tension between setting the goals for coherent policies and actually arriving at them by democratic means. But if we can increase the level of commitment to the common good and the virtues of citizenship in our nation, the ability to achieve these goals will greatly increase. It is these fundamental moral concerns that lead us as bishops to join the debate on national priorities.

D. Cooperation at the International Level

322. If our country is to guide its international economic relationships by policies that serve human dignity and justice, we must expand our understanding of the moral responsibility of citizens to serve the common good of the entire planet. Cooperation is not limited to the local, regional, or national level. Economic policy can no longer be governed by national goals alone. The fact that the "social question has become worldwide"[25] challenges us to broaden our horizons and enhance our collaboration and sense of solidarity on the global level. The cause of democracy is closely tied to the cause of economic justice. The unfinished business of the American experiment includes the

formation of new international partnerships, especially with the developing countries, based on mutual respect, cooperation, and a dedication to fundamental justice.

323. The principle of subsidiary calls for government to intervene in the economy when basic justice requires greater social coordination and regulation of economic actors and institutions. In global economic relations, however, no international institution provides this sort of coordination and regulation. The U.N. system, including the World Bank, the International Monetary Fund, and the General Agreement on Tariffs and Trade, does not possess the requisite authority. Pope John XXIII called this institutional weakness a "structural defect" in the organization of the human community. The structures of world order, including economic ones, "no longer correspond to the objective requirements of the universal common good."[26]

324. Locked together in a world of limited material resources and a growing array of common problems, we help or hurt one another by the economic policies we choose. All the economic agents in our society, therefore, must consciously and deliberately attend to the good of the whole human family. We must all work to increase the effectiveness of international agencies in addressing global problems that cannot be handled through the actions of individual countries. In particular we repeat our plea made in *The Challenge of Peace* urging "that the United States adopt a stronger supportive leadership role with respect to the United Nations."[27] In the years following World War II, the United States took the lead in establishing multilateral bodies to deal with postwar economic problems. Unfortunately, in recent years this country has taken steps that have weakened rather than strengthened multilateral approaches. This is a shortsighted policy and should be reversed if the long-term interests of an interdependent globe are to be served.[28] In devising more effective arrangements

for pursuing international economic justice, the overriding problem is how to get from where we are to where we ought to be. Progress toward that goal demands positive and often difficult action by corporations, banks, labor unions, governments, and other major actors on the international stage. But whatever the difficulty, the need to give priority to alleviating poverty in developing countries is undeniable; and the cost of continued inaction can be counted in human lives lost or stunted, talents wasted, opportunities foregone, misery and suffering prolonged, and injustice condoned.

325. Self-restraint and self-criticism by all parties are necessary first steps toward strengthening the international structures to protect the common good. Otherwise, growing interdependence will lead to conflict and increased economic threats to human dignity. This is an important long-term challenge to the economic future of this country and its place in the emerging world economic community.

Notes

Chapter I

1. Vatican Council II, *The Pastoral Constitution on the Church in the Modern World*. 33. [Note: This pastoral letter frequently refers to documents of the Second Vatican Council, papal encyclicals, and other official teachings of the Roman Catholic Church. Most of these texts have been published by the United States Catholic Conference Office of Publishing and Promotion Services; many are available in collections, though no single collection is comprehensive. See Selected Bibliography.]
2. *Pastoral Constitution*, 1.
3. See ibid., 10, 42, 43; Congregation for the Doctrine of the Faith, *Instruction on Christian Freedom and Liberation*. (Washington, D.C.: USCC Office of Publishing and Promotion Services, 1986), 34–36.
4. See Pope John Paul II, *On Human Work* (1981), 14; and Pope Paul VI, *Octogesima Adveniens* (1971), 35. See also Arthur Okun, *Equality and Efficiency: The Big Tradeoff* (Washington, D.C.: The Brookings Institution, 1975), ch. 1; Michael Walzer, *Spheres of Justice:*

A Defense of Pluralism and Equality (New York: Basic Books, 1983), ch. 4; Jon P. Gunnemann, "Capitalism and Commutative Justice," paper presented at the 1985 meeting of the Society of Christian Ethics.
5. Abraham Lincoln, Address at Dedication of National Cemetery at Gettysburg, November 9, 1863.
6. Pope John XXIII, *Peace on Earth* (1963), 130–131.
7. Synod of Bishops, *Justice in the World* (1971), 8; Pope John Paul II, *Redeemer of Man* (1979), 15.
8. U.S. Department of Labor, Bureau of Labor Statistics, *The Employment Situation: August 1985* (September 1985), Table A-1.
9. Ibid.
10. U.S. Bureau of the Census, Current Population Reports, Series P-60, 145, *Money Income and Poverty Status of Families and Persons in the United States: 1983* (Washington, D.C.: U.S. Government Printing Office, 1984), 20.
11. Greg H. Duncan, *Years of Poverty, Years of Plenty: The Changing Economic Fortunes of American Workers and Their Families* (Ann Arbor, Mich.: Institute for Social Research, University of Michigan, 1984).
12. See Pope John Paul II, *Familiaris Consortio* (1981), 46.
13. *Pastoral Constitution*, 47.
14. National Conference of Catholic Bishops, *The Challenge of Peace: God's Promise and Our Response* (Washington, D.C.: USCC Office of Publishing and Promotion Services, 1983).
15. Cardinal Joseph L. Bernardin and Cardinal John J. O'Connor, Testimony before the House Foreign Relations Committee, June 26, 1984, *Origins* 14:10 (August 10, 1984): 157.
16. *Pastoral Constitution*, 43.
17. See, for example, Peter Berger, Brigitte Berger, and Hansfried Kellner, *The Homeless Mind: Modernization and Consciousness* (New York: Vintage, 1974).
18. For a recent study of the importance and difficulty of achieving such a common language and vision see Robert N. Bellah, Richard Madsen, William M. Sullivan, Ann Swindler, and Stephen M. Tipton, *Habits of the Heart: Individualism and Commitment in American Life* (Berkeley, Calif.: University of California Press, 1985). See also Martin E. Marty, *The Public Church* (New York: Crossroads, 1981).
19. Pope John Paul XXIII, *Mater et Magistra* (1961), 219; *Pastoral Constitution*, 40.
20. Congregation for the Doctrine of the Faith, *Instruction on Certain Aspects of the Theology of Liberation* (Washington, D.C.: USCC Office of Publishing and Promotion Services, 1984); Pope Paul VI, *Octogesima Adveniens* (1971), 42.
21. *Octogesima Adveniens*, 4.
22. Administrative Committee of the National Catholic War Council, *Program of Social Reconstruction*, February 12, 1919. Other notable statements on the economy by our predecessors are *The Present Crisis*,

April 25, 1933; *Statement on Church and Social Order,* February 4, 1940; *The Economy: Human Dimensions,* November 20, 1975. These and numerous other statements of the U.S. Catholic episcopate can be found in Hugh J. Nolan, ed., *Pastoral Letters of the United States Catholic Bishops,* 4 vols. (Washington, D.C.: USCC Office of Publishing and Promotion Services, 1984).

Notes

Chapter IV

1. *Octogesima Adveniens,* 24.
2. For different analyses along these lines with quite different starting points see Martin Carnoy, Derek Shearer, and Russell Rumberger, *A New Social Contract* (New York: Harper and Row, 1983); Amatai Elzioni, *An Immodest Agenda: Reconstructing America before the Twenty-First Century* (New York: McGraw-Hill, 1983); Charles E. Lindblon, *Politics and Markets* (New York: Basic Books, 1977), esp. 346–348; George C. Lodge, *The New American Ideology* (New York: Alfred A. Knopf, 1975); Douglas Sturm, "Corporations, Constitutions, and Covenants," *Journal of the American Academy of Religion,* 41 (1973); 331–55; Lester Thurow, *The Zero-Sum Society* (New York: Basic Books, 1980), esp. ch. 1; Roberto Mangabeira Unger, *Knowledge and Politics* (New York: Free Press, 1975); George F. Will, *Statecraft as Soulcraft: What Government Does* (New York: Simon and Schuster, 1982), esp. ch. 6.
3. *Pastoral Constitution,* 68. See *Mater et Magistra,* 75–77.
4. Charles W. Powers provided a helpful discussion of these matters in a paper presented at a conference on the first draft of this pastoral letter sponsored by the Harvard University Divinity School and the Institute for Policy Studies, Cambridge, Massachusetts, March 29–31, 1985.
5. See John Paul II, "The Role of Business in a Changing Workplace," 3, *Origins* 15 (February 6, 1986): 567.
6. *Rerum Novarum,* 28. For an analysis of the relevant papal teachings on institutions of collaboration and partnership, see John Cronin, *Catholic Social Principles: The Social Teaching of the Catholic Church Applied to American Economic Life* (Milwaukee: Bruce, 1950), ch. VII; Oswald von Nell-Breuning, *Reorganization of Social Economy: The Social Encyclical Developed and Explained,* trans. Bernard W. Dempsey (Milwaukee: Bruce, 1936), chs. X–XII; Jean-Yves Calvez and Jacques Perrin, *The Church and Social Justice,* trans. J. R. Kirwan (Chicago: Regnery, 1961), ch. XIX.
7. Michael Conte, Arnold S. Tannenbaum, and Donna McCulloch, *Employee Ownership,* Research Report Series, Institute for Social Research (Ann Arbor, Mich.: University of Michigan, 1981); Robert A. Dahl, *A Preface to Economic Democracy* (Berkeley: University of California Press, 1985); Harvard Business School, "The Mondragon Cooperative Movement," case study prepared by David P. Ellerman (Cambridge, Mass.: Harvard Business School, n.d.); Robert Jackall and Henry M. Levin, eds., *Worker Cooperatives in America* (Berkeley: University of California Press, 1984); Derek Jones and Jan Svejnar, eds., *Participatory and Self-Managed Firms: Evaluating Economic Performance* (Lexington, Mass.: D. C. Heath, 1982); Irving H. Siegel and Edgar Weinberg, *Labor-Management Cooperation: The American Experience* (Kalamazoo, Mich.: W. E. Upjohn Institute for Employment Research, 1982); Stuart M. Speiser, "Broadened Capital Ownership—The Solution to Major Domestic and International Problems," *Journal of Post Keynesian Economics* VIII (1985); 426–434; Jaroslav Vanek, ed., *Self-Management: Economic Liberation of Man* (London: Penguin, 1975); Martin L. Weitzman, *The Share Economy* (Cambridge, Mass.: Harvard University Press, 1984).
8. *Program of Social Reconstruction in Justice in the Marketplace,* 381.
9. *Mater et Magistra,* 32, 77, 85–103; *On Human Work,* 14.
10. For examples of worker-owned and operated enterprises supported by the Campaign for Human Development's revolving loan fund see CHD's *Annual Report* (Washington, D.C.: USCC).
11. *Quadragesimo Anno* states the basic norm on which this conclusion is based: "It is wholly false to ascribe to property alone or to labor alone whatever has been obtained through the combined effort of both, and it is wholly unjust for either, denying the efficacy of the other, to arrogate to itself whatever has been produced" (53).
12. *On Human Work,* 12.
13. Ibid., 20. This point was well made by John Cronin twenty-five years ago: "Even if most injustice and exploitation were removed, unions would still have a legitimate place. They are the normal voice of labor, necessary to organize social life for the common good. There is positive need for such organization today, quite independently of any social evils which may prevail. Order and harmony do not happen; they are the fruit of conscious and organized effort. While we may hope that the abuses which occasioned the rise of unions may disappear, it does not thereby follow that unions will have lost their function. On the contrary, they will be freed from unpleasant, even though temporarily necessary, tasks and able to devote all their time and efforts to a better organization of social life"

Catholic Social Principles, 418. See also AFL-CIO Committee on the Evolution of Work, *The Future of Work* (Washington, D.C.: AFL-CIO, 1983).

14. For a classic discussion of the relative power of managers and shareholders see A. A. Berle and Gardiner C. Means, *The Modern Corporation and Private Property* (New York: Macmillan, 1932).

15. Peter L. Berger and Richard John Neuhaus, *To Empower People: The Role of Mediating Structures in Public Policy* (Washington, D.C.: American Enterprise Institute, 1977).

16. United States Small Business Administration, *1978 Annual Report* (Washington, D.C.: Government Printing Office, 1979).

17. For recent discussion from a variety of perspectives see: Robert Friedman and William Schweke, eds., *Expanding the Opportunity to Produce: Revitalizing the American Economy through New Enterprise Development: A Policy Reader* (Washington, D.C.: Corporation for New Enterprise Development, 1981); Jack A. Meyer, ed., *Meeting Human Needs: Toward a New Public Philosophy* (Washington, D.C.: American Enterprise Institute, 1982); Committee for Economic Development, *Jobs for the Hard-to-Employ: New Directions for a Public-Private Partnership* (New York: Committee for Economic Development, 1978); Gar Alperovitz and Jeff Faux, *Rebuilding America: A Blueprint for the New Economy* (New York: Pantheon Books, 1984).

18. Christopher Mackin, *Strategies for Local Ownership and Control: A Policy Analysis* (Somerville, Mass.: Industrial Cooperative Association, 1983).

19. *Mater et Magistra*, 59, 62.

20. *On Human Work*, 18.

21. Ibid.

22. For examples and analysis of different meanings of economic planning see Naomi Caiden and Aaron Wildavsky, *Planning and Budgeting in Poor Countries* (New York: Wiley, 1974); Robert Dahl and Charles E. Lindblom, *Politics, Economics and Welfare: Planning and Politico-Economic Systems Resolved into Basic Social Processes* (Chicago: University of Chicago Press, 1976); Stephen S. Cohen, *Modern Capitalist Planning: The French Model* (Berkeley, University of California Press, 1977); Albert Waterston, *Development Planning: Lessons of Experience* (Baltimore: Johns Hopkins Press, 1965); *Rebuilding America*, chs. 14, 15.

23. For example, many students of recent policy point out that monetary policy on the one hand and fiscal policies governing taxation and government expenditures on the other have been at odds with each other, with larger public deficits and high interest rates at the outcome. See Alice M. Rivlin, ed., *Economic Choices 1984* (Washington, D.C.: The Brookings Institution, 1984), esp. ch. 2.

24. *The Challenge of Peace*, 270–271.

25. *On the Development of Peoples*, 3.

26. *Peace on Earth*, 134–135.

27. *The Challenge of Peace*, 268.

28. See Robert O. Keohane and Joseph S. Nye, Jr., "Two Cheers for Multilateralism," *Foreign Policy* 60 (Fall 1985): 148–167.

Writing and Discussion Topics

Questions 1–6 address content, critical analysis, personal choices, ethical options, specific discipline, and interdisciplinary alternatives, respectively.

1. In this message, the bishops recommend less emphasis on competition and more on cooperation. Explain why competition could be considered an obstacle to promoting economic good?

2. What are the principle themes of the pastoral letter?

3. The bishops believe that economic pressures place tensions on family life. Do you agree or disagree? What evidence do you see that supports this position?

4. The letter discusses company closings. What are the ethical and moral ramifications of a plant or corporate closure?

5. What are some problems in today's society that would hamper the implementation of the pastoral letter? Can these problems be solved?

6. Is the bishops' letter more radical and far-reaching than some of the philosophers' positions which promote social responsibility? Compare and contrast the letter with the philosophers in this section.

Robert Benne

THE BISHOPS' LETTER: A PROTESTANT READING

◆◆◆

*R*obert Benne is the Jordan Trekler Professor of Christian Theology and Ethics at Roanoke College. He is a prolific writer in the area of Christianity, ethics, and business. A graduate of the University of Chicago, Benne criticizes the Catholic bishops for their failure to appreciate the creativity and efficiency of the United States economy. ◆

The bishops have kept their promise that their reflections on the American economy would be open to ongoing dialogue with their readers. Though they have not changed their minds about the basic thrust of their document, which in itself does not call into doubt the authenticity of the conversation, they have clearly responded to the criticism leveled by thousands of voices who have participated in the dialogue.

The second version shows marked improvements, among them, the bishops have: conveyed a more balanced view of American economic performance; learned more from the American pragmatic and reformist tradition than earlier; appreciated more readily the "market virtues" of economic freedom, initiative and productivity; emphasized more vigorously the need for economic activism among persons in the economy, including the poor (the economy is measured not only by what it does *to* and *for* people, but also by how people *participate* in it); attempted to refute the charge of statism by underscoring their commitment to cooperation among economic actors; and, most welcomed, toned down the shrill "prophetic denunciations" of the United States and its people, perhaps because of a new respect for the complexity and intractability of many serious economic issues as well as for the variety of opinions about such matters held by persons of goodwill and intelligence. They have made good their pledge that feedback would be taken seriously.

Nevertheless, the main argument is unchanged. Their fundamental ethical principle—the dignity of the human person realized in community with others—is combined with its indispensable corollary, the "preferential option for the poor," which addresses the sorry fact that too many people do not participate in that dignity in community. Standing on that principle, which they believe is a summation of the Christian moral vision, the bishops derive more specific norms for economic life and then argue that those must lead to the extension of economic democracy in America.

Economic democracy seems to mean two basic things: an elaboration of certain fundamental economic rights that will ensure that all have access to a dignified level of life, and participation in decision making in the economic process by all. This realization of economic democracy will bring closer to fruition the American commitment to democracy, which has thus far been focused on the achievement of political democracy. As the bishops put it, "These economic rights are as essential to human dignity as are the political and civil freedoms granted pride of place in the Bill of Rights of the U.S. Constitution."

In spite of the several changes that have been made in the second draft, some people are still uncomfortable about document, although they share the bishops' fundamental moral principle. Part of the discomfort is warranted, for the bishops have succeeded in drawing attention repeatedly to the serious human problems facing society—there is simply too much misery and suffering. Certainly, we ought to do more to alleviate that suffering and to move toward a more just society in which ever more people have the opportunity to participate with dignity. If the bishops can continue to make us uncomfortable by pointing to that suffering and insisting on some sort of constructive approach, their efforts will not have been in vain.

However, part of the discomfort has to do with disagreement about the specific argument of the letter, which this essay will discuss. First will be addressed questions about how one of the normative sections of the paper is handled, particularly, "Ethical Norms for Economic Life." That section contains the detailed specification of what human dignity in community really means, especially for economic life. Second will be critical rejections on the selected policy proposals made in chapters 3 and 4. Third, some disagreements will be registered with the general approach of the document; for example, its partisanship, its handling of critics and its hesitation to apply its principles to the church.

Normative Considerations

Although it is true that economic growth is recognized in the policy-issues section as indispensable for the alleviation of unemployment and poverty, one searches in vain for any discussion of economic growth in the normative sections of the document. In short, the document seems to avoid completely the issue of primarily what an economy is *for*. The letter certainly has a plethora of moral principles that hold economic actors accountable. They are to be imbued with civic friendship, they have duties to be

Reprinted with permission of Macmillan Publishing Company from *The Catholic Challenge to the American Economy*, edited by Thomas M. Gannon. Copyright © 1987 by Macmillan Publishing Company, a division of Macmillan, Inc.

commutatively, socially and distributively just, and they are called to overcome the marginalization and powerlessness of the poor. On the other hand, all persons, whether or not they are capable of contributing economically, have economic rights to life, food, clothing, shelter, rest, medical care and social security. Those who can contribute have rights to employment at an adequate wage for human dignity as well as healthful working conditions.

Besides ensuring that economic actors adhere to these rights and duties, the nation is called to moral priorities of fulfilling the basic needs of the poor, increasing active participation in economic life by those who are excluded or vulnerable, and investing wealth, talent and human energy in ways that directly benefit the poor and economically insecure.

Conversely, in the introductory section of the letter, unequal economic outcomes—employment falling on some and not others, disparities among nations, differentials between male and female incomes and poverty amid plenty—are attributed to moral failure in the economy. Inequalities are consistently attributed to injustice.

Indeed, on reading the normative sections of the letter, one would conclude that economic life is almost exclusively a moral activity. Economics *is* ethics. No doubt it is true that moral failures are present in all the problems just mentioned. It is also true that economic life as a thoroughly human activity has many moral interstices. The bishops are right in arguing that economic life has an inescapable moral dimension, especially in the face of a good deal of economic writing and business practice that tries to rule it out, mistakenly assuming that economics is exclusively a technical endeavor. However, in almost completely ignoring the technical and nonmoral values connected with the adequate working of an economy, the letter appears naive.

These weaknesses are starkly revealed in what has to be one of the most foolish statements in the letter: "They [all economic decisions, policies and institutions] must be at the service of all people, especially the poor." What does such a statement mean? When the local grocery store manager decides to purchase wholesale some fish in order to sell them to customers, how can such a decision possibly be assured to serve *all* people, especially the poor? The store manager has to serve only some people, for example, wholesalers, customers and employees. It is impossible for the manager to make an economic decision that benefits all people but especially the poor because it is only a small, limited part in

an impersonal, unconsciously coordinated market system that requires the manager to be accountable to specific people in specific ways. These discrete economic decisions cannot be based on the common good, universal benevolence, or the preferential option for the poor because, if they were, the particular service to supplier, customer and employee would soon end, for the manager would have neglected sober consideration of prices and marketing and thereby bankrupted the store by failing to make an adequate profit. In a very indirect way, however, the manager is serving many people, including many of the poor, by effectively participating in a market system that in its own impersonal and broadly utilitarian way lifts the living strategy of the majority.

This vast and dynamic American market system, operating in a relatively free and competitive way, hands out rewards and losses according to how well enterprises and persons respond to its demands. This process involves what Joseph Schumpeter called "creative destruction," where new products and services as well as new ways of producing them come to the fore while older ones are sloughed off. This process, Schumpeter avers, leads to revolutions in the means of production, which in turn, bring more and more products within reach of ordinary people, thus lifting the living standards of the majority.[1] The American economy seems to be very adept at doing what economies are fundamentally *for*—the efficient and creative combination of factors of production so that wealth is generated.

By neglecting the nonmoral, technical and instrumental values of efficiency and productivity, the bishops imply that economic activity is primarily moral and political. This has several harmful effects on the letter.

First, the letter fails to distinguish between economics and politics. The bishops are actually addressing the American political economy; they are making mostly public policy recommendations, giving very little attention to economic values and processes per se. They foster an idealistic illusion that the moral and political enterprise, mainly devoted to distribution and participation, could go on without the economic expertise and vitality that logically and chronologically take precedence.

Second, distortions in their normative approach lead them to expect too much morally of economic life. Certainly, we should expect more just outcomes in economic life, but by dissolving the inevitable tension between efficiency and equality through their failure to consider the requirements of efficiency, the bishops proliferate the moral and political demands on economic life in such a way that the goose that lays the golden egg would indeed be throttled. The letter seems to suppose that the problems of efficiency and production have been solved—all we have to do is make the process more just.

Third, this imbalance toward moralism leads to the unwise use of such concepts as "economic democracy" and "new experiments in democratic, economic decision making." Friend and foe alike have remarked how similar the bishops' proposal sounds to the platforms of European social democratic parties. While the bishops say they wish to avoid assessments of economic systems, their very list of questions to be put to economic systems exhibits a serious distrust of free market arrangements, and their commitment to economic democracy suggests a strong affinity for a moderate democratic socialism.

Clearly, Christians of goodwill and intelligence can opt for such an approach, but perhaps such partisanship is unwise in view of the difficulty those social democratic approaches have had in economic growth and job creation. That partisanship is also unnecessary because many of the letter's more specific proposals on unemployment, poverty, agriculture and the world economy need not flow from those particular ideological commitments. Many Christians will be able to affirm a good number of the specific policy proposals out of a democratic capitalist persuasion, but the socialist rhetoric could put them off.

Fourth, the rather heavy moralistic overlay at the expense of technical, practical, economic "excellence" leads to an unduly heroic ethic for lay people. There is little mention of the laity's obligation to perform cheerfully and well their daily work and thereby serve others in mundane ways. Rather, the laity are summoned to imitate the pattern of Jesus' life, take up the way of the cross, empty the self and "leave all" to follow Jesus. Now, interpreted rightly, all those injunctions have authentic Christian meaning. Further, the bishops do affirm the role of the laity in their worldly callings in the section on Christian vocation: "The vocation of all Christians is rather to draw faith and life into a vital synthesis which proclaims God's glory." The normative images, though, do not emphasize ordinary worldly excellence as a way to serve God and others.

The bishops also tend to overemphasize the amount of leeway lay economic actors have in their decision making. Lay people are more constrained by their particular place in the economic system than the bishops imply with their somewhat heroic ethic. Moreover, little Gospel comfort is given to those who are caught in the inevitable tensions between particular necessities and more universal moral aspirations, a tension that all Christians frequently experience.

In sum, the more specific, normative section of the document is flawed because it tends only to moral values and neglects the nonmoral values with which economics inescapably deals. This leads to the aforementioned unfortunate results. If one tried to keep moral and nonmoral values in a more realistic tension, different concepts than "economic democracy" and "cooperation" would be more appropriate. Also, different specific proposals would take shape. Both concepts and proposals are likely to be more consonant with American experience and ideology, and perhaps they might also be specific embodiments of the bishops' indisputable fundamental principle—the dignity of the person in community.

Policy Proposals

The policy proposals the letter makes on poverty, employment, agriculture, and the U.S. role in the world economy seem, on the whole, to be moderate and measured, especially in comparison with the normative section of the document. This is quite possibly the case because the writers are forced to take into account considerations of efficiency and practicality. The proposals are basically pragmatic and reformist, and many persons of various political philosophies can agree with at least some of them. However, there are a number of areas in which critical questions can be raised.

One wonders, for example, what all that the bishops propose would cost. The mention of dramatic increases in welfare benefits, job retraining, child care, public employment, loans for threatened farmers and development assistance, to name but a few items, raises serious questions of feasibility, especially in the light of booming federal deficits and a general loss of confidence in the government's ability to attack problems effectively. The letter can be regarded as a vision of all the things that should be done, but then the bishops have stopped with an elaboration of principles and goals. When the letter tackles practical policy, the bishops owe some estimate of the feasibility of all of these programs, or at least, they owe us a calculation of costs and of from where the additional money is to come. Without that, the letter shares the characteristic of too many church documents, that is, no realistic sense of limits.

Another worrisome problem is the letter's vagueness about whether its proposals are to be legally mandated or taken as a moral summons for all economic actors. Some proposals, such as reform of the welfare system and lessening of the tax burden on the poor, are obviously meant to entail a change in laws. How about upgrading jobs, though, and the exhortation for comparable worth, the inveighing against luxury goods (word processors, for example?) and above all, the grand proposal for a new American experiment in economic cooperation and participation? In introducing chapter IV, "A New American Experiment: Partnership for the Common Good," the bishops say that as the nation's founders took daring steps to create structures of mutual accountability within the political system, so "we believe that similar institutional steps are needed today to expand the sharing of economic power and to relate the economic system more accountably to the common good." That would suggest that their vision of partnership among all involved in the productive process, as well as those affected by it, should be legally imposed on economic enterprises.

This is a very disturbing thought because it would mandate a specific model of ownership and decision making on a highly dynamic and experimental system, and would introduce rigidity and inflexibility into that system. The exciting experiments with Japanese models, with employee ownership and management and with other schemes for making workplaces more humane are endorsed by a range of theorists, from left-wing supply-siders like Robert Reich to hard-nosed capitalists like Louis Kelso.[2] Many true believers have great faith in these efforts to enhance human values and productivity at the same time. Conclusive evidence, however, is not yet available. The American economy is characterized by a variety of ownership and management styles, all of which compete with each other in a grand experiment about which ones shall prevail.

It is wisest to allow a thousand flowers to bloom. The many different styles of ownership and management will probably survive. We should not foreclose on the experiment as the bishops tend to suggest; the secrets of economic vitality are not known fully by anyone, nor are they fully captured by any one model. Perhaps the bishops think they know too much about "true" models.

The bishops enthusiasm for partnership and participation also is too uncritical. They seem to suggest that the introduction of participatory practices will suddenly do away with conflicts of interest within firms and within industries and communities. This probably is not so. Further, in affirming a cooperative model over a competitive one, they seem unaware of the capacity for cooperating groups to exert their self-interest in powerful ways that border on monopoly. For example, auto manufacturers, their workers and their political representatives *do* cooperate in pressing for protectionist measures. In fact, Mancur Olson has argued in his *The Rise and Decline of Nations* that collusive efforts by special interests tend to substitute political favors and protection for economic performance, thus harming the overall competitive position of the nation.[3]

The suggestion here is not that these new experiments in the "pursuit of excellence" are unworthy of the bishops' interest, but rather, that too many eggs have been put in one basket, that if these experiments were to be mandated legally, they could produce a disaster for the American economy. The present experimental system, held accountable by competition, is likelier to come up with viable models.

Perhaps the bishops think that their pastoral letter on peace has solved all the debates on defense spending and foreign policy. They imply that the United States has exaggerated East-West conflicts, that the need to address domestic ills and to participate more generally in Third World economic development obviously outweighs the need to build up the military, and that political-strategic considerations in the use of foreign aid should simply stand aside before the basic needs of developing countries. All of that may be true, but it certainly is not argued in this document. Readers of the document then can find themselves asking these questions: So what if there is a real Marxist-Leninist threat in Nicaragua and El Salvador? Are only North-South dynamics going on there? So what if the Soviet Union is involved in a gigantic military buildup? Even allowing for unjustifiable waste, has not the bulk of the U.S. buildup been necessary? Ought we really to devote money to develop Cuba or Vietnam without regard to political or strategic interests? Since the bishops would draw a good deal of their money for the costs of domestic and international economic reforms from the defense budget, they perhaps owe us more reflection on priorities than they have given us within this letter.

While most of the letter's policy proposals are levelheaded and moderate, it seems clear that they generally come from the liberal side of American political philosophy. They exhibit something of the grand old tradition of New Deal liberalism: the expansion and refinement of economic rights, increased welfare, economic planning and cooperation and interventions into markets through income policy. Except for one bow to Milton Friedman's negative income tax, little attention is given to analyses and proposals from other movements of political philosophy and action such as the neoliberal, conservative and libertarian groups.

The bishops ignore those movements at their own peril, because many of the more interesting proposals for extending justice and opportunity are coming from those sources. For example, the proposal for school vouchers is fascinating. The bishops do not take it up as a means of dramatically improving access to excellent education by the poor, no doubt because they would appear to be involved in special pleading for Catholic schools. That is unfortunate, because a voucher system biased toward the poor could be an extremely important way to extend a fairer shake to them.

Widely known is that Milton Friedman (followed by a number of libertarians) has been keenly interested in eroding the near-monopoly on primary and secondary education held by the public school system. His idea is for the state to give a voucher worth a year of education to parents for each of their school-age children. The vouchers would be nontransferable, but usable in public or private schools. This would expand parents' choice and force public schools to compete on equal footing with private schools.[4]

Many telling criticisms of this proposal have been made by persons who are not simply defensive proponents of the present system. Chief among these reservations is that middle-class parents would quickly move their children into private and parochial schools on their vouchers, those schools would fill up, and then the children of disadvantaged families would be left with the public schools, which would become dumping grounds for the worst cases. That is a convincing criticism. However, what if the families of disadvantaged children (children of one-parent families below a very low income level) were given vouchers worth 150% of the cost of a year of education? Private and public schools would arrange education to help those children and appeal to their

parents because they would have an incentive to do it. Catholic and other church-related schools would have an advantage because they have had a lot of practice in these kinds of arrangements. Many poor families could then afford such an education, and the schools could afford to give it to them. Church schools would offer a more disciplined context that would emphasize moral values. They could tap the idealism of many young persons who would choose to become teachers of the disadvantaged if only they could make a living at it and work in healthy and effective environments. Meanwhile, the public schools would have to compete for their students, and poor parents would have a choice.

The worth of vouchers for private education would decline as one went up the socioeconomic scale, while all families would have vouchers worth the full amount for use in public schools. This would give incentives for middle-class families to keep their children in public schools. All across the board, the choice would be real and effective. This would not only break down the monopolies that currently help to block improvements in urban education, but would open important educational channels for the poor.

In many small town and suburban areas, these schemes would not be necessary, since disadvantaged children already have access to the same schools that more advantaged children attend. Such an approach might be tried, though, in areas where the poor have miserable opportunities. Several state legislatures such as that of Minnesota have similar plans before them. This idea illustrates an important point. Some of the most creative social policy thought is coming from conservative and even libertarian sources. Such economists as Walter Williams have many proposals that would open up access for the poor to work that are currently closed off by collusive regulation. Licensure is a key way special interest groups can cooperate to maintain monopoly conditions and freeze out unwanted entrants.[5]

Also, many economists argue that the best way to support the poor at a decent level is through direct subsidy (vouchers for fuel, medical insurance, rent) rather than trying to fix the pricing system of the market. These examples are given in order to suggest that other mechanisms are available for extending justice, ways that may be more efficient and decentralized than the kind of interventions the bishops suggest. This is to say that "economic democracy" may be related more to the expansion and power of choice than to direct participation in the economic decision-making process. While the importance of direct participation is not to be underplayed, it is even more important for the poor to have a choice of opportunities in work and in the crucial services that enhance their lives. Conservative and libertarian economists have been creative in proposing schemes that in fact support those kinds of choices. The bishops do not have to accept the philosophical underpinnings of those economists in order to accept, or at least take seriously, many of their proposals.

General Approach

The tendency to entertain only liberal analyses and policy proposals in the Catholic bishops' letter, as well as in most other mainline church statements, raises a serious question of basic approach. How helpful is it for the church to commend particular public policy options? The churches have been infatuated with this kind of witness, but it is not clear that such an approach is the wisest and most helpful to both members and nonmembers as well as the church itself. Church statements often alienate large numbers of the laity, not only because the people disagree with the positions taken by their church, but because they observe their views are often not considered by church leaders. In this regard, it seems rather ungracious of the bishops not even to mention the Lay Commission or its letter. Further, they do not consider the arguments of such writers as Murray, Auletta, Williams and Sowell.[6] They never mention Michael Novak's writing, although the bishops' committee did hear testimony from him and several other conservatives. It is as if the bishops do not want to say anything nice or even recognize the existence of their "enemies"—but the laity do in fact read such analyses. When the church does not even recognize their existence, many people become suspicious that the writers of church statements are not playing fair.

The churches might be wiser to adapt another approach in their address to most social issues, that is, "most" and not "all," because there are some issues to which the church has long-held, settled commitments. Its clarity on apartheid, for example, cannot be challenged. However, the church should maintain flexibility on how Christians might resist apartheid in South Africa; there seem to be a number of morally viable options.

Wiser and more helpful would be for the church to encourage fair moral discourse on the great issues facing us. At the outset, the church could attempt to discern the limits of permissible Christian options by identifying those positions and actions that are clearly beyond the pale of Christian moral possibility. Then, it would be helpful to identify the key analyses and policy proposals, perhaps including its own if it thinks it really has something unique to add to the discussion at that level. The church could follow up by carefully critiquing the major analyses and proposals, lifting up weaknesses and strengths. In a few cases of authentic urgency and churchly clarity, it could come out for a specific option, but this would be done relatively infrequently. In most cases, the laity could be left to make up its own mind within the range of possibilities.

Moreover, the church could become much more of a mediator of divergent opinions and interests than it has been. Like the Evangelical and Catholic academies in Germany, the American churches could spend more time and energy providing a gracious context for bringing together divergent groups and interests to facilitate conversation. These efforts might lead to the kind of partnership, cooperation and accommodation the bishops call for in their "New American Experiment" chapter, and could be more helpful than constantly taking positions on issues. Further, it would honor and support the laity in its rightful role in the practical affairs of the world.

Although clearly, the bishops have tried to apply their own moral principles to the life of the Catholic church, that effort is still unsatisfactory in regard to two important issues. The bishops insist that economic life should be characterized by democracy. They actually give very few reasons for this—they just think it would be a good thing. They also insist that economic life should be free of sexual discrimination. The reasons they give here are fairly compelling. In neither case, however, do they consider whether these challenges should be addressed to the decision-making and leadership practices of the Catholic church. There may be good reasons why these challenges should not be heeded, but there may also be good reasons why all economic decision-making cannot be democratic. In neither case have they made compelling arguments. If the bishops want to commend strongly certain principles to worldly spheres of activity, they owe us reasons why they should not as well apply to the religious.

Finally, there leaves one nagging concern. Though this chapter has referred to the letter as the bishops' letter, some people believe that it is actually their staff's letter. The bishops approve its final form, of course, but the flavor of its argument is decidedly academic rather than ecclesiastic. Such is the case with the lion's share of church statements. Without resorting to nefarious, "new class" theories it has been suggested that the domination of statements by church staffs is not unnoticed by the lay constituencies of the various churches. The bishops lose some credibility as pastoral leaders when they shift the responsibility in drafting statements to their staffs.

Conclusion

This chapter concludes with a word of praise and caution. The praise comes for the service the bishops have provided in keeping before us as Christians and as a nation the issue of deprivation in our land of plenty. This is not terribly fashionable to do, but the bishops, shrewdly drawing out the discussion through several drafts after the election of a conservative U.S. president, have succeeded in keeping a public debate going. Moreover, considering the possibilities for real disaster, the bishops have done rather well. Protestants can learn much from their seriousness and thoroughness.

Concerning the word of caution, it can be suggested that all religious communities, particularly those of the Protestant and Catholic mainstream, become more "intentional" and disciplined about the primary reason for their existence: the formation of their members into the religious and moral vision they bear. That process of formation seems to become weaker as time goes by, especially for the young. The *substance* of both Catholic and Protestant traditions is becoming fainter. Meanwhile, those communities seem increasingly focused on the *implications* of their religious and moral vision, implications that can and ought to be open to a variety of interpretations. Is the attention of the bishops and the religious professions too bound up with implications and too little with fundamental formation? If so, the moral weight of what they propose will soon dissolve because they will have too few troops for them to be taken seriously.

Notes

1. Joseph Schumpeter, *Capitalism, Socialism and Democracy* (New York: Harper and Row, 1940; 1975), p. 83.
2. Robert Reich, *The Next American Frontier* (New York: Penguin, 1984).
3. Mancur Olson, *The Rise and Decline of Nations* (New Haven: Yale University Press, 1982).
4. Milton Friedman, *Capitalism and Freedom* (Chicago: University of Chicago Press, 1962), pp. 175–187.
5. Walter Williams, *Youth and Minority Unemployment* (Palo Alto: Hoover Institution Press, 1977).
6. Charles Murray, *Losing Ground: American Social Policy, 1950–1980* (New York: Basic Books, 1984); Ken Auletta, *The Underclass* (New York: Random House, 1983); Walter Williams, *America: A Minority Viewpoint* (Palo Alto: Hoover Institution Press, 1977); Thomas Sowell, *Markets and Minorities* (Oxford: International Center for Economic Policy Studies, 1981); *Ethnic America* (New York: Basic Books, 1981), *The Economics and Politics of Race* (New York: Morrow, 1983), and *Civil Rights: Rhetoric or Reality?* (New York: Morrow, 1984).

Writing and Discussion Topics

Questions 1–6 address content, critical analysis, personal choices, ethical options, specific discipline, and interdisciplinary alternatives, respectively.

1. What does Benne say is the main argument of the bishops' letter? Why is he critical of this argument?
2. What are the major problems with the normative considerations in the bishops' letter, according to Benne?
3. Does Benne seem to ignore the seriousness of the social problems in society, or do the bishops overstate the problem?
4. According to Benne, what are the main characteristics or features of the Protestant ethic? How do these differ from the theme of the pastoral letter?
5. Are the bishops advocating a form of socialism? Does Benne tend to assume that everyone, regardless of their religious convictions, will accept the bishops' message?
6. Why does Benne disagree with the mixture of church, business, and government through new experiments in economic "democracy"?

Ronald Green

THE BISHOPS' LETTER: A JEWISH READING

*R*onald Green *is a professor at Dartmouth College and chair of the Department of Religion. He received his doctorate from Harvard University. He has published widely, including two books,* Population, Growth *and* Justice *and* Religious Reason. ♦

Ronald Green   Courtesy of Ronald Green.

The bishops' pastoral letter on the U.S. economy appears at a peculiarly uncertain moment in the history of American Jewish thinking about social and economic issues. For many decades, American Jews have strongly supported progressive initiatives in the economic and social sphere. Indeed, Jews have so often been identified with the ideals of the welfare state that, in the words of one writer, "Jewish liberalism" has been almost a redundant term.[1] Nevertheless, on several fronts, this traditional identification of Jews with progressive social and economic causes has recently been called into question.

Although Jewish voters continue to support Democratic party candidates at substantially higher rates than the other immigrant religious groups that once formed the New Deal coalition, there has been some movement among Jewish voters toward moderate Democratic, Republican and even conservative candidates.[2] More important, perhaps, is the fact that some of the most important Jewish intellectuals and activists involved in shaping both Jewish and non-Jewish thinking about economic matters are now to be found on the conservative rather than the liberal side of public debate. Such thinkers as Robert Nozick, Irving Kristol, or Milton Friedman appear to have partly replaced the Herbert Marcuses or Allard Lowensteins of a previous era.

In many ways, of course, this transformation is to be expected. As Jews have attained middle- and upper-middle-class affluence and nearly full social acceptance, some have naturally been attracted to doctrines of economic individualism and success. This transformation, however, has also created a sense of puzzlement about the Jewish past and the traditions with which many Jews have identified themselves. Recently, for example, voices have been heard saying that Jewish liberalism, especially Jewish concern for the economically disadvantaged and socially marginal, is a very recent and peripheral aspect of Jewish life and thought; that it is the product of nineteenth century European experience and Jews' opposition to the alliance of economically conservative and anti-Semitic forces arrayed against them; and that it was reinforced in America by an encounter with the nativist, isolationist and conservative economic interests that opposed the New Deal and forced Jews to the left. This Jewish liberalism, it is said, is as ephemeral as the New Deal coalition

itself, a short-lived "marriage of convenience" between an embattled ethnic group and a social ideology. If this marriage is now coming to an end, it is because changing circumstances have permitted Jews to return to the attitudes they have historically possessed: a preference for unfettered capitalistic activity, individual economic initiative and self-reliance.[3]

The remarks that follow will challenge this view. "Jewish liberalism," it will be suggested, is not a novel phenomenon, but an enduring, and indeed, almost defining aspect of this ancient tradition. Moral concern for the poor and disadvantaged has its deepest roots in the Hebrew bible, but also is reiterated in the normative sources of Jewish thinking—the Talmud, and the writings of its great medieval codifiers. More important, this concern was expressed in the daily practice and institutions of Jewish communities over many centuries.

Another way of saying this is to observe that many of the most basic themes of Jewish social thought are deeply congruent with those emphasized in the bishops' letter. Proceeding from a common foundation in biblical teaching about social justice, both traditions elaborated a rich series of shared understandings of the nature and limits of economic life, and both sought to embody these understandings in the lives of their respective communities. For this reason, a brief review of some of the major themes enunciated in the bishops' letter is a useful way of beginning a survey of Jewish teaching on these issues. Although there are some important differences in nuance between Jewish and Catholic economic ethics, the major themes announced by the bishops have corresponding importance and saliency in the traditional Jewish sources. Apart from its value to Catholics and Americans in general, the pastoral letter, therefore, performs a special service for Jewish Americans: It reminds them of some of the major ethical themes their own tradition has contributed to Western thinking in the area of social and economic life.

Themes in the Pastoral Letter

Four themes appear to predominate in the bishops' letter. These are not always singled out as such, nor are they entirely distinguishable, but they appear frequently enough to merit independent identification.

They include, first, an emphasis on human dignity, and the resulting test of an economic system in terms of what it does *for* people and what it does *to* people.[4] This theme underlies the letter's stress on the importance of individuals' participation in the economic system on the value of labor, not merely as a way of meeting material needs, but as a mode of self-realization.[5]

Second, there is the theme that the right to private property is not unqualified. This view, rooted in centuries of church teaching, holds that the goods of the earth are ordained by God as the common property of all human beings. Although private possession has penultimate legitimacy as a way of ordering use of these goods, such possession is always to be regarded as a form of "stewardship" of resources for the common good and can be limited by urgent social needs.[6]

The third theme follows directly from this—the special obligation that exists to sustain and aid the poor. Precisely because the goods of the earth are divinely ordained to *all* human beings, the poor have a right to access to the goods and opportunities needed to sustain life in dignity. Assistance to the poor is not merely an obligation of charity and private giving, but a strict demand of justice, and the test of a social system is partly how well it serves the needs of the disadvantaged. This understanding, along with other motifs drawn from the biblical and later Christian tradition, help form the "preferential option for the poor" espoused by the letter.[7]

Finally is the theme that these attitudes and obligations are not confined to only the local or even national community, but extend to humankind as a whole. Allowing for the enormous complexities that bear on economic sharing beyond the national level, the letter affirms the oneness of human moral community and the requirement of global responsibility in the economic domain.[8]

Biblical Foundations

The deep congruence between Jewish teaching and the themes of the bishops' letter has its origin in a shared heritage of biblical faith. Here are found the essential ideas and norms that shape all subsequent Jewish thinking about economic life.

The emphasis on social justice is, of course, a hallmark of prophetic faith. The beginnings of Israel as a nation stem from a battle against economic oppression at the hands of Egyptian masters, and the memory of this is reflected in the many specific covenantal requirements of justice imposed on the nation. Under the constant reminder that they were once themselves bondsmen in Egypt (Exod. 23:9; Deut. 15:15, 16:12), the Israelites were required to show special solicitude for the economically and socially "marginalized" in their midst; the poor, the slave, the orphan, the widow and the sojourner.

This concern was embodied in a series of commandments that furnish the basis for what subsequently becomes Jewish law (*halakhah*). Among other things, these commandments include: the provision for the cancellation of debts, return of alienated property and the emancipation of slaves in the Jubilee year; the requirement that the spontaneous growths of the field and garden during the Sabbatical year be left free to the poor (Exod. 23:11); that every third year a tithe—one tenth—of all products be given to the needy (Deut. 14:28-29); that at every harvest, a corner of all grain fields (Lev. 19:9, 23:22)—later interpreted as amounting to one sixtieth of the crop—as well as the gleanings, the forgotten sheaves and the imperfect and topmost clusters of grapes, be left to the poor and the stranger (Lev. 19:10). In connection with the three pilgrim festivals (Passover, Weeks and Tabernacles), when attendance at the capital was required of all families, it was ordained that the stranger, the widow and the orphan be invited to share the food of the pilgrims (Deut. 16:11-14). Special care was enjoined for the weak: The stranger was not to be oppressed, the widow and the orphan were not to be dealt with harshly (Exod. 22:20-23, 23:9; Lev. 19:23-34); a borrower was to be given loans without interest (Deut. 15:7-11) and the borrower's garment taken in pledge, was to be returned by nightfall (Exod. 22:24-26; Lev. 25:35-38).

Connected with these specific enactments and underlying them are several fundamental ideas that form part of the permanent legacy of biblical thinking about economic life. One is the idea that the most basic productive resource and most valued possession, land, belongs to God. The refrain, "The earth is the Lord's, and the fullness thereof" (Psalms 24:1) was taken literally by this tradition. While members of the community are entitled to a patrimony, this proceeds as a gift from God's hand, and in the most basic sense, God remains its owner. As Roger Brooks has observed, only this understanding explains the panoply of covenantal requirements for the distribution of the land's produce to the two landless groups: the priests and the poor. Within the biblical and later Talmudic conception, Brooks says, the ordinary Israelite is, in a sense, a "tenant farmer" for God:

> [He] works God's land and enjoys its yield, with the result that a portion of all he produces belongs to God. In order to pay this obligation, Israelites render to the priests grain as heave offering, tithes and other priestly rations. Similarly, a specific portion of the Land's yield is set aside, by chance alone, for the poor. So underlying the designation of both priestly rations is a single theory: God owns the entire Land of Israel and, because of this ownership, a portion of each crop must be paid to him as a sort of sacred tax.[9]

By attributing ownership of essential property to God, therefore, Hebrew thought essentially undermines any property claims of individual owners that run counter to social need and it provides the conceptual basis for an insistence on economic interrelatedness and obligation. Although there are small differences in the way the individual right to property is qualified in Hebrew and later Catholic thinking—the Hebrew tradition tends to stress God's ownership while Christian thinking tends to stress God's primordial establishment of common human ownership[10]—the practical implications for economic life are the same in both cases: Human owners are regarded as holding their possessions in trust and subject to the conditions of righteous stewardship.

Another key idea follows. Within this context, assistance to the poor and the marginal is not requested or encouraged, but is required. Benevolence, as Ephraim Frisch has put it, "is viewed, not as a matter of grace, but as an imperative duty."[11] It follows that the poor have a religiously grounded "right" to sustenance and support. Furthermore, whenever serious economic misery occurs, it is regarded not as the fault of the poor themselves, but as the result of a failure of moral obligation by the more fortunate. Within the prophetic world view, the belief that the poor merit their fate, a view found in some Hindu and Buddhist as well as in some later Protestant thinking, has no place. On the contrary, within the Pentateuch and prophetic writings, destitution is almost always attributed to social and economic exploitation of the weak by the strong.

Talmudic Elaborations

With the enduring shift in Jewish communal life from Israel to the communities of the diaspora following the Roman War in the year 70 a need developed to expand the Pentateuch's structure of legal regulation to cover the new circumstances of life in exile. This stimulated a process of biblical commentary and legal expansion already begun during the intertestamental "Mishnaic" period. The result was the body of legal interpretation and quasilegislation represented by the Talmud. Completed by roughly the middle of the first millennium in its extensive Babylonian version, the multivolume work itself became subject to interpretation and to a more systematic codification at the hands of such medieval commentators as Rashi, Moses Maimonides, Jacob ben Asher and Joseph Caro. By means of this vast corpus of material, the biblically established norms of social justice were systematically elaborated and implemented in the daily life of Jewish communities.[12]

On the institutional level, a considerable task faced the rabbinic sages. They had to take a body of social welfare legislation developed in what was essentially an agricultural setting and adapt it to the increasingly urban and commercial life of medieval Jewry. Had obligations to the poor been taken lightly, this transition might have permitted Jews to abandon the older requirements merely by allowing them to become irrelevant and obsolete. Instead, this older agricultural law was thoroughly adapted and reinterpreted to suit the new situation, and commandments were sometimes made even more demanding.

The practical rules elaborated in the Talmud pertaining to responsibility to the poor came under two headings: *Zedakah* and *Gemilut Hasadim*. The root meaning of *Zedakah* is "right" or "justice," and although it is sometimes translated as charity, it refers to the religiously mandated giving and support of the poor established within each autonomous Jewish community. *Gemilut Hasadim*, sometimes translated as "loving kindness," is more properly thought of as "charity" in our common, contemporary sense of the term, since it refers to those forms of voluntary almsgiving and personal service—for example, the provision of dowries for poor maidens or visitation of the sick—that go beyond the letter of legal requirement.

In the Talmud and rabbinic rulings, Zedakah was given complex legal embodiment. The traditional obligations of landowners were not forgotten, but were supplemented by a series of institutions and practices more suited to urban or village life in the diaspora. In the words of Isadore Twersky, each Talmudicly governed community "appears as a modified welfare city-state, with its special functionaries who collect the compulsory levy and act as trustees for the poor and the needy."[13] Each city, town or village, for example, was required to set up two basic funds for relief of the poor. One, the Tamchui or "plate," was designated for emergency relief and was available to transients and local poor with less than two days food at their disposal. The second, the Kuppah or "chest," was designated for the ongoing support of the community's indigent.[14] The near-universality of these institutions is suggested by Maimonides' comment that he had "never seen or heard of an Israelite community that does not have an alms fund."[15]

The collection and distribution of these funds were governed by a series of carefully detailed regulations. For example, this work was the responsibility of special administrators of charity (Gabba'ei Zedakah), individuals of outstanding integrity who served without remuneration.[16] The amount owed by each household who carefully stipulated—usually as the Ma'aser or tenth of annual income[17]—and none but orphans or nonresidents were exempt from contributing. Criteria were established that, even by modern standards, are relatively generous for determining who could receive assistance and how much they might receive. For example, a family did not have to relinquish its home or utensils to be eligible for aid.[18] Individuals who were accustomed to a higher standard of living might be given more from the fund.[19] Begging was strongly discouraged—in the effort to direct all support of the needy through the well-regulated public agency[20]—requests for aid from the plate or fund were almost always respected and not subject to rigorous scrutiny. In all cases, the governing rule was, "We must show charity even to the deceivers."[21]

Behind this extensive structure of social welfare legislation were a series of fundamental ethical conceptions that reached back to the bible. Foremost among these is the idea that material resources are not the exclusive possession of any human owner, but are goods bestowed by God and held in trust for him.[22] One consequence of this belief was the conviction that those needy persons who call on the community's assistance do so not as an appeal to others' charity, but as a right. This understanding is demonstrably exhibited by a famed Talmudic story concerning a poor man who had visited Raba. The sage asked the poor man what he usually had for dinner and the poor man replied, "Fatted chicken and old wine." "But," said Raba, "do you not feel worried that you are a burden to the community?" To which the man replied, "Do I eat what is theirs? I eat what is God's." The story concludes as Raba's sister arrives bearing a gift of fatted chicken and old wine for her brother, which the sage then offers to the poor man with apologies for his questions.[23]

A further consequence of the idea that material goods are God's possession was the view that Zedakah does not represent a favor that might be withheld but, as Frisch puts it, "an imperative obligation springing from elementary considerations of justice."[24] If, from the standpoint of the poor, assistance is a right, from the standpoint of the giver, it is a religious and legal duty. In the words of Maimonides, "Gifts to the poor are not benevolence, but debts."[25] It follows that all people (except orphans) are required to give charity. Even the poor who themselves are supported by charity are required to give a portion of what they receive.[26] The fact that we are here in a realm, not merely of voluntary and private benevolence, but of socially mandated giving, is evidenced by the fact that any who refuse to pay their legally stipulated minimum contribution to the community fund or give less than what is proper should be compelled by the court (Bet Din) to give what the court designates, and the authorities may seize their goods for this purpose.[27]

Once again, notice how similar these Jewish conceptions are to traditional Catholic teaching. As in the Catholic view, obligations to the poor belong to the domain of justice and right. Precisely because all owners of property hold their possessions as conditional grants from God, private possession has no ultimate sanctity; property rights may be overridden to meet the needs of the less fortunate of God's creatures, who just as validly receive his graciousness as do the more-fortunate property owners themselves. As in Catholic thinking, the final responsibility for effecting these rights falls on society in its collective institutions. Although Jews rarely had full political authority, their communal religious institutions were for all intents their government, and *Zedakah* was institutionally organized and enforced.

Finally, as in Catholic thinking, these socially mandated obligations did not exhaust the moral and religious responsibilities of individuals to their less-fortunate brothers and sisters. *Gemilut Hasadim*, private giving and purely voluntary service to others, began where legal obligation ended and its expression might be unlimited. According to the Talmud, *Gemilut Hasadim* comprises a wider range of human kindness than does *Zedakah*. *Zedakah* can be given only with money, while *Gemilut Hasadim* may include personal service; *Zedakah* can be given only to the poor, while *Gemilut Hasadim* both to the poor and the rich; *Zedakah* only to the living, and *Gemilut Hasadim* to the living and the dead (through service during mourning or in the preparation of the deceased for burial).[28] In rabbinic thinking, *Gemilut Hasadim* was the subject of numerous treatises and lyrical expressions of praise, regarded as one of the loftiest expressions of human compassion.[29]

Although Jewish thinking did not articulate the formal Catholic principle of subsidiary, there was, in other words, a strong conviction that impersonal social institutions must not be entirely allowed to replace forms of personal giving and neighborly concern that both express and stimulate compassion among human beings. Halakhah thus walked a fine line between the twin requirements of individual and collective responsibility. "Although the balance may be delicate and tense," Isadore Twersky observes, in the thinking of the rabbis," corporate responsibility does not eclipse individual awareness and should not dull individual sensitiveness."[30]

Mention of private giving introduces another theme in Jewish thought that has corresponding importance in Catholic teaching: the theme of human dignity as the basis of all thinking about economic life. In the bishops' letter, this theme undergirds the emphasis on participation in economic systems and the importance of work in human activity. These emphases also have resonance in Jewish thinking, as will be discussed shortly. However, the emphasis on human dignity has another, more immediate, expression in Jewish thought. It produces an intense concern with the suffering and humiliation associated with poverty or dependency and it leads to sustained efforts to minimize the humiliation associated

with the acceptance of charity or "relief." In this connection, certain forms of private giving come under critical scrutiny.

Two aspects of Jewish thought contribute to these concerns. One is the sense that poverty represents a great evil. "There is no lot which is harder than poverty," says one rabbinic commentary, and it adds, "If all troubles were assembled on one side, and poverty on the other, poverty would outweigh them all."[31] This is a somewhat typical example of rabbinic hyperbole, though it reflects the deep valuation of material well-being in a faith in which the disempowerment and low status associated with poverty are regarded as unmitigated evils, and that has no significant tradition of asceticism.[32]

A second aspect contributing to a concern for the psychological state of the poor is the almost exquisite attention Jewish thinking gives to the avoidance of inflicting shame or humiliation on another person. Recognizing that self-respect is an individual's most precious possession, the rabbis repeatedly affirmed that any conduct that publicly shames another person represents a very serious moral wrong. For example, the Talmud records R. Simeon ben Yochai as saying, "Better had a man thrown himself into a fiery furnace than publicly put his neighbor to shame."[33] In a related technique, one who publicly humiliates another is likened to a murderer: If the second sheds blood, the first causes blood to rise to the face of a fellow human being.

This concern about protecting the poor from humiliation was reflected in the rabbis' discomfort with certain forms of direct, person-to-person charity. One commentary, for example, records the remark of R. Jannai to an individual whom he saw giving money to a poor man publicly: "It had been better that you had not given him, than now that you have given him publicly and put him to shame."[34] Commenting on Psalm 41.2, the rabbis remarked that the words are not "Happy is he who gives to the poor," but "Happy is he who considers the poor," that is, the person who takes into account the feelings and self-respect of the charity recipient.[35]

To prevent the possibility of humiliation, the rabbis insisted on the primacy of the kind of "impersonal altruism"[36] represented by the community fund. When private benefaction was unavoidable, they recommended secret giving as the model of charitable endeavor.[37] One Talmudic passage gives this idea whimsical expression by speculating on the forms of the letters Gimmel and Dalet. Since the two letters together can signify "Gemol Dallim," or "Show kindness to the poor," the question is: Why is the foot of the Dalet turned toward the Gimmel? The answer offered is that the Dalet (that is, the poor) should be on hand (they should not make it necessary for the benevolent to run after them). Why is the face of the Dalet turned away from the Gimmel? So that the help should be given to him secretly, sparing him blushes.[38]

To avoid further humiliation, the rabbis always emphasized the value of loans or offers of employment over outright gifts to the needy. Indeed, Moses Maimonides codified this teaching in his listing of the "eight degrees of charity" that appears as part of his treatise on the "Portions of the Poor" in his famous code of Jewish law, the Mishneh Torah. This listing expresses many concerns. For example, spontaneous and unsolicited giving is ranked higher than mere responses to requests for aid. Secret giving is commended over public display. Maimonides, though, reserves the highest degree for the kind of aid that not only spares the feelings of the recipient, but strengthens the individual's self-respect. This is the degree of "one who upholds the hand of an Israelite reduced to poverty by handing him a gift, or entering into a partnership with him, or finds work for him, in order to strengthen his hand, so that he would have no need to beg from other people."[39] Maimonides and other commentators become active, productive members of the community. Nevertheless, they still recommend this procedure of offering loans—and sometimes even requiring modest collateral to secure them—as a humane ruse to preserve the recipient's self-respect.[40]

As in Catholic teaching, these concerns also led Jewish commentators to insist repeatedly on the importance and value of work. Although the poor have a right to support, one should make every effort to avoid dependency. According to the Talmud, for example, a father had the responsibility to teach his son a trade, and one who failed in this duty was regarded as making his son a robber.[41] Work, however menial, is superior to dependency. "Flay carcasses in the marketplace and earn wages and do not say, 'I am a priest and a great man and it is beneath my dignity," admonishes one Talmudic text.[42]

In sum, with respect to human dignity and human need, traditional Judaism, like Catholicism, traces a course through a tensely related series of issues. Recognizing the evils created by dependency, it stresses the value of work and discourages, for giver and receiver alike, perpetuating a status of charity recipient. Nevertheless, it does not allow these admonitions against dependency to become a reason for disparaging the poor or the state of poverty itself, and it never allows these admonitions to undermine the welfare rights of those in need. Disesteeming poverty, it stresses both the right of every human being in circumstances of hardship to call on the community for assistance, and the corresponding duty of the community to make this aid available without prejudice or disdain. Unifying these seemingly disparate insistences is the theme of human dignity. Above all, the moral aim of an economic system is to sustain dignity by furnishing the work and participation for self-support and, where this is not possible, the means to sustain life without damage to the self-respect of the recipient.

A final theme in the bishops' letter with which classical Jewish thinking displays important affinities concerns the scope of the obligations of justice. The bishops strongly affirmed the global extent of justice. The individual's and the community's responsibility to alleviate misery and injustice does not stop at national frontiers, but extends, in principle, to human beings everywhere. In the words of the pastoral letter, traditional Catholic teaching emphasizes "the unity of the family, the universally beneficial purpose of the goods of the earth, the need to pursue the international common good," and the imperative to pursue justice to eliminate the "shocking inequality between rich and poor."[43]

In two respects, this breadth of responsibility would seem alien to classical Jewish thought: First, because under the constrained circumstances of life, there would seem to be few occasions to be concerned about the welfare of individuals beyond the boundaries of one's local community, and second, because whatever forms of assistance existed were religiously oriented and would naturally be directed first to one's coreligionists. This tendency would seem to be accentuated by what Max Weber has termed the "pariah" status of classical Judaism: As members of a persecuted and despised minority, Jews might be expected to place priority on their duties to coreligionists and minimize ethical responsibilities to members of the larger, and often persecuting, communities around them.[44]

Even though these and other factors play a role in limiting the scope of justice in classical Jewish thought and practice, powerful tendencies are also on the other side impelling Jews to a wider, and even universal, perspective. One is the international nature of the Jewish community itself. From the earliest date, Jews recognized themselves as a part of a community of persons whose membership transcended national borders. A common culture and, perhaps even more important, a common experience of persecution and suffering, bound the members of this community to one another. In times of pogrom, Jewish communities far removed from the events could be called on to lend financial assistance to their coreligionists or to receive refugees from the centers of persecution. During the medieval period, when piracy and the holding of hostages imperiled every Jewish traveler, the ransom of captives became a preoccupation of Jewish communities everywhere.[45] Indeed, the importance of this activity was expressed in the priorities established by the rabbis for handling cases of distress: The ransom of captives received the highest priority, followed in order by the alleviation of hunger, the provision of clothes, relief of extraphysical wants and the supplying of means for poor brides to marry.[46]

Finally, from the earliest date, Jews everywhere felt an obligation to assist the small and usually impoverished community of Jews who continued to live in Israel.[47] Although the general rule was that "The poor of your own town come before the poor of any other town,"[48] this was suspended for the poor of Israel, who took precedence over all other needy persons.[49] In the ongoing and institutionalized collections for these coreligionists, a basis was established for the unprecedented support diaspora Jewry has given to the modern state of Israel.

Charitable exertions, however, were not confined to coreligionists. On the local level, obligations extended beyond the confines of the religious community. The rule was "to give to everyone who stretched out his hand."[50] From the earliest date, and with a view to harmonious relations among neighbors, Gentiles were helped from the public benevolent fund. "In a city where there are both Jews and Gentiles," the Jerusalem Talmud says, "the collectors of alms collect both from Jews and Gentiles; they feed the poor of both, bury both, comfort the mourners whether Jews or Gentiles, and they restore the lost goods of both—for the sake of peace."[51]

This is not to say that in cases of conflict, Jews did not often favor their coreligionists above others. Not only was this partly permitted by tradition, which for such specific economic obligations as the prohibition of usury imposed stricter requirements for the treatment of the fellow Jew than for the non-Jew, but it was a natural response to the conditions of persecution Jews so often faced. Nevertheless, within the sphere of economic ethics, as elsewhere, classical Jewish thought possessed a strong sense that human beings are their brothers' and sisters' keepers, that neither geographic, cultural, or religious boundaries permit standing by while another human being faces alleviable distress.

Conclusion

The correspondences between classical Jewish and Roman Catholic thinking should not be surprising. Both traditions spring from a common biblical foundation, and both have sought to mold their societies, not just religiously, but socially and economically, recognizing that religious faith goes beyond private spirituality to touch all dimensions of life in community. Nevertheless, these correspondences are worth stressing.

In many of its key themes, especially in its emphasis on the preferential option for the poor and the human purpose of economic systems, the bishops' letter has come under attack from within and without the Catholic community. Some of these criticisms have related to technical matters and have disagreed with aspects of the bishops' proposals for implementing these moral values, but other criticisms, sometimes presented under a guise of technical disagreement, have called into question the bishops' basic moral priorities. Here, the history of Jewish thinking about economic life becomes relevant. What we have seen is that Jewish thinking profoundly agrees with the priorities articulated in the bishop's letter. Not economic efficiency, but concern with the dignity of individual human beings, especially the needy and disadvantaged, has always been to the fore in Jewish thinking. The paramount moral theme has not been the right to the ownership and use of one's own property, but one's responsibility for the just stewardship of that property.

Behind all this lay a spiritual perception shared by Catholic thinking that all good fortune, whether personal or material, proceeds from God's hands. Those who have been blessed in this way, whether by health, strength, ability, or wealth, have a corresponding duty to use their resources to aid those less fortunate, and they subvert this understanding when they turn their blessings into "merited" possessions they can use to the neglect or detriment of others.

In this most basic theme of all, Jewish teaching lends its voice to the deep moral and spiritual message converted by the pastoral letter.

If Catholic teachers can take heart from the support afforded by the heritage of Jewish teaching, then Jews, too, can learn from the bishops' letter. As indicated at the outset, the American Jewish community understandably faces a period of moral and spiritual confusion. As the prophets recognized long ago, material prosperity and social status make it difficult to call to mind the plight of one's less-fortunate neighbors. This may be a reason the *Haggadah* or liturgy for the Passover ritual to this day asks Jews to distance themselves from their good fortune and to regard themselves, even momentarily, as though they were members of the generation just saved from slavery and oppression.[52] In this respect, the pastoral letter serves as a modern *Haggadah*. It reminds Jews of the deepest themes of their own tradition, and it presents to them the model of a daughter tradition whose leadership, at least, is willing to remember these themes at a time in the life of both religious communities when it may be less popular or convenient to do so.

Notes

1. Walter Block, "The Jews and Capitalism," *Vital Speeches*, February 15, 1985, p. 284.

2. The matter of trends in Jewish voting is enormously complicated. In 1980, largely because of their relative dissatisfaction with President Jimmy Carter and their attraction to the independent John Anderson, Jews appeared to have deserted the Democratic party in larger numbers than ever before. However, this trend appears to have been reversed in the 1984 election, with 66% of Jewish voters casting their ballot for Mondale versus only 32% for Reagan. In the same election, white Catholics voted 41% for Mondale versus 58% for Reagan (*The New York Times*, Sunday, November 25, 1984, section 4, p. 23). A number of explanations for this continuing Democratic affiliation have been offered, including Charles Silberman's emphasis on Jews' endemic sense of social insecurity and their corresponding "cultural liberalism" and preference for political parties that support tolerance and diversity. [For a discussion of this matter, see his *A Certain People* (New York: Summit Books, 1985), pp. 345–359.] Nevertheless, apart from the immediate fluctuations of election campaigns and the attraction offered by specific candidates, many commentators agree that deep social and economic forces are working against traditional Jewish liberalism and Jews' affiliation with less-fortunate groups in the New Deal coalition.

3. Milton Friedman, "Capitalism and the Jews," in *Religion, Economics and Social Catholic Social Thought* quoted in Block (n.1), p. 284.

4. *Catholic Social Teaching and the U.S. Economy* (second draft), Publication No. 968, Washington, D.C.: National Conference of Catholic Bishops, 1985, pp. 1, 10f.

5. Ibid., pp. 1, 22f.

6. Ibid., p. 12.

7. Ibid., pp. 8, 18.

8. Ibid., pp. 66–68.

9. Roger Brooks, *Support for the Poor in the Mishnaic Law of Agriculture: Tractate Peah* (Chico, California: Scholars Press, 1983), p. 18.

10. For a fuller discussion of the theme of common ownership of the created goods of the world as this teaching emerged in the early church, see William J. Walsh and John P. Langan, "Patristic Social Consequences—The Church and the Poor," in John C. Haughey, ed., *The Faith that Does Justice* (New York: Paulist Press, 1977), pp. 113–151.

11. Ephraim Frisch, *An Historical Survey of Jewish Philanthropy* (New York: Macmillan, 1924), p. 9.

12. Discussions of classical Jewish approaches to the issue of social welfare include Israel Abrahams, *Jewish Life in the Middle Ages* (London: Edward Goldston, 1932); Salo W. Baron, *The Jewish Community* (Philadelphia: Jewish Publication Society of America, 1942), vol. 2, chap. 16; Ephraim Frisch, *Survey of Jewish Philanthropy*; Kaufman Kohler, "The Historical Development of Jewish Charity," *Hebrew Union College and Other Addresses* (Cincinnati, 1916), pp. 229–252; Solomon Schechter, "Notes of Lectures on Jewish Philanthropy," *Studies in Judaism*, 3rd series (Philadelphia: Jewish Publication Society of America, 1934), pp. 238–276; Isadore Twersky, "Some Aspects of the Jewish Attitude Toward the Welfare State," *Tradition* 5:2 (Spring 1963), pp. 137–158. Also, the articles in the *Encyclopedia Judaica* on "Charity," "The Poor" and "Gemilut Hasadim."

13. "Some Aspects of the Jewish Attitude toward the Welfare State," *Tradition* 5:1 (Spring 1963), p. 146.

14. TB Pe'ah, 8:7. All references to the Babylonian Talmud are to the Soncino edition, I. Epstein, ed. (London: Soncino Press, 1935–520).

15. *The Code of Maimonides*, Book Seven, *The Book of Agriculture*, Isaac Klein, trans. (New Haven: Yale University Press, 1979), Treatise II, "Laws Concerning Gifts to the Poor," chap. 9, par. 3, p. 85.

16. Frisch, *Survey of Jewish Philanthropy*, p. 39.

17. To give a tenth of one's wealth to charity was regarded as a moderate contribution, a twentieth or less

was judged to be "mean." The rabbis also stipulated that during their lifetime, persons might not contribute more than one fifth of their wealth to charity lest their families suffer impoverishment, but bequests at death might exceed this amount (TB Kethubot 50a, 67b).

18. TB Pe'ah, 8:8.

19. This was done to spare them undue psychological suffering. A precedent for this practice was found in a famous Talmudic story about Hillel the Elder who provided for an impoverished but formerly well-to-do man the best of food and drink and a horse and footman for his journeys. One day, according to the story, the sage was unable to locate a footman and performed this service himself (TB Kethubot, 67b).

20. The rule was laid down that relief was to be withheld from those who went begging door to door, although a compromise was arrived at, allowing some giving to such mendicants (TB Baba Bathra, 9a).

21. Talmud Yerushalmi, Pe'ah viii, sec. 9, f. 21b, line 13. This selection from the Jerusalem Talmud is translated in Montefiore and Lowe, *A Rabbinic Anthology* p. 418. Cf. *The Code of Maimonides*, vol. 6; *The Book of Seasons*, Hyman Klein, ed. (New Haven: Yale University Press, 1961), chaps. 2, 16 (p. 462). At the same time, the rabbis repeatedly warned against deception in matters of eligibility for public relief. The constant teaching was that "if a man accepts charity and is not in need of it, his end {will be that} he will not pass out of the world before he comes to such a condition" (TB Kethubot, 68a).

22. Solomon Schechter observes that this same understanding forms the basis for the recitation of a benediction and saying grace before and after meals. According to the Talmud, "One who enjoys of the good things of this world without saying grace, is as though he robbed the Holy One. . . ." "Notes of Lectures on Jewish Philanthropy," p. 243.

23. TB Kethubot, 67b. Compare this anecdote with Ambrose's admonition to the avaricious to make restitution by giving alms: "You are not making a gift of your possessions to the poor person. You are handing over to him what is his." *Naboth* 55, quoted in Walsh and Langan (n. 10), "Patristic Social Consciousness," p. 128.

24. Frisch, *Survey of Jewish Philanthropy*, p. 79.

25. Frisch, *Survey of Jewish Philanthropy*, p. 79, paraphrasing *The Code of Maimonides*, Book Seven, Treatise II, 1:1–6 and 7:10.

26. TB Gittin, 7a. Cf. *The Code of Maimonides*, Book Seven, Treatise II, 9:18 (p. 49f.).

27. TB Kethubot, 49b; *The Code of Maimonides*, Book Seven, Treatise II, 7:10 (p. 79).

28. TB Sukkah, 49b.

29. Hence, the teaching that "Loving-kindness is much greater than charity" (TB Sukkah, 49b). For a discussion of comparisons between *Zedakah* and *Gemilut Hasadim*, see Frisch, *Survey of Jewish Philanthropy*, p. 92f.

30. Twersky, "Aspects of the Jewish Attitude," p. 149.

31. *Exodus Rabbah*, S. M. Lehrman, trans. (London: Soncino Press, 1939), Mishpatim, xxxi, 14 (p. 395).

32. Although such Jewish ascetic groups as the Essenes existed, they always constituted fringe movements within orthodox Judaism. For a fuller treatment of asceticism and the Jewish tradition, see Schechter (n. 12), "Lectures on Jewish Philanthropy," pp. 267f. This relative absence of an ascetic tradition is an important contrast to Christian thought. As a result, Judaism's heritage of social concern tends to be rooted in compassion for the poor and insistence on their rights, rather than in the kind of discomfort over attachment to material goods in Christian teaching. For a discussion of this motif, see Walsh and Langan (n. 10), "Patristic Social Consciousness," pp. 119–126.

33. TB Kethubot, 67b.

34. TB Hagigah, 5a.

35. TJ Pe'ah, 8:9, 21b.

36. This concept is borrowed from Richard Titmuss, *The Gift Relationship* (New York: Pantheon Books, 1971), chapter 13.

37. According to R. Eliezer, the "secret giver" is greater than Moses (TB Baba Bathra, 9b). The practice of secret giving is indicated in the Mishnah, in which it is said that the Temple had a chamber of "secret gifts" where donations to the poor could be deposited and collected anonymously (TB Shekalim, 5:6).

38. TB Shabbath, 104a.

39. *The Code of Maimonides*, Book Seven, Treatise II, 10:7 (p. 91). Sifre, ed. Friedmann, p. 98a, nn. 11–12. Cf. TB Baba Mezià, 31b. The Talmud records the remark of R. Abba said, in the name of R. Simeon ben Lakesh, that "He who advances a loan is greater than he who gives charity, and he who puts in capital for partnership (with the person in distress) is more meritorious than all others' (TB Shabbath, 63a).

40. "If a man has no means and does not wish to be maintained {out of poor funds} he should be granted {the sum he requires} as a loan. . . ." "If he has no means and does not wish to be maintained {out of the poor funds} he is told 'Bring a pledge and you will receive {a loan}' in order to raise thereby his {drooping} spirit" (TB Kethubot, 67b).

41. TB Kiddushin, 29b.

42. TB Pesahim, 113a.

43. *Catholic Social Teaching and the U.S. Economy* (second draft), p. 66.

44. Max Weber, *Ancient Judaism* (New York: The Free Press, 1952), chap. 13.3
45. Abrahams (n. 12), *Jewish Life in the Middle Ages*, pp. 359ff.
46. Frisch, *Survey of Jewish Philanthropy*, p. 117.
47. Baron, *The Jewish Community*, pp. 339–343.
48. TB Baba Mezi'a, 71a.
49. Joseph Karo, Shulhan Aruk, Yoreh Deàh, 251:3.
50. Frisch, *Survey of Jewish Philanthropy*, p. 117.
51. Talmud Yerushalmi, Demai, IV, sec. 6, f. 24a, line 67. Montefiore and Lowe, trans., *A Rabbinic Anthology*, p. 424, and TB Gittin, 61a.
52. "In every generation, let each man look on himself as if *he* had come forth out of Egypt." *The Passover Haggadah*, Nahum N. Glatzer, ed. (New York: Schocken Books, 1969), p. 49.

Writing and Discussion Topics

Questions 1–6 address content, critical analysis, personal choices, ethical options, specific discipline, and interdisciplinary alternatives, respectively.

1. In what ways does Green believe that Jews are in sympathy with the bishops' letter? Are these similarities sufficient to claim that Jews would agree with Roman Catholics on how the American economy should change?
2. What are possible biblical foundations for Jewish economic thought, according to Green?
3. What impresses you most about this response to the pastoral letter? What gives you cause to reject this response?
4. According to Green, a fundamental Jewish belief is the idea that "material resources are not the exclusive possession of any human owner, but are goods bestowed by God and held in trust for him." How does Green justify both the adherence and the nonadherence to this belief?
5. Explain the Jewish concept of community. How does this concept differ from the Protestant concept of community?
6. In light of the readings in this chapter, does Judaism have more in common with Roman Catholicism or Protestantism on the issue of corporate social responsibility? Evaluate the bishops' letter from all three perspectives.

Yusuf Al-Qaradawi

THE HALAL AND THE HARAM IN THE
DAILY LIFE OF THE MUSLIM
◆◆◆

Yusuf Al-Qaradawi is affiliated with the General Institute of Islamic Culture of Azhar University, which commissioned him to write The Lawful and the Prohibited in Islam, *from which this reading is excerpted. Dr Al-Qaradawi has written twenty books and is a distinguished poet.* ◆

Business Transactions

Allah Subhanahu wa Ta'ala has created human beings in a state of dependence upon one another. Each individual does not own all the things he needs; one person has something which he can spare while at the same time he may need something which others have and which they can spare. Allah has directed people toward exchanging goods and utilities through buying and selling because such transactions make social and economic life function smoothly and encourage people to be productive.

Various types of transactions and exchanges of property were current among the Arabs at the dawn of the Prophet's mission. He approved and confirmed such types of transactions which did not conflict with the principles of the *Shari'ah* and disapproved and prohibited those business practices which were against the purposes and aims of the *Shari'ah*. The prohibitions were due to specific reasons, as, for example, trading in *haram* goods, transactions involving fraud or exorbitant profits, or injustice to one of the contracting parties. . . .

The Prohibition of a Sale Involving Uncertainty

The Prophet (peace be on him) forbade any kind of transaction which could lead to a quarrel or litigation due to some uncertainty[1] or which involved an unspecific quantity to be exchanged or delivered. This includes the sort of transaction in which there is no guarantee that the seller can deliver the goods for which he receives payment. Accordingly, the Prophet (peace be on him) forbade accepting money for a stallion's or male camel's covering, for fish in water or birds in the air which one has not caught, or for the offspring of a camel still in the female's womb, since there is an element of uncertainty as to the outcome in all such transactions.

The Prophet (peace be on him) observed that people sold unripened fruits which were still in the fields or orchards; if the crop were destroyed by blight or some natural calamity, the buyer and seller would quarrel over who was to bear the loss. Hence, the Prophet (peace be on him) prohibited the sale of fruit until they were clearly in good condition,[2] unless they were to be picked on the spot. Similarly, he forbade selling ears of corn until they were white and safe from blight,[3] saying,

> "Tell me why, if Allah withholds the fruit, any of you should take his brother's property."[4]

However, not every sale involving what is unknown or uncertain is prohibited; for example, a person may buy a house without knowing the condition of its foundation or what is inside the walls. What is prohibited is selling something about which there is an obvious element of uncertainty which may lead to dispute and conflict, or may result in the unjust appropriation of other people's money. Again, if the risk of uncertainty is small—and this is determined by experience and custom—the sale is not prohibited. For example, one may sell root vegetables such as carrots, onions, and radishes while they are still in the ground, or fields of cucumbers, watermelons and the like. In the opinion of Imam Malik, all such sales of needed items in which the margin of risk is bearable are permissible.[5]

Price Manipulation

In Islam the market is to be free and permitted to respond to the natural laws of supply and demand. Thus, when the prices became high in the Prophet's time and people asked him to fix prices for them, he replied,

> Allah is the One Who fixes prices, Who withholds, Who gives lavishly, and Who provides, and I hope that when I meet Him none of you will have a claim against me for any injustice with regard to blood or property.[6]

With these words the Prophet of Islam (peace be on him) declared that unnecessary interference in the freedom of individuals is injustice and that one should meet Allah free of blame for such a thing. If,

---

From Yusuf Al-Qaradawi, *The Lawful and the Prohibited in Islam*. Copyright © 1981 American Trust Publications, Indianapolis, IN. Reprinted by permission.

[1]See the chapter on "The Prohibition of *al-Gharar* (Transactions Involving Uncertainty)" in Muslim and others.

[2]Reported by al-Bukhari and Muslim.
[3]Reported by Muslim.
[4]Reported by al-Bukhari and others.
[5]In *Al-qawa'id al-nuraniyyah*, p. 118, Ibn Taimiyyah says: "The principles laid down by (Imam) Malik concerning sales are superior to those of others, because he took them from Sa'id ibn al-Musayyib, who is the best authority on the *fiqh* (jurisprudence) of sales." Imam Ahmad bin Hanbal's opinion is close to that of Malik.
[6]Reported by Ahmad, Abu Daoud, al-Tirmidhi, Ibn Majah, al-Dari and Abu Y'ala.

however, any artificial forces, such as hoarding and manipulation of prices by certain merchants, interfere in the free market, public interest takes precedence over the freedom of such individuals. In such a situation price control becomes permissible in order to meet the needs of the society and to protect it from greedy opportunists by thwarting their schemes, for the above *hadith* does not mean that price control is prohibited regardless of the circumstances, even if it removes harm and prevents obvious injustice. Researchers among scholars have concluded that, depending on the nature of the circumstances, price control may at times be unjust and prohibited, and at other times may be just and permissible.

If price control compels people to sell their goods at a price which is not acceptable to them or denies them the reasonable profit permitted by Allah, it is *haram*. If, on the other hand, price control establishes equity among people, for example, by forcing sellers to accept a price equal to that commanded by other comparable commodities and restraining them from taking more than this, it is allowed—indeed necessary.

The *hadith* cited above relates to the first type of situation. Accordingly, if merchants are selling a commodity in the customary fashion without any wrong-doing on their part and the price subsequently rises due to the scarcity of the commodity or due to an increase in population (indicating the operation of the law of supply and demand), this circumstance is from Allah, in which case to force them to sell the commodity at a fixed price would be unjust compulsion.

In relation to the second type of situation, should the dealers in a commodity refuse to sell it, despite the fact that people are in need of it, unless they secure a price higher than its known value, they must be compelled to sell it at a price equal to the price of an equivalent commodity. Price control here means nothing more than establishing comparable prices for equivalent commodities and it is therefore in conformity with the standard of justice demanded by Allah Ta'ala. . . .[7]

Interference in the Free Market

Another practice related to hoarding which was prohibited by the Prophet (peace be on him) was a townsman's selling on behalf of a man from the desert. Scholars have explained the situation in the following manner: a stranger would bring some goods to be sold in town at the current market price. A townsman would approach him, saying, "Leave them with me for a while. I will sell them for you when the price is better." Had the non-resident himself sold his goods, he would have done so for a lower price, thereby benefitting the people, while he himself would have made a reasonable profit.

This sort of practice was very common in Arab society when Islam came. Anas says, "Sale by a resident on behalf of a desert-dweller was prohibited to us, even though he might be a blood brother."[8] From this we learn that for the Muslim the public interest takes precedence over personal relationships. Said the Prophet (peace be on him),

> A resident (of the town) must not sell for a man from the desert. If people are left alone, Allah will give them provision from one another.[9]

This significant expression of the Prophet's, "If people are left alone, Allah will give them provision from one another," establishes a basic principle in the field of commerce: that the market, its prices, and sales, should be left free to respond to internal economic forces and natural competition without manipulation. When Ibn 'Abbas was asked about the meaning of "A resident must not sell for a man from the desert," he replied, "The resident should not be a broker for him."[10] From this we understand that if someone were to inform the man from the desert about prices, proffering him good advice and telling him about prevailing market prices without charging him a commission, there would be no harm in it, for giving good advice is part of the religion; in fact, a sound *hadith* states,

> "Religion is the giving of good advice,"[11]

and,

> "If someone asks your advice, advise him."[12]

However, with regard to the broker, it is quite probable that, in a situation such as that described above, he might neglect the public interest for the sake of his own profit. . . .

---

[7]Refer to *Risalat al-hisbah* by Ibn Taimiyyah, as well as to *Al-turuq al-hikmiyyah* by Ibn al-Qayyim, p. 214 ff.
[8]Reported by al-Bukhari and Muslim.
[9]Reported by Muslim.
[10]Reported by al-Bukhari.
[11]Reported by Muslim.
[12]Reported by Ahmad.

"He Who Deceives Us Is Not of Us"

Islam prohibits every type of fraud and deception, whether it be in buying and selling or in any other matter between people. In all situations the Muslim must be honest and truthful, holding his faith dearer than any wordly gain. The Prophet (peace be on him) said,

> Both parties to a business transaction have a right to cancel it as long as they have not separated. If they tell the truth and make everything clear, they will be blessed in their transaction, but if they lie and conceal anything, the blessing will be blotted out.[13]

He also said,

> It is not permissible to sell an article without making everything (about it) clear, nor is it permissible for anyone who knows (about its defects) to refrain from mentioning them.[14]

Once, when passing by a grain merchant, the Prophet's curiosity was aroused. He thrust his hand into the heap of grain and found it wet. "What is this, O merchant?" he asked. "It is because of rain," the man replied. The Prophet (peace be on him) then said to him,

> "Why did you not put it on top so that the people could see it? He who deceives us is not of us."[15]

In another report it is said that he passed by a heap of grain which was made to look good by the merchant. The Prophet (peace be on him) put his hand into it and found it to be bad. He told the merchant,

> "Sell the good and the bad separately. He who deceives us is not of us."[16]

The Muslims of earlier times strictly observed the practices of exposing the defects of what they sold, of telling the truth, and of giving good advice. When Ibn Sirin sold a sheep, he told the buyer, "I would like to tell you about a defect it has: it kicks the fodder." And when al-Hassan bin Salih sold a slave girl he told the buyer, "Once she spat up blood." Although she had done this only once, al-Hassan's Muslim conscience required that he mention the fact, even if it resulted in his receiving a lower price. . . .

---

[13]Reported by al-Bukhari.
[14]Reported by al-Hakim and al-Bayhaqi.
[15]Reported by Muslim.
[16]Reported by Ahmad.

Partnership Between Capital and Labor

It may be said that Allah Subhanahu wa Ta'ala has distributed talents and wealth among human beings according to a wise plan of apportionment. We find many a talented and experienced individual who does not possess much wealth or none at all, while others have a great deal of money but little or no talent. Why, therefore, should not the wealthy person turn over to the one possessing talents some of his wealth to invest in a profitable business, so that the two may benefit from one another and share the profits according to some agreed-upon formula? In particular, business ventures on a large scale require the co-operation of many investors. Among the populace we find a large number of people who have savings and excess capital but who lack time or the capability of investing it. Why should not this money be pooled and placed under the management of capable people who will invest it in significant, large-scale projects?

We maintain that the Islamic *Shari'ah* did not prohibit cooperation between capital and management, or between capital and labor as these terms are understood in their Islamic legal sense. In fact, the *Shari'ah* established a firm and equitable basis for such cooperation: if the owner of capital wishes to become a partner with the working man, he must agree to share all the consequences of this partnership. The *Shari'ah* lays down the condition that in such a partnership, which is called *al-mudaribah* or *al-qirad*, the two parties should agree that they will share the profit if there is profit and loss if there is loss in a proportion agreed upon in advance. This proportion can be one-half, one-third, one-fourth, or any other proportion for one party and the remainder for the other party. Thus the partnership between capital and labor is that of two parties with joint responsibility, each having his share, whether of profit or loss, and whether much or little. If, in the balance, the losses exceed the profits, the difference is to be charged against the capital. This arrangement is not surprising, for while the owner of the capital has suffered a loss in his wealth, the working partner has lost his time and effort.

This is the law of Islam concerning partnership contracts. Conversely, were the owner of the capital to be guaranteed a fixed profit on his capital regardless of the magnitude of the profit or loss, it would be a clear violation of justice and a bias in favor of capital against investment experience and labor; it would also be contrary to the realities of investment, which always contain elements of risk. To guarantee to the person who did not toil or take any risk is the very essence of abominable usury.

The Prophet (peace be on him) forbade the type of partnership on cultivable land which was known as *al-muzara'ah* (share-cropping),[17] in which the contract would give one partner the produce of a specified area of a farm or a fixed amount of grain such as one or two tons. He prohibited this because such a transaction is similar to usury or gambling; for if the farm produced less than the specific amount or nothing at all, one partner would still get his share, while the other would suffer a total loss, which is contrary to justice. . . .

Partnership Among Owners of Capital

Just as it is lawful for the Muslim to use his own wealth for any permissible purpose or to give it to a capable experienced person to invest in a joint venture, it is also lawful for him to pool his capital with the capital of others for investment, trade, or any lawful business ventures.

There are all kinds of activities and projects, some requiring intensive labor, others intensive mental expenditure, and still others large capital. By themselves individuals may not be able to accomplish much, but when joined with others, they can achieve many things. Allah Ta'ala says,

> . . . and help each other in righteousness and God-consciousness. (5:3(2))

Any deed which produces good results for the individual or society, or which removes some evil, is righteousness, and a righteous deed becomes piety if a good intention is added to it. Islam is not content with merely allowing such joint endeavors but encourages and blesses them, promising Allah's help in this world and His reward in the Hereafter as long as these endeavors are within the sphere of what Allah has made *halal*, far removed from usury (interest) and from ambiguity, injustice, fraud, and cheating in any form. In this connection the Messenger of Allah (peace be on him) said,

> Allah's hand is over two partners as long as one of them does not cheat the other, but when he cheats his partner, He withdraws it from both.[18]

"Allah's hand" refers to His help, inspiration, and blessing. The Prophet (peace be on him) also stated in a *hadith qudsi* that Allah, the Great and Glorious says,

> I make a third with two partners as long as one of them does not cheat the other, but when he cheats him I depart from them.[19]

Razin's version adds,

> "and Satan comes."[20]

Writing and Discussion Topics

Questions 1–6 address content, critical analysis, personal choices, ethical options, specific discipline, and interdisciplinary alternatives, respectively.

1. Examine some of the basic rules of business transactions for Muslims. Do you see any quandaries associated with these rules?
2. What kind of partnership is available between capital and labor in the Islamic religion? Is this a fair arrangement? Could the bishops recommend this type of partnership?
3. From these writings, what impressions do you have about the social responsibility of business for Muslims? Specifically, would it be acceptable for someone to pollute the air or water in order to make money?
4. Why does loaning money with interest break Islamic law? What societal and religious problems can usury cause? Could this practice be adopted in other countries or in other religions?
5. Compare and contrast Islamic business morality with the business morality discussed in the Roman Catholic, Protestant, and Jewish readings.
6. Compare and contrast this piece with the writing by Ronald Green regarding Jewish scriptural business traditions. Which system would work best in America? Which would work best worldwide?

---

[17]Reported by Muslim.

[18]Reported by al-Darqutni.
[19]Reported by Abu Daoud and by al-Hakim, who calls it sound.
[20]Reported by Razin in his *Jami'ah*.

THE QUALITIES OF THE PRINCE

Machiavelli Source: Historical
Picture Service.

Niccolo Machiavelli (1469–1527) was born in Florence, Italy, to a wealthy family. He entered political office as a clerk and rose to the position of defense secretary for the Florentine republic. He became acquainted with power politics through several important diplomatic missions. The return of the Medici family caused his dismissal and he was briefly imprisoned and tortured for his unproved complicity in a plot against the Medici. Upon his release, he wrote The Prince *from which this piece is excerpted. He hoped his writings would win him a spot with the government, but that did not happen.* ♦

On Those Things for Which Men, and Particularly Princes, Are Praised or Blamed

Now there remains to be examined what should be the methods and procedures of a prince in dealing with his subjects and friends. And because I know that many have written about this, I am afraid that by writing about it again I shall be thought of as presumptuous, since in discussing this material I depart radically from the procedures of others. But since my intention is to write something useful for anyone who understands it, it seemed more suitable to me to search after the effectual truth of the matter rather than its imagined one. And many writers have imagined for themselves republics and principalities that have never been seen nor known to exist in reality, for there is such a gap between how one lives and how one ought to live that anyone who abandons what is done for what ought to be done learns his ruin rather than his preservation: for a man who wishes to make a vocation of being good at all times will come to ruin among so many who are not good. Hence it is necessary for a prince who wishes to maintain his position to learn how not to be good, and to use this knowledge or not to use it according to necessity.

Leaving aside, therefore, the imagined things concerning a prince, and taking into account those that are true, I say that all men, when they are spoken of, and particularly princes, since they are placed on a higher level, are judged by some of these qualities which bring them either blame or praise. And this is why one is considered generous, another miserly (to use a Tuscan word, since "avaricious" in our language is still used to mean one who wishes to acquire by means of theft, we call "miserly" one who excessively avoids using what he has); one is considered a giver, the other rapacious, one cruel, another merciful, one treacherous, another faithful; one effeminate and cowardly, another bold and courageous, one humane, another haughty; one lascivious, another chaste; one trustworthy, another cunning; one harsh, another lenient; one serious, another frivolous; one religious, another unbelieving, and the like. And I know that everyone will admit that it would be a very praise worthy thing to find in a prince, of the qualities mentioned above, those that are held to be good; but since it is neither possible to have them nor to observe them all completely, because human nature does not permit it, a prince must be prudent enough to know how to escape the bad reputation of those vices that would lose the state for him, and must protect himself from those that will not lose it for him, if this is possible; but if he cannot, he need not concern himself unduly if he ignores these less serious vices. And, moreover, he need not worry about incurring the bad reputation of those vices without which it would be difficult to hold his state; since, carefully taking everything into account, one will discover that something which appears to be a virtue, if pursued, will end in his destruction; while some other thing which seems to be a vice, if pursued, will result in his safety and his well-being.

On Generosity and Miserliness

Beginning, therefore, with the first of the abovementioned qualities, I say that it would be good to be considered generous; nevertheless, generosity used in such a manner as to give you a reputation for it will harm you; because if it is employed virtuously and as one should employ it, it will not be recognized and you will not avoid the reproach of its opposite. And so, if a prince wants to maintain his reputation for generosity among men, it is necessary for him not to neglect any possible means of lavish display; in so doing such a prince will always use up all his resources and he will be obliged, eventually, if he wishes to maintain his reputation for generosity, to burden the people with excessive taxes and to do everything possible to raise funds. This will begin to make him hateful to his subjects, and, becoming impoverished, he will not be much esteemed by anyone; so that, as a consequence of his generosity, having offended many and rewarded few, he will feel the effects of any slight unrest and will be ruined at the first sign of danger; recognizing this and wishing to alter his policies, he immediately runs the risk of being reproached as a miser.

A prince, therefore, unable to use this virtue of generosity in a manner which will not harm himself if he is known for it, should, if he is wise, not worry about being called a miser; for with time he will come to be considered more generous once it is evident that, as a result of his parsimony, his income is sufficient, he can defend himself from anyone who makes war against him, and he can undertake enterprises without overburdening his people, so that he comes to be generous with all those from whom he takes nothing, who are countless, and miserly with all those to whom he gives nothing, who are few. In our times we have not seen great deeds accomplished except by those who were considered miserly; all others were done away with. Pope Julius II,[1] although he made use of his reputation for generosity in order to gain the papacy, then decided not to maintain it in order to be able to wage war; the present King of France[2] has waged many wars without imposing extra taxes on his subjects, only because his habitual parsimony has provided for the additional expenditures; the present King of Spain,[3] if he had been considered generous, would not have engaged in nor won so many campaigns.

Therefore, in order not to have to rob his subjects, to be able to defend himself, not to become poor and contemptible, and not to be forced to become rapacious, a prince must consider it of little importance if he incurs the name of miser, for this is one of those vices that permits him to rule. And if someone were to say: Caesar with his generosity came to rule the empire, and many others, because they were generous and known to be so, achieved very high positions; I reply: you are either already a prince or you are on the way to becoming one; in the first instance such generosity is damaging; in the second it is very necessary to be thought generous. And Caesar was one of those who wanted to gain the principality of Rome; but if, after obtaining this, he had lived and had not moderated his expenditures, he would have destroyed that empire. And if someone were to reply: there have existed many princes who have accomplished great deeds with their armies who have been reputed to be generous; I answer you: a prince either spends his own money and that of his subjects or that of others; in the first case he must be economical; in the second he must not restrain any part of his generosity. And for that prince who goes out with his soldiers and lives by looting, sacking, and ransoms, who controls the property of others, such generosity is necessary; otherwise he would not be followed by his troops. And with what does not belong to you or to your subjects you can be a more liberal giver, as were Cyrus, Caesar, and Alexander; for spending the wealth of others does not lessen your reputation but adds to it; only the spending of your own is what harms you. And there is nothing that uses itself up faster than generosity, for as you employ it you lose the means of employing it, and you become either poor or despised or, in order to escape poverty, rapacious and hated. And above all other things a prince must guard himself against being despised and hated; and generosity leads you to both one and the other. So it is wiser to live with the reputation of a miser, which produces reproach without hatred, than to be forced to incur the reputation of rapacity, which produces reproach along with hatred, because you want to be considered as generous.

On Cruelty and Mercy and Whether It Is Better to be Loved Than to be Feared or the Contrary

Proceeding to the other qualities mentioned above, I say that every prince must desire to be considered merciful and not cruel; nevertheless, he must take care not to misuse this mercy. Cesare Borgia[4] was considered cruel; nonetheless, his cruelty had brought order to Romagna,[5] united it, restored it to peace and obedience. If we examine this carefully, we shall see that he was more merciful than the Florentine people, who, in order to avoid being considered cruel, allowed the destruction of Pistoia.[6] Therefore, a prince must not worry about the reproach of cruelty when it is a matter of keeping his subjects united and loyal; for with a very few examples of cruelty he will be more compassionate than those who, out of excessive mercy, permit disorders to continue, from which arise murders and plundering; for these usually harm the community at

---

[1] *Pope Julius II (1443–1513)* Giuliano della Rovere, pope from 1503 to 1513. Like many of the popes of the day, Julius II was also a diplomat and a general.
[2] *present King of France* Louis XII (1462–1515). He entered Italy on a successful military campaign in 1494.
[3] *present King of Spain* Ferdinand V (1452–1516). A studied politician; he and Queen Isabella (1451–1504) financed Christopher Columbus's voyage to the New World in 1492.

[4] *Cesare Borgia (1476–1507)* He was known for his brutality and lack of scruples, not to mention his exceptionally good luck. He was a firm ruler, son of Pope Alexander VI.
[5] *Romagna* Region northwest of Tuscany; includes the towns of Bologna, Ferrara, Ravenna, and Rimini. Borgia united it as his base of power in 1501.
[6] *Pistoia* A town near Florence, disturbed by a civil war in 1501 which could have been averted by strong repressive measures.

large, while the executions that come from the prince harm one individual in particular. And the new prince, above all other princes, cannot escape the reputation of being called cruel, since new states are full of dangers. And Virgil, through Dido, states "My difficult condition and the newness of my rule make me act in such a manner, and to set guards over my land on all sides."[7]

Nevertheless, a prince must be cautious in believing and in acting, nor should he be afraid of his own shadow; and he should proceed in such a manner, tempered by prudence and humanity, so that too much trust may not render him imprudent nor too much distrust render him intolerable.

From this arises an argument: whether it is better to be loved than to be feared, or the contrary. I reply that one should like to be both one and the other; but since it is difficult to join them together, it is much safer to be feared than to be loved when one of the two must be lacking. For one can generally say this about men: that they are ungrateful, fickle, simulators and deceivers, avoiders of danger, greedy for gain; and while you work for their good they are completely yours, offering you their blood, their property, their lives, and their sons, as I said earlier, when danger is far away; but when it comes nearer to you they turn away. And that prince who bases his power entirely on their words, finding himself stripped of other preparations, comes to ruin; for friendships that are acquired by a price and not by greatness and nobility of character are purchased but are not owned, and at the proper moment they cannot be spent. And men are less hesitant about harming someone who makes himself loved than one who makes himself feared because love is held together by a chain of obligation which, since men are a sorry lot, is broken on every occasion in which their own self-interest is concerned; but fear is held together by a dread of punishment which will never abandon you.

A prince must nevertheless make himself feared in such a manner that he will avoid hatred, even if he does not acquire love; since to be feared and not to be hated can very well be combined; and this will always be so when he keeps his hands off the property and the women of his citizens and his subjects.

And if he must take someone's life, he should do so when there is proper justification and manifest cause; but, above all, he should avoid the property of others; for men forget more quickly the death of their father than the loss of their patrimony. Moreover, the reasons for seizing their property are never lacking; and he who begins to live by stealing always finds a reason for taking what belongs to others; on the contrary, reasons for taking a life are rarer and disappear sooner.

But when the prince is with his armies and has under his command a multitude of troops, then it is absolutely necessary that he not worry about being considered cruel; for without that reputation he will never keep an army united or prepared for any combat. Among the praiseworthy deeds of Hannibal[8] is counted this: that, having a very large army, made up of all kinds of men, which he commanded in foreign lands, there never arose the slightest dissention, neither among themselves nor against their prince, both during his good and his bad fortune. This could not have arisen from anything other than his inhuman cruelty, which, along with his many other abilities, made him always respected and terrifying in the eyes of his soldiers; and without that, to attain the same effect, his other abilities would not have sufficed. And the writers of history having considered this matter very little, on the one hand admire these deeds of his and on the other condemn the main cause of them.

And that it be true that his other abilities would not have been sufficient can be seen from the example of Scipio, a most extraordinary man not only in his time but in all recorded history, whose armies in Spain rebelled against him; this came about from nothing other than his excessive compassion, which gave to his soldiers more liberty than military discipline allowed. For this he was censured in the senate by Fabius Maximus,[9] who called him the corruptor of the Roman militia. The Locrians,[10] having been ruined by one of Scipio's officers, were not

---

[7]The quotation is from *Aeneid* (II 563–564), the greatest Latin epic poem, written by Virgil (70–19 B.C.). Dido in the poem is a woman general who rules Carthage.

[8]**Hannibal (247–183 B.C.)** An amazingly inventive military tactician who led the Carthaginian armies against Rome for more than fifteen years. He crossed the Alps from Gaul in order to surprise Rome. He was noted for use of the ambush and for "inhuman cruelty."
[9]**Fabius Maximus (2–203 B.C.)** Roman general who fought Hannibal. He was jealous of the younger Roman general Scipio.
[10]**Locrians** Inhabitants of Locri, an Italian town settled by the Greeks in 683 B.C.

avenged by him, nor was the arrogance of that officer corrected, all because of his tolerant nature; so that someone in the senate who tried to apologize for him said that there were many men who knew how not to err better than they knew how to correct errors. Such a nature would have, in time, damaged Scipio's fame and glory if he had maintained it during the empire; but, living under the control of the senate, this harmful characteristic of his not only concealed itself but brought him fame.

I conclude, therefore, returning to the problem of being feared and loved, that since men love at their own pleasure and fear at the pleasure of the prince, a wise prince should build his foundation upon that which belongs to him, not upon that which belongs to others: he must strive only to avoid hatred, as has been said.

How a Prince Should Keep His Word

How praiseworthy it is for a prince to keep his word and to live by integrity and not by deceit everyone knows; nevertheless, one sees from the experience of our times that the princes who have accomplished great deeds are those who have cared little for keeping their promises and who have known how to manipulate the minds of men by shrewdness; and in the end they have surpassed those who laid their foundations upon honesty.

You must, therefore, know that there are two means of fighting: one according to the laws, the other with force; the first way is proper to man, the second to beasts; but because the first, in many cases, is not sufficient, it becomes necessary to have recourse to the second. Therefore, a prince must know how to use wisely the natures of the beast and the man. This policy was taught to princes allegorically by the ancient writers, who described how Achilles and many other ancient princes were given to Chiron[11] the Centaur to be raised and taught under his discipline. This can only mean that, having a half-beast and half-man as a teacher, a prince must know how to employ the nature of the one and the other; and the one without the other cannot endure.

Since, then, a prince must know how to make good use of the nature of the beast, he should choose from among the beasts the fox and the lion, for the lion cannot defend itself from traps and the fox cannot protect itself from wolves. It is therefore necessary to be a fox in order to recognize the traps and a lion in order to frighten the wolves. Those who play only the part of the lion do not understand matters. A wise ruler, therefore, cannot and should not keep his word when such an observance of faith would be to his disadvantage and when the reasons which made him promise are removed. And if men were all good, this rule would not be good; but since men are a sorry lot and will not keep their promises to you, you likewise need not keep yours to them. A prince never lacks legitimate reasons to break his promises. Of this one could cite an endless number of modern examples to show how many pacts, how many promises have been made null and void because of the infidelity of princes; and he who has known best how to use the fox has come to a better end. But it is necessary to know how to disguise this nature well and to be a great hypocrite and a liar: and men are so simpleminded and so controlled by their present necessities that one who deceives will always find another who will allow himself to be deceived.

I do not wish to remain silent about one of these recent instances. Alexander VI[12] did nothing else, he thought about nothing else, except to deceive men, and he always found the occasion to do this. And there never was a man who had more forcefulness in his oaths, who affirmed a thing with more promises, and who honored his word less; nevertheless, his tricks always succeeded perfectly since he was well acquainted with this aspect of the world.

Therefore, it is not necessary for a prince to have all of the above-mentioned qualities, but it is very necessary for him to appear to have them. Furthermore, I shall be so bold as to assert this: that having them and practicing them at all times is harmful; and appearing to have them is useful; for instance, to seem merciful, faithful, humane, forthright, religious, and to be so; but his mind should be disposed in such a way that should it become necessary not to be so, he will be able and know how to change to the contrary. And it is essential to understand this: that a prince, and especially a new prince, cannot observe all those things by which men are considered good, for in order to maintain the state he is often obliged to act against his promise, against

---

[11]**Chiron** A mythical figure, a centaur (half man, half horse). Unlike most centaurs, he was wise and benevolent, he was also a legendary physician.

[12]**Alexander VI (1431–1503)** Roderigo Borgia, pope from 1492 to 1503. He was Cesare Borgia's father and a corrupt but immensely powerful pope.

charity, against humanity, and against religion. And therefore, it is necessary that he have a mind ready to turn itself according to the way the winds of Fortune and the changeability of affairs require him; and, as I said above, as long as it is possible, he should not stray from the good, but he should know how to enter into evil when necessity commands.

A prince, therefore, must be very careful never to let anything slip from his lips which is not full of the five qualities mentioned above: he should appear, upon seeing and hearing him, to be all mercy, all faithfulness, all integrity, all kindness, all religion. And there is nothing more necessary than to seem to possess this last quality. And men in general judge more by their eyes than their hands; for everyone can see but few can feel. Everyone sees what you seem to be, few perceive what you are, and those few do not dare to contradict the opinion of the many who have the majesty of the state to defend them; and in the actions of all men, and especially of princes, where there is no impartial arbiter, one must consider the final result.[13] Let a prince therefore act to seize and to maintain the state; his methods will always be judged honorable and will be praised by all; for ordinary people are always deceived by appearances and by the outcome of a thing; and in the world there is nothing but ordinary people; and there is no room for the few, while the many have a place to lean on. A certain prince[14] of the present day, whom I shall refrain from naming, preaches nothing but peace and faith, and to both one and the other he is entirely opposed; and both, if he had put them into practice, would have cost him many times over either his reputation or his state.

On Avoiding Being Despised and Hated

But since, concerning the qualities mentioned above, I have spoken about the most important, I should like to discuss the others briefly in this general manner: that the prince, as was noted above, should think about avoiding those things which make him hated and despised; and when he has avoided this, he will have carried out his duties and will find no danger whatsoever in other vices. As I have said, what makes him hated above all else is being rapacious

and a usurper of the property and the women of his subjects; he must refrain from this; and in most cases, so long as you do not deprive them of either their property or their honor, the majority of men live happily; and you have only to deal with the ambition of a few, who can be restrained without difficulty and by many means. What makes him despised is being considered changeable, frivolous, effeminate, cowardly, irresolute; from these qualities a prince must guard himself as if from a reef, and he must strive to make everyone recognize in his actions greatness, spirit, dignity, and strength; and concerning the private affairs of his subjects, he must insist that his decision be irrevocable; and he should maintain himself in such a way that no man could imagine that he can deceive or cheat him.

That prince who projects such an opinion of himself is greatly esteemed; and it is difficult to conspire against a man with such a reputation and difficult to attack him, provided that he is understood to be of great merit and revered by his subjects. For a prince must have two fears: one, internal, concerning his subjects; the other, external, concerning foreign powers. From the latter he can defend himself by his good troops and friends; and he will always have good friends if he has good troops; and internal affairs will always be stable when external affairs are stable, provided that they are not already disturbed by a conspiracy; and even if external conditions change, if he is properly organized and lives as I have said and does not lose control of himself, he will always be able to withstand every attack, just as I said that Nabis the Spartan[15] did. But concerning his subjects, when external affairs do not change, he has to fear that they may conspire secretly: the prince secures himself from this by avoiding being hated or despised and by keeping the people satisfied with him; this is a necessary matter, as was treated above at length. And one of the most powerful remedies a prince has against conspiracies is not to be hated by the masses; for a man who plans a conspiracy always believes that he will satisfy the people by killing the prince; but when he thinks he might anger them, he cannot work up the courage to undertake such a deed; for the problems on the side of the conspirators are countless. And experience demonstrates that conspiracies have been many but few have been concluded successfully; for anyone who conspires cannot be alone,

---

[13]The Italian original, *si. guarda al tine*, has often been mistranslated as "the ends justify the means" something Machiavelli never wrote. [Translator's note]

[14]**A certain prince** Probably King Ferdinand V of Spain (1452–1516).

[15]**Nabis the Spartan (fl. 220 B.C.)** A Greek tyrant routed by Philopoemon and the Achaean League.

nor can he find companions except from amongst those whom he believes to be dissatisfied; and as soon as you have uncovered your intent to one dissatisfied man, you give him the means to make himself happy, since he can have everything he desires by uncovering the plot; so much is this so that, seeing a sure gain on the one hand and one doubtful and full of danger on the other, if he is to maintain faith with you he has to be either an unusually good friend or a completely determined enemy of the prince. And to treat the matter briefly, I say that on the part of the conspirator there is nothing but fear, jealousy, and the thought of punishment that terrifies him; but on the part of the prince there is the majesty of the principality, the laws, the defenses of friends and the state to protect him; so that, with the good will of the people added to all these things, it is impossible for anyone to be so rash as to plot against him. For, where usually a conspirator has to be afraid before he executes his evil deed, in this case he must be afraid, having the people as an enemy, even after the crime is performed, nor can he hope to find any refuge because of this.

One could cite countless examples on this subject; but I want to satisfy myself with only one which occurred during the time of our fathers. Messer Annibale Bentivogli, prince of Bologna and grandfather of the present Messer Annibale, was murdered by the Canneschi[16] family, who conspired against him; he left behind no heir except Messer Giovanni,[17] then only a baby. As soon as this murder occurred, the people rose up and killed all the Canneschi. This came about because of the good will that the house of the Bentivogli enjoyed in those days; this good will was so great that with Annibale dead, and there being no one of that family left in the city who could rule Bologna, the Bolognese people, having heard that in Florence there was one of the Bentivogli blood who was believed until that time to be the son of a blacksmith, went to Florence

to find him, and they gave him the control of that city; it was ruled by him until Messer Giovanni became of age to rule.

I conclude, therefore, that a prince must be little concerned with conspiracies when the people are well disposed toward him; but when the populace is hostile and regards him with hatred, he must fear everything and everyone. And well-organized states and wise princes have, with great diligence, taken care not to anger the nobles and to satisfy the common people and keep them contented; for this is one of the most important concerns that a prince has.

Writing and Discussion Topics

Questions 1–6 address content, critical analysis, personal choices, ethical options, specific discipline, and interdisciplinary alternatives, respectively.

1. What adjectives does Machiavelli use to describe generosity and miserliness? Which path would he advise a prince to take?
2. Would it be ethical for a corporation to follow the advice on economics Machiavelli gives to a prince? Document corporate practices that follow the Machiavellian style.
3. If you were promised that you could be wealthy and powerful as a result of following Machiavelli's advice, would you do it? What parts of his philosophy are compelling or repulsive to you?
4. Which philosopher from chapter one is most compatible with Machiavelli? Which one seems to differ the most? Explain.
5. Does a prince need to keep his word? Contrast this concept with the writings of Immanuel Kant.
6. Probably the main ethical issue advanced by *The Prince* is the consideration of ends justifying the means in any situation. Is it ethical for a corporation to be concerned only with ends and to ignore means? Use Machiavelli and other sources from this section to justify your response. Immanuel Kant should also be cited in your answer.

---

[16]***Canneschi*** Prominent family in Bologna.
[17]***Giovanni Bentivogli (1443–1508)*** Former tyrant of Bologna. In sequence he was a conspirator against, then a conspirator with Cesare Borgia.

Edwin Arlington Robinson

RICHARD CORY
◆◆◆

E dwin Arlington Robinson (1869–1935) grew up in Gardiner, Maine. He attended Harvard University for two years then returned to his hometown to write. Robinson wrote in traditional metrical forms, often using familiar and colloquial language. He was an exceptionally prolific writer; however, recognition and success came to him late in life, when he received three Pulitzer Prizes for his Collected Poems (1921), The Man Who Died Twice (1924), and Tristram (1927). ◆

Whenever Richard Cory went down town,
We people on the pavement looked at him:
He was a gentleman from sole to crown,
Clean favored, and imperially slim.

And he was always quietly arrayed,
And he was always human when he talked;
But still he fluttered pulses when he said,
"Good morning," and he glittered when he walked.

And he was rich—yes, richer than a king—
And admirably schooled in every grace:
In fine, we thought that he was everything
To make us wish that we were in his place.

So on we worked, and waited for the light,
And went without the meat, and cursed the bread;
And Richard Cory, one calm summer night,
Went home and put a bullet through his head.

Source: Edward Arlington Robinson, "Richard Cory" in *Children of the Night*. Copyright © 1897 Scribner's, New York.

Writing and Discussion Topics

Questions 1–6 address content, critical analysis, personal choices, ethical options, specific discipline, and interdisciplinary alternatives, respectively.

1. Richard Cory is a "prince" of industry in this piece. Is Cory content? Can appearances bring a full life?
2. Does American capitalism lead us to equate monetary success with happiness? How does Robinson's poem refute this notion?
3. Is anyone responsible for your happiness— your parents, your spouse, your employer, your church? Argue for the position that no one but you is responsible for your happiness.
4. What do you propose to be a solid measure of success that would ensure the greatest happiness for an individual? Use the writings of John Stuart Mill to support your answer.
5. Examine Robinson's choice of words. What tone do they give to this poem?
6. Evaluate corporate social responsibility in light of this poem. Use Friedman and the bishops' letter to support your response.

Howard Fast

THE COLD, COLD BOX

◆◆◆

H oward Fast was born and raised in New York City. He has
written numerous novels and short stories. He has received an
Emmy and a Newspaper Guild Award, as well as a Schumburg Award
for race relations. This story comes from a book of short stories entitled
Time and the Riddle. ◆

As always, the annual meeting of the Board of Directors convened at nine o'clock in the morning, on the 10th of December. Nine o'clock in the morning was a sensible and reasonable hour to begin a day's work, and long ago, the 10th of December had been chosen as a guarantee against the seduction of words. Every one of the directors would have to be home for the Christmas holiday—or its equivalent—and therefore the agenda was timed for precisely two weeks and not an hour more.

In the beginning, this had caused many late sessions, sometimes two or three days when the directors met the clock round, with no break for sleep or rest. But in time, as things fell into the proper place and orderly management replaced improvisation, each day's meeting was able to adjourn by four o'clock in the afternoon—and there were even years when the general meeting finished its work a day or two early.

By now, the meeting of the Board of Directors was very matter-of-fact and routine. The big clock on the wall of the charming and spacious meeting room was just sounding nine, its voice low and musical, as the last of the directors found their seats. They nodded pleasantly to each other, and if they were seated close to old friends, they exchanged greetings. They were completely relaxed, neither tense nor uneasy at the thought of the long meeting that lay ahead of them.

There were exactly three hundred of these directors, and they sat in a comfortable circle of many tiers of seats—in a room not unlike a small amphitheatre. Two aisles cut through to a center circle or stage about twenty feet in diameter, and there a podium was placed which allowed the speaker to turn in any direction as he spoke. Since the number of three hundred was an arbitrary one, agreed upon after a good deal of trial and error, and maintained as an excellent working size, half the seats in the meeting room were always empty. There was some talk now and then of redesigning the meeting room, but nobody ever got down to doing it and by now the empty seats were a normal part of the decor.

The membership of the Board was about equally divided between men and women. No one could serve under the age of thirty, but retirement was a matter of personal decision, and a reasonable number

of members were over seventy. Two thirds of them were in their fifties. Since the Board was responsible for an international management, it was only natural that all nations and races should be represented—black men and white men and brown men and yellow men, and all the shadings and gradations in between. Like the United Nations—they were too modest to make such a comparison themselves—they had a number of official languages (and a system of simultaneous translation), though English was most frequently used.

As a matter of fact, the Chairman of the Board who had been born in Indo-China, opened this meeting in English, which he spoke very well and with ease, and after he had welcomed them and announced the total attendance—all members present—he said:

"At the beginning of our annual meeting—and this is an established procedure, I may say—we deal with a moral and legal point, the question of Mr. Steve Kovac. We undertake this before the reading of the agenda, for we have felt that this question of Mr. Kovac is not a matter of agenda or business, but of conscience. Of our conscience, I must add, and not without humility; for Mr. Kovac is the only secret of this meeting. All else that the Board discusses, votes upon and decides or rejects, will be made public, as you know. But of Mr. Steve Kovac the world knows nothing; and each year in the past, our decision has been that the world should continue to know nothing about Mr. Kovac. Each year in the past, Mr. Kovac has been the object of a cruel and criminal action by the members of this Board. Each year in the past, it has been our decision to repeat this crime."

To these words, most of the members of the Board did not react at all—but here and there young men and women showed their surprise, bewilderment and unease, either by expressions on their faces or by low protestations of disbelief. The members of the Board were not insensitive people.

"This year, as in the past, we make this question of Mr. Kovac our first piece of business—because we cannot go onto our other business until it is decided. As in the past, we will decide whether to engage in a criminal conspiracy or not."

A young woman, a new member of the board, her face flushed and angry, rose and asked the chairman if he would yield for a question. He replied that he would.

"Am I to understand that you are serious, Mr. Chairman, or is this some sophomoric prank for the edification of new members?"

From Howard Fast, "The Cold, Cold Box," in *Time and the Riddle*. Reprinted by permission of Sterling Lord Literistic, Inc. Copyright © 1975 by Howard Fast.

"This board is not used to such descriptive terms as sophomoric, as you should know, Mrs. Ramu," he answered mildly. "I am quite serious."

The young woman sat down. She bit her lower lip and stared at her lap. A young man arose.

"Yes, Mr. Steffanson?" the chairman said pleasantly.

The young man sat down again. The older members were gravely attentive, thoughtful without impatience.

"I do not intend to choke off any discussion, and I will gladly yield to any questions," said the Chairman, "but perhaps a little more about this troublesome matter first. There are two reasons why we consider this problem each year. Firstly, because the kind of crime we have committed in the past is hardly anything to grow indifferent to; we need to be reminded; premeditated crime is a deadly threat to basic decency, and God help us if we should ever become complacent! Secondly, each year, there are new members on this board, and it is necessary that they should hear all of the facts in the case of Mr. Kovac. This year, we have seven new members. I address myself to them, but not only to them. I include all of my fellow members of this Board."

Steve Kovac (the President of the Board began) was born in Pittsburgh in the year 1913. He was one of eleven children, four of whom survived to adulthood. This was not too unusual in those days of poverty, ignorance and primitive medicine.

John Kovac, Steve Kovac's father, was a steelworker. When Steve Kovac was six years old, there was a long strike—an attempt on the part of the steelworkers to increase their wages. I am sure you are all familiar with the method of the strike, and therefore I will not elaborate.

During this strike, Steve Kovac's mother died; a year later, John Kovac fell into a vat of molten steel. The mother died of tuberculosis, a disease then incurable. The father's body was dissolved in the molten steel. I mention these things in terms of their very deep and lasting effect on the mind and character of Steve Kovac. Orphaned at the age of seven, he grew up like an animal in the jungle. Placed in a county home for orphan children, he was marked as a bad and intractable boy, beaten daily, deprived of food, punished in every way the ignorance and insensitivity of the authorities could devise. After two years of this, he ran away.

This is a very brief background to the childhood of a most remarkable man, a man of brilliance and strong character, a man of high inventive genius and grim determination. Unfortunately, the mind and personality of this man had been scarred and traumatized beyond redemption. A psychiatric analysis of this process has been prepared, and each of you will find a copy in your portfolio. It also itemizes the trials and suffering of Steve Kovac between the ages of nine and twenty—the years during which he fought to survive and to grow to adulthood.

It also gives a great many details of this time of his life—details I cannot go into. You must understand that while the question before us is related to this background, there are many other features I will deal with.

At this point, the Chairman of the Board paused to take a drink of water and to glance through his notes. The younger members of the Board glanced hurriedly at the psychiatric report; the older members remained contemplative, absorbed in their own thoughts. As many times as they had been through this, somehow it was never dull.

At the age of twenty (the Chairman resumed) Steve Kovac was working in a steel mill outside of Pittsburgh. He was friendly then with a man named Emery. This man, Emery, was alone, without family or means of support. A former coal miner, he suffered from a disease of the lungs, common to his trade. All he had in the world was a five thousand dollar insurance policy. Steve Kovac agreed to support him, and in return he made Kovac the beneficiary of the insurance policy. In those days, insurance policies were frequently the only means with which a family could survive the death of the breadwinner.

Four months later, Emery died. Years afterward, it was rumored that Kovac had hastened his death, but there is no evidence for the rumor. The five thousand dollars became the basis for Steve Kovac's subsequent fortune. Twenty-five years later, the net worth of Steve Kovac was almost three billion dollars. As an individual, he was possibly the wealthiest man in the United States of America. He was a tycoon in the steel and aluminum industries, and he controlled chemical plants, copper mines, railroads, oil refineries and dozens of associated industries. He was then forty-six years old. The year was 1959.

The story of his climb to power and wealth is unique for the generations he lived through. He was a strong, powerful, handsome man—tortured within himself, driven by an insatiable lust to revenge himself, and his father and mother too, for the poverty and suffering of his childhood. Given the traumatic factors of his childhood, his cravings for power turned psychopathic and paranoid, and he built this structure of power securely. He owned newspapers as well as airlines, television stations and publishing houses, and much more than he owned, he controlled. Thereby, he was able to keep himself out of the public eye. In any year of the fifties, you can find no more than an occasional passing reference to him in the press.

How an individual achieved this in a time of the public corporation and the "corporation man" is a singular tale of drive and ambition. Steve Kovac was ambitious, ruthless, merciless and utterly without compassion or pity. His policy was to destroy what stood in his way, if he could; if he could not, he bent it to his will in one way or another. He wrecked lives and fortunes. He framed and entrapped his competitors; he used violence when he had to—when he could not buy or bribe what he wanted. He corrupted individuals and bribed parliaments and bought governments. He erected a structure of power and wealth and control that reached out to every corner of the globe.

And then, in his forty-sixth year, at the height of his wealth and power, he discovered that he had cancer.

The chairman of the Board paused to allow the impact of the words to settle and tell. He took another drink of water. He arranged the papers in front of him.

"At this time," he said. "I propose to read to you a short extract from the diary of Dr. Jacob Frederick. I think that most of you are familiar with the work of Dr. Frederick. In any case, you know that he was elected a member of our Board. Naturally, that was a long time ago. I need only mention that Dr. Frederick was one of the many wise and patient pioneers in the work of cancer research—not only a great physician, but a great scientist. The first entry I propose to read is dated January 12, 1959."

I had an unusual visitor today (the Chairman of the Board read), Steve Kovac, the industrial tycoon. I had heard rumors to the effect of the wealth and power of this man. In himself, he is a striking individual, tall, muscular, handsome, with a broad strong face and a great mane of prematurely-white hair. He has blue eyes, a ruddy complexion, and appears to be in the prime of life and health. Of course, he is not. I examined him thoroughly. There is no hope for the man.

"Doctor," he said to me, "I want the truth. I know it already. You are not the first physician I have seen. But I also want it from you, plainly and bluntly."

I would have told him in any case. He is not the kind of a man you can lie to easily. "Very well," I said to him, "you have cancer. There is no cure for your cancer. You are going to die."

"How long?"

"We can't say. Perhaps a year."

"And if I undergo operative procedure?"

"That could prolong your life—perhaps a year or two longer if the operation is successful. But it will mean pain and incapacity."

"And there is no cure?" His surface was calm, his voice controlled; he must have labored for years to achieve that kind of surface calm and control; but underneath, I could see a very frightened and desperate man.

"None as yet."

"And the quacks and diet men and the rest—they promise cures?"

"It's easy to promise," I said. "But there isn't any cure."

"Doc," he said to me, "I don't want to die and I don't intend to die. I have worked twenty-five years to be where I am now. The tree is planted, I'm going to eat the fruit. I am young and strong—and the best years of my life are ahead of me."

When Kovac talked like that, he was convincing, even to me. It is his quality not simply to demand life, but to take. He denies the inevitable. But the fact remained.

"I can't help you, Mr. Kovac," I told him.

"But you're going to help me," he said calmly, "I came to you because you know more about cancer than any man in the world. Or so I am told."

"You have been misinformed," I said shortly. "No man knows more than anyone else. Such knowledge and work is a collective thing."

"I believe in men, not mobs. I believe you. Therefore, I am ready to pay you a fee of one million dollars if you can make it possible for me to beat this thing and live a full life span." He then reached into his coat for his wallet and took out a certified check for one million dollars. "It is yours—if I live."

I told him to return the following day—that is tomorrow. And now I have been sitting here for hours, thinking of what one million dollars would mean to my work, my hopes—indeed, through them, to all people. I have been thinking with desperation and with small result. Only one thought occurs to me. It is fantastic, but then Steve Kovac is a fantastic man.

Again, the Chairman of the Board paused and looked inquiringly at some of the younger members. They had been listening with what appeared hypnotic concentration. There were no questions and no comments.

"Then I will continue with the diary of Dr. Frederick," the Chairman said.

January 13, (the Chairman said). Steve Kovac returned at 2:00, as we had arranged. He greeted me with a confident smile.

"Doc, if you are ready to sell, I am ready to buy."

"And you really believe that you can buy life?"

"I can buy anything. It's a question of price."

"Can you buy the future?" I asked him. "Because that is where the cure for cancer lies. Do you want to buy it?"

"I'll buy it because you have decided to sell," he said flatly. "I know who I am dealing with. Make your offer, Dr. Frederick."

I made it, as fantastic as it was. I told him about my experiments with the effects of intense cold upon cancer cells. I explained that though, as yet, the experiments had not produced any cure, I had made enormous strides in the intense and speedy application of extreme cold—or, to put it more scientifically, my success in removing heat from living objects, I detailed my experiments—how I had begun with frogs and snakes, freezing them, and then removing the cold and resuming the life process at a later date; how I had experimented with mice, cats, dogs—and most recently monkeys.

He followed me and anticipated me. "How do you restore life?" he wanted to know.

"I don't restore it. The life never dies. In the absence of heat, what might be called the ripening or aging process of life is suspended, but the life remains. Time and motion are closely related; and under intense cold, motion slows and theoretically could cease—all motion, even within the atomic structure. When the motion ceases, time ceases."

"Is it painful?"

"As far as I know, it isn't. The transition is too quick."

"I'd like to see an experiment."

I told him that I had in my laboratory a spider monkey that had been frozen seven weeks ago. My assistants could attest to that. He went into the laboratory with me and watched as we successfully restored the monkey. Seemingly, it was none the worse.

"And the mind?" he asked me.

I shrugged. "I don't know. I have never attempted it with a human being."

"But you think it would work?"

"I am almost certain that it would work. I would need better and larger equipment. With some money to spend, I can improve the process—well, considerably."

He nodded and took the certified check out of his wallet. "Here is your retainer—apart from what you have to spend. Buy whatever you need, and charge it to me. Spend whatever you have to spend and buy the best. No ceiling, no limit. And when I wake up, after a cure has been discovered, there will be a second million to add to your fee. I am not a generous man, but neither am I niggardly when I buy what I want. When will you be ready?"

"Considering the prognosis of your disease," I said, "we should not delay more than five weeks. I will be ready then. Will you?"

Steve Kovac nodded. "I will be ready. There are a good many technical and legal details to work out. I have many large interests, as you may know, and this is a journey of uncertain duration. I will also take care of your own legal responsibilities."

Then he left, and it was done—possibly the strangest agreement ever entered into by a doctor and his patient. I try to think of only one thing—that I now have a million dollars to put into my work and research.

The Chairman of the Board wore pince-nez, and now he paused to wipe them. He cleared his throat, rearranged the papers on the podium once again, and explained.

You see, the plan was a simple one and a sensible one too. Since Mr. Kovac's condition could not be cured, here was a means of preserving his life and arresting the disease until science had found a cure. Timidity was never one of Mr. Kovac's qualities. He analyzed the situation, faced it, and accepted the only possible escape offered to him. So he went about placing his affairs in such order as to guarantee the success and prosperity of his enterprise while he slept—and also their return to his bidding and ownership when he awoke.

In other words, he formed a single holding company for all of his many interests. He gathered together a Board of Directors to manage that holding company in his absence, making himself president in absentia with a substitute president to preside while he was gone. He made a set of qualifying bylaws, that no president could hold office for more than two years, that the Board was to be enlarged each year and a number of other details, each of them aimed at the single goal of retaining all power to himself. And because he was not dead, but merely absent, he created a unique situation, one unprecedented in the history of finance.

This holding company was exempted from all the traditional brakes and tolls placed upon previous companies through the mechanism of death. Until Mr. Kovac returned, the holding company was immortal. Naturally, Dr. Frederick was placed upon the Board of Directors.

In other words (the Chairman of the Board concluded) that is how this Board of Directors came into being.

He allowed himself his first smile then. "Are there any questions at this point?" he asked mildly.

A new member from Japan rose and wanted to know why, if this was the case, the whole world should be told otherwise?

We thought it best (said the President). Just as we, on this Board, have great powers for progress and construction, so do we have no inconsiderable powers of concealment and alteration. The people of the United States and the United Kingdom might have accepted the knowledge that Steve Kovac brought this Board of Directors into being, but certainly in the Soviet Union and China, such knowledge might have been most disconcerting and destructive. Remember that once we had established an open trade area in the Soviet Union and had brought three of her leading government people onto our Board of Directors, our situation changed radically. We were enabled then, through a seizure of all fuel supplies on earth, to prevent the imminent outbreak of World War III.

At that point, neither the extent of our holdings nor the amount of our profits could be further concealed. I say we (the Chairman deferred modestly) but of course it was our predecessors who faced these problems. Our cash balance was larger than that of the United States Treasury, our industrial potential greater than that of any major power. Believe me, without planned intent or purpose, this Board of Directors suddenly found itself the dominant force on earth. At that point, it became desperately necessary for us to explain what we represented.

A new member from Australia rose and asked, "How long was that, Mr. Chairman, if I may inquire, after the visit of Mr. Kovac to Dr. Frederick?"

The Chairman nodded. "It was the year Dr. Frederick died—twenty-two years after the treatment began. By then, five types of cancer had already surrendered their secret to science. But there was not yet any cure for Mr. Kovac's disease."

"And all the time, the treatment had remained secret?"

"All the time," the Chairman nodded.

You see (he went on), at that time, the Board felt that the people of Earth had reached a moment of crisis and decision. A moment, I say, for the power was only momentarily in the hands of this Board. We had no armies, navies or air-fleets—all we had were a major portion of the tools of production. We knew we had not prevented war but simply staved it off. This was a Board of Directors for management, not for power, and any day the installations and plants we owned and controlled could have been torn from our grasp. That was when our very thoughtful and wise predecessors decided to embark on a vast, global propaganda campaign to convince the world that we represented a secret Parliament of the wisest and best forces of mankind—that we were in effect a Board of Directors for the complex of mankind.

And in this, we succeeded, for the television stations, the newspapers, the radio, the film and the theatre—all these were ours. And in that brief, fortunate moment, we launched our attack. We used the weapons of Steve Kovac—let us be honest and admit that. We acted as he would have acted, but out of different motives entirely.

We bought and bribed and framed. We infiltrated the parliaments of all mankind. We bought the military commanders. We dissolved the armies and navies in the name of super-weapons, and then we destroyed the super-weapons in the name of mankind. Where leaders could not be bought or bribed, we brought them into our Board. And above all, we bought control—control of every manufacturing, farming or mining unit of any consequence upon the face of the earth.

It took the Board of Directors twenty-nine years more to accomplish this; and at the end of that twenty-nine years our earth was a single complex of production for use and happiness—and if I may say so, for mankind. A semblance of national structure remained, but it was even then as ritualistic and limited as any commonwealth among the old states of the United States. Wars, armies, navies, atom bombs—all of these were only ugly memories. The era of reason and sanity began, the era of production for use and life under the single legal code of man. Thus, we have become creatures of law, equal under the law, and abiding by the law. This Board of Directors was never a government, nor is it now. It is what it proposes to be, a group management for the holding company.

Only today, the holding company and the means of mankind are inseparable. Thereby, our very great responsibility.

The Chairman of the Board wiped his face and took a few more sips of water. A new member from the United States rose and said, "But Mr. Chairman, the cure for all types of cancer was discovered sixty-two years ago."

"So it was," the Chairman agreed.

"Then, Steve Kovac—" The new member paused. She was a beautiful, sensitive woman in her middle thirties, a physicist of note and talent, and also an accomplished musician.

"You see, my dear," the Chairman said, lapsing into a most informal mode of address, pardonable only because of his years and dignity, "it faced us. When we make a law for mankind and submit to it, we must honor it. Sixty-two years ago, Steve Kovac owned the world and all its wealth and industry, a dictator beyond the dream of any dictator, a tyrant above all tyrants, a king and an emperor to dwarf all other kings and emperors—"

As he spoke, two of the older members left the meeting room. Minutes later, they returned, wheeling into the room and up to the podium a rectangular object, five feet high, seven feet long and three feet wide, the whole of it covered with a white cloth. They left it there and returned to their seats.

"—yes, he owned the world. Think of it—for the first time in history, a just peace governed the nations of mankind. Cities were being rebuilt, deserts turned into gardens, jungles cleared, poverty and crime a thing of the past. Man was standing erect, flexing his muscles, reaching out to the planets and the stars—and all of this belonged to a single savage, merciless, despotic paranoid, Steve Kovac. Then, as now, my dear associates, this Board of Directors was faced with the problem of the man to whom we owed our existence, the man who all unwittingly unified mankind and ushered in the new age of man—yes, the man who gave us the right and authority to hold and manage, the man whose property we manage. Then as now, we were faced with Steve Kovac!"

Almost theatrical in his conclusion and gestures, the Chairman of the Board stepped down from the podium and with one motion swept the cloth aside. The entire Board fixed their eyes on the cabinet where, under a glass cover, in a cold beyond all concept of cold, a man lay sleeping in what was neither life nor death, but a subjective pause in the passage of time. He was a handsome man, big and broad, ruddy of face and with a fine mane of white hair. He seemed to sleep lightly, expectantly, confidently—as if he were dreaming hungrily but pleasantly of what he would awaken to.

"Steve Kovac," the President said. "So he sleeps, from year to year, no difference, no changes. So he appeared to our predecessors sixty-two years ago, when they first had the means to cure him and the obligation to awaken him. They committed the first of sixty-two crimes; they took no action in the face of a promise, a duty, a legality and an almost sacred obligation. Can we understand them? Can we forgive them? Can we forgive the board that voted this same decision again and again? Above all, can we forgive ourselves if we stain our honor, break the law, and ignore our own inheritance of an obligation?

"I am not here to argue the question. It is never argued. The facts are presented, and then we vote. Therefore, will all those in favor of awakening Mr. Kovac raise their right hands?"

The President of the Board waited. Long moments became minutes, but no hands were raised. The two older members covered the cold, cold box and wheeled it out. The Chairman of the Board took a sip of water, and announced.

"We will now have the reading of the agenda."

Writing and Discussion Topics

Questions 1–6 address content, critical analysis, personal choices, ethical options, specific discipline, and interdisciplinary alternatives, respectively.

1. What is the rationale advanced by the Board of Directors in the conclusion of this story? Explain whether this explanation is logical or illogical.
2. Could the theme of this story suggest that money made by corporations needs to be distributed to advance social causes? Does this place the profit motive in a questionable light for wealthy corporations?
3. If you were a member of the Board of Directors, how would you vote and why?
4. Is the overall outcome of this story a moral one? Which authors in section one of this chapter would support your views?
5. How does story form help add to your understanding of the dilemma of corporate responsibility?
6. Compare and contrast the Islamic position with Fast's story.

AN ENEMY OF THE PEOPLE

Henrik Ibsen   Source:
Historical Picture Service.

H enrik Ibsen (1828–1906) was a Norwegian playwright who became known as the father of modern drama. He earned this distinction through the realistic introduction of modern social problems into his plays. He wrote twenty-six works during his fifty years as a dramatist. Some of his plays include A Doll's House, Ghosts, Hedda Gabler, The Wild Duck, Peer Gynt, and When We Dead Awaken. He spent twenty-seven years in exile in Italy and Germany, but returned to his native Norway before his death.

This excerpt is from Act One of An Enemy of the People. In this play, Dr. Stockmann has discovered that the town bath, a major income for the community, is contaminated. He has convinced some townspeople, including the press, that persons coming to the baths for health reasons are actually being poisoned. His brother, the mayor, does not want the baths closed and convinces the town that Dr. Stockmann is actually an enemy of the people. ♦

Dr. Stockmann, *goes to dining room and looks in:*
Catherine! Oh, you're home already, Petra!

Petra, *coming in:*   I just got back from school.

Mrs. Stockmann, *entering:*   Hasn't he been here yet?

Dr. Stockmann: Peter? No, but I just had a long chat with Hovstad. He's really fascinated with my discovery, and you know, it has more implications than I thought at first. Do you know what I have backing me up?

Mrs. Stockmann: What in heaven's name have you got backing you up?

Dr. Stockmann: The solid majority.

Mrs. Stockmann: Is that good?

Dr. Stockmann: Good? It's wonderful. You can't imagine the feeling, Catherine, to know that your own town feels like a brother to you. I have never felt so at home in this town since I was a boy. *A noise is heard.*

Mrs. Stockmann: That must be the front door.

Dr. Stockmann: Oh, it's Peter then. Come in.

Peter Stockmann, *entering from the hall:*   Good morning!

Dr. Stockmann: It's nice to see you, Peter.

Mrs. Stockmann: Good morning. How are you today?

Peter Stockmann: Well, so so. *To Dr. Stockmann:* I received your thesis about the condition of the springs yesterday.

Dr. Stockmann: I got your note. Did you read it?

Peter Stockmann: I read it.

Dr. Stockmann: Well, what do you have to say? *Peter Stockmann clears his throat and glances at the women.*

Mrs. Stockmann: Come on, Petra. *She and Petra leave the room at the left.*

Peter Stockmann, *after a moment:*   Thomas, was it really necessary to go into this investigation behind my back?

Dr. Stockmann: Yes. Until I was convinced myself, there was no point in—

Peter Stockmann: And now you are convinced?

Dr. Stockmann: Well, certainly. Aren't you too, Peter? *Pause.* The University chemists corroborated . . .

Peter Stockmann: You intend to present this document to the Board of Directors, officially, as the medical officer of the springs?

Dr. Stockmann: Of course, something's got to be done, and quick.

Peter Stockmann: You always use such strong expressions, Thomas. Among other things in your report you say that we *guarantee* our guests and visitors a permanent case of poisoning.

Dr. Stockmann: But, Peter, how can you describe it any other way? Imagine! Poisoned internally and externally!

Peter Stockmann: So you merrily conclude that we must build a waste-disposal plant—and reconstruct a brand-new water system from the bottom up!

Dr. Stockmann: Well, do you know some other way out? I don't.

Peter Stockmann: I took a little walk over to the city engineer this morning and in the course of conversation I sort of jokingly mentioned these changes—as something we might consider for the future, you know.

Dr. Stockmann: The future won't be soon enough, Peter.

Peter Stockmann: The engineer kind of smiled at my extravagance and gave me a few facts. I don't suppose you have taken the trouble to consider what your proposed changes would cost?

Dr. Stockmann: No, I never thought of that.

Peter Stockmann: Naturally. Your little project would come to at least three hundred thousand crowns.

Dr. Stockmann, *astonished:*   That expensive!

Peter Stockmann: Oh, don't look so upset—it's only money. The worst thing is that it would take some two years.

Dr. Stockmann: Two years?

Peter Stockmann: At the least. And what do you propose we do about the springs in the meantime? Shut them up, no doubt! Because we would have to, you know. As soon as the rumor gets around that the water is dangerous, we won't have a visitor left. So that's the picture, Thomas. You have it in your power literally to ruin your own town.

Dr. Stockmann: Now look, Peter! I don't want to ruin anything.

Peter Stockmann: Kirsten Springs are the blood supply of this town, Thomas—the only future we've got here. Now will you stop and think?

Dr. Stockmann: Good God! Well, what do you think we ought to do?

Peter Stockmann: Your report has not convinced me that the conditions are as dangerous as you try to make them.

Dr. Stockmann: Now listen; they are even worse than the report makes them out to be. Remember, summer is coming, and the warm weather!

Peter Stockmann: I think you're exaggerating. A capable physician ought to know what precautions to take.

Dr. Stockmann: And what then?

Peter Stockmann: The existing water supply for the springs is a fact, Thomas, and has got to be treated as a fact. If you are reasonable and act with discretion, the directors of the Institute will be inclined to take under consideration any means to make possible improvements, reasonably and without financial sacrifices.

Dr. Stockmann: Peter, do you imagine that I would ever agree to such trickery?

Peter Stockmann: Trickery?

Dr. Stockmann: Yes, a trick, a fraud, a lie! A treachery, a downright crime, against the public and against the whole community!

Peter Stockmann: I said before that I am not convinced that there is any actual danger.

Dr. Stockmann: Oh, you aren't? Anything else is impossible! My report is an absolute fact. The only trouble is that you and your administration were the ones who insisted that the water supply be built where it is, and now you're afraid to admit the blunder you committed. Damn it! Don't you think I can see through it all?

Peter Stockmann: All right, let's suppose that's true. Maybe I do care a little about my reputation. I will say I do it for the good of the town—without moral authority there can be no government. And that is why, Thomas, it is my duty to prevent your report from reaching the Board. Some time later I will bring up the matter for discussion. In the meantime, not a single word is to reach the public.

Dr. Stockmann: Oh, my dear Peter, do you imagine you can prevent that!

Peter Stockmann: It will be prevented.

Dr. Stockmann: It can't be. There are too many people who already know about it.

Peter Stockmann, *angered:*   Who? It can't possibly be those people from the *Daily Messenger* who—

Dr. Stockmann: Exactly. The liberal, free, and independent press will stand up and do its duty!

Peter Stockmann: You are an unbelievably irresponsible man, Thomas! Can't you imagine what consequences that is going to have for you?

Dr. Stockmann: For me?

Peter Stockmann: Yes, for you and your family.

Dr. Stockmann: What the hell are you saying now!

Peter Stockmann: I believe I have the right to think of myself as a helpful brother, Thomas.

Dr. Stockmann: You have been, and I thank you deeply for it.

Peter Stockmann: Don't mention it. I often couldn't help myself. I had hoped that by improving your finances I would be able to keep you from running completely hog wild.

Dr. Stockmann: You mean it was only for your own sake?

Peter Stockmann: Partly, yes. What do you imagine people think of an official whose closest relatives get themselves into trouble time and time again?

Dr. Stockmann: And that's what I have done?

Peter Stockmann: You do it without knowing it. You're like a man with an automatic brain—as soon as an idea breaks into your head, no matter how idiotic it may be, you get up like a sleepwalker and start writing a pamphlet about it.

Dr. Stockmann: Peter, don't you think it's a citizen's duty to share a new idea with the public?

Peter Stockmann: The public doesn't need new ideas—the public is much better off with old ideas.

Dr. Stockmann: You're not even embarrassed to say that?

Peter Stockmann: Now look, I'm going to lay this out once and for all. You're always barking about authority. If a man gives you an order he's persecuting you. Nothing is important enough to respect once you decide to revolt against your superiors. All right then, I give up. I'm not going to try to change you any more. I told you the stakes you are playing for here, and now I am going to give you an order. And I warn you, you had better obey it if you value your career.

Dr. Stockmann: What kind of an order?

Peter Stockmann: You are going to deny these rumors officially.

Dr. Stockmann: How?

Peter Stockmann: You simply say that you went into the examination of the water more thoroughly and you find that you overestimated the danger.

Dr. Stockmann: I see.

Peter Stockmann: And that you have complete confidence that whatever improvements are needed, the management will certainly take care of them.

Dr. Stockmann, *after a pause:*   My convictions come from the condition of the water. My convictions will change when the water changes, and for no other reason.

Peter Stockmann: What are you talking about convictions? You're an official, you keep your convictions to yourself!

Dr. Stockmann: To myself?

Peter Stockmann: As an official, I said. God knows, as a private person that's something else, but as a subordinate employee of the Institute, you have no right to express any convictions or personal opinions about anything connected with policy.

Dr. Stockmann: Now you listen to me. I am a doctor and a scientist—

Peter Stockmann: This has nothing to do with science!

Dr. Stockmann: Peter, I have the right to express my opinion on anything in the world!

Peter Stockmann: Not about the Institute—that I forbid.

Dr. Stockmann: You forbid!

Peter Stockmann: I forbid you as your superior, and when I give orders you obey.

Dr. Stockmann: Peter, if you weren't my brother—

Petra, *throwing the door at the left open:* Father! You aren't going to stand for this! *She enters.*

Mrs. Stockmann, *coming in after her:* Petra, Petra!

Peter Stockmann: What have you two been doing, eavesdropping?

Mrs. Stockmann: You were talking so loud we couldn't help . . .

Petra: Yes, I was eavesdropping!

Peter Stockmann: That makes me very happy.

Dr. Stockmann, *approaching his brother:* You said something to me about forbidding—

Peter Stockmann: You forced me to.

Dr. Stockmann: So you want me to spit in my own face officially—is that it?

Peter Stockmann: Why must you always be so colorful?

Dr. Stockmann: And if I don't obey?

Peter Stockmann: Then we will publish our own statement, to calm the public.

Dr. Stockmann: Good enough! And I will write against you. I will stick to what I said, and I will prove that I am right and that you are wrong, and what will you do then?

Peter Stockmann: Then I simply won't be able to prevent your dismissal.

Dr. Stockmann: What!

Petra: Father!

Peter Stockmann: Dismissed from the Institute is what I said. If you want to make war on Kirsten Springs, you have no right to be on the Board of Directors.

Dr. Stockmann, *after a pause:* You'd dare to do that?

Peter Stockmann: Oh, no, you're the daring man.

Petra: Uncle, this is a rotten way to treat a man like Father!

Mrs. Stockmann: Will you be quiet, Petra!

Peter Stockmann: So young and you've got opinions already—but that's natural. *To Mrs. Stockmann:* Catherine dear, you're probably the only sane person in this house. Knock some sense into his head, will you? Make him realize what he's driving his whole family into.

Dr. Stockmann: My family concerns nobody but myself.

Peter Stockmann: His family and his own town.

Dr. Stockmann: I'm going to show you who loves his town. The people are going to get the full stink of this corruption, Peter, and then we will see who loves his town!

Peter Stockmann: You love your town when you blindly, spitefully, stubbornly go ahead trying to cut off our most important industry?

Dr. Stockmann: That source is poisoned, man. We are getting fat by peddling filth and corruption to innocent people!

Peter Stockmann: I think this has gone beyond opinions and convictions, Thomas. A man who can throw that kind of insinuation around is nothing but a traitor to society! . . .

Writing and Discussion Topics

Questions 1–6 address content, critical analysis, personal choices, ethical options, specific discipline, and interdisciplinary alternatives, respectively.

1. Who controls the operation of the baths? Would this organization actually reject the doctor's findings about the harmful physical effects of the baths? Explain.
2. Both the mayor and his brother, Dr. Stockmann, have staked their professional reputations on the outcome of the dispute over the safety of the bath. Why is the

mayor adamant about keeping the baths open? Why is the physician willing to give up his entire career to close the baths?

3. Are you familiar with a situation involving a "whistle-blower"? Examine the consequences for the whistle-blower. Would you risk giving up your job to expose a social wrong at your place of employment?

4. How does Ibsen pit a champion of the oppressed people against the repressive force of an irrational authority? What are the ethical and political implications of this theme? Is the doctor only interested in the health problems caused by baths?

5. How does the dialogue in this play give us insight into the nature of each of the individuals? Critically examine the integrity of one of the characters.

6. Evaluate this play using the utilitarian system of ethics. How would John Stuart Mill expect the mayor to act in view of the evidence presented to him by his brother, Dr. Stockmann? How would Jesus' teachings suggest the mayor act?

Robert Almeder

MORALITY IN THE MARKETPLACE

◆◆◆

Robert Almeder Courtesy of
Robert Almeder.

R obert Almeder is a professor of philosophy at Georgia State
University, where he was awarded a Distinguished Professor
Award in 1984. His scholarship includes works in American philosophy,
ethics, and philosophy of science. He has written several books in
bioethics and has also been an editor for several philosophy journals. ◆

In order to create a climate more favorable for corporate activity, International Telephone and Telegraph allegedly contributed large sums of money to "destabilize" the duly elected government of Chile. Even though advised by the scientific community that the practice is lethal, major chemical companies reportedly continue to dump large amounts of carcinogens into the water supply of various areas and, at the same time, lobby to prevent legislation against such practices. General Motors Corporation, other automobile manufacturers, and Firestone Tire and Rubber Corporation have frequently defended themselves against the charge that they knowingly and willingly marketed a product that, owing to defective design, had been reliably predicted to kill a certain percentage of its users and, moreover, refused to recall promptly the product even when government agencies documented the large incidence of death as a result of the defective product. Finally, people often say that numerous advertising companies happily accept, and earnestly solicit, accounts to advertise cigarettes knowing full well that as a direct result of their advertising activities a certain number of people will die considerably prematurely and painfully. We need not concern ourselves with whether these and other similar charges are true because our concern here is with what might count as a justification for such corporate conduct were it to occur. There can be no question that such behavior is frequently legal. The question is whether corporate behavior should be constrained by nonlegal or moral considerations. As things presently stand, it seems to be a dogma of contemporary capitalism that the sole responsibility of business is to make as much money as legally possible. But the question is whether this view is rationally defensible.

Sometimes, although not very frequently, corporate executives will admit to the sort of behavior depicted above and then proceed proximately to justify such behavior in the name of their responsibility to the shareholders or owners (if the shareholders are not the owners) to make as much profit as is legally possible. Thereafter, less proximately and more generally, they will proceed to urge the more general utilitarian point that the increase in profit engendered by such corporate behavior begets such an unquestionable overall good for society that the

behavior in question is morally acceptable if not quite praiseworthy. More specifically, the justification in question can, and usually does, take two forms.

The first and most common form of justification consists in urging that, as long as one's corporate behavior is not illegal, the behavior will be morally acceptable because the sole purpose of being in business is to make a profit; and the rules of the marketplace are somewhat different from those in other places and must be followed if one is to make a profit. Moreover, proponents of this view hasten to add that, as Adam Smith has claimed, the greatest good for society is achieved not only by corporations seeking to act morally, or with a sense of social responsibility in their pursuit of profit, but rather by each corporation seeking to maximize its own profit, unregulated in that endeavor except by the laws of supply and demand along with whatever other laws are inherent to the competition process. Smith's view, that there is an invisible hand, as it were, directing an economy governed solely by the profit motive to the greatest good for society,[1] is still the dominant motivation and justification for those who would want an economy unregulated by any moral concern that would, or could, tend to decrease profits for some *alleged* social or moral good.

Milton Friedman, for example, has frequently asserted that the sole moral responsibility of business is to make as much profit as is legally possible; and by that he means to suggest that attempts to regulate or restrain the pursuit of profit in accordance with what some people believe to be socially desirable ends are in fact *subversive* of the common good since the greatest good for the greatest number is achieved by an economy maximally competitive and unregulated by moral rules in its pursuit of profit.[2] So, on Friedman's view, the greatest good for society is achieved by corporations acting legally, but with no further regard for what may be morally desirable; and this view begets the paradox that, *in business*, the greatest good for society can be achieved only by acting without regard for morality. Moreover, adoption of this position constitutes a fairly conscious commitment to the view that while one's personal life may well need governance by moral considerations, when pursuing profit, it is necessary that one's corporate behavior be unregulated by any moral concern other than that of making as much money as is legally possible, curiously enough, it is only in this way that society achieves the greatest good. So viewed, it is not difficult to see how a corporate executive could consistently adopt rigorous standards of morality in his or her personal life and yet feel quite comfortable in abandoning those standards in

From *Business Ethics: Corporate Values and Society,* edited by Milton Snoeyenbos, Robert Almeder, and James Humber (Buffalo, N.Y.: Prometheus Books). Copyright © 1983 by Milton Snoeyenbos, Robert Almeder, and James Humber. Reprinted by permission of the publisher.

the pursuit of profit. Albert Carr, for example, likens the conduct of business to that of playing poker.[3] As Carr would have it, moral busybodies who insist on corporations acting morally might do just as well to censure a good bluffer in poker for being deceitful. Society, of course, lacking a perspective such as Friedman's and Carr's, is only too willing to view such behavior as strongly hypocritical and fostered by an unwholesome avarice.

The second way of justifying, or defending, corporate practices that may appear morally questionable consists in urging that even if corporations were to take seriously the idea of limiting the profits because of a desire to be moral or more responsible to social needs, then corporations would be involved in the unwholesome business of selecting and implementing moral values that may not be shared by a large number of people. Besides, there is the overwhelming question of whether there can be any nonquestionable moral values or noncontroversial list of social priorities for corporations to adopt. After all, if **ethical relativism** is true, or if **ethical nihilism** is true (and philosophers can be counted upon to argue both positions), then it would be fairly silly of corporations to limit profits for what may be a quite dubious reason, namely, for being moral, when there are no clear grounds for doing it, and when it is not too clear what would count for doing it. In short, business corporations could argue (as Friedman has done)[4] that corporate actions in behalf of society's interests would require of corporations an ability to clearly determine and rank in noncontroversial ways the major needs of society; and it would not appear that this could be done successfully.

Perhaps another, and somewhat easier, way of formulating this second argument consists in urging that because philosophers generally fail to agree on what are the proper moral rules (if any), as well as on whether we should be moral, it would be imprudent to sacrifice a clear profit for a dubious or controversial moral gain. To authorize such a sacrifice would be to abandon a clear responsibility for one that is unclear or questionable.

If there are any other basic ways of justifying the sort of corporate behavior noted at the outset, I cannot imagine what they might be. So, let us examine these two modes of justification. In doing this, I hope to show that neither argument is sound and, moreover, that corporate behavior of the sort in question is clearly immoral if anything is immoral—and if nothing is immoral, then such corporate behavior is clearly contrary to the long-term interest of

a corporation. In the end, we will reflect on ways to prevent such behavior, and on what is philosophically implied by corporate willingness to act in clearly immoral ways.

II

Essentially, the first argument is that the greatest good for the greatest number will be, and can only be, achieved by corporations acting legally but unregulated by any moral concern in the pursuit of profit. As we saw earlier, the evidence for this argument rests on a fairly classical and unquestioning acceptance of Adam Smith's view that society achieves a greater good when each person is allowed to pursue her or his own self-interested ends than when each person's pursuit of self-interested ends is regulated in some way or another by moral rules or concern. But I know of no evidence Smith ever offered for this latter claim, although it seems clear that those who adopt it generally do so out of respect for the perceived good that has emerged for various modern societies as a direct result of the free enterprise system and its ability to raise the overall standard of living of all those under it.

However, there is nothing inevitable about the greatest good occurring in an unregulated economy. Indeed, we have good inductive evidence from the age of the Robber Barons that unless the profit motive is regulated in various ways (by statute or otherwise) untold social evil can (and some say *will*) occur because of the natural tendency of the system to place ever-increasing sums of money in everdecreasing numbers of hands. If all this is so, then so much the worse for all philosophical attempts to justify what would appear to be morally questionable corporate behavior on the grounds that corporate behavior, unregulated by moral concern, is necessarily or even probably productive of the greatest good for the greatest number. Moreover, a **rule utilitarian** would not be very hard pressed to show the many unsavory implications to society as a whole if society were to take seriously a rule to the effect that, provided only that one acts legally, it is morally permissible to do whatever one wants to do to achieve a profit. Some of those implications we shall discuss below before drawing a conclusion.

The second argument cited above asserts that even if we were to grant, for the sake of argument, that corporations have social responsibilities beyond that of making as much money as is legally possible for the shareholders, there would be no noncontroversial way for corporations to discover just what these responsibilities are in the order of their importance. Owing to the fact that even distinguished moral philosophers predictably disagree on what one's moral responsibilities are, if any, it would seem irresponsible to limit profits to satisfy dubious moral responsibilities.

For one thing, this argument unduly exaggerates our potential for moral disagreement. Admittedly, there might well be important disagreements among corporations (just as there could be among philosophers) as to a priority ranking of major social needs, but that does not mean that most of us could not, or would not, agree that certain things ought not be done in the name of profit even when there is no law prohibiting such acts. There will always be a few who would do anything for a profit; but that is hardly a good argument in favor of their having the moral right to do so rather than a good argument that they refuse to be moral. In sum, it is hard to see how this second argument favoring corporate moral nihilism is any better than the general argument for ethical nihilism based on the variability of ethical judgments or practices; and apart from the fact that it tacitly presupposes that morality is a matter of what we all in fact would, or should, accept, the argument is maximally counterintuitive (as I shall show) by way of suggesting that we cannot generally agree that corporations have certain clear social responsibilities to avoid certain practices. Accordingly, I would now like to argue that if anything is immoral, a certain kind of corporate behavior is quite immoral although it may not be illegal.

III

Without caring to enter into the reasons for the belief, I assume we all believe that it is wrong to kill an innocent human being for no other reason than that doing so would be more financially rewarding for the killer than if he were to earn his livelihood in some other way. Nor, I assume, should our moral feelings on this matter change depending on the amount of money involved. Killing an innocent baby for fifteen million dollars would not seem to be any less objectionable than killing it for twenty cents. It is possible, however, that some self-professing utilitarian might be tempted to argue that the killing of an innocent baby for fifteen million dollars would not be objectionable if the money were to be given to the poor; under these circumstances, greater good would be achieved by the killing of the innocent baby. But, I submit, if anybody were to argue in this fashion, his argument would be quite deficient because he has not established what he needs to establish to make his argument sound. What he needs is a clear, convincing argument that raising the standard of living of an indefinite number of poor persons by the killing of an innocent person is a greater good for all those affected by the act than if the standard of living were not raised by the killing of an innocent person. This is needed because part of what we mean by having a basic right to life is that a person's life cannot be taken from him or her without a good reason. If our utilitarian cannot provide a convincing justification for his claim that a greater good is served by killing an innocent person in order to raise the standard of living for a large number of poor people, then it is hard to see how he can have the good reason he needs to deprive an innocent person of his or her life. Now, it seems clear that there will be anything but unanimity in the moral community on the question of whether there is a greater good achieved in raising the standard of living by killing an innocent baby than in leaving the standard of living alone and not killing an innocent baby. Moreover, even if everybody were to agree that the greater good is achieved by the killing of the innocent baby, how could that be shown to be true? How does one compare the moral value of a human life with the moral value of raising the standard of living by the taking of that life? Indeed, the more one thinks about it, the more difficult it is to see just what would count as objective evidence for the claim that the greater good is achieved by the killing of the innocent baby. Accordingly, I can see nothing that would justify the utilitarian who might be tempted to argue that if the sum is large enough, and if the sum were to be used for raising the standard of living for an indefinite number of poor people, then it would be morally acceptable to kill an innocent person for money.

These reflections should not be taken to imply, however, that no utilitarian argument could justify the killing of an innocent person for money. After all, if the sum were large enough to save the lives of a large number of people who would surely die if the innocent baby were not killed, then I think one would as a rule be justified in killing the innocent baby for the sum in question. But this situation is obviously quite different from the situation in which one would attempt to justify the killing of an innocent person in order to raise the standard of living for an indefinite number of poor people. It makes sense to kill one innocent person in order to save, say, twenty innocent persons; but it makes no sense at all to kill one innocent person to raise the standard of living of an indefinite number of people. In the latter case, but not in the former, a comparison is made between things that are incomparable.

Given these considerations, it is remarkable and somewhat perplexing that certain corporations should seek to defend practices that are in fact instances of killing innocent persons for profit. Take, for example, the corporate practice of dumping known carcinogens into rivers. On Milton Friedman's view, we should not regulate or prevent such companies from dumping their effluents into the environment. Rather we should, if we like, tax the company after the effluents are in the water and then have the tax money used to clean up the environment.[5] For Friedman, and others, the fact that so many people will die as a result of this practice seems to be just part of the cost of doing business and making a profit. If there is any moral difference between such corporate practices and murdering innocent human beings for money, it is hard to see what it is. It is even more difficult to see how anyone could justify the practice and see it as no more than a business practice not to be regulated by moral concern. And there are a host of other corporate activities that are morally equivalent to deliberate killing of innocent persons for money. Such practices number among them contributing funds to "destabilize" a foreign government, advertising cigarettes, knowingly to market children's clothing having a known cancer causing agent, and refusing to recall (for fear of financial loss) goods known to be sufficiently defective to directly maim or kill a certain percentage of their unsuspecting users because of the defect. On this latter item, we are all familiar, for example, with convincingly documented charges that certain prominent automobile and tire manufacturers will knowingly market equipment sufficiently defective to increase the likelihood of death as a result of the defect and yet refuse to recall the product because the cost of recalling and repairing would have a greater adverse impact on profit than if the product were not recalled and the company paid the projected number of predictably successful suits. Of course, if the projected cost of the predictably successful suits were to outweigh the cost of recall and repair, then the product would be recalled and repaired, but not otherwise. In cases of this sort, the companies involved may admit to having certain marketing problems or a design problem, and they may even admit to having made a mistake; but, interestingly enough, they do not view themselves as immoral or as murderers for keeping their product in the marketplace when they know people are dying from it, people who would not die if the defect were corrected.

The important point is not whether in fact these practices have occurred in the past, or occur even now; there can be no doubt that such practices have occurred and do occur. Rather the point is that when companies act in such ways as a matter of policy, they must either know what they do is murder (i.e., unjustifiable killing of an innocent person), or knowing that it is murder, seek to justify it in terms of profit. And I have been arguing that it is difficult to see how any corporate manager could fail to see that these policies amount to murder for money, although there may be no civil statute against some corporate behavior. If so, then where such policies exist, we can only assume that they are designed and implemented by corporate managers who either see nothing wrong with murder for money (which is implausible) or recognize that what they do is wrong but simply refuse to act morally because it is more financially rewarding to act immorally.

Of course, it is possible that corporate executives would not recognize such acts as murder. They may, after all, view murder as a legal concept involving one noncorporate person or persons deliberately killing another noncorporate person or persons and prosecutable only under existing civil statute. If so, it is somewhat understandable how corporate executives might fail, at least psychologically, to see such corporate policies as murder rather than as, say, calculated risks, tradeoffs, or design errors. Still, for all that, the logic of the situation seems clear enough.

IV Conclusion

In addition to the fact that the only two plausible arguments favoring the Friedman doctrine are unsatisfactory, a strong case can be made for the claim that corporations *do* have a clear and noncontroversial moral responsibility not to design or implement, for reasons of profit, policies that they know, or have good reason to believe, will kill or otherwise seriously injure innocent persons affected by those policies. Moreover, we have said nothing about wage discrimination, sexism, discrimination in hiring, price fixing, price gouging, questionable but not unlawful competition, or other similar practices that some will think businesses should avoid by virtue of responsibility to society. My main concern has been to show that since we all agree that murder for money is generally wrong, and since there is no discernible difference between that and certain corporate policies that are not in fact illegal, then these corporate practices are clearly immoral (that is, they ought not to be done) and incapable of being morally justified by appeal to the Friedman doctrine since that doctrine does not admit of adequate evidential support. In itself, it is sad that this argument needs to be made and, if it were not for what appears to be a fairly strong commitment within the business community to the Friedman doctrine in the name of the unquestionable success of the free enterprise system, the argument would not need to be stated.

The fact that such practices do exist—designed and implemented by corporate managers who, for all intents and purposes, appear to be upright members of the moral community—only heightens the need for effective social prevention. Presumably, of course, any company willing to put human lives into the profit and loss column is not likely to respond to moral censure. Accordingly, I submit that perhaps the most effective way to deal with the problem of preventing such corporate behavior would consist in structuring legislation such that senior corporate managers who knowingly concur in practices of the sort listed above can effectively be tried, at their own expense, for murder, rather than censured and fined a sum to be paid out of corporate profits. This may seem a somewhat extreme or unrealistic proposal. However, it seems more unrealistic to think that aggressively competitive corporations will respond to what is morally necessary if failure to do so could be very or even minimally profitable. In short, unless we take strong and appropriate steps to prevent such practices, society will be reinforcing a destructive mode of behavior that is maximally disrespectful of human life, just as society will be reinforcing a value system that so emphasizes monetary gain as a standard of human success that murder for profit could be a corporate policy if the penalty for being caught as it were not too dear.

In the long run, of course, corporate and individual willingness to do what is clearly immoral for the sake of monetary gain is a patent commitment to a certain view about the nature of human happiness and success, a view that needs to be placed in the balance with Aristotle's reasoned argument and reflections to the effect that money and all that it brings is a means to an end, and not the sort of end in itself that will justify acting immorally to attain it. What that beautiful end is and why being moral allows us to achieve it, may well be the most rewarding and profitable subject a human being can think about. Properly understood and placed in perspective, Aristotle's view on the nature and attainment of human happiness could go a long way toward alleviating the temptation to kill for money.

In the meantime, any ardent supporter of the capitalistic system will want to see the system thrive and flourish; and this it cannot do if it invites and demands government regulation in the name of the public interest. A *strong* ideological commitment to what I have described above as the Friedman doctrine is counterproductive and not in anyone's long-range interest because it is most likely to beget an ever-increasing regulatory climate. The only way to avoid such encroaching regulation is to find ways to move the business community into the long-term view of what is in its interest, and effect ways of both determining and responding to social needs before society moves to regulate business to that end. To so move the business community is to ask business to regulate its own modes of competition in ways that may seem very difficult to achieve. Indeed, if what I have been suggesting is correct, the only kind of enduring capitalism is humane capitalism, one that is at least as socially responsible as society needs. By the same token, contrary to what is sometimes felt in the business community, the Friedman doctrine, ardently adopted for the dubious reasons generally given, will most likely undermine capitalism and motivate an economic socialism by assuring an erosive regulatory climate in a society that expects the business community to be socially responsible in ways that go beyond just making legal profits.

In sum, being socially responsible in ways that go beyond legal profit-making is by no means a dubious luxury for the capitalist in today's world. It is a necessity if capitalism is to survive at all; and, presumably, we shall all profit with the survival of a vibrant capitalism. If anything, then, rigid adherence to the Friedman doctrine is not only philosophically unjustified, and unjustifiable, it is also unprofitable in the long run, and therefore, downright subversive of the long-term common good. Unfortunately, taking the long-run view is difficult for everyone. After all, for each of us, tomorrow may not come. But living for today only does not seem to make much sense either, if that deprives us of any reasonable and happy tomorrow. Living for the future may not be the healthiest thing to do; but do it if we must, if we have good reason to think that we will have a future. The trick is to provide for the future without living in it, and that just requires being moral.[6]

Notes

1. Adam Smith, *The Wealth of Nations*, ed. Edwin Canaan (Modern Library, N.Y., 1937), p. 423.
2. Milton Friedman, "The Social Responsibility of Business Is to Increase Its Profits" *The New York Times Magazine* (September 13, 1970), pp. 33, 122–126 and "Milton Friedman Responds" *Business and Society Review* (Spring, 1972, No. 1), p. 5 ff.
3. Albert Z. Carr, "Is Business Bluffing Ethical?" *Harvard Business Review* (January-February 1968).
4. Milton Friedman, "Milton Friedman Responds" *Business and Society Review* (Spring 1972, No. 1), p. 10.
5. Milton Friedman, "Milton Friedman Responds" *Business and Society Review* (Spring 1972, No. 1), p. 10.
6. I would like to thank C. G. Luckhardt, J. Humber, R. L. Arrington, and M. Snoeyenbos for their comments and criticisms of an earlier draft.

Shortly after this paper was initially written, an Indiana superior court judge refused to dismiss a homicide indictment against the Ford Motor Company. The company was indicted on charges of reckless homicide stemming from a 1978 accident involving a 1973 Pinto in which three girls died when the car burst into flames after being slammed in the rear. This was the first case in which Ford, or any other automobile manufacturer, had been charged with a criminal offense.

The indictment went forward because the state of Indiana adopted in 1977 a criminal code provision permitting corporations to be charged with criminal acts. At the time, twenty-two other states allowed as much.

The judge, in refusing to set aside the indictment, agreed with the prosecutor's argument that the charge was based not on the Pinto design fault, but rather on the fact that Ford had permitted the car "to remain on Indiana highways knowing full well its defects."

The case went to trial, a jury trial, and Ford Motor Company was found innocent of the charges. Of course, the increasing number of states that allow corporations to fall under the criminal code is an example of social regulation that could have been avoided had corporations and corporate managers not followed so ardently the Friedman doctrine.

Writing and Discussion Topics

Questions 1–6 address content, critical analysis, personal choices, ethical options, specific discipline, and interdisciplinary alternatives, respectively.

1. Explain how illegal and immoral considerations should act as a constraint on corporate behavior.
2. What are some of the examples that Almeder gives of immoral corporate behavior? Are these practices legal? What are the differences between legal and moral practices?
3. Would you kill a baby for a large sum of money and then give the money to the poor? How would this action compare to actual corporate conduct?
4. Describe two ways that executives working for "moral corporations" justify high profits but immoral decisions.
5. Do businesses today still practice the unrestrained pursuit of profits? Why would this practice that Almeder describes run counter to the utilitarian system of ethics?
6. Compare and contrast the personal experiences of DeLorean with the theory of Almeder. How are their ethics similar and different?

Neil Chamberlain

THE UNCERTAIN RELATION BETWEEN BUSINESS AND SOCIETY

—◆◆◆—

N eil Chamberlain is a professor emeritus of the Graduate School of Business at Columbia University. He was director of the Yale Labor and Management Center and a professor of economics before moving to Columbia in 1954. He is a well-known scholar and author on the subjects of labor, management, economics, and corporate social responsibility. He has written over twenty-five books. ◆

The corporation in America was first and foremost a political expression performing a public economic function. The colonies transplanted a mercantilist European society. The central tenet of mercantilism was the integration of the social order within the nation-state, which had become the parochial and secular substitute for the declining Roman Catholic church. The advancement of the state was intended to contribute to the welfare of its people, and that political objective affected the character of the state's instrumentalities. Thus, in colonial America, no less than in the metropolitan countries of Europe, the state created corporations for public purposes. The purely private business affairs of the colonists, more restricted in scale and scope, were carried on chiefly by individuals or by unincorporated joint-stock companies of a local nature.

The Corporation in the Early United States

Neither independence nor Adam Smith's great antimercantilist polemic *The Wealth of Nations*, which emerged in the same year, wrought any radical change in public attitudes toward the corporation as a political instrument. Mercantilist views on the need for government to promote the social welfare hung on in the newly created United States for fifty years or more. No longer, however, were there the preclusive powers of an overseas imperial government, nor did the new federal government exercise much of an inhibitive role. Under the constitutional principle of states' rights, state governments moved into the business of chartering their own corporations. Each corporation required a special act of the state legislature, tailored to the specific purpose being promoted.

By the turn of the nineteenth century more than three hundred business corporations had been created. Two-thirds were concerned with inland navigation, turnpikes, and toll bridges. The remainder included insurance companies, commercial banks, and public services (e.g., administering the water supply and docks). As the historian Stuart Bruchey observed: "These business corporations were no more exclusively profit-seeking associations than the chartered joint-stock companies with which the English had pioneered in the settlement of America."

Reprinted with permission of The Free Press, a Division of Macmillan, Inc. from *Social Strategy and Corporate Structure* by Neil W. Chamberlain. Copyright © 1982 by The Trustees of Columbia University in the City of New York.

They were, in fact, quasi-public agencies of the state." He quoted a Massachusetts charter of 1818 that created "a corporation *and body politic*" for the purpose of milling flour.[1] The special privileges accorded such corporations were premised on the social services they rendered: the dedication of private capital and entrepreneurial effort to the public interest. Other investigators have underlined this political character of the early corporation. John P. Davis, in the classic two-volume history of the corporation, noted that "it was not considered justifiable to create corporations for any purpose not clearly public in nature; each application was considered by itself, and if favorably, was followed by a legislative act of incorporation."[2] Oscar Handlin commented that "at its origin in Massachusetts, the corporation was conceived as an agency of the government, endowed with public attributes, exclusive privileges, and political power, and designed to serve a social function for the State."[3]

After 1815 an increase in economic opportunity projected the country into what, in contemporary terminology, would be called the takeoff into sustained economic growth. The moving West became more closely integrated with the industrially expanding East. A surge in immigration, especially of the Irish and Germans, increased the pool of both consumers and workers. A concomitant, yeasty egalitarianism led to movements in the several states for abolition of property holder or taxpayer status to qualify for the vote; admission of new states, formed out of the western territories and populated with rugged individualists, expanded an assertive electorate.

This spread of economic opportunity gave rise to a new class of economic adventurers in single-minded pursuit of wealth. The cult of the self-made man became the national symbol. In those heady days the self-created businessman was the very embodiment of democracy, contrasting with the members of the older eastern aristocratic families who had inherited their privileges. The changed climate was not without effect on the political concept of the corporation.

First, the practice of issuing corporate charters by special legislative act came to be viewed with suspicion and distaste. For one thing, it smacked of privilege: individuals with well-placed contacts, favorable social standing, and economic advantage clearly had an inside track on a state's grant of corporate rights. Even though that grant was premised on the rendering of a public service it nevertheless entailed private profit and benefit. Egalitarian sentiment supported a legislature representing all equally.

A second shift in social attitude toward the corporation was perhaps even more important. In the spirit of the times economic development, a national objective, was a goal that could be promoted by Everyman. Adam Smith was coming into his own, winning recognition that the butcher, the baker, the candlestick maker—all seeking their private gain— were contributing to the national wealth and thus serving a public purpose. In serving a public purpose, they, too, merited the advantages of incorporation. In Davis's words, "Not only was it difficult to distinguish between public and private, but the view that individuals should have the freest possible opportunities to create wealth encouraged the presumption that every business was of public importance in the respect that it might increase the aggregate wealth of society."[4] Private enterprise had become public purpose.

The consequence for the corporation of this changing social context was remarkable. Although there had been some early flirtation with general incorporation laws, obviating the necessity of special legislative acts, movement in this direction now swelled. At least half a dozen states had passed general incorporation laws prior to the Civil War. And the notion that public purpose was served by private profit seeking gave ample rationale to this more open access to the corporate form, with its attendant advantages.

Private profit seeking has characterized societies in almost every age, as R. H. Tawney pointed out, but what was new about the nineteenth-century development, and especially its American expression, was the unabashed identification of private with public good and the widespread embrace of material advancement as embodying the highest democratic good. This value orientation shaped both American society and the American landscape. Law and business practice emphasized the privacy of person and property and gave to the corporation the constitutional rights of those persons who had formed it. After all, the federal constitution had made no special provision for such an institution. Business relations—the relations between the institutionalized person of the corporation and the real persons with whom it dealt—rested on voluntary contract, volition assumed to be equal on both sides. Such voluntary relations were largely unsupervised by the state as to their efforts on the contracting parties or on third parties—even whole communities. Cities and nature, people and resources, became appropriate arenas for the economic exploits of private adventurers, whether single entrepreneurs or incorporated associates.

Expanding Corporations and Their Impact

The consequence of this transformation of the corporation from public service provider to private profit seeker became more evident after the Civil War with the development of a national market based on an expanding transportation network. The more enterprising corporations grew in size, enlarged their financial base, and changed their organizational form and managerial functions. In effect the corporation, which sought to seize the economic opportunities offered by the amalgamation of pockets of population into a vast and virtual empire, had to pull up its local roots, separating itself from a community in which its managers were familiar civic figures, subject to the constraints of neighbors' opinions, and loosening ties with the state that issued the corporate charter. Abandoning this limited field of operations, the national corporation could obtain its charter in any state as a license to do business anywhere in the nation. Autonomous in its actions under the permissive philosophy of private initiative, the national corporation, with its subsidiaries and satellites, was free to move in and out of communities as suited its operations. With its behavior justified by the political principle that whatever contributed to economic development achieved public purposes, the national corporation could view social communities and the physical environment as malleable materials to be shaped to its own pecuniary advantage.

The enormity of this continental challenge spawned a race of titans capable of measuring up to the new standard. Cities like Detroit, Gary, Chicago, St. Louis, Omaha, and Denver could be thrown up almost like stage sets, outfitted to satisfy corporate balance sheets. Technology—building from Eli Whitney's insightful use of interchangeable parts in the early nineteenth century—was pushed at an accelerating pace; one discovery paved the way for another. In an early version of Mao's hundred blooming flowers, backyard laboratories sprang up wherever there were backyards. Soon the basement inventor was replicated on a vast scale within the nationalizing corporations: Steinmetz and General Electric became the paradigm.

New industries emerged—automobile, rubber and tire, electrical, pharmaceutical. The race of titans gave way to more impersonal and institutionalized divisions of the large corporations, each with a mission and a budget—to invent, to develop commercially, to produce efficiently and profitably, to create appetites for the more and the different. Raw and processed materials followed the same pattern—steel mills that quickly dwarfed those of England, from which they had taken their inspiration; oil derricks hastily assembled to bring the new fuel to use abundantly and quickly, if also wastefully; massive machinery, eventually towering like Gothic cathedrals in the wilderness, for the purpose of extracting coal and minerals and in the process creating mountains of slag that would be left ominously behind. Like the materials-producing industries, the new manufacturing plants generated wastes on a scale proportionate to their output. Wastes could be discharged into rivers and lakes, deposited in landfills, or buried. In some instances the violation of social amenities was blatant enough to evoke—not always effectively—resentment and resistance: automobile graveyards stacked with the rusted bodies of junked cars; nauseous odors in the vicinity of plants using certain chemicals; and water so contaminated that the chlorination to make it safe for drinking made it unpalatable. In other cases toxic wastes buried in the ground or left in dump sites found their way, after the passage of years, into underground streams, where they endangered the health of nearby residents. The potential hazard may never have been suspected: the dump was available and there were few restrictions on the private use of land (there still are not in many states).

Thus, large-scale corporate industry affected society in two ways: the direct impact of the production process on the social and natural environment—the use of people and nature as resources for the benefit of the autonomous corporation, whose private gain was identified with public good; and the health hazards, pollution, and environmental despoliation for which no corporate responsibility—until recently—was assessed since these activities breeched no right of contract or fair usage of property and were incidental to the production process, which was itself wanted (corporate profits, workers' jobs, and community taxes all being at stake).

Moreover, the adverse effects of technological processes are often disputable: "Is the routine use of antibiotics in animal feed breeding medicine-resistant bacteria that will eventually cause untreatable diseases in humans?" *Business Week* asks, "No one seems to know for sure. . . . The stakes are huge. Although the $170 million annual market for animal-use antibiotics represents insignificant fractions of the total sale of such drug giants as American Cyanamid, Pfizer, and Diamond Shamrock, it forms the backbone of their agricultural sales divisions. . . . The nagging question, however, is whether continuing the use of feed antibiotics will yield cheap meat at the expense of good health."[5] An elderly woman living near a former industrial dumpsite that harbors residual asbestos, benzine, and other toxic substances, says perplexedly: "Chemicals are everywhere. One test will show that it's dangerous, one test will show that it's not. In this day and age, who do you believe?"[6]

The knotty problem of weighing economic advantage against social disadvantage, particularly in the face of scientific uncertainty, is perhaps most clearly illustrated by the case of nuclear power. But recent years have witnessed an increasing number of like industrial dilemmas: the effect of certain spray propellants on the ozone layer; the hothouse effect of carbon dioxide from increased coal burning to conserve scarce and expensive oil; the widespread use of herbicides containing dioxin, which has been called the most powerful carcinogen known; and a Pandora's box of suggested horrors capable of being visited on humankind by genetic engineering for industrial purposes. The unknowns involved are vigorously debated by scientists.

In the face of such scientific riddles, courts have at times taken the position that "the lives and health of people . . . in the circumstances of modern industrialism, are largely beyond self-protection."[7] But if this is so, who has responsibility for the public? Is responsibility rested in the corporation, whose value system stresses autonomous decisions directed to the business's own advantage? Is responsibility rested in the hands of government agents, who would have to create a vast network to oversee all corporate activity, granting or refusing their imprimatur often on the basis of inadequate or conflicting information? Is industrialization on a large scale a force so elemental, almost like nature itself, that it cannot be controlled in any meaningful sense?

Leo Marx surveyed the attitudes of American writers of the nineteenth and twentieth centuries with respect to the impact of industrialism on society and constructed a vivid historic allegory entitled *The Machine in the Garden*.[8] From its discovery America embodied the myth of the garden—an Eden existing in reality. The myth had two versions: one, a primitivistic view—nature untouched, unspoiled, and provident; the other, a cultural view—nature left to itself tending as much to wilderness as to garden and requiring human care to realize the pastoral vision.

Into this idyllic conception of the New World intruded, in time, the machine, the steam engine, and above all, the railroad. The Industrial Revolution had started in England, it was true, but there the machine intruded into a formed, socialized setting, with classes, customs, and commerce already in place. In America, it intruded into the unspoiled Garden, the myth-dream of a recovered Eden.

For a while, the opposition between the two cultures—the pastoral and the technological—went unrecognized. The machine could be regarded as a product of the Enlightenment, enjoyed and praised for its capacity to supply harnessed power, allowing the husbandman to practice even more successfully his rural pursuit—divorced in thought from an urban, factory culture. Even when the recognition came that a machine society introduced competing values and social relations, there developed the philosophic-poetic-artistic vision of "the middle landscape." The machine could be harnessed to tasks that would improve the pastoral society—but it must be restrained at the point where, if allowed to expand further, it would itself dominate society.

Following this conception, the frontier West epitomized the barbaric wilderness of nature untamed. Europe was the overcivilized, overcommercialized, overurbanized, and overmechanized domain where the new technology had been allowed to rule. In between—geographically, psychologically, and socially—lay settled America, still in a controllable stage of development: the middle landscape avoided the undesirable extremes.

The vision was static, and as technology expanded its hold under the driving force of unrestrained individualistic competition, American writers sought to confront the vision and the reality, the machine in the garden, in a way that reconciled pastoral sensibilities with modern technological advances. But reconciliation was impossible. American literature became distinguished by the dialectic, the discomfort, the disillusion of a deeply felt need to hold fast to natural goodness in the face of irresistible institutional forces. As Marx concluded his

illuminating study: "To change the situation we require new symbols of possibility, and although the creation of those symbols is in some measure the responsibility of artists, it is in greater measure the responsibility of society. The machine's sudden entrance into the garden presents a problem that ultimately belongs not to art but to politics."[9]

Social Challenges to Corporate Autonomy

If corporate industrialism has had adverse as well as benign effects on society, requiring a reappraisal of their relationship, it is no less true that society has been undergoing transformations that have influenced the business corporation. These have largely to do with the pressures of population on resources and space. Relative scarcity has always been an issue, to be sure, but in most countries before industrialization the problem was contained by early indoctrination in an appropriate allocation of scarce goods by social class and function; since the spread of industrialization this problem has been finessed by the promise of economic growth in which all could share, even if not equally. Only within the past few decades—indeed, chiefly within the last decade—has the notion of absolute scarcity been debated. If we can safely say that few now subscribe to the concept of a definite limit on economic growth, we would have to add that many—including many reputable scientists—affirm that economic growth does have limits, even though not easily specified, and that continued indiscriminate growth may waste irreplaceable resources and permanently despoil the environment. It is the one measure of the seriousness with which we now view resource limits that air and water—once classic examples of free goods—have come to be appreciated as having their price, sometimes a high one.[10]

The soaring costs of energy in all forms have engendered the fear of a declining standard of consumption. Pressures to sustain economic growth—to maintain jobs and income, if not to add to affluence—have resulted in the use of lower quality, less accessible, higher cost raw materials (the Ricardian effect), raising prices and frustrations. The optimistic belief that new technologies will provide substitute products and processes is at best an article of faith and at worst ignores potentially damaging consequences of the substitutes (the industrialization effect just noted). There has been a growing intellectual acceptance, even in some business circles, that the rate of economic growth cannot and should not be sustained at past levels; at the same time, we are reluctant to explore the significance of this conclusion.

But one consequence seems unavoidable. If growth can no longer be counted on to provide for all the major wants, private and public, of a society, or to sustain all the peripheral members of a society at a level that keeps a lid on mutinous outbreaks, especially in congested urban centers, then *some* specification of a nation's most serious needs—its social priorities—and *some* direction as to how goods are to be allocated among society's members are needed. The appropriate word is *planning*. Planning may be comprehensive or piecemeal, compulsory or advisory, long-run or short-run, but whatever its form, planning means identifying priorities in the production and distribution of economic resources. It is here that political decision making challenges the autonomous corporation.

It was easier in an earlier day to support individualism, including economic discretion, as the expression of a more basic philosophical freedom. But in our times—in the process of change from pastoral society to massive industrialism, from small-scale, open settlements to large, packaged populations, from amateur experimentation with keys on kites to scientific applications having major impact far from their source, with populations pressing hard on resources and resorting to modern forms of massed political power to cut themselves into the distribution of consumer goods—the autonomous corporation, free as an individual in its business decisions, has become an anachronism. A philosophy of privatism that extends to the large business corporation is no longer tenable.

Corporate managers who bitterly assail the accumulating federal regulations with which they must cope contend, and with vehemence, that they have long since lost their privacy, at least since the New Deal.

> The heavily individualistic tenor of *caveat emptor* has been largely supplanted by a myriad of class-oriented consumer protection laws, and employment relations, which once were a matter of individual agreement between master and servant, have been circumscribed by regulations setting minimum wages, prescribing safety and health regulations, and prohibiting discrimination based on race, sex, age, creed, and national origin as Congress has moved to protect consumers, workers, and minorities as classes.[11]

But such protective legislation still accepts the basic premise of corporate autonomy. The legislation provides a framework within which the business firm can operate as it chooses or cease to operate if it chooses. The burden of governmental regulation has grown phenomenally in response to social pressures, proscribing certain corporate conduct but without modifying corporate objective. The difference was noted by David Rockefeller, chairman of the board of Chase Manhattan Bank: "Today, society's heightened expectations of an improved life are increasingly coming to bear upon private institutions, as well as traditional public institutions. Major corporations are being asked not merely to support, but to help devise and carry out basic strategies to eliminate social ills."[12] The Committee for Economic Development (CED), a businessman's organization, came to much the same conclusion. Maintaining that society increasingly turns to business corporations for help in solving major problems, CED explained: "Out of a mixture of public frustration and respect for the perceived efficiency of business organizations, there is a clear tendency to look to corporations to take up the slack resulting from inadequate performance of other institutions, notably government." For whatever reasons, "broadened expectations of business have been building up for some time."

> Today it is clear that the terms of the contract between society and business are, in fact, changing in substantial and important ways. Business is being asked to assume broader responsibilities to society than ever before and to serve a wider range of human values. Business enterprises, in effect, are being asked to contribute more to the quality of American life than just supplying quantities of goods and services. Inasmuch as business exists to serve society, its future will depend on the quality of management's response to the changing expectations of the public.[13]

Given their autonomy, corporations even within a regulatory framework are structured to realize profits efficiently. If this autonomy is called into question—not just through a redrafting of the regulatory contours but through a public sharing in the definition of objectives—profit efficiency, however much leavened by enlightened public relations, can no longer claim to be the singular corporate strategy. It is not so much unchecked corporate power or adverse consequences of corporate power that are at issue but the appropriate uses of corporate power, particularly with respect to major social objectives that can be presumed, on the strength of an evolving political philosophy, to take precedence over individual desires.

Public and Private Purpose

The question of society's right to override private discretion goes back to earlier attempts at social legislation—minimum wages, maximum hours, child labor restrictions, for example—in a day when individualism and voluntarism were considered the bedrock of western democracy and the U.S. Supreme Court could assert that to strike down such inhibiting legislation was not to destroy the public good but to exalt it. That issue, involving the police powers of the state, has for some time been resolved in favor of the state. The point now being raised is different. Concern has shifted from the restraint of actions the corporation *might* have initiated if its privacy has been unchecked; now the focus is on the definition of actions the corporation *actually* undertakes or *could* undertake if corporate decisions were determined by criteria that the corporation *left to itself* would not choose to follow.

The distinction can be seen when applied to America's premier industry, the automobile industry. Left to their own devices the auto manufacturers' objective would be to sell as many cars as they profitably could within whatever regulatory framework involving safety, pollution control, and gasoline conservation Congress might erect. The more cars the better. But if their objective were set in the light of social desiderata, Detroit might become involved in a vigorous effort to *reduce* the population of automobiles by developing alternative means of transportation that would satisfy public needs at lower social costs, even if the profit potential were less.

Many leaders in the corporate world have testified that large corporations are in fact being pushed to adopt new strategies involving social purpose. As the CED commented, "The evidence strongly suggests that these are solid and durable trends, not momentary frustrations or fads, and that they are likely to increase rather than diminish in the future."[14]

A New Strategy, A New Structure

Nevertheless, support for new strategies will remain largely wind and words unless there are changes in the structure of the corporation to facilitate them.

That proposition has been effectively elaborated by Alfred Chandler, Jr., in *Strategy and Structure: Chapters in the History of Industrial Enterprise.*[15] Concerned with the growth of the contemporary corporation, he concluded from a detailed examination of the period prior to World War II that changes in opportunities and needs from one period to a succeeding period dictated shifts in corporate strategy. And "there seems to be no question that a new strategy created new administrative needs."[16] Delays in developing new institutional devices perhaps reflected executive preoccupation with day-to-day affairs or failure to recognize the organizational problems impeding the success of a new strategy. Resistance to change may also have stemmed from perceived threats to the executive's own organizational or psychological security. In any event, sooner or later the needed structural change had to be forthcoming if the enterprise were to pursue the new strategy efficiently. In the period Chandler examined, new strategies were necessitated chiefly by changes in population, national income, and technology—conditions over which the individual corporation has no control but to which the corporation was obliged to adapt.

Here is where the corporation is challenged today. The changes that are compelling a new corporate strategy are to some extent a continuation of past changes on a vastly altered scale. In part they represent shifts that are more political and social than economic. In total, they demand a new corporate strategy geared to broader objectives than profit and to more specific objectives than whatever production can turn a profit. Profit is not excluded as a goal, but it is no longer exclusive.

Such a changed strategy cannot be pursued effectively without altering the corporate structure. To pretend that social purpose can simply be grafted onto the existing corporate organization is an illusion and an evasion. However, to revise the present corporate structure will not be easy: today's corporate form matured in the permissive atmosphere of the last century, when the principle of corporate privatism replaced the guiding principle of public service. Introducing social purpose depends not only on modifying the internal corporate structure but on reordering working relationships among corporations, other interest groups, and government.

Notes

1. Stuart Bruchey,"Corporation: Historical Development," in Alfred D. Chandler, Jr., Stuart Bruchey, and Louis Galambos (eds.), *The Changing Economic Order* (New York: Harcourt, 1968), p. 143.
2. John P. Davis, *Corporations* (New York: Capricorn, 1961; first published 1904), vol. II, p. 269.
3. Oscar Handlin, with Mary Flug Handlin, "Origins of the American Business Corporation," *Journal of Economic History* 5 (1945):22.
4. Davis, *Corporations*, p. 269.
5. *Business Week*, January 16, 1978, p. 55.
6. *Wall Street Journal*, May 22, 1979.
7. *United States v. Dotterweich*, 320 U.S. 277, 280 (1943), cited in *United States v. Park*, 421 U.S. 658 (1975).
8. Leo Marx, *The Machine in the Garden* (New York: Oxford University Press, 1964, 1976; citations from latter).
9. Ibid., p. 365.
10. *The Economist*, August 18, 1979, p. 34.
11. O. Lee Reed, Jr., "Comments: The Sunshine Society and the Legal Regulation of Business through Compulsory Disclosure," *American Business Law Journal* 16 (Spring 1978):87.
12. David Rockefeller, "Corporate Capacity for Public Responsibility," *Business Lawyer* 28 (March 1973):55.
13. Committee for Economic Development, *Social Responsibilities of Business Corporations* (New York: CED, 1971), p. 16.
14. *Ibid.*
15. Alfred D. Chandler, Jr., *Strategy and Structure: Chapters in the History of the Industrial Enterprise* (Cambridge: M.I.T. Press, 1962).
16. Ibid., p. 14.

Writing and Discussion Topics

Questions 1–6 address content, critical analysis, personal choices, ethical options, specific discipline, and interdisciplinary alternatives, respectively.

1. Does Chamberlain believe that corporations have out-of-date practices in the area of social responsibility? Do you agree or disagree with his assessment?
2. How have corporate structures been altered over the last two centuries? Why does Chamberlain assert that beneficial social purposes cannot be furthered without modifying corporate patterns?
3. Chamberlain points out that corporate selfishness benefits the public good only during periods of rapid economic development. Using Chamberlain as a source, explain what the American corporate system of business needs to do to serve the public interest today.
4. In this decade, many Americans are more concerned with overall quality of life than the rate of economic growth. Explain which philosophers from chapter one would agree with this concept.
5. Citing Chamberlain's article as a source, explain your beliefs on whether history repeats itself or if each age is unique. Use the theme of corporate responsibility as a focus.
6. How do the disciplines of philosophy, religion, literature, and history help you to better understand the subject of corporate social responsibility? Explain and defend your ethical position on the topic of corporate responsibility.

Recommended Readings

Backman, J., ed. *Social Responsibility and Accountability.* New York: New York University Press, 1975.

Barry, V. *Moral Issues in Business.* Belmont, Cal.: Wadsworth, 1979.

Beauchamp, T. L. *Case Studies in Business, Society, and Ethics.* Englewood Cliffs, N.J.: Prentice Hall, 1983.

DeGeorge, R., and Pichler, eds., *Ethics, Free Enterprise and Public Policy.* New York: Oxford University Press, 1978.

Donaldson, Thomas and Patricia H. Werhane, eds. *Ethical Issues in Business.* Englewood Cliffs, N.J.: Prentice Hall, 1979.

Hailey, Arthur. *The Money Changers.*

Hansberry, Lorraine. *A Raisin in the Sun.*

Held, Virginia. *Property, Profits and Economic Justice.* Belmont, Cal.: Wadsworth, 1980.

Hoffman, W. Michael, and Jennifer Mills Moore, eds. *Business Ethics.* New York: McGraw-Hill, 1984.

Hospers, John. *Libertarianism.* Los Angeles: Nash Publishing Co., 1971.

Miller, Arthur. *Death of a Salesman.*

Nozick, Robert. *Anarchy, State and Utopia.* New York: Basic Books, 1974.

Partridge, Scott H. *Cases in Business and Society.* Englewood Cliffs, N.J., 1982.

Rawls, John. *A Theory of Justice.* Cambridge: Harvard University Press, 1971.

Shakespeare, William. *The Merchant of Venice.*

Shaw, Irwin. *Rich Man Poor Man.* New York: Dell, 1970.

Snoeyenbos, Milton, Robert Almeder, and James Humber, eds. *Business Ethics.* Buffalo, N.Y.: Prometheus Books, 1983.

Recommended Periodical Readings

Carr, Albert, "Is Business Bluffing Ethical?" *Harvard Business Review* (Jan. 1968): 143–153.

Carroll, A. "Business Ethics and the Management Hierarchy." *National Forum* 58 (1978).

French, P. "The Corporation as a Moral Person," *American Philosophical Quarterly* 16 (1979).

Goldman, A. "Business Ethics: Profits, Utilities and Moral Rights." *Philosophy and Public Affairs* 9 (1980).

McGuire, J. "The Business of Business Ethics." *National Forum* 58 (1978).

Stackhouse, M. "Business and Ethics." *Hastings Center Report Supplement.* Hastings, N.Y. (1977):10–12.

INDEX

A

Abortion, 63–182
"Abortion and Equality,"
106–17
"Abortion and the Conscience
of the Nation," 74–79
"Abortion: A Personal Moral
Dilemma," 80–84
Acts and Other Events, 86
Addelson, Kathryn Pyne, 66,
98–105
A. H. Robins Corporation, 313
Albert Einstein College of
Medicine, 130
Almeder, Robert, 315, 436–42
Ambivalence of Abortion, The,
80
American Association for
Community and Junior
Colleges, 160
"American Ignorance of War,"
270–73
Analysis, 4
Ancient world, 164–67
Anshen, Melvin, 314, 358–62
Araqi, Gholam-Reza Fada'i,
186, 266–69
Aristotle, 5, 10, 44–52
Asimov, Isaac, 187, 284–85
Azhar University, 406

B

Baruch College, 212
Behavior, 4
Behemoth, 18
Benne, Robert, 314, 386–93
Bible, 12–16
Birth control devices, 313
"Bishops' Letter—A Jewish
Reading, The,"
394–404
"Bishops' Letter—A Protestant
Reading, The," 386–93
Blackmun, Harry, 65, 68–72
Bowdoin College, 348
Brooks, Gwendolyn, 67,
152–54
Brown University, 206
Bush, George, 185, 190

C

"Calvin & Hobbes," 8
"Can a Corporation Have a
Conscience," 348–56
Carnegie Institute of
Technology, 358
Carrol, Daniel E., 185, 242–50
Categorical, 9
"Categorical Imperative, The,"
9, 26–35
"Catholic Theologian at an
Abortion Clinic, A,"
124–29
Catholic University, 124
*Challenge of Peace: God's
Promise and Our
Response, The*, 232
Challenger, 313
Chamberlain, Neil, 315,
444–52
"Changing the Social Contract:
A Role for Business,"
358–62
Charmatz, Albert W., 242–50
Children of Hiroshima, 187,
290–301
Citadel, The, 148
City University of New York,
212
Clean Sites, Inc., 364
Clemens, Samuel Langhorne.
See Twain, Mark
"Cold, Cold Box, The," 315,
422–28
Collected Poems, 420
Columbia University, 358, 444
Contemplative life, 51–52
"Convention," 18–25
Cornell University, 192, 286
Corporate responsibility,
311–452
*Corporate Strategies for Social
Performance*, 358
Council for Religion in
Independent Schools,
164
"Criminals, The," 168, 175–81
Critique of Judgment, The, 26
Critique of Pure Reason, The, 26
Cronin, A. J., 67, 148–51
Cummins Engine Company,
364

D

Danner, Victor, 186, 262–64
Dante, 192
Dartmouth College, 394
"Death Is Not an End but a
Continuation," 266,
267–68
Decalogue. *See* Ten
Commandments
"Decision to Bomb Japan,
The," 187, 302–10
De Cive, 18
De Corpore Politico, 18
"Defense of Abortion, A,"
86–96
De Homine, 18
DeLorean, John, 313, 322–35
DeLorean Corporation, 322
Deontological theories, 6
Deuteronomy, 12
Disarmament, 184–85, 188
"Doctor, I Can't . . . I Won't
Have a Child," 148–51
Doll's House, A, 430
Drake University, 206

E

"Economic Justice for All: A
Pastoral Message,"
372–85
Ecumenical Institute of
Technology, 164
Egoism, 5
Emory University, 364
Enemy of the People, An, 315,
430–34
Englehardt, Elaine, 67, 160–63
Equality, 106–17
Ethics
foundations of, 7–59
introduction, 2–6
and life, 61–452
nature of, 1–59
"Ethics and Nuclear
Deterrence," 212
Etiquette, 4
Exodus, 12, 13
Exxon Corporation, 311, 312
Exxon Valdez, 311, 312

F

Farewell to Arms, A, 156
"Far Side, The," 184
Fast, Howard, 315, 422–28
Ferraro: My Story, 80
First Lady of Plains, 80
Ford Pinto, 313
For Whom the Bell Tolls, 156
*Foundations of the Metaphysics
of Morals*, 26
Francke, Linda Bird, 66, 80–84
Frankena, William K., 3
Friedman, Milton, 313, 314,
316–21

G

General Advisory Committee,
198
General Institute of Islamic
Culture, 406
General Motors, 313, 322
Georgia State University, 436
Ghosts, 430
Gilligan, Carol, 10, 54–59
Good, 5, 45–48
Goodpaster, Kenneth E., 314,
348–56
Good Samaritan, 3
Gorbachev, Mikhail S., 184,
185, 188–91
Gordon, James W., 242–50
Gordon, Linda, 67, 168–82
Gorman, Michael, 67, 164–67
Gray, Colin S., 185, 198–204
Gray, Edmund R., 314, 336–46
Greece, 63, 67, 164–67
Green, Ronald, 314, 394–404
Group think, 313
Growing Up Divorced, 80
Gunnemann, Jon P., 314,
374–70

H

"Halal and the Haram in the
Daily Life of the
Muslim, The," 406–10
Happiness, 5, 51–52
Harvard College, 364

Harvard Graduate School of
    Business
    Administration, 348
Harvard Law School, 68
Harvard University, 54, 348,
    394, 420
Hatter's Castle, 148
Hay, Robert D., 314, 336–46
Health Effect Institute, 364
Hedda Gabler, 430
Hedonism, 5
"Heinz's dilemma," 10
Hemingway, Ernest, 67, 156–59
"Hills Like White Elephants,"
    67, 156–59
Hiroshima, 187
Hiroshima University, 290
Hobbes, Thomas, 9, 18–25
"Holy War, The," 262–64
Hoover Institution, 316
"How Moral Men Make
    Immoral Decisions,"
    322–35
Hudson Institute, 198
"Humanae Vitae," 118–22

I

Ibsen, Henrik, 315, 430–34
Ichikawa, Hiroaki, 291–92
"Images of Relationship,"
    54–59
Imperative, 9
In a Different Voice:
    Psychological Theory and
    Women's Development,
    54
Indiana University, 262, 358
Industrial Revolution, 315
Inferno, The, 192
Intellectual virtue, 50–51
"Introduction to Social
    Responsibility," 336–46
Iran, 266
Islamic perspectives, 67,
    142–46, 186, 262–64,
    266–69, 315, 406–10
"Islam Is Not a Religion of
    Pacifists," 266, 267
IUD, 313

J

Jesus, 6, 9, 12–16
Jewish perspectives, 67, 130–40,
    252–60, 314, 394–404
Jihad, 262
Johns Hopkins University, 286
Johnson and Johnson, 313
Jus Naturale, 20
Justification, 4
"Just War Theory and Nuclear
    Strategy," 220–31
Juzaitis, Raymond J., 242–50

K

Kant, Immanuel, 6, 9, 26–35
Keys of the Kingdom, The, 148
Khomeini, Ayatollah Ruhollah,
    186, 266–69

Kimura, Susumu, 294–95
Kimura, Yoshihiro, 293–94
Kohlberg, Lawrence, 10

L

Lackey, Douglas P., 185,
    212–19
Lady with Carnations, A, 148
Lansing Community College,
    252
Late Night Thoughts on Listening
    to Mahler's Ninth
    Symphony, 187, 286–88
Lawful and the Prohibited in
    Islam, The, 406
Law of Nature, 21
Laws of War, 185, 206–11
Leiser, Burton M., 185, 206–11
Leviathan, 9, 18–25
Lex Naturalis, 21
Liberty, Justice, and Morals:
    Contemporary Value
    Conflicts, 206
Life, and ethics, 61–452
Lives of a Cell, The, 286
Long Island Jewish Medical
    Center Affiliation, 130
Los Alamos, New Mexico, 183,
    185, 242
Los Alamos Scientific National
    Laboratory, 242
Lovelace, Richard, 186, 278–79
Loyola Marymount University,
    336
Luke, 12

M

Machiavelli, Niccolo, 315,
    412–18
Mademoiselle, 152
Maguire, Daniel C., 66, 124–29
Mahowald, Mary B., 66,
    106–17
"Majority Opinion in Roe v.
    Wade," 68–72
Managing the Socially
    Responsible Corporation,
    358
"Man of Professional Wisdom,"
    98
Man Who Died Twice, The, 420
Marquette University, 124
Massachusetts Institute of
    Technology, 86
Matthew, 12, 13–16
Matthews, John B., Jr., 314,
    348–56
Mayo Clinic, 68
Memorial Sloan-Kettering
    Cancer Center, 286
Mill, James, 36
Mill, John Stuart, 9–10, 36–43
Milosz, Czeslaw, 186, 270–73
"Missiles and Morals: A
    Utilitarian Look at
    Nuclear Deterrence,"
    212–19
Miyata, Tetsuo, 295–99
Montini, Giovanni Battista. See
    Pope Paul VI

"Moral Case for Unilateral
    Nuclear Disarmament,
    The," 212
Morality, 2, 3, 4, 5, 6
"Morality in the Marketplace,"
    436–42
Moral Principles and Nuclear
    Weapons, 212
Moral virtue, 48–50
Morton-Thyecol, 313
Mosaic Law, 6, 9
"Mother, The," 152–54
Motivation, 4
Muslim perspective, 67,
    142–46, 186, 262–64,
    266–69, 315, 406–10
Mussallam, Basim F., 67,
    142–46

N

National Alliance of
    Businessmen, 322
National Conference of
    Catholic Bishops, 185,
    232–40, 348, 372–85
National Endowment for the
    Humanities, 160
National Institute for Policy,
    198
New England Journal of
    Medicine, 286
Newsweek, 80
New Yorker, 80
New York Times, 80
New York University, 286
"Nietzsche and Moral Change,"
    98
Non-consequentialist theories,
    6
Normal College for Women,
    274
Novak, David, 186, 252–60
"Nuclear Disarmament by the
    Year 2000," 188–91
Nuclear war, 183–310
"Nuclear Weapons and Nuclear
    Deterrence," 232–40
"Nuclear Winter, The," 185,
    192–96

O

Ohio State University, 336
On a Clear Day You Can See
    General Motors, 322
On Liberty, 36
On the Subjugation of Women,
    36
Osada, Arata, 187, 290–301

P

Pace University, 206
Pagans, 67, 164–67
"Pagan World, The," 164–67
Pahlavij, Mohammed Riza, 266
Payne, Keith, 185, 198–204
Peer Gynt, 430
Phillip of Macedonia, 44
Pirandello, Luigi, 186, 274–77

Plato, 44
Pocketful of Rye, A, 148
Pongratz, Morris B., 242–50
Pope Paul VI, 66, 118–22
Population Growth and Justice,
    394
Powers, Charles W., 314,
    374–70
Prince, The, 412–18
Princeton Theological
    Seminary, 164
Prince William Sound, 311, 312
Pro-choice, 64
"Prohibition on Birth Control,
    The," 168, 169–75
Pro-life, 64
Protestant churches, 67, 314,
    386–93

Q

Qaradawi, Yusuf Al-, 315,
    406–10
"Qualities of the Prince, The,"
    412–18
Queens Hospital Center, 130
Qur'an, 186, 266–69

R

Rational justification, 4
Reagan, Ronald, 66, 74–79
Reflection, 4
Religions, 5. See also specific
    religion
Religious Reason, 394
Resources for Responsible
    Management, 364
"Response to the US Bishops'
    Second Draft of a
    Proposed Pastoral
    Letter on War,
    Armaments, and
    Peace," 242–50
"Responsibilities of
    Corporations and Their
    Owners, The," 364–70
Responsibility, corporate. See
    Corporate responsibility
Reykjavik Summit, 184, 185
"Richard Cory," 315, 420–21
Right, 5
Right of Nature, 20
Roanoke College, 386
Robber Baron, 315
Robinson, Edwin Arlington,
    315, 420–21
Roe v. Wade, 64, 65, 68–72
Roman Catholic Church, 63,
    66, 67, 118–22, 185,
    232–40, 372–85
Rome, 63, 67
Roosevelt, Franklin D., 358
Rosner, Fred, 67, 130–40
Rutkowsk, Henry L., 242–50

S

Sagan, Carl, 185, 192–96
St. Mary's Seminary, 164
Satoh, Tomoyuki, 291
Schmeltekopf, Donald D., 6

Self-interest, 5
Self-realization, 5
Sermon on the Mount, 12,
    13–16
Sex and Society in Islam, 142
"Silly Asses," 187, 284–85
Simon, John G., 314, 374–70
Smith, Adam, 312
Smith College, 98
"Social Benefit," 36–43
"Social Responsibility of
    Business Is to Increase
    Its Profits, The,"
    316–21
Stanford University, 316
Stars Look Down, The, 148
Sterba, James P., 185, 220–31
Sumi, Shizuo, 292
Sun Also Rises, The, 156
Supreme Court. *See* United
    States Supreme Court
Survival, 185, 198–204
Swarthmore College, 168

T

Taconic Foundation, 364
Taylor, Harriet, 36
Ten Commandments, 6, 9, 12,
    13

Ten Words. *See* Ten
    Commandments
Thing of Beauty, A, 148
Think tank, 198
Thomas, Lewis, 187, 286–88
Thomson, Judith Jarvis, 66,
    86–96
"Threat of Nuclear War: Jewish
    Perspectives, The,"
    252–60
Time and the Riddle, 422–28
"To Lucasta, Going to the
    Wars," 186, 278–79
Tristram, 420
Truman, Harry S., 302
Twain, Mark, 187, 280–82
Two Worlds, 148
Tylenol, 313

U

"Uncertain Relationship
    Between Business and
    Society, The," 444–52
Union of Concerned Scientists,
    192
United States Department of
    Defense, 198
United States Supreme Court,
    64, 65, 66, 68–72

University of Arkansas, 336
University of Baltimore, 164
University of Bonn, 274
University of Cambridge, 142
University of Chicago, 106,
    316, 386
University of Minnesota, 286
University of Notre Dame, 220
University of Oklahoma, 336
University of St. Thomas, 348
University of Wisconsin at
    Madison, 168
Utah Valley Community
    College, 160
Utilitarianism, 5, 9–10, 36–43
Utilitarianism, 36–43

V

Valdez, 311, 312
"Victory Is Possible," 185,
    198–204
Villanova, 124
Virtue. *See* Intellectual virtue
    and Moral virtue
"Virtuous Activity," 44–52

W

War, 183–310
"War," 186, 274–77
"War Crimes and Crimes
    Against Humanity,"
    206–11
"War Prayer, The," 187,
    280–82
When We Dead Awaken, 430
Wild Duck, The, 430
*Woman's Right, Woman's Body:
    A Social History of Birth
    Control,* 168
Wright, J. Patrick, 322
Wrong, 5

Y

Yale Labor and Management
    Center, 444
Yale University, 168, 286, 364
Yass, Marion, 187, 302–10
Yeshiva University, 130